The Theory of Corporate Finance
Volume II

The International Library of Critical Writings in Financial Economics

Series Editor: Richard Roll
All State Professor of Economics
The Anderson School at UCLA, US

This major series presents by field outstanding selections of the most important articles across the entire spectrum of financial economics – one of the fastest growing areas in business schools and economics departments. Each collection has been prepared by a leading specialist who has written an authoritative introduction to the literature.

1. The Theory of Corporate Finance (Volumes I and II)
   Michael J. Brennan

Future titles will include:

Futures Markets (Volumes I, II and III)
A.G. Malliaris

Market Efficiency: Stock Market Behaviour in Theory and Practice
Andrew W. Lo

The Debt Market
Stephen A. Ross

Empirical Corporate Finance
Michael J. Brennan

Options Markets

Financial Markets

International Securities

Continuous Time Finance

The Theory of Corporate Finance Volume II

Edited by

Michael J. Brennan

Goldyne and Irwin Hearsh Chair in Money and Banking
The Anderson School, University of California at Los Angeles, US

and

Professor of Finance, London Business School, UK

THE INTERNATIONAL LIBRARY OF CRITICAL WRITINGS IN FINANCIAL ECONOMICS

An Elgar Reference Collection
Cheltenham, UK • Brookfield, US

© Michael J. Brennan 1996. For copyright of individual articles please refer to the Acknowledgements.

All rights reserved. No part of this publication may be reproduced, stored in a retrieval system, or transmitted in any form or by any means, electronic, mechanical, photocopying, recording, or otherwise without the prior permission of the publisher.

Published by
Edward Elgar Publishing Limited
8 Lansdown Place
Cheltenham
Glos GL50 2HU
UK

Edward Elgar Publishing Company
Old Post Road
Brookfield
Vermont 05036
US

British Library Cataloguing in Publication Data
The theory of corporate finance. (The international
  library of critical writings in financial economics ; no. 1)
  1. Corporations – Finance
  I. Brennan, Michael J.
  658.1'5

Library of Congress Cataloguing in Publication Data
The theory of corporate finance / Michael J. Brennan (ed.).
    p. cm. — (International library of critical writings in
  financial economics ; 1)
    Includes bibliographical references and index.
    1. Corporations—Finance. 2. Business enterprises—Finance.
  3. Stockholders. 4. Managerial accounting. I. Brennan, Michael J.
  II. Series.
  HG4011.T483 1996
  658.15—dc20

96-609
CIP

ISBN 1 85898 278 2 (2 volume set)

Printed in Great Britain at the University Press, Cambridge

Contents

Acknowledgements vii
An Introduction by the editor to both volumes appears in Volume I

PART I   FINANCIAL STRUCTURE AND THE REAL ASSET AND PRODUCT MARKETS
1. Sheridan Titman (1984), 'The Effect of Capital Structure on a Firm's Liquidation Decision', *Journal of Financial Economics*, **13**, 137–51   3
2. Vojislav Maksimovic and Josef Zechner (1991), 'Debt, Agency Costs, and Industry Equilibrium', *Journal of Finance*, **XLVI** (5), December, 1619–43   18
3. Andrei Shleifer and Robert W. Vishny (1992), 'Liquidation Values and Debt Capacity: A Market Equilibrium Approach', *Journal of Finance*, **XLVII** (4), September, 1343–66   43
4. Patrick Bolton and David S. Scharfstein (1990), 'A Theory of Predation Based on Agency Problems in Financial Contracting', *American Economic Review*, **80** (1), March, 93–106   67

PART II   CAPITAL INVESTMENT AND VALUATION
5. Michael J. Brennan (1990), 'Latent Assets', *Journal of Finance*, **XLV** (3), July, 709–30   83
6. Michael J. Brennan and Eduardo S. Schwartz (1985), 'Evaluating Natural Resource Investments', *Journal of Business*, **58** (2), April, 135–57   105
7. Jonathan E. Ingersoll, Jr. and Stephen A. Ross (1992), 'Waiting to Invest: Investment and Uncertainty', *Journal of Business*, **65** (1), January, 1–29   128
8. Hayne E. Leland (1994), 'Corporate Debt Value, Bond Covenants, and Optimal Capital Structure', *Journal of Finance*, **XLIX** (4), September, 1213–52   157

PART III   HEDGING, DISCLOSURE POLICY AND INSIDER TRADING
9. Peter M. deMarzo and Darrell Duffie (1991), 'Corporate Financial Hedging with Proprietary Information', *Journal of Economic Theory*, **53**, 261–86   199
10. Kenneth A. Froot, David S. Scharfstein and Jeremy C. Stein (1993), 'Risk Management: Coordinating Corporate Investment and Financing Policies', *Journal of Finance*, **XLVIII** (5), December, 1629–58   225

11. Michael J. Fishman and Kathleen M. Hagerty (1989), 'Disclosure Decisions by Firms and the Competition for Price Efficiency', *Journal of Finance*, **XLIV** (3), July, 633–46 ... 255
12. Hayne E. Leland (1992), 'Insider Trading: Should It Be Prohibited?', *Journal of Political Economy*, **100** (4), August, 859–87 ... 269

PART IV TAXES AND FINANCIAL POLICY
13. Merton H. Miller (1977), 'Debt and Taxes', *Journal of Finance*, **XXXII** (2), May, 261–75 ... 301
14. Franco Modigliani (1982), 'Debt, Dividend Policy, Taxes, Inflation and Market Valuation', *Journal of Finance*, **XXXVII** (2), May, 255–73 ... 316
15. Stephen A. Ross (1985), 'Debt and Taxes and Uncertainty', *Journal of Finance*, **LX** (3), July, 637–57 ... 335

PART V VOTING AND CONTROL
16. Sanford J. Grossman and Oliver D. Hart (1988), 'One Share–One Vote and the Market for Corporate Control', *Journal of Financial Economics*, **20**, 175–202 ... 359
17. Milton Harris and Artur Raviv (1989), 'The Design of Securities', *Journal of Financial Economics*, **24**, 255–87 ... 387

PART VI TAKEOVER CONTESTS
18. Sanford J. Grossman and Oliver D. Hart (1980), 'Takeover Bids, the Free-Rider Problem, and the Theory of the Corporation', *Bell Journal of Economics*, **11** (1), Spring, 42–64 ... 423
19. Michael J. Fishman (1989), 'Preemptive Bidding and the Role of the Medium of Exchange in Acquisitions', *Journal of Finance*, **XLIV** (1), March, 41–57 ... 446
20. David Hirshleifer and Sheridan Titman (1990), 'Share Tendering Strategies and the Success of Hostile Takeover Bids', *Journal of Political Economy*, **98** (2), 295–324 ... 463

PART VII CORPORATE BANKRUPTCY
21. Ronald M. Giammarino (1989), 'The Resolution of Financial Distress', *Review of Financial Studies*, **2** (1), 25–47 ... 495
22. Robert Gertner and David Scharfstein (1991), 'A Theory of Workouts and the Effects of Reorganization Law', *Journal of Finance*, **XLVI** (4), September, 1189–222 ... 518
23. Robert M. Mooradian (1994), 'The Effect of Bankruptcy Protection on Investment: Chapter 11 as a Screening Device', *Journal of Finance*, **XLIX** (4), September, 1403–30 ... 552

Name Index ... 581

Acknowledgements

The editor and publishers wish to thank the authors and the following publishers who have kindly given permission for the use of copyright material.

Academic Press, Inc. for article: Peter M. deMarzo and Darrell Duffie (1991), 'Corporate Financial Hedging with Proprietary Information', *Journal of Economic Theory*, **53**, 261–86.

American Economic Association for article: Patrick Bolton and David S. Scharfstein (1990), 'A Theory of Predation Based on Agency Problems in Financial Contracting', *American Economic Review*, **80** (1), March, 93–106.

American Finance Association for articles: Merton H. Miller (1977), 'Debt and Taxes', *Journal of Finance*, **XXXII** (2), May, 261–75; Franco Modigliani (1982), 'Debt, Dividend Policy, Taxes, Inflation and Market Valuation', *Journal of Finance*, **XXXVII** (2), May, 255–73; Stephen A. Ross (1985), 'Debt and Taxes and Uncertainty', *Journal of Finance*, **LX** (3), July, 637–57; Michael J. Fishman (1989), 'Preemptive Bidding and the Role of the Medium of Exchange in Acquisitions', *Journal of Finance*, **XLIV** (1), March, 41–57; Michael J. Fishman and Kathleen M. Hagerty (1989), 'Disclosure Decisions by Firms and the Competition for Price Efficiency', *Journal of Finance*, **XLIV** (3), July, 633–46; Michael J. Brennan (1990), 'Latent Assets', *Journal of Finance*, **XLV** (3), July, 709–30; Robert Gertner and David Scharfstein (1991), 'A Theory of Workouts and the Effects of Reorganization Law', *Journal of Finance*, **XLVI** (4), September, 1189–222; Vojislav Maksimovic and Josef Zechner (1991), 'Debt, Agency Costs, and Industry Equilibrium', *Journal of Finance*, **XLVI** (5), December, 1619–43; Andrei Shleifer and Robert W. Vishny (1992), 'Liquidation Values and Debt Capacity: A Market Equilibrium Approach', *Journal of Finance*, **XLVII** (4), September, 1343–66; Kenneth A. Froot, David S. Scharfstein and Jeremy C. Stein (1993), 'Risk Management: Coordinating Corporate Investment and Financing Policies', *Journal of Finance*, **XLVIII** (5), December, 1629–58; Hayne E. Leland (1994), 'Corporate Debt Value, Bond Covenants, and Optimal Capital Structure', *Journal of Finance*, **XLIX** (4), September, 1213–52; Robert M. Mooradian (1994), 'The Effect of Bankruptcy Protection on Investment: Chapter 11 as a Screening Device', *Journal of Finance*, **XLIX** (4), September, 1403–30.

Elsevier Science S.A. for articles: Sheridan Titman (1984), 'The Effect of Capital Structure on a Firm's Liquidation Decision', *Journal of Financial Economics*, **13**, 137–51; Sanford J. Grossman and Oliver D. Hart (1988), 'One Share–One Vote and the Market for Corporate Control', *Journal of Financial Economics*, **20**, 175–202; Milton Harris and Artur Raviv (1989), 'The Design of Securities', *Journal of Financial Economics*, **24**, 255–87.

Oxford University Press for article: Ronald M. Giammarino (1989), 'The Resolution of Financial Distress', *Review of Financial Studies*, **2** (1), 25–47.

RAND for article: Sanford J. Grossman and Oliver D. Hart (1980), 'Takeover Bids, the Free-Rider Problem, and the Theory of the Corporation', *Bell Journal of Economics*, **11** (1), Spring, 42–64.

University of Chicago Press for articles: Michael J. Brennan and Eduardo S. Schwartz (1985), 'Evaluating Natural Resource Investments', *Journal of Business*, **58** (2), April, 135–57; David Hirshleifer and Sheridan Titman (1990), 'Share Tendering Strategies and the Success of Hostile Takeover Bids', *Journal of Political Economy*, **98** (2), 295–324; Jonathan E. Ingersoll, Jr and Stephen A. Ross (1992), 'Waiting to Invest: Investment and Uncertainty', *Journal of Business*, **65** (1), January, 1–29; Hayne E. Leland (1992), 'Insider Trading: Should It Be Prohibited?', *Journal of Political Economy*, **100** (4), August, 859–87.

Every effort has been made to trace all the copyright holders but if any have been inadvertently overlooked the publishers will be pleased to make the necessary arrangement at the first opportunity.

In addition the publishers wish to thank the Library of the London School of Economics and Political Science and the Marshall Library of Economics, Cambridge University, for their assistance in obtaining these articles.

Part I
Financial Structure and the Real Asset and Product Markets

THE EFFECT OF CAPITAL STRUCTURE ON A FIRM'S LIQUIDATION DECISION

Sheridan TITMAN

University of California, Los Angeles, CA 90024, USA

Received August 1982, final version received November 1983

A firm's liquidation can impose costs on its customers, workers, and suppliers. An agency relationship between these individuals and the firm exists in that the liquidation decision controlled by the firm (as the agent) affects other individuals (the customers, workers, and suppliers as principals). The analysis in this paper suggests that capital structure can control the incentive/conflict problem of this relationship by serving as a pre-positioning or bonding mechanism. Appropriate selection of capital structure assures that incentives are aligned so that the firm implements the ex-ante value-maximizing liquidation policy.

1. Introduction

The issue of corporate capital structure has been widely debated since Modigliani and Miller (1958, 1963) published their seminal papers. In response to their second work, which implied that in a world with corporate taxes a firm's capital structure consists entirely of debt, researchers looked for debt-related costs, possibly arising from costly contracting, which would admit equity into the capital structure.[1] This paper explores one source of contracting costs which is indirectly related to bankruptcy.

Bankruptcy costs have been used by (among others) Kim (1978), Kraus and Litzenberger (1973), and Scott (1976), to explain the choice of capital structure.

---

*This paper is a condensed version of my Ph.D. dissertation. I wish to thank members of my dissertation committee, Dennis Epple, Scott Richard, Chester Spatt, and Rex Thompson for their many helpful comments and insights. This study also benefited from discussions with Kenneth Dunn, John Fitts, David Mayers, Richard Roll, Clifford Smith and Brett Trueman. Earlier versions of this work were presented at Carnegie-Mellon University, the University of Texas, UCLA, the University of British Columbia, the University of Pennsylvania, and the Federal Reserve Board of Governors. I received valuable comments at all of these seminars and also from faculty members at the University of California, Berkeley. Financial support from Carnegie-Mellon University and the Social Science Research Council is gratefully acknowledged.

[1]See for example, Baxter (1967), DeAngelo and Masulis (1980), Grossman and Hart (1982), Jensen and Meckling (1976), Kim (1978), Kraus and Litzenberger (1973), Miller (1977), Myers (1977), Ross (1977), Scott (1976). See Chen and Kim (1979) and Titman (1981) for a review of these articles.

The significance of these costs, however, has been disputed by Warner (1977) and Haugen and Senbet (1978). Warner, in a study of bankrupt railroads, finds that the direct costs of bankruptcy are small and concludes that they cannot explain observed capital structures. Haugen and Senbet argue that indirect costs associated with bankruptcy [as suggested by Baxter (1967)] are also unlikely to explain observed capital structures. They point out that these indirect costs are really associated with the firm going out of business, that is, liquidating. By arguing that the firm's bondholders and stockholders agree that the firm should liquidate whenever the liquidation value of the firm is greater than its operating value they conclude that liquidation costs cannot be a factor in the determination of the firm's capital structure.

The Haugen and Senbet paper makes a number of assumptions which are not realistic. First, they assume that the firm makes the liquidation choice that maximizes the total value of the firm's bonds and stock regardless of whether or not the firm is bankrupt. This implicitly assumes that the costs of forming a coalition between stockholders and bondholders are zero. Furthermore, the paper looks only at stockholders and bondholders and thus ignores an important agency relationship between these security holders (as the agents) and other associates of the firm (as principals) who can suffer costs if the firm liquidates.[2] These costs include search and retooling costs for workers and suppliers with job specific capital, and increased expenses for customers.

The model developed in this paper demonstrates that these liquidation costs, along with the conflicting incentives of bondholders and stockholders, have important implications which are relevant to the theory of optimal capital structure.[3] The specific liquidation cost examined in this model is the increased maintenance costs which are borne by the firm's customers. Recent articles in the financial press suggest that observed consumer behavior is consistent with the relevance of these costs. For example, the Wall Street Journal (October 11, 1982) reports that 'the closing of some (International Harvester) dealerships is causing a few customers to worry about getting parts and service'. Lee Iacocca is quoted as saying that because of Chrysler's need for government loan guarantees, 'its share of new car sales dropped nearly two percentage points because potential buyers feared the company would go bankrupt' (Wall Street Journal, July 23, 1981).

If the customers and other associates of a firm rationally assess its probability of liquidation, the firm will indirectly bear the imposed liquidation costs

---

[2]See Jensen and Meckling (1976), Myers (1977), and Ross (1973), for a general discussion of the agency relationship.

[3]For large corporations, very few bankruptcies lead to the total liquidation of the firm. In most cases, the firm is reorganized and continues to operate. However, the reorganized firm may make substantial changes. It may reduce the scale of its operations, drop unprofitable lines of business, and renege on implicit commitments. If the firm's customers, workers, and suppliers suffer costs as a result of these changes, then the reorganization is equivalent to a liquidation for the results that follow.

ex ante. For example, the price a consumer is willing to pay for a durable good declines as the probability of the firm's liquidation increases reflecting the increase in expected maintenance costs. A value-maximizing firm then has an incentive to adopt an enforceable policy of only liquidating in those states of nature where the value of the assets if liquidated exceeds their value if not liquidated by an amount greater than the costs imposed on its customers and other associates. However, this policy is time-inconsistent.[4] Ex post, after the firm has transacted with its customers and associates, an unconstrained value-maximizing firm will want to liquidate as soon as the liquidation value of the assets exceeds their value if not liquidated by any positive amount.

In order to guarantee implementation of its value-maximizing liquidation policy a firm must either accept constraints on its future behavior, or in some other way 'pre-position' or bond itself, to rule out actions which are rational at the future date but detrimental to its value at the current time.[5] Most previous studies which have examined methods of pre-positioning to implement time-inconsistent policies have limited their analyses to explicit contracts such as bond covenants which directly constrain behavior.[6,7] This paper suggests a method of pre-positioning which resolves the time-inconsistency problem through the choice of capital structure, without resorting to explicit constraints.

It is shown here that the capital structure choice affects the stockholders' incentives to liquidate when the firm is not bankrupt. The capital structure choice also determines in which states of nature the liquidation decision is transferred to the bondholders' control (via bankruptcy). Since bondholders have the highest priority claim to the liquidation proceeds they are more likely (than stockholders) to choose to liquidate the firm. Consequently, the capital structure the firm chooses is a determinant of the liquidation policy that it implements. The firm, therefore, by choosing the appropriate capital structure bonds itself to implement the optimal liquidation policy.

---

[4] A policy which specifies a future action which is consistent with maximization of the decision maker's objective function at the future date is called a time-consistent policy. A policy which does not have this property is time-inconsistent. The first mention of this concept appeared in a paper by Strotz (1956). Kydland (1977) shows that the time-inconsistency problem arises in dominant-player relationships, of which the agency relationship is a special case.

[5] Pre-positioning can be thought of as either a state-dependent bonding activity or as making a state-contingent pre-commitment. See Strotz and Grossman and Hart (1982) for a discussion of pre-commitment.

[6] See for example, Jensen and Meckling (1976), Myers (1977), Smith and Warner (1979) and Strotz (1956).

[7] The exceptions being, Klein, Crawford and Alchian (1978), who discuss the use of vertical integration to resolve a time-inconsistency problem which arises for reasons similar to those discussed here; Jensen and Meckling who hint at methods of pre-positioning using manager compensation and securities other than straight debt and equity; Mayers and Smith (1982) who suggest a bonding role for insurance and Grossman and Hart (1982) who devise a pre-commitment mechanism which also involves a role for capital structure.

If firms cannot issue state-contingent debt claims, they will not, in general, be able to choose capital structures which lead them to exactly implement the unconstrained optimal liquidation policy which was described above. However, this is not crucial for the theory of capital structure suggested by this model. What is important is that a firm's capital structure controls the future liquidation decision and that this, in turn, affects the terms of trade at which the firm does business with its customers, workers, and suppliers. An increase in a firm's debt level, which increases its probability of bankruptcy, will thus worsen these terms of trade to reflect the increased probability of liquidation. These less favorable terms of trade are a cost of debt financing which is relevant to the firm's capital structure decision.

The structure of the paper is as follows. In the next section a partial equilibrium model is presented which demonstrates that the optimal liquidation policy of a firm is generally time-inconsistent. The analysis in section 3 demonstrates that a firm which chooses the appropriate capital structure implements its optimal liquidation policy without using explicit liquidation contracts. The concluding section summarizes the work and discusses the testable implications of the theory.

2. The time-inconsistency of the firm's optimal liquidation policy

In the model which follows, the firm can be viewed from the perspective suggested by Alchian and Demsetz (1972) and Jensen and Meckling (1976); as a nexus for contracting relationships between the firm's different classes of security holders and its customers, workers and suppliers. However, firm value is defined in the more traditional manner as the summed values of its outstanding securities. The analysis which follows demonstrates that a value-maximizing firm's optimal liquidation policy is not, in general, time-consistent. The liquidation policy which maximizes the firm's value in period 0 specifies that the firm should act to maximize the aggregate wealth of all of its associates (including its customers, workers and suppliers) in period 1 rather than just the wealth of its security holders. These objectives are inconsistent whenever any of these outside associates suffer a cost from the firm's liquidation. Although we focus on the costs that liquidation imposes on a firm's customers, the time-inconsistency result follows if any outside associate of the firm has specific human capital or any other form of capital which becomes less valuable as a result of the firm's liquidation.

The model examines a firm which produces a machine that requires maintenance in future periods. Although the combination of the machine and the maintenance (i.e., machine services) are sold in a competitive market, the maintenance for a particular machine may be more cheaply obtained from the producer of the machine. Titman (1981) demonstrates within a general equilibrium model that this will be the case if the production of the machines and their maintenance (e.g., spare parts) exhibits joint economies of scale.[8] As a result of this, the cost of operating a machine increases if the producer liquidates.

The model has two periods. In period 0 the firm determines its production level and purchases the required quantity of the numeraire good needed for production. The firm utilizes $K(M)$ units of the numeraire good to produce M machines, where $K(M)$ is strictly convex, monotonically increasing and differentiable at all points. The machines are sold at the end of period 0 for use in period 1. In period 1, the firm either produces additional machines, or liquidates its capital, based on which of the N possible states of nature occurs. The firm's period 1 liquidation value is denoted $\delta(\theta_i)K$ in state θ_i, and its operating value in this state is denoted $V_1(\theta_i)$, where V_1 is the value the firm achieves given optimal operating decisions in period 1. The firm's liquidation policy is defined as the function $\rho(\theta_i)$, where $\rho(\theta_i) = 1$ if the firm is to liquidate in state θ_i, and $\rho(\theta_i) = 0$ if the firm plans to continue operating in this state.

Individuals in this economy derive utility from the numeraire good and from machine services. Firms act as price-takers in the sense that the total cost of obtaining the service of a given machine must equal a market determined price. The cost of obtaining this service consists of two components, the purchase price and the maintenance costs, which can differ across firms. If the machines produced by one firm cost more to operate than the machines produced by another firm, then the machines with the higher operating costs must sell for less than the machines with the lower operating costs by an amount equal to the difference in the discounted cost of operating these machines over their lives. For this reason, a firm's products will fall in value, by an amount equal to the present value of the increase in their operating cost, if the firm chooses to liquidate. If the firm chooses to liquidate in state θ_i [i.e., $\delta(\theta_i) = 1$], the machines will be worth $P[1, \theta_i]$. If however the firm chooses not to liquidate in this state [i.e., $\delta(\theta_i) = 0$], the machines will be worth $P[0, \theta_i]$, where $P[0, \theta_i] - P[1, \theta_i] = c(\theta_i)$, the cost imposed by the liquidation.

Since the value of a machine in period 1 is affected by whether or not the producer liquidates, the price that a firm's machines sell for in period 0 will reflect the firm's liquidation policy. If a complete market for state-contingent claims exists, and individuals know the price of machines in the future states, the period 0 selling price of machines, $P_0(\rho)$, can be expressed as the sum of their period 1 state-determined prices discounted by $p(\theta_i)$, the period 0

---

[8] The price of maintenance will be determined by the marginal producer. Thus, with joint economies of scale in producing the machines and their maintenance, the manufacturer of the machines is an intramarginal producer of replacement parts. The liquidation of this firm raises the cost of maintenance by the difference in the costs of the marginal supplier after versus before liquidation. Depending on their production functions, this difference in cost may either be large or small.

forward price for one unit of the numeraire good in state θ_i,

$$P_0(\rho) = \sum_{i=1}^{N} P[\rho(\theta_i), \theta_i] p(\theta_i). \qquad (1)$$

The firm's period 0 value is equal to its period 0 cash flow $[P_0(\rho)M - K(M)]$ plus the sum of its state-determined period 1 values discounted by $p(\theta_i)$. The period 1 value of the firm will be its liquidation value $[\delta(\theta_i)K(M)]$ in states of nature in which $\rho(\theta_i) = 1$ (i.e., its policy specifies liquidation) and it will be its operating value $[V_1(\theta_i)]$ in states of nature in which $\rho(\theta_i) = 0$. The assumptions of complete and competitive markets are consistent with the notion that value-maximization is the firm's goal in period 0. The following maximization problem assumes that the firm makes its production decision, as well as its period 1 liquidation policy, in period 0,

$$\max_{\{\rho, M\}} V_0 = P_0(\rho)M - K(M)$$

$$+ \sum_{i=1}^{N} [\delta(\theta_i)K(M)\rho(\theta_i) + V_1(\theta_i)(1 - \rho(\theta_i))] p(\theta_i). \qquad (2)$$

Given the convexity of $K(\ )$, an M^* exists which maximizes (2). The optimal liquidation policy $\rho(\theta_i)$ can then be found by substituting (1) into (2) and comparing the incremental increase in period 0 value for $\rho(\theta_i) = 1$ with the increase in value for $\rho(\theta_i) = 0$ for each state of nature. This comparison is expressed by the following inequality which demonstrates that the firm should liquidate in those states of nature and only those states in which

$$P[1, \theta_i]M^* + \delta(\theta_i)K(M^*) > P[0, \theta_i]M^* + V_1(\theta_i), \qquad (3a)$$

which reduces to

$$\delta(\theta_i)K(M^*) - C(\theta_i) > V_1(\theta_i), \qquad (3b)$$

where

$$C(\theta_i) = c(\theta_i)M^* = P[0, \theta_i]M^* - P[1, \theta_i]M^*.$$

The preceding analysis suggests that ex ante, before the machines are sold, a value-maximizing firm should adopt a policy of only liquidating in states of nature where the liquidating value of its assets exceeds their operating value by an amount greater than the costs imposed on its customers. The importance of the assumption that the period 1 liquidation choice was determined in period 0 can be appreciated given this result. If the firm does not prespecify the period 1 liquidation conditions in period 0, it will liquidate whenever its liquidating value exceeds its operating value. The consumers will rationally forecast this liquidation policy reflecting it in their demand prices for the machines. This will make the value of the firm lower. This creates an incentive for firms to either impose constraints on themselves or in some other way pre-position themselves so that the ex ante value-maximizing policies rather than the ex post value-maximizing decisions are made in the future.

Implementing the optimal liquidation policy would be straightforward if it were costless to write and enforce state-contingent contracts. Contracts between the firm's bondholders and stockholders would then specify that stockholders make decisions which maximize the total value of the bonds and stock. The stockholders, in turn, would write contracts with its customers which either describe conditions (i.e., states of nature) under which liquidation is permitted or, alternatively, would specify a state-contingent penalty which the firm pays its customers if it liquidates. However, in many instances state-contingent contracts are expensive to negotiate, administer, and enforce. In such instances, firms must use indirect methods of pre-positioning to implement their optimal liquidation policy. One such method is examined below.

3. Pre-positioning with capital structure

The analysis which follows assumes that the firm is controlled by wealth maximizing equityholders as long as the firm is not bankrupt.[9] If the firm becomes bankrupt, control passes to its bondholders who seek to maximize their wealth. The analysis in the last section suggests that the equity holders of such a firm have an incentive to enter into contracts which force it to make period 1 decisions which maximize the combined wealth of its bondholders, stockholders, and its customers. The cost of any deviation from such a policy will be reflected in the prices of the firm's bonds and its products and will thus be borne by the equity holders. The relevant problem facing the equity holders is then to enter into contracts with the firm's bondholders and customers which lead it to implement the optimal liquidation policy.

Writing and enforcing contracts which lead the firm to implement the optimal liquidation policy becomes especially costly when the bonds are issued before the firm's products are sold. In this case, if contracts with the bondholders do not specify otherwise, equity holders will enter into contracts with their customers which exporpriate wealth from the bondholders and lead the

[9]Jensen and Meckling (among others) have pointed out that the equity holders will not, in this case, always act to maximize the total value of the firm. However, Fama (1978) argues that firms which are subject to outside takeover must maximize total value. Grossman and Hart (1980) suggested that because of transaction costs and a free-rider problem, non-value-maximizing firms can continue to exist without offering any individual an opportunity for a profitable takeover. Titman (1981) demonstrated that this is the case even when the firm's liquidation value exceeds its operating value.

firm to liquidate in fewer states of nature than would be prescribed by the optimal policy. This can easily be seen for the case where the liquidation claim of the firm's senior securities exceeds its liquidation value. In this case, the equity holders will either offer the firm's customers excessive reimbursement payments for their liquidation costs or alternatively enter into contracts which preclude liquidation. Equity holders lose nothing from such contracts, because they stand to receive nothing from the firm's liquidation proceeds, but they gain by offering these contracts since it allows the firm to charge higher prices for its products.

The preceding discussion suggests that a firm which is sufficiently levered implements the optimal liquidation policy only if both bondholders and customers engage in contracts with the equity holders. The contracts with customers are needed to insure that the firm does not liquidate in states of nature not specified by the optimal policy. The contracts with bondholders are needed to prevent the firm from agreeing to continue operations in states of nature in which the optimal policy prescribes liquidation.

In the absence of contracting costs the number of contracts needed to implement a given policy is irrelevant. However, contracting costs are significant and firms have an incentive to structure a cost-minimizing set. The analysis which follows suggests that under certain conditions firms can eliminate the need for customer contracts by choosing the appropriate capital structure.

The analysis abstracts from the many facets of a firm's capital structure decision and examines it as one of optimally choosing two different contracts. One contract specifies the states of nature in which the firm is bankrupt, and hence controlled by its bondholders. The other contract specifies the payoff to each class of security holders in the event that the firm liquidates.[10] It is assumed in this section that equity holders have the lowest priority claim in the event of liquidation. In other words, bondholders and preferred stockholders must receive their liquidating claims, D and Pf respectively, before the equity holders can receive anything. If $D + Pf$ is greater than the liquidation value δK, then the bondholders' claims have priority over the claims of the preferred stockholders.

In contrast to the Haugen and Senbet model, bondholders and stockholders in this model do not always agree on whether or not the firm should liquidate. Stockholders have a stronger preference for continuing to operate the firm since they have the lowest priority claim to the liquidation proceeds, and bondholders tend to prefer liquidation since they have the highest priority claim to the liquidation proceeds. This conflict between the different sets of security holders allows the firm to use capital structure contracts to pre-position itself to implement a specific liquidation policy.

[10] This contract stipulates payoffs which are contingent on the firm liquidating its line of business, not on the firm going out of business. Changing lines of business without repaying the senior claimants would, therefore, constitute a default of the second contract. Smith and Warner (1979) suggest that bond covenants of this type are fairly standard.

The relation between the capital structure which is chosen and the liquidation policy which is subsequently implemented is fairly straightforward. Increasing the face value of the firm's debt or preferred stock decreases the liquidation proceeds which go to the equity holders and hence reduces the number of states of nature in which equity holders will choose to liquidate the firm. If the face value of the debt and preferred stock exceeds the liquidation value of the firm in all states of nature, the equity holders receive nothing in the event of liquidation, and thus never choose this alternative. But in this case, if the firm's liquidation value exceeds its operating value, bondholders prefer to liquidate the firm. The states of nature in which the firm liquidates are then determined by the states in which bondholders have control of the firm, that is, in those states where the firm is bankrupt.

The principal contribution of this paper is contained in the following propositions. Proposition 1 establishes conditions on the firm's capital structure contract, which if satisfied, lead the firm to implement its optimal liquidation policy. These conditions may appear to be rather complex, and they may in general be difficult to satisfy. However, as Proposition 2 demonstrates, under simplifying conditions these sufficient conditions are satisfied by a rather straightforward capital structure.

Proposition 1. *A firm will liquidate according to its optimal policy if its capital structure contracts are chosen so that*

(1) *it is bankrupt in all those states of nature and only those states of nature in which*

$$V_1(\theta_i) < \delta(\theta_i)K - C(\theta_i),$$

(2) $D \geq \delta(\theta_i)K - C(\theta_i)$ *whenever the firm is bankrupt, and*
(3) $Pf + D \geq \delta(\theta_i)K, \forall \theta_i.$

Proof. Condition (1) states that the firm is bankrupt in all those states of nature and only those states of nature in which liquidation is prescribed by the optimal policy. The second condition guarantees that the debt holders strongly prefer liquidation over continuing to operate the firm. The third condition implies that the equity holders' share of the liquidation proceeds must always be zero. These conditions indicate that equity holders never choose to liquidate in the states of nature in which they control the firm, and that bondholders always choose to liquidate the firm when it is bankrupt. Since the firm is bankrupt in all those states of nature, and only those states of nature in which liquidation is prescribed by the optimal policy, the proposition is proved. □

It should be noted that the conditions specified in the above proposition are sufficient, but are not necessary. Condition (2) will not be needed if we make the alternative assumption that debt holders choose to liquidate the firm if they are indifferent between liquidation and continuing to operate the firm but preferred stockholders prefer the liquidation alternative. Condition (3) can be weakened to allow equity holders a share of the liquidation proceeds in some states of nature as long as that share is not large enough to induce shareholders to liquidate the firm.

Preferred stock is included in this analysis because in certain cases conditions (1) and (3) cannot be satisfied simultaneously using only debt and common equity. For instance, it is not always possible to set the liquidating claims of the debt above the firm's liquidation value without causing the firm to be bankrupt in more states of nature than are specified in condition (1). By issuing preferred stock, the firm can eliminate the common stockholders' incentive to liquidate the firm without causing the firm to be bankrupt in additional states of nature.

It should be noted, however, that condition (1) can require fairly complex bankruptcy contracts. The complexity arises since the liquidating value of the firm, net of the costs imposed (i.e., $\delta K - C$), can exceed its operating value in some states of nature in which operating value is relatively high, but may be lower than its operating value in some states of nature in which operating value is relatively low. Hence, condition (1) of the above proposition cannot in general be satisfied by selecting a debt level D^* and specifying that the firm is bankrupt whenever $V_1(\theta_i) < D^*$.

The example illustrated in fig. 1 demonstrates this point. If the firm's period 1 debt obligation is less than D', it will not be bankrupt, and subsequently not

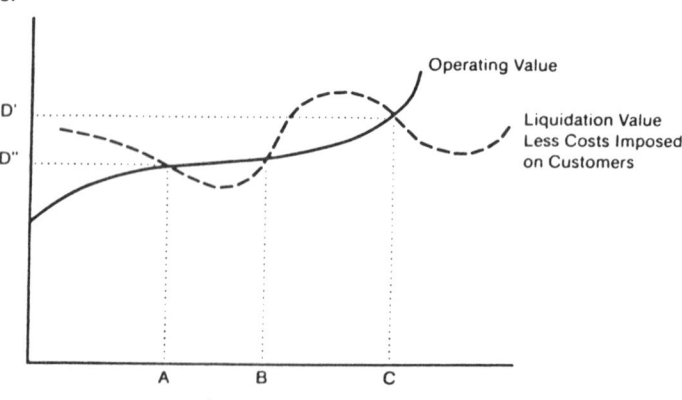

Fig. 1. The operating value of the firm ($V_1(\theta_i)$) and its liquidation value less the costs imposed on its customers $[\delta(\theta_i)K(M^*) - C(\theta_i)]$ are plotted against the state of nature θ_i, where θ_i is ordered so that $V_1(\theta_i)$ is a monotonically increasing function. This figure illustrates the case where these two values intersect twice, implying that for the relatively low operating values in the region AB, $V_1(\theta_l) > \delta(\theta_l)K(M^*) - C(\theta_l)$, and for the higher operating values in the region BC, $V_1(\theta_h) < \delta(\theta_h)K(M^*) - C(\theta_h)$. Since $V_1(\theta_h) > V_1(\theta_l)$, the firm cannot implement the optimal liquidation policy by selecting a debt level D^* and specifying that the firm is bankrupt whenever $V_1(\theta_i) < D^*$.

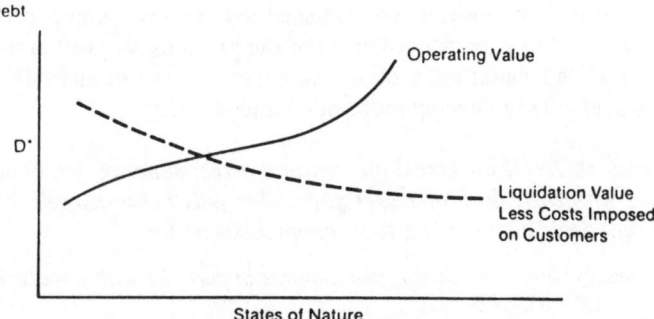

Fig. 2. As in fig. 1, the operating value of the firm ($V_1(\theta_i)$) and its liquidation value less the costs imposed on its customers $[\delta(\theta_i)K(M^*) - C(\theta_i)]$ are plotted against the state of nature θ_i, where θ_i is order so that $V_1(\theta_i)$ is a monotonically increasing function. This figure illustrates the case where these two values intersect only once. In this case the firm can implement its optimal liquidation policy by choosing a debt level D^* which equals the firm's operating value at the point of intersection and specifying that the firm is bankrupt whenever $V_1(\theta_i) < D^*$.

liquidating, in all states of nature in which $V_1(\theta_i) < \delta(\theta_i)K(M^*) - C(\theta_i)$. Conversely, if the firm's debt obligation exceeds D'', it will be bankrupt, and subsequently liquidating, in some period 1 states of nature in which $V_1(\theta_i) > \delta(\theta_i)K(M^*) - C(\theta_i)$. Since D' exceeds D'', no state-independent debt obligation will lead the firm to implement its optimal liquidation policy.

In reality, firms can at least partially determine the states of nature in which they will be bankrupt by properly selecting the maturity and seniority structure of their debt and by writing the appropriate bond covenants.[11] In general, it would be prohibitively costly to write capital structure contracts which exactly implement the optimal policy. Nevertheless, since the capital structure does determine the firm's liquidation policy, that structure which implements the best of the feasible policies will be chosen. Capital structure will, in this case, only partially resolve the time-inconsistency problem.

Under certain conditions, very simple capital structure contracts implement the optimal liquidation policy. If one could say, for instance, that $V_1(\theta_i) - \delta(\theta_i)K(M^*) + C(\theta_i)$ is positive in all states of nature in which V_1 exceeds some $\hat{V}$ and is negative in all states in which V_1 is less than $\hat{V}$, the conditions in

---

[11]An article by Bulow and Shoven (1978) discusses how the mix between short-term and long-term debt and the priority of these claims affect whether or not a firm becomes bankrupt in a particular state of nature. They demonstrate that a bank which holds a substantial portion of a firm's short-term loans will either renew the loans and prevent bankruptcy or call in the loans forcing the firm into default depending on, among other things, the relative size of the loan and its priority in the event of bankruptcy. Smith and Warner (1979), in the context of a problem much different than the one examined in this paper, discuss the use of various types of bond covenants. These covenants allow the firm to predetermine the states of nature in which it is in default for reasons other than the non-payment of the interest or the principle on its debt.

the previous proposition are satisfied by a very simple capital structure contract. In this case, condition (1) of the previous proposition is satisfied if D equals $\hat{V}$ and bankruptcy occurs whenever V_1 is less than D. This point is illustrated in the following proposition and in fig. 2.

Proposition 2. If δK and C are constant across states of nature and bankruptcy occurs whenever the firm's operating value falls below its debt obligations, the firm will liquidate according to its optimal policy if it

(a) *issues short term debt which matures in period 1 with a maturity value equal to $\delta K - C$, and*
(2) *issues preferred stock in an amount where $Pf \geq C$.*

Proof. The reader can easily verify that the above capital structure satisfies conditions (1) and (2) from the previous proposition. The firm, therefore, implements its optimal liquidation policy. □

The particular capital structure described in the preceding proposition is not necessarily the only one which implements the optimal liquidation policy; perhaps long-term debt can be substituted for the firm's preferred stock.[12] The capital structure was chosen for its simplicity rather than its realism. The proposition demonstrates that under certain conditions, a firm can guarantee implementation of its value-maximizing liquidation policy without using state-contingent contracts.

It should be noted that both under the simplifying assumptions of Proposition 2 and the more general assumption of Proposition 1, that the capital structure method for pre-positioning uses fewer contracts than the alternative involving liquidation contracts with customers, and is thus probably less expensive to enact. If this is actually the case, then the preceding analysis provides a positive theory of capital structure which accounts for the use of debt, equity, and possibly preferred stock. An important and potentially testable implication of this theory is that, ceteris paribus, firms which impose relatively large costs on their customers in the event of liquidation, and thus wish to pre-position so that they liquidate in only a few states of nature, choose low levels of debt which lead them to be bankrupt in only those few states of nature.[13]

---

[12] In this simplified example, the optimal liquidation policy will also be implemented with a capital structure consisting of short-term debt with a maturity value equal to $\delta K - C$, and subordinated long-term debt with a liquidation claim equal to C. It would be misleading to present this result without also determining the consequences of a dynamic process in which long-term debt eventually becomes short-term debt. The two period model presented in this paper is incapable of discerning these consequences.

[13] This assumes that the number of states in which a firm is bankrupt is a monotonically increasing function of its debt level. This assumption seems intuitively correct, but the reader should be aware of the discussion in Miller (1977) regarding income bonds for a dissenting opinion.

The role of bankruptcy in this theory can be viewed within the context of more traditional theories of capital structure which assume that bankruptcy is costly. Bankruptcy is costly in this model if the firm issues more debt and subsequently goes bankrupt and then liquidates in states of nature in which liquidation is inconsistent with its optimal policy.[14] The cost of being bankrupt and then liquidating in a state not prescribed by the firm's optimal policy is the difference between its operating value and its liquidation value net of the costs imposed on its customers. The firm bears this cost, in the form of lower prices for its products, in period 0. Bankruptcy in an additional period 1 state θ_i will thus lower a firm's period 0 value by the following amount if it affects its liquidation decision. This can be obtained from eqs. (1) and (2) in section 2,

$$BC(\theta_i) = [V_1(\theta_i) - \delta(\theta_i)K + C(\theta_i)] p(\theta_i). \tag{4}$$

4. Conclusion

This paper examines an agency relationship between a firm (as the agent) and its customers (as principals) who suffer costs if the firm liquidates. It is shown that the firm indirectly bears the liquidation costs which it imposes on its customers in future states of nature in the form of lower prices for its products in the current period. Because of this, the liquidation policy which maximizes a firm's current value takes into account the costs which it imposes on its customers in the future if it liquidates. However, an unconstrained value-maximizing firm will not carry out this policy in the future period but will instead choose to liquidate whenever its liquidation value exceeds its operating value.

The firm's capital structure choice was shown to provide a method by which the firm can pre-position or bond itself so that the optimal liquidation policy is implemented. Appropriate selection of capital structure assures that equity holders continue to operate the firm when it is not bankrupt, and that the firm is bankrupt and controlled by bondholders who choose to liquidate the firm in those states of nature, and only those states, in which liquidation is consistent with the optimal policy.

The analysis in this paper ignored other factors such as other types of agency costs, direct bankruptcy costs, and taxes which influence a firm's capital structure choice. These factors cause the firm to choose a different capital structure than would be optimal from the consideration of the above liquidation policy incentives alone. A tax gain from leveraging, for example, causes the firm to issue additional debt, and hence go bankrupt in states of nature in which

---

[14]A bankrupt firm will not always choose to liquidate. A firm which is bankrupt in a state of nature in which $V_1 > \delta K$ will not liquidate and hence will not suffer these liquidation related bankruptcy costs in this state.

liquidation is not prescribed by the above policy. Bankruptcy in these additional states of nature will be costly since it either leads the firm to implement a suboptimal liquidation policy or alternatively, forces the firm to write additional contracts with its customers. These costs must be considered along with the other costs and benefits of debt financing in the choice of the firm's optimal capital structure.

The developed theory of optimal capital structure has potentially testable cross-sectional implications. It predicts which firms should be highly levered and which should lever very little. According to the theory, firms (such as computer and automobile companies) which can potentially impose high costs on their customers and business associates in the event that they liquidate choose capital structures with relatively low debt/equity ratios. Conversely, firm (such as hotels and retail establishments) which impose relatively low costs on their customers and business associates in the event that they liquidate choose high debt/equity ratios.

There is very little published empirical work in the area of optimal capital structure. This probability reflects the absence of testable hypotheses generated from prior theoretical work in this area. Schwartz and Aronson (1967), Scott (1973), and Scott and Martin (1975), found that industry groupings explained a statistically significant proportion of the variance of observed capital structures. This finding is consistent with the theory suggested in this paper but is also consistent with almost any theory of capital structure imaginable. Clearly, additional empirical research on this subject is needed.

References

Alchian, A. and H. Demsetz, 1972, Production information costs, and economic organization, American Economic Review 62, 777–795.
Baxter, N., 1967, Leverage, risk of ruin and the cost of capital, Journal of Finance 22, 395–403.
Bulow, J. and J. Shoven, 1978, The bankruptcy decision, Bell Journal of Economics 9, 437–456.
Chen, A. and H. Kim, 1979, Theories of corporate debt policy: A synthesis, Journal of Finance 34, 371–384.
DeAngelo, H. and R. Masulis, 1980, Optimal capital structure under corporate and personal taxation, Journal of Financial Economics 8, 3–29.
Fama, E.F., 1978, The effects of a firm's investment and financing decisions on the welfare of its security holders, American Economic Review 68, 272–284.
Grossman, S. and O. Hart, 1980, Takeover bids, the free-rider problem, and the theory of the corporation, Bell Journal of Economics 11, 42–64.
Grossman, S. and O. Hart, 1982, Corporate financial structure and managerial incentives, in: J. McCall, ed., The economics of information and uncertainty (University of Chicago Press, Chicago, IL).
Haugen, R. and L. Senbet, 1978, The insignificance of bankruptcy costs to the theory of optimal capital structure, The Journal of Finance 33, 383–393.
Jensen, M. and W. Meckling, 1976, Theory of the firm: Managerial behavior, agency costs and ownership structure, Journal of Financial Economics 3, 305–360.
Kim, H., 1978, A mean-variance theory of optimal capital structure and corporate debt capacity, Journal of Finance 33, 45–64.
Klein, B., R. Crawford and A. Alchian, 1978, Vertical integration, appropriable rents, and the competitive contracting process, Journal of Law and Economics 21, 297–326.

Kraus, A. and R. Litzenberger, 1973, A state preference model of optimal financial leverage, Journal of Finance, 911-921.
Kydland, F., 1977, Equilibrium solutions in dynamic dominant-player models, Journal of Economic Theory 15, 307-324.
Mayers, D. and C. Smith, 1982, On the corporate demand for insurance, Journal of Business 55, 281-296.
Miller, M., 1977, Debt and taxes, Journal of Finance 32, 261-275.
Modigliani, F. and M. Miller, 1958, The cost of capital, corporation finance and the theory of investment, American Economics Review 48, 261-297.
Modigliani, F. and M. Miller, 1963, Corporation income taxes and the cost of capital: A correction, American Economic Review 53, 433-443.
Myers, S., 1977, Determinants of corporate borrowing, Journal of Financial Economics 4, 147-176.
Ross, S., 1973, The economic theory of agency: The principal's problem, American Economic Review 63, 134-139.
Ross, S., 1977, The determination of financial structure: The incentive-signalling approach, Bell Journal of Economics 8, 23-40.
Schwartz, E. and J. Aronson, 1967, Some surrogate evidence in support of the concept of optimal financial structure, Journal of Finance 22, 10-19.
Scott, D., 1973, Evidence on the importance of financial structure, Financial Management, 45-50.
Scott, D. and J. Martin, 1975, Industry influence on financial structure, Financial Management, 67-73.
Scott, J., 1976, A theory of optimal capital structure, Bell Journal of Economics, Spring, 33-54.
Smith, C. and J. Warner, 1979, On financial contracting: An analysis of bond covenants, Journal of Financial Economics 7, 117-161.
Strotz, R., 1956, Myopia and inconsistency in dynamic utility maximization, Review of Economic Studies 62, 165-180.
Titman, S., 1981, The effect of capital structure on a firm's liquidation decision, Unpublished Ph.D. dissertation (Carnegie-Mellon University, Pittsburgh, PA).
Warner, J., 1977, Bankruptcy costs: Some evidence, Journal of Finance 32, 337-347.

Debt, Agency Costs, and Industry Equilibrium

VOJISLAV MAKSIMOVIC and JOSEF ZECHNER*

ABSTRACT

We show that risk characteristics of projects' cash flows are endogenously determined by the investment decisions of all firms in an industry. As a result, in reasonable settings, financial structures which create incentives to expropriate debtholders by increasing risk are shown not to reduce value in an industry equilibrium. Without taxes, capital structure is irrelevant for individual firms despite its effect on the equityholders' incentives, but the maximum total amount of debt in the industry is determinate. Allowing for a corporate tax advantage of debt, capital structure becomes relevant but firms are indifferent between distinct alternative debt levels.

THE EFFECT OF FIRMS' financial structures on subsequent investment and output decisions has recently received considerable attention in the finance literature. The central insight that equityholders control the firm's investment and production decisions and in general do not maximize the value of a levered firm has been applied to the analysis of risk shifting, underinvestment, and firms' abilities to enter into optimal contracts with their customers.[1] Existing models of firms' financial structures and their effect on investment decisions are generally based on a single-firm framework and do not take into account the relationship between project cash flows and the investment decisions of all firms in the industry.[2] In this paper we allow the distribution of investment projects within an industry to adjust and show that this generates new insights and reverses several key results of single-firm agency cost models. The new predictions conform with well documented

---

*Faculty of Commerce and Business Administration, University of British Columbia. We wish to thank Michael Fishman, David Hirshleifer, Darrell Lee, Art Raviv, Eduardo Schwartz, Sheridan Titman, Keith Wong, and the participants of Finance Workshops at Berkeley, British Columbia, Carnegie Mellon, University of Chicago, University of Columbia, University of Guelph, INSEAD, London Business School, Maryland, Minnesota, Stanford, USC, UC Irvine, Vanderbilt University, Wharton, the Federal Reserve Bank at Philadelphia and the 1990 WFA and AFA meetings. We are grateful for financial support from the Canadian Social Science and Humanities Research Council, Operating Grant number 410-91-0794.

[1] The original contributions are Jensen and Meckling (1976) and Myers (1977). See Green (1984, 1986), Haugen and Senbet (1981), and Williams (1987) for an analysis of the risk shifting incentive of debt and perquisites consumption. Titman (1984) examines the effect of financial leverage on contracts with customers. For a survey of this literature up to the early eighties see the monograph by Barnea, Haugen, and Senbet (1985).

[2] One exception are the contributions on industries in which firms behave strategically by Allen (1986), Brander and Lewis (1986), and Maksimovic (1986, 1988).

empirical evidence which cannot be explained by single-firm agency models. In particular, we derive the following main results.

First, we demonstrate that the risk of a project's cash flows is endogenously determined by the investment decisions of all firms in the industry. As the number of firms adopting a given production technology increases, the price of the good sold more closely reflects their production cost. Thus, these firms become better hedged against changes in the cost of production and generate less risky cash flows.[3] Since technologies with higher expected costs of producing output are adopted by fewer firms, this implies that they exhibit riskier cash flows than low-cost technologies.

Second, our analysis shows that, in reasonable settings, financial structures which create incentives to shift risk, and which appear to reduce the value of the firm when viewed in isolation, do not lower value when the distribution of projects in the industry is taken into account. In equilibrium the aggregate amount of debt in an industry adjusts, inducing investment decisions, such that the values of low-risk and high-risk projects are equal. As a result, although an individual firm's financial structure can influence investment decisions, it does not affect firm value.

Third, when we allow for a tax advantage of debt, the resulting capital structure equilibrium is asymmetric. Some firms issue low amounts of debt, foregoing debt-related tax shields but committing to the subsequent choice of the less risky project with higher pre-tax cash flows. Other firms issue large amounts of debt, capturing large tax benefits but creating incentives to subsequently choose the riskier project with lower pre-tax cash flows. In equilibrium, individual firms are indifferent between a low leverage ratio and choice of the project with higher expected pre-tax cash flows or a higher leverage ratio and choice of the project with lower expected pre-tax cash flows. The aggregate number of firms choosing a particular financial structure is endogenous.

Fourth, we demonstrate that the principal determinants of firms' financial structures such as the corporate tax rate not only have a direct effect on firms' decisions but also change the equilibrium distribution of investment projects in the industry. This affects the cash flows generated by alternative projects and thus, indirectly, firms' capital structure choices. For example, an increase in the corporate tax rate leads to an increase in the number of firms choosing the riskier investment since it supports a higher debt level. This changes the risky project's cash flow distribution and, as we demonstrate, tends to lower the project's debt capacity.

Incorporating industry equilibrium conditions into the analysis explains empirical findings which are considered to be inconsistent with static agency theories in a single-firm framework. First, in contrast to existing agency models, our model predicts that even within industries debt ratios will vary widely. This accords well with empirical observations by, for example, Rem-

---

[3] Throughout the remainder of this paper we use the terms investment project and production technology interchangeably.

mers, Stonehill, Wright, and Beekhuesen (1974) and Bradley, Jarrell, and Kim (1984).[4] Second, our model with corporate taxes predicts a negative relationship between profitability as measured by earnings before interest and taxes (EBIT) and leverage. Firms with high debt levels realize higher debt tax shields but choose projects with lower EBIT than firms with low debt levels. This prediction is consistent with numerous empirical studies such as Titman and Wessels (1988) and Long and Malitz (1985).[5] Finally, our analysis suggests that firms with high debt levels choose technologies with risky cash flows. The empirical evidence on this relationship is less determinate. While Castanias (1983) and Baskin (1989) find that firms' debt levels and the riskiness of cash flows are positively related, Titman and Wessels (1988) and Bradley, Jarrell, and Kim (1984) find an insignificant or a negative relationship.

Our results on agency costs of debt can be compared to those of Miller (1977) on taxes. In Miller's model firms are indifferent between alternative capital structures because in equilibrium the corporate tax advantage of debt is offset by its personal tax disadvantage. In our model the corporate tax advantage of debt is offset by the disadvantage of subsequent distortions of equityholders' incentives. Thus, before making their investment decisions individual firms are indifferent between alternative capital structures, but the aggregate amount of debt in the industry is determined in equilibrium.[6]

The analysis in this paper is also related to the contributions on the effect of financial structure on product market decisions by Allen (1986), Brander and Lewis (1986), and Maksimovic (1986, 1990). In this literature it is demonstrated that in imperfectly competitive industries, where firms act strategically in the product market, the choice of financial structures affects firms' optimal output levels. Our paper derives the distribution of financial structures within an industry in which firms behave as price-takers. The model also builds on the literature on input substitution under uncertainty by Blair (1974), Abel (1983), and de Meza (1986). In particular, de Meza (1986) models the effect of cost uncertainty on firms' technology choices in an industry equilibrium. We extend this literature by addressing the conflicts of interest between classes of security holders and the effect of financial structure on the equilibrium.

---

[4] Bradley, Jarrell, and Kim (1984) find that when leverage ratios of non-regulated firms are regressed on SIC codes, the R^2 of these regressions is less than 0.25. The observation that apparently similar firms exhibit a wide variation of capital structures has also been made by Myers (1984, p. 589). Alternative explanations for this variation are provided by Myers (1984) and by Fischer, Heinkel, and Zechner (1989) in a dynamic model of optimal capital structure.

[5] Other corroborating studies include Chudson (1945), Arditti (1967), Carleton and Silberman (1977), Nakamura and Nakamura (1982), Kester (1986), Baskin (1989), and Myers (1990). Kim and Maksimovic (1990) find in a study of the airline industry that firms with high financial leverage use more input per unit of output, and are therefore less efficient, than firms with low debt levels.

[6] A major difference between our framework and that of Miller (1977) is that in Miller's model investment decisions are fixed exogenously whereas in our model firms make their investment choices subsequent to their capital structure decisions.

In Section I we introduce the model and show that financial structure is irrelevant in a competitive equilibrium. The effect of a corporate tax advantage of debt is analyzed in Section II, and we summarize our findings in Section III. The proofs of all propositions are contained in the Appendix.

I. The Model Without Taxes

A. Overview

In this section we analyze the effect of financial structure on subsequent investment and production decisions in the absence of taxes. As in the single-firm case, a firm's financial structure generally affects equityholders' incentives to choose between alternative investment projects. However, when the decisions of other firms in an industry are taken into account, the effect of asset substitution on firm value differs from that in a single-firm framework. This occurs because, as de Meza (1986) demonstrates, it may be optimal for different firms to use projects with different risk profiles. In such cases financial structure affects investment decisions but may not alter firm value.

To see this, assume that there exist two alternative production technologies with the same expected costs but whose cost shocks are imperfectly correlated.[7] Suppose that, initially, all firms choose the same technology. Then competitive behavior implies that the price of the output will be highly correlated with this technology's cost shocks. Now consider a single firm's incentives to adopt the alternative technology. The price of the good sold will not be highly correlated with this deviating firm's cost shocks. In those states in which the deviating firm's production cost is lower than that of its rivals, it can increase its production and hence its profit. By contrast, in states in which the deviating firm has higher production costs, it will find it optimal to decrease production. The option to adjust the production quantity implies that profits are convex in the difference between prices and costs. Since, as discussed above, this difference is more variable for the deviating firm, its *expected* profit is higher. The option feature becomes less valuable if more firms deviate and adopt the alternative technology. In equilibrium the number of firms choosing each technology adjusts until their expected values are equated and an individual firm is indifferent between alternative technologies. This intuition generalizes to cases in which production technologies have different expected costs. The number of firms adopting each project again adjusts until their net present values are the same. However, the riskiness of projects' cash flows differs.

---

[7] Imperfect correlation of production costs may occur for a variety of reasons. Examples are difference in exposure to energy prices of alternative technologies, uncertainties about a new production process, imperfect and segmented input markets, or the need to enter into long-term contracts, if, say, one of the investments employs unionized labor. For a detailed example of the use of different technologies in the same industry see Henderson's (1988) discussion of the manufacture of photolithographic alignment equipment used in the production of microchips.

Now consider how the firm's project choice is affected by its financial structure. The equityholders of firms with risky debt have an incentive to choose the riskier investment. If there are too many firms with risky debt, the value of the riskier investment will fall below that of the less risky project. This creates incentives for some firms to reduce their debt levels and subsequently invest in the less risky project. In equilibrium the distribution of capital structures must adjust until no firm can increase its value by altering its equityholders' incentives to invest so that each individual firm is indifferent between alternative financial structures.[8] In the remainder of this section we introduce the model and formalize the above intuition.

B. The Model

We assume an industry in which a large number, n, of competing firms produce a homogeneous good, each firm perceiving the price as given. There are three dates. At time t_0 firms' original owners choose a financial structure consisting of equity and pure discount debt with face value D. At time t_1 equityholders select an investment project which determines the (possibly stochastic) cost of production at time t_2. The investment decision and the subsequent cost of production are not publicly observable and thus, cannot be contracted upon.[9]

After all uncertainty has been resolved, equityholders decide how much to produce at time t_2.[10] The output is sold and the resulting cash flows are distributed to security holders. To simplify the exposition we make the standard assumptions of risk neutrality and a zero interest rate. We analyze the problem recursively and begin with the production decision at time t_2.

B.1. The Time t_2 Production Decision

Each firm is assumed to be a price taker. There is no uncertainty remaining at time t_2 and equityholders face the following maximization problem:

$$\max_{q} pq - C(q, P), \qquad (1)$$

---

[8] The main result here is that, in equilibrium, risky debt does not lower firm value. However, in the absence of taxes, there are no incentives for firms to issue debt either. We demonstrate in Section II how our analysis extends to the case where taxes provide a motive for firms to issue debt.

[9] For tractability we model uncertainty in a very simple way so that, in the model presented below, firms' cash flows could be used to infer the equityholders' investment decisions. This would allow agents to write forcing contracts where equityholders commit to a specific investment decision. In general, however, the cash flow distributions of alternative investment projects will have overlapping supports and therefore investors cannot perfectly infer the equityholders' preceding investment decisions from the final cash flows. Forcing contracts are therefore ruled out in the following analysis. More complex contracts contingent on final cash flows are discussed in Section III.

[10] We make the assumption that *all* uncertainty is removed before time t_2 only for expositional clarity. It is important, however, that equityholders receive some signal regarding the cost of production before they decide on the quantities produced. This will in general be sufficient to give rise to the option feature discussed above.

where $C(q, P)$ denotes the cost of producing q units of the good if project P is in place. The market price of the good, p, depends on the total quantity of the good produced, Q, and is given by

$$p = a - bQ. \tag{2}$$

B.2. The Time t_1 Investment Decision

The investment choice at time t_1 affects the costs of production at time t_2. We assume that these costs are not perfectly correlated across different technologies. To keep the analysis tractable each firm has access to one of only two investment projects, $P \in \{NS, S\}$, each of which requires an investment of I_P and enables the firm to produce the good.[11] The costs of production are *stochastic* for project S whereas they are *non-stochastic* for project NS.[12] The stochastic costs of project S are assumed to be the only source of uncertainty. There are two equiprobable states of nature and the marginal cost of producing with project S, $MC(S)$, in each state is[13]

$$MC(S) = \begin{cases} k - h + \gamma q \text{ in state } L \\ k + h + \gamma q \text{ in state } H. \end{cases} \tag{3}$$

We refer to states L and H as the "low-cost" and the "high-cost" state, respectively, since the marginal cost of technology S is low in state L and high in state H.[14]

For investment project NS the marginal cost function is state independent:

$$MC(NS) = k + \gamma q. \tag{4}$$

From equations (3) and (4) it follows that the technology with the lower initial investment, I_P, has lower expected total costs of producing any given quantity of the good.[15] We therefore refer to this technology as the efficient

---

[11] Equityholders may also be able to affect the risk of future cash flows by other means. For example, they could make risky side-bets by taking positions in financial markets. As long as the claims against the firm resulting from such side-bets are junior to the bondholders' claim, equityholders have no incentives to take such actions. Thus, if the bond indenture specifies me-first rules, exploitation of bondholders can only occur by substituting assets and altering the production technology.

[12] It is not important for our analysis to assume one technology with non-stochastic production costs. All principal results still obtain as long as the production costs of the alternative technologies are not perfectly correlated.

[13] The intuition underlying the results below extends to cases with many states or many technologies. Analyzing these more general cases increases the notational complexity considerably and does not generate significant new insights.

[14] We have also investigated the case in which there exists one non-stochastic cost technology and several stochastic cost technologies. If the stochastic cost technologies' marginal costs of producing are perfectly correlated and are given by equation (3) with different h parameters, then only two technologies are employed in equilibrium. The non-stochastic cost technology is always chosen. Which one of the stochastic cost technologies is chosen depends on their respective required capital outlays and h parameters.

[15] We have also analyzed the case where the intercept term k of the marginal cost function was allowed to differ across projects. In this case the lower-cost project has a lower k. This alternative specification of differences in the efficiency of the projects generates results analogous to the ones reported below.

technology and to the alternative, that is the technology with the higher initial investment outlay, as the inefficient technology.

Define π_P^θ as the firm's profit in state $\theta \in \{H, L\}$ given that project P is in place. Profits differ across states for two reasons. First, the stochastic production costs have a direct effect on the profits of those firms with project S. Second, the stochastic production costs affect the price of the good sold and thus make the profits of firms with project NS risky as well.

The value of the firm's equity as a function of the investment choice is given by

$$E(D, S) = \tfrac{1}{2}\{\max[\pi_S^L - D, 0] + \max[\pi_S^H - D, 0]\} - I_S \quad (5a)$$

$$E(D, NS) = \tfrac{1}{2}\{\max[\pi_{NS}^L - D, 0] + \max[\pi_{NS}^H - D, 0]\} - I_{NS} \quad (5b)$$

where D is the firm's face value of debt and π_P^θ denotes the firm's profit, derived in the Appendix.

The equityholders choose the investment project that maximizes the value of their securities and thus solve the following problem at time t_1:

$$\max_{P \in \{S, NS\}} E(D, P). \quad (6)$$

Inspection of equations (5a) and (5b) reveals that the choice of investment projects generally depends on the firm's debt level. We now endogenize the capital structure decision at time t_0.

B.3. The Time t_0 Capital Structure Decision

At time t_0 the firms' owners will choose a financial structure that maximizes the total value of the firm, taking into account the investment choice implied by the capital structure decision. Thus the equityholders' maximization problem at time t_0 is given by

$$\max_D V(P(D)) = E(D, P(D)) + B(D, P(D)) \quad (7)$$

where $V(P(D))$, $E(D, P(D))$ and $B(D, P(D))$ denote the values of the firm and its equity and debt securities, respectively, which depend on the face value of debt and the firm's project choice. The latter is itself a function of the firm's debt level.

C. Financial Structure and Industry Equilibrium

In an industry equilibrium the number of firms choosing each project adjusts until the expected profits from the two projects are equal.[16] In this section we derive the distribution of projects and characterize the equilibrium financial structures which support it. More specifically, we proceed as follows. (i) We first derive the equilibrium number of firms choosing projects S and NS. (ii) For this equilibrium distribution of projects we characterize the

---
[16] If not, some firms can increase their values by changing their capital structures and thereby altering the equityholders' investment decisions.

riskiness of cash flows generated by each project. (iii) We then derive equityholders' project choice as a function of the firm's debt level; and, finally, (iv) we characterize the equilibrium distributions of firms' debt levels that support investment decisions derived in (i).

C.1. The Equilibrium Distribution of Project Choices

As discussed above, if production costs are not perfectly correlated, a project can be employed in equilibrium even if it requires a higher initial investment. As long as there is one state in which the project has lower production costs than the alternative project, it may be profitable for some firms to adopt it. In equilibrium, the number of firms choosing each project will adjust such that the higher investment outlay of the project will just be offset by the higher profits in the state(s) in which its production costs are lower. The equilibrium number of firms choosing projects S and NS is derived in Proposition 1 by finding the number of firms which equates the total values of the two projects.[17] Define $I^* \equiv I_S - I_{NS}$.

Proposition 1: *If the difference between the required investments is sufficiently small then $\hat{f}$ firms choose project S and the remaining $n - \hat{f}$ firms choose project NS where*

$$\hat{f} = \frac{(h^2 - 2\gamma I^*)(bn + \gamma)}{2bh^2}.$$

If $I^* > \dfrac{h^2}{2\gamma}$, then all firms choose project NS and if $I^* < \dfrac{h^2}{2\gamma}\dfrac{\gamma - nb}{\gamma + nb}$, then all firms choose project S.

For the distribution of projects derived in Proposition 1 the projects' expected cash flows, net of the initial investment, are equal.[18] In general, however, the riskiness of these cash flows differs across technologies and, therefore, equityholders of levered firms are not indifferent between projects. Thus, in order to analyze equityholders' investment decisions, we first need to determine the riskiness of the cash flows generated by the alternative investments.[19]

C.2. The Riskiness of Project Cash Flows

In contrast to the analysis in a single-firm context, the riskiness of a project is endogenous and depends on the equilibrium number of firms choosing each investment project. To understand this result intuitively, suppose that a given firm faces an unexpectedly high cost of production. If most other firms in the industry have chosen the same production technology

---

[17] de Meza (1986) derives a similar result for the case in which the initial investment is zero.

[18] In general the distribution of projects derived in Proposition 1 does not maximize consumer surplus. It can be shown that consumer surplus is maximized if all n firms choose technology S. For a discussion of consumers' gains and price uncertainty see Waugh (1944).

[19] Throughout the remainder of the paper we focus on the case in which each technology is chosen by at least one firm.

and therefore face the same shock in production costs, then the higher production costs will be reflected in a higher price of the goods sold. This reduces the sensitivity of the firm's profits to stochastic changes in production costs. By contrast, if the firm is the only firm or one of few firms in the industry affected by this increase in costs, prices will not reflect the higher production costs and the firm's profits will fall significantly. The same intuition holds for the alternative case where a firm's cost of producing a given quantity of the good is lower than that of its competitors. If this firm is one of few firms realizing this cost advantage, then its profits will be large. If the firm shares this cost advantage with a large number of other firms, then the positive effect on profits will be smaller. Thus, the relative magnitudes of projects' cash flows depend on the total number of firms choosing each project. It follows from Proposition 1 that, as a project becomes relatively less cost efficient due to an increase in the initial investment, I_P, it is chosen by fewer firms. Together with the above discussion this implies that the maximum cash flow from the inefficient project exceeds the maximum cash flow from the efficient project and the minimum cash flow from the inefficient project is lower than the minimum cash flow from the efficient project. This result is stated formally for $I^* > 0$ in Lemma 1.

Lemma 1: *In equilibrium* $\pi_S^L > \pi_{NS}^H > \pi_{NS}^L > \pi_S^H$.

The ranking of profits in Lemma 1 implies a direct relationship between the risk of net cash flows, defined as profits net of initial investment, and efficiency. Less cost-efficient projects exhibit riskier net cash flows. By contrast, low-cost projects are chosen by more firms and therefore generate less risky net cash flows. This is so even if the unit cost of production associated with this project is more variable than that of the alternative project. The next proposition formalizes this result.

Proposition 2: *In equilibrium the net cash flows of the inefficient project are riskier in the sense of Rothschild and Stiglitz (1970) than the net cash flows of the efficient project.*

We can now analyze how an individual firm's financial structure affects the equityholders' investment incentives, taking as given the equilibrium distribution of projects derived in Proposition 1. Proposition 2 implies that an asset substitution problem exists when projects are not equally cost efficient, i.e., if $I_S \neq I_{NS}$, and we focus on this case. To simplify the analysis we assume throughout the remainder of the paper that $I_S > I_{NS} = 0$, i.e., that technology S is less efficient.[20]

---

[20] For the general case where $I_{NS} > 0$, the debt levels of firms choosing project NS have to satisfy an additional constraint: the expected payments to equityholders must exceed the cost of the project, I_{NS}. Assuming $I_{NS} = 0$ allows us to drop this constraint. In a previous version of the paper we have also derived the results for the case where $I^* < 0$. As shown in Proposition 2, technology NS is then riskier. In that case all the following results still obtain with technologies S and NS interchanged.

C.3. Project Choice as a Function of the Debt Level

Since in equilibrium the expected profits from each investment project are equal, equityholders only choose the less risky project if the debt claims are riskless under both investment choices. If debt is risky, equityholders strictly prefer the riskier project. Thus, there exists an upper bound on the debt level that is consistent with the subsequent choice of the low-risk investment project. The relationship between a firm's debt level and the equityholders' incentives to choose a particular project is derived in the following proposition. Define $D^{max} = \pi_S^L - 2I_S$.

Proposition 3: Equityholders of firms with riskless debt, i.e., $D \le \pi_S^H$, are indifferent between projects S and NS. Equityholders of firms with face values of debt $\pi_S^H < D \le D^{max}$ strictly prefer project S and their debt is risky. Equityholders of firms with debt face values greater than D^{max} do not invest.

The effect of a firm's financial structure on the equityholders' investment incentives is illustrated in Figure 1. The total value of the firm as a function of the face value of debt is given by the horizontal line $V(D, S) = V(D, NS)$.

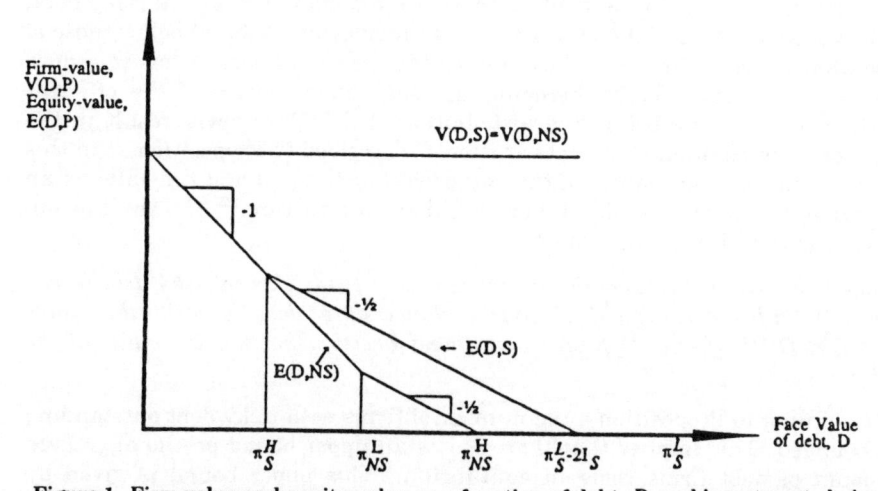

Figure 1. Firm value and equity value as a function of debt, D, and investment choice, $P \in \{S, NS\}$ for the case without taxes and $I_S > I_{NS} = 0$. I_S, I_{NS} denote the initial capital outlays for projects S and NS, respectively; D denotes the face value of debt; $V(D, P)$, $E(D, P)$ are, respectively, the total value of the firm and the value of equity, as a function of its debt level, D, and its project choice, P; π_P^θ denotes project P's profit in state θ, where $\theta \in \{H, L\}$ and the two states are equally likely. The ordering of the cash flows is derived in Lemma 1 and in the proof of Proposition 2. As the face value of debt increases, the value of the equity decreases with a slope of -1 if the debt is riskless, while it decreases with a slope of $-\frac{1}{2}$ if the debt is risky. For project S, debt is risky if D exceeds π_S^H. For project NS debt is risky if D exceeds π_{NS}^L. Thus, for $D > \pi_S^H$, the equity value for project S exceeds the corresponding equity value for project NS. Equityholders of firms with $D > \pi_S^H$ therefore prefer project S. In equilibrium, the total value of firms adopting project S or NS is equal.

The equity value is a decreasing function of the debt level. For debt levels below π_S^H, debt is riskless irrespective of the investment choice and thus the equity values are the same for both investment projects. For debt levels between π_S^H and π_{NS}^L debt is still riskless for project NS but already risky for project S. Thus, over this range, $E(D, S)$ decreases less rapidly than $E(D, NS)$. Finally, for debt levels greater than π_{NS}^L, debt is risky for both investment projects and the slopes of $E(D, S)$ and $E(D, NS)$ are the same. For debt levels greater than or equal to π_{NS}^H the equity only has value if project S is chosen. If the debt level exceeds $\pi_S^L - 2I_S$, equityholders do not have an incentive to invest. Thus, if the face value of debt is less than or equal to π_S^H, equityholders are indifferent between projects S and NS. For debt face values greater than π_S^H, equityholders find it in their own best interest to choose project S.[21]

C.4. The Equilibrium Distribution of Financial Structures

We next analyze the equilibrium distributions of debt levels in the industry such that at time t_0 no firm can increase value by altering its financial structure and thereby affecting equityholders' subsequent investment incentives. As we have shown in Proposition 3, equityholders of those firms with risky debt outstanding have an incentive to subsequently choose the less efficient and riskier investment. If there are too many firms with risky debt, the expected profits of the less efficient technology are reduced below those of the alternative technology. This creates incentives for some firms to reduce their debt levels, thereby inducing the subsequent choice of the efficient technology. In equilibrium the distribution of debt levels will result in the first best distribution of projects at time t_1 described in Proposition 1. In this case the net present values of the two projects are equal and the value of an individual firm does not depend on its financial structure.[22] The equilibrium is characterized in Proposition 4.

Proposition 4: *In equilibrium not more than $\hat{f}$ firms choose risky debt levels, i.e., $D > \pi_S^H$. An individual firm's choice of a debt level in the range $0 \leq D \leq D^{\max}$ affects its future investment decision but not the value of the firm.*

According to Proposition 4 the number of firms with risky debt outstanding is bounded. This implies that there exists an upper bound on the aggregate amount of debt firms issue in equilibrium. This upper bound is given by $\hat{f} D^{\max} + (n - \hat{f})\pi_S^H$.

In this section we have demonstrated that first best investment decisions can be achieved even if some firms issue risky debt, creating incentives for equityholders to choose the riskier project. The specific distribution of pro-

---

[21] In the model we do not formally allow equityholders to invest in more than one production technology. However, even if we allow firms to do this, it can be shown that it is not sequentially rational for equityholders of firms with risky debt to employ both technologies simultaneously.

[22] As stated in Proposition 4 below, debt levels are irrelevant for $0 \leq D \leq D^{\max}$. If $D > D^{\max}$ equityholders do not invest at time t_1 and the firm value is zero.

jects and financial structures depends on the assumed model structure, i.e., linear demand and marginal cost curves and that only the constant in the marginal cost function is affected by the state. However, the result, that firms are indifferent between alternative financial structures as long as the efficiencies of the technologies only differ within a range, will generally be robust with respect to these assumptions. In the next section we extend the analysis and introduce a motive for firms to issue debt by allowing for a corporate tax advantage of debt.

II. The Model with Corporate Taxes

In Section I the only potential effect of the capital structure decision on firm value was by altering investment incentives. In this section we generalize the analysis and introduce corporate taxes. With taxes the value of the firm is affected by the amount of debt-related tax shields and, as a result, the firm's capital structure is no longer completely irrelevant. We show, however, that firms are indifferent between (i) restricting the amount of debt to a critical level and subsequently investing in a project that maximizes before-tax profits and (ii) choosing a high debt level and investing in a less efficient project with lower before-tax profits. In equilibrium the lower before-tax profit from the "inferior" investment is exactly offset by the interest tax deduction. Thus, although the complete irrelevance result derived above no longer holds with taxes, firms are still indifferent between distinct alternative financial structures.

To simplify the exposition, we do not consider personal taxes and assume that total payments to debtholders are deductible from the corporate tax base.[23] Let τ denote the corporate tax rate. Then the quantity produced at time t_2 is obtained by

$$\max_q [pq - C(q, P)](1 - \tau).$$

Thus, the optimal output produced at time t_2 is unaffected by the proportional corporate tax. The equity values at time t_1 are now given by

$$E(D, S) = (1 - \tau)\{^1\!/_2[\max[\pi_S^L - D, 0] + \max[\pi_S^H - D, 0]] - I_S\} \quad (10a)$$

$$E(D, NS) = (1 - \tau)\{^1\!/_2[\max[\pi_{NS}^L - D, 0] + \max[\pi_{NS}^H - D, 0]]\} \quad (10b)$$

where π_P^θ denotes the profits before corporate tax and before debt payments and where it is assumed that the initial investment outlay can be depreciated

---

[23] In a more realistic framework, the tax benefit of debt would only be realized on the interest portion of the debt payments. As shown by Talmor, Haugen, and Barnea (1985) and Zechner and Swoboda (1986), the distinction between interest and principal becomes important when tax shields can be lost due to depreciation and/or other non-cash charges. In the context of our model, making only interest payments tax deductible would not alter the following results.

immediately for tax purposes so that the after-tax investment outlay is given by $(1 - \tau)I_S$.[24]

Equilibrium at time t_0 requires that no firm can increase its value by changing its capital structure. In the absence of a corporate tax advantage of debt, the differential cash flows generated by alternative investment projects must compensate investors for the difference in the initial capital outlay. With corporate taxes investors also take into account differences in the tax shields generated by alternative investments. These differences affect firms' after-tax profits and therefore alter the equilibrium distribution of projects in an industry. The following proposition derives the equilibrium number of firms choosing the risky and the riskless investment projects.[25]

Proposition 5: *The number of firms choosing investment project S, $\hat{f}^\tau$, is given by*

$$\hat{f}^\tau = \hat{f} + \frac{\gamma E[\Delta TS](bn + \gamma)}{bh^2(1 - \tau)},$$

where $\hat{f}$ denotes the number of firms choosing project S in the absence of taxes and ΔTS is the difference in the corporate tax shields generated by the two alternative investment projects:

$$E[\Delta TS] = E[TS(D_S)] - E[TS(D_{NS})],$$
$$E[TS(D_S)] = \tfrac{1}{2}\tau\{\min[\pi_S^L, D_S] + \min[\pi_S^H, D_S]\} \text{ and}$$
$$E[TS(D_{NS})] = \tfrac{1}{2}\tau\{\min[\pi_{NS}^L, D_{NS}] + \min[\pi_{NS}^H, D_{NS}]\}.$$

It is apparent from Proposition 5 that the number of firms choosing a particular technology can be higher or lower than in the no-tax case, depending on the sign of the difference in the expected tax shields. In particular, if the less efficient project realizes larger tax shields, the number of firms adopting it will be greater than that without taxes.

[24] There are several ways of modeling the tax shields arising due to the initial investment outlay. Equations (10a) and (10b) reflect our assumption that the investment, I_P, can be depreciated and leads to an immediate tax refund to equityholders of τI_P. Alternatively, one could assume that the tax benefit from deducting the investment is realized at time t_2. In this case, at time t_2, the tax authorities reduce the firm's tax liabilities by τI_P. (This might lead to negative tax payments, especially for firms with technology S in state h. "Negative tax payments" can occur in a world in which losses can be carried back and/or tax shields can be sold to other corporations.) Then equityholders of firms choosing technology S pay the cost of the investment, but only receive the benefits of its tax deductibility in the no-default states, i.e., in state L. The corresponding equity value is then given by $E(D, S) = \tfrac{1}{2}\{\pi_S^L - D - \tau(\pi_S^L - D - I_S)\} + \tfrac{1}{2} \times 0$. Thus, the fact that the tax deductibility of I_S does not benefit the equityholders in state H increases the expected after-tax investment cost of technology S. While this would affect the specific numbers of firms choosing each project, modeling this effect does not qualitatively alter any of our results in Propositions 5 and 6.

[25] As in the previous section we focus on interior equilibria where $0 < \hat{f}^\tau < n$.

Next we can again relate a firm's financial structure to its investment choice. In the presence of a tax advantage of debt and holding investment decisions constant, the initial owners of a firm prefer to be fully debt financed. However, high debt levels are inconsistent with the subsequent choice of the less risky project. As a result, we obtain an asymmetric equilibrium in which some firms are highly levered and the equityholders of these firms choose the risky investment project. Equityholders of other firms will choose lower debt levels, thereby committing to the less risky project. The following proposition derives this result formally.

Proposition 6: *Firms which choose the less efficient technology issue debt with a higher face value than firms choosing the efficient technology. Specifically, $D_S = \pi_S^L - 2I_S$, $D_{NS} = \pi_{NS}^L + \pi_{NS}^H - \pi_S^L + 2I_S$ and $D_S > D_{NS}$.*

The optimal debt levels derived in Proposition 6 have the following properties. Firms choosing project S issue risky debt.[26] For these firms the optimal face value of debt is $D_S = \pi_S^L - 2I_S$, the highest debt level consistent with subsequent investment. If the face value of debt exceeds this value, then equityholders would "underinvest" and neither project would be chosen. The debt of firms with face values D_{NS} is riskless if project NS is chosen but risky if project S is adopted.[27] At the debt level D_{NS} defined in Proposition 6, equityholders are exactly indifferent between exploiting debtholders by choosing technology S and choosing the more efficient technology NS. For any debt level below D_{NS}, firms would unnecessarily forego debt tax shields.

Two Corollaries follow from Proposition 6.

Corollary 1: *Firms choosing the inefficient technology issue debt with a higher market value.*

Corollary 2: *Firms choosing the inefficient technology realize higher expected tax shields than firms choosing the efficient technology: $E[TS(D_S)] > E[TS(D_{NS})]$.*

Thus, firms that choose the risky project have higher amounts of debt outstanding and also realize higher expected tax shields. This result together with the expression for $\hat{f}^\tau$ in Proposition 5 implies that taxes increase the number of firms that choose the inefficient technology. In equilibrium the higher value of debt tax shields is offset by the fact that the profits before interest and taxes of the inefficient technology are lower.

A. Capital Structure Effects of Changing Corporate Tax Rates

The distributions of investment projects and firms' equilibrium financial structures depend on exogenous parameters such as the corporate tax rate, τ, and the uncertainty of the production cost captured by the parameter, h. In

---

[26] It is shown in Lemma 2 in the Appendix that $\pi_S^L - 2I_S > \pi_{NS}^H$. Since the profit definitions imply that $\pi_{NS}^H > \pi_S^H$, debt with a face value of $D_S = \pi_S^L - 2I_S$ is risky.

[27] This is true since, as shown in Lemma 2 in the Appendix, $\pi_{NS}^L - \pi_S^L + 2I_S < 0$, implying that $D_{NS} = \pi_{NS}^L + \pi_{NS}^H - \pi_S^L + 2I_S < \pi_{NS}^L$, i.e., debt with this face value is riskless if project NS is chosen.

an industry equilibrium, changing each one of these parameters has two effects. First, there is a direct effect on firms' optimal capital structures, holding the investment decisions of other firms constant. Second, a change in a parameter affects the equilibrium distribution of projects and thereby their risk characteristics. This second effect on optimal capital structure cannot be captured by models focusing on single firm. In this section we examine the interaction of both effects.

As an example consider the effect of an increase in the corporate tax rate on firms' financial structures. Holding the distribution of before-tax cash flows of projects S and NS constant, this change in the corporate tax rate increases the difference in the value of the tax shields generated by the two projects. Each individual firm then has an incentive to raise the face value of debt to $D = D_S$, and choose project S. This corresponds to the first effect discussed above. However, as an increasing number of firms do this, they alter the distribution of projects in the industry and thereby the projects' cash flows. In the new equilibrium, more firms choose technology S, but individual firms are again indifferent between the two alternative projects. Since in the new equilibrium more firms choose project S, the cash flows generated by this production technology are less risky, i.e., its highest profit, π_S^L, decreases and its lowest profit increases. Since the face value of debt issued by firms choosing technology S, $D_S = D^{\max}$, depends on the highest profit, and is equal to $\pi_S^L - 2I_S$, it decreases with the corporate tax rate. The opposite is true for the debt level of firms which plan to select technology NS, D_{NS}. The intuition for this result relies on the fact that the less risky project S's cash flows are, the smaller are the gains to equityholders from shifting to this project. This raises the debt level that can be chosen while still committing to the low risk project. This implies a positive relationship between corporate taxes and the optimal debt level D_{NS}. Thus, if the distribution of firms' investment decisions is endogenous, then there is no simple relationship between corporate taxes and optimal debt levels. While some firms will increase their debt levels as a response to higher tax rates, other firms lower the face value of debt issued. These results are formally stated in Proposition 7.

Proposition 7:

(a) The number of firms adopting the inefficient project increases with the corporate tax rate: $d\hat{f}^\tau/d\tau > 0$.

(b) The optimal debt face value of firms choosing the inefficient project decreases with the corporate tax rate and the optimal debt face value of firms choosing the efficient project increases with the corporate tax rate: $dD_S/d\tau < 0$ and $dD_{NS}/d\tau > 0$.

III. Conclusions

This paper shows that the analysis of important dimensions of the agency problems associated with debt requires a multi-firm framework. In an industry equilibrium the riskiness of a project's cash flows is determined endogenously and depends on the investment decisions of all firms. In equilibrium those investment projects with higher expected costs of producing output are chosen by fewer firms and generate riskier cash flows. Although debt provides incentives for asset substitution, we provide a reasonable setting where individual firms are indifferent between alternative financial structures as long as the difference in efficiency of the alternative technologies does not exceed a given bound. In equilibrium the number of firms with high leverage ratios adjusts so that initial firm owners are indifferent between the choice of a high debt level and subsequent investment in the risky project and a low debt level and subsequent investment in the low risk project. We show that, in the absence of a tax advantage of debt, capital structure affects investment decisions but not the value of the firm. The latter result provides an analog to Miller's (1977) tax equilibrium for the case of agency costs.

If we allow for a tax advantage of debt, individual firms are no longer indifferent between all alternative financial structures. In the absence of agency costs, firms would now wish to become fully debt financed. However, large amounts of debt create incentives to subsequently invest in the riskier project. As a result, some firms find it optimal to limit their debt issues and thus commit to invest in the less risky project. In equilibrium the cash flow from the low risk project compensates firms for the foregone tax shields. Individual firms are indifferent between issuing the maximum amount of debt consistent with the subsequent choice of the less risky project and becoming highly levered and choosing the riskier project.

The model of financial structure in this paper provides several empirical predictions. First, our model suggests that, even when the financial structure affects the equityholders' incentives to invest, firms in the same industry are indifferent between alternative financial structures. This is consistent with empirical findings indicating that apparently similar firms in the same industry exhibit diverse financial structures.

Second, as discussed above, the riskiness of an investment project depends on the decisions of all firms in the industry. A firm adopting a technology chosen by most of its competitors is partly hedged against shocks in its production costs since they will be reflected in the price of the goods sold. This natural hedge is not available for deviant firms. Thus, the cash flows of firms adopting a technology which is chosen by a minority of firms should be more volatile.

Third, we demonstrate that changes in the corporate tax rate can have a surprising effect on firms' optimal debt level because the value of tax shields influences the equilibrium distribution of projects in the industry. Increasing the corporate tax rate makes the project with the higher debt capacity more attractive and, consequently, it is chosen by more firms. This tends to lower the highest cash flows generated by this project and thus decreases the debt capacity of firms choosing this project. Thus, firms that choose the risky project decrease their debt levels as the corporate tax rate increases. By contrast we show that firms choosing the low risk project are able to increase their debt level as a response to an increase in the tax rate.

Fourth, the model suggests a link between technology choice and financial structure. Within an industry, firms that adopt the technology chosen by the majority of firms generate higher expected earnings before interest and taxes and are less levered than firms that deviate and adopt a technology which is only chosen by few firms.

The analysis of this paper has focused on the choice between alternative production technologies. Our analysis of an industry equilibrium can also be extended to explore the effect of financial structure on other operating decisions. For example, consider an industry in which the relative demand for high quality and low quality product lines is uncertain. Then there may exist an equilibrium in which some firms produce high quality lines and others produce low quality lines. Firms' financial structures may affect equityholders' decision whether to produce high or low quality goods, but for the individual firm the choice between high leverage and low leverage will be a matter of indifference.

Appendix

Derivation of Firms' Profits: Firms maximize profits in each state by producing until marginal cost is equal to the price of the good. The profits are then equal to the difference between revenues and costs at that quantity. For example, in state L a firm with technology S will produce the quantity q_S^L such that $p_L = k - h + \gamma q_S^L$, where p_L denotes the price of the good in state L. The firm's profit in this state is then given by

$$\pi_S^L = p_L q_S^L - \int_0^{q_S^L} MC(S, L) \, dq.$$

Substituting for q_S^L and $MC(S, L)$ and integrating yields $\pi_S^L = (p_L - k + h)^2/2\gamma$. Similarly, we obtain

$$\pi_S^H = \frac{(p_H - k - h)^2}{2\gamma}; \quad \pi_{NS}^L = \frac{(p_L - k)^2}{2\gamma}; \quad \pi_{NS}^H = \frac{(p_H - k)^2}{2\gamma},$$

where p_H denotes the price of the good in state H.

Proof of Proposition 1: The total firm values for projects S and NS are given by

$$V(S) = \tfrac{1}{2}[\pi_S^L + \pi_S^H] - I_S \tag{A1}$$

and

$$V(NS) = \tfrac{1}{2}[\pi_{NS}^L + \pi_{NS}^H] - I_{NS}. \tag{A2}$$

In equilibrium the values of the two projects must be equal. Equating expressions (A1) and (A2) yields

$$h[p_L - p_H] + h^2 = 2\gamma I^*$$

or
$$p_L - p_H = 2\gamma I^*/h - h, \tag{A3}$$

where $I^* = I_S - I_{NS}$. Let the equilibrium number of firms choosing investment project S be $\hat{f}$. The prices in each state can be determined by equating the aggregate output in each state with the quantity demanded, yielding

$$p_L = \frac{a\gamma + b(nk - h\hat{f})}{bn + \gamma} \tag{A4}$$

$$p_H = \frac{a\gamma + b(nk + h\hat{f})}{bn + \gamma}. \tag{A5}$$

Subtracting the expression for p_H from the expression for p_L, we obtain

$$p_L - p_H = \frac{-2bh\hat{f}}{bn + \gamma}. \tag{A6}$$

Equating expressions (A3) and (A6), we solve for $\hat{f}$

$$\hat{f} = \frac{(h^2 - 2\gamma I^*)(bn + \gamma)}{2bh^2}. \tag{A7}$$

For the above solution to be feasible we need $0 < \hat{f} < n$. These inequalities lead to the following condition

$$\frac{h^2}{2\gamma} > I^* > \frac{h^2}{2\gamma} \frac{\gamma - nb}{\gamma + nb}.$$

If $I^* > \dfrac{h^2}{2\gamma}$ then all firms choose project NS and if $I^* < \dfrac{h^2}{2\gamma} \dfrac{\gamma - nb}{\gamma + nb}$ then all firms choose project S.

Proof of Lemma 1: Assume that $I^* > 0$. Since it follows directly from the profit definitions that $\pi_{NS}^H > \pi_{NS}^L$, we only need to show that $\pi_{NS}^L > \pi_S^H$ and $\pi_S^L > \pi_{NS}^H$. Substituting for π_{NS}^L and π_S^H, the first inequality can be written as

$$\frac{(p_L - k)^2}{2\gamma} > \frac{(p_H - k - h)^2}{2\gamma}.$$

For this to hold requires $p_L - p_H > -h$. Substituting for p_H and p_L from (A4) and (A5) we obtain

$$\hat{f} < \frac{bn + \gamma}{2b}.$$

Substituting for $\hat{f}$ from (A7) we obtain the condition that

$$\hat{f} = \frac{(h^2 - 2\gamma I^*)(bn + \gamma)}{2bh^2} < \frac{bn + \gamma}{2b},$$

which holds for $I^* > 0$. The proof of the second inequality, $\pi_S^L > \pi_{NS}^H$, is analogous.

Proof of Proposition 2: We prove this proposition for $I^* > 0$. We demonstrate that, net of differential capital investments, the cash flows of project S are a mean preserving spread of cash flows of project NS. Define $\bar{\pi}_P^\theta$ as the net cash flows of project P in state θ, $\bar{\pi}_P^\theta \equiv \pi_P^\theta - I_P$. Recall that in equilibrium expected net cash flows are equal:

$$\tfrac{1}{2}[\bar{\pi}_S^H + \bar{\pi}_S^L] = \tfrac{1}{2}[\bar{\pi}_{NS}^H + \bar{\pi}_{NS}^L]. \tag{A8}$$

We have shown above that $\pi_S^H < \pi_{NS}^L$ which, for $I_S > I_{NS}$, implies $\bar{\pi}_S^H < \bar{\pi}_{NS}^L$. Thus, the equilibrium condition (A8) requires that $\bar{\pi}_S^L > \bar{\pi}_{NS}^H$ and, as a result, the net cash flows of the inefficient project S are a mean preserving spread of the net cash flows of project NS and are therefore riskier in a Rothschild and Stiglitz sense. The proof for $I^* < 0$ is analogous.

The following lemma will be used in the proof of Proposition 3.

Lemma 2: Assume that $I_S > I_{NS} = 0$. Then the following inequality holds in equilibrium: $\pi_S^L - \pi_{NS}^H > 2I_S$.

Proof: For $I_S > I_{NS} = 0$ it follows from Lemma 1 that $\pi_S^H < \pi_{NS}^L$. Then, for equation (A8) to hold, this requires that $\pi_S^L > \pi_{NS}^H + 2I_S$.

Proof of Proposition 3: Proposition 2 and Lemma 2 imply that $\pi_S^H < \pi_{NS}^L < \pi_{NS}^H < \pi_S^L - 2I_S$. Then, if $D \leq \pi_S^H$ debt is riskless. Since in equilibrium $V(D, S) = V(D, NS)$, equityholders of firms with riskless debt are indifferent between projects S and NS. For $\pi_S^H < D \leq D^{\max}$, debt is risky if project S is chosen. For this case Proposition 2 implies that $E(D, S) > E(D, NS)$. Thus, for these debt levels equityholders prefer the risky investment project S. For $D > D^{\max}$, investing in technology S is a negative net present value project for the equityholders and, thus, for these debt levels they do not invest.

Proof of Proposition 4: Assume that f firms choose debt levels $D \geq \pi_S^H$ and that $f \leq \hat{f}$. We start by showing that this distribution of financial structures is an equilibrium. Conjecture the following investment decisions. The f firms with risky debt (i.e., $D \geq \pi_S^H$) outstanding all choose project S. $n - \hat{f}$ firms with riskless debt (i.e., $D < \pi_S^H$) choose project NS and $\hat{f} - f$ firms with riskless debt choose project S. The total number of firms choosing project S is therefore equal to $\hat{f}$ which implies that $V(D, S) = V(D, NS)$. For this distribution of projects, it follows from Proposition 3 that the above conjectured investment decisions are sequentially rational for equityholders. There is no incentive for any firm to change its capital structure or investment decision.

Next we prove that if more than $\hat{f}$ firms choose debt levels $D \geq \pi_S^H$, there does not exist an equilibrium. It follows from Proposition 1 that the values of the two projects are equal if and only if $\hat{f}$ firms adopt technology S and $n - \hat{f}$ firms adopt technology NS. Proposition 3 implies that, with this distribution of projects, equityholders of firms with $D > \pi_S^H$ have an incentive to select project S. If more than $\hat{f}$ firms have such high debt levels, then this contradicts the equilibrium condition in Proposition 1 that only $\hat{f}$ firms choose project S. Thus, if more than $\hat{f}$ firms choose debt levels $D \geq \pi_S^H$, the values of the two projects cannot be equal and some firms lower their debt levels to induce a change in the subsequent investment decision.

We have now demonstrated that not more than $\hat{f}$ firms issue risky debt and that in equilibrium $\hat{f}$ firms choose project S and $n - \hat{f}$ firms choose project NS. In this case the values of the two projects are equal but the investment decision of an individual firm depends on its debt level according to Proposition 3.

Proof of Proposition 5: In equilibrium $V(D_S, S) = V(D_{NS}, NS)$:

$$\tfrac{1}{2}[\pi_S^H + \pi_S^L - 2I_S](1 - \tau) + E[TS(D_S)]$$
$$= \tfrac{1}{2}[\pi_{NS}^H + \pi_{NS}^L](1 - \tau) + E[TS(D_{NS})]. \tag{A9}$$

The first term on the left-hand side of equation (A9) denotes the after-tax net-present value of an all-equity financed firm choosing project S. The second term reflects the corporate tax savings due to issuing debt with a face value of D_S. A similar interpretation can be given to the right-hand side of equation (A9) for firms choosing project NS.

Substituting the definitions of firms' pre-tax profits and simplifying yields

$$p_L - p_H = \frac{2\gamma(I_S(1 - \tau) - E[\Delta TS])}{h(1 - \tau)} - h \tag{A10}$$

where ΔTS is defined in the statement of the Proposition. Since taxes do not affect the production decision, equation (A6) also holds with taxes. Equating the expressions for $p_L - p_H$ from equations (A6) and (A10) yields

$$\hat{f}^\tau = \frac{(h^2(1 - \tau) + 2\gamma(E[\Delta TS] - I_S(1 - \tau)))(bn + \gamma)}{2bh^2(1 - \tau)}. \tag{A11}$$

Substituting the expression for $\hat{f}$ from Proposition 1 and noting that $I_{NS} = 0$ yields the result.

The following Lemma will be used in the proof of Proposition 6.

Lemma 3: In equilibrium the following condition holds: $\pi_S^L - \pi_{NS}^H > 2I_S$.

Proof: There are two cases to consider depending on whether $E[\Delta TS]$ is greater or less than zero.

Assume first that $E[\Delta TS] < 0$. Then $(E[\Delta TS] - I_S(1 - \tau)) < 0$ which implies from (A10) that $p_L - p_H > -h$. Using the definitions of firm profits, it then follows that $\pi_S^H < \pi_{NS}^L$. Inspection of equilibrium condition (A9) reveals that the inequalities $\pi_S^H < \pi_{NS}^L$ and $E[\Delta TS] < 0$ imply that $\pi_S^L - \pi_{NS}^H - 2I_S > 0$.

Second, assume that $E[\Delta TS] > 0$. To construct a contradiction, assume that $\pi_S^L - \pi_{NS}^H - 2I_S < 0$. Then firms adopting the NS project can be fully debt financed without creating an incentive to switch to project S, so that now $D_{NS} = \pi_{NS}^H$ and $D_S = \pi_S^L - 2I_S$. Then

$$E[\Delta TS] = \tfrac{1}{2}\tau[(\pi_S^H + \pi_S^L - 2I_S) - (\pi_{NS}^L + \pi_{NS}^H)]. \qquad (A12)$$

However, using the condition $V(D_S, S) - V(D_{NS}, NS)$, equation (A12) implies that $E[\Delta TS] < 0$, contradicting the initial assumption that $E[\Delta TS] > 0$. Thus $\pi_S^L - \pi_{NS}^H - 2I_S > 0$.

Proof of Proposition 6: We first conjecture that $\hat{f}^\tau$ firms choose project S and $n - \hat{f}^\tau$ firms choose project NS. Then we verify this conjecture and show that for this distribution of projects, $\hat{f}^\tau$ firms issue debt with face value $D = D_S$ and subsequently choose project S and $n - \hat{f}^\tau$ firms issue debt with face value $D = D_{NS}$ and subsequently choose project NS.

We first prove that $D_S = \pi_S^L - 2I_S$. This is the highest feasible debt level for firms that choose project S.[28] Note that, holding the project choice constant, the tax advantage of debt implies that $dV(D, P)/dD > 0$. Thus, if it is incentive compatible, i.e., if equityholders of firms with debt levels $D = \pi_S^L - 2I_S$ invest in project S, it is optimal at time t_0 to set $D_S = \pi_S^L - 2I_S$. Since it has been shown in Lemma 3 that the highest profit of technology NS, π_{NS}^H is less than $\pi_S^L - 2I_S$, equityholders of firms with debt levels $D_S = \pi_S^L - 2I_S$ have no incentive to switch to technology NS. Thus it is optimal for $\hat{f}^\tau$ firms to set $D_S = \pi_S^L - 2I_S$ and subsequently select project S.

Next we prove that $D_{NS} = \pi_{NS}^L + \pi_{NS}^H - \pi_S^L + 2I_S$. We first conjecture that

$$\pi_{NS}^L > D_{NS} > \pi_S^H. \qquad (A13)$$

Then incentive compatibility requires that $E(D_{NS}, NS) \geq E(D_{NS}, S)$,

$$\frac{1-\tau}{2}(\pi_{NS}^L + \pi_{NS}^H) - D_{NS}(1 - \tau) \geq \frac{1-\tau}{2}(\pi_S^L - D_{NS}) - I_S(1 - \tau)$$

or that

$$D_{NS} \leq \pi_{NS}^L + \pi_{NS}^H - \pi_S^L + 2I_S.$$

Since, for a given investment choice, $dV/dD > 0$, the above condition must hold as an equality at the optimal debt level. Thus the result that $D_{NS} = \pi_{NS}^L + \pi_{NS}^H - \pi_S^L + 2I_S$ follows from the conjecture in (A13). We must therefore prove that the conjecture is fulfilled in equilibrium. The first inequality in (A13) states that

$$\pi_{NS}^L > D_{NS} = \pi_{NS}^L + \pi_{NS}^H - \pi_S^L + 2I_S$$

---

[28] Higher face values of debt would imply that equityholders cannot expect to recover their initial investment. For such debt levels equityholders would therefore default immediately.

or
$$\pi_S^L - \pi_{NS}^H - 2I_S > 0.$$

This has been shown to hold in Lemma 3.

The second inequality in (A13) states that
$$D_{NS} = \pi_{NS}^L + \pi_{NS}^H - \pi_S^L + 2I_S > \pi_S^H$$
or
$$\pi_{NS}^L + \pi_{NS}^H - \left[\pi_S^L + \pi_S^H - 2I_S\right] > 0.$$

In equilibrium the firm values must be equal:
$$\pi_{NS}^L + \pi_{NS}^H - \left[\pi_S^L + \pi_S^H - 2I_S + \frac{2E[\Delta TS]}{1-\tau}\right] = 0. \quad (A14)$$

Thus, if $E[\Delta TS] > 0$, then the second inequality in (A13) holds. Therefore we will now show that $E[\Delta TS] > 0$. It follows from the definitions of D_S and D_{NS} that
$$E[TS(D_S)] = \tfrac{1}{2}\tau\left[\pi_S^H + \pi_S^L - 2I_S\right]$$
$$E[TS(D_{NS})] \leq \tfrac{1}{2}\tau\left[\pi_{NS}^H + \pi_{NS}^L\right].$$

To obtain a contradiction, assume that $E[\Delta TS] \leq 0$. Then the equilibrium condition (A14) implies that
$$\pi_S^L + \pi_S^H - 2I_S \geq \pi_{NS}^L + \pi_{NS}^H.$$

But this inequality implies that
$$E[TS(D_S)] - E[TS(D_{NS})] > 0,$$
which contradicts our initial assumption that $E[\Delta TS] \leq 0$. Thus, $E[\Delta TS] > 0$ and the second inequality in (A13) holds. As a result $D_{NS} = \pi_{NS}^L + \pi_{NS}^H - \pi_S^L - 2I_S$. From (A13) it follows that $D_S > D_{NS}$.

Proof of Corollary 1: In equilibrium, $V(D_S, S) = V(D_{NS}, NS)$. Thus, to prove the corollary, it is sufficient to show that $E(D_S, S) < E(D_{NS}, NS)$. It follows from the definition of D_S and D_{NS} that
$$E(D_S, S) = 0$$
$$E(D_{NS}, NS) = \frac{1-\tau}{2}\left[2(\pi_S^L - 2I_S) - (\pi_{NS}^L + \pi_{NS}^H)\right] > 0,$$
where the inequality follows from Lemma 3 that $\pi_S^L - 2I_S > \pi_{NS}^H$, and the profit definition implying that $\pi_{NS}^H > \pi_{NS}^L$.

Proof of Corollary 2: The proof of Corollary 2 is contained in the proof of Proposition 6 above.

Proof of Proposition 7: Before proving the proposition we first derive the expressions for $E[\Delta TS]$ in terms of p_H and p_L. The definition of $E[\Delta TS]$ in Proposition 5 and the definitions of D_S and D_{NS} in Proposition 6 imply that

$$E[TS(D_S)] = \tfrac{1}{2}\tau[\pi_S^L - 2I_S + \pi_S^H]$$

$$E[TS(D_{NS})] = \tau[\pi_{NS}^L + \pi_{NS}^H - \pi_S^L + 2I_S]$$

and, therefore,

$$E[\Delta TS] = \tau\left[\frac{3\pi_S^L}{2} + \frac{\pi_S^H}{2} - \pi_{NS}^L - \pi_{NS}^H - 3I_S\right].$$

Substituting the expressions for the profits we get

$$E[\Delta TS] = \frac{\tau}{4\gamma}\{(p_L - k)^2 - (p_H - k)^2$$

$$+ 6(p_L - k)h + 4h^2 - 2(p_H - k)h\} - 3\tau I_S. \quad (A15)$$

We first show that $d\hat{f}^\tau/d\tau > 0$. From Proposition 5 the expression for $\hat{f}^\tau$ is given by

$$\hat{f}^\tau = \frac{bn + \gamma}{2b} + \frac{\gamma(E[\Delta TS] - I_S(1-\tau))(bn + \gamma)}{bh^2(1-\tau)}.$$

Differentiating with respect to the corporate tax rate yields

$$\frac{d\hat{f}^\tau}{d\tau} = \frac{\gamma(bn + \gamma)}{bh^2(1-\tau)^2}\left[E[\Delta TS] + (1-\tau)\frac{dE[\Delta TS]}{d\tau}\right]. \quad (A16)$$

To determine the sign of $d\hat{f}/d\tau$ we need to sign $E[\Delta TS]$ and $\dfrac{dE[\Delta TS]}{d\tau}$. In Corollary 2 it is shown that $E[\Delta TS] > 0$. Differentiating (A15) with respect to the corporate tax rate we obtain

$$\frac{dE[\Delta TS]}{d\tau} = \frac{\tau}{4\gamma}\left[2(p_L - k)\frac{dp_L}{d\tau} - 2(p_H - k)\frac{dp_H}{d\tau} + 6h\frac{dp_L}{d\tau} - 2h\frac{dp_H}{d\tau}\right]$$

$$+ \frac{1}{\tau}E[\Delta TS]. \quad (A17)$$

From the expressions for p_L and p_H, (A4) and (A5), we obtain

$$\frac{dp_L}{d\tau} = -bh\frac{d\hat{f}^\tau/d\tau}{bn + \gamma} = -\frac{dp_H}{d\tau}. \quad (A18)$$

Substituting for $\dfrac{dp_L}{d\tau}$ and $\dfrac{dp_H}{d\tau}$ from (A18) into (A17) and then solving (A16) yields $d\hat{f}^\tau/d\tau > 0$.

Proof that $dD_S/d\tau < 0$: Substituting the definition for π_S^L into the expression for D_S derived in Proposition 6 we obtain

$$D_S = \frac{(p_L - k + h)^2}{2\gamma} - 2I_S.$$

Differentiating with respect to the corporate tax rate yields

$$\frac{dD_S}{d\tau} = \frac{1}{\gamma}(p_L - k + h)\frac{dp_L}{d\tau}.$$

Substituting for $dp_L/d\tau$ from (A18) and recognizing that $d\hat{f}^\tau/d\tau > 0$,

$$\frac{dp_L}{d\tau} = \frac{-bhd\hat{f}^\tau/d\tau}{bn + \gamma} < 0 \qquad (A19)$$

which implies that $\dfrac{dD_S}{d\tau} < 0$.

Proof that $dD_{NS}/d\tau > 0$: Substituting the definition for π_{NS}^L, π_{NS}^H, and π_S^L into the expression for D_{NS} derived in Proposition 6 and simplifying we obtain

$$D_{NS} = \frac{(p_H - k)^2}{2\gamma} - \frac{(p_L - k)h}{\gamma} - \frac{h^2}{2\gamma} + 2I_S.$$

Differentiating with respect to the tax rate yields

$$\frac{dD_{NS}}{d\tau} = \frac{1}{\gamma}\left[(p_H - k)\frac{dp_H}{d\tau} - h\frac{dp_L}{d\tau}\right] > 0,$$

where we have used the results that $dp_H/d\tau > 0$ and $dp_L/d\tau < 0$ from expressions (A18) and (A19).

REFERENCES

Abel, A., 1983, Energy price uncertainty and optimal factor intensity: A mean-variance analysis, *Econometrica* 51, 1839–1845.

Allen, F., 1986, Capital structure and imperfect competition in product markets, Discussion paper, University of Pennsylvania.

Arditti, F. D., 1967, Risk and the required rate of return on equity, *Journal of Finance* 23, 19–36.

Barnea A., Haugen, R. A., and L. W. Senbet, 1985, Agency problems and financial contracting, (Prentice-Hall, Inc., Englewood Cliffs, NJ).

Baskin, J., 1989, An empirical investigation of the pecking order hypothesis, *Financial Management* 18, 26–35.

Blair, R. D., 1974, Random input prices and the theory of the firm, *Economic Inquiry* 12, 214–226.

Bradley, M., G. Jarrell, and E. H. Kim, 1984, On the existence of an optimal capital structure, *Journal of Finance* 39, 857–878.

Brander, J. and T. Lewis, 1986, Oligopoly and financial structure: the limited liability effect, *American Economic Review* 76, 956–971.

Carleton, W. and I. Silberman, 1977, Joint determination of rate of return and capital structure: An econometric analysis, *Journal of Finance* 32, 811-821.

Castanias, R., 1983, Bankruptcy risk and optimal capital structure, *Journal of Finance* 38, 1617-1635.

Chudson, 1945, *The Pattern of Corporate Financial Structure*, (NBER, New York, NY).

de Meza, D., 1986, Safety in conformity but profits in deviance, *Canadian Journal of Economics* 19, 261-269.

Fischer, E. O., R. Heinkel, and J. Zechner, 1989, Dynamic capital structure choice: Theory and tests, *Journal of Finance* 44, 19-40.

Green, R., 1984, Investment incentives, debt and warrants, *Journal of Financial Economics* 13, 115-136.

—— and E. Talmor, 1986, Asset substitution and the agency costs of debt financing, *Journal of Banking and Finance* 10, 391-399.

Haugen, R. A. and L. W. Senbet, 1981, Resolving agency problems of external capital through options, *Journal of Finance* 36, 629-647.

Henderson, R., 1988, The failure of established firms in the face of technical change: A study of the photolithographic alignment industry, Ph.D. thesis, Harvard University.

Jensen, M. and W. Meckling, 1976, Theory of the firm: Managerial behavior, agency costs and ownership structure, *Journal of Financial Economics* 3, 305-360.

Kester, W. C., 1986, Capital and ownership structure: a comparison of United States and Japanese manufacturing corporations, *Financial Management* 15, 5-16.

Kim, M. and V. Maksimovic, 1990, Debt and input misallocation, *Journal of Finance* 45, 795-816.

Long, M. S. and E. B. Malitz, 1985, Investment patterns and financial leverage, in: B. Friedman (ed), *Corporate Capital Structures in the United States*, University of Chicago Press, Chicago, IL.

Maksimovic, V., 1986, Optimal capital structure in a stochastic oligopoly, Ph.D. thesis, Harvard University.

——, 1988, Capital structure in a repeated oligopoly, *Rand Journal of Economics* 19, 389-407.

——, 1990, Product market imperfections and loan commitments, *Journal of Finance* 45, 1641-1653.

Miller, M., 1977, Debt and taxes, *Journal of Finance* 32, 261-275.

Myers, S. C., 1977, Determinants of corporate borrowing, *Journal of Financial Economics* 9, 147-175.

——, 1984, The capital structure puzzle, *Journal of Finance* 39, 575-592.

——, 1990, Still searching for the optimal capital structure, in: Kopcke, R. and E. Rosengren (eds), Are the distinctions between debt and equity disappearing? Federal Reserve Bank of Boston Conference Series 33.

Nakamura, A. and M. Nakamura, 1982, On the firm's production, capital structure and demand for debt, *Review of Economics and Statistics* 64, 384-393.

Remmers, L., A. Stonehill, R. Wright, and T. Beekhuesen, 1974, Industry and size as debt ratio determinants in manufacturing internationally, *Financial Management* 3, 24-32.

Rothschild, M. and J. Stiglitz, 1970, Increasing risk I: A definition, *Journal of Economic Theory* 2, 225-243.

Talmor, E., R. Haugen, and A. Barnea, 1985, The value of the tax subsidy on risky debt, *Journal of Business* 58, 191-202.

Titman, S., 1984, The effect of capital structure on a firm's liquidation decision, *Journal of Financial Economics* 13, 137-151.

—— and R. Wessels, 1988, The determinants of capital structure choice, *Journal of Finance* 43, 1-19.

Waugh, F. V., 1944, Does the consumer benefit from price instability? *Quarterly Journal of Economics* 58, 602-614.

Williams, J., 1987, Perquisites, risk, and capital structure, *Journal of Finance* 42, 29-48.

Zechner, J. and P. Swoboda, 1986, The critical implicit tax rate and capital structure, *Journal of Banking and Finance* 10, 327-341.

Liquidation Values and Debt Capacity: A Market Equilibrium Approach

ANDREI SHLEIFER and ROBERT W. VISHNY*

ABSTRACT

We explore the determinants of liquidation values of assets, particularly focusing on the potential buyers of assets. When a firm in financial distress needs to sell assets, its industry peers are likely to be experiencing problems themselves, leading to asset sales at prices below value in best use. Such illiquidity makes assets cheap in bad times, and so ex ante is a significant private cost of leverage. We use this focus on asset buyers to explain variation in debt capacity across industries and over the business cycle, as well as the rise in U.S. corporate leverage in the 1980s.

HOW DO FIRMS CHOOSE debt levels, and why do firms or even whole industries sometimes change how much debt they have? Why, for example, have American firms increased their leverage in the 1980s (Bernanke and Campbell (1988), Warshawsky (1990)), and why has this debt increase been the greatest in some industries, such as food and timber? Despite substantial progress in research on leverage, these questions remain largely open. In this paper, we explore an approach to debt capacity based on the cost of asset sales. We argue that the focus on asset sales and liquidations helps clarify the cross-sectional determinants of leverage, as well as why debt increased in the 1980s.

Williamson (1988) stresses the link between debt capacity and the liquidation value of assets. He argues that assets which are redeployable—have alternative uses—also have high liquidation values. For example, commercial land can be used for many different purposes. Such assets are good candidates for debt finance because, if they are managed improperly, the manager will be unable to pay the debt, and then creditors will take the assets away from him and redeploy them. Williamson thus identifies one important determinant of liquidation value and debt capacity, namely, asset redeployability.[1]

---

*From Harvard University and The University of Chicago, respectively. We are grateful to Douglas Diamond, Eugene Fama, Robert Gertner, Milton Harris, Glenn Hubbard, Steven Kaplan, Robert McDonald, Merton Miller, Raghuram Rajan, Artur Raviv, Howard Zimmerman, and especially to Harry DeAngelo and René Stulz, for helpful comments. We are also grateful to the National Science Foundation, Bradley and Sloan Foundations, and Dimensional Fund Advisors for financial support.

[1] Harris and Raviv (1990), Hart and Moore (1989), Diamond (1991), and Hart (1991) present models in which liquidation value appears as an exogenously given factor in determining debt capacity. Only Harris and Raviv (1990) treat liquidation value as a central parameter of their model. Unlike Williamson (1988), none of these papers discuss the determinants of the liquidation value, which is the central focus of our work.

Unfortunately, most assets in the world are quite specialized and, therefore, are not redeployable. Oil rigs, brand name food products, pharmaceutical patents, and steel plants have no reasonable uses other than the one they are destined for. When such assets are sold, they have to be sold to someone who will use them in approximately the same way. Williamson does not address the problem of such sales. This paper analyzes what prices non-redeployable assets fetch in asset sales or liquidations relative to their value in best use. We call this difference between price and value in best use *asset illiquidity*. We argue that many assets are often illiquid, i.e., fetch prices below values in best use when liquidated, and that asset illiquidity has important implications for capital structure.

The principal reason for asset illiquidity—and the principal contribution of this paper—is the *general equilibrium* aspect of asset sales. When firms have trouble meeting debt payments and sell assets or are liquidated, the highest valuation potential buyers of these assets are likely to be other firms in the industry. But these firms are themselves likely to have trouble meeting their debt payments at the time assets are put up for sale as long as the shock that causes the seller's distress is industry- or economy-wide. When they themselves are hurting, these industry buyers are unlikely to be able to raise funds to buy the distressed firms' assets. Even if industry buyers can raise funds, in many cases antitrust and other government regulations might prevent them from purchasing the liquidated assets of competitors. Because of credit constraints and government regulation of industry buyers, assets would have to be sold to industry outsiders who don't know how to manage them well, face agency costs of hiring specialists to run these assets, and, moreover, fear overpaying because they cannot value the assets properly. When industry buyers cannot buy the assets and industry outsiders face significant costs of acquiring and managing the assets, assets in liquidation fetch prices below value in best use, which is the value when managed by specialists.

This result contrasts with the view expressed by many academic lawyers (e.g., Baird (1986)) that conducting an immediate auction is the best way to allocate the assets of distressed firms. The idea behind this claim is that auctions allocate the assets to the highest value user for the price equal to the second highest fundamental valuation. If the first and second highest valuations are reasonably close, then the auction price will be close to fundamental value in best user. In our model, in contrast, illiquid assets are not always allocated to the highest fundamental valuation users, and the auction price will not necessarily be close to the value in best use. This implies that forced liquidations can have significant private costs to the asset seller as well as significant social costs to the extent that the assets do not end up owned by the highest value user. Despite these costs, complete or partial liquidation will, in some cases, be the least costly of the various alternatives which include debt rescheduling and new equity issues. In other cases, the least costly strategy will be to continue operating under formal bankruptcy protection. We agree with Easterbrook (1990) that the policy of automatic auctions for the assets of distressed firms, without the possibility of Chapter 11 protection, is not theoretically sound.

Our approach implies that liquidated assets are underpriced in recessions and therefore suggests that asset illiquidity is a potentially important cost of leverage. As a result, asset liquidity helps explain cross-sectional and time series financing patterns. Harris and Raviv (1991) exhaustively surveyed the theoretical literature on optimal capital structure and catalogued the relevant empirical work. While some studies have identified characteristics of individual assets that predict higher leverage, such as "tangibility" and R & D intensity, none have focused on the "general equilibrium" (industry, legal, and macroeconomic) factors that determine which assets are liquid and therefore have a higher debt capacity. Perhaps more importantly, no other work has explained major shifts in borrowing behavior over short periods of time, such as those that occurred in the United States in the 1980s.

The first section of the paper explains the effects we have in mind, using an example of a bankrupt farmer. Section II presents a formal model, which builds on Stulz (1990) and Hart (1991). Section III discusses some extensions of the basic model. Section IV looks at the implications of the analysis for cross-sectional financing patterns, Section V presents the time series implications, and Section VI focuses on the specific case of the takeover wave and leverage increase in the 1980s. Section VII presents our conclusions.

I. Determinants of Asset Liquidity: An Example

To fix ideas, consider a heavily indebted farmer whose farm is not currently generating a sufficient cash flow to cover his interest payments. Suppose that this farmer cannot reschedule his debt, issue new equity, or borrow more. He might not be able to reschedule the debt because his banker is not sure that he is really competent, and would like to foreclose and auction off the property rather than wait. He might be unable to issue new securities because of debt overhang, studied by Myers (1977), Hart and Moore (1989), and Hart (1991), and also used in the model below. Or it might be a consequence of adverse selection problems facing the potential buyers of securities, as suggested by Myers and Majluf (1984). When the farmer cannot keep the creditors away by raising more cash, the farm is liquidated.

There are three distinct types of potential buyers of the land. It can be sold to an outsider who would convert it to "alternative" use, such as a baseball field. It could be sold to a neighbor who would farm it himself. Or it could be sold to a financial "deep pocket" investor who would hire the current or some other farmer to farm the land, at least until he could resell it. This list of buyer types pretty much exhausts the relevant set for most assets.

Suppose that the asset, namely farmland, is converted to another use, such as the baseball field. If the land is as valuable as a baseball field as it is as a farm, this solution is very attractive in that the farmer gets a price close to the value in best use, especially if there are several bidders. Such land would be fungible, or "redeployable" in Williamson's (1988) language, and as such would be very liquid. But of course farms and other assets virtually never have alternative uses as good as the current use. The buyer in liquidation would most likely have to use the land for farming.

The most likely high valuation buyer is one of the neighboring farmers. These buyers have the enormous advantage of knowing the quality of the land and perhaps even the quality of the current farmer. The adverse selection problems that might plague outsiders interested in the farm are much less important for the neighbors. Moreover, the neighbors can work the land themselves, thereby avoiding the agency problems resulting from hiring employees. In fact if the neighbors are actually allowed to bid for the farm and if they can borrow at attractive terms, they are likely to buy the farm. Competition among neighbors would ensure a price close to value in best use, making the land liquid.

Unfortunately, in many cases, the neighbors might not be able to bid or able to borrow at attractive terms. First, neighbors might be legally excluded from bidding because of government limits on farm size (this is obviously more relevant in the case of antitrust restrictions on companies). In addition, unless the farmer got in trouble for some *idiosyncratic* reason such as mismanagement, the neighbors are likely to have cash flow problems of their own at the time the farmer is distressed. They might therefore simply be unable to borrow to buy the farm, as our model below illustrates. When the neighbors cannot participate, or when they face credit constraints, the land has be sold to a "deep pocket" industry outsider, who by definition does not face as severe a credit constraint as the farmer's neighbors.

This outsider, however, faces his own set of extra costs of buying the farm. He must worry about the quality of the farm, which he knows little about, and so is afraid to overpay. In addition, he cannot run the farm himself, and so must hire either the current farmer or someone else to run it. The agency cost further reduces the value to him relative to the value to the neighbors. Because of these adverse selection and moral hazard problems, the price that a deep pocket outsider will pay for the farm will be lower than the neighbors would pay if they were not constrained. As a result, the land will sell at a low price to the inefficient operator: a case of illiquidity.

The moral of the story is that the general equilibrium problem—namely, that the highest valuation buyers are likely not to be able to bid for the land —will lead to the sale of land to inefficient managers at prices below value in best use. The prospect of ex post losses of this type generates an ex ante incentive to adjust leverage to mitigate the possibility of forced asset sales at prices below value in best use.

II. The Model

A. Overview

Our model is closely related to the work of Jensen (1986), Hart and Moore (1989, 1990), Harris and Raviv (1990), Stulz (1990), and Diamond (1991). The actual formulation builds on Hart (1991).[2] To describe the model simply, suppose we have an industry with two firms, and there are two future states of the world: prosperity and depression. In prosperity, each firm has a *negative* NPV investment project that its managers would like to undertake for their own personal benefit. Investors would like to keep firms from undertaking these projects. To do that, investors create a *debt overhang* using senior long-term debt as well as short-term debt. The short-term debt forces the firm to come to the capital market when it wants to invest, even if its cash flow is high. Long-term debt, in contrast, ensures that the firm cannot borrow in prosperity when it wants to invest because of the debt overhang. Hart thus extends the insight of Myers (1977) to show that long-term debt can be used to prevent firms from borrowing.

Although this combination of long- and short-term debt keeps both firms from investing in prosperity, it has a cost in the recession. Suppose that one firm is hit harder by the recession and so cannot afford to pay its short-term debt. Because of the long-term debt overhang, it cannot borrow to continue its operations. Moreover, assume that the debt cannot be rescheduled and that the firm is forced into liquidation.[3] Suppose that the best buyer is the other firm in the industry. But remember that the second firm itself has both short- and long-term debt, and so is most probably unable to borrow to acquire the first firm. The debt that keeps the second firm from investing in prosperity also keeps it from buying the assets of the liquidating firm in the recession. In the extreme, the second firm might be near or in liquidation itself! When the second firm cannot buy the assets of the liquidated firm, they get sold to someone outside the industry who might be an inferior operator but does not have the debt overhang. In the depression then, assets are sold to an inferior operator because the better users (other firms in the industry) are constrained in the capital market. The model thus delivers our result that optimal capital structures can lead to costly liquidation in some states of the world because all the best users of the assets are credit constrained at the same time.

B. Details of the Model

The model has three periods, 0, 1, and 2. There are two firms in the industry. The capital structure is determined in period 0; uncertainty is resolved in period 1, when firms have to make further decisions as well as receive and pay out some cash flow; and finally in period 2 additional cash flows are received. There are two states of the world, prosperity and depression, and uncertainty about the state is resolved in period 1. In prosperity, each firm gets a negative NPV investment opportunity that its managers

---

[2] Another type of credit constraints model focuses on imperfect information (Bernanke and Gertler (1989)); Froot and Stein (1991); Gertler and Hubbard (1988); Greenwald, Stiglitz, and Weiss (1984); Myers and Majluf (1984)). We believe that this approach, when applied to liquidation, would yield results similar to the ones reported here.

[3] We discuss this assumption in Section IV.

want to take; hence, the agency problem. For simplicity, we assume that such an opportunity does not arise in the depression.

So far, the two firms are completely symmetrical. However, we assume that, in the depression, one firm is hit harder than the other with a low cash flow. As a result, the possibility arises that the harder hit firm (the seller) is liquidated, and sold to the other firm in the industry (the buyer) or an industry outsider. A key distinction between the insider and the outsider is that the cash flow of the assets of the seller in period 2 is higher under ownership by the insider. This may be because the insider is just a better operator, or because the outsider faces a bigger agency problem of hiring a manager to run these assets. We will also assume that the outsider has no debt overhang, and so can bid the full value of the firm under his management. As a result, the outsider might get the liquidating firm even if he values it less than the credit-constrained insider.

We first consider the capital structure of the selling firm, then the capital structure of the buying firm and finally the liquidation equilibrium. Figure 1 summarizes the timing of cash flows and decisions of the selling firm. Our notation is as follows. R is the future payoff from the investment, while I is the cost of the investment. Y is cash flow from existing assets. Superscripts refer to states, either prosperity or depression, while subscripts refer to periods 1 or 2. Note also that we assume the riskless interest rate is zero.

We make three substantive assumptions about parameter values:

Assumption S1: *Investment in prosperity has negative net present value*:

$$R^P < I^P.$$

Assumption S2: *Period 1 cash flow is higher in prosperity even net of the investment*:

$$Y_1^D < Y_1^P - I^P.$$

Assumption S3: *The overall cash flow is higher in prosperity than in the depression even net of the negative NPV investment*:

$$Y_1^P + Y_2^P + R^P - I^P > Y_2^D + Y_1^D.$$

Assumption S1 represents the agency problem and creates the need to use capital structure to control self-interested investments by management. Without S1, there is no need to use debt in the model. Assumptions S2 and S3 both say that prosperity is a much better state of the world than depression. Together they imply that a capital structure which is stringent enough to constrain managers from making bad investments in prosperity will actually put the firm into financial difficulty in the depression. If these assumptions do not hold, there will exist a capital structure that alleviates the agency costs in prosperity without entailing any distress costs in the depression. For example, if S3 holds but S2 does not, the optimal capital structure will call for a level of short-term debt that prevents the investment in prosperity but is still low enough that the firm can repay the short-term

Liquidation Values and Debt Capacity

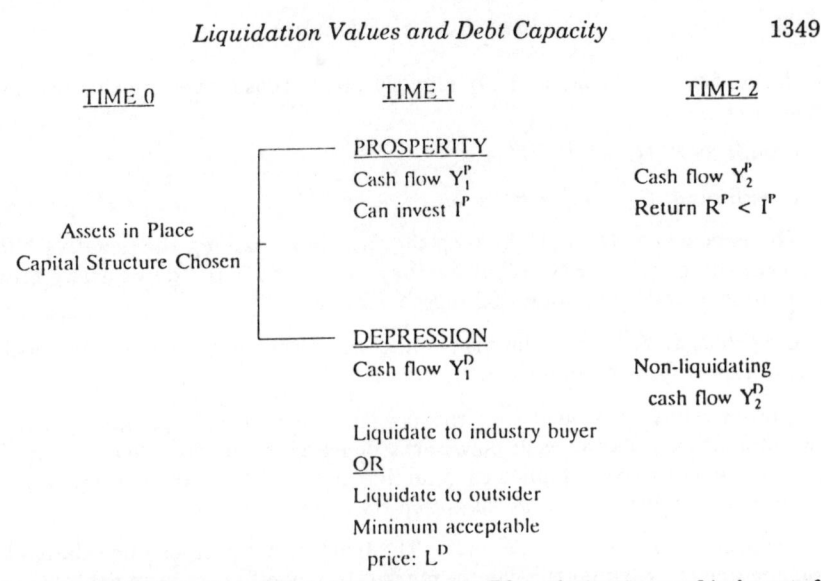

```
TIME 0                    TIME 1                      TIME 2

                          PROSPERITY
                          Cash flow $Y_1^P$           Cash flow $Y_2^P$
                          Can invest $I^P$            Return $R^P < I^P$
Assets in Place
Capital Structure Chosen

                          DEPRESSION
                          Cash flow $Y_1^D$           Non-liquidating
                                                      cash flow $Y_2^D$
                          Liquidate to industry buyer
                          OR
                          Liquidate to outsider
                          Minimum acceptable
                            price: $L^D$
```

Figure 1. Timing for the seller. R is the future payoff from the investment, I is the cost of the investment, and Y is cash flow from existing assets. Superscripts denote states (either prosperity or depression) and subscripts denote time periods.

debt out of period 1 cash flow in depression. Conversely, if S2 holds but S3 does not, the first best can be obtained using long-term debt to constrain investment.

Hart (1991) studies the optimal period 0 capital structure when complete state-contingent contracts cannot be written. He shows that the capital structure that maximizes the wealth of period 0 shareholders, under Assumptions S1–S3, consists of senior debt D_2 due in period 2 and debt D_1 due in period 1. The function of junior short-term debt is to bring the firm to the capital market in period 1 rather than let it invest from the internal cash flow. Hart (1991) assumes that this debt cannot be rescheduled; we discuss this assumption in Section III. The function of senior long-term debt is to create debt overhang, so that a firm with a negative NPV investment opportunity cannot raise more money by issuing new securities. Both the long-term and the short-term debt, then, are used to discipline the management.

To prevent investment in period 1, these debt levels must meet the following conditions in prosperity:

Condition 1: $I^P > Y_1^P - D_1$: After paying debt, the firm does not have enough to invest without raising capital.

Condition 2: $I^P - Y_1^P + D_1 > Y_2^P + R^P - D_2$: Senior debt overhang precludes the firm from raising enough capital to invest.

Provided it pays initial investors to prevent the wasteful investment in prosperity (Condition 7 below), the optimal capital structure in this model calls for debt levels D_1 and D_2 slightly above those given by Conditions 1 and 2, i.e.,

Condition 3: $D_1 = Y_1^P - I^P + \epsilon$.

Condition 4: $D_2 = Y_2^P + R^P + \delta$.

The debt levels D_1 and D_2 keep the firm from making the negative NPV investment in prosperity. What do they imply about the depression? First, Condition 1 and Assumption S2 together imply

Condition 5: $Y_1^D < D_1$: The firm cannot meet the debt payments out of the current cash flow in depression.

Since we have assumed that the period 1 cash flow in prosperity net of investment exceeds the cash flow in the depression, the need to go to capital markets in prosperity implies the inability to pay debt in the depression.

Second, Condition 2 and Assumption S3 together imply

Condition 6: $D_1 - Y_1^D > Y_2^D - D_2$: The firm cannot postpone liquidation by raising enough cash on the capital market to pay off short-term debt.

Again, since prosperity even with the bad investment is more profitable than depression, a debt overhang that keeps the firm from making the bad investment in prosperity also prevents it from raising enough money to delay liquidation in the depression. In this model, then, so long as depression is sufficiently inferior to prosperity, the firm is turned over to the creditors in the depression.

Following Hart (1991), we assume that the creditors liquidate the firm when it defaults on its short-term debt (we discuss this assumption in the next section). The main question of our analysis is at what price the firm is liquidated in the depression. From the viewpoint of the seller, the only constraint on that price is that it be high enough for the capital structure described above to be optimal. That is, the gains from avoiding the investment in prosperity must outweigh the losses from liquidation, rather than continuation, in the depression. The condition is:

Condition 7: $\Pi^P(I^P - R^P) \geq \Pi^D(Y_2^D - L^D)$,

where Π^P and Π^D are probability of prosperity and depression, respectively. This means that the minimum acceptable price, L^D, is:

Condition 8: $L^D = Y_2^D - \dfrac{\Pi^P}{\Pi^D}(I^P - R^P)$.

Note that liquidation in this model may well take place at a price below the value of second period cash flow under the incumbent, Y_2^D, for reasons of debt overhang.

Hart (1991), as well as the rest of the literature, assumes that the actual liquidation value is exogenous. Our paper endogenizes this value. We assume that there are two potential buyers of the assets of the seller. First, there is

Liquidation Values and Debt Capacity

an industry outsider, who can generate a second period cash flow C_{out} from these assets. We assume that this outsider does not face debt overhang and so can bid up to C_{out} for the assets. Second, there is the industry insider, "the buyer," who can generate a second period cash flow $C_{ins} > C_{out}$ from the assets of the selling firm. Although the industry insider has a higher fundamental valuation of the liquidating firm's assets, he might not be able to pay this valuation because of his own debt overhang. The next question then is, how much can he pay?

To answer this question, we need to analyze the problem of the buyer. We treat the buyer almost symmetrically to the seller, except that we use small letters. So, the timing of the buyer, presented in Figure 2, is virtually the same, except that the period 2 problem in the depression is whether to buy the liquidating firm.

Assumptions B1 and B3 parallel the assumptions for the seller and are used for the same reasons:

Assumption B1: *Investment in prosperity has negative net present value*:

$$r^P < i^P.$$

Assumption B3: *The overall cash flow is higher in prosperity than in the depression even net of the negative NPV investment*:

$$y_1^P + y_2^P + r^P - i^P > y_2^D + y_1^D.$$

However, Assumption S2 for the seller is now replaced by:

Assumption B2: $0 < y_1^D - y_1^P + i^P < C_{out}.$

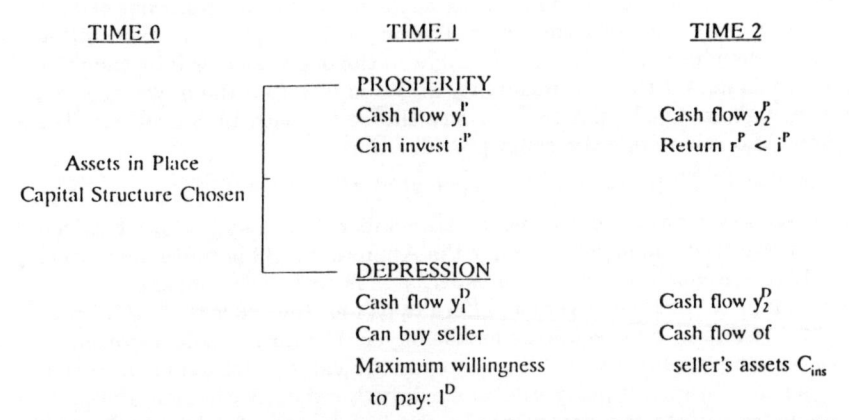

TIME 0	TIME 1	TIME 2
Assets in Place Capital Structure Chosen	PROSPERITY Cash flow y_1^P Can invest i^P	Cash flow y_2^P Return $r^P < i^P$
	DEPRESSION Cash flow y_1^D Can buy seller Maximum willingness to pay: I^D	Cash flow y_2^D Cash flow of seller's assets C_{ins}

Figure 2. Timing for the industry buyer. r is the future payoff from the investment, i is the cost of the investment, and y is cash flow from existing assets. Superscripts denote states (either prosperity or depression) and subscripts denote time periods.

The first part of the inequality is the reverse of S2; it will imply that the buyer's cash flow in the depression is high enough that he does not have to be liquidated. This assumption captures our key distinction between the buyer and the seller, namely that the former is hit less hard in the depression. If the first part of the inequality in B2 is reversed, the buyer like the seller will be liquidated and our result that assets are allocated to low valuation buyers would be even stronger. The second part of the inequality in B2 will imply that the buyer does not have enough internal cash flow to buy the seller's assets for C_{out}, the outsider's valuation. If the buyer wants to get the seller's assets in the depression, he must go to the external capital market. In equilibrium, in fact, he would sometimes not be able to raise cash there either, because of debt overhang.

Denote debt levels by d_1 for short-term debt, and d_2 for senior long-term debt. Then the levels necessary to keep the buyer from investing in prosperity satisfy:

Condition 9: $i^P > y_1^P - d_1$: the buyer needs to come to the capital market in prosperity in order to invest; and

Condition 10: $i^P - y_1^P + d_1 > y_2^P + r^P - d_2$: Debt level is too high to raise money to invest.

These conditions, of course, are exactly the same as 1 and 2 for the seller. The minimum debt levels d_1 and d_2 that satisfy 9 and 10 and so keep the firm from investing in prosperity are the same as those given by 3 and 4 for the seller:

Condition 11: $d_1 = y_1^P - i^P + \epsilon$.

Condition 12: $d_2 = y_2^P + r^P + \delta$.

Can the buyer burdened with d_1 and d_2 acquire the seller in the depression? Let l^D denote the *maximum* price such that the buyer can raise enough money to pay this price for the seller. The buyer can acquire the seller either if he has enough cash flow to do it outright in the depression or if he can raise money to do it. But the first inequality in B2 implies that the buyer does not have enough internal cash flow to buy the seller without borrowing. The buyer can borrow to buy the seller provided that:

Condition 13: $l^D < (y_1^D + y_2^D) - (y_1^P + y_2^P + r^P - i^P) + C_{ins}$.

This is the key condition of the model. Remember that the difference between the first two terms is negative under the Assumption B3 because depression cash flows are much lower than prosperity cash flows. This means that the maximum price that the buyer can afford to pay for the seller is strictly lower than the cash flow of the seller under the buyer. The reason is debt overhang: the buyer simply cannot raise money to pay the value of the seller under his management. In fact, if prosperity is much better than depression, the price the industry insider can pay might be much below the fundamental value under his management. In sum, the buyer can only buy the liquidating firm in the depression if the price is below l_D given by Condition 13.

Before analyzing who buys the firm in liquidation, we should remember that there is also a condition that says that it is in the interest of the initial owners of the buyer to create the debt overhang to avoid investment in prosperity. This condition is parallel to Condition 7 for the seller. The gains to avoiding such an investment must exceed the losses from not getting the liquidating firm in prosperity, i.e.,

Condition 14: $\Pi^P(i^P - r^P) > \Pi^D(C_{ins} - \text{liquidation price})$.

If the liquidating firm can be gotten for a price so low that Condition 14 fails, then the buyer's shareholders will not impose the debt overhang in period 0 because of the possibility of making a very cheap acquisition in the depression.[4]

So who gets the liquidating firm? If l^D, the maximum price that the industry buyer can pay, exceeds the cash flow under the outsider, C_{out}, then this industry insider gets the firm for the price C_{out}. He is the more efficient of the two buyers, although he might still be less efficient than the incumbent. In this case of the nonbinding debt-overhang, assets do move to the more efficient of the two potential buyers. One way to interpret this case is that the seller experiences an idiosyncratic shock, or perhaps a much more severe version of the aggregate shock than other firms in the industry, and so one of these firms manages to raise capital and acquire his assets.

The case of most interest, however, is when the maximum price l^D that the buyer can pay, given by Condition 13, is below the cash flow C_{out} under the outsider, but still high enough that it is optimal for the buyer's investors to impose debt overhang (i.e., Condition 14 holds). This can occur even though the cash flow under the industry buyer exceeds the cash flow under the outsider. The firm is then sold to the outsider, who has a lower fundamental valuation but does not face credit constraints, rather than to the high valuation industry insider who has a heavy debt overhang. The firm is thus sold for a price below the second highest fundamental valuation and does not end up in the hands of the highest valuation buyer.

The liquidation price will be l^D given by Condition 13, as the industry insider loses the auction to the outsider, who ends up paying the insider's maximum ability to pay. This will be the equilibrium assuming that, at this price, the buyer and the seller are both willing to put in place the debt overhang capital structure, i.e., if Conditions 7 and 14 hold. The conclusion of this model, then, is that liquidation need not bring in the second highest fundamental valuation, but might instead bring in a lower price.

In the case we have focused on above, both the buyer and the seller choose to have debt overhang, and so there is an interior debt level for both the

---

[4] Consistent with our assumptions for the seller, we do not allow renegotiation of the buyer's debt agreement once the state is revealed and the purchase opportunity becomes available. This no-renegotiation assumption is discussed in detail later on. For now, suffice it to say that this assumption is meant to capture the difficulty in overcoming a debt overhang in the presence of many dispersed creditors or significant information asymmetries.

buyer and the seller. These debt levels depend on the cash flows of the firms, and on the parameters of their investment opportunities in prosperity. So long as the equilibrium continues to be in the range where both firms use debt overhang, the levels of debt are independent of the liquidation price. However, when the liquidation price falls or rises enough, there may be a change in regimes and it may no longer be optimal for both firms to have debt overhang. For example, as $i^P - r^P$ falls, optimal debt overhang of the industry buyer rises, the liquidation price falls, and so at some point the owners of the seller might choose to move to the no-debt capital structure. In this discontinuous way, optimal debt levels of the seller fall as the liquidity of its assets falls. In a more general model with more states, one can imagine a continuously changing capital structure, with falling levels of debt as liquidation value falls and investors would choose to allow negative NPV investments in more states rather than have more frequent liquidations. Our model thus reflects an important general principle: optimal leverage or debt capacity falls as liquidation value falls.

Interesting results also obtain for the parameter values at which it does not pay for both the seller and the industry buyer to have debt overhang. For some parameter values, there are two equilibria. In the first equilibrium, the buyer has a debt overhang to prevent investment in prosperity, so he cannot pay much for the liquidating firm in the depression. The liquidating firm, if it were to have debt overhang, would then get sold in depression to the industry outsider at a price equal to what the insider with the overhang can pay. Faced with the prospect of such a low price in liquidation, investors in the selling firm choose to have no debt and to allow the negative NPV investment in prosperity. This in turn makes it very attractive for the industry buyer to have a lot of debt, since the first firm is not even for sale in the depression and nothing is given up by having more debt. In this equilibrium, the buyer has a lot of debt, and the seller has none.

But there is also a second possible equilibrium here. In this equilibrium, the seller has a debt overhang, and is liquidated in the depression. The buyer, however, recognizes that there is an opportunity to buy the liquidating firm in the depression at a price equal to the cash flow under the industry outsider, and therefore chooses to forego the debt overhang just to take this opportunity. The optimal debt level for the industry buyer is 0. In turn, the fact that the industry buyer is there to pay the relatively high price for the assets makes it attractive for the seller to have more debt. In this equilibrium, the seller has a lot of debt, and the industry buyer has none.

This case of two equilibria suggests the notion of an *industry debt capacity* in this model. While each individual firm can have a high or a low debt level depending on which equilibrium obtains, the aggregate industry debt level is approximately the same (if the buyer and the seller are similar). Either the buyer has a lot of debt, in which case the seller chooses to have none and so avoids liquidation, or the seller has a lot of debt in which case the buyer avoids debt to be ready to acquire the seller. But it would not be an equilibrium, for these parameter values, either for both firms to have a lot of debt or for neither to have debt. The industry debt capacity reflects the desirability of both, avoiding some wasteful investment in the industry, and also of preventing the sale of liquidating firms to industry outsiders. The existence of an industry debt capacity, even when the debt capacity of any individual firm may vary widely depending on which equilibrium obtains, is perhaps the clearest example of the general equilibrium effect operating in this model.

C. Discussion of Illiquidity

The conclusion of the model is that the price of an asset in liquidation might fall below value in best use because some or all industry buyers have trouble raising funds. This result relies on the assumption that the shock is either industry- or economy-wide. An idiosyncratic adverse shock to the cash flow would not have the same effect. If the seller suffers a bad idiosyncratic shock, but other firms in the industry do not, these other firms will not have a debt overhang and will compete to drive the asset price in liquidation up to the fundamental value in best use. In fact, it is trivial to extend the model to allow for idiosyncratic shocks, in which case the seller is sold to the industry buyer if he experiences an adverse idiosyncratic shock, and to the outsider if the whole industry suffers. In the first case, there is no private or social loss from liquidation, but in the second case both the private and the social loss may be large.

The airline industry illustrates the crucial distinction between idiosyncratic and industry-wide shocks in this model. When in the mid-1980s some firms in the industry experienced idiosyncratic problems, such as Peoples' Express with overexpansion or Eastern with unions, their gates, routes, and planes were easily acquired by other airlines. More recently, when Eastern and Pan Am put their assets up for sale at a time when other airlines were themselves losing money, the potential buyers could not borrow money as easily and assets appeared to be selling at more "distressed prices." For example, in December 1991 United bought bankrupt Pan Am's Latin American routes for $135 million compared to the $215 million it had offered in late August and $342 million paid earlier to Eastern by American for similar routes.

The institution of airline leasing seems to be designed partly to avoid fire sales of assets: airlines can stop their leasing contracts when they lose money rather than dump airplanes on the market which has no debt capacity. Even leasing companies, however, have a limited debt capacity and, therefore, cannot absorb all the planes put on the market when an industry suffers an adverse shock.

The oil shipping business offers another interesting example. As cash flows from that business temporarily plummeted in the mid-1980s and owners could not meet their debt payments, many tankers were selling for scrap value. At that time, astute investors from outside the industry bought some tankers and mothballed them. Mothballing the tankers may well have been the socially efficient strategy, but it seems likely that the sellers of the tankers bore a substantial private cost because they had to sell in a distressed situation where most of the informed potential buyers had little access to capital. At least in an ex post sense, the cost to the tanker sellers was large. Outside investors appear to have made a 700 percent return on their tanker investments over a five-year period.

The airline and shipping industries illustrate the critical role of deep pocket investors in maintaining some degree of asset liquidity during industry and economy wide recessions. We expect that in bad times pools of outside money will be organized to buy the distressed assets and hold them until the industry or the economy recovers. This process would certainly reduce the private costs of illiquidity. Unfortunately, the deep pocket industry outsiders often face substantial agency and informational deterrents to aggressive investment in particular industries. In addition, when the whole economy is in a recession, many potential industries compete for the funds of deep pocket investors, which raises their opportunity costs of committing funds to particular sectors. The pools of outside money are thus unlikely to eliminate the private costs of asset illiquidity. The social costs of management by industry outsiders remain as well, although these are lower when deep pocket investors develop some industry expertise.

It is important to stress that in many cases credit constraints of industry buyers, such as those resulting from debt overhang, are not the only factor that prevents them from buying distressed industry assets. Another potentially important barrier is regulation. For example, the United States Department of Transportation has historically prevented foreign airlines from buying assets of U.S. airlines, reducing the access of high valuation buyers to these assets and therefore reducing their prices. More importantly, antitrust regulation is an important factor that often prevents industry buyers from buying industry assets. In the 1960s, for example, it was virtually impossible to sell assets to competitors because of aggressive antitrust enforcement. These regulations have a similar effect to credit constraints: they reduce the liquidity of assets and the debt capacity for the firms in the industry.

III. Asset Sales More Generally

The model has provided a bare-bones illustration of how assets could be sold to a buyer with a low fundamental valuation. By focusing on the costs of asset sales, the model has missed some important issues. In particular, why do firms often *choose* to sell assets when debt rescheduling or raising new securities are potential alternatives? After all, asset sales are only one of several options a firm can pursue, and they must have some good properties to be chosen so often.

A firm that does not have enough cash to meet its interest payments, or is nearing that condition, has several options. It can try to reschedule its debt, either voluntarily or in Chapter 11; it can try to raise cash by issuing new debt or equity; or it can sell assets. All these options are costly. Consider first debt rescheduling. In our analysis and in Hart (1991), it is simply disallowed by assumption. However, in this model it would sometimes pay the short-term creditors of the seller to postpone debt repayment if the liquidation is very costly, since even as junior creditors they could negotiate a mutually advantageous deal with the seller. It would also sometimes pay the short-term creditors of the industry buyer to postpone debt repayment because the acquisition of the seller is so lucrative. Debt rescheduling must have some costs that are not explicitly modeled to be avoided in these circumstances.

Several such costs have been discussed in the literature. First, debt rescheduling might require difficult and costly coordination between multiple creditors (Gertner and Scharfstein (1991)). Second, creditors might worry about the asset substitution problem, namely that the managers will take extra risks if the loan maturities are extended (Jensen and Meckling (1976)). These creditors would rather force liquidation than wait and risk the complete depreciation of their collateral, especially in the face of their inferior knowledge about future investment prospects and profitability. Third, creditors may suspect that the problems of the firm stem from bad management. This prospect also makes them wary of rescheduling and granting management more time. For all these reasons, debt rescheduling is often difficult.

What about new security issues? In our model, a security issue is simply impossible because the debt overhang from the senior long-term debt is so severe that no new securities can be issued. More generally, the uncertainty of the new security buyers about the value of the assets in place, including the quality of management, also raises the cost of security issues (Myers and Majluf (1984)). Finally, like the creditors who are wary of rescheduling the debt, buyers of new securities have to worry that the managers will squander the new cash rather than use it productively. Issuing new securities, then, is also an expensive option for the firm.

Asset sales can better deal with some of the problems that plague debt rescheduling and new security issues, and therefore sometimes become the most attractive choice.

First, proceeds from asset sales are typically used to repay debt. In fact, bond covenants often require that proceeds from the sale of assets be used to pay down debt (Smith and Warner (1979), p. 127). As a result, asset sales alleviate the asset substitution problem, since creditors get cash today rather than waiting and fully exposing themselves to the riskiness of the firm.

Second, because proceeds from asset sales not only substitute for fresh credit but also reduce creditors' exposure, creditors do not have to worry as much about the quality of the management or of its projects. Hence, the asymmetric information problem which plagues new security issues and debt rescheduling is also less severe. While asset buyers from the industry must still put a value on a portion of the firm's assets in these transactions, these are precisely the agents most capable of doing so. A key advantage of asset sales over other ways of obtaining cash or credit in financial distress is that the informational asymmetries are likely to be much smaller when dealing with informed industry insiders.

Third, because control over the assets is turned over to the buyers when assets are sold, these buyers, unlike the buyers of new securities, do not have to worry as much about agency problems in the management of the assets.

Fourth, when asset sales generate substantial proceeds and some debt is repaid, the need for extracting concessions from many dispersed creditors is eliminated. Also, the number of creditors, and therefore the number of conflicts between creditors, usually falls. In this way as well, asset sales might be preferred to rescheduling.

Finally, when a firm sells assets that are valuable, but do not generate current cash flow, it can relieve its debt burden without sacrificing its current income, or its ability to service other debt in the near future. Such assets might include businesses that are temporarily losing money, as well as growth businesses. Of course, if the industry buyers are themselves credit constrained, assets with high fundamental values but low current cash flows would sell at the largest discounts to their values: they would be the least liquid. But assuming that credit constraints are the tightest on the liquidating firm, it is probably still attractive to sell these assets. By doing so, this firm can avoid default not just immediately, but in the near future as well.

Overall, in some cases asset sales can lessen conflicts between creditors, reduce the asset substitution problem, control agency costs, and alleviate the informational asymmetry between the firm and outsiders, all without sacrificing the firm's ability to survive in the future. In these cases, they are the cheapest—though not a free—way to avoid complete liquidation and keep the creditors at bay. Of course, when the firm's assets are sufficiently illiquid, debt rescheduling or the issue of new securities might be the preferred alternatives, expensive as they are.

IV. Asset Liquidity and Debt Capacity

Our model explains how asset illiquidity reduces the optimal amount of debt in the capital structure. While having more debt prevents inefficient investment, it also causes more frequent costly liquidation. The result might be an interior level of debt that trades off these benefits and costs. This logic has substantial implications for the cross-section of financing patterns. Specifically, illiquid assets are poor candidates for debt finance, and vice versa for liquid assets. Asset liquidity creates debt capacity because liquid assets are in effect better collateral.

It is hard to know how big the illiquidity costs of distress are. Real estate appraisers typically assume that the rapid sale of real estate leads to price discounts of 15 to 25 percent relative to the orderly sale that might take several months. Kaplan (1989) cites Merrill Lynch estimates that the distressed sale of the Campeau retail empire would bring about 68 percent of what an orderly sale would bring. The New York Times reported that the rapid sale discount on the Trump Shuttle may be as much as 50 percent. Holland (1990) cites discounts of 50 to 70 percent off normal prices in a case study of liquidation of assets of a machine tool manufacturer.

Liquidation Values and Debt Capacity

In addition to suggesting that debt capacity is limited, our approach has a variety of implications for cross-sectional financing patterns. Liquid assets should be more extensively financed by debt. Williamson (1988) has argued that "redeployable" assets are liquid and thus are good candidates for debt finance, but this is only part of the story. Our model predicts that growth assets such as high technology firms and cyclical assets such as steel and chemical firms are illiquid because industry buyers of these assets are likely to be themselves severely credit constrained when the owners of these assets need to sell. Industry buyers of cyclical assets are constrained because they are hit by the same macroeconomic shock. Industry buyers of growth assets are virtually always credit constrained because they have so little cash relative to the value of these assets. Cyclical and growth assets are therefore poor candidates for debt finance, unless they are readily understood by deep pocket investors outside the industry.

Growth and cyclical assets are usually considered to be poor candidates for debt finance because they have a high probability of a low cash flow and default on debt. But even an asset with a reasonable chance of default may have a high debt capacity if it can be easily sold for fundamental value when default occurs. If, on the other hand, cyclical and growth assets are extremely illiquid in a recession, costs of financial distress are large, and financing these assets with debt is costly. Airline gates and routes, tankers and industrial equipment are, ceteris paribus, poor candidates for debt finance precisely because industry buyers are themselves in trouble in a recession, and so these assets are highly illiquid. Illiquidity is an important reason for low debt capacity of cyclical and growth assets.

The theory also predicts that smaller firms are ceteris paribus better candidates for debt finance. The caveat is important because small firms might be uninteresting to very many buyers, since they are too specialized, in which case the thin market reason for illiquidity might be more important than credit constraints of buyers. The way to test this prediction is to look at an industry where firms of different sizes operate together, and to see if smaller ones have more debt. Chan and Chen (1991) find that, within industry, smaller firms are more leveraged than larger firms, although they do not distinguish firms that freely choose high leverage from firms who temporarily have leverage above the long-run optimum level due to a large unanticipated drop in market value.

The theory also predicts that conglomerates are better candidates for debt finance than pure plays of the same size. This is true for several reasons other than the usual reason that conglomerates tend to have lower cash flow volatility and therefore a lower probability of not being able to meet debt payments. First, a conglomerate in need of cash has the option of selling assets in several different industries. This allows the conglomerate to avoid selling assets whose underlying industries are illiquid as long as it has sufficient assets in liquid industries. Second, a conglomerate has the option of selling its assets off in smaller, more liquid pieces without adversely affecting either the value of the divested assets or the assets kept in the firm. The ease of separability and the smaller degree of synergy between pieces of the firm give the conglomerate more flexibility to sell off some pieces of the firm while retaining control of others. This argument also applies to firms that are not literally conglomerates. All other things being equal, a business consisting of a loose affiliation of different parts should have a higher debt capacity. For example, a company whose principal assets are 10 cable franchises in different cities has more flexibility in selling off assets and would therefore have more debt capacity than a similar-sized company operating in only one city.

V. Changes in Liquidity Over Time

Our discussion thus far has focused on cross-sectional variation in liquidity and in debt capacity. Liquidity also changes over time. Optimal debt levels are determined not by today's liquidity, but by liquidity over some planning horizon during which the asset might be sold. Investors must then make forecasts of future liquidity to establish the optimal capital structure.

How persistent is asset liquidity? For most assets without alternative uses, two key determinants of liquidity are participation and cash flow of industry buyers. Constraints on participation by industry buyers tend to be determined by laws and institutions, and so probably change slowly. Corporate cash flows tend to be fairly persistent as well, largely because the conditions in an industry and in the economy typically change slowly.[5] Corporate cash reserves are probably even more persistent than cash flows, since stocks change less rapidly than flows. Because industry buyer participation and cash flow are persistent, liquidity would tend to be fairly persistent as well. If an asset is liquid today, people probably expect it to be liquid for a couple of years. Today's liquidity is then generally associated with today's debt capacity.

Although liquidity should be persistent, it should also change over time. Changes in liquidity lead to changes in the optimal debt level. High markets are generally believed to be liquid and low markets to be illiquid. That is, fundamental values rise at the same time as prices come closer to fundamental values. Housing markets and markets for companies illustrate this principle. Below, we offer some reasons why high markets are liquid markets.

A. Why High Markets Are Liquid Markets

The most important reason that liquidity changes over time, and that high liquidity goes together with high asset values, is that industry cash flows drive both value and liquidity. In particular, industry cash flows change dramatically over the business cycle. When the cash flows of industry *buyers* are high, they are more likely to be able to finance asset acquisitions. This raises the liquidity of these assets. Also, fundamental values of assets rise with their *own* cash flows. In part, this is because current cash flows are part of the value, but also because cash flows are likely to be persistent, and so buyers extrapolate current cash flow levels into the future.

---

[5] For evidence on the high persistence of output over time, see Cochrane (1988).

Liquidation Values and Debt Capacity

We see, then, that the fundamental value of an asset rises with its own cash flow, and its liquidity rises with its potential buyers' cash flow. When cash flows of the asset and of its potential buyers rise at the same time, as they would in an industry or general business upturn, both fundamental values and liquidity rise. In such markets, prices are high both because fundamental values are high, and because prices assets fetch are closer to these values since industry buyers are able to finance their purchases. High markets are thus liquid markets. A lot of transactions often take place in such markets, since sellers are willing to part with their assets at prices close to already high fundamental values even without financial distress. In low markets, in contrast, sellers get prices below already-low fundamentals because assets are illiquid. As a result, fewer transactions take place and those that do tend to be forced liquidations.

Another key determinant of both fundamental values and liquidity is the number of potential buyers. Changes in government regulation, such as antitrust policy or limitations on foreign investment, can bring more industry buyers into the market. In real estate markets, lower mortgage rates can be the source of new buyers. If some of these new buyers are high valuation buyers, the influx has the effect of raising fundamental values. But the entry of new buyers also raises the liquidity of the assets. Hence, a broadening of the set of buyers simultaneously increases asset prices and asset liquidity, and accounts for the coincidence of high markets with liquid markets. As liquidity rises, debt capacity rises as well because of the possibility of reselling to one of the many new buyers.

B. Self-Fulfilling Liquidity and Debt Capacity

In our discussion so far, we have focused on exogenous changes, such as those in cash flow or in the number of buyers, as the reasons for increased liquidity and debt capacity. But to some extent, these processes are self-reinforcing. When liquidity increases, by definition assets sell at prices closer to their values under best management. Someone who wants to buy a different asset from the one he owns can sell it at a price close to value in best use and buy another one. Such buyers would tend to avoid an illiquid market because they would not be sure that they can sell their own assets on good terms. As such, buyers enter the market in the belief that they can easily resell this or some other asset should the need arise; they each help to increase liquidity further and their beliefs thus become self-fulfilling.

This analysis might be germane to housing markets, where people might try to buy houses only if they know that they can sell theirs on attractive terms. When a housing market is liquid, many people are willing to be buyers and sellers, reinforcing this liquidity. In contrast, when a market is illiquid, people do not become buyers because they can't sell their old house at a good price, and so the market stays illiquid. In liquid markets, there are many transactions, high prices, and high debt capacity because the resale market is good. The reverse is true in illiquid markets. Similarly, corporations might trade divisions to find best matches in liquid markets because they know they can sell poor matches, and abstain from trading in illiquid markets, thus keeping them illiquid.

There is an additional important feedback from debt capacity to liquidity. People borrow and banks lend in liquid markets because resale is attractive. But resale is made more attractive by the ability of future buyers to borrow. So the ability to borrow increases liquidity, which in turn raises the ability to borrow. In our real estate example, buyers might choose debt finance precisely because they know that if they need to resell, other buyers would have access to debt finance. In this way, not only does liquidity create debt capacity, but debt capacity creates liquidity.

These feedback effects might be strong enough to generate multiple equilibria. In one equilibrium, assets are illiquid and are not bought with debt because buyers recognize that, if assets need to be resold, other buyers could not themselves borrow at attractive terms. In another equilibrium, assets are liquid and buyers use debt to finance them because they expect they can resell them to other buyers who will also have access to debt at attractive terms. People can borrow solely because others they trade with can borrow. In principle, these two equilibria can coexist, holding constant both the number of potential buyers and the cash flow. Widespread belief in high liquidity and debt capacity can be self-fulfilling.

VI. Takeover Waves and Leverage Increases: The Experience of the 1980s

One application of our theory is to takeover waves. Asset acquisitions—such as takeovers, selloffs and divestitures—are highly procyclical (Golbe and White (1988)). This fact is surprising unless one focuses on asset liquidity. If assets sell for their fundamental values, and if capital markets are perfect, there need be no cyclical pattern to acquisitions. If, in addition, forced liquidations are an important source of acquisitions, acquisitions should be *countercyclical*. In fact, we observe the opposite.

Asset liquidity helps account for the evidence. In recessions, many asset buyers are credit constrained and cannot pay the fundamental values for the assets. Sellers should then try to postpone the sale of assets until markets become more liquid. It is not so much that fundamental values are low when cash flows are low, but that prices are even lower than fundamental values when cash flows are low. By comparison, when cash flows are high, sellers can get prices close to fundamental values since buyers are not credit constrained. Sellers should therefore be willing to part with their assets more readily. The resulting volume of transactions is procyclical.

High corporate cash flows have characterized every takeover wave in this century. In the 1980s, however, an additional reason for increased liquidity was the rise in the number of buyers. Before 1986, the General Utilities doctrine combined with accelerated depreciation provided a tax reason for churning assets. In addition, there has been an influx of foreign acquirers, particularly in food, chemical, electronics, and financial services industries. Most importantly, much of the increase in the takeover activity in the 1980s was in horizontal mergers owing to relaxation of antitrust enforcement. Bhagat et al. (1990) show that, once selloffs are accounted for, over 70 percent of the assets of targets of hostile takeovers end up in the hands of firms in the same industry as these assets.

The increase in the number and the cash flow of industry buyers raised liquidity and debt capacity, since firms could more easily take on debt expecting that they could sell assets and divisions at close to fundamental values if they could not meet interest payments. In fact, many loans during this period were made with a clear understanding that cash flow was insufficient to pay interest from the beginning and assets must be sold to pay down debt. Asset sales were not an unlikely contingency, but a certainty for these loans. Asset liquidity was therefore essential for these loans to be made. In this way, the liquid market for firms and divisions made possible large increases in bank debt and junk bond financing in the 1980s (Bernanke and Campbell (1988), Warshawsky (1990)). Enhanced liquidity made debt financing more attractive both in takeovers and for all companies that might think about asset sales.

Many of the leveraged acquisitions of the 1980s would not have been possible were it not for the liquid market for divisions. This new active market for large firms and their divisions—spawned in part by the relaxation of antitrust enforcement and in part by financial innovation—created the possibilities for debt finance conditional on rapid resale of assets, a practice often essential for leveraged buyouts (LBOs). Bhagat et al. (1990) document that on average 30 percent of assets were sold following a hostile takeover in the 1980s; this average is 40 percent for LBOs. Bustup takeovers are the extreme example of borrowing in anticipation of selling assets. Debt finance in anticipation of a resale of parts in a liquid market made the takeover wave of the 1980s so extensive and so concentrated among the large companies.

When companies were not optimally managed, their assets could be sold at prices above their values as part of these companies. In this case, the costs of a forced liquidation were actually *negative*, since assets could be sold for more than their status quo values. The increased liquidity of the market for assets raised division prices in divestitures, thus increasing the profitability of busting up mismanaged conglomerates. In this way, increased liquidity might have encouraged more efficiency improvements.

The view that the liquidity in the market for corporate assets increased debt capacity contrasts with the conventional view. That view credits junk bonds and other financial innovations with increased takeovers since junk bonds permitted the raiders to attack large companies. Our view is that the liquidity of the market for companies helped generate the growth of the junk bond market. First, takeover waves have taken place during many economic booms, and many takeovers were financed with debt before junk bonds became popular. Second, junk bond financing of takeovers did not really become significant until 1985, several years after the takeover wave of the

1980s became big (Kaplan and Stein (1990)). This fact suggests that taking on junk debt became attractive only after the market for assets became liquid enough. Liquidity seems to have created debt capacity and not just the other way around in the 1980s takeovers, although of course there were important feedback effects as well.

At the end of the 1980s, LBOs and the use of junk bonds declined sharply. Some of the causes of this decline were probably exogenous, such as the forecasted recession, the collapse of Drexel and of prices in the junk bond market, and the troubles of some visible LBOs such as Campeau and Southland. In addition, investors, scared by the few bad episodes, no longer expected markets for divisions to be liquid, and these expectations seemed to become self-fulfilling.

The troubles of the junk bond market meant that new LBOs could not be easily financed and old ones refinanced. But even seasoned LBOs that did not rely on further junk bond financing ran into trouble because their assets became illiquid. Many of these LBOs counted on asset sales to pay down debt (Kaplan and Stein (1991)). Asset illiquidity reduced proceeds from asset sales below previously expected levels, making debt repayment more difficult. In addition, asset illiquidity further weakened the junk bond market, since investors in junk bonds relied on asset sales for principal repayments. The troubles of the junk bond market and declines in asset liquidity reinforced each other, since asset liquidity depends on financing, and financing relies on liquidity. Highly-leveraged transactions will probably resume only when markets for corporate assets become more liquid.

VII. Conclusion

Asset liquidity is an important determinant of the costs of financial distress. This paper has focused on economy- and industry-wide determinants of asset liquidity. Our main conclusions are as follows:

(1) Asset liquidation—through an auction or other sale—does not necessarily allocate assets to the highest value users. As a result, assets with no alternative uses can fetch prices below value in best use when sold during an industry- or an economy-wide recession or when industry buyers are prevented from bidding by regulation. Such fire sales can have substantial private and social costs.

(2) Optimal debt levels are limited by asset illiquidity. For example, even holding cash flow volatility constant, cyclical and growth assets have a lower optimal level of debt finance. Similarly, conglomerates and multi-division firms have a higher optimal debt level at the same level of cash flow volatility.

(3) The optimal leverage of a firm depends on the leverage of other firms in its industry. An industry might have an optimal debt capacity even when its individual firms do not.

(4) Asset liquidity and therefore optimal debt levels change over time. High markets tend to be liquid markets. Beliefs in high liquidity of assets can be self-fulfilling.
(5) Well-documented increases in leverage in the 1980s, both by firms involved in corporate control transactions and by other firms, were attributable at least in part to the liquid market for corporate divisions. This liquid market for divisions was in turn the result of exogenous factors such as relaxed antitrust enforcement and the influx of foreign buyers as well as of an important self-reinforcing component. The widespread expectation of future liquidity and debt capacity created current liquidity and debt capacity.

REFERENCES

Baird, D., 1986, The uneasy case for corporate reorganization, *Journal of Legal Studies* 15, 127-147.
Bernanke, B. and J. Y. Campbell, 1988, Is there a corporate debt crisis? *Brookings Papers on Economic Activity*, 83-125.
Bernanke, B. and M. Gertler, 1989, Agency costs, collateral, and business fluctuations, *American Economic Review* 79, 14-31.
Bhagat, S., A. Shleifer, and R. W. Vishny, 1990, Hostile takeovers in the 1980s: The return to corporate specialization, *Brookings Papers on Economic Activity: Microeconomics*, 1-84.
Chan, K. C. and N. F. Chen, 1991, Structural and return characteristics of small and large firms, *Journal of Finance* 46, 1467-1484.
Cochrane, J. H., 1988, How big is the random walk in GNP? *Journal of Political Economy* 96, 893-920.
Diamond, D. W., 1991, Debt maturity structure and liquidity risk, *Quarterly Journal of Economics* 106, 709-738.
Easterbrook, F. H., 1990, Is corporate bankruptcy efficient? *Journal of Financial Economics*, 27, 411-418.
Froot, K. and J. C. Stein, 1991, Exchange rates and foreign direct investment: An imperfect capital markets approach, *Quarterly Journal of Economics* 106, 1191-1218.
Gertler M. and R. G. Hubbard, 1988, Financial factors in business fluctuations, *Financial Market Volatility* (Federal Reserve Bank of Kansas City).
Gertner R. and D. S. Scharfstein, 1991, A theory of workouts and the effects of reorganization law, *Journal of Finance* 46, 1189-1222.
Golbe, D. L. and L. J. White, 1988, A time series analysis of mergers and acquisitions in the U.S. economy, in Alan J. Auerbach, ed.: *Corporate Takeovers: Causes and Consequences* (University of Chicago Press, Chicago).
Greenwald, B., J. E. Stiglitz, and A. Weiss, 1984, Information imperfections in the capital market and economic fluctuations, *American Economic Review* 74, 174-199.
Harris, M. and A. Raviv, 1990, Capital structure and the informational role of debt, *Journal of Finance* 45, 321-349.
———, 1991, The theory of capital structure, *Journal of Finance* 46, 297-355.
Hart, O., 1991, Theories of optimal capital structure: A principal-agent perspective, Paper prepared for the Brookings Conference on Takeovers, LBO's, and Changing Corporate Forms.
——— and J. Moore, 1989, Default and renegotiation: A dynamic model of debt, MIT Department of Economics Working Paper.
———, 1990, A theory of corporate financial structure based on the seniority of claims, MIT Working Paper 560.

Holland, M., 1990, *When the Machine Stopped* (Harvard Business School Press, Cambridge, MA).

Jensen, M. C., 1986, Agency costs of free cash flow, corporate finance and takeovers, *American Economic Review* 76, 323–329.

——— and W. H. Meckling, 1976, Theory of the firm: Managerial behavior, agency costs and ownership structure, *Journal of Financial Economics* 3, 305–360.

Kaplan, S. N., 1989, Campeau's acquisition of federated: Value destroyed or value added? *Journal of Financial Economics* 25, 191–212.

——— and J. C. Stein, 1990, How risky is debt in highly leveraged transactions: Evidence from public recapitalizations, *Journal of Financial Economics* 27, 215–246.

———, 1991, The evolution of buyout pricing and financial structure in the 1980s, Mimeo, University of Chicago.

Myers, S. C., 1977, Determinants of corporate borrowing, *Journal of Financial Economics* 5, 147–175.

———, 1984, The capital structure puzzle, *Journal of Finance* 39, 575–92.

——— and N. Majluf, 1984, Corporate financing and investment decisions when firms have information that investors do not have, *Journal of Financial Economics* 13, 187–221.

Smith, C. W., Jr., and J. B. Warner, 1979, On financial contracting: An analysis of bond covenants, *Journal of Financial Economics* 7, 117–162.

Stulz, René, 1990, Managerial discretion and optimal financing policies, *Journal of Financial Economics*, 26, 3–27.

Warshawsky, M., 1990, Is there a corporate debt crisis? Another look, Finance and Economics Discussion Series Paper No. 110 (Federal Reserve Board).

Williamson, O. E., 1988, Corporate finance and corporate governance, *Journal of Finance* 43, 567–592.

[4]

A Theory of Predation Based on Agency Problems in Financial Contracting

By PATRICK BOLTON AND DAVID S. SCHARFSTEIN*

By committing to terminate funding if a firm's performance is poor, investors can mitigate managerial incentive problems. These optimal financial constraints, however, encourage rivals to ensure that a firm's performance is poor; this raises the chance that the financial constraints become binding and induce exit. We analyze the optimal financial contract in light of this predatory threat. The optimal contract balances the benefits of deterring predation by relaxing financial constraints against the cost of exacerbating incentive problems. (JEL 610)

In this paper, we present a theory of predation based on agency problems in financial contracting. Our work is closest in spirit to the "long-purse" (or "deep-pockets") theory of predation, in which cash-rich firms drive their financially constrained competitors out of business by reducing their rivals' cash flow.[1] Although the existing theory is suggestive, it begs important questions. Why are firms financially constrained? And, even if firms are financially constrained, why don't creditors lift these constraints under the threat of predation?

We attempt to answer these questions. In Section I, we present a model (which is of independent interest) in which financial constraints emerge endogenously as a way of mitigating incentive problems. We argue that the commitment to terminate a firm's funding if its performance is poor ensures that the firm does not divert resources to itself at the expense of investors. This termination threat, however, is costly in a competitive environment. Rival firms then have an incentive to ensure that the firm's performance is indeed poor. This increases the likelihood that investors cut off funding, and induces premature exit.

In Section II, we analyze the optimal contract when firms and investors take this cost into account. In general, the optimal response to predation is to lower the sensitivity of the refinancing decision to firm performance. There are two ways of doing this. One is to increase the likelihood that the firm is refinanced if it performs poorly; the other is to lower the likelihood that the firm remains in operation even if it performs well. Both strategies reduce the benefit of predation by lowering the effect of predation on the likelihood of exit. We identify conditions under which each of these strategies is optimal.

There is a tradeoff between deterring predation and mitigating incentive problems; reducing the sensitivity of the refinancing decision discourages predation, but exacerbates the incentive problem. Depending on the importance of the incentive problem relative to the predation threat, the equilibrium optimal contract may or may not deter predation.

We are by no means the first to present a theory of rational predation. In the existing models of rational predation,[2] one firm tries

---

*Department of Economics, Harvard University, Cambridge, MA 02138 and Sloan School of Management, MIT, Cambridge, MA 02139. This paper is a revised version of "Agency Problems, Financial Contracting, and Predation." For helpful comments, we thank Drew Fudenberg, Oliver Hart, Patrick Rey, Julio Rotemberg, Jean Tirole, the anonymous referees, and seminar participants at Harvard, MIT, and the European Conference on Information Economics in Madrid.

[1] See, for example, John McGee (1958), Lester Telser (1966), Jean-Pierre Benoit (1984), and Jean Tirole (1988).

[2] See for example, Steven Salop and Carl Shapiro (1982), David Scharfstein (1984), and Garth Saloner (1987). These papers draw much from the early work of Paul Milgrom and John Roberts (1982) on rational limit-pricing.

to convince its rivals that it would be unprofitable to remain in the industry; predation changes rivals' beliefs about industry demand or the predator's costs. In our model, there is common knowledge that production in each period is a positive net present value investment. Thus, predation need not be effective by changing rivals' beliefs, but rather by adversely affecting the agency relationship between the firm and its creditors. Drew Fudenberg and Jean Tirole (1986) have also argued that agency problems between creditors and the firm can result in financial constraints that induce predatory behavior by rivals. Their model differs from ours in that they consider only a sequence of one-period contracts and do not consider optimal responses to predation.

Our paper is also related to the recent work on the interaction between product-market competition and the capital market. James Brander and Tracy Lewis (1986) and Vojislav Maksimovic (1986) are among the earliest papers. They point out that because equity holders receive only the residual above a fixed debt obligation, the marginal production incentives of managers who maximize the value of equity depends on the debt-equity ratio. Therefore, investors can use capital structure to induce managers to compete more agressively, in the process affecting product-market equilibrium. There are two drawbacks of their work. First, it restricts attention to a subset of feasible financial instruments; under a broader set of instruments, product-market equilibrium would be very different. Our paper, in contrast, derives the set of feasible contracts from first principles and analyzes optimal contracts within that set. Second, in these papers, financial structure plays no role other than through its effect on product-market strategy. In our analysis, financial policy also affects agency problems within the firm.

These papers are similar in spirit to the work of John Vickers (1985) and Chaim Fershtman and Kenneth Judd (1987a,b) who analyze the effect of managerial incentive contracting (rather than financial contracting) on product-market competition. Like Brander and Lewis's model, firms gain competitive advantage by altering managerial objectives. For example, by basing compensation on sales, shareholders can induce the manager to produce more output. This may have strategic value if firms compete in a Cournot environment. Unlike Brander and Lewis's model, but like ours, the latter Fershtman and Judd paper analyzes optimal contracts. These contracts serve the dual function of mitigating agency problems and affecting product-market competition.

On a formal level, our basic framework is similar to work by Roger Myerson (1982) and Michael Katz (1987). These papers consider incentive problems between a principal and an agent in which the agent's performance both influences and is influenced by other parties. Although Myerson's development is in an abstract principal-agent setting and Katz's main application is to bargaining, this framework seems particularly well-suited to analyze the interaction between product-market competition and the capital market.

An important implication of our approach is that financial structure affects firms' financing costs as well as their gross profitability. Information and incentive problems in the capital market can determine the structure of the product market. This is in contrast to most models, in which capital structure only affects financing costs.[3]

Finally, we note that the dynamic nature of our of financial contracting has some novel features. We assume that contracts cannot be made directly contingent on profits. To induce managers to pay out cash flows to investors, the firm is liquated when its payouts are low. Liquidation occurs although it is inefficient, and the threat of liquidation is credible. The optimal dynamic financial contracts that we describe resemble standard debt contracts in many ways.

I. Contracting Without Predation

There are two firms labeled A and B, who compete in periods 1 and 2. At the beginning of each period, both firms incur a fixed cost,

---

[3] This is also a feature of Robert Gertner, Robert Gibbons, and Scharfstein (1988). In that paper capital structure decisions can convey information to both the capital and product markets.

F. The firms differ with respect to how they finance this cost. Firm A has a "deep pocket," a stock of internally generated funds which it can use to finance this cost. In contrast, firm B has a "shallow pocket"; it must raise all funds from the capital market.

The first step in our analysis is to characterize the contractual relationship between firm B and its sources of capital. We assume that there is one investor who makes a take-it-or-leave-it contract offer to firm B at the initial date 0, which firm B accepts if the contract provides nonnegative expected value. The assumption that the investor rather than the firm has all the bargaining power may seem unrealistic. This is particularly so for a firm issuing public debt or equity in a well-functioning capital market with many competing investors. However, young companies requiring venture capital, or older ones placing private debt or equity, are likely to bargain with investors. In reality, neither side has all the bargaining power; our assumption simply sharpens our results without affecting their essential character. Indeed, it will become clear below that the termination threat must be part of any feasible contract regardless of the competitive structure of the capital market.

Firm B's gross profit (before financing costs) in each period is either π_1 or π_2, where $\pi_1 < \pi_2$. At the beginning of each period, all players believe that $\pi = \pi_1$ with probability θ. Thus, we are assuming that profits are independently distributed across periods. We make this assumption to distinguish our results from models of predation (based on the limit-pricing model of Milgrom and Roberts, 1982) in which the incumbent firm tries to convince the entrant that it would be unprofitable to remain in the industry. These models rest on the assumption that the entrant's profits are positively serially correlated. As we argue below, we would strengthen our results by assuming that profits are positively correlated.

For simplicity, we assume that the discount rate is zero. We also assume that $\pi_1 <$ F: with positive probability the investment loses money. Later we analyze the model under the assumption that $\pi_1 > F$ and argue that in that case as well the termination threat is valuable (although the analysis raises some other issues). In both cases, the expected net present value of the investment is positive:

$$\bar{\pi} \equiv \theta \pi_1 + (1 - \theta) \pi_2 > F.$$

The agency problem we analyze stems from the impossibility of making financial contracts explicitly contingent on realized profit. There are two alternative interpretations of this assumption. One is that at the end of each period, the firm privately observes profit. The other is that profit is observable but not verifiable; although both the firm and investor can observe profit, the courts cannot, and hence these parties cannot write an enforceable profit-contingent contract.[4]

We do assume that the investor can force the firm pay out a minimum of π_1 in each period. If the courts know that this is the minimum possible profit, then a contract of this form is feasible. This assumption amounts to the claim that π_1 is the verifiable component of profit and the residual $\pi_2 - \pi_1$ is the non-verifiable component.

There are at least three reasons for assuming that contracts cannot be made fully contingent on realized profit. First, it is often difficult to judge whether particular expenses are necessary; what look like justifiable expenses may really be managerial perquisites with no productive value. Thus, there is scope for managers to divert resources away from investors to themselves. A second, related reason is that the firm might be affiliated with another firm, thus providing some flexibility in the joint allocation of costs and revenues. Finally, from a methodological perspective, the assumption that profits are not observable generates simple and intuitive results that generalize to a wide variety of

---

[4] In many situations, the latter interpretation is more plausible; an investor is often closely involved in the firm's operations, whereas the courts are not. Irregular accounting practices can make it difficult for outside parties to know the firm's true profitability. Although these assumptions have the same implications in the basic model we analyze, they will have different implications if renegotiation is possible. We discuss this in more detail in Section II, Part B.

realistic agency models. One such model is discussed in Section II, Part B.[5]

In a one-period model, the investor would not invest in the firm. To see this, let R_i be the transfer from the firm to the investor at date 1 if the manager reports that profit is π_i, $i = 1, 2$. Assuming limited liability protects the firm and its managers, and that the firm has no other assets, R_i can be no greater than π_i. Clearly, it will report the profit level that minimizes financing costs. Since $R_i \leq \pi_i$, at date 1 the investor can receive at most $\pi_1 < F$ and hence would always lose money. If instead the relationship lasts for two periods, the investor can control whether the firm receives financing in the second period. The investor can threaten to cut off funding in the second period if the firm defaults in the first. This threat induces the firm to pay more than π_1 in the first period. Note that this threat is credible; since $\pi_1 - F < 0$, no investor wishes to finance the firm in the second period.

Formally, we analyze the contract-design problem as a direct revelation game, in which the terms of the contract are based on the firm's report of its profit. In particular, suppose the investor gives the firm F dollars at date 0 to fund first-period production. As in the above one-period model, let R_i be the transfer at date 1 if the firm reports profits of π_i in the first period. Let $\beta_i \in [0,1]$ be the probability that the investor gives the firm F dollars at date 1 to fund second-period production if the firm reports π_i in the first period.[6] We assume that without this second-round financing the firm lacks the necessary funds to operate in the second period.[7] Finally, let R_{ij} be the transfer from the firm to the investor at date 2 if the first-period report is π_i and the second-period report is π_j.

It is clear from the argument presented above for the one-period model that $R_{i1} = R_{i2}$; the second-period transfer cannot depend on second-period profit because the firm would always report the profit level corresponding to the lower transfer. Thus, let R^i be the second-period transfer if the first-period reported profit is π_i. It follows from the limited liability assumption that $R^i \leq \pi_i - R_i + \pi_1$; the second-period transfer cannot exceed the surplus cash from the first period, $\pi_i - R_i$, plus the minimum profit in the second period, π_1.[8]

The optimal contract maximizes the expected profits of the investor subject to the following constraints: (1) the firm truthfully reveals its profit at dates 1 and 2 (incentive compatibility); (2) the contract does not violate limited liability; (3) the firm opts to sign the contract at date 0 (individual rationality). Formally, the problem is the following:

$$\text{Maximize}_{\{\beta_i, R_i, R^i\}} -F + \theta\left[R_1 + \beta_1(R^1 - F)\right]$$
$$+ (1-\theta)\left[R_2 + \beta_2(R^2 - F)\right],$$

subject to

(1) $\quad \pi_2 - R_2 + \beta_2(\bar{\pi} - R^2)$
$$\geq \pi_2 - R_1 + \beta_1(\bar{\pi} - R^1);$$

(2) $\quad \pi_i \geq R_i,$

(2') $\quad \pi_i - R_i + \pi_1 \geq R^i, \quad i = 1, 2;$

(3) $\quad \theta\left[\pi_1 - R_1 + \beta_1(\bar{\pi} - R^1)\right]$
$$+ (1-\theta)\left[\pi_2 - R_2 + \beta_2(\bar{\pi} - R^2)\right]$$
$$\geq 0.$$

---

[5] Robert Townsend (1979) and Douglas Gale and Martin Hellwig (1985) present models in which investors and firms can write profit-contingent contracts for some finite cost; this contrasts with our assumption of infinite costs. Below, we discuss the relationship between these models and ours.

[6] For now, we are assuming that there exists an enforceable randomization scheme. We discuss this assumption in greater detail below.

[7] One can show that this amounts to assuming that $\pi_2 - \pi_1 < F$.

[8] Implicit in this formulation is the assumption that the firm must keep profits (net of transfers to the investor) in the firm between dates 1 and 2, but that at the end of period 2 any profit left over can be consumed by the entrepreneur. This is consistent with the assumption that profits cannot be observed.

The incentive-compatibility constraint (1) ensures that when profit is high the firm does not report that profit is low. If profit is π_2, the firm receives some surplus in the first period if it reports π_1 since $R_1 \leq \pi_1 < \pi_2$; however, by setting $\beta_1 < \beta_2$ the investor makes it costly for the firm to report π_1, since the firm generally receives surplus in the second period.

We have omitted the incentive-compatibility constraint ensuring that the firm reports π_1 rather than π_2. We demonstrate later that this constraint is not binding. Note also that the limited-liability constraints (2) and (2') imply that the individual-rationality constraint (3) is not binding.

The following two lemmas, which we prove in the Appendix, simplify analysis of the optimal contract.

LEMMA 1: *The incentive compatibility constraint (1) is binding at an optimum.*

LEMMA 2: *There exists an optimal contract in which second-period transfers, R^1 and R^2, equal π_1.*

Lemma 1 is a typical feature of contracting problems. Lemma 2 establishes that the investor can receive at most π_1 from the firm in the second period because there is no termination threat at that time.

These two lemmas simplify the maximization problem to

(4) $\quad$ Maximize $- F + R_1$

$\qquad + \beta_2(1 - \theta)(\bar{\pi} - F)$

$\qquad - \beta_1[\theta F + (1 - \theta)\bar{\pi} - \pi_1],$

subject to the limited-liability constraint, $\pi_i \geq R_i$, $i = 1, 2$.

Let $\{R_1^*, \beta_1^*, R_2^*, \beta_2^*\}$ denote the optimal contract. It follows immediately that $R_1^* = \pi_1$ and $\beta_2^* = 1$. Moreover, because both F and $\bar{\pi}$ exceed π_1, the last bracketed term is positive. Thus, $\beta_1^* = 0$. It then follows from the incentive-compatibility constraint (1) that $R_2^* = \bar{\pi}$. Finally, this contract satisfies the limited-liability constraints and (given that $R_2^* = \bar{\pi} > \pi_1$) the omitted incentive constraint.[9]

There are two reasons why the investor cuts off funding if the firm reports low profits. First, the investor avoids losing $F - \pi_1$ in the second period. Second, it induces the firm to report profits truthfully, enabling the investor to extract more surplus from the firm in the first period. To see this, note that the incentive constraint implies

(5) $\quad R_2^* = \pi_1 + (1 - \beta_1)(\bar{\pi} - \pi_1).$

The term $\bar{\pi} - \pi_1$, is the firm's expected surplus in the second period given it operates then. By reporting π_1 rather than π_2, the firm reduces by $(1 - \beta_1)$ the probability that it receives this surplus. A marginal reduction in β_1 therefore lowers by $\bar{\pi} - \pi_1$ the expected value of reporting π_1. Hence, it increases by $\bar{\pi} - \pi_1$ the amount the investor can require the firm to pay when it reports profit of π_2.

Finally, we must determine the conditions under which the investor earns nonnegative profit. Given the optimal contract, the investor's expected profits are $\pi_1 - F + (1 - \theta)(\bar{\pi} - F)$. Thus, for the investor to invest at date 0, F can be no greater than $\bar{\pi} - (\bar{\pi} - \pi_1)/(2 - \theta)$. As a result, some positive net present value projects may not be funded.

We summarize these results in the following proposition.

PROPOSITION 1: *The investor invests at date 0, if and only if $F < \bar{\pi} - (\bar{\pi} - \pi_1)/(2 - \theta)$. In this case, $R_1^* = \pi_1$, $\beta_1^* = 0$, $R_2^* = \bar{\pi}$, $\beta_2^* = 1$; the firm operates in the second period if and only if its first-period profits are π_2.*

The proposition implies that there is an *ex post* inefficiency; the firm is liquidated when first-period profit is π_1 even though

---

[9] Note that the firm weakly prefers to announce the true profit, when first-period profit is π_1. If the firm reports π_2, it is unable to make its first-period payment. In this case, the investor is paid π_1 and does not refinance the firm. The firm is then indifferent between the profit reports, in which case we assume that it reports its true profit.

$\bar{\pi} > F$ and it is efficient to operate.[10] It is natural to ask whether, at date 1, after first-period profit of π_1 is realized, the two parties wish to tear up the original contract and renegotiate a mutually beneficial arrangement. Note, however, that although it is efficient to produce, the most the investor can receive from the firm is $\pi_1 < F$. Thus, it is impossible to negotiate around the contractually specified inefficiency and no other investor would be willing to lend money. *Our results therefore do not depend on the assumption that renegotiation is impossible or that other investors are irrational.*[11]

A. Discussion

The main point of the analysis is that a firm's performance affects its financing costs *and* its access to capital. This result is quite general and captures an important feature of corporate-financing arrangements. For example, in venture-capital financing the venture capitalist rarely provides the entrepreneur with enough capital up front to see a new product from its early test-marketing stage to full-scale production. (See William Sahlman, 1986.) Instead, typical venture-financing arrangements take the form of "staged capital commitment." Initially, the venture capitalist provides enough money to finance the firm's start-up needs like research and product development. Conditional on the firm's performance in this early stage, the venture capitalist may provide further financing to fund test-marketing, and then full-scale production.

There are at least two reasons why such contracts are used. First, they mitigate adverse selection problems. Entrepreneurs who have confidence in the venture accept contracts of this form more willingly because they know that when they return for more funding it will be at favorable terms. This point is similar to Mark Flannery's (1986) explanation of short-term debt and Benjamin Hermalin's (1986) argument that more able workers will sign short-term contracts to signal their ability. Second, staged financing arrangements reduce incentive problems between entrepreneurs and financiers. Requiring the firm to return to the venture capitalist for further funding limits the extent to which management can pursue its own interests (like consuming excess cash) at the expense of the venture capitalist. Our model formalizes this second benefit of staged capital commitment.

The model applies to more than just venture capital. Any disbursement of corporate funds through, for example, debt payments, dividends, or share repurchases, increases the chance that the firm will be unable to finance investment internally and must return to the capital market for further financing. And, as argued above, the commitment to go back to the capital market can increase value either through the information it conveys or its effect on managerial incentives. Michael Jensen (1986) has made a similar point: forcing managers to pay out cash prevents them from spending free cash flow on unprofitable investment projects.

Joseph Stiglitz and Andrew Weiss (1983) have also argued that the termination threat is an effective incentive device. Their analysis, however, differs from ours in two ways: the contracts they consider are not optimal; and the incentive problem concerns the choice of project riskiness rather than the observability of profits.

Finally, the agency problem we analyzed is related to the one-period models of Townsend (1979) and Gale and Hellwig (1985). In these models, the investor has a costly inspection technology that enables him to make payments contingent on profits. The optimal contract specifies that if the firm reports low enough profits, then the investor inspects and confiscates all of the firm's profits. Thus, inspection in these models plays the same role as the termination

---

[10] This result is reminiscent of Townsend (1982) where an inefficiency in the second period facilitates trade in the first period. Like our model, trade cannot be supported if there is only one period.

[11] A more subtle set of questions arise if the firm reports π_1, when profits are really π_2 and then tries to renegotiate the contract. We turn to this question in the next section.

threat.[12] There is one important difference, however. In the inspection models it is never optimal for the investor to inspect once the firm has reported low profits even though the contract calls for him to do so; at this point, the investor knows the firm's profits and need not inspect. Thus, the inspection threat is not credible. In contrast, the termination threat in our model is credible; since $\pi_1 < F$, the investor always prefers to cut off funds when the firm's profits are low.[13]

B. Extensions

Other Agency Problems. Our model focuses on a particular agency problem, which enables us to make our point in the simplest possible way. We believe that the termination threat is useful for a wide variety of agency problems. The following example exhibits how this basic idea extends to the familiar effort-elicitation model of agency. This model also shows that our results do not depend on the assumption that profits are privately observed.

Suppose there are two periods of production and that in each period the manager can "work" or "shirk." By working, the risk neutral manager increases the probability that profit is π_2, but he incurs a utility cost. If the manager has limited wealth or is protected by limited liability, investors cannot sell him the entire firm (which is otherwise the optimal solution to the moral-hazard problem when the manager is risk neutral). This implies that if there is only one period of production, the manager must receive some expected surplus to induce him to work. (See Sappington, 1983, for a result along these lines.) This is analogous to the result in the one-period model considered above in which the firm receives an expected surplus of $\bar{\pi} - \pi_1$. The manager, therefore, bears a cost if the firm is not refinanced. Thus, the threat of not refinancing the firm raises the cost of shirking; the investor can then induce greater effort at lower cost.

Correlation in Profits. In this model, profits are independently distributed across periods. Thus, unlike many multiperiod agency models, the principal (investor) learns nothing about the agent's (firm's) profitability over time. We can extend the model to the case where profits are positively serially correlated. In fact, this strengthens our results. Let $E(\pi|\pi_i)$ be expected second-period profits conditional on first-period profits, π_i. With positive serial correlation, $E(\pi|\pi_2) > \bar{\pi}$ and $E(\pi|\pi_2) > E(\pi|\pi_1)$. It is straightforward to establish that the optimal contract sets $\beta_1^* = 0$, $\beta_2^* = 1$, $R_1^* = \pi_1$, and $R_2^* = E(\pi|\pi_2)$. Since the firm's expected surplus in period 2 is greater when first-period profit is π_2, it loses more if it is not refinanced. This reduces the manager's incentive to underreport profits and enables the investor to extract more rent from the firm.[14]

Capacity Expansion. So far we have interpreted β_i as the probability of refinancing. Alternatively, we can interpret β_i as a capacity-expansion parameter; the investor commits to a staged capital-expansion plan contingent on the firm's first-period performance. By this we mean that if profits are π_i, the investor gives the firm enough money to increase capacity by an amount $\beta_i F$. We assume this increases expected profits by $\beta_i \bar{\pi}$.[15] Under this interpretation, we drop the constraint $\beta_i \in [0,1]$, and suppose that β_i lies in some interval $[\underline{\beta}, \bar{\beta}]$. These assumptions preserve the basic structure of our model. Thus, the investor sets $\beta_1 < \beta_2$ to mitigate incentive problems.

---

[12] In our model, if inspection costs are finite, one can show that the investor would never simultaneously use both inspection and the refinancing threat. So if inspection costs are high enough, only the refinancing threat is used.

[13] We are grateful to Julio Rotemberg for pointing out this difference between the models.

[14] If the firm's profits are negatively correlated over time, it loses less if it is not refinanced and it is more difficult for the investor to extract rent from the firm. However, situations in which profits are negatively correlated over time seem rather implausible.

[15] The assumption that expected profits are linear in β is strong, but it could be relaxed without much difficulty.

Renegotiation. The model assumes that renegotiation is not feasible. Suppose instead that after profits are realized the firm and investor can renegotiate mutually beneficial changes in the contract. Further, suppose that profits are observable to both parties (although not verifiable).

If profits are π_2 but the firm reports π_1, under the terms of the contract the firm is not supposed to receive any further financing. However, the firm has leftover cash of $\pi_2 - \pi_1$. Thus, if $\pi_2 - \pi_1 > F$, the firm can finance second-period investment with its own funds. In this case, it is impossible to induce the firm to pay more than π_1 in the first period and thus no investor would finance investment.[16]

This result rests on the assumption that investors cannot enforce a covenant restricting further investment by the firm; however, if investment is verifiable, such a covenant is feasible. Thus, suppose the investor and firm agree on this covenant at date 0 and suppose the firm decides to report π_1 when its profit is π_2. Without permission from the investor, the firm is prohibited from further investment and is forced to liquidate.

Liquidation, however, is inefficient and we would expect the parties to renegotiate around this covenant. Thus, whether the firm is willing to deviate (by reporting π_1 rather than π_2) depends on the outcome of the renegotiation process. If the firm has none of the bargaining power, the most it stands to gain from deviating is $\pi_2 - \pi_1$, which is exactly what it would get if it did not deviate. Since the firm is indifferent between the two alternatives, we can assume it would report profits truthfully. If, instead, the firm has some of the bargaining power during renegotiation, it can extract some of the efficiency gains and thus will earn more than $\pi_2 - \pi_1$ from deviating. Thus, the contract is not "renegotiation-proof" and not incentive compatible.

---

[16] Note that if profit is indeed π_1 there are no excess funds so that the firm cannot invest in violation of the prohibition.

A renegotiation-proof can be designed, however. Suppose that the firm stands to gain a fraction, α, of the efficiency gain from investing, $\bar{\pi} - F$. Then instead of requiring the firm to pay $\bar{\pi}$ if it reports π_2, a renegotiation proof contract requires the firm to pay $\bar{\pi} - \alpha(\bar{\pi} - F)$; this makes the firm indifferent between reporting π_2 truthfully and reporting π_1 and then renegotiating.

The more bargaining power the investor has (the greater is α), the less the investor can require the firm to pay when it reports profit of π_2. If α is large enough so that the firm has most of the bargaining power then the renegotiation-proof payment is so low that the investor cannot cover his financing costs. For example, if α equals one, the firm pays F when profit is π_2 and π_1 when profit is π_1; these payments are not enough to cover the investor's costs. In this case, the possibility of renegotiation at date 1 drives out investment at date 0. There is, however, a wide range of parameter values for which the threat of renegotiation does not affect investment behavior.

The same analysis essentially applies when $\pi_2 - \pi_1 < F$. The only difference is that in this case the firm need not write a covenant against further investment since the firm must return to the investor to raise additional funds. The investor may be willing to lend because the firm has collateral of $\pi_2 - \pi_1$. By reducing the required payment when profit is π_2, the investor can ensure that the contract is renegotiation proof. It may, also, be efficient to restrict the firm from borrowing funds elsewhere because such borrowing induces competition among creditors and transfers some of the bargaining power to the firm.

Other Extensions. The results are easily generalized to a continuum of profit levels. One can show that if first-period profits are greater than $\bar{\pi}$, $\beta = 1$ and the firm pays back $\bar{\pi}$ in the first period. If profits are below $\bar{\pi}$ the firm pays back all of its first-period profits and it is refinanced with some probability between zero and one; the greater the firm's profits the greater the likelihood it is refinanced. In many ways, this contract resembles a debt contract: the firm is supposed to pay back $\bar{\pi}$; if it does not, all of its profits are paid over to the creditor and there is some chance that the firm is liquidated.

One can also extend the model to assume that there is competition among investors at date 0 so that effectively the firm has all the bargaining power initially. In this case one can show that the contract involves $\beta_2^* = 1$ and $1 > \beta_1^* > 0$. The termination threat will still be used, but to a lesser extent and the contract will be more efficient.

II. Predation and the Optimal Contract

In this section we model explicitly the interaction between the firm's financial policy and product-market competition. To begin, suppose the investor and firm B ignore the existence of firm A when designing an optimal financial contract; they assume that (stochastic) profits are exogenous. In this case, the financial contract is as described above. But, this makes it attractive for firm A to prey. If firm A can lower firm B's expected first-period profit (say, by reducing its price or increasing its advertising), then it can increase the probability that firm B exits. Firm A will do so if the costs of taking such actions are less than the expected benefits of becoming a monopolist.

To formalize these ideas, we model predation as follows: for a cost $c > 0$, firm A can increase from θ to μ the probability that firm B earns low profit, π_1, in period 1. If firm B exits, firm A becomes a monopolist and its second-period expected profits are π^m. If, instead, firm B remains in the market, firm A's expected profits are π^d. Thus, given a contract in which the pair $(\beta_1, \beta_2) = (0,1)$, the expected benefits of predation are $(\mu - \theta)(\pi^m - \pi^d)$. It preys provided $(\mu - \theta)(\pi^m - \pi^d) > c$, or defining $\Delta \equiv c/[(\mu - \theta)(\pi^m - \pi^d)]$, if $\Delta < 1$. If it does prey, the investor's expected profits are $\pi_1 - F + (1 - \mu)(\bar{\pi} - F)$.

More generally, given any financial contract of firm B, firm A preys if $(\beta_2 - \beta_1)(\mu - \theta)(\pi^m - \pi^d) > c$ or $(\beta_2 - \beta_1) > \Delta$. Hence, the benefits of predation depend on firm B's financial contract. Note that when the investors of firm B ignore the possibility of predation, they maximize the benefit of predation to firm A, since $\beta_2 - \beta_1$ is largest when $\beta_2 = 1$ and $\beta_1 = 0$. *The contract that minimizes agency problems, maximizes the rival's incentive to prey.* To make the analysis interesting, we assume for the remainder of the paper that the parameters are such that if $\beta_2 = 1$ and $\beta_1 = 0$, it is optimal to prey, that is, $\Delta < 1$.

To analyze the effect of financial contracting on product-market equilibrium we need to make two further informational assumptions. First, we assume that the courts cannot observe firm A's predatory action. This is a reasonable assumption in light of the difficulties legal scholars and economists have encountered in defining predation. And, even if a reasonable definition of predation did exist, the information that the courts would need to use it could make enforcement unworkable. For example, the courts would need detailed knowledge of demand functions to know whether a firm's advertising and pricing policies were predatory.[17]

Given that the court cannot observe predation, firm B and the investors cannot make the contract contingent on the predatory action of firm A. Notice that we do allow firm B and its investors to observe firm A's predatory actions. This distinguishes our model from signaling (Milgrom and Roberts, 1982) and signal-jamming (Fudenberg and Tirole, 1986) models of predation which rely on the assumption that predation is not observable.

Our second informational assumption concerns the observability by firm A of the contract between firm B and its investors. If the predator can observe the contract, then the investor can use the contract to influence firm A's actions. By reducing the sensitivity of the refinancing decision to first-period profit, that is, reducing the difference be-

---

[17]See, for example, Paul Joskow and Alvin Klevorick (1979) for one attempt at defining predation and a discussion of the difficulties in doing so. See Scharfstein (1984) for a model which takes account of the costs of detecting predation.

tween β_2 and β_1, the investor reduces the gains from predation. For small enough values of $(\beta_2 - \beta_1)$ he deters predation. He can do so by strengthening the commitment to refinance the firm, that is, increasing β_1. In the extreme, he can deter predation by setting $\beta_2 = \beta_1 = 1$. That is, the investor can give firm B a "deep pocket," a commitment of resources to finance investment in both periods. Alternatively, the investor can deter predation by refinancing the firm less often, that is, reducing β_2. We refer to this as a "shallow-pocket" strategy.

In many cases it is reasonable to suppose that contracts are observable; for example, the Securities and Exchange Commission requires all publicly held firms to disclose information on their financial structure. For privately held companies, however, there is no disclosure requirement. It may be more reasonable to assume that for these firms financial contracts cannot be observed. We therefore consider the two cases of observable and unobservable contracts.[18]

A. Observable Contracts

If contracts are observable, the investor can ensure that firm A does not prey by writing a contract that satisfies the following "no-predation constraint":

(6) $(\beta_2 - \beta_1)(\mu - \theta)(\pi^m - \pi^d) \leq c$, or

(6') $(\beta_2 - \beta_1) \leq \Delta$.

That is, the investor can deter predation by reducing the sensitivity of the contract to firm B's performance.

Recall that our formulation assumes that there exists a public randomization technology enabling the investor to set $\beta_i \in (0,1)$. Without such a technology, the investor is restricted to deterministic schemes. This means the only feasible contract in which the firm enters must set $(\beta_1, \beta_2) = (0,1)$. Thus, one cannot deter predation in this case. This strengthens our point that preda-

[18]For more discussion of the different implications of contract observability, see Katz (1987).

tion can occur as an equilibrium phenomenon.

To determine the efficient contractual response to predation if randomization is feasible (or if we interpret β as a capacity-expansion parameter), we first analyze the optimal contract that deters predation. We then compare this contract to the optimal contract given predation. The investor chooses the contract with the higher payoff, provided it earns nonnegative profit.

The optimal predation-deterring contract solves the following program:

$$\max_{\{\beta_1, R_i\}} - F + \theta[R_1 + \beta_1(\pi_1 - F)] + (1 - \theta)[R_2 + \beta_2(\pi_1 - F)],$$

subject to the incentive constraint (1), the limited-liability constraint (2), and the no-predation constraint (6').

This maximization problem is identical to the problem analyzed in Section I except for the constraint (6') which ensures that no predation occurs in the first period. At an optimum, this constraint is binding and $\beta_2 - \beta_1 = \Delta$; otherwise, the optimal solution would be $\beta_2 = 1$, $\beta_1 = 0$, firm A would prey, and the constraint would be violated. Observing that, as before, $R_1 = \pi_1$, the binding incentive constraint (1) becomes $R_2 = \Delta \bar{\pi} + (1 - \Delta)\pi_1$. Substituting these equalities into the objective function, we reduce the maximization problem to

$$\max - F + \beta_1(\pi_1 - F) + (1 - \theta)\Delta(\bar{\pi} - F).$$

It then follows that $\beta_1^* = 0$ and $\beta_2^* = \Delta$; *the investor optimally deters predation by lowering the probability that the firm is refinanced when its profits are high*. This deters predation because there is little incentive for firm A to pay a cost, c, to ensure that profits are low. But, why lower β_2 rather than increase β_1? A change in either of these two variables has the same effect on the no predation constraint and the incentive constraint. However, increasing β_1 is costly because it increases the probability that the investor loses $F - \pi_1$ in the second period, whereas lowering β_2 reduces this probability.

Finally, note that the expected profit from following this predation-deterring strategy is $\pi_1 - F + (1-\theta)\Delta(\bar{\pi} - F)$. Thus, conditional on entering, firm B chooses to deter predation provided $(1-\theta)\Delta > 1 - \mu$. And, if $\pi_1 - F + \max\{(1-\theta)\Delta, 1-\mu\}(\bar{\pi} - F) > 0$, it will be profitable to enter. We summarize these results below.

PROPOSITION 2: *Firm B enters if and only if*

$$\pi_1 - F + \max\{(1-\theta)\Delta, 1-\mu\}(\bar{\pi} - F) \geq 0.$$

If B enters, and $(1-\theta)\Delta \geq 1 - \mu$, the optimal contract deters predation. In this case, $\beta_1^* = 0$, $R_1^* = \pi_1$, $\beta_2^* = \Delta$, and $R_2^* = \Delta\bar{\pi} + (1-\Delta)\pi_1 < \bar{\pi}$. If firm B enters and $(1-\theta)\Delta < 1 - \mu$, the contract is as given in Proposition 1 and firm A preys.

The striking result that the shallow-pocket strategy optimally deters predation depends on the assumption that $\pi_1 < F$. Suppose instead that $\pi_1 > F$. By setting $\beta_1 = 0$, the investor is able to extract more surplus from the firm in the first period, but he foregoes positive surplus of $\pi_1 - F$ in the second period. Provided π_1 is not too large, the optimal contract still sets $(\beta_1, \beta_2) = (0,1)$.[19]

In the presence of a predatory threat, however, $\beta_2 - \beta_1$, must equal Δ to deter predation. But, here the investor earns positive profit in the second period. So rather than reduce β_2, β_1 should be increased; this increases the probability that the investor earns a profit of $\pi_1 - F$ in the second period. In this case, a deep pocket is the optimal response to the predatory threat.

Note, however, that if $\pi_1 > F$ it is inefficient for firm B to exit in the second period. Thus, if the contract calls for the firm to be liquidated in the second period when its first-period profits are low, the investor and the firm may be able to renegotiate a more efficient arrangement in which the firm remains in operation and the two parties split the surplus $\pi_1 - F$. If bargaining is efficient, firm B would never exit and firm A has no incentive to prey.

There are reasons to believe, however, that efficient renegotiation may not always occur. First, it can be in the investor's interest to ensure that such renegotiation is infeasible even though it encourages predation. By doing so, he may be able to extract more surplus from the firm in the first period. One way of committing not to renegotiate is to bring in other investors to finance the firm. If each has only a small stake and there are costs of negotiation, then none will have an incentive to renegotiate even though it would be efficient to do so if there were only one investor.[20] Second, our model assumes symmetric information about future profitability. A more realistic model would allow for the possibility of asymmetric information in which case bargaining is more likely to break down.

B. *Unobservable Contracts*

The assumption that contracts are observable may be inappropriate in some circumstances. There are no financial disclosure requirements for privately held firms, so it may be impossible for outsiders to observe a firm's contractual relationship with its creditors. Thus, we also investigate the case in which firm A cannot observe the contract signed by firm B and the investor. Instead, firm A must make a rational conjecture about the chosen contract.

When contracts are unobservable, it is as if the investor and the predator play a simultaneous move game.[21] (We can ignore firm B

---

[19] The precise condition, discussed in more detail in an earlier version of our paper, is that $\theta F + (1-\theta)\pi - F > 0$. This can be seen from inspection of (4) in the text.

[20] For example, small bondholders do not typically participate in financial renegotiations. Bankruptcy law recognizes this difficulty and provides a mechanism for facilitating renegotiation through the Chapter 11 reorganization process.

[21] Note, however, that we continue to assume that firm B signs the contract before firm A decides whether to prey. It might be argued that if the contract is signed first it would be in the interest of firm A to reveal its contract. But, as Katz points out in a related context, if the observed contract is not efficient, the two parties

because its actions follow trivially from the contract the investor chooses.) Firm A's strategy set is composed of two pure strategies: "prey," which we denote by P, and "do not prey," which we denote by NP. The investor's strategy set is essentially a choice of a pair $(\beta_1, \beta_2) \in [0,1]^2$. (We can ignore R_1 and R_2 since firm A is only concerned with the probabilities of refinancing, β_1 and β_2.)

We now establish that if firm B enters, in equilibrium $(\beta_1^*, \beta_2^*) = (0,1)$ and firm A preys. Given any strategy by firm A (and hence any probability of π_1, μ or θ) it is optimal to set $(\beta_1, \beta_2) = (0,1)$, $R_1 = \pi_1$, and $R_2 = \bar{\pi}$; this is a dominant strategy. Firm A's optimal response is then to prey. This forms the unique Nash equilibrium if firm B enters.

With observable contracts, firm B can credibly precommit to a contract that deters predation. But, when contracts are not observable, so that A must conjecture what contract B signed, firm B always wishes to set $(\beta_1, \beta_2) = (0,1)$; no precommitment is possible.

Thus, if contracts are not observable, firm B will enter provided its profits upon entry, $\pi_1 - F + (1-\mu)(\bar{\pi} - F)$, are positive. Note that firm B enters (weakly) less often when contracts are unobservable. These results are summarized in the following proposition.

PROPOSITION 3: *Firm B enters if and only if $\pi_1 - F + (1-\mu)(\bar{\pi} - F) > 0$. If the firm enters, the contract is as given in Proposition 1 and firm A preys.*

This result, like Proposition 2, is sensitive to the assumption that $\pi_1 < F$. If instead $\pi_1 > F$, in general the optimal (β_1, β_2) pair is a function of the probability of π_1 and hence whether firm A preys. Therefore, $(\beta_1, \beta_2) = (0,1)$ is not necessarily a dominant strategy. Given that firm A preys and the probability of π_1 is μ, the optimal response by firm B may be to set $\beta_1 = \beta_2 = 1$. But if this is true, it is not in the interest of firm A to

---

will have an incentive to privately annul the advertised contract and write a new one.

prey. Similarly, if firm A does not prey, it may be optimal to set $(\beta_1, \beta_2) = (0,1)$; but then firm A has an incentive to prey. As a result, there may be no pure strategy equilibrium. One can show, however, that there is a mixed strategy equilibrium in which firm A preys with positive probability and firm B sets $\beta_1 = 1 - \Delta$ and $\beta_2 = 1$.[22] Thus, in equilibrium, the investor partially deters predation.

III. Concluding Remarks

The central argument of this paper is that agency problems in financial contracting can give rise to rational predation. The financial contract that minimizes agency problems also maximizes rivals' incentives to prey. As a result, there is a tradeoff between deterring predation and mitigating incentive problems: reducing the sensitivity of the refinancing decision to the firm's performance discourages predation, but exacerbates the incentive problem. In equilibrium, whether financial contracts deter predation depends on the relative importance of these two effects.

Our theory of predation departs from the existing literature which views predation as an attempt to convince rivals that it would be unprofitable to remain in the industry. In our model, everyone knows it is profitable for the rival to remain in the industry. Nevertheless, predation induces liquidation and exit because it adversely affects the agency relationship between the rival's investors and manager.

Although our model narrowly focuses on predation, we believe that the model provides a useful starting point to analyze a broader set of issues concerning competitive interaction among firms with agency problems and financial constraints. For example, our model suggests that an important determinant of product-market success is the degree to which firms can finance investment with internally generated funds. This is in

---

[22] More details of this argument can be found in an earlier version of our paper issued as a Sloan Working Paper No. 1986-88.

contrast to standard models of dynamic competition in which the only relevant consideration is the total capital stock and not the way in which it was acquired. The impliction of our model are consistent with Gordon Donaldson's (1984) findings that one reason managers prefer internal sources of funds is that it enhances their ability to compete in product markets.

In addition, our model suggests that certain types of product-market competition can increase managerial incentive problems within the firm. As implied by our model, the reliance on external financing exposes the firm to cutthroat competition. This may force the firm to rely more on internal sources of capital than on external ones. But, this reduces the extent to which outside investors monitor the firm and increases the possibility of managerial slack. Thus, external financing comes with costs and benefits: on the one hand, it disciplines management, but on the other, it makes the firm vulnerable in its product markets.

APPENDIX

LEMMA 1: *The incentive-compatibility constraint* (1) *is binding.*

PROOF: Suppose to the contrary that (1) is slack and that the only constraints are (2) and (2'). We establish that the optimal solution to this relaxed program violates (1).

First note that since (1) is slack, we need not be concerned with the effect of $\{\beta_1, R_1, R_1\}$ on the optimal choice of $\{\beta_2, R_2, R_2\}$ and vice versa. Thus, the maximization problem can be written:

Maximize $R_t + \beta_t R^t - \beta_t F$
$\{\beta_t, R_t, R^t\}$

subject to

(A1) $\qquad R_t \leq \pi_t$

(A2) $\qquad R_t + R^t \leq \pi_t + \pi_1$. $\qquad \square$

At an optimum to this program, $R_t = \pi_t$ and $R^t = \pi_1$. This is true in the case where $\beta_t < 1$ because given the constraint on the total payments (A2), it is optimal to shift more of the payment to the first period when it will be received with certainty. If $\beta_t = 1$, any division of payments satisfying $R_t + R^t = \pi_t + \pi_1$ is optimal and we may as well set $R_t = \pi_t$ and $R_t = \pi_1$. (Note that given $\beta_t = 1$ the division of payments between R_t and R^t has no effect on the incentive-compatibility constraint.)

The incentive constraint (1) therefore simplifies to

$$\beta_2(\bar{\pi} - \pi_1) \geq \pi_2 - \pi_1 + \beta_1(\bar{\pi} - \pi_1).$$

It is easily seen that for all feasible values of β_1 and β_2 the inequality cannot be satisfied. Thus the incentive constraint is violated at the optimum of the relaxed program, establishing the contradiction.

LEMMA 2: $R^1 = R^2 = \pi_1$ *is a part of an optimal contract.*

PROOF: Substituting the incentive constraint (1) into the objective function yields the new objective function:

$$-F + R_1 + \beta_1 \big[R^1 - \theta F - (1-\theta)\bar{\pi} \big]$$

$$+ (1-\theta)\beta_2(\bar{\pi} - F).$$

It follows that $\beta_2 = 1$. Hence only the sum, $R^2 + R_2$, and not the individual values R^2 and R_2 affects the objective function and the incentive constraint. Thus we can set $R^2 = \pi_1$. If $\beta_1 = 1$ the same can be said for R_1 and R^1. If $\beta_1 < 1$, R_1 and R^1 will be chosen to maximize $R_1 + \beta_1 R^1$ since it simultaneously maximizes the objective function and relaxes the incentive constraint. This expression is maximized subject to the limited-liability constraints by setting $R_1 = R^1 = \pi_1$. This completes the proof. $\qquad \square$

REFERENCES

Benoit, Jean-Pierre, "Financially Constrained Entry in a Game with Incomplete Information," *Rand Journal of Economics*, Winter 1984, *15*, 490–99.

Bolton, Patrick and Scharfstein, David S., "Agency Problems, Financial Contracting, and Predation," Sloan Working Paper 1988-86, MIT, February 1988.

Brander, James A. and Lewis, Tracy R., "Oligopoly and Financial Structure," *American Economic Review*, December 1986, *76*, 956–70.

Donaldson, Gordon, *Managing Corporate Wealth*, New York: Praeger, 1984.

Fershtman, Chaim and Judd, Kenneth L., "Equilibrium Incentives in Oligopoly," *American Economic Review*, December 1987, *77*, 927–40.

_____, "Strategic Incentive Manipulation in Rivalrous Agency," Northwestern University, 1987.

Flannery, Mark, "Asymmetric Information

and Risky Debt Maturity Choice," *Journal of Finance*, March 1986, *41*, 19-38.

Fudenberg, Drew and Tirole, Jean, "A 'Signal-Jamming' Theory of Predation," *Rand Journal of Economics*, Autumn 1986, *17*, 366-76.

Gale, Douglas and Hellwig, Martin, "Incentive-Compatible Debt Contracts: The One Period Case," *Review of Economic Studies*, October 1985, *52*, 647-64.

Gertner, Robert, Gibbons, Robert and Scharfstein, David, "Simultaneous Signalling to the Capital and Product Markets," *Rand Journal of Economics*, Spring 1988, *19*, 173-90.

Hermalin, Benjamin, "Adverse Selection and Contract Length," MIT, 1986.

Jensen, Michael C., "Agency Costs of Free Cash Flow, Corporate Finance, and Takeovers," *American Economic Review*, May 1986, *76*, 323-29.

Joskow, Paul L. and Klevorick, Alvin K., "A Framework for Analyzing Predatory Pricing Policy," *Yale Law Journal*, December 1979, *89*, 213-70.

Katz, Michael L., "Game-Playing Agents: Contracts as Precommitments," Princeton University, 1987.

Maksimovic, Vojislav, "Capital Structure in a Stochastic Oligopoly," unpublished doctoral dissertation, Harvard University, 1986.

McGee, John, "Predatory Price Cutting: The Standard Oil (N.J.) Case," *Journal of Law and Economics*, October 1958, *1*, 137-69.

Milgrom, Paul and Roberts, John, "Limit Pricing and Entry under Incomplete Information," *Econometrica*, March 1982, *50*, 443-60.

Myerson, Roger B., "Optimal Coordination Mechanisms in Generalized Principal-Agent Problems," *Journal of Mathematical Economics*, June 1982, *10*, 67-81.

Ordover, Janusz A. and Willig, Robert D., "An Economic Definition of Predation: Pricing and Product Innovation," *Yale Law Journal*, November 1981, *91*, 8-53.

Sahlman, William, "Note on Financial Contracting: Deals," Harvard Business School, 1986.

Saloner, Garth, "Predation, Mergers, and Imperfect Information," *Rand Journal of Economics*, Summer 1987, *18*, 165-87.

Salop, Steven and Shapiro, Carl, "A Guide to Test-Market Predation," Princeton University, 1982.

Sappington, David E. M., "Limited Liability Contracts between Principal and Agent," *Journal of Economic Theory*, February 1983, *29*, 1-21.

Scharfstein, David S., "A Policy to Prevent Rational Test-Market Predation," *Rand Journal of Economics*, Summer 1984, *15*, 229-43.

Telser, Lester G., "Cutthroat Competition and the Long Purse," *Journal of Law and Economics*, October 1966, *9*, 259-277.

Tirole, Jean, *The Theory of Industrial Organization*, Cambridge: MIT Press, 1988.

Townsend, Robert, "Optimal Contracts and Competitive Markets with Costly State Verification," *Journal of Economic Theory*, October 1979, *21*, 265-93.

_____, "Optimal Multiperiod Contracts and the Gain from Enduring Relationships Under Private Information," *Journal of Political Economy*, December 1982, *90*, 1166-86.

Vickers, John, "Delegation and the Theory of the Firm," *Economic Journal*, Supplement 1985, *95*, 138-47.

Part II
Capital Investment and Valuation

Latent Assets

MICHAEL J. BRENNAN*

IT IS NOW A commonplace that corporate insiders possess an informational advantage over investors at large. On the one hand, the imperfect observability of the actions of corporate managements and of corporate investment opportunities has given rise to a now extensive literature on the problems of agency and adverse selection that arise in the corporate context. On the other, since Ross (1972) there has been considerable interest in the possibility of signaling resolutions to the problems arising from the superior information of management about corporate prospects. Nevertheless, it seems that signaling can provide only a partial resolution of the information asymmetry, and in this paper I want to consider some implications of the fact that it is costly for investors at large to determine the value of the assets held by the corporation. At the risk of oversimplification I shall distinguish between those assets whose values are known and agreed on by investors and reflected in share prices and those assets whose values are not reflected in share prices; the latter I shall refer to as latent assets. Investor rationality requires that the expected value of latent assets for any given firm be equal to zero, so that latent assets may be negative as well as positive.

Systematic evidence that share prices do not always fully reflect the value of assets held for corporations is hard to come by, not least because of the tenuous relation between our valuation models for most assets and observable variables. Nevertheless, there is considerable anecdotal and indirect evidence to this effect. For example, the substantial bid premia that are observed in the current wave of takeovers constitute prima facie evidence of the existence of latent assets, even though the premia themselves may be made possible by tax and operating efficiencies and wealth redistributions rather than the exploration of undervaluation. Thus a bid premium of 30% of the pre-bid market price can be consistent with the market knowing that the value of the assets in their alternative use is 30% higher than in their current use, only if the market assigns a zero probability to the emergence of the bid—that seems unreasonable. If the market assigns only a 20% probability to the bid, then a 30% bid premium implies that the assets are worth 49% more in the alternative than in the current use—but then a 20% probability seems implausibly low, and a 50% probability implies an 86% differential.[1] If investors can be so ignorant of the value of assets in alternative

---

* Anderson Graduate School of Management, UCLA. I thank Phelim Boyle, Craig Holden, Tim Opler, Richard Roll, Mark Rubinstein, and particularly Julian Franks and Alan Kraus for helpful comments on an earlier draft. The usual disclaimer applies.

[1] Let A denote the value of assets in current use and V their value to a bidder. If M is the current market value of the firm then $M = pV + (1-p)A$, where p is the probability of a succesful bid. The example in the text assumes $V = 1.3M$.

uses it is reasonable to assume that they have less than perfect information about their values in current use. Further evidence to this effect lies in stock price reactions to many corporate announcements.

I shall consider the implications of latent assets from two perspectives. First I shall take an extreme case in which investors are unable to observe the value of the firm's assets at any cost, and consider some implications of this for corporate policy. In doing so I shall offer an explanation for a problem that has puzzled me for some time—namely the fact that gold mines are widely exploited despite the fact that standard present value analyses generally imply that it is optimal to defer exploitation indefinitely. Generalizing from the example of the gold mine, I shall argue that the latency of asset values induces firms to convert them into cash when they are positive, even when it is costly to do so—and conversely, to postpone realization when they are negative, even when that is costly. Among other things, our results point to the dangers of making inferences from stock price reactions to the announcement of corporate decisions, without giving due attention to the objective of the management.

Secondly, I shall consider the other extreme case in which corporate policies are fixed, but investors are able to acquire information about the value of latent assets at a cost. The main point I shall stress here is the interdependence of individual information acquisition decisions. In a market populated by small investors, the advantage to any individual of acquiring information about the latent assets of a firm may be very small if those assets have a low current yield and no other investor acquires the same information. On the other hand, if many other investors acquire the same information the share price will adjust to reflect it, rewarding those who acquired the information first. Thus, while too much information acquisition activity will compete away the rewards to acquiring information as in the classical efficient market, too little information acquisition activity also may make it not worthwhile for any individual to undertake it. What is true about information acquisition is also true about modes of analysis. If the market follows a demonstrably inappropriate procedure in valuing a particular asset, the rewards to having the correct procedure may yet be small, unless others can be persuaded of the superiority of your approach, and this may be difficult since, by definition, it does not correspond to market prices as well as the conventional procedure. Pity the man who alone knows how to value gold mines, for his reward shall be slight. Thus, I argue, market prices may reflect a large element of convention without there existing a strong tendency for this to be corrected. Of course there are some corrective forces. First among these is the activity of corporations themselves which have so far held fixed. To the extent that assets remain latent or under-valued by the market, there will be an incentive for managements to convert them to cash or run the risk of being acquired by someone else who will convert them. Thus the market for corporate control exerts a corrective force and even tends to increase the incentives for private information acquisition by hastening the day when the rewards of such activity will be enjoyed. Secondly, there are obviously benefits to our atomistic investors of coordinating their information gathering activities to ensure that when latent assets are discovered there is sufficient investment activity that the asset values come to be reflected in market prices. Strict coordination of investment, as in the mutual fund form, will not do the trick, for then the group claiming the information has an obvious incentive to misrepresent, since it will also have taken a position in the securities. However, a "disinterested" third party which is paid only for information acquisition, and gains a reputation for accuracy, may be able to provide the degree of coordination across investors necessary for its information to be quickly and profitably reflected in security prices. Brokerage house analysts provide a possible example.

I. The Gold Mine

My thinking about latent assets was stimulated by a puzzle that arose some years ago in developing with Eduardo Schwartz a model for valuing mineral resources.[2] A distinguishing feature of these assets is the highly unpredictable nature of the price of the extracted resource which, we argued, makes application of traditional valuation techniques extremely difficult. At the same time, this unpredictability provides the impetus for the development of futures markets, and these in turn provide information that can be used to infer the risk adjusted expected price change of the extracted mineral. Although we have used this model quite successfully, it had one embarrassing feature when applied to gold—it was very difficult to find parameter values that would make it optimal to extract the gold at all.

The reason for this apparent perversity is not hard to find. Stocks of gold in the world far exceed commercial inventory needs, and the bulk of the gold is held by individuals and central banks for investment purposes. This means that gold is an asset like a share of common stock, except that it does not pay a dividend.[3] Therefore, the present value of an ounce of gold deliverable at any time in the future is equal to the current spot price. However, it takes resources to extract the gold from the mine; and, assuming that the cost of extraction is rising at a rate less than the rate of interest, it will always pay to defer extraction. So our advice to owners of gold mines was always the same: "Wait!"[4] This makes perfectly good sense when it is just as good to own shares in a gold mine as it is to own the bullion directly.

Nevertheless, we observe that in practice most firms do extract the gold. In an opportunistic compromise between the descriptive and the prescriptive we added a knob to our model that could make this the optimal policy: we allowed for the possibility that the mine could be expropriated without compensation.[5] This

---

[2] See Brennan and Schwartz (1985).

[3] Nor does it cost much to store. In what follows we shall neglect storage costs. Other commodities that are held for commercial purposes are said to yield "convenience services" which correspond to the dividend on a share of common stock. See Brennan (1958).

[4] Keynes (1936) also though it was a (social) mistake to extract the gold: "··· the form of digging holes in the ground known as gold mining, which not only adds nothing whatever to the real wealth of the world, but involves the disutility of labour ···"

When I offered this same advice to a friend who was promoting a gold mine he thought it so laughable that he used to repeat it as evidence of the folly into which one could be led by excessive ratiocination.

[5] Our position was similar to that of Coleridge who one remarked to his dinner partner, "Madam, I accept your conclusion, but you must allow me to provide the logic for it."

means that the mine itself is no longer such a good store of value as the bullion itself. There are other considerations that may also serve to induce immediate extraction; for example, a government which is anxious to get its hands on the tax and royalty revenues from the mine may award a lease which will lapse if the mine is not developed. Rather than pursue these possibilities I shall focus on the asymmetry of the information between corporate insiders and investors about the value of the resource.

Asymmetry of information about the true value of a firm's assets seems particularly likely when those assets consist of a mineral resource, for not only is it difficult to communicate the raw information on which the valuation of the deposit depends and difficult to interpret those data, but there is also always the possibility that the information communicated is incomplete[6]: the market for unused gold mines suffers from much the same problems as the market for used cars. The information asymmetry will include such matters as amounts and grades of ore, costs of extraction and so on. In order to capture the information asymmetry in a simple fashion, we shall assume that it is common knowledge that the mine contains a unit of gold and that the gold can be extracted instantaneously, but that the cost of extraction is known only to management. We shall assume that the management of the mine is precluded from any signaling activities that would reveal its private information; in the appendix we consider a scenario in which the management can reveal its private information by precommitting to an output policy.[7]

Let g denote the current price of a unit of gold, which is also the value of a unit deliverable for sure at any time in the future, and let $M(s)$ denote the market value of the firm at time s. We assume that the future price path of the gold is known with certainty and that management maximizes a weighted average of present values of future stock prices:

$$\max \alpha \int_0^\infty e^{-(\alpha+r)s} M(s) \, ds, \qquad (1)$$

where r is the interest rate and α is a parameter.

Let τ denote the date on which the gold is extracted from the mine. Since this cannot be signaled in advance, all firms with unexploited mines will be valued identically. Without loss of generality, we may write the value of such a firm as

$$M(s) = g e^{rs} - Q(s), \qquad s < \tau, \qquad (2)$$

where $Q(s)$ is the present value at time s of the expected future costs of extraction

---

[6] See discussion by Grossman and Hart (1980). When one gold mining company was bid for, a commentator remarked: "It (Newmont Gold Mining Company) may also be a company of sizeable *hidden* value." *Los Angeles Times*, September 20, 1989 (emphasis added).

[7] Gold loans whose repayments are in bullion or bullion equivalent are a recent innovation which may function as precommitment devices. Such loans typically carry interest rates of 1.5–3% and are used to finance mine development. Note that while these loans provide a price hedge for the producer, this cannot be their sole purpose for such hedges are available more cheaply in the futures market. Since lenders send in their own analysts to evaluate a mine before making a loan, the size and yield on the loan also serve as signals of the quality of the mine. For a formal model of third party information production see Thakor (1982).

and ge^{rs} is the price of gold at time s, since under certainty the price will appreciate at the riskless rate. Note that since no firm will extract the gold if the cost of extraction exceeds the current gold price, it must be the case that $M(s) \geq 0$, or

$$Q(s) \leq ge^{rs}. \tag{3}$$

Extraction costs grow continuously over time at the known rate m. For ease of reference we shall refer to the extraction costs measured at time 0 as the real cost of extraction and denote it by C. Consider then a firm that extracts the gold at time τ. Its value at that time, $M^*(\tau)$, is equal to the difference between the value of the gold and the, now known, cost of extraction:

$$M^*(\tau) = ge^{r\tau} - Ce^{m\tau}. \tag{4}$$

Finally, for $s > \tau$, the true value of the firm is known so that

$$M(s) = M^*(\tau)e^{r(s-\tau)}. \tag{5}$$

Substituting for $M(s)$ and $M^*(s)$ from equations (2), (4) and (5) in (1), the objective function of the firm may be written as

$$\max_{\tau} V = g - \alpha \int_0^{\tau} Q(s)e^{-(\alpha+r)s}\,ds - Ce^{-(\alpha+r-m)\tau}. \tag{6}$$

The first and second order conditions for a maximum in (6) are

$$V' = -\alpha Q(\tau)e^{-(\alpha+r)\tau} + (\alpha + r - m)Ce^{-(\alpha+r-m)\tau} = 0, \tag{7}$$

$$V'' = [\alpha(\alpha+r)Q - \alpha Q' - (\alpha+r-m)^2 Ce^{m\tau}]e^{-(\alpha+r)\tau} < 0. \tag{8}$$

Solving the first order condition (7) for $C(t)$, the real cost of a mine for which it is optimal to produce at time t:

$$C(t) = \left(\frac{\alpha}{\alpha + r - m}\right)Q(t)e^{-mt}. \tag{9}$$

So

$$Q(0) = \left(\frac{\alpha + r - m}{\alpha}\right)C(0),$$

where $C(0)$ is the cost of the producing mine at time 0.

Then, substituting from (9) in (8), the second order condition may be written as

$$Q'/Q > m. \tag{10}$$

Under risk neutrality, equilibrium in the capital market requires that the expected rate of increase in the value of unexploited mines be equal to the risk-free interest rate. This expected rate of increase has two components—the rate of increase in the value of mines which remain unexploited, M', and the instantaneous capital gain or loss on a mine when it is brought into production, $(M^* - M)$, times the proportional rate at which new mines are brought into production. This rate is equal to the product of the hazard rate of the cost distribution function,[8] $h(C)$, and the time derivative of the real cost of the currently producing mine, $C'(t)$. Thus the condition for equilibrium in the capital market may be written as

$$(M^* - M)hC' + M' = Mr. \tag{11}$$

In order to complete the characterization of the equilibrium, it is necessary to specify the probability distribution function for the costs. For analytical convenience we take this as

$$F(C) = 1 - a/C^k, \quad a > 0, \quad C > a^{1/k}. \tag{12}$$

This implies the hazard rate function $h(C) = k/C$. Then, computing M' from equation (2), and substituting for h and for M and M^* from (2) and (4) in (11) and using (9), we obtain

$$\eta(C'/C)Q - Q' + rQ = 0, \tag{13}$$

where $\eta \equiv k(r - m)/(\alpha + r - m) > 0$. But from (9) $C'/C = Q'/Q - m$, so that (13) may be written as

$$Q'/Q = (r - m\eta)/(1 - \eta) \equiv \gamma. \tag{14}$$

It may be verified that $\gamma > m$ as required by the second order condition (10) if $r > m$.[9]

The solution to equation (14) may be written as[10]

$$Q(t) = Q(0)e^{\gamma t}, \tag{15}$$

where $Q(0)$ is the present value at time 0 of the expected future costs of extraction, given that the cost of the mine which is producing at time t satisfies condition (18). Define $f(C) \equiv akC^{-(1+k)}$, the density function of extraction costs. Then $Q(0)$ may be written as

$$Q(0) = \int_0^\infty C(t)e^{(m-r)t}f[C(t)]\,dt. \tag{16}$$

Then, substituting for $f(\ )$ and for $C(t)$ from (9), and using (15) it is seen that

$$Q(0)^{1+k} = \left(\frac{\alpha}{\alpha + r - m}\right)^{-k} ak \int_0^\infty \exp\{\{m - r + k(m - \gamma)\}t\}\,dt, \tag{17}$$

or

$$Q(0) = \left[\left(\frac{\alpha}{\alpha + r - m}\right)^{-k} \frac{ak}{[k(\gamma - m) + r - m]}\right]^{1/(1+k)}. \tag{18}$$

---

[8] The fraction of mines producing in the interval $(t, t + dt)$ is $|F[C(t + dt)] - F[C(t)]||1 - F[C(t)]|^{-1}$, where F is the distribution function of real costs. Taking limits, this may be written as $h[C(t)]C'(t)dt$, where $h(C) \equiv F'(C)/(1 - F(C))$ is the hazard rate and primes denote derivatives.

[9] Note that this is just the condition required for it to be costly to advance production.

[10] In the interest of tractability we are assuming that all mines are expected to produce eventually. Alternatively, $Q(0)$ could be determined by the assumption that all mines, if they are to produce, must do so by some final date T^*.

Latent Assets

The cost of the mine which produces at time t in equilibrium is given by equation (9) where $Q(t)$ is defined by equations (15) and (18).

All mines with real costs less than $C(0)$ produce immediately at time 0. The remaining mines defer production until their cost satisfies condition (9). Thus in equilibrium the current cost of the currently producing mine rises at the rate γ. Each mine finds it worthwhile to postpone production until the cost of further postponement due to continuing as a member of the remaining pool of high cost mines exceeds the cost of advancing production. Since, under symmetric information, it would be optimal to postpone production indefinitely, the timing of production can be regarded as a costly "signal" of firm type. Then the model is one of dynamic costly signaling in which firms reveal their types sequentially. However, to treat the act of production as a costly signal is to strain usage, and the equilibrium is perhaps better described as one of sequential type revelation. In any case, we note that in this model the announcement of production is greeted with an immediate increase in the stock price, as the cost of production of the currently producing firm is a fraction $\mu \equiv \alpha/(\alpha + r - m) < 1$ of the present value of the costs of the average firm which is yet to produce.

Our results thus far rely on the somewhat ad hoc specification of the firm's objective function (1). It is instructive to consider how our results change if the firms pursue a more classical policy of (market) value maximization. Under a policy of value maximization, a mine with real cost C will produce if and only if its cost of extraction does not exceed $Q(s)$:

$$Ce^{ms} \le Q(s). \tag{19}$$

To avoid technical difficulties, it is convenient to assume that each firm follows a policy of *virtual* continuous value maximization, so that a firm with initial cost $C(t)$ produces at time t where

$$C(t) = \mu Q(t)e^{-mt} \tag{20}$$

and $\mu < 1$. This policy approaches continuous value maximization as $\mu \to 1$.

Suppose that the probability distribution of mine costs is given as before by expression (12). Then, noting the similarity between expressions (9) and (20) which determine the optimal production policies under the two policies, it is apparent that the equilibrium under value maximization is identical to that derived above when $\alpha/(\alpha + r - m) = \mu$. In particular, the optimal production policy is given by (20), where

$$Q(0) = \mu^{-k}\left[\frac{ak}{k(\gamma - m) + (r - m)}\right]^{1/(1+k)}, \tag{21}$$

$$Q(t) = Q(0)e^{\gamma t}, \tag{22}$$

and $\gamma = (r - m\eta)/(1 - \eta)$, where $\eta = k(1 - \mu)$. Thus as $\mu \to 1$, $\gamma \to r$, and the current cost of the currently producing mine grows at a rate approaching the riskless interest rate. Moreover, since $C(t)e^{mt} \to Q(t)$ as $\mu \to 1$, as the policy

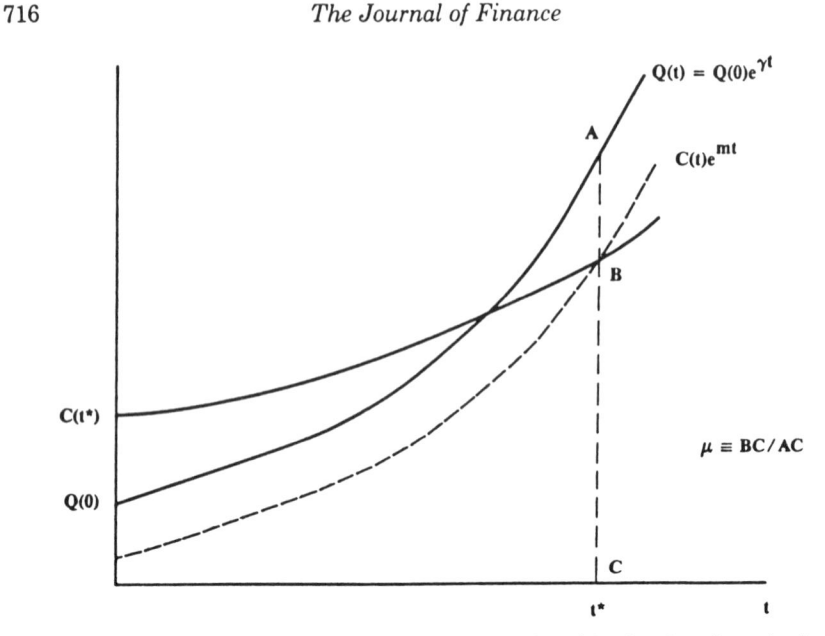

Figure 1. **Equilibrium extraction policy for alternative objective functions.** A mine with real cost $C(t^*)$ produces at t^*, where its cost of extraction is a fraction μ of the present value of the average costs of extraction of remaining undeveloped mines, $Q(t^*)$. Under objective function (1), $\mu = \alpha/(\alpha + r - m)$; under value maximization, $\mu \to 1$.

approaches that of pure value maximization, the capital gain on the announcement of production approaches zero.[11]

Figure 1 illustrates the nature of the equilibrium under the alternative objective functions. The ratio of the distances $AB:AC$ is equal to $\mu \equiv \alpha/(\alpha + r - m)$. This represents the ratio of the average cost imputed by the market to unexploited mines to the cost of the currently producing mine.

The mines in our model are atomistic, each producing unit output. Real mines correspond to collections of these mines. The model thus predicts that within a given mine the low cost ore will tend to be exploited first, which corresponds with the conventional view, though for different reasons.

II. Generalization from the Gold Mine Example

We have shown that, even under a policy of value maximization the classical NPV rule need not emerge as the criterion of (private) investment optimality under conditions of information asymmetry. Once again we see how critical is the assumption of symmetric information for the simple decision rules yielded by the classical theory of corporate finance; unfortunately, the decision rules which emerge from informational considerations seem much harder to imple-

---

[11] Note that market value maximization in this case is not equivalent to full information value maximization because of the effect of the (non)-production decision on investor perceptions. For a similar point in a different context see Rotemberg and Scharfstein (1989).

Latent Assets

ment,[12] and while our result has been derived under the assumption that the firm has no means of signaling its quality, it seems likely that a similar result will emerge so long as there is any residual uncertainty about the quality of the mine.

Our analysis yields in principle a test of whether or not firms follow a policy of value maximization. A non-zero price reaction to the announcement that a mine is to be put into production is inconsistent with value maximization, and if the alternative is the objective function (1) which is a generalization of the type usually found in signaling models,[13] then the price reaction may be used to estimate the discount factor, α.[14]

Although we have considered a gold mine for reasons of analytical tractability,[15] similar results follow in more complex settings, and the gold mine example is intended as a parable of a more general phenomenon of latent, or only partially observed, asset values. As we saw, the effect of latency was to induce managers to realize the asset value early by converting it into cash whose value is universally observable. Other authors have suggested the possibility of a similar outcome,[16] and the financial press contains frequent references to hidden or latent assets.[17]

McConnell and Muscarella (1985) report that stock prices react positively to the announcement of investment projects; this is consistent with the view that the value of the investment opportunities is known only imperfectly to the market. Our theory then suggests that if management places any weight on the current stock price in their objective function, then these opportunities will be exploited too early relative to the usual NPV criterion.

Similarly, Klein (1986) reports that announcements of asset sales are accompanied by positive stock price rections.[18] Again, if the current stock price is an element of the managerial objective function, it follows that asset sales are at least partially motivated by the desire to signal value, and that they will be made even when the sale price does not reflect the full value of the asset. In the model of the previous section, the lower is the discount factor α the more weight is placed on the current stock price and the earlier are the mines exploited. It follows that an exogenous shock that decreases α, such as a sudden threat of takeover, can be expected to trigger increased asset disposals that are costly to

---

[12] See Heinkel (1978), Miller and Rock (1985), and Constantinides and Grundy (1989) have also presented models in which informational considerations affect investment policy. Dividend policy, capital structure decisions, and optimal call strategies inter alia are all affected by similar considerations.

[13] See Miller and Rock, op. cit, and Harris and Raviv (1985) for example. For a criticism of these objective functions see Dybvig and Zender (1987).

[14] Farrow (1985) provides evidence that actual resource extraction policies are inconsistent with value maximization.

[15] This allowed us to ignore the effect of timing on the present value of the revenues.

[16] Stein (1988) has developed a model somewhat similar to ours, in which for certain parameter values, managers may advance the exploitation of a resource in order to forestall a takeover. Narayanan (1985) presents a model in which the manager chooses projects with short payback periods in order to signal his own ability.

[17] The *Wall Street Journal* (January 20, 1989) in an article on "Hidden Assets" in Japan reported that many U.S. companies were sitting on "potential gold mines," that some companies were moving to "reap value" from these assets, while some bankers wonder if "companies are moving too hastily to reap one time gains."

[18] Interestingly, the positive reaction is only for announcements in which the sale price is specified.

the firm. The takeover threat forces the incumbent management to prove the value of its assets, and the only way in which this can be accomplished is by sale.

It has been suggested that real estate holdings which have relatively low yields may be difficult for the market to reflect accurately in share prices.[19] Consider for example an industrial company that owns its own head office building, or a chain of supermarkets that owns its stores. Ownership will contribute to earnings only by the amount of the rent savings, and it may be difficult for investors to distinguish that part of earnings which is implicitly rental income and should be capitalized at a low rate from that which arises from industrial or grocery product sales and should be capitalized at a higher rate.[20] We might therefore expect those companies whose stock prices do not fully reflect the value of their real estate holdings to sell them and lease them back, even if it is costly to do so.[21] And we might expect a positive stock price reaction to the announcement of such transactions even though the transaction has a negative net present value for, as we argued above, the stock price will depend on whether the firm is continuously maximizing its stock price.

As a final example of a class of assets which may be hard for the market to value, consider the net pension assets of a company which depend on the value of the pension rights held by employees. Prior to the tax imposed by the Miscellaneous Revenue Act of 1988, terminations of defined benefit plans were not infrequent; Alderson and Chen (1986) find a positive stock price response to the announcement of plan termination; this is consistent with the values of pension assets being only partially known to the market and the management maximizing an objective function similar to expression (1). On the other hand, Vanderhei (1987) finds a positive stock price response for only part of his sample, and Bruner, Harrington, and Marshall (1987) find no abnormal returns. While the lack of a stock price response may be interpreted in terms of market efficiency and certain theories of pension property rights, it should be noted that it is consistent also with the hypothesis that investors do not possess detailed knowledge of individual plans, but that firm managements follow policies of market value maximization. This points to the care that must be taken in interpreting event studies when the event in question is a corporate action.[22]

Our analysis of the extraction policy of the gold mine has rested on the assumption that it was not possible for the firm to communicate information about its costs to investors. This is not an unreasonable assumption so long as the investors are small. However, it is not plausible for large investors who might buy up the whole mine. How is our analysis changed by the existence of large investors who can assess mine costs? If the large investors are individuals, then they do not have an incentive to buy up high cost mines that are just about to

---

[19] Hite et al. (1987) report that firm liquidations are frequently associated with management complaints of "undervaluation of natural resources and real estate holdings, assets that had appreciated in relation to their historical cost carrying value" (p. 233).

[20] We shall argue below that, depending on the convention, it may not be worthwhile for the individual investor to make such calculations.

[21] "Investors can profit from real estate ··· provided a company exploits the value of its holdings. It can do this by swelling, leveraging, or upgrading properties ···." Heard on the street. *Wall Street Journal*, January 29, 1989.

[22] A similar point is made by Acharya (1988) and by Eckbo, Maksimovic, and Williams (1989).

produce and to hold them out of production, thereby reducing the present value of the extraction costs. More generally, it seems that large investors or corporate insiders may have an advantage in operating latent assets, since such investors need not concern themselves with market values.[23] Note that this does not apply to large *corporate* investors who must themselves be concerned about market values unless they in turn are owned by large individual investors. Thus a firm will be worth more if it is controlled by a large investor who is concerned with intrinsic value as well as market value.[24] And second, a firm will be worth more if it is owned by the managers rather than publicly held, since it will then be free to pursue the goal of intrinsic value maximization. This accords well with the popular view that firms go private in order to free themselves from the pressures for short term performance that a stock market quotation engenders. Of course in practice there are riskbearing costs associated with management ownership and dominant shareholdings; therefore, these are not necessarily optimal ownership arrangements.

III. Equilibrium Information Collection in a Market of Small Investors

Let us turn now from the problem of a firm which owns latent assets to the incentives for individual investors to collect information about firm asset values when it is costly to do so. The main point I shall make in this section is that for long-lived assets the incentive for an individual investor to collect information may depend heavily upon whether other investors are collecting information and that, as a result, there may exist more than one equilibrium, in only one of which investors collect information; in the other equilibrium the assets remain latent.

Assume without loss of generality that each of N individual investors can collect information about the latent asset value of any one of M firms at a cost c, but that this information cannot be communicated credibly to other investors. Consider then an overlapping generations economy in which each generation lives for three, not necessarily equally spaced periods, and a new generation is born every second period at t, $t + 2$, $t + 4$, etc.[25] In the first period of life (period t) generation i ($i = t/2 + 1$) uses its labor income to purchase shares from the previous generation, which in turn uses the proceeds for consumption. Labor

---

[23] Of course, they must be concerned with market values when they come to sell, but there is a presumption that market value maximization will not be a continual concern to them as it is to the management of a firm owned by small investors. It is possible that a managerial policy of acquiring latent assets, rather than simply agency costs, accounts in part for the association between undistributed cash flow and premiums in going private transactions observed by Lehn and Poulson (1989).

[24] This complements the theory of Shleifer and Vishny (1986) which also predicts that firms will be worth more when there is a large shareholder.

[25] The intent of this assumption is to represent the short decision horizon of most investors. The effect of this is to make non-income yielding assets whose value cannot be realized by sale or borrowing and which cannot appear on a balance sheet for, say, 10 years essentially valueless. Even institutional investors with long apparent horizons may have short effective horizons because of agency problems which induce frequent monitoring of the investment manager's performance.

DeLong, Shleifer, Summers, and Waldmann (1989) also employ an overlapping generations assumption to develop a model in which market values depart from fundamentals. However, in their model the departure is caused by the existence of noise traders. Common, and essential to both models, is the market incompleteness captured by the overlapping generations assumption.

Table I
Overlapping Generations Model with Information Production

	Generation i			Generation $(i+1)$
Time	t	$t+1$	$t+2$	$t+3$
Firm Assets	$a_{i-1} + l_{i-1}$ $+l_i$	$a_i + l_i$	$a_i + l_i$ $+l_{i+1}$	$a_{i+1} + l_{i+1}$
Generation i	Receives labor income. Purchases shares from generation ($i-1$). Purchases information about l_i.	Receives information about l_i purchased at t. Trades.	Sells shares to ($i+1$). Consumes. Dies.	
Share Price: Reflects l_i?	No	Not at open. At close if $j > m$ investors purchased information.	If reflected at $(t+1)$ or publicly revealed (probability:μ).	Yes
Share Price: At open*		$a_i - D(1+r)^2$		$a_{i+1} - D(1+r)^2$
At close:				
if l_i reflected		$a_i + l_i - D$	$a_i + (l_i - D)(1+r)$	
if l_i not reflected		$a_i - D$	$a_i - D(1+r)$	

*If different from closing price.

income in the first period of life may also be used to purchase information about the latent asset values of individual firms: this information becomes available at random times during trade in the second period. In the second period ($t+1$) individuals suffer random wealth shocks that induce them to trade; at this time individuals who purchased information in the first period may use it to trade as it becomes available. Individuals are assumed to be risk neutral, but to be restricted in the amounts they can purchase or sell short. The key assumption we shall make is that the market price of a firm does not reflect the private information of investors in the second period, until there is some minimum number of investors informed about the firm. In the third period ($t+2$) the current generation sells its shares to the new generation of individuals, consumes, and dies.

The information structure of the model is illustrated in Table I. In the first period of life of generation i, time t, a fraction f of firms are endowed with latent assets, $l_i/(1+r)$, where $l_i = \pm \Pi$ with equal probability, and r is the riskless interest rate; latent assets yield no current return but appreciate in value at the riskless interest rate. At the beginning of $(t+1)$, before trade occurs, the value of latent assets held by the firm in generation $i-1$ is revealed if it is not already known to its investors. Hence the public assets of the firm (in the second period of life of generation i) at time $t+1$, a_i,[26] are equal to the sum of the public and latent assets from the previous generation: $a_i = a_{i-1} + l_{i-1}$. Public assets yield a

[26] All asset values are expressed on a per share basis.

Latent Assets

certain return each period equal to the interest rate. Information about l_i becomes available at random times during trading at period $t + 1$ to all investors who paid the information acquisition cost c at time t.

For simplicity we shall assume that share prices react in a discontinuous fashion to the purchases and sales of informed investors. In particular, we assume that each informed investor is able to buy/sell a maximum of one share, and that the share price does not reflect the private information until m shares have been purchased/sold by the informed, at which point the price changes to reflect the private information[27] which is thereby revealed.

If the latent asset value l_i is not reflected in the share price as a result of trading at time $t + 1$, there is an (exogenous) probability, μ, that the value will be revealed prior to the opening of trading at $t + 2$; failing this, the latent asset value will certainly be revealed prior to the opening of trading at $t + 2$ (period 2 of generation $i + 1$). The important feature of the model for our purposes is that information about latent asset values may not be reflected in asset values until the next generation.

Note that uninformed investors lose on average by trading with the informed in period 2, because informed investors are more likely to be sellers of shares with latent liabilities (<0), and purchasers of shares with latent assets. Let the expected loss per share for the uninformed from trading with the informed in the second period of life be d, and denote by D the value of the perpetuity of these expected losses, $D \equiv d/R$ where $R \equiv [(1 + r)^2 - 1]$. Then it may be verified that the following is an equilibrium: The share price at the open of trade at $t + 1$ is given by $a_i - D(1 + r)^2$. The price at the close of trade at $t + 2$, if the latent asset value has not been revealed by trade, is $a_i - D$. If the latent asset value has been revealed, the price is $a_i + l_i - D$. Similarly, the price at $t + 2$ is $a_i - D(1 + r)$ if the latent asset value has not been revealed, and $a_i + l_i(1 + r) - D(1 + r)$ if it has. Finally, the price at the open of trade at $t + 3$ of the following generation is $a_{i+1} - D(1 + r)^2$.

An informed investor who is able to transact at the opening price at $t + 1$ will realize an immediate expected profit of $f\Pi$ if l_i is revealed in the course of trading. Given our assumption about price adjustment, if j, the number of investors who acquire information about a frim, exceeds m, the first m of them will realize an expected profit of $f\Pi$ when the price adjusts after the transaction of investor m, while the remaining $(j - m)$ will realize no profit since they will not be able to transact at the full information price. Therefore, if there are $j \geq m$ informed investors, the expected profit per investor from price adjustment in period 2 is $f\Pi(m/j)$. If $j < m$, there will be no price adjustment in period 2; however, informed investors may yet profit from asset value revelation in period $t + 2$. The present value of the expected profit (as of period 2) is $\mu f\Pi$ where μ is the previously defined exogenous probability of value revelation in period $t + 2$.

Define η_{jt} as the probability that exactly j investors in generation t become informed about a particular firm. Then V, the Period 2 present value of the expected reward to becoming informed about a particular firm, given that a

---

[27] The model can be thought of as a simplification of that of Diamond and Verrecchia (1987), which has the same implications for information collection in our intertemporal setting.

fraction f of firms have latent assets, may be written as

$$V = f\Pi[\sum_{j \geq m} \eta_{jt}(m/j) + \mu \sum_{j < m} \eta_{jt}]. \tag{23}$$

The first term in the parentheses corresponds to the event that at least m investors are informed about the firm, so that its value is revealed in the course of trading at $(t + 1)$; the second term corresponds to the possibility of a public announcement of the latent asset value at $(t + 2)$. We consider a stationary environment in which M, the number of firms, and N, the number of individuals who decide to become informed, are time invariant. It is assumed that each individual acquires information about no more than one firm and that firm is chosen at random. Then the probability that a given firm is chosen by a particular investor is M^{-1}, and the distribution of the number of investors who become informed about any firm is binomial, where N is the number of trials, and M^{-1} is the probability of success on a given trial.

Under these assumptions V is a function of N, the number of investors who decide to become informed, and may be written as

$$V(N) = f\Pi [\sum_{j=m}^{N} b_j(M/j) + \mu \sum_{j=1}^{m-1} b_j], \tag{24}$$

where $\eta_{jt} = b(N, j, M^{-1}) \equiv b_j$, the binomal probability of j successes in N trials.

Equilibrium in the market for information requires that all those who acquire information earn an expected return that compensates them for the cost of acquiring information, and that there be no incentive for further information acquisition: the equilibrium number of investors who acquire information, N^e, must satisfy

$$V(N^e) \geq \hat{c} \equiv c(1 + r), \quad V(N^e + 1) < \hat{c}. \tag{25}$$

At low levels of N, and for small μ, $V(N)$ is increasing, because an increase in the number of informed investors increases the probability that the price will reflect that latent asset value. However, for larger N the probability of immediate price adjustment is already high, and further increases in N tend simply to increase the number of informed individuals over whom the reward of the price adjustment must be spread.

Figure 2 illustrates the two possible types of equilibria in the market for information. The $V(N)$ schedule is drawn for $\mu = 0$ and for $\mu > \hat{c}/f\pi$.[28] When $\mu = 0$, $V(N) = 0$ for $N < m$, because there is no possibility of price adjustment in the current generation; $V(N)$ increases at first for $N > m$ as the probability of price adjustment increases, but eventually turns down as the increase in the number of individuals among whom the fruits of price adjustment must be shared outweighs the increased probability of adjustment. $V(N)$ is a strictly increasing function of μ as shown, and for sufficiently large μ will be a monotone negative function of N.

It is helpful to distinguish two types of market according to the probability of exogenous information revelation. If $\mu > \hat{c}/f\Pi$, there is only one equilibrium in

---

[28] It is also possible that the $V(N)$ schedule is everywhere below $\hat{c}$. In that case it is never worth collecting information.

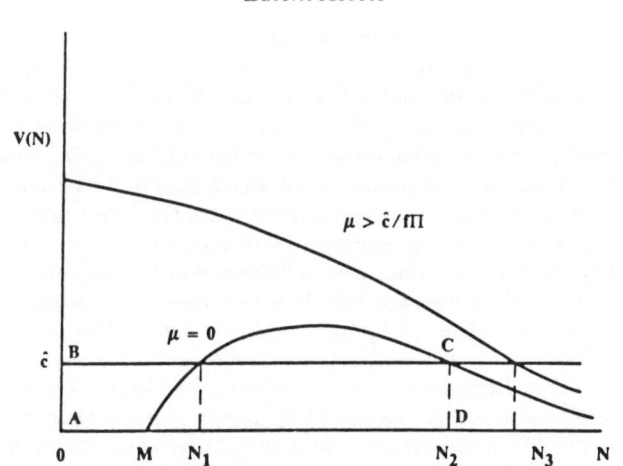

Figure 2. Equilibrium in the market for information acquisition.

the market for information at $N = N_3$. We might describe the security market in such an information gathering equilibrium as stochastically efficient since the probability that the period $(t + 1)$ closing price reflects the value of the firm's latent assets is $B(N_3, m; M^{-1})$ where $B(\ )$ is the probability of m or more successes in N trials. Note that as the cost of information acquisition approaches zero, $N_1 \to \infty$ and the probability that security prices fully reflect asset values approaches unity.

Consider the situation on the other hand when μ, the probability of exogenous information revelation, is low: $\mu < \hat{c}/f\Pi$. Now there exist two equilibria. $N = 0$ is an "informationless" equilibrium. In this equilibrium it is not worthwhile for anyone to gather information because no one else is gathering information and there is no way to profit from price adjustment. There is also an information gathering equilibrium at $N = N_2$; note that $N = N_1$ is not an equilibrium since at that point there is an incentive for additional investors to become informed.

The first lesson of this simple model is that there may be externalities to the collection of information in securities markets. For example, if oil company shares do not reflect the option value of reserves that can only be developed profitably at a higher oil price, there may be no incentive for individual analysts to estimate the value of these reserves and share prices may continue to ignore them. Nor will this problem be rectified by a single large investor (not included in our model) buying up the whole company unless this investor has an investment horizon which stretches over into the next generation.

While in this model we have made a simple distinction between assets whose values are publicly known and assets which are latent or observable only at a cost, it should be clear that almost all assets possess aspects of latency, and that the uncertainty surrounding corporate asset values can be progressively reduced as the cost incurred in investigation is increased. Our analysis suggests that it may not be worthwhile for an individual to invest heavily in information acquisition unless a sufficient number of other investors are also doing so.

Second, since there is more than one possible equilibrium, the particular equilibrium that prevails may be a matter of convention or of historical accident. For example, it has often been noted that the discounts from net asset value of closed end investment companies show considerable intertemporal variation. However, as Thompson (1978) has shown, the rewards from buying "underpriced" funds are quite modest, because prices do not adjust rapidly[29]—because not many investors attempt to arbitrage these securities. If, on the other hand, there were a well-agreed-on-formula for the appropriate discount based on expense ratios, investment performance, etc., then it is at least possible that there would exist an equilibrium in which it was worthwhile for investors to estimate the appropriate discount and adjustments to this would be rapid. The now abandoned proposal for Unbundled Securities Units may represent a case in which the bad equilibrium prevailed. Reputedly this innovation failed because of concern that the market for USUs would be insufficiently liquid, causing them to trade at a discount to the underlying securities. There is another equilibrium in which the USUs are regarded as perfect substitutes for the underlying security, thereby gain liquidity, and are priced as perfect substitutes.[30]

Third, note that in an information gathering equilibrium the number of individuals who collect information at time t is an increasing function of μ, the probability of exogenous information revelation at $t + 2$. The reason for this of course is that the greater the value of μ, the higher the probability that the asset will trade at its full information value during the life of the current generation, so that purchasers will realize the true full information value rather than handing the asset on to the following generation at a price which does not reflect this information. In a more general model, the higher the income stream and the longer the individual investor horizon, the higher is the proportion of the return realized by the investor that depends on fundamentals and the lower the proportion that depends on the terminal price; consequently, the greater is the incentive to collect information. Thus we should expect the prices of high payout assets to reflect the underlying asset values more precisely than those of low payout assets, ceteris paribus.

Consider next the determinants of D, the expected discount from asset value at which shares trade at the end of period $(t + 1)$. First, note that in an informationless equilibrium the discount will be zero, for then uninformed investors would experience no adverse selection in their period $(t + 2)$ trading. In the information gathering equilibrium informed investors exactly recoup their information costs by trading with the uninformed. Hence d, the expected trading losses of the uninformed per period per share, are equal to $(N_e/M)\hat{c}$ where N_e is the equilibrium number of informed investors. Hence the discount from asset value, D, is given by

$$D = \frac{N^e \hat{c}}{MR}, \qquad (26)$$

where $R \equiv (1 + r)^2 - 1$, is the two period interest rate.[31]

---

[29] A similar point has been made by Summers (1986).

[30] Cornell and Shapiro (1989) present an interesting example of the failure of arbitrage in the U.S. Treasury bond market.

[31] See also Heinkel and Kraus (1987) for a model of differential returns to insiders and outsiders.

Equation (26) implies that the discount from asset value is proportional to the area of the rectangle $ABCD$ in Figure 2. Since, from equation (24), the expected reward to information collection, V, is increasing in both $f\Pi$ and μ, it follows from inspection of Figure 2 that in an information gathering equilibrium D, the expected discount from asset value, is an increasing function of

(i) the uncertainty about latent asset value, as measured by $f\Pi$, since the greater is this uncertainty, the greater is the adverse selection problem faced by the uninformed. It follows that value maximizing firms have an incentive to reveal their values as accurately as possible.[32]
(ii) μ, the probability that the value of the latent assets will be revealed in period $t + 2$. Not surprisingly, information that is not likely to be revealed does not pose a threat to the uninformed.

It seems likely that information acquisition costs, c, would be higher for multidivisional conglomerate firms which are spread across unrelated industries. Although the effect of c on the discount is ambiguous, it is at least possible in this model that the diversified conglomerate pays a valuation penalty on account of the difficulty of evaluating its assets.

IV. Conventional Valuation

In the model of Section IV, share values may fail to reflect intrinsic values for two distinct reasons. First, the shares may be valued in an informationless equilibrium in which there is no incentive for individuals to collect information because an insufficient number of other individuals are collecting information. Second, in an informed equilibrium, the cost of information collection must be extracted from the uninformed: responding to their resulting losses from adverse selection, the uninformed will be willing to pay less than the expected value of the assets for the shares they purchase. There is also a third way in which prices may fail to reflect fundamental values, for the particular informed equilibrium that prevails may also be a matter of convention—the market may systematically employ the "wrong" model to value a particular class of securities, and yet there may be no natural forces tending to return the market to the "right" model.

To see this, assume now that the value of the latent asset, l is normally distributed with mean zero and variance, σ_1^2, and suppose that there exists a noisy signal of l:

$$s = l + \epsilon, \qquad (27)$$

where $\epsilon = N(0, \sigma_\epsilon^2)$. s may be thought of as the valuation implied by an inappropriate model. Assume that the cost of observing l or the noisy signal is c, the same for both.

Then from equation (24) and the properties of the normal distribution it follows that $V'(N)$, the expected reward of observing l when N investors observe l is

$$V'(N) = f\sigma_1 \sqrt{\frac{2}{\pi}} \{\textstyle\sum_{j=m}^{N} b_j(m/j) + \mu \sum_{j=1}^{m-1} b_j\}. \qquad (24')$$

---

[32] Cf. Diamond (1985) and Ross (1989).

Consider next $V^s(N)$, the expected return from observing the noisy signal s when N investors also observe the same signal. If m investors acquire information about the same firm, the time period $(t + 1)$ price adjustment will be equal to $\hat{l} \equiv E[l \mid s]$, then the expected additional price change at time $(t + 2)$, conditional on information revelation and the signal will be zero. If no information is revealed in the course of trading at $(t + 1)$, the expected profit conditional on information revelation at $(t + 2)$ for an investor who received the signal s is $|E[l \mid s]| \equiv |\hat{l}|$. Thus $V^s(N)$ is given by

$$V^s(N) = f\sigma_1 \sqrt{\frac{2k}{\pi}} \{\sum_{j=m}^{N} b_j(m/j) + \mu \sum_{j=1}^{m-1} b_j\}, \tag{28}$$

where $E[|\hat{l}|] = \sigma_1 \sqrt{\frac{2k}{\pi}}$ and $k = \sigma_1^2/(\sigma_1^2 + \sigma_\epsilon^2)$. Comparing (24') and (28), it is seen that for all N $V^l(N) > V^s(N)$, so that given the number of investors who collect information, they would, not surprisingly, be better off collecting information about l rather than about s, the noisy signal of l. Despite this, we shall see that if N investors are collecting information about s, it may not pay any of them to switch to collection of information about l.

An individual who knows l will make an expected profit of $|E[\hat{l} \mid l]|$ in Period 2 if m or more investors collect information about s,[33] and, if the information is revealed at $(t + 2)$, will make a further profit whose expected value is $|E[l - \hat{l} \mid l]|$. If the price does not adjust at $(t + 1)$, then his or her profit at $(t + 2)$, conditional on information revelation, is $|l|$. Thus $\phi(N)$, the expected reward to collecting information about l when N investors collect information about s is given by

$$\phi(N) = f\{\sum_{j=m}^{N} b_j[(m/j)E[|E[\hat{l} \mid l]|] + \mu E[|E[l - \hat{l} \mid l]|]]$$
$$+ \mu \sum_{j=1}^{m-1} b_j E[|l|]\}, \tag{29}$$

where b_j is the binomial probability that j investors collect information about s.

Using the properties of the normal distribution, this may be written as

$$\phi(N) = f\sigma_1 \sqrt{\frac{2}{\pi}} \{\sum_{j=m}^{N} b_j[km/j + \mu(1 - k)] + \mu \sum_{j=1}^{m-1} b_j\}. \tag{30}$$

Thus, the incentive for an individual to collect information about s, or to use the "wrong" model, rather than collect information about l is proportional to

$$\sum_{j=m}^{N} b_j[(m/j)(\sqrt{k} - k) - \mu(1 - k)] - \mu \sum_{j=1}^{m} b_j(1 - \sqrt{k}), \tag{31}$$

and this expression may clearly be positive for small μ—it is more likely to be positive the less noisy the signal (the larger is k).

The incentive to deviate from the equilibrium convention of collecting information on the noisy signal or imperfect model, s, is increasing in μ because the

---

[33] We are assuming that our deviant individual has no effect on price setting.

higher is μ the greater is the probability that the payoff received by the current generation will depend upon the underlying fundamentals rather than the noise signal s. Similarly, the more noisy is the signal, the greater is the incentive to deviate by collecting information on the underlying asset value, because the more noisy is the signal the greater is the reward from knowing the underlying asset value if it is revealed at $t + 2$; offsetting this is the consideration that the noisier is the signal, the less useful is knowledge of the underlying asset value for predicting the change in price during trading at $t + 1$; nevertheless, it can be shown that the former effect outweighs the latter.

Thus, we have shown that it may be advantageous for an investor to stick with the conventional valuation model even though that model is incorrect in the sense that there may be another model which predicts the asset payoffs better. The reason for this paradox of course is that the investor has only limited interest in the ultimate asset payoffs—he is also interested in the resale value of the asset, and that may depend on the conventional valuation model. Note that this result does not depend on the cost of information since we have assumed that the cost of both signals is the same.[34]

It is an interesting empirical issue whether asset market values are ever based on inferior valuation models. This will not be easy to determine, because for few assets is there a close relation between theoretical values and observable variables. Nevertheless, Modigliani and Cohn (1979) have suggested that the whole market was undervalued at times of high inflation because of mistaken conventions in treating real and nominal interest rates, and this hypothesis may be tested. As another example, consider gold again. Casual empiricism suggests that gold mines are valued by traditional discounting of expected net cash flows, although it is well known that the present value of an ounce of gold deliverable in the future is exactly equal to the current spot price. The question then is whether the difference between the value of gold computed at the current spot price and the value obtained by discounting projected sales revenues adds explanatory power to a regression in which the market value is the dependent variable and conventional brokerage house valuations are the independent variable.

V. Summary and Conclusion

We have considered the implications of costly information acquisition by investors from two perspectives. First, we have shown, using the parable of the gold mine, that if market prices do not reflect asset values and the managerial objective function places any weight on the current market price, then there will be an incentive to realize asset values early. We also showed that the market price reaction to the announcement of an asset realization will depend on the precise managerial objective function, and that in particular there will be no price reaction if the manager continuously maximizes the current stock price. If the cost of following such a policy is high, there will be a substantial advantage to

---

[34] The result is similar to sunspot theories of asset market equilibrium.

being owned by a single large investor or by management, since this will shift concern from the market price.

Second, we showed that in a market of small investors the rewards of information collection will depend in a non-monotonic fashion on the number of investors who collect information, since this will affect not only the frequency with which mispriced assets can be discovered, but also the speed at which the pricing discrepancies are eliminated and their discoverers rewarded. Thus it is possible to have equilibria in which assets remain latent despite relatively small information acquisition costs. Such situations create incentives for both managers and large investors who can gain control to convert assets to cash to demonstrate values. The externalities to the collection of information suggest that there may be advantages for small investors in delegating their information acquisition to a single entity; not only does this allow a sharing of costs, but also, by coordinating the investment decisions of the investors, ensures that the information acquired will be rapidly reflected in market prices to their mutual advantage.[35] It is possible that brokerage house analysts play such a role.

Appendix: An Equilibrium with Precommitment

Assume that the manager of the mine can precommit to an extraction policy and that the cost of extraction is not publicly observable. Then, if the interest rate is r, the real cost of extraction is C, and the rate of growth in the nominal cost of extraction is $m < r$, the intrinsic value of time 0 of a mine which is committed to producing at time τ is $g - Ce^{(m-r)\tau}$. Let $V(\tau)$ denote the market value at time 0 of a mine which precommits to producing at time τ, and assume that the manager of the mine maximizes a weighted average of the current market value of the mine and its intrinsic value:[36]

$$\max_{\tau} \alpha V(\tau) + (1 - \alpha)[g - (e^{(m-r)\tau}]. \tag{A1}$$

The first and second order conditions for a maximum in this problem are

$$\alpha V' - (1 - \alpha)(m - r)Ce^{(m-r)\tau} = 0, \tag{A2}$$

$$\alpha V'' - (1 - \alpha(m - r)^2)Ce^{(m-r)\tau} < 0. \tag{A3}$$

Rational expectations require that the market value be equal to the intrinsic value:

$$V(\tau) = g - C(\tau)e^{(m-r)\tau}, \tag{A4}$$

where $C(\tau)$ is the real (time 0) cost of a mine that precommits to produce at time τ in equilibrium. Differentiating expression (A4) with respect to τ,

$$V' = -[C'(\tau) + (m - r)C(\tau)]e^{(m-r)\tau}. \tag{A5}$$

---

[35] Of course, to keep individual investors in the coalition, it will be necessary to randomize the order in which they receive the information. This differs from the randomization of messages by a monopoly information supplier in Admati and Pfleiderer (1986).

[36] This type of objective function which is virtually canonical in models of this kind contrasts with the market value maximization role considered in the body of the paper.

Substitution for V' from (A5) in condition (A2) yields, after some simplification:

$$\alpha C' = (r - m)C. \tag{A6}$$

Solving (A6) and imposing the condition that the lowest cost mine produces immediately, yields the equilibrium time to produce schedule:

$$\tau(c) = \left(\frac{\alpha}{r - m}\right)\ln(C/\underline{C}), \tag{A7}$$

where $\underline{C} \leq g$ is the real extraction cost of the lowest cost mine.

The equilibrium valuation schedule is obtained by solving (A7) for $C(\tau)$ and substituting in (A4):

$$V(\tau) = g - \underline{C} \exp\{(r - m)(1 - \alpha)\tau/\alpha\}. \tag{A8}$$

It can be shown that this schedule satisfies the second order condition (A3), and that (A8) is the unique valuation schedule to satisfy the Cho-Kreps (1987) Intuitive Criterion. Finally, we can calculate the market value assigned to a mine with initial cost C by subsituting for $\tau(C)$ from (A7) in (A8) to obtain

$$V(C) = g - \underline{C}^{\alpha}C^{1-\alpha}. \tag{A9}$$

As with the model without precommitment presented in the text, the information asymmetry induces early extraction, and it is the mines with the lowest cost that produce first. Thus the equilibrium in qualitatively similar to that of Section II.

REFERENCES

Acharya, S., 1988, A generalized econometric model and tests of a signalling hypothesis, *Journal of Finance* 43, 413–430.

Alderson, M., and K. C. Chen, 1986, Excess asset reversions and shareholder wealth, *Journal of Finance* 41, 225–241.

Brennan, M. J., 1958, The supply of storage, *American Economic Review* 48, 50–72.

——— and E. S. Schwartz, 1985, Evaluating natural resource investments, *Journal of Business* 58, 135–158.

Bruner, R. F., D. R. Harrington and S. B. Marshall, 1987, A test of ownership of excess pension assets, Unpublished manuscript, Darden School.

Butz, D. A., 1989, A theory of bust-up takeovers and takeover defenses, Unpublished manuscript, UCLA.

Cho, I. K. and D. M. Kreps, 1987, Signalling games and stable equilibria, *Quarterly Journal of Economics* 101, 179–221.

Constantinides, G. M. and B. D. Grundy, 1989, Optimal investment with stock repurchase and financing as signals, *Review of Financial Studies* Forthcoming.

Cornell, B. and A. C. Shapiro, 1989, The mispricing of U.S. Treasury bonds: A case study, *Review of Financial Studies* Forthcoming.

DeLong, J. B., A. Shleifer, L. H. Summers, and R. J. Waldmann, 1989, The size and incidence of the losses from noise trading, *Journal of Finance* 44, 681–698.

Diamond, D. W., 1985, Optimal release of information by firms, *Journal of Finance* 40, 1071–1094.

——— and R. E. Verrecchia, 1987, Constraints on short-selling and asset price adjustment to private information, *Journal of Financial Economics* 18, 277–312.

Dybvig, P. H. and J. F. Zender, 1987, Capital structure and dividend irrelevance, Unpublished manuscript.

Eckbo, B. E., V. Maksimovic, and J. Williams, 1990, Cross-sectional models in event studies: Econometric issues with an application to horizontal mergers, *Review of Financial Studies* Forthcoming.

Farrow, S., 1985, Testing the efficiency of extraction from a stock resource, *Journal of Political Economy* 93, 452-487.

Grossman, S. J. and O. D. Hart, 1980, Disclosure law and takeover bids, *Journal of Finance* 35, 323-334.

Harris, M. and A. Raviv, 1985, A sequential signalling model of convertible debt call policy, *Journal of Finance* 40, 1263-1281.

——— and A. Raviv, 1988, Corporate control contests and capital structure, *Journal of Financial Economics* 20, 55-86.

Heinkel, R., 1978, Dividend policy as a signal of firm value, in: *Essays on Financial Markets with Imperfect Information*. Ph.D. dissertation, Berkeley.

——— and A. Kraus, 1987, The effect of insider trading on average rates of return, *Canadian Journal of Economics* 20, 588-611.

Hite, G., J. E. Owens, and R. C. Rogers, 1987, The market for interfirm asset sales, *Journal of Financial Economics* 18, 229-252.

Jensen, M. C., 1986, Agency costs of free cash flow, corporate finance and takeovers, *American Economic Review* 76, 323-329.

Keynes, J. M., 1936, *The General Theory of Employment, Interest, and Money* (MacMillan, London).

Klein, A., 1986, The timing and substance of divestiture announcements: Individual, simultaneous, and cumulative effects, *Journal of Finance* 41, 685-695.

Lehn, K. and A. Poulsen, 1989, Free cash flow and stockholder gains in going private transactions, *Journal of Finance* 44, 771-787.

McConnell, J. J. and C. J. Muscarella, 1985, Corporate capital expenditure decisions and the market value of the firm, *Journal of Financial Economics* 14, 399-422.

Miller, M. H. and K. Rock, 1985, Dividend policy under asymmetric information, *Journal of Finance* 40, 1031-1051.

Modigliani, F. and R. A. Cohn, 1979, Inflation and the stock market, *Financial Analysts Journal* 35, 24-44.

Morck, R., A. Shleifer, and R. Vishny, 1988, Management ownership and market valuation: An empirical analysis, *Journal of Financial Economics* 20, 293-316.

Narayanan, M. P., 1985, Observability and the payback criterion, *Journal of Business* 58, 309-323.

Ross, S. A., 1972, The determination of financial structure: The incentive-signalling approach, *The Bell Journal of Economics* 8, 23-40.

———, 1989, Information and volatility: The no-arbitrage martingale approach to timing and resolution irrelevancy, *Journal of Finance* 44, 1-17.

Rotemberg, J. J. and D. S. Scharfstein, 1989, Shareholder value maximization and product market competition, *Review of Financial Studies* Forthcoming.

Scholes, M. S., G. P. Wilson, and M. A. Wolfson, 1989, Tax planning, regulatory capital planning, and financial reporting strategy for commercial banks, G.S.B., Stanford.

Shleifer, A. and R. W. Vishny, 1986, Large shareholders and corporate control, *Journal of Political Economy* 94, 461-488.

Stein, J., 1988, Takeover threats and managerial myopia, *Journal of Political Economy* 96, 61-80.

Stulz, R., 1988, Managerial control of voting rights: Financing policies and the market for corporate control, *Journal of Financial Economics* 20, 25-54.

Summers, L., 1986, Does the stock market rationally reflect fundamental values?, *Journal of Finance* 41, 591-600.

Thakor, A. V., 1982, An exploration of competitive signalling equilibria with third party information, *Journal of Finance* 37, 717-739.

Thompson, R., 1978, The information content of discounts and premiums on closed end fund shares, *Journal of Financial Economics* 6, 151-186.

Vanderhei, J., 1987, The effect of voluntary termination of overfunded pension plans on shareholder wealth, *Journal of Risk and Insurance* 131-156.

[6]

Michael J. Brennan
Eduardo S. Schwartz
University of British Columbia

Evaluating Natural Resource Investments*

Notwithstanding impressive advances in the theory of finance over the past 2 decades, practical procedures for capital budgeting have evolved only slowly. The standard technique, which has remained unchanged in essentials since it was originally proposed (see Dean 1951; Bierman and Smidt 1960), derives from a simple adaptation of the Fisher (1907) model of valuation under certainty: under this technique, expected cash flows from an investment project are discounted at a rate deemed appropriate to their risk, and the resulting present value is compared with the cost of the project. This standard textbook technique reflects modern theoretical developments only insofar as estimates of the discount rate may be obtained from crude application of single period asset pricing theory (but see Brennan 1973; Bogue and Roll 1974; Turnbull 1977; Constantinides 1978).

The inadequacy of this approach to capital budgeting is widely acknowledged, although not widely discussed. Its obvious deficiency is its

The evaluation of mining and other natural resource projects is made particularly difficult by the high degree of uncertainty attaching to output prices. It is shown that the techniques of continuous time arbitrage and stochastic control theory may be used not only to value such projects but also to determine the optimal policies for developing, managing, and abandoning them. The approach may be adapted to a wide variety of contexts outside the natural resource sector where uncertainty about future project revenues is a paramount concern.

---

* Research support from the Corporate Finance Division of the Department of Finance, Ottawa, is gratefully acknowledged. We especially thank the referee whose insightful comments have enabled us to eliminate several errors and to improve the presentation. We also thank Robert Pyndyck, Rene Stulz, Suresh Sundaresan, Merton Miller, and participants at seminars in London, Stockholm, Stanford, and Los Angeles.

(*Journal of Business*, 1985, vol. 58, no. 2)
© 1985 by The University of Chicago. All rights reserved.
0021-9398/85/5802-0004$01.50

total neglect of the stochastic nature of output prices and of possible managerial responses to price variations. While price uncertainty is unimportant in applications for which the relevant prices are reasonably predictable, it is of paramount importance in many natural resource industries, where price swings of 25%–40% per year are not uncommon.[1] Under such conditions the practice of replacing distributions of future prices by their expected values is likely to cause errors in the calculation both of expected cash flows and of appropriate discount rates and thereby to lead to suboptimal investment decisions.

The model for the evaluation of investment projects presented in this paper treats output prices as stochastic. While this makes it particularly suitable for analyzing natural resource investment projects, where uncertain prices are a particular concern, the model may be applied in other contexts also. The model also takes explicit account of managerial control over the output rate, which is assumed to be variable in response to the output price; moreover, the possibility that a project may be closed down or even abandoned if output prices fall far enough is also considered. Variation in risk and the discount rate due both to depletion of the resource and to stochastic variation in the output price are explicitly taken into account in deriving the equilibrium condition underlying the valuation model.

Two essentially distinct approaches may be taken to the general problem of valuing the uncertain cash flow stream generated by an investment project. First, the market equilibrium approach requires both complete specification of the stochastic properties of the cash flow stream and an underlying model of capital equilibrium whose parameters are known.[2] A general limitation of this approach is that it is difficult to devise adequately powerful tests of the model of market equilibrium and to obtain refined estimates of the model parameters. In the present instance, the market equilibrium approach is further hampered by the difficulty of determining the stochastic properties of the cash flow stream that depend on the stochastic process of the output price: as we have already remarked, it is often very difficult to estimate the expected rate of change in commodity prices. Therefore in this paper we resort to a second approach, which yields the value of one security relative to the value of a portfolio of other traded securities.

Our approach is to find a self-financing portfolio whose cash flows replicate those which are to be valued.[3] The present value of the cash

---

1. Bodie and Rosansky (1980) report that the standard deviation of annual changes in futures prices over the period 1950–76 was 25.6% for silver, 47.2% for copper, and 25.2% for platinum.

2. See, e.g., the framework developed by Cox, Ingersoll, and Ross (1978); this was used by Brennan and Schwartz (1982a, 1982b) to analyze the valuation of regulated public utilities.

3. A self-financing portfolio has the property that its value at any time is exactly equal to the value of the investment and cash flow distributions required at that time. See

flow stream is then equal to the current value of this replicating portfolio. When a replicating self-financing portfolio can be constructed, our approach offers several advantages over the market equilibrium approach; not only does it obviate the need for a discount rate derived from an inadequately supported model of market equilibrium but, most important in the current context, it eliminates the need for estimates of the expected rate of change of the underlying cash flow and therefore of the output price.

Construction of the requisite replicating self-financing portfolio rests on the assumption that the convenience yield on the output commodity can be written as a function of the output price alone and that the interest rate is nonstochastic. These assumptions suffice to yield a deterministic relation between the spot and futures price of the commodity, and the cash flows from the project can then be replicated by a self-financing portfolio of riskless bills and futures contracts.

Specific limitations of the valuation model include the assumptions that the resource to be exploited is homogeneous and of a known amount, that costs are known, and that interest rates are nonstochastic. Any one of these assumptions may be relaxed at the expense of adding one further dimension to the state space on which the model is defined: as a practical matter it would be difficult to obtain tractable results if more than one of these assumptions were relaxed at a time. While the model as presented here presupposes the existence of a futures market in the output commodity, it would be straightforward to derive an analogous model in a general equilibrium context similar to that employed by Brennan and Schwartz (1982a, 1982b).

To allow for dependence of the output rate on the stochastic output price the capital budgeting decision is modeled as a problem of stochastic optimal control. Stochastic optimal control theory has been applied to the investment decision in a general context by Constantinides (1978), and in the specific context of a regulated public utility by Brennan and Schwartz (1982a, 1982b). Dothan and Williams (1980) have also analyzed the capital-budgeting decision within a similar framework. Pindyck (1980), like us, applies stochastic optimal control to the problem of the optimal exploitation of an exhaustible resource under uncertainty. In some respects Pindyck's analysis is more general than ours: in particular, he allows the level of reserves of the resource to vary stochastically and to be influenced by exploration activities. On the other hand, by confining his attention to risk-neutral firms he neglects the issues of risk and valuation that are the focus of the capital-budgeting decision and of this paper. Other writers who have recognized the importance of the option whether or not to exploit a natural

---

Harrison and Kreps (1979). The notion of a replicating self-financing portfolio is closely related to the option-pricing models of Black and Scholes (1973) and Merton (1973).

resource, which is inherent in the ownership of the resource, include Tourinho (1979); Brock, Rothschild, and Stiglitz (1982); and Paddock, Siegel, and Smith (1982). These writers have not however analyzed the present value of the decision to exploit a given resource or the optimal operating policy for a given facility, as we do, and Brock et al. do not exploit the arbitrage implications of a replicating self-financing portfolio.

Miller and Upton (1985) develop and test empirically a model for the valuation of natural resources based on the Hotelling model. Although it is close in spirit to our model, in that the spot price of the commodity is a sufficient statistic for the value of the mine, unlike ours their model assumes no upper limit on the output rate and ignores the possibility of closing and reopening the mine in response to current market conditions. As they point out this may be a good approximation when output prices exceed extraction costs by a wide margin, just as the value of a stock option approaches its intrinsic value when it is deep in the money.

The general type of model presented here lends itself to use in a number of related contexts—most obviously, to corporations considering when, whether, and how, to develop a given resource; to financial analysts concerned with the valuation of such corporations; and to policymakers concerned with the social costs of layoffs in cyclical industries and with policies to avert them. The model is well suited to analysis of the effects of alternative taxation, royalty, and subsidy policies on investment, employment, and unemployment in the natural resource sector.

Section I develops a general model for valuing the cash flows from a natural resource investment. A specialized version of the general model is presented in Section II. Under the assumption of an inexhaustible resource the model allows for only a single feasible operating rate when the project is operating but includes the possibility of costs of closing and reopening the project. Section III discusses a numerical example based on the general model. Section IV considers the problem, previously raised by Tourinho (1979), of the optimal timing of natural resource investments. Section V discusses briefly the application of the model to the analysis of fixed price long term purchase contracts for natural resources.

I. The General Valuation Model

The first step in analyzing an investment project is to determine the present value of the future cash flows it will generate and to compare this present value with the required investment. If the present value exceeds the investment a further decision is whether to proceed with the project immediately or to wait. We shall postpone consideration of this second, dynamic aspect of the capital-budgeting decision until Section III and in this and the following section will restrict our attention to the problem of determining the present value of the cash flows from a project. In this section we develop a general model, a specialization of which is considered in Section II.

To focus discussion we will suppose that the project under consideration is a mine that will produce a single homogeneous commodity, whose spot price, S, is determined competitively and is assumed to follow the exogenously given continuous stochastic process

$$\frac{dS}{S} = \mu \, dt + \sigma \, dz, \qquad (1)$$

where dz is the increment to a standard Gauss-Wiener process; σ, the instantaneous standard deviation of the spot price, is assumed to be known; and μ, the local trend in the price, may be stochastic.

As a preliminary to developing the valuation model it will prove useful to consider the relation between spot and futures prices and the convenience yield on the commodity. The convenience yield is the flow of services that accrues to an owner of the physical commodity but not to the owner of a contract for future delivery of the commodity (see Kaldor 1939; Working 1948; Brennan 1958; Telser 1958). Most obviously, the owner of the physical commodity is able to choose where it will be stored and when to liquidate the inventory. Recognizing the time lost and the costs incurred in transporting a commodity from one location to another, the convenience yield may be thought of as the value of being able to profit from temporary local shortages of the commodity through ownership of the physical commodity. The profit may arise either from local price variations or from the ability to maintain a production process as a result of ownership of an inventory of raw material.[4]

The convenience yield will depend on the identity of the individual holding the inventory and in equilibrium inventories will be held by individuals for whom the marginal convenience yield net of any physical storage costs is highest. We assume that a positive amount of the commodity is always held in inventory, and note that competition among potential storers will ensure that the net convenience yield of the marginal unit of inventory will be the same across all individuals who hold positive inventories. This marginal (net) convenience yield can be expected to be inversely proportional to the amount of the commodity held in inventory. Moreover, when stocks of the physical commodity are high, not only will the marginal convenience yield tend to be low, but so also will be the spot price S, and conversely when

---

4. Cootner (1967, p. 65) defines the convenience yield of inventory as "the present value of an increased income stream expected as a result of conveniently large inventories." This contrasts with our definition of the convenience yield as a flow.

stocks of the physical commodity are low. We make the simplifying assumption that the marginal net convenience yield of the commodity can be written as a function of the current spot price and time, $C(S, t)$. Detailed modeling of the behavior of the convenience yield is beyond the scope of this paper, and in the interest of tractability we shall sometimes assume simply that the convenience yield is proportional to the current spot price.

Our assumption that the convenience yield is a function only of the current spot price, together with the further assumption which we maintain throughout the paper, that the interest rate is a constant, ρ, suffices to yield a determinate relation between the spot and futures prices of the commodity. Thus let $F(S, \tau)$ represent the futures price at time t for delivery of one unit of the commodity at time T where $\tau = T - t$. The instantaneous change in the futures prices is given from Ito's lemma by

$$dF = (-F_\tau + \tfrac{1}{2} F_{SS} \sigma^2 S^2) \, dt + F_S \, dS. \tag{2}$$

Then consider the instantaneous rate of return earned by an individual who purchases one unit of the commodity and goes short $(F_S)^{-1}$ futures contracts. Since entering the futures contract involves no receipt or outlay of funds, his instantaneous return per dollar of investment including the marginal net convenience yield, using (2), is

$$\frac{dS}{S} + \frac{C(S)dt}{S} - (SF_S)^{-1} dF$$
$$= (SF_S)^{-1} [F_S C(S) - \tfrac{1}{2} F_{SS} \sigma^2 S^2 + F_\tau] \, dt. \tag{3}$$

Since this return to nonstochastic and since $C(S)$ is defined as the (net) convenience yield of the marginal unit of inventory, it follows that the return must be equal to the riskless return $\rho \, dt$. Setting the right hand side of (3) equal to $\rho \, dt$, we obtain the partial differential equation

$$\tfrac{1}{2} F_{SS} \sigma^2 S^2 + F_S (\rho S - C) - F_\tau = 0. \tag{4}$$

Thus the futures price is given by the solution to (4) subject to the boundary condition

$$F(S, 0) = S. \tag{5}$$

This establishes that the futures price is a function of the current spot price and the time to maturity. Moreover, the parameters of the convenience yield function may be estimated directly from the relation between spot and futures prices. If the convenience yield is proportional to the spot price,

$$C(S, t) = cS, \tag{6}$$

Evaluating Natural Resource Investments

then following Ross (1978) the futures price is given by

$$F(S, \tau) = Se^{(\rho - c)\tau}, \tag{7}$$

independent of the stochastic process of the spot price. For more general specifications of the convenience yield it is necessary to solve (4) and (5) directly.

Finally, using (4) in expression (2), the instantaneous change in the futures price may be expressed in terms of the convenience yield and the instantaneous change in the spot price as

$$dF = F_S[S(\mu - \rho) + C]dt + F_S S\sigma \, dz. \tag{8}$$

We are now in a position to derive the partial differential equation that must be satisfied by the value of the mine and to characterize the optimal output policy of the mine.

The output rate of the mine, q, is assumed to be costlessly variable between the upper and lower bounds $\bar{q}$ and $\underline{q}$.[5] The output rate can be reduced below $\underline{q}$ only by closing the mine, and it is costly both to close the mine and to open it again. For this reason the value of the mine will depend on whether it is currently open or closed. The value of the mine will also depend on the current commodity price, S; the physical inventory in the mine, Q; calendar time, t; and the mine operating policy, ϕ. We write the value of the mine as

$$H \equiv H(S, Q, t; j, \phi). \tag{9}$$

The indicator variable j takes the value one if the mine is open and zero if it is closed. The operating policy is described by the function determining the output rate when the mine is open $q(S, Q, t)$, and three critical commodity output prices: $S_1(Q, t)$ is the output price at which the mine is closed down or abandoned if it was previously open; $S_2(Q, t)$ is the price at which the mine is opened up if it was previously closed; $S_0(Q, t)$ is the price at which the mine is abandoned if it is already closed. The distinction between closure and abandonment is that a closed mine incurs fixed maintenance costs but may be opened up again. An abandoned mine incurs no costs but is assumed to be permanently abandoned. It is assumed that abandonment involves no costs.

Applying Ito's lemma to (9), the instantaneous change in the value of the mine is given by

$$dH = H_S \, dS + H_Q \, dQ + H_t \, dt + \tfrac{1}{2} H_{SS}(dS)^2, \tag{10}$$

---

5. These bounds may depend on the amount of inventory remaining in the mine and time.

where the instantaneous change in the mine inventory is determined by the output rate

$$dQ = -q\, dt. \qquad (11)$$

The after-tax cash flow, or continuous dividend rate, from the mine is

$$q(S - A) - M(1 - j) - \lambda_j H - T, \qquad (12)$$

where

$A(q, Q, t)$ is the average cash cost rate of producing at the rate q at time t when the mine inventory is Q;

$M(t)$ is the after-tax fixed-cost rate of maintaining the mine at time t when it is closed;

$\lambda_j (j = 0, 1)$ is proportional rate of tax on the value of the mine when it is closed and open; and

$T(q,Q,S,t)$ is the total income tax and royalties levied on the mine when it is operating. While alternative forms are possible we shall assume that the tax function is

$$T(q, Q, S, t) = t_1 qS + \max\{t_2 q[S(1 - t_1) - A], 0\}, \qquad (13)$$

where

t_1 is the royalty rate and t_2 is the income tax rate.[6]

The parameters λ_0 and λ_1 are interpreted most simply as property tax rates. However an alternative interpretation may be apposite in some contexts: they may represent the intensities of Poisson processes governing the event of uncompensated expropriation of the owners of the mine. Then the expected loss rate from expropriation is $\lambda_j H$ and expression (12) represents the cash flow net of the expected cost of expropriation. Under this interpretation the arbitrage strategy outlined below is not entirely risk free; however, we shall assume that there is no risk premium associated with the possibility of expropriation.

To derive the differential equation governing the value of the mine under the output policy ϕ consider the return to a portfolio consisting of a long position in the mine and a short position in (H_S/F_S) futures contracts. The return on the mine is given by (10)–(12) and the change in the futures price is given by (8). Combining these and using (1), the return on this portfolio is

$$\tfrac{1}{2}\sigma^2 S^2 H_{SS} - qH_Q + H_t + q(S - A) \\ - M(1 - j) - T - \lambda_j H + (\rho S - C) H_s. \qquad (14)$$

---

6. For simplicity we have ignored depreciation tax allowances.

Ignoring the possibility of expropriation, this return is nonstochastic, and to avoid riskless arbitrage opportunities it must be equal to the riskless return on the value of the investment. Setting expression (14) equal to the riskless return ρH, the value of the mine must satisfy the partial differential equation

$$\tfrac{1}{2}\sigma^2 S^2 H_{SS} + (\rho S - C)H_S - qH_Q + H_t + q(S - A) - M(1 - j) - T$$
$$- (\rho + \lambda_j) H = 0 \qquad (15)$$
$$(j = 0, 1).$$

The mine value satisfies (15) for any operating policy $\phi \equiv \{q, S_0, S_1, S_2\}$. Under the value maximizing operating policy $\phi^* = \{q^*, S_0^*, S_1^*, S_2^*\}$, the values of the mine when open, $V(S, Q, t)$, and when closed, $W(S, Q, t)$ are given by

$$V(S, Q, t) \equiv \max_{\phi} H(S, Q, t; 1, \phi) \qquad (16)$$

$$W(S, Q, t) \equiv \max_{\phi} H(S, Q, t; 0, \phi). \qquad (17)$$

The value-maximizing output and the value of the mine under the value-maximizing policy satisfy the two equations

$$\max_{q \in (q, \bar{q})} [\tfrac{1}{2}\sigma^2 S^2 V_{SS} + (\rho S - C)V_S - qV_Q$$
$$+ V_t + q(S - A) - T - (\rho + \lambda_1)V] = 0, \qquad (18)$$

$$\tfrac{1}{2}\sigma^2 S^2 W_{SS} + (\rho S - C) W_S + W_t - M - (\rho + \lambda_0)W = 0 \qquad (19)$$

(see Merton 1971, theorem 1; Fleming and Rishel 1975, chap. 6; Cox, Ingersoll, and Ross 1978, lemma 1).

Since the policies regarding opening, closing, and abandoning the mine are known to investors, we have

$$W(S_0^*, Q, t) = 0 \qquad (20)$$

$$V(S_1^*, Q, t) = \max[W(S_1^*, Q, t) - K_1(Q, t), 0] \qquad (21)$$

$$W(S_2^*, Q, t) = V(S_2^*, Q, t) - K_2(Q, t) \qquad (22)$$

where $K_1(\cdot)$ and $K_2(\cdot)$ are the cost of closing and opening the mine respectively. Assuming that the value of an exhausted mine is zero we also have the boundary condition

$$W(S, 0, t) = V(S, 0, t) = 0. \qquad (23)$$

Finally, since S_0^*, S_1^*, S_2^* are chosen to maximize the value of the mine it follows from the Merton-Samuelson high-contact condition (Samuelson 1965; Merton 1973) that

$$W_S(S_0^*, Q, t) = 0; \qquad (24)$$

$$V_S(S\dagger, Q, t) = \begin{cases} W_S(S\dagger, Q, t) & \text{if } W(S\dagger, Q, t) - K_1(Q, t) \geq 0, \\ 0 & \text{if } W(S\dagger, Q, t) - K_1(Q, t) < 0; \end{cases} \quad (25)$$

$$W_S(S_2^*, Q, t) = V_S(S_2^*, Q, t). \quad (26)$$

The value of the mine depends on calendar time only because the costs A, M, K_1, and K_2 and the convenience yield C depend on time. If there is a constant rate of inflation π in all of these and if $C(S, t)$ may be written as κS, then equations (18)–(26) may be simplified as follows:

Define the deflated variables

$$a(q, Q) = A(q, Q, t) e^{-\pi t},$$

$$f = M(t) e^{-\pi t},$$

$$k_1(Q) = K_1(Q, t) e^{-\pi t}, \quad k_2(Q) = K_2(Q, t) e^{-\pi t},$$

$$s = S e^{-\pi t},$$

$$v(s, Q) = V(S, Q, t) e^{-\pi t},$$

$$w(s, Q) = W(S, Q, t) e^{-\pi t}.$$

Then it may be verified that the deflated value of the mine satisfies

$$\max_{q \in (q, \bar{q})} [½ \sigma^2 s^2 v_{ss} + (r - \kappa) s v_s - q v_Q \quad (27)$$
$$+ q(s - a) - \tau - (r + \lambda_1) v] = 0,$$

$$½ \sigma^2 s^2 w_{ss} + (r - \kappa) s w_s - f - (r + \lambda_0) w = 0, \quad (28)$$

where $\quad r = \rho - \pi$ is the real interest rate,

$$\tau = t_1 q s + \max \{t_2 q [s(1 - t_1) - a], 0\}; \quad (29)$$

$$w(s_0^*, Q) = 0; \quad (30)$$

$$v(s\dagger, Q) = \max[w(s\dagger, Q) - k_1(Q), 0]; \quad (31)$$

$$w(s_2^*, Q) = v(s_2^*, Q) - k_2(Q); \quad (32)$$

$$w(s, 0) = v(s, 0) = 0; \quad (33)$$

$$w_s(s_0^*, Q) = 0; \quad (34)$$

$$v_s(s\dagger, Q) = \begin{cases} w_s(s\dagger, Q) & \text{if } w(s\dagger, Q, t) - k_1(Q, t) \geq 0, \\ 0 & \text{if } w(s\dagger, Q, t) - k_1(Q, t) < 0; \end{cases} \quad (35)$$

$$w_s(s_2^*, Q) = v_s(s_2^*, Q). \quad (36)$$

Equations (27)–(36) constitute the general model for the value of a mine. They suffice to determine not only the (deflated) value of the mine when open and closed, but also the optimal policies for opening, closing, and abandoning the mine and for setting the output rates. In general there exists no analytic solution to the valuation model, though it is straightforward to solve it numerically. In the next section we present a simplified version of the model.

II. The Infinite Resource Case

To obtain a model that is analytically tractable we assume that the physical inventory of the commodity in the mine, Q, is infinite. This infinite resource assumption enables us to replace the partial differential equations (27) and (28) for the value of the mine with ordinary differential equations, since the mine inventory, Q, is no longer a relevant state variable. To facilitate the analysis further we assume that the tax system allows for full loss offset so that (29) becomes

$$\tau(q, s) = t_1 qs + t_2 q[s(1 - t_1) - a]. \tag{29'}$$

Finally, we assume that the mine has only two possible operating rates, q^* when it is open, and zero when it is closed; furthermore, because it is costly to open or close the mine, costs must be incurred in moving from one output rate to the other.[7]

Under the foregoing assumptions the (deflated) value of the mine when it is open and operating at the rate q^* satisfies the ordinary differential equation

$$\tfrac{1}{2} \sigma^2 s^2 v_{ss} + (r - \kappa) s v_s + ms - n - (r + \lambda)v = 0, \tag{37}$$

where $m = q^*(1 - t_1)(1 - t_2)$, and $n = q^* a(1 - t_2)$.

If we assume that f, the periodic maintenance cost for a closed mine, is equal to zero, then the value of the mine when closed satisfies the corresponding differential equation

$$\tfrac{1}{2} \sigma^2 s^2 w_{ss} + (r - \kappa) s w_s - (r + \lambda)w = 0. \tag{38}$$

The boundary conditions are obtained by ignoring Q in (31), (32), (35), and (36) and by setting $w(0) = 0$.[8]

The complete solutions to equations (37) and (38) are

$$w(s) = \beta_1 s^{\gamma_1} + \beta_2 s^{\gamma_2}, \tag{39}$$

$$v(s) = \beta_3 s^{\gamma_1} + \beta_4 s^{\gamma_2} + \frac{ms}{\lambda + \kappa} - \frac{n}{r + \lambda}, \tag{40}$$

---

7. The App. develops the model under the neoclassical assumption of a continuously variable output rate with convex costs.

8. In the absence of maintenance costs it is never optimal to abandon a closed mine so long as there is a possibility that it will be optimal to reopen it. Hence $w(0) = 0$ and $w(s) > 0$ for $s > 0$.

where the β's are constants to be determined by the boundary conditions and

$$\gamma_1 = \alpha_1 + \alpha_2, \quad \gamma_2 = \alpha_1 - \alpha_2,$$

$$\alpha_1 = \frac{1}{2} - \frac{r - \kappa}{\sigma^2}, \quad \alpha_2 = \left[\alpha_1^2 + \frac{2(r + \lambda)}{\sigma^2}\right]^{1/2}.$$

If we assume that $(r + \lambda) > 0$,[9] then $\beta_2 = 0$ since γ_2 is negative and $w(s)$ must remain finite as s approaches zero. Similarly, since $\gamma_1 > 1$, $\beta_3 = 0$ if we impose the requirement that v/s remain finite as $s \to \infty$. Thus the value of the mine when closed is given by $w(s) = \beta_1 s^{\gamma_1}$, and the value when open is

$$v(s) = \beta_4 s^{\gamma_2} + \frac{ms}{\lambda + \kappa} - \frac{n}{r + \lambda}. \tag{41}$$

If the possibility of closing the mine when output prices are low is ignored, the value of the mine is given by the last two terms in (41); thus the first term represents the value of the closure option.

The remaining constants β_1 and β_4, as well as the optimal policy for closing and opening the mine represented by the output prices s_1^* and s_2^*, are determined by conditions (31), (32), (35), and (36), which imply that

$$\beta_1 = \frac{d\, s_2^*(\gamma_2 - 1) + b\gamma_2}{(\gamma_2 - \gamma_1)\, s_2^{*\gamma_1}}, \quad \beta_4 = \frac{d\, s_2^*(\gamma_1 - 1) + b\gamma_1}{(\gamma_2 - \gamma_1)\, s_1^{*\gamma_2}},$$

$$s_2^* = \gamma_2(e - bx^{\gamma_1})/(x^{\gamma_1} - x)\, d\,(\gamma_2 - 1),$$

$$\frac{s_1^*}{s_2^*} = x,$$

where $e = k_1 - n/(r + \lambda)$, $b = -k_2 - n/(r + \lambda)$, $d = m/(\lambda + \kappa)$, and x, the ratio of the commodity prices at which the mine is closed and opened, is the solution to the nonlinear equation

$$\frac{(x^{\gamma_2} - x)(\gamma_1 - 1)}{\gamma_1(e - bx^{\gamma_2})} = \frac{(x^{\gamma_1} - x)(\gamma_2 - 1)}{\gamma_2(e - bx^{\gamma_1})}. \tag{42}$$

The solution is illustrated in figure 1. In this figure the dotted line represents the present value of the cash flows from the mine assuming that it can never be shut down; this is obtained by setting $\beta_4 = 0$ in equation (42). Since $\gamma_2 < 0$, the value of the closure option diminishes and approaches zero for high output prices. For very low output prices the mine is worth more when it is closed than when it is open and making losses because of the cost of closure. However, for higher output prices the mine is worth more when open, and at the commodity

9. This is necessary for the present value of the future costs to be finite.

Evaluating Natural Resource Investments

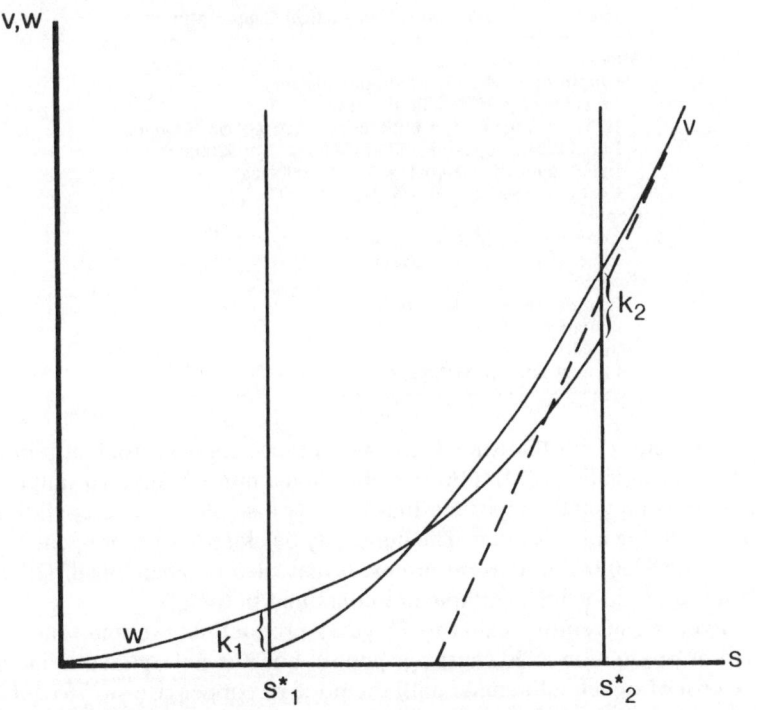

FIG. 1.—Mine value when open (v) and closed (w) as a function of the commodity price (s); k_1: cost of closing mine; k_2: cost of opening mine.

price s_2^* it is worth just enough more to warrant the outlay k_2 to open it. It is clear from the figure and can be demonstrated analytically that as the costs of opening and closing the mine approach zero, s_1^* and s_2^* approach the same value and the mine value schedule becomes a single curve. On the other hand, as the cost of mine closure becomes very large the closure option becomes worthless, and in the limit the value schedule for the open mine approaches the dotted line. Changes in the cost of mine closure, brought about for example by government regulation, will alter the optimal policy for closing the mine, s_1^*: however, they will also affect the original decision to invest in the mine by changing the present value of the future cash flows. Such effects, or those induced by changes in the tax regime, are readily analyzed in the context of this simplified model or the general model of the previous section.

III. An Example

To illustrate the nature of our solution we consider a mine example based on the stylized facts for copper. In this example there is a finite

TABLE 1   Data for a Hypothetical Copper Mine

Mine:
  Output rate (q^*): 10 million pounds/year
  Inventory (Q): 150 million pounds
  Initial average cost of production $a(q^*, Q)$: $0.50/pound
  Initial cost of opening and closing (k_1, k_2): $200,000
  Initial maintenance costs (f): $500,000/year
  Cost inflation rate (π): 8%/year
Copper:
  Convenience yield (κ): 1%/year
  Price variance (σ^2): 8%/year
Taxes:
  Real estate (λ_1, λ_2): 2%/year
  Income (t_2): 50%
  Royalty (t_1): 0%
  Interest rate (ρ): 10%/year

mine inventory so that the stochastic optimal control problem represented by equations (27)–(36) must be solved numerically. To simplify matters somewhat we assume that there is a single feasible operating rate when the mine is open. The mine may be closed down or opened at a cost of $200,000 in current prices; it may also be abandoned. Other data required for this example are contained in table 1.[10]

Given an inventory equal to 15 years production, we find that the cost of production is 50 cents per pound, but it is not optimal to incur the cost of opening the mine until the price of copper rises to 76 cents. On the other hand, if the mine is already open and operating, it is not optimal to close it down until the copper price drops to 44 cents. Finally, the mine should be abandoned if the price drops below 20 cents. Obviously these critical prices depend on the assumed costs of opening, closing, and maintaining the mine: they also depend upon the remaining inventory in the mine. The greater the inventory in the mine the greater is the incentive to extract the copper immediately, since the opportunity cost of immediate extraction falls as the expected life of the mine increases. Thus the greater the inventory the lower is the price at which the mine is opened and closed and, since the mine value is a nondecreasing function of the inventory, the lower the price at which it is abandoned.

Table 2 summarizes the results when the mine has a 15-year inventory. Columns 1 and 3 give the present values of the future cash flows from the mine, assuming that it is open and closed, respectively, for different copper prices. These are the relevant values for the investment decision. Column 4 gives the value of the mine assuming that it

---

10. The variance rate and convenience yield used in table 1 compare with a variance rate for COMEX monthly settlement prices for copper of 7.8% per year for 1971–82 and an average convenience yield of 0.7% per year computed from annual data on the May contract for the same period, using eq. (7).

Evaluating Natural Resource Investments

TABLE 2 Value of Copper Mine for Different Copper Prices

Copper Price ($/pound) (1)	Mine Value ($ million) Open (2)	Mine Value ($ million) Closed (3)	Value of Fixed-Output-Rate Mine ($ million) (4)	Value of Closure Option ($ million) (5)	Risk (6)	Value of Mine under Certainty, $\sigma^2 = 0$ ($ million) (7)
.30	(1.25)*	1.45	.38	1.07		0
.40	(4.15)*	4.35	3.12	1.23		0
.50	7.95	8.11	7.22	.89	.75	1.85†
.60	12.52	12.49	12.01	.51	.66	7.84†
.70	17.56	17.38	17.19	.37	.59	13.87†
.80	22.88	(22.68)†	22.61	.27	.54	19.91†
.90	28.38	(28.18)†	28.18	.20	.50	25.94†
1.00	34.01	(33.81)†	33.85	.16	.47	31.98†

* Optimal to close mine
† Optimal to open mine

cannot be closed down but must be operated at the rate of 10 million pounds per year until the inventory is exhausted in 15 years. The difference between column 4 and the greater of the values shown in columns 2 and 3 represents the value of the option to close down or abandon the mine if the price of copper falls far enough. The value of this closure option is shown in column 5: it amounts to 12% of the value of the fixed-output-rate mine when the copper price is equal to the variable cost of 50 cents per pound; of course this would represent a much higher proportion of the *net* present value of an investment in the mine.

Column 6 of the table reports the instantaneous risk of the mine at different copper prices. This is the instantaneous standard deviation of the mine value, defined as $(v_s/v)\sigma s$ when the mine is open and $(w_s/w)\sigma s$ when the mine is closed. As we would expect, the risk of the mine decreases as the copper price and hence the operating margin increases. Since the copper price is stochastic, so also is the risk of the mine and the instantaneous rate of return required by investors, pointing to the dangers of assuming a single discount rate in a present value analysis.

Ownership of a mine that is not currently operating involves three distinct types of decision possibilities or options: first, the decision to begin operations; second, the decision to close the mine when it is currently operating (and possibly to reopen it later), which we have referred to as the closure option; and third, the decision to abandon the mine early, before the inventory is exhausted.

The decision to begin operations depends in our model on the current spot price of the commodity and the mine inventory. When there is no uncertainty, so that the time path of the commodity price is deterministic, the optimal decision rule for beginning operations can be expressed in calendar time (and the mine inventory). This certainty case, which has been analyzed extensively under the rubric of the "timing option" (see, e.g., Solow 1974), corresponds to column 7, of table 2: this gives the value of the closed mine under the assumption of certainty, which may be contrasted with the uncertainty case of column 3. For our parameter values it is never optimal under certainty to close or abandon the mine, once it is open, before the inventory is exhausted,[11] so that the closure and early abandonment options are worthless. When the commodity price is in the neighborhood of the production costs the elimination of uncertainty reduces the value of the mine dramatically. Of course this depends on the particular values of the convenience yield and other parameters.

IV. The Investment Decision

Thus far, only the valuation of the cash flows from an investment project has been considered. The investment decision itself requires that a comparison be made between the present value of the project cash flows and the initial investment needed for the project. Continuing with the example of a mine, $V(S, Q^*, t)$ represents the (nominal) value at time t of a completed operating mine with inventory Q^* when the current output price is S; $V(\cdot)$ is equal to the present value of the cash flows that will be realized from the mine under the optimal operating policy. Similarly, let $I(S, Q^*, t)$ represent the investment required to construct an operating mine with inventory Q^* on a particular property: the amount of this initial investment may obviously depend on calendar time and upon the size of the mine as represented by Q^*, and S is included as an argument for the sake of generality. Then, assuming that construction lags can be neglected, the net present value (NPV) at time t of constructing the mine immediately is given by

$$\text{NPV}(S, Q^*, t) = V(S, Q^*, t) - I(S, Q^*, t). \tag{43}$$

However, once the possibility of postponing an investment decision is recognized, it is clear that it is not in general optimal to proceed with construction simply because the net present value of construction is positive: there is a "timing option" and it may pay to wait in the expectation that the net present value of construction will increase. This dynamic aspect of the investment decision is closely related to the problem of determining the optimal strategy for exercising an option on a share of common stock: the right to make the investment decision and to appropriate the resulting net present value is the ownership right in the undeveloped mine property, and the value of this ownership right corresponds to the value of the stock option.

Define $X(S, Q^*, t)$ as the value of the ownership right to an unde-

---

11. Because the commodity price is increasing faster than the production costs.

veloped mine with inventory Q^* at time t when the current output price is S. The stochastic process for $X(\cdot)$ is obtained from Ito's lemma, using the assumption about the stochastic process for S embodied in expression (1). Then the arbitrage argument used to derive the differential equation (15) for the value of a completed mine may be repeated to show that $X(\cdot)$ must satisfy the partial differential equation

$$\tfrac{1}{2}\sigma^2 S^2 X_{ss} + (\rho S - C)X_s + X_t - (\rho + \lambda)X = 0, \qquad (44)$$

where, as before, λ represents either the rate of tax on the value of the property or the intensity of a Poisson process governing the event of expropriation.[12]

Since the origin is an absorbing state for the commodity price, S, we have the boundary condition

$$X(0, Q^*, t) = 0, \qquad (45)$$

and if the ownership rights are in the form of a lease which expires at time T, then

$$X(S, Q^*, T) = 0. \qquad (46)$$

Assuming that the size of the mine inventory, Q^*, is predetermined by technical and geological factors, the optimal strategy for investment can be characterized in terms of a time dependent schedule of output prices $S^I(t)$ such that

$$X(S^I, Q^*, t) = V(S^I, Q^*, t) - I(S^I, Q^*, t), \qquad (47)$$

$$X_S(S^I, Q^*, t) = V_S(S^I, Q^*, t) - I_S(S^I, Q^*, t). \qquad (48)$$

Equation (47) states simply that the value of the property is equal to the net present value of the investment at the time it is made. Equation (48) is the Merton-Samuelson high-contact or envelope condition for a maximizing choice of S^I.

If the amount of the accessible inventory in the mine, Q^*, depends on the amount of the initial investment instead of being determined exogenously, then we have the additional value-maximizing condition to determine the size of the initial mine inventory, Q^*:

$$V_Q(S^I, Q^*, t) = I_Q(S^I, Q^*, t). \qquad (49)$$

Thus the optimal investment strategy is obtained by solving the partial differential equation (44) for the value of the ownership right, subject to boundary conditions (45)–(49). The optimal time to invest is determined by the series of critical output prices $S^I(t)$ described by (47) and (48); the optimal amount to invest is determined by the first order condition (49). Note that the boundary conditions for this problem

---

12. An alternative assumption is that all costs inflate at the common rate π; this would convert (44) into an *ordinary* differential eq. for the deflated mine value $x = Xe^{-\pi t}$.

involve $V(S, Q, t)$, the present value of the cash flows from a completed mine. Thus solving the cash flow valuation problem is a prerequisite for the investment decision analysis described in this section.

V. Long-Term Supply Contracts

It is not uncommon for the outputs of natural resource investments to be sold under long-term contracts that fix the price of the commodity but leave the purchase rate at least partially to the discretion of the purchaser. Where they exist, such contracts must be taken into account in valuing ongoing projects. Therefore in this section we show briefly how these contracts may be valued and the equilibrium contract price determined.

Let $Y(S, t; p, T)$ denote the value at time t of a particular contract to purchase the commodity up to time T at the contract price p, when the current spot price of the commodity is S. The contract is assumed to permit the purchaser to vary the price rate, q, between the lower and upper bounds $\underline{q}$ and $\bar{q}$. Since the commodity is by assumption available for purchase at the prevailing spot price S, ownership of the contract yields an instantaneous benefit or cash flow $q(S - p)$.

Using Ito's lemma and the stochastic process for S, the instantaneous change in the value of the contract is given by

$$dY = (\tfrac{1}{2} \sigma^2 S^2 Y_{ss} + Y_t)dt + Y_s \, dS. \tag{50}$$

Then an arbitrage argument analogous to that presented in Section I implies that the value of the contract must satisfy the partial differential equation:

$$\max_{q \in (\underline{q}, \bar{q})} [\tfrac{1}{2} \sigma^2 S^2 Y_{ss} + (\rho S - C)Y_s + Y_t + q(S - p) - \rho Y] = 0. \tag{51}$$

The value of the contract at maturity, $t = T$, is equal to zero, so that

$$Y(S, T; p, T) = 0. \tag{52}$$

In addition, the origin is an absorbing state for the spot price S. This implies that if $S = 0$, the holder of the contract must incur certain losses at the rate $\underline{q}p$ up to the maturity of the contract, so that

$$Y(0, t; p, T) = \frac{-p\underline{q}}{\rho} [1 - e^{-\rho(T-t)}]. \tag{53}$$

Finally, for sufficiently high values of S, the value of the right to vary the purchase rate approaches zero and the value of the contract approaches that of a series of forward contracts to purchase at the rate $\bar{q}$

at the fixed price p. Noting that forward and futures prices are equivalent when the interest rate is nonstochastic (see Cox et al. 1981; Jarrow and Oldfield 1981; Richard and Sundaresan 1981), this implies that

$$\lim_{s \to \infty} \frac{\partial Y(S, t;\ p, T)}{\partial S} = \frac{\partial}{\partial S} \int_0^{T-t} \bar{q}\, F(S, \tau)\, d\tau, \qquad (54)$$

where $F(S, \tau)$ is the futures price for delivery in τ periods as defined previously.

The equilibrium contract price (or price schedule) is that which makes the value of the contract at inception equal to zero, given the prevailing spot price, S, and maturity, T. Writing the equilibrium contract price as $p^*(S, T)$, we have

$$Y[S, 0;\ p^*(S, T), T] = 0 \qquad (55)$$

In general there does not exist a closed-form solution for $Y(\cdot)$ or $p^*(\cdot)$. However, if the convenience yield can be written as $C(s) = \kappa S$, then closed-form solutions may be obtained in two special cases.

First, if the purchaser has no discretion over the purchase rate, so that $\bar{q} = \underline{q} = q^*$, then the contract is equivalent to a series of forward contracts with value given by[13]

$$Y(S, t;\ p, T) = q^* \left\{ \frac{S}{\kappa} [1 - e^{-\kappa(T-t)}] - \frac{p}{\rho} [1 - e^{-\rho(T-t)}] \right\}. \qquad (56)$$

This implies that the equilibrium contract price is

$$p^*(S, T) = \frac{\rho S}{\kappa} \left(\frac{1 - e^{-\kappa T}}{1 - e^{-\rho T}} \right). \qquad (57)$$

Second, if the contract has an infinite maturity, the value of the contract is equal to the sum of the values of two assets we have already valued: a perpetual contract to purchase the commodity at the fixed rate $\underline{q}$ and a mine with infinite inventory, an average cost of production p, feasible production rates $\bar{q} - \underline{q}$, and with no taxes, maintenance costs, or costs of opening and closing. The former may be valued using equation (56) and the latter is a special case of Section II.[14] It can then be shown that

$$Y(S, t;\ p, \infty) = \begin{cases} \beta_1 S^{\gamma_1} + \underline{q}\left(\dfrac{S}{\kappa} - \dfrac{p}{\rho}\right), & S < p \\[1em] \beta_4 S^{\gamma_2} = \bar{q}\left(\dfrac{S}{\kappa} - \dfrac{p}{\rho}\right), & S \geq p, \end{cases} \qquad (58)$$

---

13. We thank the referee for this point.

14. As the referee remarks, this contract is equivalent to a perpetuity of European options on the commodity.

where

$$\beta_1 = \frac{1}{2\alpha_2\kappa}\left[1 - \gamma_2\left(\frac{\rho - \kappa}{\rho}\right)\right]q^d p^{1-\gamma_1},$$

$$\beta_4 = \frac{1}{2\alpha_2\kappa}\left[1 - \frac{\gamma_1}{\rho}(\rho - \kappa)\right]q^d p^{1-\gamma_2},$$

$$q^d = \bar{q} - \underline{q},$$

and γ_1, γ_2, and α_2 are as defined following equation (40). The equilibrium price $p^*(S, \tau)$ is found from the nonlinear equation obtained by setting either of the expressions (58) equal to zero.

VI. Conclusion

We have shown in the paper how assets whose cash flows depend on highly variable output prices may be valued and how the optimal policies for managing them may be determined by exploiting the properties of replicating self-financing portfolios. The explicit analysis rests on the assumption that such portfolios may be formed by trading in futures contracts in the output commodity, but the general approach can also be developed in a general equilibrium context if the relevant futures markets do not exist.

In addition to providing a rich set of empirical predictions for empirical research, this framework should be useful for the analysis of capital-budgeting decisions in a wide variety of situations in which the distribution of future cash flows is not given exogenously but must be determined by future management decisions.

Appendix

In contrast to the assumption of Section II that there are only two feasible output rates, zero and q^*, and that it is costly to shift from one to the other, we assume in this case that the output rate is continuously and costlessly variable between zero and $\bar{q}$; in keeping with this assumption, costs of opening and closing the mine are neglected and this renders the distinction between an open and a closed mine otiose.

We assume that no costs are incurred if the output rate is zero and that for positive output rates the total cost per unit time of the output rate q is $c(q) = q \cdot a(q) = a_0 + a_1 q + a_2 q^2$, where $a_1, a_2 > 0$; this represents a (linearly) increasing marginal cost schedule.

Using these assumptions in equation (27), the optimal output policy and the value of the mine satisfy

$$\tfrac{1}{2}\sigma^2 s^2 v_{ss} + (r - \kappa)vs + (1 - t_2)\max_{q \in (0,\bar{q})}[(1 - t_1)qs - a_0 - a_1 q - a_2 q^2, 0] - (r + \lambda)v = 0. \tag{A1}$$

Carrying out the maximization we find that the optimal output policy is

$$q^*(s) = \begin{cases} \bar{q} & s > \bar{s} \\ \dfrac{(1-t_1)s - a_1}{2a_2} & \bar{s} > s > s^* \\ 0 & s \leq s^*, \end{cases}$$

where $s^* = (a_1 + 2\sqrt{a_0 a_2})/(1 - t_1)$ and $\bar{s} = (a_1 + 2a_2\bar{q})/(1 - t_1)$. Thus the optimal output policy maximizes the instantaneous profit rate; since the profit rate is zero when the output rate is zero, the output rate is positive whenever the net-of-royalty output price exceeds the minimum average cost of production.

The after-tax cash flow from the mine under the optimal output policy, $p(s)$, is given by

$$p(s) = \begin{cases} (1 - t_2)[(1 - t_1)\bar{q}s - a_0 - a_1\bar{q} - a_2\bar{q}^2] & s > \bar{s}, \\ (1 - t_2)\dfrac{(1 - t_1)(s - a_1)^2}{4a_2 - a_0} & \bar{s} > s > s^*, \\ 0 & s \leq s^*. \end{cases}$$

When $p(s)$ is substituted for the maximand in equation (A1), the complete solutions for the three regions are

$$v(s) = \beta_1 s^{\gamma_1} + \beta_2 s^{\gamma_2} \qquad s \leq s^*, \qquad (A2)$$

$$v(s) = \beta_3 s^{\gamma_1} + \beta_4 s^{\gamma_2} + \delta(s) \qquad \bar{s} > s > s^*, \qquad (A3)$$

$$v(s) = \beta_5 s^{\gamma_1} + \beta_6 s^{\gamma_2} + \dfrac{ms}{\lambda + \kappa} - \dfrac{n}{r + \lambda} \qquad s > \bar{s}, \qquad (A4)$$

where

$$\delta(s) = \dfrac{(1 - t_2)}{r + \lambda}\left[\dfrac{a_1^2}{4a_2} - a_0\right] - \left[\dfrac{a_1(1 - t_1)(1 - t_2)}{2a_2(\lambda + c)}\right]s,$$

$$+ \left[\dfrac{(1 - t_1)^2(1 - t_2)}{4a_2(\lambda + 2c - \sigma^2 - r)}\right]s^2,$$

$$m = \bar{q}(1 - t_1)(1 - t_2),$$

$$n = (1 - t_2)(a_0 + a_1\bar{q} + a_2\bar{q}^2).$$

Variables γ_1 and γ_2 are as defined following equation (40), and the coefficients β_i ($i = 1, \ldots, 6$) are constants determined as follows. As in the case of Section II the requirements that v and v/s remain finite for very small and very large s, respectively, imply that $\beta_2 = \beta_5 = 0$. The remaining four constants are obtained by solving the four linear equations yielded by imposing the condition that the valuation schedule $v(s)$ be continuous and have a finite second derivative at s^* and $\bar{s}$:

$$\beta_1 s^{*\gamma_1} = \beta_3 s^{*\gamma_1} + \beta_4 s^{*\gamma_2} + \delta(s^*), \qquad (A5)$$

$$\gamma_1 \beta_1 s^{*\gamma_1 - 1} = \gamma_1 \beta_3 s^{*\gamma_1 - 1} + \gamma_2 \beta_4 s^{*\gamma_2 - 1} + \delta'(s^*), \qquad (A6)$$

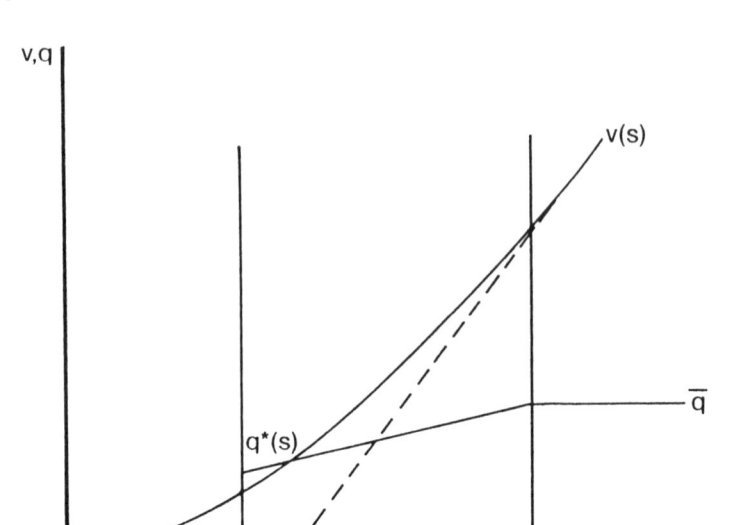

FIG. 2.—Case ii: Mine value (v) and optimal output as a function of the output price (s).

$$\beta_3 \bar{s}^{\gamma_1} + \beta_4 \bar{s}^{\gamma_2} + \delta(\bar{s}) = \beta_6 \bar{s}^{\gamma_2} + \frac{m\bar{s}}{\lambda + \kappa} - \frac{n}{r + \lambda}, \qquad (A7)$$

$$\gamma_1 \beta_3 \bar{s}^{\gamma_1 - 1} + \gamma_2 \beta_4 \bar{s}^{\gamma_2 - 1} + \delta'(\bar{s}) = \gamma_2 \beta_6 \bar{s}^{\gamma_2 - 1} + \frac{m}{\lambda + \kappa}. \qquad (A8)$$

Thus the value of the mine is given by the solution to equations (A2)–(A8) with $\beta_2 = \beta_5 = 0$. Since the equation system (A5)–(A8) is linear it is a straightforward if tedious task to obtain an explicit valuation expression which may be used for comparative statics. The valuation schedule and the optimal output policy are illustrated in figure 2. In this figure the dotted line corresponds to the value of the mine if it is required to operate perpetually at its maximum rate $\bar{q}$: thus the difference between the $v(s)$ schedule and this line represents the value of the option to vary the output rate in response to changing output prices.

References

Bierman, H., and Smidt, S. 1960. *The Capital Budgeting Decision.* New York: Macmillan.
Black, F., and Scholes, M. 1973. The pricing of options and corporate liabilities. *Journal of Political Economy* 81 (May–June): 637–54.
Bodie, Z., and Rosansky, V. I. 1980. Risk and return in commodity futures. *Financial Analysts Journal* 36 (May–June): 27–40.
Bogue M. C., and Roll, R. 1974. Capital budgeting of risky projects with imperfect markets for physical capital. *Journal of Finance* 29 (May): 601–13.
Brennan, M. J. 1958. The supply of storage. *American Economic Review* 48 (March): 50–72.
Brennan, M. J. 1973. An approach to the valuation of uncertain income streams. *Journal of Finance* 28 (July): 661–73.

Evaluating Natural Resource Investments   **157**

Brennan, M. J., and Schwartz, E. S. 1982a. Consistent regulatory policy under uncertainty. *Bell Journal of Economics* 13 (Autumn): 506–21.
Brennan, M. J., and Schwartz, E. S. 1982b. Regulation and corporate investment policy. *Journal of Finance* 37 (May): 289–300.
Brock, W. A.; Rothschild, M.; and Stiglitz, J. E. 1982. Stochastic capital theory. Financial Research Center Memorandum no. 40. Princeton, N.J.: Princeton University, April.
Constantinides, G. M. 1978. Market risk adjustment in project valuation. *Journal of Finance* 33 (May): 603–16.
Cootner, P. 1967. Speculation and hedging. *Food Research Institute Studies* 7 (Suppl.): 65–106.
Cox, J. C.; Ingersoll, J. E.; and Ross, S. A. 1978. A theory of the term structure of interest rates. Research Paper no. 468. Stanford, Calif.: Stanford University.
Cox, J. C.; Ingersoll, J. E.; and Ross, S. A. 1981. The relation between forward prices and futures prices. *Journal of Financial Economics* 9 (December): 321–46.
Dean, Joel 1951. *Capital Budgeting; Top Management Policy on Plant Equipment and Product Development.* New York: Columbia University.
Dothan, U., and Williams, J. 1980. Term-risk structures and the valuation of projects. *Journal of Financial and Quantitative Analysis* 15 (November): 875–906.
Fama, E. F. 1977. Risk-adjusted discount rates and capital budgeting under uncertainty. *Journal of Financial Economics* 5 (August): 3–24.
Fisher, Irving. 1907. *The Rate of Interest: Its Nature, Determination and Relation to Economic Phenomena.* New York: Macmillan.
Fleming, W. H., and Rishel, R. W. 1975. *Deterministic and Stochastic Optimal Control.* New York: Springer-Verlag.
Harrison, J. M., and Kreps, D. M. 1979. Martingales and arbitrage in multiperiod securities markets. *Journal of Economic Theory* 20:381–408.
Jarrow, R. A., and Oldfield, G. S. 1981. Forward contracts and futures contracts. *Journal of Financial Economics* 9 (December): 373–82.
Kaldor, N. 1939. Speculation and economic stability. *Review of Economic Studies* 7:1–27.
Merton, R. C. 1971. Optimum consumption and portfolio rules in a continuous time model. *Journal of Economic Theory* 3 (December): 373–413.
Merton, R. 1973. The theory of rational option pricing. *Bell Journal of Economic and Management Science* 4 (Spring): 141–83.
Miller, M. H., and Upton, C. W. 1985. A test of the Hotelling valuation principle. *Journal of Political Economy* 93 (February): in press.
Myers, S. C., and Turnbull, S. M. 1977. Capital budgeting and the capital asset pricing model: Good news and bad news. *Journal of Finance* 32 (May): 321–32.
Paddock, J. L.; Siegel, D. R.; and Smith, J. L. 1982. Option valuation of claims on physical assets: The case of off-shore petroleum leases. Unpublished manuscript. Evanston, Ill.: Northwestern University.
Pindyck, R. S. 1980. Uncertainty and exhaustible resource markets. *Journal of Political Economy* 88 (December): 1203–25.
Richard, S. F., and Sundaresan, M. 1981. A continuous time equilibrium model of forward prices and futures prices in a multigood economy. *Journal of Financial Economics* 9 (December): 347–72.
Ross, S. A. 1978. A simple approach to the valuation of risky streams. *Journal of Business* 51 (July): 453–75.
Samuelson, P. A. 1965. Rational theory of warrant pricing. *Industrial Management Review* 6 (Spring): 3–31.
Solow, R. M. 1974. The economics of resources or the resources of economics. *American Economic Review* 64 (May): 1–14.
Telser, L. G. 1958. Futures trading and the storage of cotton and wheat. In A. E. Peck, ed., *Selected Writings on Future Markets.* Chicago, 1977.
Tourinho, O. A. F. 1979. The option value of reserves of natural resources. Unpublished manuscript. Berkeley: University of California.
Working, H. 1948. The theory of price of storage. *Journal of Farm Economics* 30:1–28. Reprinted in *Selected Writings of Holbrook Working.* Chicago: Chicago Board of Trade, 1977.

Jonathan E. Ingersoll, Jr.
Stephen A. Ross
Yale University

Waiting to Invest: Investment and Uncertainty*

I. Introduction

One of the first things we learn when we begin to study finance is the simple rule that we should take an investment if it has a positive net present value (NPV) and reject it if its NPV is negative. Later we learn how to compute present values with risk adjustments, but the rule remains essentially the same. The theory becomes a bit fuzzier when investment budgets are limited and, more important, when some investment decisions have implications for other projects. Unfortunately, the ubiquitous nature of this latter situation is seldom made very clear. While we do recognize as a formal matter that decision making is altered if undertaking an investment alters the remaining set of available projects, the full implications of this alteration have not been adequately studied.

For example, suppose that the 1-year risk-free interest rate is 10% and that an investment is available that will require just $100 and will return $112 for certain in 1 year. Should this investment be undertaken? An unqualified answer of yes to this question entails tacit assumptions that

The textbook analysis that accepts all projects with positive net present values as positive is quite generally wrong. The ability to delay a project means that almost every project competes with itself postponed. With uncertain interest rates, even the simplest of projects has an option value. The effect of interest-rate uncertainty on the optimal delay of investment is sizable. This implies that the rate of aggregate investment will depend on both the level of the real interest rate and the degree of interest-rate uncertainty. Furthermore, it is not necessarily true that investment rises with a fall in interest rates.

* We are grateful to Doug Diamond, Phil Dybvig, Steve Heston, and the referee for comments on earlier drafts of this article. We would also like to thank the participants in workshops at the University of California, Berkeley, Massachusetts Institute of Technology, Stanford University, University of California, Los Angeles, University of Chicago, and Washington University.

(*Journal of Business*, 1992, vol. 65, no. 1)
© 1992 by The University of Chicago. All rights reserved.
0021-9398/92/6501-0001$01.50

are quite unsatisfactory for most investment projects. Suppose, for instance, that the yield curve is downward sloping with an interest rate 1 year from today of 7% (known with certainty). Instead of taking the investment now, we could wait a year and make the investment then. Taking on the investment today results in an NPV of 112/1.1 − 100 = 1.82. In contrast, the NPV today of undertaking the investment 1 year from today is

$$\text{NPV} = \left(\frac{112}{1.07} - 100\right)\frac{1}{1.1} = 4.25.$$

If in making the investment today we lose the opportunity to take on the same project in the future, then the project competes with itself delayed in time. In deciding to take an investment by looking at only its NPV, the standard textbook solution tacitly assumes that doing so will in no way affect other investment opportunities. Since a project generally competes with itself when delayed, the textbook assumption is generally false. Notice, too, that the usual intuition concerning the "time value of money" can be quite misleading in such situations. While it is true that postponing the project delays the receipt of its positive NPV, it is not true that we are better off taking the project now rather than delaying it since delaying postpones the investment commitment as well.

Of course, with a flat, nonstochastic yield curve we would indeed be better off taking the project now, and this sort of paradox could not occur. But that brings up the even more interesting phenomenon that is the central focus of this article, the effect of interest-rate uncertainty on the timing of investment.

Assume that the yield curve is flat at a 10% interest rate, and consider a second project with a return of $109 1 year after it is undertaken. If interest rates were certain to stay at 10% forever, then the project would be valueless, but this is not true if the future development of interest rates is uncertain. If there is any possibility that the 1-year interest rate may fall below 9%, then rights to the project will have value today. And should we undertake the project if the yield curve is flat at a 7% interest rate? Not necessarily. With a sufficiently uncertain environment, even though the project now has a positive NPV, it might pay to wait and hope for a decline in interest rates.

Furthermore, the greater the uncertainty about futures rates, the more likely it is that the interest rate will fall below 9% in the near future, and the greater the value of these rights. In other words, even though the project itself has no option characteristics—it is certain to repay $1.09 1 year after an investment of $1 is made—the uncertainty in interest rates, and in pricing more generally, gives it an option-like feature.

We are not the first to recognize that delaying a project can be desirable, but we are the first to observe that this need have nothing to do with changes in the cash flows of the project itself or with the effects of certain changes in interest rates. The earliest neoclassical studies were concerned either with examples where a falling term structure favored delay or with the projects whose cash flows changed in a deterministic way over time.

Marglin (1967) provides a nice analysis of the case in which the cash flows of a project change in a known and deterministic fashion when it is delayed. He shows that the optimal rule is to undertake the project at the future time that maximizes the current NPV.

More recent analyses deal with projects with uncertain cash flows whose uncertainty is resolved by waiting. McDonald and Siegel (1986) consider irreversible investments with benefits and initial outlays that both follow diffusion processes. They apply option-pricing techniques to show that the project is undertaken when the NPV is sufficiently high. Bernanke (1983), while not using option-pricing techniques, models the flow of information on cash flows to find the optimal delay policy. Brennan and Schwartz (1985) and Ekern (1988) evaluate resource development problems in which the project explicitly contains an option to undertake investment after uncertainty about oil prices is resolved. Titman's (1985) analysis of development options on vacant land is a particularly novel use of these techniques to show why real estate development may be delayed.

By contrast with this literature, the central theme of our work is that, even for the simplest projects with deterministic cash flows, interest-rate uncertainty has a significant effect on investment. While uncertain changes in cash flows and learning can cause some projects to be delayed, the effect of interest rate uncertainty is ubiquitous and critical to understanding investment at the macroeconomic level. In particular, then, even naive investors who ignore the embedded options in their projects and use simple certainty equivalent cash flow projections may well be sensitive to the options inherent in possible changes in financing costs.

Section II of this article develops some models that allow us to explore the effect on investment decisions of the stochastic process governing interest rates. Section III examines the effect of changes in interest rates and uncertainty on the timing of investment decisions. We will see that uncertainty has an important and measurable influence on investment. Section IV explores these results in more general stochastic models. In this section we show that investment may actually fall when interest rates decline even when we restrict our attention to the simplest single period investments that avoid the "Cambridge controversy" associated with multiple internal rates of return. Section V, however, derives a general result that describes a sufficient condition for an investment to be postponed (aggregate investment to decline) when uncertainty increases. The models of these sections treat uncertainty in a rational context, and, as such, they are compatible additions to the literature on rational expectations macroeconomics. The final section briefly concludes this article by summarizing the major findings and considering some future directions for research.

II. A Simple Model of Investment with a Stochastic Interest Rate

To concentrate on the effects of interest rates on investment we consider first the simplest of investment projects. The project returns $1 (real) at time $t + T$ when a commitment of I dollars is made at time t.[1] There is no uncertainty as to the amount or timing of this return. No additional resources or expenditures apart from the commitment of I are required either to maintain rights to the investment before the commitment is made or to sustain the project during the time t through $t + T$ and assure its payoff. The project can only be undertaken once and is indivisible. In addition, committing to this investment has no effect on any other investment projects or on the capacity to undertake them.

Let $P(t) - I \equiv \hat{E}[\exp(-\int_t^{t+T} r(s)ds)] - I$ denote the NPV of the project if the investment commitment of I is made at time t where $\hat{E}$ denotes expectations with respect to the risk adjusted (equivalent martingale) stochastic process. It follows that the optimal time to invest in this project is the solution to

$$\sup \hat{E}\left([P(\tilde{\tau}) - I]\exp\left[-\int_0^{\tilde{\tau}} \tilde{r}(s)\, ds \right]\right), \qquad (1)$$

where $\tilde{\tau}$ is a (random) stopping time for the stochastic process driving the term structure.[2]

With a flat, nonstochastic yield curve, the NPV of the investment does not change with time, and it is optimal to invest immediately if the project's NPV is positive and no investment should ever be undertaken if the NPV is negative. For a nonstochastic but sloped yield

---

1. This analysis is also directly applicable if r is the nominal interest rate and the payoff and commitment are fixed at $1 and I in nominal terms. It is equally valid in either real or nominal terms if r is the appropriate risk-adjusted discount rate for a risky project with an *expected* payoff of $1. In the last case, however, the random payoff must have a constant expected value of $1 regardless of the level of the interest rate.

2. A random variable τ is a *stopping time* with respect to a stochastic process $\langle x(t) \rangle$ if for all t the event $\tau = t$ is determined by the path $\langle x(s) \rangle_0^t$; that is, the event of "stopping" must not be anticipatory but be solely determined by the history up to that point.

curve, the first-order necessary condition for a maximum is

$$\frac{I}{P(t^*)} = \frac{r(t^* + T)}{r(t^*)}.\qquad(2)$$

As the NPV must be positive when the project is undertaken [$P(t^*) > I$], a falling yield curve [$r(t^*) > r(t^* + T)$] is a necessary condition for the postponement of investment in a certain environment. For an uncertain economy, the problem is conceptually the same.

Before examining this very general problem, it will be useful to consider it under a particular parameterized model of real interest rates. We assume that changes in the (real) instantaneous interest rate, r, satisfy the Itô equation

$$dr = \sigma\sqrt{r}\,d\omega,\qquad(3)$$

where σ is constant. This process restricts the one in Cox, Ingersoll, and Ross (1985b) to a zero-expected change rather than their more general mean-reverting drift. We have chosen this special case of their process both to simplify our analysis and to focus on the effects of interest-rate uncertainty. Clearly, there will be a tendency to delay (accelerate) investment when the interest rate is expected to fall (rise), ceteris paribus. By setting the drift to zero we can concentrate on the effects of uncertainty and not expected rate movements on investment decisions. The qualitative properties of this example would also be true with their more general drift term.

As shown in Cox, Ingersoll, and Ross (1985a, 1985b), the price of any interest-rate contingent claim satisfies the equation

$$\frac{1}{2}\sigma^2 r F_{rr} + \lambda r F_r - rF + F_t + C(r,t) = 0,\qquad(4)$$

where C is the net cash paid out to the claim. In this equation, λ measures the price of interest-rate risk; that is, for an asset with price p, $E(dp) = (rp - \lambda r \partial p/\partial r - C)dt$. As $\partial p/\partial r < 0$ for bonds, $\lambda > 0$ corresponds to the case of positive term premia. Equation (4) is equivalent to pricing by assuming the local expectations hypothesis $\hat{E}(dp/p) = r\,dt$, where $\hat{E}$ denotes the expectation with respect to the martingale (or "risk neutral") interest-rate dynamics $dr = \lambda r\,dt + \sigma\sqrt{r}\,d\omega$. We will assume that λ is a constant.

While traditional capital budgeting theory might erroneously suggest that this investment should be taken as soon as its NPV is positive, a misreading of option-pricing theory suggests the opposite extreme—the paradox that this option to invest should never be exercised. The underlying asset (a point-input, point-output investment) pays no dividends or other disbursements while the option is alive, and we know that it is never optimal to exercise a call option on a stock with no cash dividend until it expires (see Merton 1973).

Such reasoning is faulty in this case because the underlying asset of the investment option is not like other assets. Compare this asset—that is, the value of the project at the time the commitment is made—to a zero-coupon bond with the same original maturity. As time passes, the price of the bond changes with changes in the interest rate *and* increases as its maturity shortens. Only the first effect is present in the potential investment. As long as the commitment is not made, the project's payoff comes no closer, so its present value does not tend to rise. As a consequence, the present value of the investment will tend to lag behind the value of the zero-coupon bond. This lag in value is similar to the drain in price created by a continuous dividend stream[3] and provides an incentive for "early exercise."

To determine the optimal investment policy and the value of the project, we break the problem into two parts. First, we determine the project's value *after* the investment commitment has been made and before the payoff has been realized. Second, we determine the value of the *right* to take on the project *before* the commitment has been made.

Once the commitment, I, has been made, the investment is identical to a T-period zero-coupon bond with a real face value of \$1. Let $P(r; T)$ denote this value for a T-period project (from Cox, Ingersoll, and Ross 1985b):

$$P(r; T) = e^{-b(T)r},$$

where

$$b(T) \equiv \frac{2(e^{\gamma T} - 1)}{(\gamma - \lambda)(e^{\gamma T} - 1) + 2\gamma}, \quad \gamma \equiv \sqrt{\lambda^2 + 2\sigma^2}. \tag{5}$$

If the interest rate is r, then at the time the commitment is made the net present value of the project is $P(r; T) - I$. The value of the rights to the project must be at least this large, but, as in the case of most options, the value alive will exceed this "when-exercised" amount. Clearly the optimal "exercise" policy will be of the form

$$\text{invest if} \quad r \leq r^*,$$

$$\text{wait if} \quad r > r^*,$$

3. The change in value of an investment opportunity of duration T is

$$\frac{dF}{F} = \left(\frac{1}{2}\sigma^2 r F_{rr} + \lambda r F_r\right)\frac{1}{F}.$$

From (4), this is equal to $r - F_t/F$. As $F_t > 0$, this falls short of the expected (under the risk-neutral probabilities) rate of price increase r, of any asset. In this context, the term F_t/F can be thought of as a dividend.

where the acceptance (exercise) rate, r^*, must be determined as part of the investment decision process.[4]

The *optimal acceptance rate*, r^*, is a free boundary. For any choice of r^* we can solve for the right's value. The optimal r^* is chosen to maximize the option's value, which implies that the high-contact or smooth-pasting condition will also be satisfied (see Merton 1973).

Let $R(r; T, I)$ denote the value of perpetual, one-time *rights* to the project, that is, the total NPV including the right to postpone investing until it is optimal to do so. Value R satisfies the standard pricing equation (4), but because we have assumed that the right to invest never expires or otherwise alters over time (except, of course, when the commitment is made), $R_t = 0$. The boundary conditions are $R(r^*) = P(r^*, T) - I$, $\lim_{r \to \infty} R(r) = 0$, and the high-contact condition $R'(r^*) = \partial P(r^*, T)/\partial r$. The general solution to (4) (with $P_t = 0$) is exponential, and applying the boundary conditions yields[5]

$$R(r; T, I) = \left(\frac{v - b(T)}{vI}\right)^{v/b(T)} \left(\frac{b(T)I}{v - b(T)}\right) e^{-vr}, \qquad (6)$$

where

$$v \equiv \frac{\lambda + \gamma}{\sigma^2}.$$

The acceptance interest rate at which the commitment to the project is made

$$r^*(T, I) = \frac{1}{b(T)} \log\left(\frac{v - b(T)}{vI}\right). \qquad (7)$$

The acceptance rate differs from the break-even rate. The latter is the

---

4. The project acceptance rule will not be this simple for more general stochastic processes or projects. These issues are discussed below. Note that $P(r; T)$ is decreasing in r with $P(0; T) = 1$, so that any project with a required commitment, I, less than one will have a positive net present value for sufficiently small interest rates. This assures that the right to invest in all projects with $I < 1$ will be positive. This feature does not hold for the mean-reverting process in Cox et al. (1985b). In their model, bond prices are given by $P(r; T) = \alpha(T)\exp[-\beta(T)r]$, where $\alpha(T) < 1$. Thus, projects of duration T with $I \leq \alpha(T)$ will never be accepted even if the interest rate falls to zero.

5. This solution is valid for $I \leq [v - b(T)]/v$, since $b(T)$ is increasing in T and $b(\infty) = 2/(\gamma - \lambda) = (\lambda + \gamma)/\sigma^2 = v$, and the right-hand side of this inequality is positive. Thus, for I sufficiently small, the inequality is satisfied. If I is too large so that this inequality is violated, waiting is better than investing at any positive r. In this case, the investment is made when the interest rate drops to zero. Since $P(0; T) - I = 1 - I$ (which is positive by assumption), the NPV of the project is positive when $r = 0$. Furthermore, as r cannot become negative, there is no reason to wait any longer. In this case, the value of the right to invest is $R(r) = (1 - I)e^{-vr}$.

instantaneous spot rate at which the project has a zero NPV[6]

$$r^0(T, I) = -\frac{1}{b(T)} \log I. \tag{8}$$

From (7) and (8),

$$r^*(T, I) = r^0 + \frac{1}{b(T)} \log\left(\frac{v - b(T)}{v}\right) < r^0, \tag{9}$$

which means that the project is only undertaken when it is some distance "in the money" and not at the break-even point.

The rights value can also be expressed explicitly in terms of the acceptance rate as

$$R(r) = e^{-v(r-r^*)}[e^{-b(T)r^*} - 1]. \tag{10}$$

The second term in this expression will be recognized as the NPV of the project when it is undertaken at the acceptance rate, r^*. The first term measures the discounting due to waiting. That is, $e^{-v(r-r^*)} = \hat{E}[\exp(-\int_t^{\tau(r^*)} r(s)\,ds)|r(t) = r]$, where $\tau(r^*)$ is the first time that r falls to r^*.[7]

Figure 1 illustrates a typical case, plotting the value of the rights to the project (solid line) and its NPV when undertaken (dashed line) as a function of the interest rate. The break-even rate is the value of r for which the NPV is zero. The acceptance interest rate is at the tangency of the two curves. Note that even though the NPV can be negative, the rights to the project never have a negative value.

Table 1 shows the value of the rights to a project for various maturities and break-even rates. The first panel gives the value of the rights to the project at the break-even rate when its current NPV (if undertaken) is zero, that is, $R(r^0)$. The second panel gives the NPV of the project (and also the value of the rights) at the point where it is optimal to invest (that is, it gives $R(r^*) = P(r^*; T) - I$). The parameter values used as $\lambda = 0$ (no term premia) and $\sigma = 0.025$. As shown in the table, the latter corresponds to an annual standard deviation of changes in

---

6. Note that r^0 is not the project's internal rate of return. The break-even rate, r^0, is an instantaneous rate, but the project lasts for T periods, so its internal rate of return is the T-period rate at which it has a zero NPV. This is $\rho_T^0 = -(1/T)\log I = [b(T)/T]r^0(T, I)$. Similarly, the acceptance rate r^* for a project is the acceptance level of the *short-term* interest rate and not the T-period rate. The acceptance T-period rate for a given project is $\rho_T^* = [b(T)/T]r^*(T, I)$. These two T-period rates differ from their instantaneous counterparts because of positive or negative term premia and because, even in the absence of term premia and drift, the yield curve has a tendency to slope downward due to Jensen's inequality.

7. The term $\hat{E}[\exp(-\int_t^{\tau(r^*)} r(s)\,ds)]$ will be recognized as the value of a claim that pays $1 the first time the interest rate falls to r^*. This can be verified either by computing the expectation or verifying that $F(r; r^*) = e^{-v(r-r^*)}$ satisfies the fundamental pricing equation (4) subject to $F(r; r^*) = 1$.

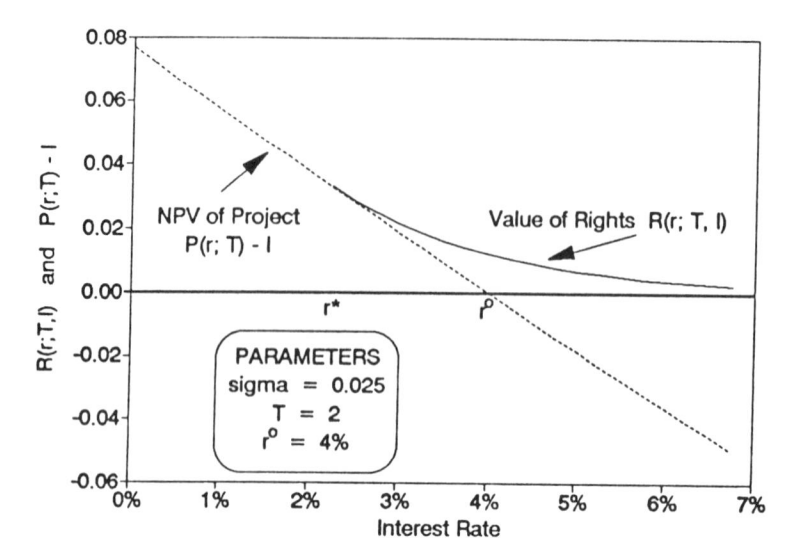

[Figure: Plot showing NPV of Project P(r; T) - I as a dashed declining line and Value of Rights R(r; T, I) as a solid curve, with x-axis Interest Rate from 0% to 7% and y-axis from -0.06 to 0.08. Parameters: sigma = 0.025, T = 2, r⁰ = 4%. Points r* and r⁰ are marked on the x-axis.]

FIG. 1.—Value of rights and NPV of project

the real interest rate in the range of 35–66 basis points. There has been substantial debate in the literature about the exact stochastic behavior of the real interest rate, but we believe this value to be a conservative one that will understate the option value to the rights.

The values in this table might appear to be small. For example, for 5-year projects, the value of the right to postpone investment until the optimal time is in the range of only 2–3 cents per dollar of payoff. But recall under traditional capital budgeting theory the project would be accepted when its NPV was zero, so it would contribute no value beyond repaying its investment. To put these numbers in proper perspective, note that investing in a 5-year project with a break-even rate of 4% requires an input of 0.819. However, from table 1, giving up the right to take this project in the future has an additional opportunity cost of 0.028. The realized rate of return based on this effective total commitment of 0.819 + 0.028 = 0.847 is only 3.331%, so it does not pay to accept this project even when the interest rate is significantly below 4%.[8]

This model lends itself to a variety of comparative static results. Obviously, the greater the interest rate, the further it is from r^*, and, ceteris paribus, the longer will be the time until the investment is undertaken. This causes the rights value of the project to drop, $\partial R/\partial r$

---

8. This calculation is for intuitive purposes only. It does not give the acceptance rate since we have only examined the value of the rights to the project at the project's break-even rate.

TABLE 1 Value of Rights to a Project at the Break-even and Acceptance Rates for Different Durations, T, and Break-even Rates, r^0, with $\sigma = .025$ and No Term Premia ($\lambda = 0$)

A. The Value of Rights to the Project at the Interest Rate Where Its NPV Is Zero
$R(r^0; T; I(r^0))$

			r^0			
T	2.0%	3.0%	4.0%	5.0%	6.0%	7.0%
1	.006	.006	.006	.006	.006	.006
2	.013	.012	.012	.012	.012	.012
5	.031	.029	.028	.026	.025	.024
10	.058	.052	.048	.043	.039	.035
15	.082	.071	.061	.053	.046	.039
20	.103	.085	.070	.058	.048	.039
25	.122	.096	.076	.060	.048	.038
50	.191	.128	.086	.058	.039	.026

B. The Value of Rights to the Project (Its NPV) at the Interest Rate Where the Investment Is Made
$R(r^*; T, I(r^0)) = P(r^*; T) - I$

			r^0			
T	2.0%	3.0%	4.0%	5.0%	6.0%	7.0%
1	.018	.017	.017	.017	.017	.017
2	.035	.035	.034	.033	.032	.032
5	.088	.083	.079	.075	.072	.068
10	.174	.158	.143	.129	.117	.106
15	.254	.225	.195	.168	.145	.125
20	.319	.289	.238	.197	.162	.134
25	.375	.351	.278	.219	.173	.137
50	.551	.699	.489	.328	.219	.147
SD (Δr) (in %)[a]	.35	.43	.50	.56	.61	.66

[a] Annual standard deviation of the real interest rate in percentage points at the level of r^0; i.e., $\sigma\sqrt{r^0}$.

< 0. This finding is consistent with classicial economic theory that predicts investment will fall when real interest rates rise.

In cross-project comparisons, we find that R decreases with an increase in either the commitment required, I, or the duration, T; that is, $\partial R/\partial I < 0$, and $\partial R/\partial T \leq 0$.[9] The intuition for the first result is that the NPV of the investment, when undertaken, decreases with an increase in I so that the value of the right to invest should also decrease. This intuition is also a feature of the duration comparative static—increasing T decreases the NPV of the project when undertaken—but there is an opposite force as well. Projects of longer dura-

---

9. The inequality is strict, $\partial R/\partial T < 0$, except when $I \geq [v - b(T)]/v$, implying $r^* = 0$. See n. 5 above.

tions will have present values that are more volatile. Ceteris paribus, the higher volatility of the underlying asset makes the option to invest in the longer duration project more valuable. The first effect dominates here.

For many applications it is more convenient to think in terms of duration, T, and return, r^0. Viewed this way, an increase in the break-even rate is similar to a decrease in I, and so it increases the value of the project, $\partial R/\partial r^0|_T > 0$. In contrast, increasing T holding r^0 fixed is ambiguous, $\partial R/\partial T|_{r^0} \leq 0$. The latter comparative static is indeterminate in sign because raising T while holding r^0 fixed has a smaller impact on NPV than raising T holding I fixed. This permits the volatility effect to dominate under some circumstances. (It is these latter comparative statistics which are illustrated in table 1.)

III. The Optimal Timing of the Investment and a Characterization of the Acceptance Rate

Apart from valuing the option to invest the issue of primary concern is the effect of interest-rate uncertainty on the propensity to undertake or postpone investment. That is, we wish to know how interest-rate uncertainty affects the accept-reject decisions.

In a static economy, a project is accepted if and only if its NPV is positive. This rule is unambiguously correct because NPVs never change in a static economy. For the simple point-input, point-output projects considered here, the NPV rule is the same as the internal rate of return (IRR) rule of accepting all projects with internal rates of return greater than the interest rate and rejecting those with lower IRRs. But this is *not* the acceptance criterion just developed. In our model, the acceptance interest rate is less than the break-even rate. How does the acceptance rate differ for different projects?

The acceptance rate decreases with the commitment, I, and the duration, T; $\partial r^*/\partial I \leq 0$ and $\partial r^*/\partial T \leq 0$.[10] These results are not surprising, however, as the break-even rate, r^0, also falls with an increase in I or T. A more relevant measure of waiting is the "in-the-money" difference $r^0 - r^*$. This measure is unaffected by I and widens with an increase in project duration, T. Since the NPVs of projects with longer durations are more volatile, this last result confirms the intuition from option-pricing theory that, when choosing among "equally profitable" projects, firms should commit sooner to those of shorter durations.

The effect of changes in the interest-rate variance in this model requires a tedious calculation of how the acceptance interest rate r^* changes with σ. The result is $\partial r^*/\partial \sigma \leq 0$ (with the inequality holding strictly whenever $r^* > 0$ and the project is undertaken at a positive

---

10. Again, the inequalities are strict except when $r^* = 0$.

TABLE 2 Difference between the Break-even Rate and the Acceptance Interest Rate with No Term Premia ($\lambda = 0$)[a], in %
$r^0 - r^*$

T	.0025	.005	.010	.025	.050
1	.177	.354	.710	1.784	3.600
2	.177	.355	.712	1.800	3.667
5	.178	.357	.720	1.851	3.886
10	.178	.360	.733	1.943	4.319
15	.179	.363	.747	2.046	4.840
20	.180	.367	.762	2.160	5.451
25	.181	.370	.777	2.284	6.150
50	.185	.389	.864	3.075	10.760
SD (Δr) (in %)[b]	.05	.10	.20	.50	1.00

[a] The difference between r^0 and r^* is independent of the break-even rate r^0 except when $r^* = 0$. Thus, when the table gives a value for $r^0 - r^*$ which is greater than r^0, the acceptance rate should be interpreted as zero.

[b] Annual standard deviation of the real interest rate in percentage points at a level of 4%; i.e., $\sigma\sqrt{4\%}$.

interest rate), giving $\partial R/\partial \sigma > 0$. This derivative indicates that the rights value of the project is higher in a more uncertain economy as we would expect from option-pricing theory. Interpreting this in the usual comparative static fashion, we can conclude that economies with a higher variance will have a lower acceptance rate at which a given investment is undertaken. In other words, the higher σ, the longer the economy is willing to wait to invest before investing in a given project, and, ceteris paribus, the less investment there will be.

This is not the same, though, as concluding that an increase in uncertainty—even as measured by the variance of local changes in the interest rate—will lower investment. We have solved only for the optimal investment schedule in a model with a fixed σ. This limits our interpretation of shifts in the variance to the comparative economy analysis considered above.

Table 2 shows the difference between the break-even and acceptance interest rates, $r^0 - r^*$, for projects of differing maturities and for various volatilities. This difference is independent of the break-even rate, r^0, and the commitment, I, so these numbers are appropriate for all projects of a given maturity regardless of any differing profitabilities.[11]

Perhaps the most obvious feature of table 2 is that the differences,

---

11. The only exception is for projects with acceptance rates of zero; i.e., those for which $I \leq [v - b(T)]/v$. The acceptance rate cannot be negative, so the difference $r^0 - r^*$ is bounded by r^0. The entries in table 2 should be so interpreted for projects with low break-even rates.

$r^0 - r^*$, are roughly independent of the duration of the investment project unless the volatility is high. At first this might seem strange. Since the value of a long duration project is more volatile than that of a shorter project, it might seem that the option value of waiting should be higher for it as well causing r^* to be lower. But this intuition is incomplete. Long duration projects do have more option value because of their higher volatility, but this extra interest-rate sensitivity also means that a given drop in the interest rate below r^0 causes a long duration project to be more "in the money" so the cost of further postponement is also higher for it.

We also see that the difference between the break-even and acceptance rates, $r^0 - r^*$, is roughly proportional to σ for the short duration ($T < 10$) projects. An interesting consequence of this is that the waiting time is insensitive to the value of σ. The values of σ used in the table correspond to standard deviations of absolute changes in the interest rate over a range of 5–100 basis points per year when the real rate is at 4%. Throughout this range in values for σ, differences between the break-even and acceptance interest rates for 1-year projects are almost exactly three and a half times as large as the annual standard deviation of interest-rate changes regardless of the value of the parameter σ. For 15-year projects, the range of the differences in rates is from three and a half to almost five times the annual standard deviation. Thus, regardless of the actual volatility of the real interest rate, it would appear that the effect of optimal timing investment is a material one.[12]

The cause of this "invariance" can be seen by comparing the costs and benefits of waiting. The benefit of waiting is the difference between the lower current NPV and the higher NPV at the time the project is optimally undertaken. To first order, this benefit is proportional to T and the difference $r^0 - r^*$. The cost of waiting is forgone present value. This depends on the length of the postponement and the average discount rate over the time. To first order, this cost is proportional to the waiting time. As the benefit of waiting is roughly independent of σ (given r^*) and at the margin the cost and benefit are matched, it is natural that the waiting time is roughly independent of σ as well.

There are several additional factors we have not yet considered that could have substantial effects on the value of waiting to undertake projects and their acceptance rates. These are term premia in long rates, expiration or alteration of the option to invest, alternative stochastic processes, and estimation error. Positive-term premia or an

---

12. There has been substantial debate in the literature about the possible constancy of the real interest rate; thus, the question of the correct value for σ cannot be easily answered. Whatever the actual volatility of the real interest rate, however, it is the appropriate standard of measurement for determining the disparity of the acceptance and break-even rates.

TABLE 3 Difference between the Break-even Rate and the Acceptance Interest Rate with Positive Term Premia ($\lambda = .0065$) in %[a]
$r^0 - r^*$

	σ				
T	.0025	.005	.010	.025	.050
1	.045	.155	.454	1.483	3.279
2	.045	.155	.455	1.495	3.335
5	.045	.156	.458	1.530	3.519
10	.045	.156	.464	1.596	3.886
15	.045	.157	.470	1.669	4.333
20	.045	.158	.477	1.752	4.863
25	.045	.159	.483	1.844	5.475
50	.046	.163	.523	2.447	9.603
SD (Δr) (in %)[b]	.05	.10	.20	.50	1.00

[a] The difference between r^0 and r^* is independent of the break-even rate r^0 except when $r^* = 0$. Thus, when the table gives a value for $r^0 - r^*$ that is greater than r^0, the acceptance rate should be interpreted as zero. For $\lambda = .0065$, the term premium on a 15-year asset is approximately 10% of the prevailing interest rate (exactly 10% when $\sigma = .025$). Thus, if the instantaneous interest rate is 4%, a 15-year default-free asset will have an expected rate of return of 4.4%.
[b] Annual standard deviation of the real interest rate in percentage points at a level of 4%; i.e., $\sigma\sqrt{4\%}$.

expiration of the option to invest will decrease the value of the rights option. The effects of different stochastic processes are ambiguous, and a full study is beyond the scope of this article.[13]

A. Term Premia Effects

Positive term premia ($\lambda > 0$) mean that long-term rates are high relative to the instantaneous rate. Usually, higher interest rates result in greater call option values owing to the time-value savings on payment of the striking price; however, here a higher T-period rate will also decrease the net present value of the project, $P(\cdot) - I$. This latter effect dominates, and $\partial R/\partial \lambda < 0$.[14]

Table 3 shows the difference $r^0 - r^*$ when there are term premia. The value of λ used corresponds to an expected rate of return on 15-year default-free assets that is approximately 10% higher than the

---

13. The ambiguity arises because altering the stochastic interest rate process changes both the value of the investment when undertaken and the value of waiting. One obvious alteration in the stochastic process is to include mean reversion as in Cox et al. (1985b), i.e., $dr = \kappa(\mu - r)dt + \sigma\sqrt{r}\,d\omega$. If μ is less than the acceptance interest rate for no mean reversion, then we might expect that mean reversion would reduce this acceptance value since the interest rate has a tendency to fall while the investment option is still alive. Whether this would increase waiting *time* is another question since the interest rate would tend to decrease faster as well.

14. When viewed in the equivalent martingale economy, a higher λ indicates a greater expected increase in the interest rate. Thus, with a higher λ it is more important to make the investment before the "likely" rise in the interest rate. See also Cox et al.'s (1985b) discussion of options on zero-coupon bonds.

instantaneous rate and an expectation on 30-year assets that is approximately 20% higher (e.g., expected returns of 4.4% and 4.8%, respectively, when the real rate is 4%). Again there is no consensus about the appropriate number to use.[15] Although positive term premia raise the acceptance interest rates toward the break-even rates because they make the opportunity cost of waiting higher, there are still substantial benefits to waiting. For example, for 15-year projects, the acceptance interest rates are still from 0.9 to 4.3 annual standard deviations below the break-even rates when the interest rate is 4%.

B. Expiration of the Rights

So far we have assumed that the rights to a given project are perpetual and in no way alter over time. In general, this will not be strictly applicable. Demand for the output could weaken or strengthen with changes in taste. Technological advances could make the project obsolete. Expiration of patents or research by competitors might reduce the productive advantages (and hence the NPV) of the project.

Consideration of all these modifications is beyond the scope of this article. Some of them, such as changes in demand, have little to do with the effects of varying interest rates on investment.[16] Here we confine our attention to a simple expiration of the rights to the project at a known time in the future. This might be a reasonable description of the effects of a patent or franchise. More important, it should also give us a good first idea of the effects of research and development and obsolescence on optimal waiting.

Let s denote the remaining time before the rights to a project expire. When they expire, the commitment either must be made immediately, or the project must be abandoned forever. The project itself is the same as before with a required commitment of I and a return of $1 after T years. As before, there will be an acceptance interest rate at or below which the project commitment is made. However, now this acceptance rate, $r^*(s)$, will change over time with the maturity of the rights option. When there is a very long time until expiration, the project commitment will not be made unless the interest rate is close to the level previously computed for infinitely lived rights, $r^*(s) \approx r^*(\infty)$ for large s. When there is only a short time until expiration, the acceptance rate will be close to the break-even rate, $r^*(s) \approx r^0$ for small s.

---

15. The Ibbotson Associates (1987) data indicate that the averge return on long-term *nominal* bonds has exceeded the Treasury-bill rate by 1.2 percentage points over the period 1926–86. We know of no evidence either for or against term premia in long-term real rates.

16. Changes in demand or project obsolescence could be modeled by allowing the payoff on the project to be stochastic. This is the general approach adopted by McDonald and Siegel (1986).

TABLE 4 The Acceptance Interest Rate, $r^*(s)$, for Finite-lived, s, Rights to Projects with Break-even Rates, r^0, of 4% and Differing Durations, T, for $\sigma = .0005$ and $.0025$ and No Term Premia ($\lambda = 0$)

$r^*(s)$ (in %)

	$\sigma = .005$			$\sigma = .025$		
s	$T = 1$	$T = 5$	$T = 10$	$T = 1$	$T = 5$	$T = 10$
0	4.00	4.00	4.00	4.00	4.00	4.00
¼	3.90	3.90	3.90	3.54	3.49	3.46
½	3.87	3.87	3.87	3.39	3.34	3.30
¾	3.85	3.85	3.85	3.29	3.24	3.20
1	3.84	3.84	3.83	3.22	3.17	3.12
2	3.80	3.80	3.80	3.02	2.97	2.91
5	3.75	3.75	3.75	2.74	2.68	2.62
10	3.72	3.71	3.71	2.54	2.49	2.41
15	3.70	3.69	3.69	2.44	2.39	2.31
∞	3.65	3.64	3.64	2.22	2.15	2.06

$$\frac{r^0 - r^*(s)}{r^0 - r^*(\infty)}$$

0	.00	.00	.00	.00	.00	.00
¼	.29	.29	.29	.26	.27	.28
½	.37	.37	.37	.34	.35	.36
¾	.42	.42	.42	.40	.41	.41
1	.46	.46	.46	.44	.45	.45
2	.56	.56	.56	.55	.56	.56
5	.70	.70	.71	.71	.71	.71
10	.80	.80	.81	.82	.82	.82
15	.86	.86	.86	.87	.87	.87
∞	1.00	1.00	1.00	1.00	1.00	1.00

The value of one-time, finite-lived rights to the project satisfies the standard valuation equation (4) with the time derivative term subject to the boundary conditions, $R[r^*(s), s] = P[r^*(s), T] - I$, $R(r, 0) = \max[0, P(r; T) - I]$, and $\partial R[r^*(s), s]/\partial r = \partial P[r^*(s); T]/\partial r$. This free boundary problem is similar to the finite-maturity American put problem in option pricing and similarly has no known closed-form solution. It does, however, yield readily to numerical methods. We used an explicit finite difference approach whose results are summarized in table 4 and figure 2.[17]

Table 4 shows the acceptance interest rate as a function of the time to expiration, s, for projects with durations of 1, 5, and 10 years. In the left three columns, the interest rate process has a very small standard deviation, approximately 10 basis points per year ($\sigma = 0.005$). In the right three columns, the standard deviation is approximately 50 basis

---

17. See Brennan and Schwartz (1978) for a discussion of the explicit and implicit finite difference numerical procedures for solving problems of this type.

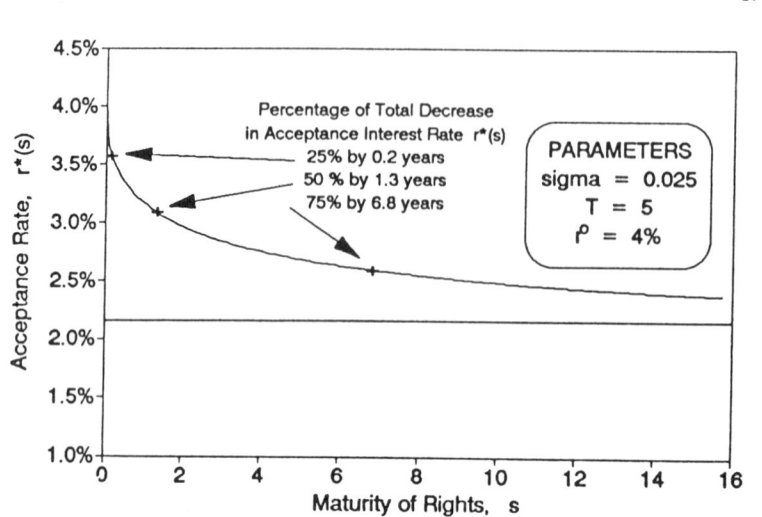

[Figure 2 shows a decreasing curve of acceptance rate r*(s) vs. maturity of rights s, from about 4% down toward 2%, with annotations: "Percentage of Total Decrease in Acceptance Interest Rate r*(s): 25% by 0.2 years, 50% by 1.3 years, 75% by 6.8 years" and parameters: sigma = 0.025, T = 5, r⁰ = 4%.]

Fig. 2.—Acceptance interest rate for finite-lived rights

points per year ($\sigma = 0.025$). In each case, the break-even rate, r^0, is 4%, and there are no term premia.

Figure 2 shows the acceptance rate as a function of maturity for a 5-year project with a break-even rate of 4% when $\sigma = 0.025$. Note the strong initial decline in the acceptance rate. The acceptance rate decreased from r^0 by 66 basis points to 3.34% with a rights maturity of only 1/2 year. This 66-basis-point drop is more than one-third of the total decline, from r^0 to $r^*(\infty)$, of 185 basis points. Similarly, the acceptance rate has achieved almost three-quarters of its total decrease by a maturity of 5 years.

The second panel of table 4 gives the ratio $[r^0 - r^*(s)]/[r^0 - r^*(\infty)]$, which measures the fraction of the total decrease in the acceptance rate for various maturities. Note the extreme similarity in these patterns. All of the acceptance rates have achieved more than one-quarter of their total decrease before a maturity of 3 months, almost one-half of their total decrease by $s = 1$ year, and more than 80% of their total decrease by $s = 10$ years.

Summarizing these findings, we see that the proper investment rule can be substantially different from the classical NPV rule even for projects that can be postponed only for a relatively short period.

C. Estimation Error

In all of the analysis so far, we have assumed that the decision maker is fully informed about the problem and, in particular, has precise information about all of the parameters. This will seldom be the case in practice, and determining the optimal time to invest will involve some inferences. Estimation and its attendant errors will have two types of effects. First, the computed values of the project and the rights may be mismeasured, and, second, the optimal acceptance policy will be imperfect. The latter will also affect the calculated value of the rights.

The former error is involved in any type of capital budgeting problem—imperfect estimates of the payoff, the investment, or the duration of the project will lead to imperfect estimates of the value. The usual solution is to take the expectation of the payoffs and investments.[18] When properly discounted, this gives an *unbiased* estimate of value. In fact, we usually just think of this as *the* value as we have no better estimate.

The latter type of error, an inferior acceptance policy, is not so easily corrected. If imperfect information prevents an exact determination of the optimal acceptance policy, then generally an unbiased acceptance policy is *not* a best alternate choice.

Suppose that errors in the measurement of the payoff, the required investment, the project's duration, or the parameters of the interest-rate process have led to an estimate of the acceptance rate, $\hat{r}^*$, which differs from the optimal rate, r^*. The value of the rights under this suboptimal policy is[19]

$$R(r; \hat{r}^*) = e^{-v(r-\hat{r}^*)}[e^{-b(t)\hat{r}^*} - 1]. \quad (11)$$

This equation gives the true value of the rights for the suboptimal policy in the absence of measurement error and not the value as assessed by the decision maker.

Since r^* is the value-maximizing acceptance rate, the rights value is smaller for any other choice of acceptance rate, be it higher or lower, $R(r; \hat{r}^*) \le R(r; r^*)$. Figure 3 illustrates the rights value for a 2-year, 4% break-even project. It plots the rights value as a function of the acceptance rate, $\hat{r}^*$, as a percent of full rights value; that is,

$$\frac{R(r; \hat{r}^*)}{R(r; r^*)} = e^{-v(r^*-\hat{r}^*)} \frac{e^{-b(T)\hat{r}^*} - 1}{e^{-b(T)r^*} - 1}. \quad (12)$$

Note the asymmetry in this ratio. The value falls off much more sharply for acceptance above r^* than it does for acceptance below r^*. For example, acceptance at 3.2% (1% above r^*) is worth 77.5% of the

---

18. Note that in traditional capital budgeting theory, uncertainty about the time of the payoff is transformed to uncertainty about the amount of distinct payoffs. For example, if a $100 payoff occurs at time 1 or 3 with a 50% probability for each, we do *not* value this as $100/(1 + \rho)^{E[t]}$. Rather, we change the time uncertainty to payoff uncertainty, a 50/50 chance at zero or 100 in each year 1 and 3 and value it as $(1/2) \cdot 100/(1 + \rho) + (1/2) \cdot 100/(1 + \rho)^3$.

19. See eq. (10) and n. 7 above.

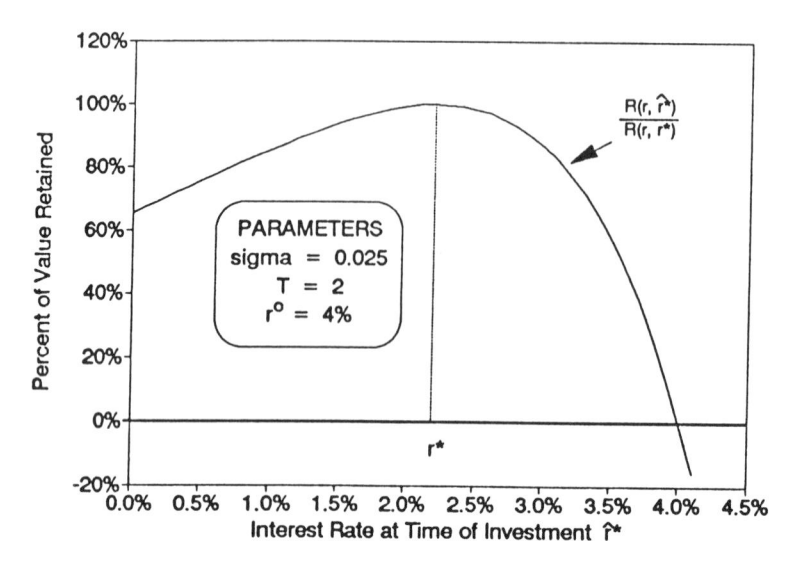

FIG. 3.—Rights value for suboptimal policies

optimal value, but acceptance at 1.2%, the same 100 basis points below the optimal rate, retains 89.7% of the optimal value.

The practical importance of this asymmetry is that a decision maker does not want to compute an unbiased estimate of the optimal acceptance rate. Instead, the estimate should be adjusted toward lower rates since erring on the low side is substantially less costly than erring high. This result is true for all point-input, point-output projects for all variance levels.[20]

IV. General Projects and Interest-Rate Processes

The simple structure of the solution in this model is as much a function of the nature of the investment as it is of the simple model for the evolution of the interest rate. In our model, the project entails a single cash outflow, followed by a single cash inflow. As is well known, this type of project has a single internal rate of return (or break-even rate, r^0). As we have just seen, there is also a single acceptance interest rate, r^*, defining a region $r \leq r^* < r^0$ in which the investment will be made.

---

20. It is also true of all projects that are positively weighted portfolios of point-input, point-output projects (e.g., any project with a single investment followed by nonnegative cash flows). It does not hold true for all other stochastic processes, however. For example, for the interest-rate process, $dr = \sigma r^{3/2} d\omega$, the asymmetry works in the other direction.

This same single acceptance rate characterization and most of the qualitative properties of our model remain valid for any project whose NPV is decreasing in the interest rate. Let $N(r)$ denote the NPV of a project when the commitment investment is made at an interest rate of r. The value of perpetual, one-time rights to this project will satisfy (4) subject to $R(r^*) = N(r^*)$ and the high contact condition $R'(r^*) = N'(r^*)$. The general discount factor for waiting until the interest rate drops from r to $\bar{r}$ is (as in eq. [10]) $\hat{E}[\exp(-\int_0^{\tau(\bar{r})} r(t)\, dt] = \exp[-v(r - \bar{r})]$, so

$$R(r) = \sup_{\bar{r}} e^{-v(r-\bar{r})} N(\bar{r}), \qquad (13)$$

and r^* is the maximizing argument. If the NPV function $N(r)$ can be expressed analytically, then (13) is a simple calculus problem for determining r^* and then $R(r)$. Even when no analytical solution for $N(r)$ is known, the numerical solution of (13) should be much simpler than for (4).

The procedure just described will give an answer for many investment problems, but a very accurate approximation can be obtained even more easily. To do this, we first determine the break-even rate for the project. The break-even rate r^0 satisfies

$$\sum_{t=0}^{T} X_t e^{-b(t) r^0} = 0, \qquad (14)$$

where X_t is the net cash flow (including current and future investment requirements) at time t.[21] The acceptance interest rate, r^*, for the project will fall short of the break-even rate by approximately the same amount as it does for a point-input, point-output project whose duration matches the project's average maturity.

For example, consider a 50-year annuity with a break-even rate of 4%. If $\sigma = 0.025$ (a standard deviation of 50 basis points per year in changes in the real rate at $r = 4\%$), then the optimal acceptance rate is 1.613%. Table 2 shows that the acceptance rate for point-input, point-output projects range from 1.784% to 3.075% below r^0. An equally weighted average of these differences is 2.343%, giving an approximate acceptance rate of 1.657%—an error of 4.4 basis points. Now consider a second project also with a break-even rate of 4% and cash flows growing at 5% per year. The optimal acceptance rate for this project is 1.397%. A weighted average of the differences, $r^0 - r^*$, with weights proportional to the cash flows gives an approximate acceptance rate of 1.399%—an error of two-tenths of a basis point.

---

21. Equation (14) will be recognized as analogous to an IRR calculation. As discussed earlier, the break-even rate is an instantaneous rate that, apart from term premium and Jensen's inequality considerations, is equal to the project's IRR.

With a smaller interest-rate variance, both these approximations are even better. At larger interest rate variances, they are somewhat worse; however, the variance of the real interest rate probably does not exceed that used in this example.

To understand why this method works, note that a project with multiple cash flows and a break-even rate of r^0 can be considered a portfolio of point-input, point-output miniprojects. The miniproject with duration t has a payoff of X_t and an initial investment of $I^t = e^{-b(t)r^0}X_t$.[22] If the duration t miniproject could be undertaken separately, then it would be accepted when the interest rate fell to $r_t^* = \log[(v - b(t)X_t)/vI^t]/b(t)$, as given in (7). In general, these acceptance rates will differ for each miniproject, and some compromise must be adopted as the entire project must be accepted. In tables 2 and 3 we saw that the difference between the break-even rate and the acceptance rate was nearly identical for all point-input, point-output projects differing only in duration. Therefore, the range in acceptance rates will be very small, and some interest rate near the average will be optimal.

At first, one might guess that the option value would vanish for very long projects with level cash flows. For these projects, postponing the investment delays the receipt of each cash flow, which is almost the same as losing the first one (exactly so for a perpetuity with constant cash flows). However, postponing the project also defers the investment commitment, which is a positive effect.

Certainly, it is possible to construct examples for which the option to delay is negligible in value. One illustration is an infinite project with cash flows growing at a rapid rate. In this case, postponing not only delays receipt of each flow but also loses a period's growth.

Now, consider an investment with multiple internal rates of return (and break-even rates). Without giving a formal proof, it can be shown that there may be multiple "acceptance ranges" for the interest rate. In these ranges the investment will be undertaken, and outside of them it will be postponed. Consequently, there may be occasions when an increase in interest rates will lead to the acceptance of a particular investment.

This is illustrated in figure 4. The project depicted has three break-even rates and three acceptance rates. If the interest rate falls to r_3^*, the project will be undertaken. However, if rights to the project are first acquired when the interest rate is in the region (r_1^*, r_2^*), then either a decrease of the interest rate to r_1^* or an increase to r_2^* will cause the project to be taken.[23]

---

22. By construction, $\Sigma_t I^t = -X_0$, so the initial cash flow is fully accounted for.

23. The existence of multiple internal rates of return (or break-even rates) is necessary but not sufficient for multiple acceptance rates. If, e.g., the "hump" in the NPV curve in fig. 3 between 7% and 10% were smaller, there would be only a single acceptance rate (near r_1^*) with the $R(r)$ curve lying completely above this hump.

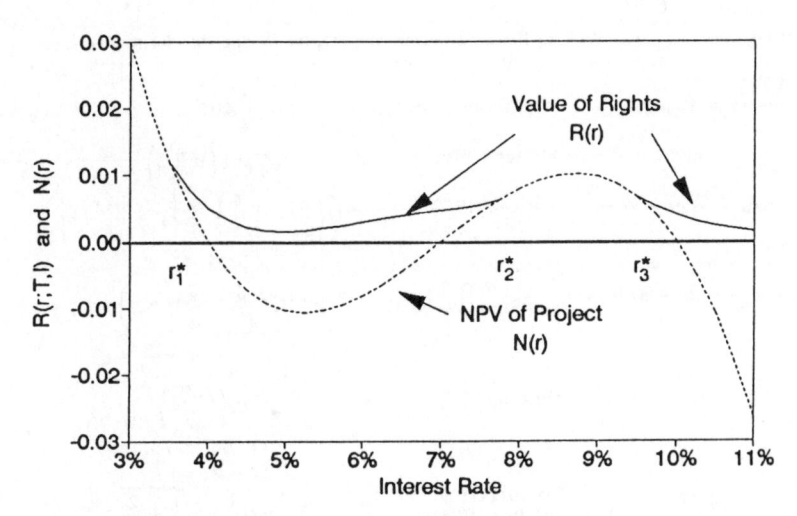

FIG. 4.—Value of rights and NPV of project multiple acceptance regions

Of course, there is nothing really new that our model or the presence of interest-rate uncertainty has to add to this old issue. The ability to construct a capital aggregate in the neoclassical fashion and the attendant Cambridge controversies remain in this model as they do in nonstochastic worlds. In what follows, we will continue to avoid these issues by considering only simple investment projects.

The same general results hold for any other single-state variable-interest-rate diffusion process. The value of one-time, perpetual rights to a project whose net present value is $N(r)$ (a decreasing function) if it is accepted when the interest rate is r is

$$\sup_{\bar{r}} \Phi(r, \bar{r}) N(\bar{r}), \qquad (15)$$

where $\Phi(r, \bar{r}) = \hat{E}[\exp(-\int_0^{\tau(\bar{r})} r(s)\, ds)]$ is the waiting time discount factor for the stochastic process. Table 5 gives the optimal waiting discount factor, for a variety of interest-rate processes that have appeared in the literature.[24]

V. General Results on Investment

If the results at the end of the previous section are disappointing, there are still a number of strong conjectures that one might be tempted to make about the effects on investment of changes in the level of interest rates or in uncertainty. In this section we will present counterexamples

---

24. The waiting time discount function $\Phi(r, \bar{r})$ solves the fundamental pricing eq. (4) suitably modified for the stochastic process in question subject to $\Phi(r, \bar{r}) = 1$.

TABLE 5 The Waiting Discount Factor $\phi(r; r^*)$, for Various Stochastic Processes

Risk-adjusted Stochastic Process	Source	$\phi(r)^a$
$\sigma\, d\omega$	Merton (1970)	$\sqrt{r}\, K_{1/3}\left(\dfrac{(2r)^{3/2}}{3\sigma}\right)$
$\kappa(\mu - r)\, dt + \sigma\, d\omega$	Vasicek (1977)	$e^{-r/\kappa} U\left(\dfrac{\mu}{2\kappa} - \dfrac{\sigma^2}{4\kappa^3}, \dfrac{1}{2}, \dfrac{\kappa}{\sigma^2}\left[\mu - \dfrac{\sigma^2}{\kappa^2} - r\right]^2\right)$
$\sigma\sqrt{r}\, d\omega$	this paper	$e^{-\sqrt{2}\, r/\sigma}$
$\kappa(\mu - r)\, dt + \sigma\sqrt{r}\, d\omega$	Cox, Ingersoll, and Ross (1985b)	$e^{\beta r} U\left(\dfrac{2\kappa\mu}{\sigma^2}, -\dfrac{\kappa\mu}{\alpha\sigma^2}, 2\alpha r\right)$, $\alpha \equiv \sqrt{\dfrac{\kappa^2}{\sigma^4} + \dfrac{2}{\sigma^2}},\ \beta \equiv \dfrac{\kappa}{\sigma^2} - \alpha$
$\sigma r\, d\omega$	Dothan (1978)	$\sqrt{r}\, K_1\left(\dfrac{2\sqrt{2r}}{\sigma}\right)$
$\kappa r(\mu - r)\, dt + \sigma r\, d\omega$	Merton (1975)	$U\left(\dfrac{1}{\kappa}, \dfrac{2\kappa\mu}{\sigma^2}, \dfrac{2\kappa r}{\sigma^2}\right)$
$\sigma r^{3/2}\, d\omega$	Cox, Ingersoll, and Ross (1980)	$r^\eta,\ \eta \equiv \dfrac{1}{2} - \sqrt{\dfrac{1}{4} + \dfrac{2}{\sigma^2}}$
$\kappa r(\mu - r)\, dt + \sigma r^{3/2}\, d\omega$	Cox, Ingersoll, and Ross (1985b)	$r^{-\delta} M\left(\delta, 2\delta + 2 + \dfrac{2\kappa}{\sigma^2}, \dfrac{2\kappa\mu}{\sigma^2 r}\right)$, $\delta \equiv \dfrac{1 + 2\kappa/\sigma^2}{2}\left(\sqrt{1 + \dfrac{8}{\sigma^2 + 2\kappa}} - 1\right)$

NOTE.—For each of the risk-adjusted stochastic processes below, the value when the interest rate is currently r for a $1 payment the first time the interest rate falls to r^* is $\Phi(r; r^*) = \phi(r)/\phi(r^*)$; $\Phi(r; r^*)$ satisfies the fundamental pricing equation (4) subject to $\Phi(r; r^*) = 1$.

[a] $M(a, b, x)$ and $U(a, b, x)$ are confluent hypergeometric functions of the first and second type; $K_\nu(x)$ is a modified Bessel function of the second type. See Abramowitz and Stegum (1965).

to some plausible conjectures and a positive theorem on the effect of an increase in uncertainty.

To discuss the more general results in this section we must shift our focus so that the random event of concern is not a particular interest rate or Markov state but the entire sample path of interest rates. We will denote the sample path of interest rates over the interval $[0, t]$ by $\langle r(s)\rangle_0^t$.

First, we will consider a monotone shift in the sample path. How will investment differ under two stochastic processes, one of which stochastically dominates the other? That is, we wish to compare investment for two processes $\langle r(s)\rangle_0^t$ and $\langle r'(s)\rangle_0^t$ whose difference $\langle h(s)\rangle_0^t \equiv \langle r'(s)\rangle_0^t - \langle r(s)\rangle_0^t$ is negative for all t with probability one.

It might be thought that such a (static) decrease in the level of interest rates for all periods would accelerate investment because each project would be more in the money. But recall that a decrease in interest rates also lowers the cost of waiting. The following example shows that the impact on investment of a monotone shift in interest rates is ambiguous.

Consider a T-period project in an economy in which the instantaneous interest rate is constant at $r = a$ over the interval $[0, \tau]$ with $\tau \geq T$ and will be constant at $r = b$ after τ. The value of taking the project today is $R_0 = e^{-aT} - I$ (assuming this to be positive). The value of waiting until time τ is[25]

$$R_\tau = e^{-a\tau}(e^{-bT} - 1). \tag{16}$$

Suppose that there is a uniform downward shift in interest rates from a and b to $a - h$ and $b - h$. Now the value of investing today is $R_0 = e^{-(a-h)T} - I$, and the value of waiting until τ is

$$R_\tau^h = e^{-(a-h)\tau}(e^{-(b-h)T} - 1). \tag{17}$$

For the parameter values $\tau = T = 1, I = 0.8, a = 22\%, b = 21\%, h = 6\%$, we have $R_0 = 0.0025$ and $R_\tau = 0.0085$, so the investment should be deferred until τ. For the shifted process, $R_0 = 0.0521$ while $R_\tau = 0.0517$, so the investment should be made immediately. In this case the uniform downward shift in the yield curve accelerated investment as we anticipated.

In contrast, for the parameter values $\tau = T = 1, I = 0.5, a = 12\%, b = 7\%$, and $h = 2\%$, we have $R_0 = 0.387$ and $R_\tau = 0.383$, so the investment should be made at time 0. For the shifted process, $R_0 = 0.405$ while $R_\tau = 0.408$, so the investment should be deferred. In this case the uniform downward shift in the yield curve caused a postponement in investment.

When combined with the results of the previous section on the impact of a change in the current short rate of interest, this example leaves the question of the impact of interest-rate changes very much unanswered. Of course, it might be possible to refine our conjectures in an effort to obtain more definitive results. For instance, in the example above, the yield curve was falling. Perhaps, then, by restricting our attention to rising yield curves we might be able to obtain a general result. Unfortunately, in the presence of uncertainty, such results would be difficult to obtain. Suppose that the yield curve is rising and that uncertainty is also increasing over time. The rise in the yield curve might make us favor investing now, but the increase in uncertainty over time will reduce or even eliminate the benefit. Thus, either result is possible.

The effect of changes in uncertainty is also ambiguous. On the one hand, an increase in the uncertainty about interest rates will raise the option value of waiting. On the other hand, it also raises the current

---

25. It can be shown that, if it is preferable to wait rather than to invest today (i.e., if b is sufficiently lower than a), then it will be optimal to wait until time τ to invest. In addition, if $R_0 > 0$, then $R_\tau > 0$.

value of undertaking the investment since the discounted value is a convex function of the interest-rate path.

We can avoid this difficulty if we define an increase in the riskiness of the interest-rate path in the proper way. Before introducing this notion of risk, we will restate the general investment decision problem.

For our simple point-input, point-output investment project, following a stopping time rule τ will lead to a value of

$$R_\tau = \hat{E}\left\{\exp\left(-\int_0^{\tilde{\tau}} \tilde{r}(s)\,ds\right) \times \left[\exp\left(-\int_{\tilde{\tau}}^{\tilde{\tau}+T} \tilde{r}(s)\,ds\right) - 1\right]\right\}, \quad (18)$$

where the expectation is taken over the sample path $\langle r(s)\rangle$ and the realization of the stopping $\tilde{\tau}$. The value of the project, including the right to delay optimally, is $R = \sup_\tau \hat{E}[R_\tau] \geq R_\tau$. Assuming that $R > 0$ (i.e., the probability of investing sometime is not zero), the investment will be made at time 0 only if $R_0 = R$, where the zero subscript denotes that stopping time rule of investing immediately. The investment will be delayed to some later time if $R_0 < R$.

The general notion of increased riskiness in the interest rate process that we shall use is similar to the Rothschild-Stiglitz (1970, 1971) notion of increased risk—the mean-preserving spread. However, we are treating an entire stochastic path rather than a single random variable. Therefore, our "spread" must also be a stochastic path. In addition, in place of mean preservation we will require present value preservation.[26] Thus, we wish to add to the interest rate, at every point in time t, a random variable that is sufficiently conditionally independent of the entire path of interest rates before and a portion of the path after t and that does not change the discount factor for time t.

DEFINITION. An interest-rate path $\langle r'(t)\rangle$ will be said to be a *neutral spread* of an interest-rate path $\langle r(t)\rangle$ if the difference between the two paths $h(t) \equiv r'(t) - r(t)$ satisfies

$$\hat{E}\left[\exp\left(-\int_0^t h(s)\,ds\,|\,\langle r(s)\rangle_0^t\right)\right] = 1 \quad \forall t. \quad (19)$$

---

26. It is easy to demonstrate that adding a mean-preserving spread (with respect to the martingale measure) to the interest-rate path is insufficient to derive an unambiguous impact on investment. If we add a mean-preserving spread $\langle m(t)\rangle$ to the interest-rate path, then the discount factor for every time t is increased,

$$\hat{E}\left[\exp\left(-\int_0^t [r(s) + m(s)]\,ds\right)\right] = \hat{E}\left[\hat{E}\left(\exp\left[-\int_0^t m(s)\,ds\right]\bigg|\langle r(s)\rangle_0^t\right)\exp\left(-\int_0^t r(s)\,ds\right)\right]$$

$$> \hat{E}\left[\exp\left(-\int_0^t r(s)\,ds\right)\right],$$

by Jensen's inequality since $\hat{E}[m(t)|\langle r(s)\rangle] = 0$, and e^{-x} is a convex function. Increasing every discount factor is equivalent to decreasing all interest rates. As we have already seen, this has an ambiguous effect on investment.

That is, a spread $h(s)$ is a neutral spread if it has no change on the present value of default-free payments occurring at time t conditional on the original interest-rate path up through time t, for all t.

An example of a neutral spread of a diffusion process $\langle r(t) \rangle$ is $\langle r(t) + h(t) \rangle$, where $h(t)$ is a diffusion independent of the interest-rate process with

$$dh = \sigma_h^2 t \, dt + \sigma_h d\omega_h, \quad (20)$$

with $h(0) = 0$, and $E[d\omega_h \cdot d\omega] = 0$. In this case, $h(t)$ is normally distributed with mean $(1/2)\sigma_h^2 t^2$ and variance $\sigma_h^2 t$. The integral $H(t) \equiv \int_0^t h(s) \, ds$ also has a normal distribution with mean $(1/6)\sigma_h^2 t^3$ and variance $(1/3)\sigma_h^2 t^3$. Therefore, $e^{-H(t)}$ is independent of the interest-rate path and distributed lognormally with mean one.

We can now state our general result about the effects of increased interest-rate uncertainty on investment.

THEOREM. The addition of a neutral spread to the interest-rate path makes the postponement of any investment weakly more desirable. That is, if some project was going to be delayed under the original process, then it will still be delayed; however, if a given investment was about to be made, it might be better to postpone it under the spread interest-rate process.

Proof. After the neutral spread the value of undertaking an investment today is unaltered:

$$R_0^h = \hat{E}\left[\exp\left(-\int_0^T [r(s) + h(s)]ds\right)\right] - I$$

$$= \hat{E}\left(\exp\left(-\int_0^T r(s)\,ds\right) \hat{E}\left[\exp\left(-\int_0^T h(s)\,ds\right) \Big| \langle r(s) \rangle_0^T \right]\right) - I \quad (21)$$

$$= \hat{E}\left[\exp\left(-\int_0^T r(s)\,ds\right)\right] - I = R_0.$$

The second line follows by taking the expectation first by conditioning on $\langle r(s) \rangle_0^T$. Since $\int_0^T r(s)\,ds$ is certain conditional on $\langle r(s) \rangle_0^T$, the term including it may be removed from the conditional expectation. The last line follows because the conditional expectation is unity by the definition of a neutral spread.

The value of delaying, however, can be increased and will not decrease. Let τ_h^* be the optimal stopping time without the neutral spread imposed. Then the value under the spread process of using the previous optimal rule cannot be greater than the value under the optimal rule. By definition, the optimal rule leads to at least as high a value for the rights to the project as any other rule including, in particular,

τ^*, the optimal rule under the original process—that is, $R^h \equiv \sup_\tau R^h_\tau \geq R^h_{\tau^*}$. Therefore,

$$R^h \geq R^h_{\tau^*}$$

$$= \hat{E}\left(\exp\left\{-\int_0^{\tau^*}[r(s) + h(s)]\,ds\right\}\right.$$

$$\left.\cdot \left\{\exp\left(-\int_{\tau^*}^{\tau^*+T}[r(s) + h(s)]\,ds\right) - I\right\}\right)$$

$$= \hat{E}\left(\exp\left(-\int_0^{\tau^*+T} r(s)\,ds\right)\right) \tag{22}$$

$$\cdot \hat{E}\left\{\exp\left(-\int_0^{\tau^*+T} h(s)\,ds\right)\bigg|\langle r(s)\rangle_0^{\tau^*+T}\right\}$$

$$- I\hat{E}\left(\exp\left(-\int_0^{\tau^*} r(s)\,ds\right)\right.$$

$$\left.\cdot \hat{E}\left\{\exp\left(-\int_0^{\tau^*} h(s)\,ds\right)\bigg|\langle r(s)\rangle_0^{\tau^*}\right\}\right) = R.$$

The third line follows by separating the terms and first taking expectations conditional on $\langle r(s)\rangle_0^{\tau^*+T}$ and $\langle r(s)\rangle_0^{\tau^*}$. Again the integrals over r are certain with the conditioning and may be removed. The remaining conditional expectations are unity by the definition of a neutral spread. Q.E.D.

VI. Conclusion

Perhaps what is most remarkable about the analysis of this article is the rather profound implication it has for the real world of investment decision making. It is simply no longer the case that investment decisions should be governed by the common NPV rule—and certainly not large-scale investments.

Our results have nothing to do with the usual addition of option-like features to the investment projects themselves; rather, we have shown that, in an uncertain economy, nearly all investment projects have option rights values. This is true even for those projects with little or no uncertainty about their cash flows.

We should also note that our analysis provides a rather simple rationale for setting corporate hurdle rates above the cost of capital. With uncertain interest rates, an investment should not be undertaken until its projected rate of return is substantially in excess of its break-even rate. This provides a complementary explanation to that of Antle and Eppen (1985), who stress the unobservable appropriation of slack by managers, and Holmström and Weiss (1985), who are concerned with the manager's risk aversion induced by human capital considerations. The extent to which these explain the observed phenomenon is an empirical issue.

While we have developed the theoretical implications of interest-rate uncertainty, many problems remain. Having highlighted the importance of uncertainty, it is most pressing to substitute a model with stochastic uncertainty for the comparative dynamics analysis developed above. This would enable us to examine the macroeconomic implications of innovations in uncertainty in a rational anticipations model. We will make some steps toward this goal in a companion paper that empirically examines the relations between uncertainty and aggregate investment. A second goal would be to examine the applicability of these techniques to the full range of investment decisions in finance, including abandonment, replacement, and tax effects. If the results of this article prove important, then such analyses could lead to a complete rethinking of our rules for investment decision making.

References

Abramowitz, Milton, and Stegum, Irene. 1965. *Handbook of Mathematical Functions with Formulas, Graphs, and Mathematical Tables.* New York: Dover.
Antle, Rick, and Eppen, Gary. 1985. Capital rationing and organizational slack in capital budgeting. *Management Science* 31 (February): 163–74.
Bernanke, Ben S. 1983. Irreversibility, uncertainty, and cyclical investment. *Quarterly Journal of Economics* 98 (February): 85–106.
Brennan, Michael J., and Schwartz, Eduardo S. 1978. Finite difference methods and jump processes arising in the pricing of contingent claims: A synthesis. *Journal of Financial and Quantitative Analysis* 13 (September): 461–74.
Brennan, Michael J., and Schwartz, Eduardo S. 1985. Evaluating natural resource investments. *Journal of Business* 58 (April): 135–57.
Cox, John C.; Ingersoll, Jonathan E., Jr.; and Ross, Stephen A. 1980. An analysis of variable rate loan contracts. *Journal of Finance* 35 (May): 389–403.
Cox, John C.; Ingersoll, Jonathan E., Jr.; and Ross, Stephen A. 1985a. An intertemporal general equilibrium model of asset prices. *Econometrica* 53 (March): 363–84.
Cox, John C.; Ingersoll, Jonathan E., Jr.; and Ross, Stephen A. 1985b. A theory of the term structure of interest rates. *Econometrica* 53 (March): 385–407.
Dothan, Uri. 1978. On the term structure of interest rates. *Journal of Financial Economics* 6 (March): 59–69.
Ekern, Steinar. 1988. An option pricing approach to evaluating petroleum projects. *Energy Economics* 10 (April): 91–99.
Holmström, Bengt, and Weiss, Laurence. 1985. Managerial incentives, investment and aggregate implications: Scale effects. *Review of Economic Studies* 52 (July): 403–25.
Ibbotson Associates. 1987. *Stocks, Bonds, Bills, and Inflation 1987 Yearbook.* Chicago: Ibbotson Associates, Inc.
McDonald, Robert, and Siegel, Daniel R. 1986. The value of waiting to invest. *Quarterly Journal of Economics* 101 (November): 707–27.
Marglin, Stephen. 1967. *Approaches to Dynamic Investment Planning.* Amsterdam: North-Holland.

Merton, Robert C. 1970. A dynamic general equilibrium model of the asset market and its application to the pricing of the capital structure of the firm. Chapter 11 in *Continuous-Time Finance*. Cambridge, Mass.: Basil Blackwell.

Merton, Robert C. 1973. Theory of rational option pricing. *Bell Journal of Economics and Management Science* 4 (Spring): 141–83.

Merton, Robert C. 1975. An asymptotic theory of growth under uncertainty. *Review of Economic Studies* 42 (July): 375–93.

Rothschild, Michael, and Stiglitz, Joseph. 1970. Increasing risk I: A definition. *Journal of Economic Theory* 2 (September): 225–43.

Rothschild, Michael, and Stiglitz, Joseph. 1971. Increasing risk II: Its economic consequences. *Journal of Economic Theory* 3 (January): 66–84.

Titman, Sheridan. 1985. Urban land prices under uncertainty. *American Economic Review* 75 (June): 505–14.

Vasicek, Oldrich. 1977. An equilibrium characterization of the term structure. *Journal of Financial Economics* 5 (November): 177–88.

# Corporate Debt Value, Bond Covenants, and Optimal Capital Structure

HAYNE E. LELAND*

ABSTRACT

This article examines corporate debt values and capital structure in a unified analytical framework. It derives *closed-form* results for the value of long-term risky debt and yield spreads, and for optimal capital structure, when firm asset value follows a diffusion process with constant volatility. Debt values and optimal leverage are explicitly linked to firm risk, taxes, bankruptcy costs, risk-free interest rates, payout rates, and bond covenants. The results elucidate the different behavior of junk bonds versus investment-grade bonds, and aspects of asset substitution, debt repurchase, and debt renegotiation.

THE VALUE OF CORPORATE debt and capital structure are interlinked variables. Debt values (and therefore yield spreads) cannot be determined without knowing the firm's capital structure, which affects the potential for default and bankruptcy. But capital structure cannot be optimized without knowing the effect of leverage on debt value.

This article examines corporate debt values and optimal capital structure in a unified analytical framework. It derives *closed-form* results relating the value of long-term corporate debt and optimal capital structure to firm risk, taxes, bankruptcy costs, bond covenants, and other parameters when firm asset value follows a diffusion process with constant volatility.

Traditional capital structure theory, pioneered by Modigliani and Miller (1958), holds that taxes are an important determinant of optimal capital structure.[1] As leverage increases, the tax advantage of debt eventually will be offset by an increased cost of debt, reflecting the greater likelihood of financial distress.[2] While identifying some prime determinants of optimal capital

---

*Haas School of Business, University of California, Berkeley. The author thanks Ronald Anderson, Fischer Black, Arnoud Boot, Michael Brennan, Philip Dybvig, Julian Franks, Robert Gertner, William Perraudin, Matthew Spiegel, Suresh Sundaresan, Ivo Welch, and especially Rob Heinkel and Klaus Toft for helpful comments. The referee and the editor, René Stulz, provided many valuable suggestions.

[1] Personal as well as corporate taxes will affect the tax benefits to leverage (Miller (1977)). Disagreement remains as to the precise value of net tax benefits.

[2] The costs of financial distress include bankruptcy costs and agency problems associated with risky debt. See, for example, Altman (1984), Asquith, Gertner, and Sharfstein (1991), Harris and Raviv (1991), Jensen and Meckling (1976), Myers and Majluf (1984), Titman and Wessels (1988), and Warner (1977).

structure, this theory has been less useful in practice because it provides qualitative guidance only.[3]

Brennan and Schwartz (1978) provide the first quantitative examination of optimal leverage. They utilize numerical techniques to determine optimal leverage when a firm's unlevered value follows a diffusion process with constant volatility.[4] Although an important beginning, the Brennan and Schwartz analysis has three limitations.

First and most importantly, their numerical approach precludes general closed-form solutions for the value of risky debt and optimal leverage. Numerical examples suggest some possible comparative static results but cannot claim generality.

Second, their analysis focuses on the special case in which bankruptcy is triggered when the firm's asset value falls to the debt's principal value. This provision approximates debt with a positive net-worth covenant. But it is by no means the only—or even the typical—situation.[5] We shall show that alternative bankruptcy-triggering conditions, including endogenously determined ones, lead to very different debt values and optimal capital structure.

Finally, Brennan and Schwartz (1978) consider changes in financial structure that last only until the bonds mature. A maturity date is required for their numerical algorithm; permanent capital structure changes are not explicitly analyzed.[6]

This article considers two possible bankruptcy determinants. The first is when bankruptcy is triggered (endogenously) by the inability of the firm to raise sufficient equity capital to meet its current debt obligations. The second is the Brennan and Schwartz case with a positive net-worth covenant. Debt with such a covenant will be termed *protected debt*.

We can derive closed-form results by examining corporate securities that depend on underlying firm value but are otherwise time independent. Yet debt securities generally have a specified maturity date and therefore have time-dependent cash flows and values. Time independence nonetheless can be justified, perhaps as an approximation, in at least two ways. First, if debt has sufficiently long maturity, the return of principal effectively has no value and

---

[3] Baxter (1967), Kraus and Litzenberger (1973), and Scott (1976) offer general analyses balancing tax advantages with the costs of financial distress, but their results have not provided directly usable formulas to determine optimal capital structure. For an alternative view on the determinants of capital structure, see Myers (1984).

[4] Kim (1978) also presents numerical examples of optimal capital structure, based on a mean-variance model. His model is less parsimonious, as knowledge of the joint distribution of market and firm returns is required.

[5] Minimum net-worth requirements are not uncommon in short-term debt contracts, but are rare in long-term debt instruments (also see Smith and Warner (1979)). In a later and more complex model, Brennan and Schwartz (1984) offer some examples with alternative bankruptcy conditions.

[6] Brennan and Schwartz do look at some examples when T becomes large. The relative insensitivity of these examples to T, as T exceeds 25 years, suggests that our limiting closed-form results for infinite maturity debt will be good approximations for debt with long but finite maturity.

Debt Value, Bond Covenants, and Optimal Capital Structure

can be ignored.[7] Very long time horizons for fixed obligations are not new, either in theory or in practice. The original Modigliani and Miller (1958) argument assumes debt with infinite maturity. Merton (1974) and Black and Cox (1976) look at infinite maturity debt in an explicitly dynamic model. Since 1752 the Bank of England has, on occasion, issued Consols, bonds promising a fixed coupon with no final maturity date. And preferred stock typically pays a fixed dividend without time limit.

An alternative time-independent environment is when, at each moment, the debt matures but is rolled over at a fixed interest rate (or fixed premium to a reference risk-free rate) unless terminated because of failure to meet a minimum value, such as a positive net-worth covenant. As we discuss later, this environment bears resemblance to some revolving credit agreements.

Time independence permits the derivation of closed-form solutions for risky debt value, given capital structure. These results extend those of Merton (1974) and Black and Cox (1976) to include taxes, bankruptcy costs, and protective covenants (if any). They are then used to derive closed-form solutions for optimal capital structure.[8] The analysis addresses the following questions:

- How do yield spreads on corporate debt depend on leverage, firm risk, taxes, payouts, protective covenants, and bankruptcy costs?
- Do high-risk ("junk") bond values behave in qualitatively different ways than investment-grade bond values?
- What is the optimal amount of leverage, and how does this depend on risk-free interest rates, firm risk, taxes, protective covenants, and bankruptcy costs?

---

[7] For 30-year debt, the final repayment of principal represents 1.5 percent of debt value when the interest rate is 15 percent, and 5.7 percent of value when the interest rate is 10 percent. Recently, a number of firms have issued 50-year debt, and one firm (Disney) has issued 100-year debt.

[8] Recently I have become aware of important related work by Anderson and Sundaresan (1992), Longstaff and Schwartz (1992), and Mella and Perraudin (1993). Anderson and Sundaresan (1992) focus on risky debt in a binomial framework. Using numerical examples, they examine the choice of debtors to discontinue coupon payments prior to bankruptcy and show that this may explain the sizable default premiums found in bond prices (see Jones, Mason, and Rosenfeld (1984), and Sarig and Warga (1989)). They do not examine optimal capital structure.

Longstaff and Schwartz (1992) derive solutions for risky debt values with finite maturity and with stochastic risk-free interest rates. Their key assumption is that bankruptcy is triggered whenever firm value, V, falls to an exogenously given level, K, (our V_B), which is time independent. This is a strong assumption for finite maturity debt, whose debt service payments are time dependent. Equation (14) below shows that V_B depends on the risk-free interest rate, suggesting that an endogenously determined K should depend upon the (stochastic) interest rate. Longstaff and Schwartz (1992) do not consider optimal capital structure.

Mella and Perraudin's approach more closely parallels this article, with endogenously determined bankruptcy levels. However, firm value is driven by a random product selling price whose drift as well as volatility must be specified, as must the firm's cost structure. (See also Fries, Miller, and Perraudin (1993)). Like Anderson and Sundaresan (1992), the article considers an endogenous decision to continue service debt.

- How does a positive net-worth covenant affect the potential for agency problems between bondholders and stockholders?
- When can debt renegotiation be expected prior to bankruptcy, and can renegotiation achieve results that debt repurchase cannot?

The model follows Modigliani and Miller (1958), Merton (1974), and Brennan and Schwartz (1978) in assuming (i) that the activities of the firm are unchanged by financial structure, and (ii) that capital structure decisions, once made, are not subsequently changed.

Much of the recent literature in corporate finance examines possible variants to assumption (i): see, for example, the survey by Harris and Raviv (1991). A particularly important variant is the "asset substitution" problem, where shareholders of highly leveraged firms may transfer value to themselves from bondholders by choosing riskier activities. If the appropriate functional form were known, feedback from capital structure to volatility could be captured in an extension of our model, at the likely cost of losing closed-form results.[9] But a simpler model that ignores such potential feedback still serves some important purposes:

1) Taxes and bankruptcy costs will importantly condition optimal capital structure even if asset substitution can occur; knowing these relationships in a basic model will provide useful insights for more complex situations.
2) The potential magnitude of the asset substitution problem can be identified by knowing how sensitive debt and equity values are to the risk of the activities chosen.
3) Bond covenants may directly limit opportunities for firms to alter the risk of their activities. In other cases, bond covenants may indirectly limit asset substitution by reducing potential conflicts of interest between stockholders and bondholders. Section VII below shows that a positive net worth requirement can eliminate the firm's incentive to increase risk.

Our second major assumption is that the face value of debt, once issued, remains static through time. This is not as unreasonable as it might appear. In Section VIII, we show that additional debt issuance will hurt current debtholders; it is typically proscribed by bond covenants. We further show that marginal debt reductions via repurchases will hurt current stockholders. These considerations may preclude continuous changes in the outstanding amount of debt, even if refinancing costs are zero.

---

[9] Mello and Parsons (1992), using a numerical approach similar to Brennan and Schwartz (1978) but including operating decisions of a (mining) firm, contrast decisions that maximize equity value with those that maximize the total value of the firm. They associate the difference in resulting values with agency costs and present an example showing the effect of these costs on optimal leverage. Mauer and Triantis (1993) also use the Brennan and Schwartz (1978) approach to examine the interaction of investment decisions and corporate financing policies.

Debt Value, Bond Covenants, and Optimal Capital Structure

However, large (discontinuous) debt repurchases via tender offers *may* under certain circumstances benefit both stock and bondholders, if refinancing costs are not excessive. A dynamic model of capital structure capturing these possibilities is desirable but considerably more difficult. First steps in this direction have been made in important work by Kane, Marcus, and McDonald (1984) and Fischer, Heinkel, and Zechner (1989). Their analyses pose several difficulties, which we avoid by adopting the static assumption shared with earlier authors.[10]

The structure of the article is as follows. Section I develops a simple dynamic model of a levered firm, and derives values for time-independent securities. Sections II and III consider debt value and optimal leverage when bankruptcy is determined endogenously. Sections IV and V consider debt value and optimal leverage when bankruptcy is triggered by a positive net-worth covenant. Section VI considers some alternative assumptions about tax deductibility, cash payouts by the firm, and the absolute priority of payments in bankruptcy. Section VII addresses agency problems and asset substitution, while Section VIII considers aspects of debt repurchase and renegotiation. Section IX concludes.

I. A Model of Time-Independent Security Values

Consider a firm whose activities have value V which follows a diffusion process with constant volatility of rate of return:

$$dV/V = \mu(V,t)dt + \sigma dW, \tag{1}$$

where W is a standard Brownian motion. We shall refer to V as the "asset value" of the firm.[11] The stochastic process of V is assumed to be unaffected by the financial structure of the firm. Thus any net cash outflows associated with the choice of leverage (e.g., coupons after tax benefits) must be financed by selling additional equity.[12]

Following Modigliani and Miller (1957), Merton (1974), Black and Cox (1976), and Brennan and Schwartz (1978), we assume that a riskless asset

---

[10] In Fischer, Heinkel, and Zechner (1989), the value of an unlevered firm (their *A*) cannot be exogenous, since it depends on the optimally levered firm value less costs of readjustment (see their p. 25). Since closed-form solutions are not available for the restructuring boundaries, they do not offer closed-form equations for risky debt value and optimal capital structure.

[11] We leave unanswered the delicate question of whether V, which could be associated with the value of an unlevered firm, is a traded asset. An alternative approach is to note that if equity, E, is a traded security, its process could be used to *define* a process, V, through equation (13) below, using Ito's Lemma. Our assumption that V has constant volatility will restrict the permissible process of E.

[12] This is consistent with bond covenants that restrict firms from selling assets. Brennan and Schwartz (1978) also make this assumption, although Merton (1974) does not. In Section VI.*B*, we consider how our results are affected by relaxing this assumption.

exists that pays a constant rate of interest r. This permits us to focus on the *risk structure* of interest rates directly.[13]

Now consider any claim on the firm that continuously pays a nonnegative coupon, C, per instant of time when the firm is solvent. Denote the value of such a claim by $F(V, t)$. When the firm finances the net cost of the coupon by issuing additional equity, it is well known (e.g., Black and Cox (1976)) that any such asset's value must satisfy the partial differential equation

$$(1/2)\sigma^2 V^2 F_{VV}(V,t) + rVF_V(V,t) - rF(V,t) + F_t(V,t) + C = 0 \quad (2)$$

with boundary conditions determined by payments at maturity, and by payments in bankruptcy should this happen prior to maturity.[14] In general, there exist no closed-form solutions to equation (2) for arbitrary boundary conditions. Hence Brennan and Schwartz (1978) resort to computer analysis of some examples. However, when securities have no explicit time dependence, the term $F_t(V, t) = 0$ and equation (2) becomes an ordinary differential equation with $F(V)$ satisfying

$$(1/2)\sigma^2 V^2 F_{VV}(V) + rVF_V(V) - rF(V) + C = 0. \quad (3)$$

Equation (3) has the general solution

$$F(V) = A_0 + A_1 V + A_2 V^{-X}, \quad (4)$$

where

$$X = 2r/\sigma^2 \quad (5)$$

and the constants A_0, A_1, and A_2 are determined by boundary conditions. *Any* time-independent claim with an equity-financed constant payout $C \geq 0$ must have this functional form. We turn now to examining specific securities.

Debt promises a perpetual coupon payment, C, whose level remains constant unless the firm declares bankruptcy. The value of debt can be expressed as $D(V; C)$. For simplicity, however, we will suppress the coupon as an argument and simply write debt value as $D(V)$. Let V_B denote the level of asset value at which bankruptcy is declared. (Note that we again suppress the argument C.) If bankruptcy occurs, a fraction $0 \leq \alpha \leq 1$ of value will be

---

[13] Extensions of numerical bond valuation to include interest rate risk are provided in Brennan and Schwartz (1980) and Kim, Ramaswamy, and Sundaresan (1993). They find that the yield spreads between corporate and Treasury bonds are quite insensitive to interest rate uncertainty.

[14] More generally, if net payouts by the firm not financed by further equity issuance are denoted $P(V, t)$, and $C(V, t)$ represents the payout flow to security F, then

$$(1/2)\sigma^2(V,t)V^2 F_{VV}(V,t) + [rV - P(V,t)]F_V(V,t) - rF(V,t) + F_t(V,t) + C(V,t) = 0.$$

Note that $\sigma^2(V, t)$ could be of the form $\sigma^2[C(V, t), V, t]$, reflecting possible asset substitution.

Equation (2) requires that V, or an asset perfectly correlated (locally) with V, such as equity, be traded. See also footnote 11.

Debt Value, Bond Covenants, and Optimal Capital Structure 1219

lost to bankruptcy costs, leaving debtholders with value $(1 - \alpha)V_B$ and stockholders with nothing.[15]

Later we show how the bankruptcy value, V_B, is determined, given alternative debt covenants. For the moment regard it as fixed. Since the value of debt is of the form in equation (4), we must determine the constants A_0, A_1, and A_2. Boundary conditions are:

$$\text{At } V = V_B, \quad D(V) = (1 - \alpha)V_B \qquad (6\text{i})$$

$$\text{As } V \to \infty, \quad D(V) \to C/r. \qquad (6\text{ii})$$

Condition (6ii) holds because bankruptcy becomes irrelevant as V becomes large, and the value of debt approaches the value of the capitalized coupon (and therefore the value of risk-free debt).

From equation (4), it is immediately apparent using equation (6ii) that $A_1 = 0$. Because $V^{-X} \to 0$ as $V \to \infty$, this with equation (6ii) implies that $A_0 = C/r$. Finally, $A_2 = [(1 - \alpha)V_B - C/r]V_B^X$, using equation (6i). Thus

$$D(V) = C/r + [(1 - \alpha)V_B - C/r][V/V_B]^{-X}. \qquad (7)$$

Equation (7) can also be written as $D(V) = [1 - p_B](C/r) + p_B[(1 - \alpha)V_B]$, where $p_B \equiv (V/V_B)^{-X}$ has the interpretation of the present value of \$1 contingent on future bankruptcy (i.e., V falling to V_B).[16]

Equation (7) represents a straightforward extension of Black and Cox (1976) to include bankruptcy costs.[17] But we shall see later that taxes affect the value, V_B, when bankruptcy is determined endogenously. Both taxes and bankruptcy costs are important determinants of debt value in this case.

Debt issuance affects the total value of the firm in two ways. First, it reduces firm value because of possible bankruptcy costs. Second, it increases firm value due to the tax deductibility of the interest payments, C. The value of both these effects will depend upon the level of firm value, V, and are time independent. Therefore they can be valued as if they were time-independent securities.

First, consider a security that pays no coupon, but has value equal to the bankruptcy costs αV_B at $V = V_B$. This security has current value, denoted

---

[15] We focus on bankruptcy costs that are proportional to asset value when bankruptcy is declared. Alternatives such as constant bankruptcy costs could readily be explored within the framework developed. Deviations from absolute priority (in which bondholders do not receive all remaining value) can also be incorporated in the boundary conditions; we do so in Section VI.C. Franks and Torous (1989) and Eberhart, Moore, and Roenfeldt (1990) document deviations from the absolute priority rule.

[16] More exactly,

$$p_B = \int_0^\infty \exp(-rt) f(t; V, V_B) \, dt,$$

where $f(t; V, V_B)$ is the density of the first passage time from V to V_B, when the process for V has drift equal to the risk-free interest rate, r.

[17] Merton (1974) derives a different formula for the case where $\alpha = 0$. This is because he assumes the firm liquidates assets to pay coupons.

$BC(V)$, that reflects the market value of a claim to αV_B should bankruptcy occur. Because its returns are time independent, it too must satisfy equation (4) with boundary conditions

$$\text{At } V = V_B, \quad BC(V) = \alpha V_B \tag{8i}$$

$$\text{As } V \to \infty, \quad BC(V) \to 0 \tag{8ii}$$

In this case equation (4) has solution

$$BC(V) = \alpha V_B (V/V_B)^{-X}. \tag{9}$$

BC is a decreasing, strictly convex function of V. Again, note the reinterpretation of equation (9) as $BC = p_B[\alpha V_B]$: the current value of bankruptcy costs is their magnitude if bankruptcy occurs, times the present value of \$1 conditional on future bankruptcy. Subsequent expressions will have similar interpretations.

Now consider the value of tax benefits associated with debt financing. These benefits resemble a security that pays a constant coupon equal to the tax-sheltering value of interest payments (τC) as long as the firm is solvent and pays nothing in bankruptcy. This security's value, $TB(V)$, equals the value of the tax benefit of debt. It too is time independent and therefore must satisfy equation (4) with boundary conditions

$$\text{At } V = V_B, \quad TB(V) = 0 \tag{10i}$$

$$\text{As } V \to \infty, \quad TB(V) = \tau C/r. \tag{10ii}$$

Equation (10i) reflects the loss of the tax benefits if the firm declares bankruptcy. Equation (10ii) reflects the fact that, as bankruptcy becomes increasingly unlikely in the relevant future, the value of tax benefits approaches the capitalized value of the tax benefit flow, τC. Using equation (4) and the boundary conditions above gives

$$TB(V) = \tau C/r - (\tau C/r)(V/V_B)^{-X}. \tag{11}$$

Tax benefits are an increasing, strictly concave function of V.

Note that the value of tax benefits, equation (11), presumes that the firm *always* benefits fully (in amount τC) from the tax deductibility of coupon payments when it is solvent. But under U.S. tax codes, to benefit fully the firm must have earnings before interest and taxes (EBIT) that is at least as large as the coupon payment, C.[18] An alternative approach, in which EBIT is related to asset value, V, and tax benefits may be lost when the firm is solvent (but close to bankruptcy), is considered in Section VI.A.

---

[18] The losses associated with interest payments exceeding EBIT may be carried forward, but lose time value, and may lose all value if the firm goes bankrupt. (Reorganizations under Chapter 11 of the Bankruptcy Code may carry forward some tax benefits. This could be modeled by a boundary condition, equation (10i), with a positive value.)

Debt Value, Bond Covenants, and Optimal Capital Structure

The total value of the firm, $v(V)$, reflects three terms: the firm's asset value, plus the value of the tax deduction of coupon payments, less the value of bankruptcy costs:

$$v(V) = V + TB(V) - BC(V)$$
$$= V + (\tau C/r)\left[1 - (V/V_B)^{-X}\right] - \alpha V_B(V/V_B)^{-X}. \quad (12)$$

Note that v is strictly concave in asset value, V, when $C > 0$ and either $\alpha > 0$ or $\tau > 0$. Note also that if $\alpha > 0$ and $\tau > 0$, then $v(V) < V$ as $V \to V_B$, and $v(V) > V$ as $V \to \infty$. This coupled with concavity implies that v is (proportionately) more volatile than V at low values of V and is less volatile at high values.

The value of equity is the total value of the firm less the value of debt:

$$E(V) = v(V) - D(V)$$
$$= V - (1 - \tau)C/r + [(1 - \tau)C/r - V_B][V/V_B]^{-X}. \quad (13)$$

We see from equation (14) below that when V_B is endogenously determined, $[(1 - \tau)C/r - V_B] > 0$, implying that $E(V)$ is a convex function of V. This reflects the "option-like" nature of equity, even when debt has an infinite horizon. When V_B is determined by a positive net worth requirement, however, we show in Section V that equity may be a *concave* function of V. This has important ramifications for agency problems associated with asset substitution, which are examined in Section VII. Finally, Ito's Lemma can be used to show that the volatility of equity's rate of return declines as V (and therefore E) rises. Stock option pricing models would need to reflect this nonconstant volatility, as well as the possibility that E reaches zero with positive probability.

Equations (7) and (13) indicate the importance of V_B in determining the values of debt and equity. In the following sections, we consider alternative bankruptcy-triggering scenarios.

II. Debt with No Protective Covenants: The Endogenous Bankruptcy Case

If the firm is not otherwise constrained by covenants, bankruptcy will occur only when the firm cannot meet the required (instantaneous) coupon payment by issuing additional equity: that is, when equity value falls to zero.[19] However, *any* level of asset value, V_B, that triggers bankruptcy will imply

---

[19] In continuous time, the coupon (Cdt) paid over the infinitesimal interval, dt, is itself infinitesimal. Therefore the value of equity simply needs to be positive to avoid bankruptcy over the next instant. In discrete time, where the time between periods, δt, is of a fixed size, the value of equity at each period must exceed the coupon ($C\delta t$) to be paid that period.

It is sometimes assumed that bankruptcy is triggered by a cashflow shortage. This can be criticized, because, if equity value remains, a firm will always be motivated and able to issue additional equity to cover the shortage, rather than declare bankruptcy. Positive equity value rather than positive cashflow seems to be the essential element when bankruptcy is endogenously determined.

that the value of equity is zero at that asset value, given the absolute priority rule.

When V_B can be chosen by the firm (rather than imposed by a covenant such as positive net-worth requirement), it can be seen from equation (12) that total firm value, v, will be maximized by setting V_B as low as possible. Limited liability of equity, however, prevents V_B from being arbitrarily small: $E(V)$ must be nonnegative for all values of $V \geq V_B$. From equation (13), $E(V)$ is strictly convex in V when $V_B < (1 - \tau)C/r$. Thus the lowest possible value for V_B consistent with positive equity value for all $V > V_B$ is such that $dE/dV|_{V=V_B} = 0$: a "smooth-pasting" or "low contact" condition at $V = V_B$. (This choice of bankruptcy level can also be shown to maximize the value of equity at any level of V: $dE/dV_B = 0$[20]). Differentiating equation (13) with respect to V, setting this expression equal to zero with $V = V_B$, and solving for V_B gives

$$V_B = [(1 - \tau)C/r][X/(1 + X)] = (1 - \tau)C/(r + 0.5\sigma^2), \qquad (14)$$

where the second line uses equation (5). Since $V_B < (1 - \tau)C/r$, equity is indeed convex in V.

Observe that the asset value, V_B, at which bankruptcy occurs

a) is proportional to the coupon, C;
b) is independent of the current asset value, V;
c) decreases as the corporate tax rate, τ, increases;
d) is independent of bankruptcy costs, α;
e) decreases as the risk-free interest rate, r, rises; and
f) decreases with increases in the riskiness of the firm, σ^2.

The results above also describe the behavior of total firm value at bankruptcy, $v_B \equiv v[V_B] = (1 - \alpha)V_B$, except that v_B falls as bankruptcy cost, α, increases. The fact that asset value, V, does not affect v_B means that the bankruptcy level of total firm market value can be estimated from the coupon, C, (plus parameters r, σ_2, α, and τ), without needing to know the firm's current asset value.[21]

Substituting equation (14) into equations (7), (12), and (13) gives

$$D(V) = (C/r)\left[1 - (C/V)^X k\right] \qquad (15)$$

$$v(V) = V + (\tau C/r)\left[1 - (C/V)^X h\right] \qquad (16)$$

$$E(V) = V - (1 - \tau)(C/r)\left[1 - (C/V)^X m\right] \qquad (17)$$

---

[20] See also Merton (1973; footnote 60). The equivalence of the two conditions suggests that the endogenously set V_B is incentive compatible in the following sense. Ex ante (before debt issuance), stockholders will wish to maximize firm value subject to the limited liability of equity. The ex ante optimal V_B achieves this by satisfying the smooth-pasting condition. Ex post, equity holders will have no incentive to declare bankruptcy at a different V, since V_B also satisfies the ex post optimal condition for maximizing equity value.

[21] Knowledge of the market value of equity, E, and debt, D, in addition to C, combined with equations (7), (13), and (14), permits calculation of a unique V and α given r, τ, and σ. Alternatively, α and σ can be recovered, given r, τ, and V.

where

$$m = [(1 - \tau)X/r(1 + X)]^X/(1 + X)$$
$$h = [1 + X + \alpha(1 - \tau)X/\tau]m$$
$$k = [1 + X - (1 - \alpha)(1 - \tau)X]m.$$

The interest rate paid by risky debt, $R(C/V)$, can be derived directly from dividing C by $D(V)$, giving

$$R(C/V) = C/D(V) = rK(C/V), \tag{18}$$

where

$$K(C/V) = \left[1 - (C/V)^X k\right]^{-1}.$$

The interest rate depends positively on the *ratio* of the coupon, C, to firm asset value, V. Note $K(C/V)$ has the interpretation of a risk-adjustment factor (multiplying the risk-free rate) that the firm must pay to compensate bondholders for the risks assumed. The yield spread is $R(C/V) - r = r(C/V)^X k/[1 - (C/V)^X k]$.

The values above are derived for an arbitrary level of the coupon, C. Section III examines the *optimal* choice of coupon (and leverage) for unprotected debt. But first, we examine the behavior of unprotected debt values and yield premiums for an arbitrary coupon level.

A. The Comparative Statics of Debt Value (D(V))

Equation (15) extends Black and Cox's (1976) results to include the effects of taxes and bankruptcy on debt value. Row 1 of Table I summarizes the comparative statics of debt value. Not surprisingly, larger bankruptcy costs decrease the value of debt. Less obvious is that an increase in the corporate tax rate will raise debt value, through lowering the bankruptcy level, V_B.[22]

More surprising still are the results when taxes or bankruptcy costs are positive and firm asset value, V, nears the bankruptcy level, V_B. Table I indicates that the effects of increases in the coupon, firm riskiness, and the risk-free rate become reversed from what is expected. An increase in coupon can *lower* debt value. An increase in firm risk can *raise* debt value, as can an increase in the risk-free rate. Thus *the behavior of "junk" bonds (or "fallen angels") differs significantly from the behavior of investment-grade bonds when bankruptcy costs and/or taxes are positive.*[23]

To understand these results, first consider the presence of positive bankruptcy costs. If V is close to V_B, the value of debt will be very sensitive to such costs. Lowering V_B will raise the value of debt since bankruptcy costs

---

[22] These comparative static results presume that other parameters (including V) remain at their current level, the usual ceteris paribus assumption. Note, however, that a change in the corporate tax rate might affect V as well.

[23] The ratios of V/V_B (or C/V) at which the various behaviors are reversed are not identical. Of course, these ratios may not correspond to Wall Street's definition of "junk" bonds.

Table I
Comparative Statics of Financial Variables: Unprotected Debt

This table describes properties of the equations describing debt value, D, the interest, R, paid on debt, the yield spread of the debt over the risk-free rate $(R - r)$, the total firm value, v, and the value of equity, E, when debt is *not* protected by a positive net-worth covenant. V is the firm's asset value, V_B is the endogenously determined value at which bankruptcy is declared, C is the coupon paid on debt, σ^2 is the variance of the asset return, r is the risk-free interest rate, α is the fraction of asset value lost if bankruptcy occurs, and τ is the corporate tax rate.

			Limit As		Sign of Change in Instrument for an Increase in:			
Variable	Homogeneity	Shape	$V \to \infty$	$V \to V_B$	C	σ^2	r	α	τ	V
D	Degree 1 in V, C	Concave in V, C	C/r	$\dfrac{C(1-\alpha)(1-\tau)}{(r+0.5\sigma^2)}$	>0; $<0^*$ as $V \to V_B$	<0; $>0^*$ as $V \to V_B$	<0; $>0^*$ as $V \to V_B$	<0	>0	>0
R	Degree 0 in V, C	Convex in V/C	r	$\dfrac{(r+0.5\sigma^2)}{(1-\alpha)(1-\tau)}$	>0	>0; $<0^*$ as $V \to V_B$	>0; $<0^*$ as $V \to V_B$	>0	<0	<0
$R-r$	Degree 0 in V, C	Convex in V/C	0	$[0.5\sigma^2 + r(\alpha+\tau-\alpha\tau)]/[(1-\alpha)(1-\tau)]$	>0	>0; $<0^*$ as $V \to V_B$	<0	>0	<0	<0
v	Degree 1 in V, C	Concave in V, C	$V + \tau C/r$	$\dfrac{C(1-\alpha)(1-\tau)}{(r+0.5\sigma^2)}$	>0; $<0^*$ as $V \to V_B$	<0; $>0^*$ as $V \to V_B$	<0; $>0^*$ as $V \to V_B$	<0	>0	>0
E	Degree 1 in V, C	Convex in V, C	$V - (1-\tau)C/r$	0	<0	>0	>0	0	>0	>0

*Sign reversal as $V \to V_B$ only if α and/or $\tau > 0$.

Debt Value, Bond Covenants, and Optimal Capital Structure

will be less imminent. From equation (14), higher asset volatility, higher risk-free interest rates, or lower coupon, C, will all serve to lower V_B. For values of V close to V_B, this positive effect on $D(V)$ will dominate. Even if there are no direct bankruptcy costs, the event of bankruptcy causes the value of the tax shield to be lost when $\tau > 0$, and the previous conclusions continue to hold.

The fact that $D(V)$ is eventually decreasing as the coupon rises implies that debt value reaches a maximum, $D_{max}(V)$, for a finite coupon, $C_{max}(V)$. We can naturally think of D_{max} as the *debt capacity* of the firm. Differentiating equation (15) with respect to C, setting the resulting equation equal to zero and solving for C gives

$$C_{max}(V) = V[(1 + X)k]^{-1/X} \qquad (19)$$

Substituting this into equation (15) and simplifying gives

$$D_{max}(V) = V[Xk^{-1/X}(1 + X)^{-(1+1/X)}]/r. \qquad (20)$$

The debt capacity of a firm is proportional to asset value, V, and falls with increases in firm risk, σ^2, and bankruptcy costs, α. Debt capacity rises with increases in the corporate tax rate, τ, and the risk-free rate, r.

Figures 1 and 2 show the relationship between debt value and the coupon

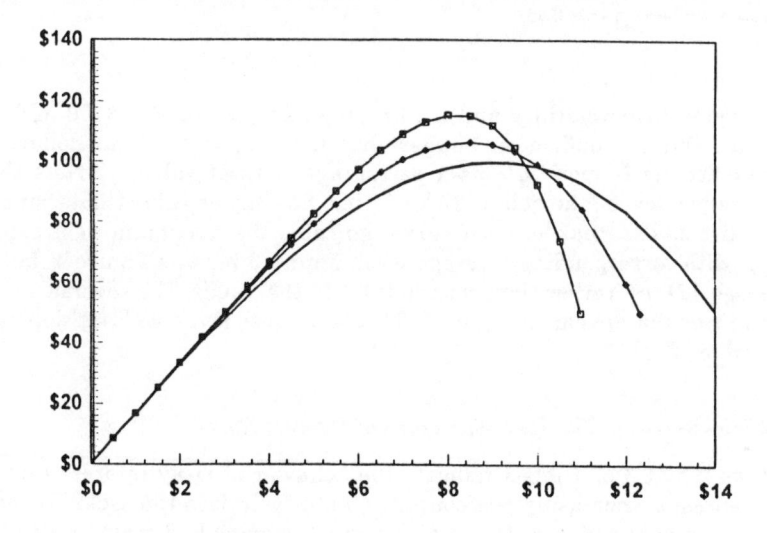

Figure 1. Debt value as a function of the coupon, when debt is unprotected. The lines plot the value of unprotected debt, D, at varying coupon levels C, for three levels of asset volatility, σ: 15 percent (*open square*), 20 percent (*filled diamond*), and 25 percent (*solid line*). It is assumed that the risk-free interest rate $r = 6.0\%$, bankruptcy costs are 50 percent ($\alpha = 0.5$), and the corporate tax rate is 35 percent ($\tau = 0.35$).

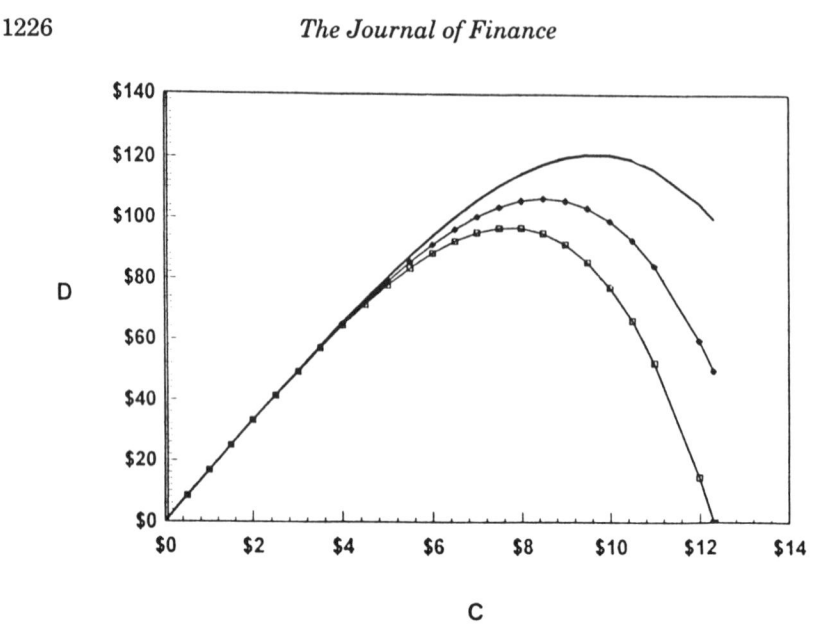

Figure 2. Debt value as a function of the coupon, when debt is unprotected. The lines plot the value of unprotected debt, D, at varying coupon levels, C, for three levels of bankruptcy costs: 0 (*solid line*), 50 percent (*filled diamond*), and 100 percent (*open square*) ($\alpha = 0$, 0.5, and 1, respectively). It is assumed that the risk-free interest rate $r = 6.0$ percent and the corporate tax rate is 35 percent ($\tau = 0.35$).

for varying firm volatility and bankruptcy costs, when $V = \$100$ and $r = 6$ percent. Our normalization implies that the coupon level (in dollars) also represents the coupon *rate* as a percentage of asset value, V. Note that at high coupon levels, the debt of riskier firms has higher value than that of less risky firms. The peak of each curve indicates the maximum debt capacity, D_{max}, with corresponding leverage level. Figure 3 repeats Figure 1, but with leverage, $[D/v]$, rather than coupon level on the x-axis. The reversals seen in Figure 1 do not appear in Figure 3. This is because leverage itself depends on the value of debt.

B. Yield Spreads: The Risk Structure of Interest Rates

Rows 2 and 3 of Table I indicate the behavior of risky interest rates and yield spreads. Increasing the coupon, C, always raises the yield spread. An increase in bankruptcy costs, α, also raises the spread, although a rise in the corporate tax rate will lower the spread because debt value will rise. Related to our earlier discussion, we observe the surprising result that *junk bond yield spreads may actually decline when firm riskiness increases.* Of course, this holds only for junk bonds: the yield spread on investment-grade debt will increase when firm risk rises. Also note that junk bond interest rates may

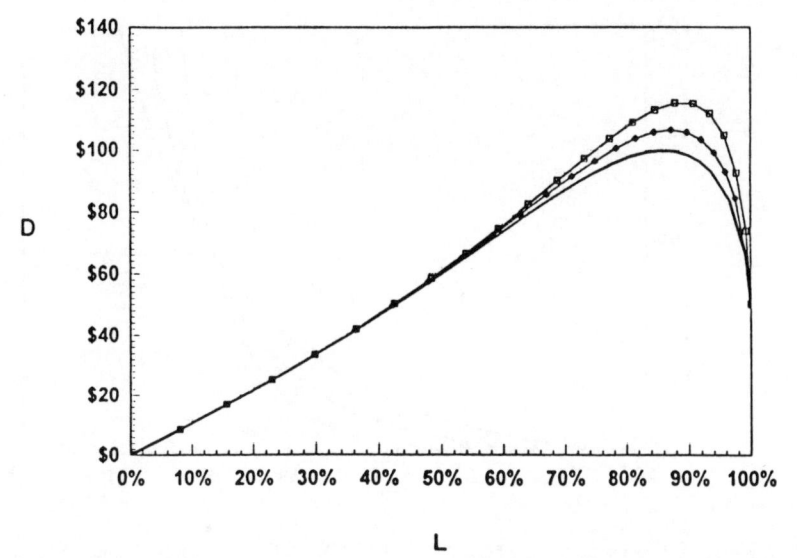

Debt Value, Bond Covenants, and Optimal Capital Structure

Figure 3. Debt value as a function of the leverage, when debt is unprotected. The lines plot the value of unprotected debt, D, at varying leverage ratios, L, for three levels of asset volatility, σ: 15 percent (*open square*), 20 percent (*filled diamond*), and 25 percent (*solid line*). It is assumed that the risk-free interest rate $r = 6.0\%$, bankruptcy costs are 50 percent ($\alpha = 0.5$), and the corporate tax rate is 35 percent ($\tau = 0.35$).

actually fall when the risk-free rate increases. Figures 4 and 5 plot yield spreads against coupon level and leverage, respectively, as asset value risk changes.

Observe that $R(C/V) \to (r + 0.5\sigma^2)$ as $V \to V_B$ when $\alpha = \tau = 0$. That is, long-term risky debt will never have a yield exceeding the risk-free rate by more than $0.5\sigma^2$ if there are no bankruptcy costs or tax benefits to debt.[24] Observing a yield spread greater than this on corporate long-term debt implies the presence of bankruptcy costs, taxes, or both.[25]

C. *The Comparative Statics of Firm Value (v(V)) and Equity Value (E(V))*

Row 4 of Table I indicates the comparative statics of total firm value. Again observe the perverse behavior of total firm value for firms with junk debt. In the presence of bankruptcy costs and/or corporate taxes, total firm value

---

[24] A firm whose asset value has an annual standard deviation of 20 percent, for example, would have debt whose yield spread *never* exceeds two percent. It has been argued that the tax advantage to debt may be nil (Miller (1977)). For arguments that bankruptcy costs may be small, see Warner (1977) (who focuses on direct costs only) and Haugen and Senbet (1988).

[25] When the firm has several debt issues, junior debt could have higher rates. But the weighted average cost of debt will be limited to $r + 0.5\sigma^2$ in this case.

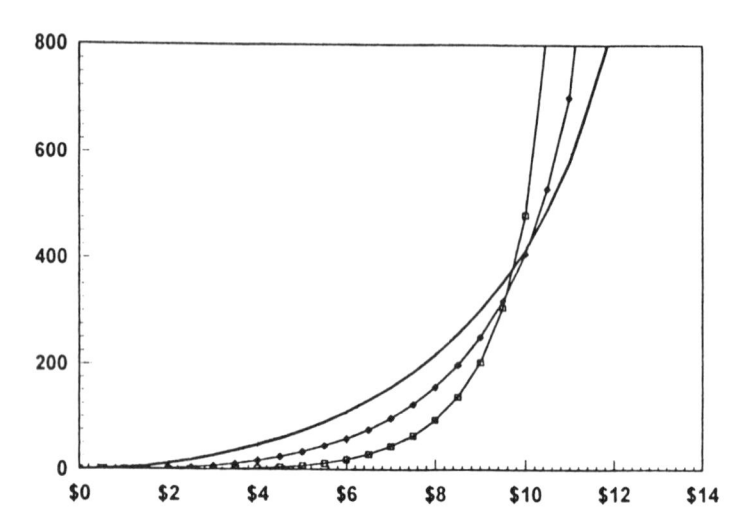

Figure 4. Yield spreads on unprotected debt as a function of the coupon. The lines plot the yield spread, YS (in basis points/year), the amount the firm's debt yield exceeds the risk-free rate, as a function of the coupon, C, for varying levels of asset volatility, σ: 15 percent (*open square*), 20 percent (*filled diamond*), and 25 percent (*solid line*). It is assumed that the risk-free interest rate $r = 6.0$ percent, bankruptcy costs are 50 percent ($\alpha = 0.5$), and the corporate tax rate is 35 percent ($\tau = 0.35$).

may rise as firm riskiness increases. Rising risk-free rates may also lead total firm value to increase. The values of firms with investment-grade debt will not exhibit such behavior. Figure 6 and Figure 7 illustrate total firm value, v, as a function of the coupon level C and the leverage D/v, respectively. Optimal leverage is the ratio at which each curve reaches its peak.

Row 5 of Table I indicates the behavior of equity value. Unlike debt, there are no reversals of comparative static results when V is close to V_B. The fact that bankruptcy costs do not affect equity value is perhaps surprising, but it reflects the fact that, given the coupon, C, debtholders bear all bankruptcy costs. In Section III we show that the *optimal* coupon and debt-equity ratio do depend upon α, and that initial equity holders ultimately are hurt by greater bankruptcy costs.

III. Optimal Leverage with Unprotected Debt

Consider now the coupon rate, C, which maximizes the total value, v, of the firm, given current asset value, V. Differentiating equation (16) with respect to C, setting the derivative equal to zero and solving for the optimal coupon,

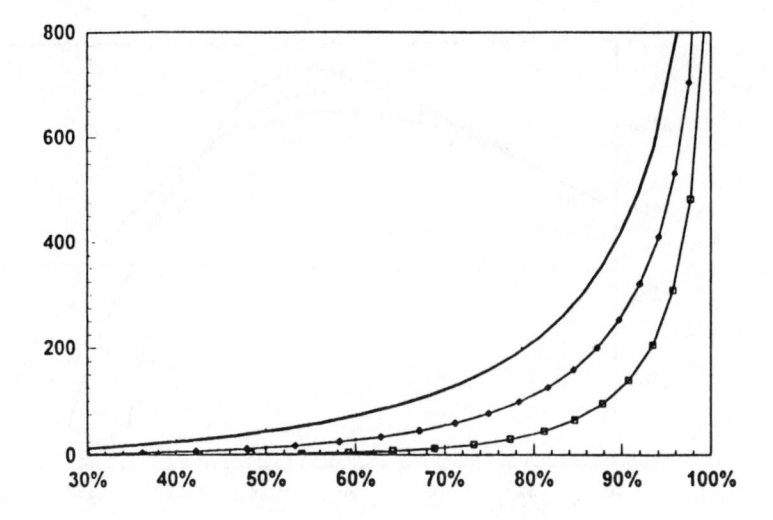

Debt Value, Bond Covenants, and Optimal Capital Structure 1229

Figure 5. Yield spreads on unprotected debt as a function of the leverage. The lines plot the yield spread, YS (in basis points/year), the amount the firm's debt yield exceeds the risk-free rate, as a function of the leverage, L, for varying levels of asset volatility, σ: 15 percent (*open square*), 20 percent (*filled diamond*), and 25 percent (*solid line*). It is assumed that the risk-free interest rate $r = 6.0$ percent, bankruptcy costs are 50 percent ($\alpha = 0.5$), and the corporate tax rate is 35 percent ($\tau = 0.35$).

C^*, as a function of asset value, V, gives:

$$C^*(V) = V[(1 + X)h]^{-1/X} \qquad (21)$$

Note that $h > k$, implying $C^*(V) < C_{max}(V)$. Substituting $C^*(V)$ into equations (15), (16), (18), and (14) gives

$$D^*(V) = V[(1 + X)h]^{-1/X}\{1 - k[(1 + X)h]^{-1}\}/r \qquad (22)$$

$$v^*(V) = V\{1 + (\tau/r)[(1 + X)h]^{-1/X}[X/(1 + X)]\} \qquad (23)$$

$$R^* = r[(1 + X)h]/[(1 + X)h - k] \qquad (24)$$

$$V_B^*(V) = V(m/h)^{1/X} \qquad (25)$$

Table II indicates the comparative statics of these variables plus optimal leverage $L^* = D^*/v^*$ and equity $E^* = v^* - D^*$. While most results are consistent with what is expected, a few merit comment.

The optimal coupon C^* is a U-shaped function of firm riskiness, as illustrated in Figure 8. Firms with little business risk, or very large risk, will optimally commit to pay sizable coupons. Firms with intermediate levels of risk will promise smaller coupons. However, the optimal leverage ratios of riskier firms will always be less than those of less risky firms, as can be seen

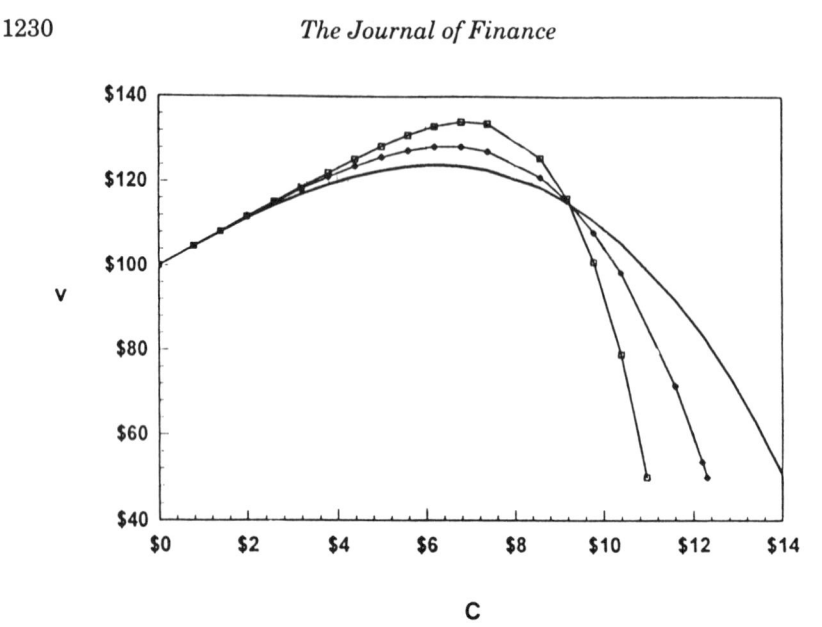

Figure 6. Total firm value as function of the coupon, when debt is unprotected. The lines plot total firm value, v, at varying coupon levels, C, for three levels of asset volatility, σ: 15 percent (*open square*), 20 percent (*filled diamond*), and 25 percent (*solid line*). It is assumed that the risk-free interest rate $r = 6.0$ percent, bankruptcy costs are 50 percent ($\alpha = 0.5$), and the corporate tax rate is 35 percent ($\tau = 0.35$).

by observing the maximal firm values in Figure 7. The potential gains in moving from no leverage to optimal leverage (where $v = v^*$) are considerable. For reasonable parameter levels, optimizing financial structure can increase firm value by as much as 25 to 40 percent over a firm with no leverage.

Our results confirm Brennan and Schwartz's (1978) observation that optimal leverage is less than 100 percent even when bankruptcy costs are zero. Too high leverage risks bankruptcy—and while there are no bankruptcy costs, the tax deductibility of coupon payments is lost.

Leverage of about 75 to 95 percent is optimal for firms with low-to-moderate levels of asset value risk and moderate bankruptcy costs.[26] Even firms with high risks and high bankruptcy costs should have leverage on the order of 50 to 60 percent, when the effective tax rate is 35 percent. Optimal

---

[26] It is of interest that many of the leveraged buyouts of the 1980s created capital structures that had 95 percent leverage or more. And targets were often firms with relatively stable value (low σ^2). Our analysis indicates these firms will reap maximal benefits from increased leverage. Subsequent leverage reduction by many of these firms could in part be explained by the substantial fall in interest rates, which reduces the optimal leverage ratio.

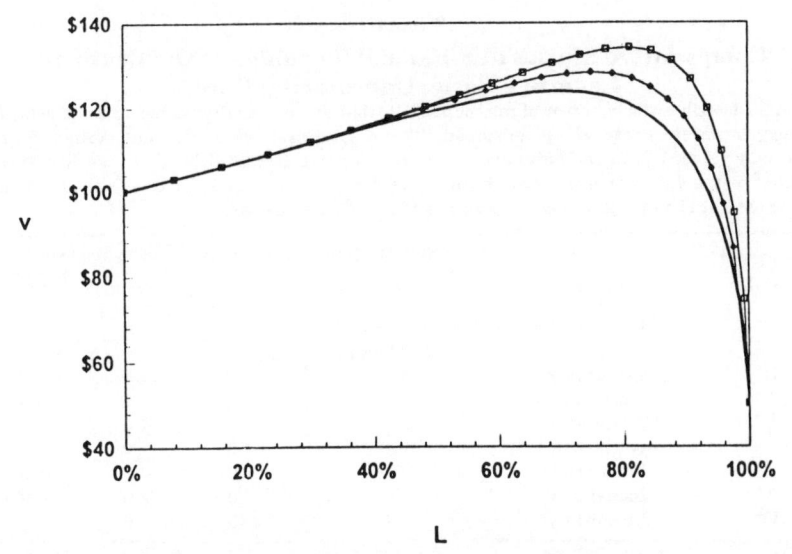

Debt Value, Bond Covenants, and Optimal Capital Structure

Figure 7. Total firm value as function of the leverage, when debt is unprotected. The lines plot total firm value, v, at varying levels of leverage L, for three levels of asset volatility, σ: 15 percent (*open square*), 20 percent (*filled diamond*), and 25 percent (*solid line*). It is assumed that the risk-free interest rate $r = 6.0$ percent, bankruptcy costs are 50 percent ($\alpha = 0.5$), and the corporate tax rate is 35 percent ($\tau = 0.35$).

leverage ratios drop by 5 to 25 percent when the effective tax rate is 15 percent, with the more pronounced falls at high volatility levels.[27] Variations of our assumptions that lead to lower optimal leverage ratios are discussed in Section VI.

The behavior of the yield spread at the optimal leverage ratio exhibits one surprise. Increased bankruptcy costs might be thought to increase interest rates. Indeed they do—but only if the coupon is fixed. As bankruptcy costs rise, the optimal coupon C^* falls. The probability of bankruptcy is then less and the yield spread decreases. Figure 9 illustrates yield spreads at the optimal leverage as a function of bankruptcy costs, α, and asset risk, σ.

Higher risk-free interest rates might also be expected to reduce the optimal amount of borrowing, but they do not: the added tax shield when interest rates are high more than offsets the greater costs of borrowing. This could be destabilizing, since supply would normally be expected to decrease as interest

---

[27] Following Miller (1977), if the effective personal tax rate on stock returns (reflecting tax deferment) were 20 percent, the tax rate on bond income were 40 percent, and the corporate tax rate 35 percent, the effective tax advantage of debt is $[1 - (1 - 0.35)(1 - 0.20)/(1 - 0.40)] = 0.133$, or slightly less than 15 percent.

Table II
Comparative Statics of Financial Variables at the Optimal Leverage Ratio: Unprotected Debt

This table describes the behavior of the coupon, C^*, that maximizes firm value, and the debt, D^*, leverage, L^*, interest rate, R^*, yield spread, $R^* - r$, total firm value, v^*, equity value, E^*, and bankruptcy value, V_B^*, at the optimal coupon level, for unprotected debt. (V is the firm's asset value, σ^2 is the variance of the asset return, r is the risk-free interest rate, α is the fraction of asset value lost if bankruptcy occurs, and τ is the corporate tax rate.

Variable	Shape	Sign of Change in Variable for an Increase in:			
		σ^2	r	α	τ
C^*	Linear in V	< 0, σ^2 small; > 0, σ^2 large	> 0	< 0	> 0
D^*	Linear in V	< 0	> 0	< 0	> 0
L^*	Invariant to V	< 0	> 0	< 0	> 0
R^*	Invariant to V	> 0	> 0	< 0	> 0
$R^* - r$	Invariant to V	> 0	< 0	< 0	> 0
v^*	Linear in V	< 0	> 0	< 0	> 0
E^*	Linear in V	> 0	< 0	> 0	< 0[a]
V_B^*	Linear in V	< 0	> 0	< 0	> 0[a]

[a] No effect if $\alpha = 0$.

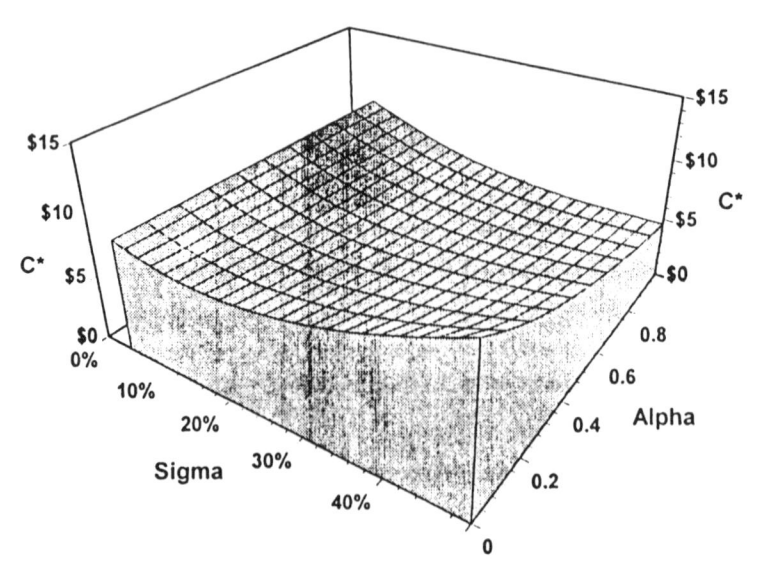

Figure 8. The optimal coupon as a function of firm risk and bankruptcy costs. The surface plots the optimal coupon, C^*, at varying levels of firm risk, σ, and bankruptcy costs, α. It is assumed that the risk-free interest rate $r = 6.0$ percent and the corporate tax rate is 35 percent ($\tau = 0.35$).

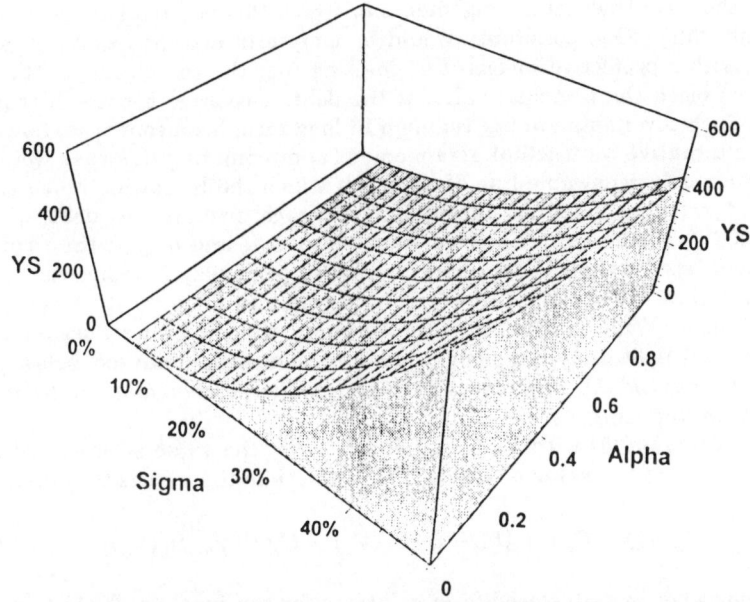

Debt Value, Bond Covenants, and Optimal Capital Structure   1233

Figure 9. The yield spread as a function of firm risk and bankruptcy costs. The surface plots the yield spread, YS, the difference between the yield on the firm's debt (at the optimal coupon, C^*) and the risk-free interest rate, r, for varying levels of firm risk, σ, and bankruptcy costs, α. It is assumed that the risk-free interest rate $r = 6.0$ percent and the corporate tax rate is 35 percent ($\tau = 0.35$).

rates rise.[28] Despite the greater borrowing, the yield spread at the optimal leverage actually falls slightly as the risk-free interest rate increases.

IV. Positive Net-Worth Covenants and the Value of Protected Debt

Consider now the case in which debt remains outstanding without time limit unless bankruptcy is triggered by the value of the firm's assets falling beneath the principal value of debt, denoted P. We presume the principal value coincides with the market value of the debt when it is issued, denoted D_0. Thus $V_B = D_0$.[29]

---

[28] Note that an increase in r might well cause a decline in V. If so, it is possible that the desired amount of borrowing (which is proportional to V) could decline even though optimal leverage rises.

[29] It must be verified that the $V_B = D_0$ is consistent with the value of equity remaining positive at all levels $V \geq V_B$. This requires that D_0 exceed the level in equation (14) satisfying the smooth-pasting conditions. In fact, this is always the case at the optimal protected debt coupon level, and is satisfied at all but extremely high initial coupon levels. We limit our examination of protected debt to coupon levels for which the minimum net-worth requirement (rather than equation (14)) is the determinant of V_B.

Are there contractual arrangements in which this is a realistic description of bankruptcy? One possibility would be long-term debt as examined previously, with a protective covenant stipulating that the asset value of the firm always exceed the principal value of the debt: a positive net-worth requirement. Such covenants are not common in long-term bond contracts, however.

An alternative contractual arrangement approximating this case would be a continuously renewable line of credit, in which the borrowing amount and interest rate are fixed at inception.[30] At each instant the debt will be extended ("rolled over" at a fixed interest rate) if and only if the firm has sufficient asset value, V, to repay the loan's principal, P; otherwise bankruptcy occurs.[31] Thus the roll-over process proxies for a positive net-worth requirement. With this latter interpretation, the differences between the unprotected debt analyzed above and protected debt analyzed below *may capture many of the differences between long-term debt and (rolled over) short-term financing.*

From equation (7) with $V_B = D_0$, we can write the value of protected debt as a function of the value of assets, V_0, at the time the debt is initiated:

$$D_0(V_0) = C/r + [(1 - \alpha)D_0(V_0) - C/r][V_0/D_0(V_0)]^{-X} \qquad (26)$$

Except when $\alpha = 0$, closed-form solutions for the function $D_0(V_0)$ satisfying equation (26) have not been found. However, we can easily solve this equation numerically to determine the value, D_0, of the debt, given initial values, V_0 and C (as before we suppress the argument C). Note that the function $D_0(V_0)$ is homogeneous of degree one in V_0 and C. Also note that equation (26) gives the value of protected debt only at the initial asset value, V_0. Equation (7) with $V_B = D_0(V_0)$ gives protected debt value as a function of asset value, V.

Figures 10 and 11 illustrate the behavior of protected debt value as the coupon and leverage change, for $V = V_0 = 100$. They should be compared with Figures 1 and 3. We observe that the surprising behavior of unprotected "junk" debt does not hold for protected debt, even when the debt exhibits considerable risk. Unlike the unprotected case, the value of debt increases with the coupon at all levels of C. And increased firm risk or a higher risk-free interest rate always lowers debt value. This is because the bankruptcy-triggering value, V_B, is determined exogenously rather than endogenously.

---

[30] We assume the firm will never choose to borrow less than the stipulated credit line amount. The fact that most credit lines are tied to a floating rate is not important here, since the risk-free rate is assumed to be constant. It is important that the interest rate paid by the firm be independent of the firm's asset value V (providing $V \geq V_B$) after the initial agreement is reached.

[31] Many lines of credit have a "paydown" provision, requiring that the amount borrowed must be reduced to zero at least once per year. A firm will fail to meet this provision if its (market) value of assets is less than the loan principal. Also note that Merton (1974) requires $V \geq P$ at maturity to avoid default on a pure-discount bond: the firm must have positive net worth at maturity or bankruptcy occurs.

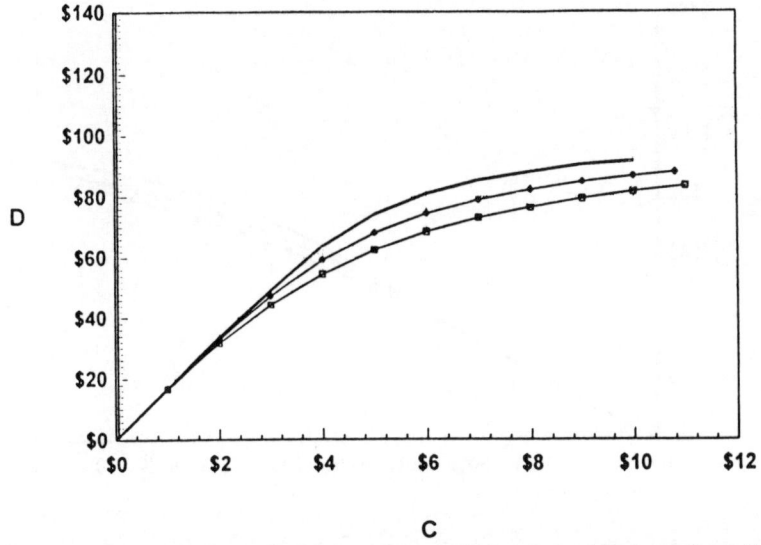

Debt Value, Bond Covenants, and Optimal Capital Structure

Figure 10. Debt value as a function of the coupon, when debt is protected by a minimum net-worth requirement. The lines plot the value of protected debt, D, at varying coupon levels, C, for three levels of asset volatility, σ: 15 percent (*solid line*), 20 percent (*filled diamond*), and 25 percent (*open square*). It is assumed that the risk-free interest rate $r = 6.0$ percent, bankruptcy costs are 50 percent ($\alpha = 0.5$), and the corporate tax rate is 35 percent ($\tau = 0.35$).

When there are no bankruptcy costs ($\alpha = 0$),
a) Protected debt is riskless and pays the risk-free rate, r.
b) For any C, the value of the tax shield with protected debt is less than the tax shield with unprotected debt.
c) For any C, the bankruptcy-triggering value of assets, V_B, for protected debt exceeds the V_B for unprotected debt.

Protected debt is riskless when $\alpha = 0$ because the firm's asset value is constantly monitored. Should asset value fall to the principal value, bankruptcy is declared and, because there are no bankruptcy costs, debtholders receive their full principal value. In this case, for a given coupon, C, the value of protected debt always exceeds that of unprotected debt. Further, $V_B = P = D_0(V_0) = C/r$. This exceeds the bankruptcy-triggering value, equation (14), of assets for unprotected debt, and implies smaller tax benefits from equation (11).

When bankruptcy costs are positive ($\alpha > 0$), the results change markedly. For a given coupon, C, protected debt may have a lesser value than unprotected debt (and therefore may pay a higher interest rate). This follows because bankruptcy will occur more frequently when debt is protected, because V_B is higher in the protected case, and bankruptcy costs will be

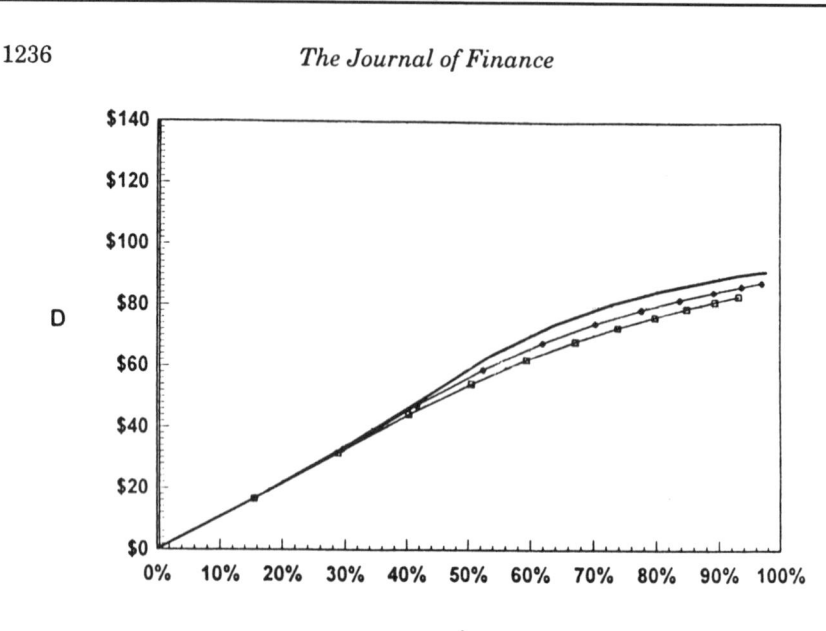

Figure 11. Debt value as a function of the leverage, when debt is protected by a minimum net-worth requirement. The lines plot the value of protected debt, D, at varying leverage ratios, L, for three levels of asset volatility, σ: 15 percent (*solid line*), 20 percent (*filled diamond*), and 25 percent (*open square*). It is assumed that the risk-free interest rate $r = 6.0$ percent, bankruptcy costs are 50 percent ($\alpha = 0.5$), and the corporate tax rate is 35 percent ($\tau = 0.35$).

incurred when $\alpha > 0$. Figure 12, when compared with Figure 5, shows yield spreads to be substantially higher for protected debt when $\alpha = 0.5$, except at extreme leverage ratios.

V. Optimal Leverage with Protected Debt

We now use a simple search procedure to find the coupon, C^*, that maximizes the total value, v, of the firm with protected debt. Figure 13, compared with Figure 7, illustrates that maximal firm value occurs at lower leverage when debt is protected.

For a reasonable range of parameters, we find that

a) Optimal leverage for protected debt is substantially less than for unprotected debt.
b) The interest rate paid at the optimum leverage is less for protected debt, even when bankruptcy costs are positive ($\alpha > 0$).
c) The maximum value of the firm (and therefore the benefit from leverage) is less when protected debt is used.

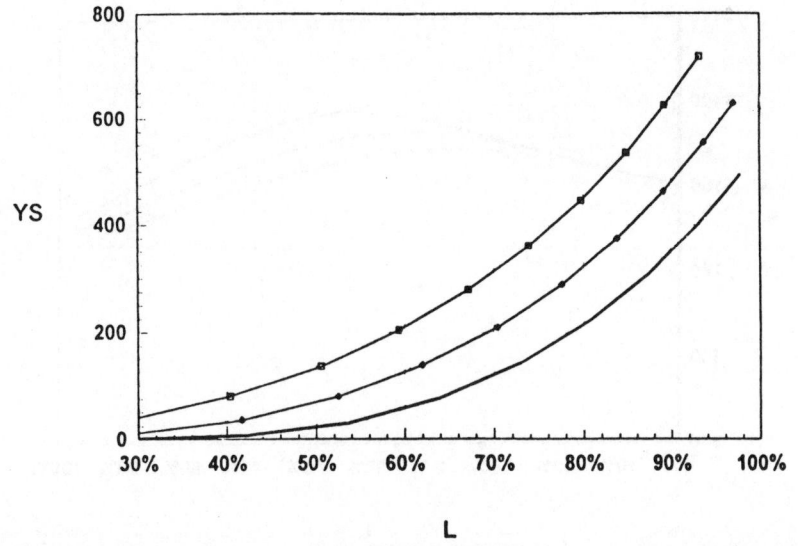

Debt Value, Bond Covenants, and Optimal Capital Structure

Figure 12. Yield spreads on protected debt as a function of the leverage. The lines plot the yield spread, *YS* (in basis points/year), the amount the firm's debt yield exceeds the risk-free rate, as a function of the leverage, *L*, for varying levels of asset volatility, σ: 15 percent (*solid line*), 20 percent (*filled diamond*), and 25 percent (*open square*). It is assumed that the risk-free interest rate $r = 6.0$ percent, bankruptcy costs are 50 percent ($\alpha = 0.5$), and the corporate tax rate is 35% ($\tau = 0.35$).

d) The maximal benefits of unprotected over protected debt increase as:
- Corporate taxes increase
- Interest rates are higher
- Bankruptcy costs are lower

A closer examination of numerical results reveals that *the optimal bankruptcy level V_B^* is the same for both protected and unprotected debt*, when bankruptcy costs are zero. We know, however, the closed-form solution for unprotected debt's optimal bankruptcy level, V_B, from equation (25). Since $D_0 = V_B$, this in turn suggests a closed-form solution for the optimal value of protected debt and related values when bankruptcy costs are zero and $V = V_0$:

$$D_0^*(V_0) = V_B^*(V_0) = V_0(m/h)^{1/X} \qquad (27)$$

Because protected debt is risk free when $\alpha = 0$, it also follows that

$$C^*(V_0) = rD_0^*(V_0) = rV_B^*(V_0) = rV_0(m/h)^{1/X} \qquad (28)$$

$$v^*(V_0) = V_0 + [\tau C^*(V_0)/r]\left\{1 - [C^*(V_0)/V_0]^X h\right\} \qquad (29)$$

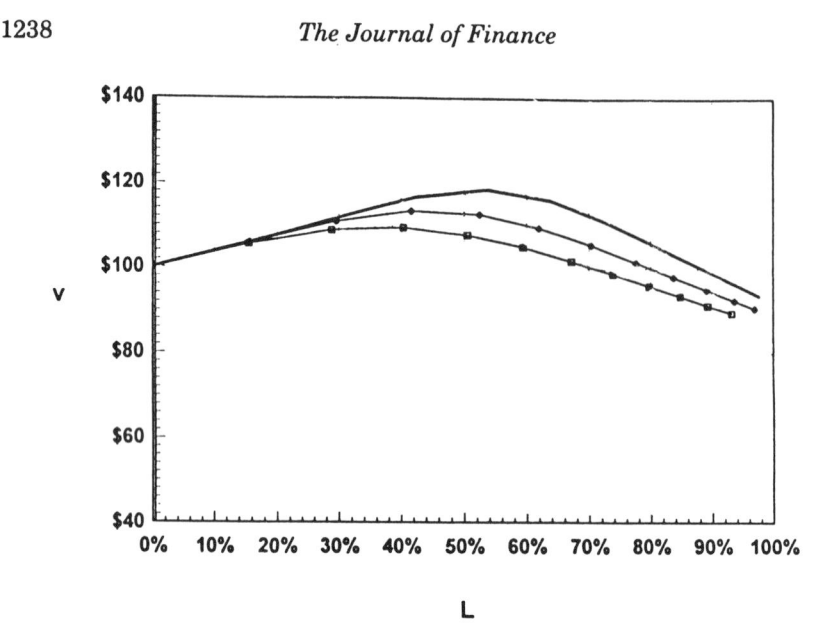

[Graph: Total firm value V (y-axis, $40–$140) vs leverage L (x-axis, 0%–100%), three curves for σ = 15%, 20%, 25%]

Figure 13. Total firm value as function of the leverage, when debt is protected. The lines plot total firm value, v, at varying levels of leverage, L, for three levels of asset volatility, σ: 15 percent (*solid line*), 20 percent (*filled diamond*), and 25 percent (*open square*). It is assumed that the risk-free interest rate $r = 6.0$ percent, bankruptcy costs are 50 percent ($\alpha = 0.5$), and the corporate tax rate is 35 percent ($\tau = 0.35$).

Recall that equations (27) to (29) hold only for the protected debt case with no bankruptcy costs. We have not been able to find closed-form solutions when $\alpha > 0$. Equation (28) implies that $[(1 - \tau)(C^*/r) - V_B^*] = -\tau C^*/r < 0$, when $\alpha = 0$. From equation (13), this implies that *equity is a strictly concave function of V*. By continuity, equity will be concave when α is close to zero. And in the numerical example considered in Section VI, equity is strictly concave in V for all α.

The observed comparative statics of optimal protected debt value (and related values) are given in Table III. There are some important differences with the comparative statics of optimal unprotected debt value. The debt yield and the yield spread at the optimum rise rather than fall as bankruptcy costs rise. The yield spread also increases as the risk-free interest rate rises, although the magnitude is small. The optimal leverage ratio, (D^*/v^*), *declines* as the corporate tax rate increases, when bankruptcy costs are low. Optimal debt, D^*, increases with τ, but (unlike the unprotected debt case) increases less rapidly than v^*.

VI. Discussion and Variations: Debt Value and Capital Structure

Our analysis has determined optimal leverage ratios and associated yield spreads in a variety of environments, for both long-term unprotected debt

Debt Value, Bond Covenants, and Optimal Capital Structure   1239

Table III
Comparative Statics of Financial Variables at the Optimal Leverage Ratio: Protected Debt

This table describes the behavior of the coupon, C^*, that maximizes firm value, and the debt, D^*, leverage, L^*, interest rate, R^*, yield spread, $R^* - r$, total firm value, v^*, equity value, E^*, and bankruptcy value, V_B^*, at the optimal coupon level, for debt protected by a positive net-worth covenant. V is the firm's asset value, σ^2 is the variance of asset returns, r is the risk-free interest rate, α is the fraction of asset value lost if bankruptcy occurs, and τ is the corporate tax rate.

Variable	Shape	σ^2	r	α	τ
C^*	Linear in V	$< 0^b$	> 0	< 0	$> 0^a$
D^*	Linear in V	< 0	> 0	< 0	$> 0^a$
L^*	Invariant to V	< 0	> 0	< 0	< 0, α small[b]; > 0, α large
R^*	Invariant to V	$> 0^a$	> 0	$> 0^b$	$> 0^a$
$R^* - r$	Invariant to V	$> 0^a$	$> 0^b$	$> 0^b$	$> 0^a$
v^*	Linear in V	< 0	> 0	< 0	> 0
E^*	Linear in V	> 0	< 0	> 0	> 0, α small[b]; < 0, α large
V_B^*	Linear in V	< 0	> 0	< 0	$> 0^a$

[a] No effect if $\alpha = 0$.
[b] Represents different behavior from unprotected debt.

and protected (or continuously rolled-over) debt. It is of interest to compare these results with typical leverage ratios and yield spreads in the United States. Leverage in companies with highly rated debt is generally less than 40 percent. Yields of investment-grade corporate bonds have exceeded Treasury bond yields by a minimum of 15 basis points (bps), and a maximum of 215 bps from 1926 to 1986. The average yield spread over this period was 77 bps.[32] These spreads reflect finite-maturity debt and also reflect the fact that corporate debt typically is callable. Call provisions may add about 25 bps to the annual cost of corporate debt.[33] Subtracting 25 bps from the average yield spread of 77 bps to eliminate the impact of call provisions gives an adjusted historical yield spread of about 52 bps.

We examine a base case where the volatility of the firm's assets is 20 percent, the corporate tax rate is 35 percent, the risk-free rate is 6 percent, and bankruptcy costs are 50 percent. In this case, optimal leverage with unprotected debt is 75 percent and the yield spread is 75 bps. The optimally

---
[32] As reported by Kim, Ramaswamy, and Sundaresan (1993); see also Sarig and Warga (1989).
[33] Kim, Ramaswamy, and Sundaresan (1993) estimate a call premium of 22 bps using a numerical example.

levered firm's equity is volatile, with a 57 percent annual standard deviation. Reducing the effective tax rate would reduce optimal leverage and the yield spread. For example, with an effective tax rate of 15 percent, optimal leverage is 59 percent, and the yield spread is 35 bps. Equity volatility is lower, but still substantial.

It is clear that, based on our assumptions thus far, the analysis of unprotected debt suggests optimal leverage considerably in excess of current practice. This could be construed as a criticism of current management rather than the model. Managers may be loath to pay out "free cash flow" (see Jensen (1986)); the wave of leveraged buyouts in the late 1980s suggests that firm value may be raised by using greater leverage (see Kaplan (1989) and Leland (1989)). However, the model's predicted yield spreads seem low given the suggested high leverage.

Optimal leverage ratios and yield spreads for protected debt are more consistent with historical ratios. In the base case, optimal leverage is 45 percent and the yield spread is 45 bps. Equity has a 34 percent annual standard deviation, which is a bit higher than the historical average equity risk of a single firm of about 30 percent.

We now consider how variations in the assumptions may affect the nature of optimal leverage and yield spreads, in both the unprotected and protected cases.

A. No Tax Shelter for Interest Payments When Value Falls

We have assumed that the deductibility of interest payments generates tax savings at all values above the bankruptcy level. But as firm asset value drops, it is quite possible that profits will be less than the coupon payout and tax savings will not be fully realized (or will be substantially postponed). If lesser tax benefits are available, the optimal leverage ratio declines.

In Appendix A, we extend the analysis to allow for no tax benefits whenever $V < V_T$, where V_T is an exogenously specified level of firm asset value.[34] In the base case considered above, optimal leverage falls from 75 to 70 percent, and the yield spread at the optimal leverage rises from 75 to 87 bps, when $V_T = 90$, i.e., 90 percent of the current asset value.

A possible criticism of the above approach is that V_T does not depend upon the amount of debt the firm has issued. Consider an alternative scenario in which higher profit is needed if higher coupon payments are to be fully deductible. For example, assume that the rate of EBIT is related to asset value as follows:

$$\text{EBIT} = (V - 60)/6. \tag{30}$$

Thus gross profit before interest drops to zero when V falls to 60 and represents one-sixth of asset value in excess of 60. Further, assume that

---

[34] We do not allow tax loss carryforwards in this analysis, since they would introduce a form of time (and path) dependence. Thus, we may overstate the loss of tax shields: the "truth" perhaps lies somewhere between the previous results and the results of this analysis.

Debt Value, Bond Covenants, and Optimal Capital Structure

coupon payments, C, can be deducted from profit (for tax purposes) only if EBIT $- C \geq 0$. (We ignore partial deductibility.) It then follows that

$$V_T = 60 + 6C. \tag{31}$$

In contrast with the previous scenario, greater debt now has a greater likelihood of losing its tax benefits.[35] Optimal leverage falls to 65 percent. The yield spread falls to 61 bps, reflecting the lesser leverage. Equity volatility remains high at 51 percent. In the case of protected debt, the loss of tax deductibility has a much smaller effect on optimal leverage and yield spread. As expected, the loss of tax deductibility reduces the maximum value of the firm in all cases.

B. Net Cash Payouts by the Firm

Following Brennan and Schwartz (1978) and others, we have focused on the case where the firm has no net cash outflows resulting from payments to bondholders or stockholders. We now change this assumption.[36] Net cash outflows may occur because dividends are paid to shareholders, and/or because after-tax coupon expenses are being paid, without fully offsetting equity financing. In this latter case, assets are being liquidated and the scale of the firm's activities is clearly affected by the extent of debt financing.

To keep matters analytically tractable, we consider only cash outflows that are proportional to firm asset value, where the proportion, d, may depend on the coupon paid on debt. Equation (3) is replaced by

$$(1/2)\sigma^2 V^2 F_{VV}(V) + (r-d)VF_V(V) - rF(V) + C = 0, \tag{32}$$

with general solution

$$F(V, t) = A_0 + A_1 V^{-Y} + A_2 V^{-X}, \tag{33}$$

where

$$X = \left\{(r - d - 0.5\sigma^2) + \left[(r - d - 0.5\sigma^2)^2 + 2\sigma^2 r\right]^{1/2}\right\}/\sigma^2 \tag{34}$$

$$Y = \left\{(r - d - 0.5\sigma^2) - \left[(r - d - 0.5\sigma^2)^2 + 2\sigma^2 r\right]^{1/2}\right\}/\sigma^2. \tag{35}$$

Boundary conditions remain unchanged, implying $A_1 = 0$ as before since $Y \leq -1$. Therefore, solutions for all security values will have exactly the same functional form as before, but with the exponent, X, given by equation (34) rather than equation (5).

When $d = 0.01$, a one-percent payout on asset value (equivalent to approximately a 3 percent dividend on equity value, given the leverage of the base

---

[35] In the base case the optimal coupon falls to $5.08, implying V_T is about 90, as above.
[36] The reader may wonder how equity value could be positive if the firm never pays dividends. But our earlier assumption is *not* that firms never pay dividends—rather, there is no net cash outflow: any cash dividends must be financed by issuing new equity. Like Black and Scholes (1973), our model is a partial equilibrium one, and simply assumes the process for V.

case), the optimal leverage falls from 75 to 74 percent, and the yield spread rises from 75 to 86 bps. But what if payouts also depend upon the coupon being paid to debtholders? Consider the case where the proportional payout is sufficient to cover the after-tax cost of debt when it is initially offered.[37] Normalizing the initial value of V to 100 implies a payout $d = (1 - \tau)C/100$, or $0.0065C$ in the above example. Any dividend payout would be in addition to this amount. For the base case above, we search over coupon levels, C, that maximize v, subject to the constraint that $d = 0.0065C + 0.01$. This reduces optimal leverage from 75 to 64 percent and increases the yield spread at the optimum from 75 to 124 bps. The volatility of equity falls from 57 to 42 percent. In the case of protected debt, optimal leverage falls from 45 to 36 percent, the yield spread increases from 45 to 49 bps, and the volatility of equity falls from 34 to 29 percent.

The maximum firm value drops from $128.4 to $122.0 with unprotected debt, and from $113.3 to $110.0 with protected debt. This decrease in maximal value reflects the fact that bankruptcy is more likely with cash payouts, with a resulting loss of tax benefits. Therefore, ex ante, *shareholders (as well as bondholders) benefit from a covenant that prevents the firm from selling assets to meet coupon payments.* It is not surprising that many debt instruments have such a preventive covenant. But if such a covenant cannot be written (or cannot be enforced), shareholders will benefit (at bondholders' expense) from the firm selling assets to pay coupons *after* the debt has been issued. Recognizing this incentive, debtholders will pay less for debt and the optimal leverage will fall as indicated above.

C. Absolute Priority Not Respected

We have assumed that debtholders receive all assets (after costs) if bankruptcy occurs, and stockholders none: the "absolute priority" rule. Now consider a simple alternative, where debtholders receive some fraction $(1 - b)$ of remaining assets, $(1 - \alpha)V_B$, while equity holders receive $b(1 - \alpha)V_B$.[38] This will affect debt value in two ways: debtholders will receive less value if bankruptcy occurs, and bankruptcy will occur at a different level V_B.

It can readily be shown that equation (7) will be replaced by

$$D(V) = C/r + [(1 - b)(1 - \alpha)V_B - C/r][V/V_B]^{-X}, \qquad (36)$$

---

[37] Note that as value falls, the proportional payout will no longer completely cover the after-tax coupon—some equity financing becomes necessary. This may not be unreasonable, since bondholders will become increasingly sensitive to liquidation of assets as firm value approaches the bankruptcy level.

[38] Franks and Torous (1989) estimate that deviations in favor of equity holders in Chapter 11 reorganizations are only 2.3 percent of the value of the reorganized firm. Eberhart, Moore, and Roenfeldt (1990) estimate average equity deviations of 7.8 percent for their sample of Chapter 11 firms. We choose a 10 percent deviation as an upper bound for this effect.

Debt Value, Bond Covenants, and Optimal Capital Structure

and equation (14) will be replaced by

$$V_B = (1 - \tau)C/[r(1 - b + \alpha b)][X/(1 + X)]. \tag{37}$$

For the base case with unprotected debt, deviations from absolute priority of 10 percent ($b = 0.1$) cause the optimal leverage ratio to fall from 75 to 72 percent. The yield spread remains at 75 bps. The effect of deviations from absolute priority are also minor when debt is protected: leverage remains unchanged at 45 percent, while the yield spread rises from 45 to 51 bps.

D. All of the Above

As a final exercise, consider the base case where, in addition, (i) dividends equal 3 percent of equity value; (ii) after-tax coupon payments are *not* initially financed with additional equity; (iii) coupon payments are not tax deductible when $V < V_T = 60 + 6C$; and (iv) there is a 10 percent deviation from absolute priority ($b = 0.1$). When these conditions hold simultaneously, the optimal leverage with unprotected debt falls to 47 percent and the yield spread is 69 bps. The annual standard deviation of equity is 36 percent. For protected debt, the optimal leverage falls to 32 percent, the yield spread is 52 bps and the standard deviation of equity is 29 percent. These last numbers seem quite in line with historical yield spreads, leverage ratios, and equity risks.

VII. Protected versus Unprotected Debt: Potential Agency Problems

Our results suggest that optimal leverage ratios are lower when debt is protected, and that the maximal gains to leverage are less. This raises a key question: why should firms issue protected debt? The answer may lie with agency problems created by debt, and asset substitution in particular. Jensen and Meckling (1976) argue that equity holders would prefer to make the firm's activities riskier, ceteris paribus, so as to increase equity value at the expense of debt value. The expected cost to debtholders will be passed back to equity holders in a rational expectations equilibrium, through lower prices on newly issued debt.

Higher firm asset risk tends to benefit equity holders when equity is a strictly convex function of firm asset value, V. And equity is strictly convex in V when debt is unprotected. In Section V, however, it was shown that equity may be a strictly *concave* function of V when debt has a positive net-worth covenant. With protected debt, stockholders may *not* have an incentive to increase firm risk at debtholders' expense.

To illustrate our point, consider the base case above with different levels of asset volatility. If debt is unprotected, the optimal coupon is $6.50, firm value is $128.4, and V_B is $52.8. If debt is protected, the optimal coupon is $3.26, firm value is $113.3, and V_B is $50.6. Assume that, ex post, managers can raise the risk of the firm's assets from the current annual standard deviation

Table IV
Values of Protected and Unprotected Debt and Equity for Different Levels of Risk

This table gives the values of debt and equity for both unprotected and protected debt, when the coupon (in each case) is chosen to maximize total firm value given a 20 percent asset volatility, but asset volatility may be increased by management to higher levels.

	Unprotected Debt		Protected Debt	
Asset Volatility (%)	Debt Value ($)	Equity Value ($)	Debt Value ($)	Equity Value ($)
20	96.3	32.1	50.6	62.7
40	70.4	45.9	36.9	55.5
60	52.6	59.1	31.2	52.5

of 20 percent—with no change in current asset value V. Will they be motivated to engage in such "asset substitution"? Using equations (7) and (13), and recalling from equation (14) that V_B will change when debt is unprotected but not when debt is protected, gives the results reported in Table IV.

Debtholders are hurt by higher risk. In the case of unprotected debt, equity value is enhanced by greater risk. Without covenants to prevent such a change, it will always be in the interest of equityholders to increase risk. *But the opposite is true when debt is protected by a positive net worth covenant*: in this case, increasing risk lowers equity value as well as debt value.[39]

In the absence of protective covenants, investors recognize that shareholders will wish to raise asset volatility to the maximum (60 percent). They will pay only $52.6 for the debt, and total firm value will be $111.7. If the firm offers protected debt, investors recognize that shareholders will have no interest in increasing firm risk, and total firm value will be $113.30. The firm maximizes value by issuing protected rather than unprotected debt. (Even if the firm initially chose to issue the amount of unprotected debt optimal for a 60 percent volatility, the total firm value would be $112.1—less than the maximal value with protected debt.)

A reevaluation of the belief that asset substitution is always advantageous for equity holders seems warranted. It is true for unprotected debt, but it is false in the case examined here, when debt is protected by a positive net-worth covenant. Both debt and equity are concave functions of asset value

---

[39] The difference in behavior as σ changes reflects the convexity (concavity) of equity in V when debt is unprotected (protected). In addition, V_B changes in the unprotected case as σ changes. This latter effect explains the curious result in Section II.A, that (for V close to V_B) an increase in firm risk can raise unprotected debt value. Thus, there is yet a further anomaly with unprotected debt: at the brink of bankruptcy (and only there), both debtholders and stockholders wish to increase firm risk!

Debt Value, Bond Covenants, and Optimal Capital Structure

in this case.[40] The greater incentive compatibility of protected debt may well explain its prevalence (or the prevalence of short-term financing), despite the fact that, ceteris paribus, it exploits the tax advantage of debt less effectively.

VIII. Restructuring via Debt Repurchase or Debt Renegotiation: Some Preliminary Thoughts

The preceding analysis has assumed that the coupon, C, of the debt issue is fixed through time. In the absence of transactions costs, restructuring by continuous readjustments of C would seem to be desirable to maximize total firm value as V fluctuates. However, we shall see that continuous readjustments of C by debt repurchase (issuance) may be blocked by stockholders (debtholders).[41] *Debt renegotiation* may be required to maximize total firm value in these cases.

To prove this contention, first consider the firm selling a small amount of additional debt, thereby increasing the current debt service by dC. This will change the total value of debt by

$$dD = (\partial D/\partial C)dC. \qquad (38)$$

But this total value change will be shared by current and new debtholders. New debtholders will hold a fraction dC/C of the total debt value, leaving current debtholders with value

$$(D + dD)(1 - dC/C) = D + dD - (D/C)dC, \qquad (39)$$

(ignoring terms of $O(dC^2)$). The change from D, the current debtholders' value before the debt issuance, is

$$[(\partial D/\partial C) - (D/C)]dC < 0 \quad \text{for } dC > 0, \qquad (40)$$

with the inequality resulting from the concavity of D in C and the fact that $D = 0$ when $C = 0$. This "dilution" result holds for arbitrary initial V and C, implying current *debtholders will always resist increasing the total coupon payments through additional debt issuance*, even though such sales may increase the value of equity and the firm. This resistance is frequently codified in debt covenants that restrict additional debt issuance at greater or equal seniority.[42]

---

[40] This, of course, is consistent with the earlier result, equation (12), where total firm value, v, is concave in V. Concavity of v follows from the concavity of tax benefits and convexity of bankruptcy costs (which are subtracted).

[41] We consider debt issuance/repurchase for capital restructuring only. Any funds raised by debt issuance will be used to retire equity, and vice-versa. Debt raised for new investment, or retired by asset sales, are asset-changing decisions that are not considered here.

[42] Our analysis assumes a single class of debt, implying that newly issued debt has the same seniority in the event of bankruptcy. Even if the newly issued debt is junior to the current debt, it will reduce the value of the current debt by raising V_B. A full analysis of multiple classes of debt securities is beyond the scope of the present article.

A related result on debt repurchase is perhaps more surprising: current shareholders will always resist *decreasing* the coupon, C, by repurchasing current debt (in small amounts) on the open market. To prove this, consider a small decrease, $dC < 0$, and its effect on current shareholders. The total value of equity will change by

$$dE = (\partial E / \partial C) dC \tag{41}$$

The cost of retiring debt will equal the value of the fraction of debt retired, or $-D(dC/C)$. This cost must be financed with newly issued equity, whose value is included in the change in total equity value above. Current shareholders will therefore have equity value

$$E + dE + D(dC/C), \tag{42}$$

implying a change in value to current shareholders of

$$[(\partial E / \partial C) + (D/C)] dC, \tag{43}$$

using equation (41). For unprotected debt, it follows from equations (15) and (17) that $[(\partial E / \partial C) + (D/C)] > 0$, implying that the change in equity value to the original shareholders is negative when $dC < 0$. This result holds for arbitrary initial V and C. Therefore, it will never be optimal for the firm's shareholders to restructure by retiring unprotected debt via small open market repurchases financed by new equity.[43] In Appendix B, we show that the result also holds for small repurchases of protected debt, when the coupon is near its optimal level.

To illustrate the arguments above, consider the base case with unprotected debt. With $V = \$100$, the optimal coupon is $\$6.50$ and $V_B = \$52.80$. Assume this coupon level has been chosen by the firm. Now let V drop from $\$100$ to $\$90$. Using equations (7) and (13) to compute the current values of debt and equity gives: $D = \$91.79$, $E = \$23.14$, and $v = \$114.93$. The firm's total value can now be increased by reducing debt. The firm should cut its coupon by 10 percent to $\$5.85$, since C^* is proportional to V, which has fallen from $\$100$ to $\$90$. This would increase the total firm value from $\$114.93$ to $\$115.60$.

But consider the firm repurchasing 10 percent of its debt to achieve the new optimal leverage. The coupon is reduced from $\$6.50$ to $\$5.85$, and V_B falls by 10 percent to $\$47.52$. The firm must pay (at least) $\$9.18$ to retire 10 percent of the bonds whose value is $\$91.79$ prior to repurchase.[44] It will raise this amount by issuing additional stock worth $\$9.18$. Again using equations (7) and (13) to compute debt and equity values with the lower coupon gives: $D = \$86.65$, and $E = \$28.95$.

---

[43] This debt repurchase result holds even if there are multiple classes of debt. Stockholders might benefit from retiring debt via asset sales, but this would violate the assumption that the asset value, V, is independent of the firm's capital structure.

[44] Note that debt becomes more valuable per unit, as the coupon is reduced. We are assuming here that the entire amount of repurchase can be effected at the lowest (i.e., current) price. Any higher price would magnify the losses to equity holders.

Debtholders are clearly better off, having received payments of $9.18 to retire 10 percent of their holdings, plus retaining holdings worth $86.65. The original equity holders have had their stock diluted: $9.18 of stock—the amount raised to pay the debtholders—now belongs to new shareholders, leaving the original shareholders with stock worth $28.95 − $9.18 = $19.77. This is less than the $23.14 value of their shares prior to repurchase. Although the total value of the firm would be increased by the restructuring, *equity holders cannot benefit from the repurchase, and will want to block such refinancing*. This problem results from an externality: when debt is reduced, its "quality" is improved. Investors who continue to hold the firm's debt receive a windfall gain from the debt repurchase.

The example shows that restructuring through debt repurchases or sales may not be possible, although such changes could increase total firm value. To capture such potential increases, changes in the terms of the debtholders' securities (or "side payments") will be required. These types of restructurings will be labeled *debt renegotiation*. In our example, replacing current debt with convertible debt may be used to achieve the optimal coupon level. By agreeing to exchange the current debt for debt with coupon $5.85 (worth $86.65), plus a convertibility privilege into stock worth (say) $5.50, debtholders receive a security worth $92.15. This exceeds the $91.79 value of the current debt paying a $6.50 coupon, so bondholders will benefit. Stockholders will also benefit by the rise in the equity value of $5.81 ($28.95 − $23.14) less the $5.50 value of the convertibility option given bondholders.

Renegotiation of unprotected debt is particularly simple when bankruptcy is imminent (V is close to V_B), and $C > C_{max}(V)$. In this case, a small reduction in the coupon will increase the value of both debt and equity—with no further compensation to bondholders (such as the convertibility privilege) being required. The firm may be able to reduce its coupon payment all the way to $C^*(V)$ with no additional payments to bondholders if the value of debt $D^*(V)$ at the optimal coupon is greater than the value of debt $D(V)$ when the renegotiation begins. This assumes stockholders can credibly make a "take-it-or-leave-it" offer to bondholders. Note that the firm may wait until the brink of bankruptcy before renegotiating, since this will minimize $D(V)$.

IX. Conclusion

By assuming a debt structure with time-independent payouts, we have been able to develop closed-form solutions for the value of debt and for optimal capital structure. This permits a detailed analysis of the behavior of bond prices and optimal debt-equity ratios as firm asset value, risk, taxes, interest rates, bond covenants, payout rates, and bankruptcy costs change.

The analysis examines two types of bonds: those that are protected by a positive net-worth covenant, and those that are not. The distinction is critical in determining when bankruptcy is triggered, which in turn affects bond values and optimal leverage. To be rolled over, short-term financing typically requires that the firm maintain positive net worth. Therefore short-term financing seems to correspond to our model of protected debt. Long-term debt, in contrast, rarely has positive net-worth covenants; it seems closer to our model of unprotected debt.

Our results indicate that protected debt values and unprotected "investment grade" debt values behave very much as expected. Unprotected "junk" bonds exhibit quite different behavior. For example, an increase in firm risk will increase debt value, as will a decrease in the coupon. Such behavior is not exhibited by protected "junk" bonds.

Two curious aspects of optimal leverage are observed. First, a rise in the risk-free interest rate (increasing the cost of debt financing) leads to a *greater* optimal debt level. Higher interest rates generate greater tax benefits, which in turn dictate more debt despite its higher cost. Second, the optimal debt for firms with higher bankruptcy costs may carry a *lower* interest rate than for firms with lower bankruptcy costs. This is because firms will choose significantly lower optimal leverage when bankruptcy costs are substantial, making debt less risky. This result does not hold for protected debt: higher bankruptcy costs imply higher interest rates at the optimal leverage.

Optimal leverage, yield ratios, and equity risk are well within historical norms for protected debt. But optimal leverage seems high (and/or yield spreads seem low) for unprotected debt. Variants of the basic assumptions, discussed in Section VI, are needed for unprotected debt to fall within historical norms. The most important modification is dropping the requirement that payouts to bondholders be externally financed.

Issuing debt without protective net-worth covenants yields greater tax benefits and would seem to dominate issuing protected debt. However, this conclusion may be reversed if firms have the ability to increase the riskiness of their activities through "asset substitution." Increasing risk will transfer value from bondholders to stockholders when debt is unprotected, leading cautious bondholders to demand higher interest rates even when the firm currently has low risk. But such costs typically are not incurred when firms issue protected debt: stockholders will *not* gain by increasing firm risk when debt is protected by a positive net-worth covenant, and bondholders will not need to demand higher interest rates in anticipation of riskier firm activities. Protected debt may be the preferred form of financing in these situations, despite having lower potential tax benefits.

Our results offer some preliminary insights on debt repurchases and on debt renegotiations. The former cannot be used to adjust leverage continuously to its optimal level: bondholders will block further debt issuance, and shareholders will block (marginal) debt reductions. Debt renegotiation can achieve simultaneous increases in debt and equity value. But the costly nature of renegotiation suggests it would be suboptimal to do so continuously (see Fischer, Heinkel, and Zechner (1989)). Our analysis shows that it may be desirable for shareholders to wait until the brink of bankruptcy before renegotiating. When bankruptcy is neared, a reduction in coupon payments to the optimal level may benefit both stockholders and bondholders, without additional side payments.

Although we have not emphasized equity values, our analysis also provides some interesting insights. Equity return volatility will be stochastic, changing with the level of firm asset value, V. This (and the possibility of bankruptcy) has important ramifications for option pricing.[45]

The model can be extended in several further dimensions. Multiple classes of long-term debt can be analyzed, recognizing that payments to the various classes of debtholders when bankruptcy occurs are determined by seniority. More difficult extensions will include finite-lived debt, dynamic restructuring, and a stochastic term structure of risk-free interest rates.

Appendix A

We assume in this case that instantaneous tax benefits = 0 whenever $V \leq V_T$. There are no carryforwards. Differential equation (3) with $C = 0$ has solution:

$$TB(V) = A_1 V + A_2 V^{-X}, \quad V_B < V \leq V_T. \tag{44}$$

Differential equation (3) with instantaneous tax benefit τC realized has solution:

$$TB(V) = (\tau C/r) + B_2 V^{-X}, \quad V \geq V_T. \tag{45}$$

$TB(V)$ must satisfy:

$$TB[V_B] = A_1 V_B + A_2 V_B^{-X} = 0 \tag{46}$$

$$TB(V_T) = A_1 V_T + A_2 V_T^{-X} = (\tau C/r) + B_2 V_T^{-X} \tag{47}$$

$$TB'(V_T) = A_1 - X A_2 V_T^{-X-1} = -X B_2 V_T^{-X-1} \tag{48}$$

Solutions:

$$A_1 = (\tau C/r)(X/(X+1))(1/V_T) \tag{49}$$

$$A_2 = -(\tau C/r)(X/(X+1))(V_B^{X+1}/V_T) \tag{50}$$

$$B_2 = -(\tau C/r)(X/(X+1))(1/V_T)(V_B^{X+1} + (1/X)V_T^{X+1}) \tag{51}$$

Substituting for tax benefits from equation (44) into equation (13) for equity gives, for $V \leq V_T$,

$$E = v - D = V + A_1 V + A_2 V^{-X} - C/r - [V_B - (C/r)](V/V_B)^{-X}. \tag{52}$$

To find V_B, we again set $dE/dV|_{V=V_B} = 0$:

dE/dV

$$= 1 + A_1 - X A_2 V^{-X-1} + X[V_B - (C/r)](V/V_B)^{-X-1}(1/V_B) = 0. \tag{53}$$

---
[45] Preliminary work on this question has been done by Klaus Toft (1993).

Evaluating equation (53) at $V = V_B$:

$$1 + A_1 - XA_2 V_B^{-X-1} + X - (C/r)(X/V_B) = 0. \tag{54}$$

Substituting for A_1 and A_2 gives

$$V_B = CV_T X / [rV_T(1 + X) + \tau CX]. \tag{55}$$

D can be computed from equation (7); and

$$v = V + (\tau C/r) + B_2 V^{-X} - \alpha V_B (V/V_B)^{-X}, \quad V > V_T. \tag{56}$$

Note we can rewrite the expression for V_B as

$$V_B = \underline{V}_B V_T / [(1 - \tau) V_T + \tau \underline{V}_B] > \underline{V}_B \tag{57}$$

with the last inequality holding since $V_T > \underline{V}_B$, where $\underline{V}_B$ satisfies equation (14).

Appendix B

Parallel to the discussion following equation (43), we know that shareholders will reject a buyback of debt (i.e., $dC < 0$) if $[(\partial E/\partial C) + (D/C)] > 0$. Since $E = v - D$,

$$[(\partial E/\partial C) + (D/C)] = \{\partial v/\partial C - [(\partial D/\partial C) - (D/C)]\}. \tag{58}$$

Define V^* as the firm asset value at which the current coupon would be optimal for protected debt, i.e., for which $\partial v(V^*)/\partial C = 0$. From equation (40), it follows that $[(\partial D/\partial C) - (D/C)]$ will be strictly negative, and therefore equation (58) will be strictly positive when $\partial v/\partial C = 0$. Continuity implies that there exists a neighborhood of values, V, around the value V^*, for which equation (58) is strictly positive. For all $V < V^*$ in this neighborhood, firm value, v, would be increased by lowering the coupon, since the optimal coupon is decreasing in V. But because equation (58) is positive in this neighborhood, current stockholders' equity value will fall when $dC < 0$ and shareholders will resist reducing the coupon to its optimal level.

REFERENCES

Altman, E., 1984, A further empirical investigation of the bankruptcy cost question, *Journal of Finance* 39, 1067–1090.

Anderson, R., and S. Sundaresan, 1992, Design and valuation of debt contracts, Working paper, Universite Catholique de Louvain.

Asquith, P., R. Gertner, and D. Scharfstein, 1991, Anatomy of financial distress: An examination of junk bond issuers, Working paper, University of Chicago.

Baxter, N., 1967, Leverage, risk of ruin, and the cost of capital, *Journal of Finance* 22, 395–403.

Black, F., and J. Cox, 1976, Valuing corporate securities: Some effects of bond indenture provisions, *Journal of Finance* 31, 351–367.

Debt Value, Bond Covenants, and Optimal Capital Structure   1251

Black, F., and M. Scholes, 1973, The pricing of options and corporate liabilities, *Journal of Political Economy* 81, 637-654.

Brennan, M., and E. Schwartz, 1978, Corporate income taxes, valuation, and the problem of optimal capital structure, *Journal of Business* 51, 103-114.

———, 1980, Analyzing convertible bonds, *Journal of Financial and Quantitative Analysis* 15, 907-932.

———, 1984, Optimal financial policy and firm valuation, *Journal of Finance* 39, 593-607.

Eberhart, A., W. Moore, and R. Roenfeldt, 1990, Security pricing and deviations from the absolute priority rule in bankruptcy proceedings, *Journal of Finance* 45, 1457-1469.

Fischer, E., R. Heinkel, and J. Zechner, 1989, Dynamic capital structure choice: Theory and tests, *Journal of Finance* 44, 19-40.

Franks, J., and W. Torous, 1989, An empirical investigation of firms in reorganization, *Journal of Finance* 44, 747-779.

Fries, S., M. H. Miller, and W. Perraudin, 1993, Pricing bond default premia in a competitive industry equilibrium with costs of entry and exit, Working paper, University of Cambridge.

Harris, M., and A. Raviv, 1991, The theory of capital structure, *Journal of Finance* 44, 297-355.

Haugen, R., and L. Senbet, 1978, The insignificance of bankruptcy costs to the theory of optimal capital structure, *Journal of Finance* 33, 383-392.

Jensen, M., and W. Meckling, 1976, Theory of the firm: Managerial behavior, agency costs, and ownership structure, *Journal of Financial Economics* 4, 305-360.

Jensen, M., 1986, The agency costs of free cash flow: Corporate finance and takeovers, *American Economic Review* 76, 323-329.

Jones, E., S. Mason, and E. Rosenfeld, 1984, Contingent claims analysis of corporate capital structures: An empirical investigation, *Journal of Finance* 39, 611-625.

Kane, A., A. Marcus, and R. McDonald, 1984, How big is the tax advantage to debt?, *Journal of Finance* 39, 841-852.

Kaplan, S., 1989, Management buyouts: Evidence on taxes as a source of value, *Journal of Finance* 44, 611-632.

Kim, E. H., 1978, A mean-variance theory of optimal capital structure and corporate debt capacity, *Journal of Finance* 33, 45-64.

Kim, I., K. Ramaswamy, and S. Sundaresan, 1993, Does default risk in coupons affect the valuation of corporate bonds?: A contingent claims model, *Financial Management* 22, 117-131.

Kraus, A., and R. Litzenberger, 1973, A state-preference model of optimal financial leverage, *Journal of Finance* 28, 911-922.

Leland, H., 1989, LBOs and taxes: No one to blame but ourselves?, *California Management Review* 32, 19-28.

Longstaff, F., and E. Schwartz, 1992, Valuing risky debt: A new approach, Working paper, University of California, Los Angeles.

Mauer, D., and A. Triantis, 1993, Interactions of investment decisions and corporate financing policies, Working paper, University of Wisconsin.

Mella, P., and W. Perraudin, 1993, Strategic debt service, Working paper, University of Cambridge.

Mello, A., and J. Parsons, 1992, The agency costs of debt, *Journal of Finance* 47, 1887-1904.

Merton, R., 1973, A rational theory of option pricing, *Bell Journal of Economics and Management Science* 4, 141-183.

———, 1974, On the pricing of corporate debt: The risk structure of interest rates, *Journal of Finance* 29, 449-469.

Miller, M., 1977, Debt and taxes, *Journal of Finance* 32, 261-275.

Modigliani, F., and M. Miller, 1958, The cost of capital, corporation finance and the theory of investment, *American Economic Review* 48, 267-297.

Myers, S., 1984, The capital structure puzzle, *Journal of Finance* 39, 575-592.

———, and N. Majluf, 1984, Corporate financing and investment decisions when firms have information that investors do not have, *Journal of Financial Economics* 5, 187-221.

Sarig, O., and A. Warga, 1989, Some empirical estimates of the risk structure of interest rates, *Journal of Finance* 44, 1351–1360.

Scott, J., 1976, A theory of optimal capital structure, *Bell Journal of Economics and Management Science* 7, 33–54.

Smith, C., and J. Warner, 1979, On financial contracting: An analysis of bond covenants, *Journal of Financial Economics* 7, 117–161.

Titman, S., and R. Wessels, 1988, The determinants of capital structure choice, *Journal of Finance* 43, 1–20.

Toft, K., 1993, Options on leveraged equity with default risk, Working paper, Haas School of Business, University of California, Berkeley.

Warner, J., 1977, Bankruptcy costs: Some evidence, *Journal of Finance* 32, 337–347.

Part III
Hedging, Disclosure Policy and Insider Trading

Corporate Financial Hedging with Proprietary Information

Peter M. DeMarzo

Kellogg Graduate School of Management, Northwestern University, Evanston, Illinois 60208

AND

Darrell Duffie[†]

Graduate School of Business, Stanford University, Stanford, California 94305

Received March 6, 1989; revised July 31, 1990

If a firm has information pertinent to its own dividend stream that is not made available to its shareholders, it may be in the interests of the firm and its shareholders to adopt a financial hedging policy. This is in contrast with the Modigliani–Miller Theorem, which implies that, with informational symmetry, such financial hedging is irrelevant. In certain cases, hedging policies are identified that are unanimously supported by shareholders. *Journal of Economic Literature* Classification Numbers: 021, 022, 026, 313, 521.   © 1991 Academic Press, Inc.

1. Introduction

The purpose of this paper is to demonstrate that, if a firm has information pertinent to its own dividend stream that is not made available to its shareholders, it may be in the interests of its shareholders for the firm to adopt an appropriate financial hedging policy. Moreover, though markets are incomplete, circumstances are identified in which there exist optimal hedging policies that are unanimously supported by all shareholders of the firm. Finally, even though hedging may be costly (i.e., a risk premium must be paid), these policies typically call for the firm to hedge the risk "completely."

---

* We acknowledge the comments and discussion provided by Karen Van Nuys, Peter Hammond, David Hirshleifer, Hayne Leland, David Starrett, and an anonymous referee.

[†] The support of Batterymarch Financial Management is gratefully acknowledged.

Our results are in direct contrast with the Modigliani–Miller (MM) theory [20], which implies that with informational symmetry and the usual perfect market assumptions, corporate financial policy has no effect on firm value. This theory is based on the presumption that any financial strategy the firm might adopt could equally well be adopted pro rata by its shareholders, implying its irrelevance in markets without transactions costs, bankruptcy costs, taxes, principal-agent effects, and similar "imperfections." (For a general form of the MM theory, see DeMarzo [7]; for work indicating cases in which it may not apply, see Miller [19].)

In practice, publicly traded firms commonly pay a great deal of attention to their financial policies and, in particular, account for the bulk of hedging positions in futures and forward markets. While many different practical considerations might justify this behavior, it seems worthwhile to model one in particular: Firms have proprietary information. The privacy of this information may be of strategic importance in the firm's marketplace, or may merely be due to the cost of disseminating up-to-date news on the corporation's production plans and other ventures. In any case, it is impossible for shareholders to adopt for themselves financial strategies that are based on information they do not have. The firm, however, may hedge on their behalf.

Private information held by managers of firms has been shown to overturn the MM conclusions in other settings as well. In particular, Jensen and Meckling [16] discuss the implications of a firm's capital structure on managerial incentives when managers' actions are not fully observable by shareholders. Also, Ross [21] shows the firm's capital structure decision may signal information to shareholders regarding the firm's prospects. Both these lines of research are very different than the motives for hedging considered here. First, we consider a case in which managers act on behalf of shareholders, and ignore problems of managerial incentive "misalignment." Second, we assume that the actual hedging portfolio held by a firm is not directly observable by shareholders, and hence is not used to signal information (shareholders may, however, infer information from price changes in securities markets).

Our results demonstrate that with regard to a financial hedging policy, there are circumstances for which unanimous agreement by shareholders can be attained. Moreover, the optimal policies we identify typically involve complete hedging of any "spanned" risk by the firm. This is true even for cases in which hedging is costly, in that futures contracts trade at their expected value plus some non-zero risk premium. Since any individual's portfolio would not be completely hedged under such circumstances, such policies imply the firm acts as though it were "infinitely" risk averse with regard to its financial policy. This contrasts with the production decisions of the firm, which generally would be made from a more risk neutral perspective. This behavioral dichotomy raises serious doubts regarding approaches to modeling firm objectives via a concave firm "utility" function. (See also Drèze [11] on this point.)

This paper is based on the intuition that the elimination of noise in a firm's dividend stream is unanimously supported by shareholders. In order to make succinct statements, however, we must in certain cases rely on the strong assumption that dividends include noise (with respect to the information available to shareholders) that is spanned by financial markets, given the information known to the firm. Our conclusions are thus related to the intuition of the spanning literature regarding production decisions, beginning with Diamond [9] and Ekern and Wilson [13], and extended by Leland [17]. They have shown that production changes within the span of existing markets are consistently evaluated by shareholders. Alternatively, in the absence of spanning, such shareholder unanimity regarding a redistribution of the firm's dividend stream is generically impossible (see DeMarzo [8], Duffie and Shafer [12], and Geanakoplos, Magill, Quinzii, and Drèze [14]).

A key premise of the paper is that there exist situations in which the firm chooses not to inform its shareholders of financial risks that they could otherwise hedge on security markets. Since shareholders do not known how to hedge these risks, they want the firm to hedge on their behalf. We only examine situations in which the firm hedges in a way that is unanimously supported by its shareholders, and thus the decision of the firm not to inform its shareholders of these risks is not to the shareholders' detriment, both in the competitive sense, and in a social welfare sense. Nevertheless, this still begs the question of why the firm holds propriety information in the first place.

We have not found a convenient way to model natural incentives for propriety information without obscuring our conclusions with additional interaction effects. For example, one of the incentives we allude to, but do not model, is the possibility that shareholders have some conflict of interest, being perhaps shareholders of other firms that could make strategic use of the proprietary information of the firm in question. Our model is competitive, and does not address these strategic effects.

For a different motivation for proprietary information, also non-competitive and also not modeled in this paper, suppose the firm wishes to take an asset position "silently," so as not to inform the rest of the market of the potential movement up or down the supply curve for the asset. In other words, the firm acts monopolistically, realizing that its own spot market commitments, when actually purchased or sold, will move the equilibrium price for those assets against itself. The firm can hedge against those effects by taking an offsetting, or partially offsetting, futures position. In many cases, a firm may try to do this silently by dealing with different brokers and gradually assuming a position without drawing attention to its intentions. By informing shareholders, the firm reveals its intent to purchase or sell, and forces the firm to bear the full costs of its impact on the supply curve for its target assets, rather than sharing some of those costs with the other side of its futures positions. Once again, we do not attempt to build these rather complicated effects into our model.

Finally, although there is nothing in our model that would suggest this, it is costly for firms to share their production plans and future spot market commitments with their shareholders on an ongoing basis. Moreover, there would often be time lags between the date on which a firm commits to its production plan and the dates that shareholders could individually hedge these plans.

The remainder of the paper proceeds as follows: Section 2 outlines the primitive notions in the model in a simple two-period setting under uncertainty. In order to provide some contrasting background to our results, Section 3 reviews the standard MM theory in our setting. Section 4 presents the basic idea that we have to offer in the bluntest possible terms; hopefully the reader will find the assumptions in later sections more palatable. Section 5 presents our notion of unanimously supported corporate financial hedging strategies. In Section 6, which could be viewed as the principal body of our results, we present unanimously supported hedging strategies in various settings. Finally, Section 7 shows that when firms adopt such financial hedging policies, the resulting equilibrium allocations are in fact constrained Pareto optimal. Concluding remarks are made in Section 8.

2. THE MODEL

For ease of exposition, we will examine a simple two-period economy with a single consumption good. In the first period, financial markets are open, and agents may trade securities and shares of firms. These securities and stocks entitle the agents to receive payoffs of the consumption good contingent upon the state of the economy, which is initially unknown. In the second period, this uncertain state is realized, and agents receive payoffs according to their portfolios. We formalize this model below.

2.1. *Agents*

We assume that the state of the economy is an element ω drawn from a set Ω, where the probability space $(\Omega, \mathscr{F}, \mathscr{P})$ is common knowledge. Let L denote the set of bounded, real-valued random variables on this space. Conditional expectation statements throughout the paper are implicitly "almost surely."

There is a finite set I of agents. A consumption plan for agent $i \in I$ is a random variable $c_i \in L$, where we interpret $c_i(\omega)$ as consumption in state ω. The preferences of agent i are described by a Von Neumann–Morgenstern utility function. That is, a consumption plan c has the utility

$$U_i(c) \equiv \mathbf{E}[u_i(c)|\mathcal{H}_i],$$

where u_i is strictly increasing, differentiable, and concave, and $\mathcal{H}_i \subset \mathcal{F}$ is the σ-algebra representing the information available to agent i.

Each agent $i \in I$ is initially endowed with some random consumption e_i. The agent also learns some information in the first period (which may be relevant to this endowment variable) that is represented by a signal s_i, a random variable (valued in some measurable signal space whose nature varies with the context). The set of all agents' signals is denoted s_I.

2.2. Securities and Shareholdings

Agents may exchange contingent consumption plans by purchasing or selling shares of firms or other securities in the first period.

There is a finite set J of firms; each firm $j \in J$ pays a random consumption dividend $D_j \in L$ in the second period. Agents are initially endowed with shares $\bar{\theta}^i_j$, $i \in I$, such that $\sum_{i \in I} \bar{\theta}^i_j = 1$ for each firm j. Agents may buy or sell these shares for some price $v_j \in L$ in the first period.

Also available for trade in this economy is a finite set F of securities. Each share of a security $f \in F$ entitles (obligates) the holder to a contingent claim (payment) represented by the random variable $Z_f \in L$. These securities are in zero net supply; agents initially hold no shares. They may purchase or sell any security f in the first period at a price of $p_f \in L$ per share.

One element of F represents a bond. Each share of the bond provides 1 unit of consumption in the second period, independent of the state. Since agents' preferences are monotonic, the bond must always trade for a positive price in equilibrium; hence we may designate the bond as numeraire in the first period.

2.3. Portfolio Problem

Given the above set of assets available for trade, the first period portfolio problem for agent i can be described as

$$(P_i) \max_{\theta, \varphi, b, c} \quad U_i(c),$$
$$\text{subject to} \quad b + \theta v + \varphi p \leq \bar{\theta}^i v,$$
$$c = e_i + b + \theta D + \varphi Z,$$

where b is the number of bonds purchased, D is the (column) vector of firms' dividends, v is the vector of firms' share prices, θ is the (row) vector of the agent's stock portfolio, and similarly for Z, p, and φ, which correspond to the assets in F other than the bond. Since b, θ, and φ are chosen after agent's information s_i and prices (v, p) are observed, these choices are contingent on these random variables; that is, they are $\mathcal{H}_i$-measurable, where $\mathcal{H}_i = \sigma(s_i, v, p)$ is the σ-algebra representing the information available to agent i.

The monotonicity of agents' preferences implies that the first periods budget constraint is always strictly binding, so that

$$b_i = (\bar{\theta}^i - \theta^i)v - \varphi^i p$$

at any optimal solution.

We will adopt the assumption that agents have rational expectations; in particular, they use all of the information available to them from prices. Hence, the portfolio problem is rewritten as

$$(P_i) \max_{\theta, \varphi} \quad E[u_i(c) | s_i, v, p],$$
$$\text{where} \quad c = e_i + \bar{\theta}^i v + \theta(D - v) + \varphi(Z - p).$$

Note that this formulation of the problem is consistent with an interpretation of the zero-net-supply securities as futures contracts. In this case, one may think of the stochastic payoff Z_f as the future "spot" price, and p_f as the contract price, determined in the first period but paid in the second. This terminology will occasionally be used for interpretation of the results.

Finally, the assumed concavity of the utility function allows us to characterize the optimal portfolio choice for agent i in terms of simple first order conditions:

LEMMA 1. *The portfolio (θ, φ) solves (P_i) if and only if*:

$$E[u_i'(c_i)(D - v) | s_i, v, p] = 0, \tag{1}$$

$$E[u_i'(c_i)(Z - p) | s_i, v, p] = 0. \tag{2}$$

Proof. Since c_i, D, and Z are bounded, and u_i is concave, "differentiation inside the expectation" is justified, and the usual first and second order condition for optimization apply. ∎

2.4. *Firms*

We assume that firms' production decisions have been made and that each firm $j \in J$ produces output $Y_j \in L$. In the first period, the firm privately

HEDGING WITH PROPRIETARY INFORMATION

observes a signal represented by some random variable s_j. Let s_J denote the set of consisting of all firms' signals.

Aside from its productive output, each firm may generate revenues via its financial policy. Specifically, after observing its signal s_j, firm j may choose to hold a portfolio φ^j of securities and finance its purchases with b_j bonds. That is, it may hold any security portfolio (φ^j, b_j) subject to the first period budget balancing constraint

$$b_j + \varphi^j p = 0. \tag{3}$$

Given such a portfolio, the dividend of the firm is the sum of its productive and financial revenues. That is,

$$D_j = Y_j + \varphi^j Z + b_j.$$

Since the firm chooses its financial strategy after observing its signal, a *hedging strategy* for firm j is a portfolio (φ^j, b_j) that is $\sigma(s_j, v, p)$-measurable and bounded. For notational emphasis on the fact that φ^j depends on the information revealed by s_j in addition to the public information revealed by (v, p), we will often write $\varphi^j(s_j)$ for the portfolio outcome given the signal s_j. Thus, using the budget equation to solve for bond purchases,

$$D_j = Y_j + \varphi^j(s_j)(Z - p). \tag{4}$$

2.5. *Equilibrium*

An equilibrium for this economy will be specified with respect to an exogeneously given production and hedging strategy on the part of firms. Thus, the economy is described by

$$\langle (\Omega, \mathscr{F}, \mathscr{P}), (u_i, e_i, \theta^i, s_i), (Y_j, s_j, \varphi^j), Z \rangle,$$

where φ^j is the hedging strategy of firm j.

An equilibrium for this economy is given by a set of portfolios and prices

$$\langle (\theta^i, \varphi^i), v, p \rangle$$

such that

1. Agents optimize conditional on their information:

    (θ^i, φ^i) is $\sigma(s_i, v, p)$-measurable and solves (P_i) given signal s_i and prices v and p;

2. Markets clear:

$$\sum_{i \in I} \theta^i = \sum_{i \in I} \theta^i$$

$$\sum_{i \in I} \varphi^i + \sum_{j \in J} \varphi^j = 0;$$

3. Prices are demand-measurable:

$$(v, p) \text{ is } \sigma\left(s_I \cup \left\{\sum_{j \in J} \varphi^j\right\}\right)\text{-measurable.}$$

The last condition, demand-measurable prices, is simply a weak condition necessary to rule out "perverse" equilibria in which prices reveal information not contained in agents' and firms' demands. The crucial assumption is that agents should not be able to infer the portfolio choice of each firm by observing security prices.

Although this paper is not concerned with proving the existence of equilibria, our results apply only in equilibrium, so some comments on existence are in order. Under dimensionality restrictions, Allen [2] demonstrates the existence of fully revealing rational expectations equilibria, that is, equilibria in which prices reveal all private information. (This is true, in particular, with a finite number of states of the world.) A fully revealing equilibrium is fairly unnatural, and in any case trivializes the results in this paper. (We have therefore left the cardinality of Ω unrestricted.)

In order to demonstrate partially revealing equilibria, on the other hand, it has so far been found necessary to (i) make severe restrictions on utility functions, as in Ausubel [5], or (ii) introduce noise, for example in the form of un-modeled supply perturbations or garbled observations of prices, as in Allen [3], Anderson and Sonnenschein [4], Admati [1], and other papers, or (iii) allow a relaxation, as in MacAllister [18], of the rational expectations assumption that prices are given by a function of the underlying state of the world that is later revealed to be correct. While these alternative routes to partially revealing equilibrium with asymmetric information may eventually be replaced by a more general set of assumptions or definition of equilibrium, the results in this paper apply in any of these sorts of models, so long as individual agent optimality is characterized by the usual first order conditions.

As a final remark on the question of existence, our results are of interest even if individual agents are symmetrically informed, so long as they have incomplete information about the signals and choices of the firm. Since the firms' choices are taken as given in the model, we can therefore claim the existence of equilibrium with symmetrically informed agents under standard technical regularity conditions by referring to the available results on random Walrasian equilibria. (The object here is merely a $\sigma(s_I \cup \{\sum_{i \in J} \varphi^j\})$-measurable selection from the Walrasian correspondence defined on Ω, which provides an equilibrium state-by-state.) Yannelis [24], for example, obtains and surveys selection results of this variety.

3. Modigliani–Miller Theorem

The MM Theorem states that, in a world of perfect information, the financial policies of firms have no effect on equilibrium prices and allocations. In the context of this paper, however, firms may make financial decisions based on information not available to shareholders, violating the MM hypothesis. Any financial decision of the firm that is observed by agents, however, has no effect on the resulting equilibria. That is, if we define

$$\sigma_P \equiv \bigcap_{i \in I} \sigma(s_i, v, p),$$

so that σ_P represents the information commonly known to all agents in equilibrium, the following version of the MM Theorem holds:

THEOREM 2. *Suppose that, given hedging policies φ^j, the economy has an equilibrium $\langle (\theta^i, \varphi^i), v, p \rangle$. Then, if firms adopt new hedging strategies $\hat{\varphi}^j$ such that $\hat{\varphi}^j - \varphi^j$ is σ_P-measurable, the economy has a new equilibrium with identical prices, consumption plans, and firm ownership, and with the new security portfolios*

$$\hat{\varphi}_i = \varphi^i - \sum_{j \in J} \theta^i_j (\hat{\varphi}^j - \varphi^j).$$

Proof. Obviously, since firm ownership has not changed, the market for firms' shares still clears. Also, since $\sum_i \varphi^i + \sum_j \varphi^j = 0$ in the initial equilibrium,

$$\sum_{i \in I} \hat{\varphi}^i = \sum_{i \in I} \varphi^i - \sum_{j \in J} (\hat{\varphi}^j - \varphi^j) = -\sum_{j \in J} \hat{\varphi}^j,$$

so that securities markets still clear. Next, the new consumption is given by

$$\hat{c}_i = e_i + \theta^i v + \theta^i (\hat{D} - v) + \hat{\varphi}^i (Z - p)$$

$$= e_i + \theta^i v + \theta^i (\hat{D} - v) + \left[\varphi^i - \sum_{j \in J} \theta^i_j (\hat{\varphi}^j - \varphi^j) \right] (Z - p).$$

But $\hat{D}_j = D_j + (\hat{\varphi}^j - \varphi^j)(Z - p)$, so that

$$\theta^i(\hat{D} - v) = \theta^i(D - v) + \sum_{j \in J} \theta^i_j(\hat{\varphi}^j - \varphi^j)(Z - p).$$

Therefore,

$$\hat{c}_i = e_i + \theta^i v + \theta^i(D - v) + \varphi^i(Z - p) = c_i,$$

and consumption plans are unchanged. The optimality condition (2) is therefore unchanged. Since $\sigma_{\hat{p}} \subset \sigma(s_i, v, p)$, the new portfolios are feasible for the agents and

$$E[u'_i(c_i)(\hat{D} - v) | s_i, v, p] = E[u'_i(c_i)(D - v) | s_i, v, p]$$
$$+ (\hat{\varphi}^j - \varphi^j) E[u'_i(c_i)(Z - p) | s_i, v, p] = 0,$$

so condition (1) is also satisfied and agent optimization is guaranteed. ∎

Of course, we are most interested here in cases for which this theorem is not directly applicable; that is, cases in which the firms' hedging policies depend upon information that is not publicly known. Theorem 2 does imply, however, that results regarding any particular hedging policy actually apply to a whole equivalence class of policies, those generated by adding to a given policy any publicly known policy.

4. An Example: Cancellable Risk

This section presents a special case clearly illustrating the possibility of corporate hedging policies that are unanimously supported by shareholders.

Suppose the set F of securities can be partitioned into two sets F_1 and F_2 such that the corresponding payoff vectors Z_1 and Z_2 are independent. Further, suppose that subset F_1 represents risks that are held in a random amount by each firm, yet "cancel out" across firms. That is, suppose

1. $Y_j = G_j + s_j Z_1$, for real-valued s_j, for each firm $j \in J$,
2. (G, s) and Z_1 are independent, and,
3. $\sum_{j \in J} s_j = 0$.[1]

Finally, suppose that Z_1 and any agent's endowment e_i are independent. If firm j adopts the hedging strategy $\varphi^j_1(s_j) = -s_j$, then $D_j = G_j + s_j p$ is

---

[1] For this cancellation assumption, one might make formal arguments in a different model with infinitely many firms using the law of large numbers.

independent of Z_1. If agents choose portfolios with $\varphi_1^i = 0$, their consumption plans will also be independent of Z_1. It is easy to check that such an equilibrium exists with, from Eq. (2), $p_1 = E[Z_1]$.

Now consider an alternative hedging policy $\hat{\varphi}_1^j$ for firm j, generating the new output

$$\hat{D}_j = D_j + (\hat{\varphi}_1^j - \varphi_1^j)(Z_1 - p_1).$$

Since $\hat{D}_j$ is a mean-preserving spread of D_j, a risk averse shareholder is worse off with $\hat{\varphi}^j$, as shown by Rothschild and Stiglitz [22]. Hence, the original hedging strategy is unanimously supported by the firm's shareholders.

5. Shareholder Unanimity

Since we are interested in determining whether the shareholders of a firm unanimously approve of a given hedging strategy it has undertaken, we must first examine the preferences held by shareholders over such strategies. Intuitively, a shareholder of a firm agrees with a particular hedging strategy if, given control of the firm, that shareholder would choose to adopt the same policy. Formally,

DEFINITION 1. *The hedging policy φ^j is optimal for shareholder i if, taking prices as given, it solves the following problem:*

$$(P_{ij})\ \max_{\theta,\varphi,\varphi^j(\cdot)}\quad E[u_i(c)|s_i, v, p],$$

where

$$c = e_i + \theta^i v + \theta(D - v) + \varphi(Z - p),$$

$$D_j = Y_j + \varphi^j(s_j)(Z - p).$$

This definition allows shareholder i to choose the firm's policy *after* observing s_i, making this notion of optimality stronger than if the policy is chosen ex-ante.

Suppose shareholder i holds a non-zero share of firm j. Then allowing i to choose j's hedging strategy allows i to hedge her own portfolio using both her own information and the firm's. This suggests that this optimality condition may be characterized by adjusting the first order condition (2) of the shareholder's hedging problem in order to account for the firm's information. This is verified in the following theorem:

THEOREM 3. *Given an equilibrium with $\theta_j^i \neq 0$, the hedging policy φ^j of firm j is optimal for shareholder i if and only if*

$$E[u_i'(c_i)(Z - p)|s_j, s_i, v, p] = 0. \tag{5}$$

Proof. Clearly, Eq. (5) is implied by the first order condition for the optimality of φ^j in (P_{ij}) when $\theta'_j \neq 0$. Thus, we must demonstrate sufficiency. Unfortunately, the problem (P_{ij}) is not convex (the constraints involve a product of portfolios), so a first-order approach does not apply. Consider, however, the alternative problem

$$(P'_{ij}) \max_{\theta, \varphi(\cdot)} \quad E[u_i(c)|s_i, v, p],$$

where $\quad c = e_i + \theta^i v + \theta(D - v) + \varphi(s_j)(Z - p),$

$$D_j = Y_j.$$

It is easy to check that the feasible consumption plans under (P'_{ij}) contain those under (P_{ij}). Thus, if a consumption plan solves (P'_{ij}), it must also solve (P_{ij}) if feasible. Problem (P'_{ij}) is convex, so optimality is implied by the first order conditions

$$E[u'_i(c_i)(D - v)|s_i, v, p] = 0,$$
$$E[u'_i(c_i)(Z - p)|s_j, s_i, v, p] = 0.$$

Since the first condition is already guaranteed in equilibrium, the second is sufficient for optimality of the firm's hedging policy, which completes the theorem. ∎

This result motivates the following definition, to be used shortly.

DEFINITION 2. The hedging policy of firm j is *unanimously supported* by its shareholders if Eq. (5) holds in equilibrium for each shareholder i of the firm.

Indeed, in the proofs that follow, we will often verify the even stronger condition

$$E[u'_i(c_i)(Z - p)|s] = 0, \qquad (6)$$

which implies Eq. (5) since $\sigma(s_j, s_i, v, p) \subset \sigma(s)$, where $s = s_I \cup s_J$.

6. OPTIMAL HEDGING POLICIES

Given the specification of the model so far, agents would typically have an incentive to make their portfolios contingent on all available information. For example, each component of s might yield additional information about a given agent's endowment. Since we wish to investigate motives for hedging based on the firm's proprietary knowledge of its own production risks, we must explicitly rule out these secondary effects. In order to do so, we first introduce a notion of "non-informativeness."

Recall that random variables A and B are conditionally independent relative to random variable C if, for any measurable subsets S_A and S_B of the respective ranges of A and B,

$$\mathscr{P}(A \in S_A, B \in S_B | C) = \mathscr{P}(A \in S_A | C) \mathscr{P}(B \in S_B | C).$$

Further, such conditional independence (and integrability) implies that

$$E[A | B, C] = E[A | C],$$

which reflects the intuition that B provides no additional information about A, once C is known. See Chung [6] for further reference.

This idea of conditional independence can be interpreted most simply in the case of random variables with a joint normal distribution. In this case, A and B are conditionally independent relative to C if and only if

$$\operatorname{cov}_C(A, B) \equiv E[AB | C] - E[A | C] E[B | C] = 0;$$

that is, if and only if A and B are conditionally uncorrelated, given C.[2]

We will use the notion of conditional independence to make assumptions that rule out secondary motives for trading on information that is unrelated to production risks. For instance, suppose that s_j is informative about e_i or Z to agent i. Then i has an incentive to adapt the hedging strategy of firm j so as to hedge i's own endowment. Consider also the case that s_h is informative about e_i or Z to agent i, for some agent $h \neq i$. Again, agent i would have an incentive to use the firm's financial policy to hedge i's own endowment, since the information s_j of the firm might, through prices, yield better information about s_h. These effects motivate the following:

Assumption A. For each agent i, s and (e_i, Z) are conditionally independent relative to s_i.

Note that, in the case of joint normality of the random variables, this condition is equivalent to the statement that for all agents i and any agent or firm h,

$$\operatorname{cov}_{s_i}(s_h, e_i) = \operatorname{cov}_{s_i}(s_h, Z) = 0.$$

Thus, conditional on i's own information, the signals of other agents and firms are not informative about agent i's endowment or the payoffs of the futures contracts.

---
[2] Though we do not use this assumption of joint normality for our results, we often restate our independence conditions using it to provide a more natural interpretation.

We also choose to rule out situations in which other agents have information about a firm j's production risks in addition to that known by firm j itself. In that case, agents might again have a purely informational demand to control other firms' hedging policies, since the information of those other firms could, together with prices, be informative about the risks of firm j. Finally, we also suppose that the firms are not "disadvantaged" in their hedging decisions due to poor information about futures payoffs. Thus, we make the following assumption:

Assumption B. For each firm j, s and (Y, Z) are conditionally independent relative to s_j.

Thus, the information of other agents and firms is not informative to firm j about its own production risk and hedging possibilities.

6.1. CARA Utility

Suppose all agents' preferences can be represented by utility functions with constant absolute risk aversion (CARA). This implies that

$$u_i(c) = -e^{-r_i c}$$

for some positive constant r_i.

Next, suppose that the risks faced by firms are "decomposable" in the following sense:

DEFINITION 3. The production payoff of firm j is *decomposable* if

$$Y_j = G_j + \alpha^j(s_j)Z + M_j,$$

such that for each agent i, (s, M) and (e_i, Z, G) are conditionally independent relative to s_i; that is, s and M are not informative in each agents' decision to hedge G.

Under the assumption of joint normality, decomposability requires that s and G be conditionally uncorrelated given the agent's information, and similarly that M and (e_i, Z, G) be conditionally uncorrelated given the agent's information. Thus, decomposability implies that the firm's private information does not pertain to the component G of production, but only to a component of production that is "spanned" by the existing securities, $\alpha^j Z$, together with a third component M_j. This third, unspanned component, however, is uncorrelated with the other factors affecting the agent's consumption (i.e., e_i, Z, and G) given the agent's own information.

Decomposability substantially strengthens our initial assumptions, but still admits certain interesting cases:

EXAMPLE 1. Suppose firms have private information regarding the magnitudes of payments to be made in, say, various foreign currencies, and suppose currency futures are available. In this case, we take s_j to be a row vector of the same dimension as Z, the currency spot prices, and suppose that $Y_j = G_j + s_j Z$. More generally, if the futures contracts only approximately hedge this risk, we might have

$$Y_j = G_j + \alpha^j Z + \gamma^j \varepsilon_j,$$

with $s_i \equiv (\alpha^i, \gamma^i)$. This production Y_j is decomposable if, for each agent i, (s, ε) and (e_i, Z, G) are conditionally independent relative to s_i. Under the additional assumption of joint normality, this condition becomes

$$\operatorname{cov}_{s_i}(s_h, G_j) = 0,$$

$$\operatorname{cov}_{s_i}(e_i, \varepsilon_k) = \operatorname{cov}_{s_i}(Z_f, \varepsilon_k) = \operatorname{cov}_{s_i}(G_j, \varepsilon_k) = 0$$

for any i, h, j, k, and f.

Again, decomposability essentially implies that the private information of the firm only pertains to components of the dividend stream that are either spanned by the futures market, or are otherwise independent of variables of interest to the agents. If the firm completely hedges the spanned risk by adopting the futures position $\varphi^j = -\alpha^j$, its dividend stream is

$$D_j = G_j + \alpha^j p + M_j = G_j + \hat{M}_j, \tag{7}$$

where the residual $\hat{M}_j$ is viewed by each shareholder as an independent "wealth shock." Under the assumption of CARA utility, such a wealth shock has no effect on shareholders' "risk preferences," and hence the agents do not wish to make their portfolios contingent on this shock. This intuition leads to the following theorem regarding optimal hedging strategies:

THEOREM 4. *Suppose agents have CARA utility and firms' production payoffs are decomposable (Definition 3). Then, in equilibrium, shareholders unanimously support the hedging policy $\varphi^j \equiv -\alpha^j$.*

Proof. It is enough to verify that Eq. (5) holds for each agent i. Indeed, we will demonstrate the stronger condition

$$E[u_i'(c_i)(Z - p) | s] = 0.$$

Decomposability implies $D = G + \hat{M}$ from Eq. (7), so that $c_i = e_i + \hat{\theta}'v + \theta^i(G + \hat{M} - v) + \varphi^i(Z - p)$. Thus,

$$u_i'(c_i) = r_i \exp[-r_i(e_i + (\hat{\theta}^i - \theta^i)v + \varphi^i(Z - p) + \theta^i G + \theta^i \hat{M})],$$

and (6) can be rewritten

$$E[r_i \exp[-r_i(e_i + (\hat{\theta}^i - \theta^i)v + \varphi^i(Z - p) + \theta^i G + \theta^i \hat{M})](Z - p)|s] = 0.$$

From the definition of decomposability, $\hat{M}$ and (G, Z, e_i) are conditionally independent relative to s_i, so that we may factor the above as the product of $E[r_i \exp[-r_i \theta^i \hat{M}]|s]$ and

$$E[\exp[-r_i(e_i + (\hat{\theta}^i - \theta^i)v + \varphi^i(Z - p) + \theta^i G)](Z - p)|s],$$

so that (6) holds if and only if

$$E[\exp[-r_i(e_i + (\hat{\theta}^i - \theta^i)v + \varphi^i(Z - p) + \theta^i G)](Z - p)|s] = 0.$$

Since s is not informative about (e_i, Z, G) given s_i (by decomposability), this is equivalent to

$$E[\exp[-r_i(e_i + (\hat{\theta}^i - \theta^i)v + \varphi^i(Z - p) + \theta^i G)](Z - p)|s_i] = 0.$$

Multiplying by $E[r_i \exp(-r_i \theta^i \hat{M})|s_i]$ yields the equivalent equality

$$E[u_i'(c_i)(Z - p)|s_i] = 0,$$

which is clearly implied by the equilibrium condition for the agent's optimization problem,

$$E[u_i'(c_i)(Z - p)|s_i, v, p] = 0.$$

Thus, Eq. (6) is satisfied for all shareholders, and unanimous support follows. ∎

6.2. "Quadratic" Utility

In this section we consider economies in which all agents have quadratic utility in a neighborhood of equilibrium consumption c_i, in the sense that, after a suitable linear transformation of u_i,

$$u_i'(c_i) = a_i - c_i, \tag{8}$$

for some positive constant a_i.

In this case it is natural to define a "full hedging" policy as the conditional L^2 projection of the risk onto the space spanned by the securities.

DEFINITION 4. The *full hedging policy* of firm j is given by

$$\varphi^j(s_j)' = -E[(Z-p)(Z-p)'|s_j]^{-1}E[Y_j(Z-p)|s_j].$$

Given this definition, we have the following result regarding shareholder unanimity:

THEOREM 5. *Suppose agents have quadratic utility in a neighborhood of equilibrium consumption; that is, (8) holds. Then shareholders unanimously support full hedging policies in equilibrium.*

Proof. First, we demonstrate condition (6) for all shareholders:

$$E[u_i'(c_i)(Z-p)|s] = 0.$$

Since $c_i = e_i + \bar{\theta}^i v + \theta^i(D-v) + \varphi^i(Z-p)$, Eq. (6) can be written, using (8), as

$$E([a_i - e_i - (\bar{\theta}^i - \theta^i)v - \varphi^i(Z-p)](Z-p)|s)$$
$$- \sum_{j \in J} \theta_j^i E[D_j(Z-p)|s] = 0. \quad (9)$$

By Assumption A, s is not informative about (e_i, Z) given s_i, so that

$$E([a_i - e_i - (\bar{\theta}^i - \theta^i)v - \varphi^i(Z-p)](Z-p)|s)$$
$$= E([a_i - e_i - (\bar{\theta}^i - \theta^i)v - \varphi^i(Z-p)](Z-p)|s_i).$$

Further, the full hedging policy of the firms implies that

$$E[D_j(Z-p)|s] = E([Y_j + \varphi^j(Z-p)](Z-p)|s)$$
$$= E[Y_j(Z-p)|s] + E[(Z-p)(Z-p)'|s]\,\varphi^{j'}$$
$$= E[Y_j(Z-p)|s] + E[(Z-p)(Z-p)'|s_j]\,\varphi^{j'}$$
$$= E[Y_j(Z-p)|s] - E[Y_j(Z-p)|s_j]$$
$$= 0,$$

where the last equations follow since s is not informative about (Y_j, Z) given s_j, by Assumption B. Thus, both terms in the sum (9) are s_i-measurable, so that (6) is equivalent to

$$E[u_i'(c_i)(Z-p)|s_i] = 0,$$

which is implied by the equilibrium condition (2) for shareholders. Hence unanimity holds. ∎

As noted in Section 3, this unanimity result extends to any hedging policy of the firm that differs from the full hedging policy φ^j in a manner that is publicly known. In order to demonstrate that this characterization is necessary as well as sufficient for unanimity, and additional assumption is required:

Assumption C. For each realization of the agents' information s, the conditional distribution of Z is non-degenerate; that is, the matrix $E[ZZ'|s]$ is positive definite for all s.

Essentially, this assumption requires that in no state of the world can any agent know the payoff of a portfolio $\varphi \neq 0$ with certainty. This allows the following characterization:

COROLLARY 6. *Under the conditions of Theorem 5 and Assumption C, consider an alternative hedging policy $\hat{\varphi}^j$ for firm j that differs from the full hedging policy φ^j. In equilibrium, this hedging policy is unanimously supported by the shareholders of firm j if and only if, for each shareholder i with $\theta_j^i \neq 0$, $\hat{\varphi}^j - \varphi^j$ is measurable with respect to $\sigma(s_i, v, p)$, the information of shareholder i.*

Proof. If firm j adopts an alternative hedging policy $\hat{\varphi}^j$, we have

$$E[u_i'(c_i)(Z-p)|s_i, v, p] - E[u_i'(c_i)(Z-p)|s_j, s_i, v, p]$$
$$= \theta_j^i E[(Z-p)(Z-p)'|s_i](\hat{\varphi}^j - \varphi^j - E[\hat{\varphi}^j - \varphi^j|s_i, v, p])'.$$

Thus, in equilibrium, this policy is optimal for shareholder i if and only if

$$\theta_j^i E[(Z-p)(Z-p)'|s_i](\hat{\varphi}^j - \varphi^j - E[\hat{\varphi}^j - \varphi^j|s_i, v, p])' = 0. \quad (10)$$

By hypothesis, $\theta_j^i \neq 0$, and from Assumption C, $E[(Z-p)(Z-p)'|s_i]$ is positive definite for any s_i. Hence (10) is equivalent to

$$\hat{\varphi}^j - \varphi^j = E[\hat{\varphi}^j - \varphi^j|s_i, v, p],$$

which is precisely the condition that $\hat{\varphi}^j - \varphi^j$ be $\sigma(s_i, v, p)$-measurable. ∎

6.3. Partial Disclosure

The previous sections have required substantial restrictions on the form of shareholders' preferences in order to demonstrate unanimously supported hedging policies. One might expect, however, that in the case where production includes a component of risk that is completely spanned by the securities markets, shareholders would prefer the firm to hedge these risks. This intuition may fail since, even if the firm were to hedge such risks, it would still hold proprietary information as to the market value of its portfolio. Since this market value affects shareholder wealth, unless agents' risk preferences are independent of wealth (for example, CARA utility), or unless the wealth effects are identical across shareholders (as is the case with quadratic utility), shareholders disagree about the firm's optimal response to such information.

In this section we consider cases in which the firm may communicate a limited amount of information to its shareholders costlessly. Obviously, if the firm can communicate its signal s_j, there is no role for a firm's hedging policy since shareholders are perfectly informed and can adjust their own portfolios to suit their needs, as was shown in the MM results of Section 3. If information is proprietary or costly to disseminate, there may be some partial disclosure that recovers unanimity for certain financial hedging strategies of benefit to shareholders. As the above discussion suggests, it may be particularly convenient for the firm to reveal the total market value of the hedged risk.

DEFINITION 5. *The private information s_j of firm j is reducible with respect to a hedging strategy φ^j if, given the associated dividends*

$$D_j = Y_j + \varphi^j(s_j)(Z-p),$$

for any agent i, s and (e_i, Z, D) are conditionally independent relative to s_i; that is, the signal s is not informative for each agent's hedging decision.

If we impose the additional assumption of joint normality, then reducibility holds if s and D_j are conditionally uncorrelated given the agent's own information. While this condition is unlikely to be satisfied in general, it will hold in the case of "spanned" risk if the shareholders are informed of the market value of the risk:

EXAMPLE 2. Consider again the foreign currency risk case in Example 1, with $Y_j = G_j + s_j Z$. Consider the hedging strategy $\varphi^j = -s_j$, which yields $D_j = G_j + s_j p$. Reducibility of s_j with respect to φ^j is satisfied if the shareholders of the firm know the magnitude $s_j p \equiv -b_j$; that is, if shareholders know the total market value of the foreign change risk, but not necessarily the particular currency commitments of the firm.

The following theorem is immediate:

THEOREM 7. *Suppose the private information of firms is reducible with respect to hedging policies (φ^j). Then, in equilibrium, shareholders unanimously support these hedging policies.*

Proof. By hypothesis, s is not informative about (e_i, Z, D) given s_i. Since c_i is a function of (e_i, Z, D), so is $u_i'(c_i)(Z-p)$, implying that

$$E[u_i'(c_i)(Z-p)|s] = E[u_i'(c_i)(Z-p)|s_i].$$

Hence, the unanimity condition (6) is equivalent to the shareholder's equilibrium optimality condition (2), and the theorem holds. ∎

Again, Theorem 2 implies that alternative policies which differ from φ^j in a publicly known fashion are also unanimously supported in equilibrium. With the further assumption of non-degeneracy of Z, we show that this characterization is complete:

COROLLARY 8. *Under the conditions of Theorem 7 and Assumption C, consider an alternative hedging policy $\hat{\varphi}^j$ for firm j. In equilibrium, this hedging policy is unanimously supported by the shareholders of firm j if and only if, for each shareholder i with $\theta_j^i \neq 0$, $\hat{\varphi}^j - \varphi^j$ is measurable with respect to $\sigma(s_i, v, p)$, the information of shareholder i.*

Proof. Suppose firm j instead adopts a policy $\hat{\varphi}^j$. The resulting dividend is

$$\hat{D}_j = Y_j + \varphi^j(Z-p) + (\hat{\varphi}^j - \varphi^j)(Z-p) = D_j + (\hat{\varphi}^j - \varphi^j)(Z-p),$$

and the equilibrium consumption of shareholder i is

$$c_i = e_i + \theta^i v + \theta^i(D-v) + \varphi^i(Z-p) + \theta_j^i(\hat{\varphi}^j - \varphi^j)(Z-p).$$

If shareholder i could instruct the firm to adopt the hedging policy φ^j, and adjust her own portfolio φ^i to be, instead,

$$\tilde{\varphi}^i \equiv \varphi^i + \theta_j^i E[\hat{\varphi}^j - \varphi^j | s_i, v, p],$$

then her new consumption $\tilde{c}_i$ would satisfy

$$c_i = \tilde{c}_i + \theta_j^i[\hat{\varphi}^j - \varphi^j - E(\hat{\varphi}^j - \varphi^j | s_i, v, p)](Z-p).$$

This implies that $E[c_i | \tilde{c}_i, s_i, v, p] = \tilde{c}_i$, so that, by the strict version of Jensen's Inequality, unless $\tilde{c}_i = c_i$, $E[u(c_i)|s_i, v, p] < E[u(\tilde{c}_i)|s_i, v, p]$. The condition $\tilde{c}_i = c_i$ is, however, equivalent to

$$\theta_j^i[\hat{\varphi}^j - \varphi^j - E(\hat{\varphi}^j - \varphi^j | s_i, v, p)](Z-p) = 0,$$

which, upon post-multiplying by $Z-p$ and taking the expectation with respect to s, becomes exactly Eq. (10). Hence, the remainder of the proof follows as in that of Corollary 6. ∎

A simple application of this result applies to cases in which a firm adopts "random" or "noisy" hedging policies; that is, chooses a portfolio φ^i based on a signal s_j that is independent of the other variables in the model. Our result implies that shareholders unanimously support the elimination of such noisy portfolio choices by the firm.

7. Constrained Optimality

In this section we analyze efficiency properties of equilibria in which firms adopt "optimal" hedging policies. Since markets are incomplete, one cannot hope to achieve full Pareto optimality via market allocations. There are, nevertheless, useful second-best notions of constrained optimality. For example, in the spirit of Diamond [9], we may suppose that a social planner has available all of the information known to agents in the first period and has the ability to choose any *market feasible* allocation; that is, any allocation achievable through an appropriate distribution of firms' shares and securities.

DEFINITION 6 (Second-Best Optimality). *An allocation* (θ, φ, b) *is second-best Pareto optimal if it solves the following optimization problem for some positive constants* (λ_i):

$$(P_2)\ \max_{\theta, \varphi, b}\quad E\left[\sum_{i \in I} \lambda_i u_i(c_i) \big| s\right],$$

where $\quad c_i = e_i + b_i + \theta^i Y + \varphi^i Z,\ i \in I,$

subject to $\quad \sum_i \theta^i = \sum_i \bar{\theta}^i,$

$$\sum_i \varphi^i = 0,\ \sum_i b_i = 0.$$

THEOREM 9. *A feasible allocation is second-best Pareto optimal if and only if the following conditions hold for some prices* (v, p) *and for all agents* $i \in I$:

$$E[u_i'(c_i)(Y-v)|s] = 0, \qquad (11)$$

$$E[u_i'(c_i)(Z-p)|s] = 0. \qquad (12)$$

Proof. Since problem (P_2) is convex, it can be characterized by the first order conditions:

$$E[\lambda_i u_i'(c_i)|s] = \beta_b,$$
$$E[\lambda_i u_i'(c_i) Y|s] = \beta_\theta,$$
$$E[\lambda_i u_i'(c_i) Z|s] = \beta_\varphi,$$

where $(\beta_b, \beta_v, \beta_\varphi)$ are the Lagrange multipliers for the corresponding constraints, with $\beta_b > 0$. This can be reduced to the above Eqs. (11) and (12) upon substitution of v for β_v/β_b and p for β_φ/β_b. ∎

Having characterized the conditions for a second-best allocation, we now demonstrate that such an allocation is achieved when firms' private information is reducible with respect to their hedging policies. This result is somewhat related to the work of Diamond [9] and others establishing the constrained optimality of stock market equilibria when production possibilities are spanned by existing markets, since the reducibility assumption is, in some sense, a "spanning" assumption about the nature of the private information.

THEOREM 10. *Suppose the private information of firms is reducible with respect to hedging strategies (φ^j), as defined in Section 6.3. Then, in an equilibrium in which firms adopt these strategies, the equilibrium allocation is second-best Pareto optimal.*

Proof. From Theorem 7, condition (12) is satisfied in equilibrium, and we only need to check condition (11). As was argued in the earlier proof, however, c_i is a function of (e_i, Z, D), so that s is not informative about $u_i'(c_i)(D - v)$ given s_i. This implies that

$$E[u_i'(c_i)(D-v)|s] = E[u_i'(c_i)(D-v)|s_i] = 0,$$

where the equality follows from the agents' optimization condition (1). Next, since $Y_j = D_j - \varphi^j(Z - p)$,

$$\begin{aligned}E[u_i'(c_i)(Y_j - v_j)|s] &= E[u_i'(c_i)(D_j - \varphi^j(Z-p) - v_j)|s] \\ &= E[u_i'(c_i)(D_j - v_j)|s] - \varphi^j E[u_i'(c_i)(Z-p)|s] \\ &= 0.\end{aligned}$$

Hence, both conditions are satisfied and the allocation is indeed second-best Pareto optimal. ∎

8. Concluding Remarks

In this section we comment on several possible extensions and generalizations of the results in the paper:

Weaker Criteria than Unanimity. This paper has adopted the strongest possible notion of shareholder agreement with a particular financial hedging policy: shareholder unanimity. Obviously, such a strict criterion calls for strict assumptions on the nature of the firm's risks and private information in order to obtain clear results. One could weaken this criterion in a variety of ways. For example, one could compare the current policy only with the alternative of doing nothing, and then ask whether it is preferred by a majority of the shareholdes (weighted by their holdings). This would allow one to make statements about a much broader class of production/information structures, though it would likely involve a concomitant loss in precision.

Firm Control and Objectives. Thus far, this paper has made no explicit mention of the objectives of the firm with regard to its financial policy. Under the assumption that control of the firm ultimately rests with its shareholders, the unanimity criterion developed here is rather compelling. This argument would also hold if firms were controlled by managers whose compensation depends linearly on the performance of the firm. If managers' compensation is a non-linear function of output, however, managers' and shareholders' interests would likely be in conflict, and we would not expect managers whose actions are only partially observable to implement the "optimal" hedging strategies discussed here.

Competitive Value Maximization. An alternative approach to resolving the firm's decision problem is to suppose that firms attempt to maximize their market value. With complete markets, this is done by supposing that firms make plans taking market prices as given. With incomplete markets, however, prices do not exist for all contingent commodities, so in order to maximize value, firms must conjecture prices. If we assume that firms act competitively with respect to prices, the most natural approach is to suppose that firms conjecture some "state" prices that are consistent with existing market prices. That is, firm j conjectures positive state prices $q^j \in L$ such that

$$E[q^j(D-v)|\sigma_c] = 0,$$
$$E[q^j(Z-p)|\sigma_c] = 0,$$

where $\sigma_c \equiv \bigcap_k \sigma(s_k)$ is the information commonly known to all agents and firms. If firm j assumes its share price is generated according to such state prices, a value-maximizing portfolio choice is one that maximizes

$$E[q^j[Y_j + \varphi^j(Z-p)]|s_j, v, p].$$

Thus, a value-maximizing equilibrium may be characterized by the condition

$$E[q^j(Z-p)|s_j, v, p] = 0$$

for each firm. Clearly, this condition cannot be expected to hold if arbitrary conjectures by firms are allowed, since they may then posit an arbitrary relationship between the state prices q^j and their information s_j. If agents are symmetrically informed, however, so that $\sigma(s_i) = \sigma_c$, and if the conjectures q^j are restricted to be measurable with respect to the consumption profile $(c_i)_{i \in I}$, then in the case of reducible information described in Section 6.3, the given hedging policies are indeed value maximizing.

Value Maximization with Quadratic Utility. In the case of quadratic utility, a stronger statement can be made regarding value maximization since it is possible to calculate directly the general equilibrium share values corresponding to a particular financial policy. In particular, if shareholders are symmetrically informed so that $\sigma(s_i) = \sigma_c$, then the equilibrium value of firm j is given by the formula, $v_j = \mathrm{E}[u'(\sum_i c_i) D_j | \sigma_c]$, where u is a quadratic utility function with $u'(c) = \sum_i a_i - c$. Since any financial policy by the firm does not change aggregate consumption but only redistributes it, a hedging policy maximizes the *general equilibrium share value* of the firm if and only if

$$\mathrm{E}\left[u'\left(\sum_i c_i\right)(Z-p) | s_j, v, p \right] = 0. \tag{13}$$

However, if firms adopt the full hedging strategies of Section 6.2, (13) can be shown to hold, exactly as in the proof of Theorem 5, so that firms are value maximizing in this strong sense.

Hedging with Common Stock. The analysis of the preceding sections could be generalized to allow firms to hedge by trading shares of other firms as well as securities. In this case,

$$D_j = Y_j + \theta^j(D-v) + \varphi^j(Z-p),$$

so that dividends must be simultaneously determined. If we define θ^J to be the matrix with row j equal to θ^j, then dividends can be calculated as follows, assuming the matrix $I - \theta^J$ is non-singular:

$$D = v + (I - \theta^J)^{-1}(Y-v) + \varphi^j(Z-p).$$

It can then be shown that the "unanimity" condition of Section 5 can be generalized to include the condition that

$$\mathrm{E}[u'_i(c_i)(D-v) | s_j, s_i, v, p] = 0$$

for each agent $i \in I$. The basic analysis of the paper can then be conducted in a similar fashion.

Interaction with Production. Throughout this paper, the production decisions of the firms have been taken as given. A natural extension would be to endogenize these production decisions and explore the interaction that might result when both production and financial policies are determined simultaneously. Such an extension might permit a generalization of the "spanning" literature, in a similar manner to that by Leland [17], and thus allow firms to evaluate unambiguously a broader class of production alternatives.

Multi-period, Multi-good Economies. Another obvious extension of the model presented in this paper would be to add multiple commodities and multiple time periods. Expanding the commodity space should in no way change the basic analysis of the paper, once asset payoffs are converted to a common numeraire, taking relative prices as given. Extending the time horizon of the model would also not affect the basic results, though it would introduce the possibility of intertemporal dividend smoothing, in addition to the intratemporal smoothing considered here. Also, the information revealed by the current period dividends of the firm may be quite important, as suggested by the "partial disclosure" results of Section 6.3.

In conclusion, it seems that the approach taken here yields insight into an aspect of corporate financial policy that has received relatively little attention in the debate and analysis that has arisen since Modigliani and Miller's original challenge.

References

1. A. ADMATI, A noisy rational expectations equilibrium for multi-asset securities markets, *Econometrica* 53 (1985), 629–657.
2. B. ALLEN, Generic existence of completely revealing equilibria for economies with uncertainty when prices convery information, *Econometrica* 49 (1981), 1173–1199.
3. B. ALLEN, The existence of fully rational expectations approximate equilibria with noisy price observations, *J. Econ. Theory* 37 (1985), 267–285.
4. R. ANDERSON AND H. SONNENSCHEIN, On the existence of rational expectations equilibrium, *J. Econ. Theory* 26 (1982), 261–278.
5. L. AUSUBEL, Partiallly-revealing rational expectations equilibrium in a competitive economy, *J. Econ. Theory* 50 (1990), 93–126.
6. K. L. CHUNG, "A Course in Probability Theory," Academic Press, New York, 1974.
7. P. M. DeMARZO, An extension of the Modigliani–Miller theorem to stochastic economies with incomplete markets and fully interdependent securities, *J. Econ. Theory* 45 (1988), 353–369.
8. P. M. DeMARZO, "Majority Voting and Corporate Control: The rule of the Dominant Shareholder," Technical Report, Stanford University, 1988.
9. P. A. DIAMOND, The role of a stock market in a general equilibrium model with technological uncertainty, *Amer. Econ. Rev.* 57 (1967), 759–776.
10. Deleted.
11. J. H. DRÈZE, (Uncertainty and) The firm in general equilibrium theory, *Econ. J.* 95 (1985), 1–20.

12. D. DUFFIE AND W. SHAFER, "Equilibrium and the Role of the Firm in Incomplete Markets," Technical Report 915, Graduate School of Business, Stanford University, 1986.
13. S. EKERN AND R. WILSON, On the theory of the firm in an economy with incomplete markets, *Bell J. Econ. Management Sci.* **5** (1974), 171–180.
14. J. GEANAKOPLOS, M. MAGILL, M. QUINZII, AND J. DRÈZE, "Generic Inefficiency of Stock Market Equilibrium when Markets are Incomplete," MRG Working Paper M8735, Department of Economics, University of Southern California, 1987.
15. Deleted.
16. M. JENSEN AND W. MECKLING, The theory of the firm: Managerial behaviour, agency costs, and capital structure, *J. Finan. Econ.* **3** (1976), 305–360.
17. H. LELAND, Information, managerial choice, and stockholder unanimity, *Rev. Econ. Stud.* **45** (1978), 527–534.
18. P. MCALLISTER, Rational behavior and rational expectations, *J. Econ. Theory* **52** (1990), 332–363.
19. M. H. MILLER, The Modigliani-Miller propositions after thirty years, *J. Econ. Perspectives* **2** (1988), 99–120.
20. F. MODIGLIANI AND M. MILLER, The cost of capital, corporation finance, and the theory of investment, *Amer. Econ. Rev.* **48** (1958), 261–297.
21. S. A. ROSS, The determination of financial structure: The incentive signalling approach, *Bell J. Econ.* **8** (1977), 23–40.
22. M. ROTHSCHILD AND J. STIGLITZ, Increasing risk. I. A definition, *J. Econ. Theory* **2** (1970), 225–243.
23. Deleted.
24. N. YANNELIS, "Random Preferences, Random Maximal Elements, and the Existence of Random Equilibria," mimeo, Department of Economics, University of Minnesota, 1986.

Risk Management: Coordinating Corporate Investment and Financing Policies

KENNETH A. FROOT, DAVID S. SCHARFSTEIN, and JEREMY C. STEIN*

ABSTRACT

This paper develops a general framework for analyzing corporate risk management policies. We begin by observing that if external sources of finance are more costly to corporations than internally generated funds, there will typically be a benefit to hedging: hedging adds value to the extent that it helps ensure that a corporation has sufficient internal funds available to take advantage of attractive investment opportunities. We then argue that this simple observation has wide ranging implications for the design of risk management strategies. We delineate how these strategies should depend on such factors as shocks to investment and financing opportunities. We also discuss exchange rate hedging strategies for multinationals, as well as strategies involving "nonlinear" instruments like options.

CORPORATIONS TAKE RISK MANAGEMENT very seriously—recent surveys find that risk management is ranked by financial executives as one of their most important objectives.[1] Given its real-world prominence, one might guess that the topic of risk management would command a great deal of attention from researchers in finance, and that practitioners would therefore have a well-developed body of wisdom from which to draw in formulating hedging strategies.

Such a guess would, however, be at best only partially correct. Finance theory does do a good job of instructing firms on the implementation of hedges. For example, if a refining company decides that it wants to use options to reduce its exposure to oil prices by a certain amount, a Black-Scholes type model can help the company calculate the number of contracts needed. Indeed, there is an extensive literature that covers numerous practical aspects of what might be termed "hedging mechanics," from the computation of hedge ratios to the institutional peculiarities of individual contracts.

Unfortunately, finance theory has had much less clear cut guidance to offer on the logically prior questions of hedging strategy: What sorts of risks

---

* Froot is from Harvard and NBER, Scharfstein is from MIT and NBER, and Stein is from MIT and NBER. We thank Don Lessard, Tim Luehrman, André Perold, Raghuram Rajan, Julio Rotemberg, and Stew Myers for helpful discussions. We are also grateful to the IFSRC and the Center for Energy Policy Research at MIT, the Department of Research at Harvard Business School, the National Science Foundation, and Batterymarch Financial Management for generous financial support.

[1] See Rawls and Smithson (1990).

should be hedged? Should they be hedged partially or fully? What kinds of instruments will best accomplish the hedging objectives? Answering these questions is difficult because, paradoxically, the same arbitrage logic that helps the refining company calculate option deltas also implies that there may be no reason for it to engage in hedging activity in the first place. According to the Modigliani-Miller paradigm, buying and selling oil options contracts cannot alter the company's value, since individual investors in the company's stock can always buy and sell such contracts themselves if they care to adjust their exposure to oil prices.

It is not that there are no stories to explain why firms might wish to hedge. Indeed, a number of potential rationales for hedging have been developed recently, by, among others, Stulz (1984), Smith and Stulz (1985), Smith, Smithson, and Wilford (1990), Stulz (1990), Breeden and Viswanathan (1990), and Lessard (1990). However, it seems fair to say that there is not yet a single, accepted framework which can be used to guide hedging strategies.[2] In part, this gap arises precisely because previous work has focused on why hedging can make sense, rather than on how much or what sort of hedging is optimal for a particular firm. Indeed, much of the previous work has the extreme implication that firms should hedge fully—completely insulating their market values from hedgeable risks.

In this paper, we illustrate how optimal risk management strategies can be designed in a variety of settings. To do so, we build on one strand of the previous work on hedging—that which examines the implications of capital market imperfections. Broadly speaking, this work argues that if capital market imperfections make externally obtained funds more expensive than those generated internally, they can generate a rationale for risk management.

The basic logic can be understood as follows. If a firm does not hedge, there will be some variability in the cash flows generated by assets in place. Simple accounting implies that this variability in internal cash flow must result in either: (a) variability in the amount of money raised externally, or (b) variability in the amount of investment. Variability in investment will generally be undesirable, to the extent that there are diminishing marginal returns to investment (i.e., to the extent that output is a concave function of investment). If the supply of external finance were perfectly elastic, the optimal ex post solution would thus be to leave investment plans unaltered in the face of variations in internal cash flow, taking up all the slack by changing the quantity of outside money raised. Unfortunately, this approach no longer works well if the marginal cost of funds goes up with the amount raised externally. Now a shortfall in cash may be met with some increase in outside financing, but also some decrease in investment. Thus variability

---

[2] This gap in knowledge is illustrated in the most recent edition of Brealey and Myers's (1991) textbook. Brealey and Myers do devote an entire chapter to the topic of "Hedging Financial Risk," but the chapter focuses almost exclusively on questions relating to hedging implementation. Less than one page is devoted to discussing the potential goals of hedging strategies.

in cash flows now disturbs both investment and financing plans in a way that is costly to the firm. To the extent that hedging can reduce this variability in cash flows, it can increase the value of the firm.

A prominent example of this line of reasoning is Lessard (1990).[3] Lessard writes: "...the most compelling arguments for hedging lie in ensuring the firm's ability to meet two critical sets of cash flow commitments: (1) the exercise prices of their operating options reflected in their growth opportunities (for example, the R & D or promotion budgets) and (2) their dividends... The growth options argument hinges on the observation that, in the case of a funding shortfall relative to investment opportunities, raising external capital will be costly."

The model that we develop below is very much in the spirit of this verbal argument. However, it takes the argument a couple of steps farther: rather than simply demonstrating that there is a role for hedging, we are able to show how a firm's optimal hedging strategy—in terms of both the amount of hedging and the instruments used—depends on the nature of its investment and financing opportunities. Or put differently, we illustrate how a well-designed risk management program can enable a firm to optimally coordinate its investment and financing policies.

The plan of the paper is as follows. In Section I, we briefly sketch several other explanations of corporate risk management that have been offered. In Section II, we present our model in its most elemental form, and use it to demonstrate the basic rationale for hedging. We then examine a series of practical applications of our framework. In Section III, we extend the model to show how optimal hedge ratios can be calculated as a function of shocks to investment and financing opportunities. Section IV considers the question of optimal currency hedging by multinationals that have investment opportunities in more than one country. Section V examines "nonlinear" hedging strategies that make use of options and other complex hedging instruments. Section VI briefly outlines a few further extensions. Section VII examines the empirical implications of the theory, and Section VIII concludes.

I. Other Rationales for Corporate Risk Management

A. Managerial Motives

Stulz (1984) argues that corporate hedging is an outgrowth of the risk aversion of managers. While outside stockholders' ability to diversify will effectively make them indifferent to the amount of hedging activity undertaken, the same cannot be said for managers, who may hold a relatively large portion of their wealth in the firm's stock. Thus managers can be made strictly better off (without costing outside shareholders anything) by reducing the variance of total firm value.

---

[3] Closely related rationales for hedging include Froot, Scharfstein, and Stein (1989), Smith, Smithson, and Wilford (1990), and Stulz (1990). These papers are discussed in detail below.

One weakness of the Stulz theory is that it implicitly relies on the assumption that managers face significant costs when trading in hedging contracts for their own account—otherwise, they would be able to adjust the risks they face without having to involve the firm directly in any hedging activities. At the same time, unless one also introduces transactions costs to hedging at the corporate level, the Stulz theory makes the extreme prediction that firms will hedge as much as possible—that is, until the variance of stock prices is minimized.

A very different managerial theory of hedging, based on asymmetric information, is put forward by Breeden and Viswanathan (1990) and DeMarzo and Duffie (1992). In both of these models, the labor market revises its opinions about the ability of managers based on their firms' performance. This can lead some managers to undertake hedges in an attempt to influence the labor market's perception.

B. Taxes

Smith and Stulz (1985) argue that if taxes are a convex function of earnings, it will generally be optimal for firms to hedge. The logic is straightforward—convexity implies that a more volatile earnings stream leads to higher expected taxes than a less volatile earnings stream. Convexity in the tax function is quite plausible for some firms, particularly those who face a significant probability of negative earnings and are unable to carry forward 100 percent of their tax losses to subsequent periods.

C. Costs of Financial Distress and Debt Capacity

For a given level of debt, hedging can reduce the probability that a firm will find itself in a situation where it is unable to repay that debt. Thus if financial distress is costly, and if there is an advantage to having debt in the capital structure (say due to taxes or agency problems associated with "free cash flow") hedging may be used as a means to increase debt capacity. The simplest variant of this argument, put forth by Smith and Stulz (1985), simply assumes that bankruptcy involves some exogenous transactions costs.

D. Capital Market Imperfections and Inefficient Investment

A more sophisticated version of the argument invokes Myers's (1977) "debt overhang" underinvestment effect to endogenize the costs of financial distress. This rationale for hedging (or equivalently, for using debt indexed to exogenous sources of risk) is given by Froot, Scharfstein, and Stein (1989) in the context of highly indebted less developed countries. The same basic point is made in a corporate finance setting by Smith, Smithson, and Wilford (1990). Stulz (1990) also argues that hedging can add value by reducing the investment distortions associated with debt finance.[4]

---

[4] A somewhat related paper is Diamond (1984). In his model of financial intermediation, "hedging" (actually diversification) mitigates incentive problems associated with debt finance.

We view these debt overhang explanations for hedging to be very close cousins of those presented both in Lessard (1990) and in our model below. Although the exact mechanism is somewhat different, all the theories rely on the basic observation that, without hedging, firms may be forced to underinvest in some states of the world because it is costly or impossible to raise external finance.

II. The Basic Paradigm

A. *A Simple Model of the Benefits to Hedging*

As stated above, hedging is beneficial if it can allow a firm to avoid unnecessary fluctuations in either investment spending or funds raised from outside investors. To illustrate this point, it is best to begin with a very simple and general framework. Afterwards, we demonstrate how this simple framework corresponds to a well-known optimizing model of costly external finance.

Consider a firm which faces a two-period investment/financing decision. In the first period the firm has an amount of liquid assets, w. At this time the firm must choose its investment expenditures and external financing needs. In the second period, the output from the investment is realized and outside investors are repaid.

On the investment side, let the net present value of investment expenditures be given by

$$F(I) = f(I) - I, \qquad (1)$$

where I is investment, $f(I)$ is the subsequent expected level of output, $f' > 0$ and $f'' < 0$.[5] For notational simplicity we assume the discount rate is equal to zero.

As will become clear, the company prefers to finance investment with internal funds first before turning to external sources. Therefore, the company will raise from outside investors an amount e, so that

$$I = w + e. \qquad (2)$$

Given the discount rate of zero, outside investors require an expected repayment of e in the second period.

We assume, however, that there are additional (deadweight) costs to the firm of external finance, which we denote by C. (Per dollar raised, these funds therefore cost C/e above the riskless rate.) These costs could arise from a number of sources. First, they could originate in costs of bankruptcy and financial distress, which include direct costs (e.g., legal fees) as well as

---

[5] The most natural interpretation of the concavity of $f(I)$ is that there are technological decreasing returns to scale. However, if the corporate tax system is progressive, then $f(I)$ will be concave even with constant technological returns to scale. Of course, taxes will impact the hedging decision in other ways since they affect not only the returns on *new* investment ($f(I)$), but also the returns on existing assets; see the discussion in Section I.B above.

indirect costs (e.g., decreased product-market competitiveness and underinvestment). Second, such costs could arise from informational asymmetries between managers and outside investors. Or, to the extent that managers are not full residual claimants, there may be agency costs associated with motivating and monitoring managers who resort to certain types of outside finance. Finally, managers may obtain private benefits from limiting their dependence on external investors. Thus even if there are no observable costs to external finance, management may *act* as though external financing has real economic costs.[6]

Regardless of which interpretation one chooses, the deadweight costs should be an increasing function of the amount of external finance. We represent these costs as $C = C(e)$ and note that $C_e \geq 0$.[7]

The issue of hedging arises when first-period wealth, w, is random. To the extent that there are marketable risks that are correlated with w, the firm may attempt to alter the distribution of w by undertaking hedging transactions in period zero. For simplicity, we make the extreme assumption that all the fluctuations in w are completely hedgeable, and furthermore that hedging has no effect on the expected level of w.[8] Given this assumption, complete hedging will clearly be beneficial if and only if profits are a concave function of internal wealth.[9]

To explore the impact of hedging on optimal financing and investment decisions, we solve the model backwards, starting with the firm's first-period investment decision. The firm enters the first period with internal resources of w and chooses investment (and thereby the amount of external financing, $e = I - w$) to maximize net expected profits:

$$P(w) = \max_I F(I) - C(e). \tag{3}$$

The first-order condition for this problem is

$$F_I = f_I - 1 = C_e, \tag{4}$$

---

[6] On costs of external finance, see e.g., Townsend (1979), Myers and Majluf (1984), Jensen and Meckling (1976), and Myers (1977) among many others.

[7] A more general formulation of these costs would allow them to depend also on the scale of the investment project undertaken, $C = C(I, e)$. This would make it possible for a firm to lower its per dollar costs of external finance by undertaking larger investment projects. The qualitative nature of our results is unaffected (although the exposition is somewhat complicated) by using this more general formulation. As we discuss below, either formulation can be rationalized in an optimal contracting framework.

[8] In order for fluctuations in w to be completely hedgeable (with default-free contracts) we need to assume that w is costlessly observable and verifiable. For example, w might represent a firm's exposure to gold price risk because the firm holds 100 bricks of gold. In this case, the exposure can be hedged if market participants can verify that the firm actually owns the bricks. For a discussion of how credit risks could interfere with hedging transactions, see footnotes 19, 28, and 31. The additional assumption that hedging does not affect the expected future level of w would follow from risk neutrality on the part of investors. It is straightforward to extend our analysis to the case where systematic risk is priced in equilibrium.

[9] Concavity of the profit function is clearly a necessary condition for *any* model in which hedging raises value.

where we have used the fact that, in the second period when w is given, $de/dI = 1$. Equation (4) implies that there is underinvestment—the optimal level of investment, I^*, is below the first-best level, which would set $f_I = 1$.

Moving to period zero, the firm chooses its hedging policy to maximize expected profits. As noted above, random fluctuations in w reduce expected profits if $P(w)$ is a concave function. Using the first-order condition in (4), the second derivative of profits is given by

$$P_{ww} = f_{II}\left(\frac{dI^*}{dw}\right)^2 - C_{ee}\left(\frac{dI^*}{dw} - 1\right)^2, \tag{5}$$

where f_{II} and C_{ee} are evaluated at $I = I^*$. If this expression is globally negative, then hedging raises average profits. Equation (5) can be rewritten by applying the implicit function theorem to (4) to yield[10]

$$P_{ww} = f_{II}\frac{dI^*}{dw}. \tag{6}$$

Equation (6) clarifies the sense in which hedging activity is determined by the interaction of investment and financing considerations. If hedging is to be beneficial, two conditions must *both* be satisfied: (i) marginal returns on investment must be decreasing, and (ii) the level of internal wealth must have a positive impact on the optimal level of investment. The latter condition is a ubiquitous feature of models of external finance in the face of information and/or incentive problems. Furthermore, there is substantial empirical evidence suggesting that corporate investment is indeed sensitive to levels of internal cash flow.[11]

Two simple examples may help to further develop the intuition behind equations (5) and (6). In the first, assume that a company has no access at all to financial markets. In this case, C is always equal to zero in equilibrium, and any variation in w is reflected one-for-one in changes in investment, $dI^*/dw = 1$. Equations (5) and (6) then tell us that $P_{ww} = f_{II}$: the concavity of the profit function comes solely from the concavity of the production technology.

In the second polar example, investment is completely fixed (e.g., the company has only one indivisible investment project with high returns). Now any fluctuations in internal funds translate one-for-one into fluctuations in the amount of external funds that must be raised, $dI^*/dw = 0$. Equation (5)

---

[10] The first-order condition (4) and the implicit function theorem together imply that I^*, satisfies

$$\frac{dI^*}{dw} = \frac{-C_{ee}}{f_{II} - C_{ee}},$$

at $I = I^*$. We assume that the second-order conditions with respect to investment are satisfied, so that the denominator of this expression is always negative.

[11] See, for example, Fazzari, Hubbard, and Petersen (1988), and Hoshi, Kashyap, and Scharfstein (1991).

then says that the concavity of the profit function comes exclusively from the convexity of the C function, i.e., $P_{ww} = -C_{ee}$.

Clearly, for intermediate cases—those in which $0 < dI^*/dw < 1$—the concavity of the profit function will come from both the concavity of the investment technology and the convexity of the financing cost function. Another way to see this is to substitute out dI^*/dw from equation (5), yielding

$$P_{ww} = \frac{-f_{II}C_{ee}}{f_{II} - C_{ee}}. \tag{7}$$

Equation (7) illustrates again that hedging is driven by an interaction between investment and financing considerations (as represented by f_{II} and C_{ee}, respectively).

Thus far we have used an arbitrary specification for the C function to establish conditions under which hedging is value increasing. However, it is unclear whether those conditions (i.e., the requirement that $C_{ee} \geq 0$) would emerge naturally if we derived the C function from an optimizing model with rational agents. Next, we examine an important class of such models, and demonstrate that the required convexity in C obtains under a wide range of parameterizations.

B. Hedging in an Optimal Contracting Model

The model we adopt is a variant of the costly-state-verification (CSV) approach developed by Townsend (1979) and Gale and Hellwig (1985). As we shall see, the prescription that companies should hedge takes the form of a simple and fairly weak restriction on the specification of this CSV model. Moreover, we are able to rewrite the $C(e)$ function explicitly in terms of parameters of the CSV model.

As before, we assume that in the first period a firm can invest an amount I, which yields a gross payoff of $f(I)$ in the second period. Also in the second period, the firm generates *additional* random cash flows of x from its preexisting assets. The cumulative distribution and density of x are given by $G(x)$ and $g(x)$, respectively.

As in the Townsend and Gale-Hellwig models, we assume that cash flows are costlessly observable to company insiders, but are observable to external creditors only at some cost. In particular, we suppose that the cash flows from the *existing* assets can be observed at a cost c, but that it is infinitely costly to observe the cash flows from the new investment project. As is well known, when $c > 0$, the optimal contract between outside investors and the company will be a standard debt contract. In return for receiving e in the first period, the company is required to repay in the second period a state-invariant amount D. If the company fails to perform, creditors pay the monitoring costs, then observe—and keep for themselves—company profits. States in which monitoring occurs can be interpreted as bankruptcy.

Our formulation of the CSV model is slightly different from that in Townsend and Gale-Hellwig: we suppose that a set of preexisting assets entirely determines the firm's capacity for external finance, so that this capacity is unaffected by the current investment spending. This parallels our setup in Section II.A above, where we assume that new investment spending has no independent effect on deadweight costs for a given level of external finance. That is, in both models C can be represented simply as $C(e)$. This assumption simplifies our analysis, but does not affect the basic results.[12]

Under these circumstances, the company chooses investment and outside financing to maximize

$$L \equiv \max_{I,D} f(I) + \int_D^\infty (x - D)g(x)dx, \qquad (8)$$

subject to a nonnegative profit constraint for outside investors:

$$\int_{-\infty}^D (x - c)g(x)dx + \int_D^\infty Dg(x)dx \geq I - w. \qquad (9)$$

The first-order conditions for this constrained optimization problem are

$$\frac{\partial L}{\partial D} = (\lambda - 1)(1 - G(D)) - \lambda cg(D) = 0, \qquad (10)$$

$$\frac{\partial L}{\partial I} = f_I - \lambda = 0, \qquad (11)$$

where λ is the Lagrange multiplier on constraint (9).

Equations (10) and (11) together imply that the firm sets I^* such that

$$f_I = \frac{1 - G(D)}{1 - G(D) - cg(D)} \geq 1. \qquad (12)$$

If there are no deadweight costs ($c = 0$) the firm sets investment efficiently ($f_I = 1$). However, if $c > 0$, then the firm underinvests, setting $f_I > 1$.[13] Underinvestment occurs in this model because an increase in I necessitates an increase in D, which raises the probability of bankruptcy. At the optimum, the firm reduces investment from the first-best level in order to economize on deadweight costs.

In this setup, there is a direct correspondence between expected deadweight costs of external finance and the probability of bankruptcy:

$$C(e) = cG(D), \qquad (13)$$

where equation (9) implicitly defines the function $D = D(e)$.

---

[12] One way to rationalize this assumption would be to suppose that the assets in place are comprised of physical capital that has some value in liquidation, whereas the new investment is in intangible assets (e.g., R & D, market share, etc.) that have no value in liquidation.

[13] This analysis assumes that there exists an optimally chosen D such that $1 - G(D) - cg(D) > 0$ and that investors' zero-profit constraint (9) is satisfied. Otherwise, there would be no solution to the problem in (8), and no investment would take place.

One can verify that the first-order condition, $F_I = C_e + 1$, derived in Section II.A, is identical to (12) above. From equation (11), it is clear that the expected shadow value of an additional dollar of internal wealth ($L_w = \lambda$) is equal to the marginal return on investment, which is given by f_I.

As before, hedging raises the value of the company if profits are concave in internal wealth, i.e., $L_{ww} = d\lambda/dw = F_{II} dI^*/dw < 0$. (Note that this is the same condition we derived in equation (6) for our reduced form model.) Totally differentiating equations (9) through (11) and solving for dI^*/dw, we can show that a sufficient condition for $dI^*/dw > 0 \forall x$ is that the hazard rate $g(x)/1 - G(x)$ is strictly increasing in x. This is a fairly weak condition, and is satisfied for the normal, exponential, and uniform distributions, among others.[14] Thus, when $f_{II} < 0$ and the hazard rate of $G(\ )$ is increasing, hedging is optimal in this CSV framework.

III. Optimal Hedging with Changing Investment and Financing Opportunities

So far our results create a very simplistic picture of optimal hedging policies—firms with increasing marginal costs of external finance should always fully hedge their cash flows. In this section, we extend our analysis to incorporate randomness in both investment and financing opportunities. As will be seen, these considerations lead to a richer range of solutions to the optimal hedging problem.

A. Changing Investment Opportunities

In the discussion above, we have assumed that a firm's investment opportunities were nonstochastic, and thus independent of the cash flows from its assets in place. In many cases, however, this assumption is unrealistic. For example, a company engaged in oil exploration and development will find that both its current cash flows (i.e., the net revenues from its already developed fields) and the marginal product of additional investments (i.e., expenditures on further exploration) decline when the price of oil falls. For such a company, hedging against oil price declines is less valuable—even without hedging, the supply of internal funds tends to match the demand for funds.

It is straightforward to extend the analysis of the previous section to address the question of the optimal hedge ratio in a world of changing investment opportunities. If we focus for the moment on linear hedging strategies (i.e., forward sales or purchases), the hedging decision can be modelled by writing internal funds as[15]

$$w = w_0(h + (1 - h)\epsilon), \qquad (14)$$

---

[14] The same restriction on the hazard rate also implies that $C_{ee} > 0$. This can be seen by twice differentiating equation (13), and then by noting that equation (9) implicitly defines $D = D(e)$.

[15] In Section V below, we consider alternative, nonlinear hedging strategies that involve instruments such as options.

where h is the "hedge ratio" chosen by the firm, and ϵ is the primitive source of uncertainty.[16] To keep things simple, we assume that ϵ—the return on the risky asset—is distributed normally, with a mean of 1 and a variance of σ^2.[17]

To model changing investment opportunities, we redefine profits as

$$F(I) = \theta f(I) - I, \tag{15}$$

with $\theta = \alpha(\epsilon - \bar{\epsilon}) + 1$. In this formulation, α is a measure of the correlation between investment opportunities and the risk to be hedged.

In period zero, the firm must choose h to maximize expected profits:

$$\max_h E[P(w)], \tag{16}$$

where the expectation is taken with respect to ϵ. The first-order condition for this problem is

$$E\left[P_w \frac{dw}{dh}\right] = 0. \tag{17}$$

Equation (17) simplifies to

$$E[P_w(1 - \epsilon)] = 0, \tag{18}$$

which can be written as

$$\text{cov}(P_w, \epsilon) = 0. \tag{19}$$

Equation (19) says that the optimal hedge ratio insulates the marginal value of internal wealth (P_w) from fluctuations in the variable to be hedged. Notice that this is *not* necessarily the same as insulating the total value of the firm, P, from such fluctuations.

To simplify the covariance term, we use a second-order Taylor series approximation (which is exact if the asset's return, ϵ, is normally distributed) with respect to h around $\epsilon = 1$.[18] Equation (19) and a little algebra then yield the optimal hedge ratio

$$h^* = 1 + \alpha \frac{E[f_I P_{ww}/\theta f_{II}]}{w_0 \bar{P}_{ww}}, \tag{20}$$

where a bar over a variable implies that an expectation has been taken with respect to ϵ, e.g., $\bar{P}_{ww} = E[P_{ww}]$.

[16] To see what (14) implies for actual futures positions and prices, define x_0 as the current futures price and q_1 as the future spot price of the variable in question. The variable ϵ then corresponds to $\epsilon = (q_1/x_0)$ and a hedging position of h corresponds to selling $h(w_0/x_0)$ futures contracts.

[17] Assuming that the mean of ϵ is one implies, as before, that the expected level of wealth is unaffected by the amount of hedging.

[18] If x and y are normally distributed, and $a(\ )$ and $b(\ )$ are differentiable functions, then $\text{cov}(a(x), b(y)) = E_x[a_x]E_y[b_y]\text{cov}(x, y)$. See Rubinstein (1976) for a proof. Note that if we were to assume that ϵ is log-normally distributed (with the same mean and variance as above), we would arrive at results very similar to those given throughout the paper.

The last term in equation (20) takes account of the direct effect of ϵ on output. Clearly, if $\alpha = 0$ (i.e., there is no correlation between investment opportunities and the availability of internal funds), it is optimal to hedge fully (i.e., $h^* = 1$), as in Section II above.

If $\alpha > 0$, the firm will not want to hedge as much. To see why, note that when ϵ is low, the firm may be low on cash, but doesn't need much, since it has few attractive investment opportunities. Conversely, when ϵ is high, the firm has good investment opportunities and therefore needs the additional cash generated internally. This logic implies that there is less to be gained from a hedge which transfers funds from high ϵ states to low ϵ states. Thus, the more sensitive are investment opportunities to ϵ, the smaller is the optimal hedge ratio.

It should be emphasized that in this case ($\alpha > 0$), the firm chooses *not* to insulate fully either its cash flows or market value from fluctuations in ϵ. In the example of the oil company mentioned above, the optimal hedging strategy would involve leaving the stock price exposed to oil price fluctuations. This conclusion differs from that of many other papers, which often imply complete insulation.

It should also be noted that according to equation (20), h^* need not necessarily be between zero and one. The possibility of $h^* < 0$ arises when investment opportunities are extremely sensitive to the risk variable. In that case it may make sense for a firm to actually *increase* its exposure to the variable in question, so as to have sufficient cash when ϵ is high and very large investments are required. Conversely, optimal hedge ratios greater than one will arise when investment opportunities are negatively correlated with current cash flows. In this case it makes sense to "overhedge," so as to have more cash when ϵ is low.[19]

To build some further intuition for why companies with different investment opportunities might implement different hedging strategies, consider the following example. Suppose there are two companies engaged in natural resource exploration and extraction. Company g is a gold company. It currently owns developed mines which produce 100 units of gold in period one at zero marginal cost. Thus company g's period one cash flows are $100\tilde{p}_g$, where $\tilde{p}_g$ is the random price of gold.

---

[19] Note that while $h^* < 0$ or $h^* > 1$ may (according to equation (20)) be optimal for the firm, such positions may implicitly leave the firm with negative first-period resources in some states. As a consequence, the capital market may no longer charge default-free prices for futures contracts, because these contracts can now involve credit risk. For example, a firm with initial wealth consisting of nothing but 100 gold bricks may not be able to buy more *on net*, because it has no nongold collateral. (That firm would have no resources to pay for the additional purchases if the price of gold were to fall to zero.) Similarly, a firm that sells futures contracts for more than the equivalent of 100 gold bricks might be unable to make good on its position when gold prices rise sufficiently. This entire credit risk issue disappears, however, if we are willing to assume that the investment function satisfies the Inada conditions, i.e., that the marginal product of investment is infinite at $I = 0$. In this case the optimal hedge ratio in equation (20) endogenously ensures that firm resources (and hence investment) are positive in all states.

Coordinating Investment and Financing Policies

Company g also has the opportunity to invest in additional exploration activities in period one. If it spends an amount I on exploration, it discovers undeveloped lodes containing $f_g(I)$ units of gold. Before the gold can be extracted, however, a further *per unit* development cost of c_g must be paid in period two. Thus, the net returns to an exploration investment of I are given by $(\tilde{p}_g - c_g)f_g(I) - I$.

Company o is an oil company. In most respects it is very similar to company g. Its period one cash flows are $100\tilde{p}_o$, and it is assumed that $\tilde{p}_o$ has the same distribution as $\tilde{p}_g$. Thus, both companies face exactly the same risks with regard to the nature of their period one cash flow.

Company o also can uncover undeveloped reserves containing $f_o(I)$ units of oil by spending an amount I on exploration in period one. Company o's development costs are higher than company g's—it must pay $c_o > c_g$ in period two to develop the new reserves before they can be extracted. Thus, the net returns to an exploration investment of I are given by $(\tilde{p}_o - c_o)f_o(I) - I$. To preserve comparability across the two companies, it is further assumed that $f_o(I) = (\bar{p} - c_g/\bar{p} - c_o)f_g(I)$, where $\bar{p}$ is the mean of both price distributions. This implies that in the "base case" where commodity prices equal their means, both companies have the same marginal product of capital at any given level of investment.

The key difference between company o and company g is the fact that higher development costs make company o's investment opportunities *more leveraged* with respect to commodity prices. For example, if $c_g = 0$ and $c_o = 50$, the marginal product of capital for the gold company falls by 10 percent when gold prices fall from 100 to 90. However, the marginal product of capital for the oil company falls by *20 percent* when oil prices fall from 100 to 90.

In the terminology of the above model, this difference in technology can be represented as a higher value of the parameter α for the oil company. Thus, the two companies should pursue different hedging strategies, with company g hedging more than company o. In other words, company o should leave its market value more exposed to fluctuations in oil prices than company g because its investment opportunities are more sensitive to the price of oil.

B. Changing Financing Opportunities

Up to now, we have assumed that the supply schedule for external finance—given by the $C(e)$ function—is exogenously fixed and insensitive to the risks impacting the firm's cash flows. However, it seems quite possible that negative shocks to a firm's current cash flows might also make it more costly for the firm to raise money from outside investors. If this is the case, it may make sense for the firm to hedge more than it otherwise would. This will allow the firm to fund its investments while making *less* use of external finance in bad times than in good times.[20]

---

[20] We thank Tim Luehrman for suggesting this case to us.

We can formalize this insight by generalizing the C function to be $C(e, \phi)$, where ϕ is given by $\delta(\epsilon - \bar{\epsilon}) + 1$. Such a generalization emerges naturally from the CSV model sketched in Section II.B. Suppose that instead of yielding x, the assets already in place yield ϕx. That is, the eventual proceeds from assets in place are correlated with the risk variable ϵ, and δ measures the strength of this correlation. As long as the distribution of x satisfies the increasing hazard rate property, then the $C(e, \phi)$ function that emerges from the CSV setting has the feature that $C_{e\phi} < 0$ (for fixed first-period wealth). This simply means that marginal costs of external finance, C_e, are lower for higher realization of ϵ.

If we assume for the moment that α—which measures the correlation of *investment* opportunities with ϵ—is zero, we can derive an expression that gives us the pure effect of changing financing opportunities on the hedge ratio. The methodology is the same as before. In particular, the first-order condition in (19) still applies. But now the optimal hedge ratio is given by

$$h^* = 1 + \delta \frac{\bar{C}_{e\phi}}{w_0 \bar{P}_{ww}}. \tag{21}$$

Given that $C_{e\phi} < 0$, the optimal hedge ratio is greater than one, with the effect being greater the more sensitive are assets in place to the risk variable ϵ. Again, the intuition is that hedging must now allow the firm to fund its investments and yet conserve on borrowing at those times when external finance is most expensive.[21]

However, even with a nonstochastic production technology (i.e., $\alpha = 0$), it is no longer true that investment is completely insulated from shocks to ϵ. This is purely a consequence of the fact that we are restricting ourselves to linear hedging strategies. Nonstochastic investment would (by the firm's first-order conditions) require that, once the hedge is in place, C_e be independent of ϕ. This generally cannot be accomplished using futures alone. In Section V below, we argue that if options are available, the firm will indeed wish to construct a hedging strategy that leads to nonstochastic investment.

IV. Risk Management for Multinationals

Our framework also has implications for multinational companies' risk management strategies.[22] Multinationals have sales and production opportunities in a number of different countries. In addition, the goods that they produce at any given location may either be targeted for local consumption

---

[21] In this particular case, there is no default risk associated with the futures position that implements the desired hedge ratio. The futures position will only incur large losses in those states where assets in place are extremely valuable. In such states the funds that can be raised against assets in place ensure that the firm will make good on its future position.

[22] Conversations with Don Lessard were especially helpful in motivating the work in this section. See Adler and Dumas (1983) for an overview of the traditional arguments for hedging exchange rate risk.

Coordinating Investment and Financing Policies

(i.e., nontradeable goods, such as McDonald's hamburgers) or for worldwide markets (i.e., tradeable goods, such as semiconductors). These factors complicate the hedging problem for multinational corporations.

We begin with a quite general framework which builds on that of the previous sections. Assume that the multinational can invest in two locations, "home" and "abroad," and that profits are given by

$$P(w) = f^H(I^H) + \theta f^A(I^A) - I^H - \gamma I^A - C(e) \qquad (22)$$

where $\theta = \alpha(\epsilon - \bar{\epsilon}) + 1$, $\gamma = \beta(\epsilon - \bar{\epsilon}) + 1$, and the production functions, $f^i(I^i)$, $i = A, H$ are increasing and concave. In this expression, ϵ now represents the home currency price of the foreign currency, and α and β are parameters (between zero and one) which index the sensitivity of foreign revenues and foreign investment costs to the exchange rate.[23] Implicitly, equation (22) treats the domestic currency as the numeraire.[24]

It is easiest to build an understanding of equation (22) by examining several special cases:

Case 1: Exchange rate exposure for both investment costs and revenues from foreign operations, $\alpha = \beta = 1$. This case might correspond to situations where both the outputs and the investment inputs are nontraded goods.[25] An example might be Euro-Disney in France, since local factors are required to begin operations.

Case 2: Exchange rate exposure for foreign investment costs but no exchange rate exposure for either foreign or domestic revenues, $\alpha = 0$ and $\beta = 1$. This case might correspond to a situation where the output from both plants is sold at the same price on the domestic market.[26] An example might be ball bearings, which can be produced using primarily local factors, but which are sold on a global market.

Case 3: No exchange rate exposure for investment costs but exchange rate exposure for foreign revenues, $\alpha = 1$ and $\beta = 0$. This case might correspond, as above, to a situation where the outputs are nontraded goods. However, now the investment inputs used in both locations are purchased on a single domestic market at the same price. An example might be a construction company, like Bechtel, which makes heavy use of construction equipment that is sold on a global market.

---

[23] Note that our earlier formulation in Section III can be interpreted as a degenerate case of equation (22), with $\beta = 0$ and I^H fixed at zero—i.e., no investment in one of the two countries.

[24] In this formulation, the external borrowing facility is also denominated in the home currency. In terms of CSV model developed in Section II.B, this amounts to assuming that the payoff x on the preexisting asset is home currency denominated. Thus, we are suppressing the issues relating to changing financing opportunities raised in Section III.B.

[25] Effectively, this assumes that the foreign currency price of nontradeable goods is not affected by exchange rate changes.

[26] This will be correct provided that this domestic currency price is constant.

In order to finance these different investments, the firm requires external finance of an amount

$$e = I^H + \gamma I^A - w. \qquad (23)$$

Maintaining our focus on linear hedging strategies, w continues to be given by equation (14) above. In this formulation, a hedge ratio of one means that period zero wealth, w_0, is held entirely in the domestic currency. In contrast, a hedge ratio of zero means that wealth is held entirely in the foreign currency.

Using arguments analogous to those developed above, we can solve for the optimal hedge ratio. (See the Appendix for a sketch of the derivation.)

$$h^* = 1 + \frac{E\left[(\alpha\gamma - \beta\theta)f_I^A P_{ww}/\theta f_{II}^A\right]}{w_0 \bar{P}_{ww}} - \beta \frac{E\left[I^A P_{ww}\right]}{w_0 \bar{P}_{ww}}, \qquad (24)$$

where

$$P_{ww} = \frac{f_{II}^H \theta f_{II}^A C_{ee}}{C_{ee}(\gamma^2 f_{II}^H + \theta f_{II}^A) - \theta f_{II}^H f_{II}^A} < 0. \qquad (25)$$

There are two basic components of the optimal hedge ratio in (24). First, there is a slightly more complex version of the "changing investment opportunity set" term,

$$\frac{E\left[(\alpha\gamma - \beta\theta)f_I^A P_{ww}/\theta f_{II}^A\right]}{w_0 \bar{P}_{ww}},$$

which effectively captures the *net* exchange rate exposure of foreign investment profitability. Second, there is a new "lock-in" term, $\beta(E[I^A P_{ww}]/w_0 \bar{P}_{ww})$, which is, loosely speaking, driven by the expected size of the foreign investment relative to internal wealth.

We can understand this lock-in term better by focusing on Case 1 above, where $\alpha = \beta = 1$. In this case (or in any case with $\alpha = \beta$), (24) can be simplified considerably—the changing investment opportunity set term disappears completely, and the lock-in term itself becomes easier to interpret. In particular, we demonstrate in the Appendix that:

PROPOSITION 1: *If $\alpha = \beta$, then the optimal hedging strategy is such that investment in both locations is independent of the exchange rate:* $I^H(\epsilon) = \bar{I}^H$; *and* $I^A(\epsilon) = \bar{I}^A \forall \epsilon$. *This hedging strategy is given by* $h^* = 1 - \beta \bar{I}^A/w_0$.

To understand the intuition behind the proposition, imagine that the company did not hedge at all but that the actual realization of the exchange rate coincided with its expectation, $\epsilon = \bar{\epsilon}$.[27] One could then solve for the optimal first-period levels of investment. What hedging does is to *assure* that

---

[27] Note that with $\bar{\epsilon} = 1$, the expected future spot rate is equal to the forward rate.

domestic and foreign investment will always be at exactly these levels, regardless of the actual realization of the exchange rate. In other words, hedging *locks in* the ability to carry out a predetermined (as of period zero) investment plan, where that plan is based on the expected future exchange rate.

In Case 2, with $\alpha = 0$ and $\beta = 1$, the lock-in term remains. However, it takes on a more complicated form, since I^A and P_{ww} are now random variables, and it is no longer generally true that $E[I^A P_{ww}] = \bar{I}^A \bar{P}_{ww}$. In addition, the hedge ratio is increased by the changing investment opportunity set term,

$$\frac{-E[f_I^A P_{ww}/f_{II}^A]}{w_0 \bar{P}_{ww}}.$$

This term implies that it is optimal to hold relatively *more* of the domestic currency than in Case 1. The logic is similar to that developed in Section III above. When the domestic currency depreciates, investments abroad become less attractive due to higher input costs. Thus, less foreign investment is warranted, and there is less need to hold foreign currency as a hedge against such an outcome.

Finally, in Case 3, with $\alpha = 1$ and $\beta = 0$, there is no lock-in effect. Because the price of foreign investment is insensitive to the exchange rate, it is unnecessary to hold foreign currency to guarantee a given level of foreign investment. At the same time, it is still worthwhile to hold *some* wealth in the form of foreign currency. This is because the correlation of net investment opportunities with the value of the domestic currency is now *negative*—when the domestic currency depreciates, returns on foreign investment are now *high*.

V. Nonlinear Hedging Strategies

Thus far we have restricted our attention to hedges which employ only forward or future contracts. With these instruments, the sensitivity of internal wealth to changes in the risk variable to be hedged is constrained to be a constant. That is, $dw/d\epsilon = (1 - h)w_0$, which is independent of the realization of ϵ. While such linear hedges can add value, they generally will not *maximize* value if other, nonlinear instruments, such as options, are available. Options effectively create the possibility for hedge ratios to be "customized" on a state-by-state basis.

To see why a firm might want its hedge ratios to be sensitive to the realization of ϵ, let us return to our oil company example. We argued that the oil company's investment opportunities become less attractive when the price of oil falls, and that this militated in favor of leaving its cash flows somewhat exposed to these fluctuations. But suppose we use futures to pick a single, state-independent hedge ratio, and that this hedge ratio results in the oil company cutting capital investment expenditures by 2 percent for every 1 percent decline in the price of oil. This might make good sense for small fluctuations in oil prices—perhaps the company's level of investment *should* be cut by 20 percent when oil prices fall by 10 percent. But it may not make equally good sense for the company to completely eliminate its investment spending when oil prices fall by 50 percent.

If this is the case, the oil company may wish to do some of its hedging with options. For example, by adding out-of-the-money puts on oil to its futures-hedging position, the company can give itself relatively more protection against large decreases in the price of oil than against small decreases. (Similarly, the company might also write out-of-the-money calls on oil, if a linear hedging strategy results in "too much" cash for very large increases in the price of oil.)

We can develop the general logic for nonlinear hedging strategies using the same basic setup as in Section IV. We denote the frequency distribution of the random variable, ϵ, by $p(\epsilon)$. If we assume complete markets, the firm's hedging problem now becomes one of choosing a profile for wealth across states of nature, $w^* = w^*(\epsilon)$, to maximize expected profits:

$$\max_{w(\epsilon)} \int_\epsilon P(\epsilon, w(\epsilon)) p(\epsilon) d\epsilon, \tag{26}$$

subject to the "fair pricing" constraint that hedging cannot change the expected level of wealth,

$$\int_\epsilon w(\epsilon) p(\epsilon) d\epsilon = w_0, \tag{27}$$

and to the first-order conditions for domestic and foreign investment (which are given in equations (A1) and (A2) of the Appendix.[28]

The first-order condition for the constrained optimization problem in (26) is given by

$$P_w = \lambda, \tag{28}$$

where λ is the Lagrange multiplier on the constraint (27). Equation (28) says that the optimal hedging policy equalizes the shadow value of internal wealth across states. By smoothing the impact of costly external finance in this way, the firm has optimally matched the cash demand of investment with the supply of internal funds.

Equation (28) implicitly defines an optimal level of internal wealth in every state. Note that because λ is constant, the implicit function theorem can be applied to (28), which after some algebra yields an expression for the optimal

---

[28] It is also important to check whether the candidate solution that emerges from (26) and (27) involves negative wealth in any states. If so, then an additional, nonnegativity constraint on internal wealth, $w \geq 0, \forall \epsilon$, might also be imposed in the maximization problem, in order to address the concerns about credit risk raised in footnote 19.

hedge ratio in each state:

$$\frac{dw^*(\epsilon)}{d\epsilon} = \frac{P_{w\epsilon}}{-P_{ww}} = -(\alpha\gamma - \beta\theta)\frac{f_I^A}{w_0 \theta f_{II}^A} + \frac{\beta I^A}{w_0}, \qquad (29)$$

where $w^* = w^*(\epsilon)$ describes the optimal level of wealth for every value of ϵ. The expression on the right-hand side of (29) can be shown to be a function (denoted by $l = l(w(\epsilon), \epsilon)$, of both internal wealth and ϵ:

$$\frac{dw^*(\epsilon)}{d\epsilon} = -(\alpha\gamma - \beta\theta)\frac{f_I^A}{w_0 \theta f_{II}^A} + \frac{\beta I^A}{w_0} = l(w^*(\epsilon), \epsilon). \qquad (30)$$

This expression defines the basic differential equation which the optimal level of wealth must satisfy. The constraint (27) provides the restriction that ties down the constant of integration.

One can use (29) to see when the first-best hedge can be attained using only futures contracts. In such cases, it must be that $(dw^*/d\epsilon)$ is a constant. Thus, making use of the results of Proposition 1, we have:

PROPOSITION 2: *With $\alpha = \beta$, futures contracts alone can provide value-maximizing hedges. In all other cases, options may be required to obtain the value-maximizing hedge.*

Futures hedging alone is thus optimal: (i) in the simple models of Section II with fixed investment and financing opportunities (i.e., with α, δ, and β equal to zero); and (ii) in our multinational setup of Section IV whenever there is the complete lock-in described in Proposition 1. In contrast, options will be needed for implementing the optimal hedges when either $\alpha \neq \beta$ or when there are state-dependent financing opportunities ($\delta \neq 0$) as in Section III.B. In the latter case, the use of options allows investment to be completely insulated from shocks to financing opportunities.[29]

For those cases in which options are required, equation (29) implicitly yields a recipe for the number of options to be purchased at different strike prices. While the first derivative of wealth, $(dw^*/d\epsilon)$, gives us the optimal exposure to ϵ, it is the *second* derivative, $(d^2w^*/d\epsilon^2)$, that describes the "density" of the options position at each strike price in the optimal hedge portfolio. Intuitively, an option at a strike price of $\hat{\epsilon}$ is indispensible for *changing* the degree of exposure at the point where $\epsilon = \hat{\epsilon}$. Thus, for example, if there are regions in which $(d^2w^*/d\epsilon^2)$ is large and positive, a substantial number of call options with strike prices in that region should be added. In contrast, for regions in which the hedge ratio is constant, $(d^2w^*/d\epsilon^2) = 0$, no additional options are required.

[29] To see this, note that with nonstochastic production technology, $F_I = P_w$, which by (28) is a constant.

Table I
Hypothetical Hedging Strategies and Investment Spending
(with Initial Wealth of 10)

			Net Funds Available for Investment			
State	Probability	Optimal Investment Spending	No Hedging (1)	Optimal Futures Hedge (2)	Payoffs to First-Best Options (3)	First-Best Hedge with Options (2) + (3) − cost
1	1/3	6	5	6	1	6 + 1 − 1 = 6
2	1/3	9	10	10	0	10 + 0 − 1 = 9
3	1/3	15	15	14	2	14 + 2 − 1 = 15
Total cost of options				−1/3 − 2/3 = −1		

To see the role for options more concretely, consider the following numerical example. Suppose that there are three equally probable states of nature, 1, 2, and 3, and that a firm's first-best levels of investment (i.e., that for which $f_I = 1$) are 6, 9, and 15, in each state respectively. Suppose also that at any level of investment below 6, the firm will be unable to compete and will be forced into bankruptcy, and that the firm has no access to external finance. Finally, suppose that internal wealth is initially equal to 10, and that a no-hedging strategy yields 5, 10, and 15 of internal funds available for investment. (See Table I for a schematic.)

If the firm has only futures contracts available to it, it can increase state one internal wealth only through an equivalent reduction in state three wealth. Its optimal hedge will therefore be predicated on protecting revenues in the lowest state, and will lead to an internal wealth configuration of something like 6, 10, and 14. This is a better profile than without hedging, but it does not generate first-best levels of investment.

Now suppose that options become available. With its futures hedge in place, the firm has excess cash in state two and insufficient cash in state three. The value-maximizing hedging strategy therefore involves buying 1 state one "put" option (which pays 1 in state one and zero otherwise) and 2 state three "call" options (each of which pay 1 in state three or zero otherwise). Because each option costs 1/3, their total cost is 1, which exactly eliminates the previously existing excess cash balance in state two. (See Table I.) Options are therefore valuable when value-maximizing hedge ratios are not constant.[30]

VI. Further Extensions

Although we have explored a number of applications of our basic risk management paradigm, several interesting questions remain. In this section,

---

[30] By put-call parity, one can achieve an equivalent hedge by using only the put (or call) option together with a different quantity of futures, or by using options alone.

we briefly sketch some additional extensions, focusing on the basic intuition and leaving the formal development for future work.

A. Intertemporal Hedging Considerations

Since the model developed above is essentially a static one—there is only a single period during which investment takes place—we have not addressed any of the potentially important intertemporal issues associated with risk management.

To see how intertemporal considerations can complicate matters, suppose that at each of N dates, the firm has a random cash flow and *a nonstochastic* investment opportunity. (The simplest model in Section II.A is just a special case of this with $N = 1$.)

Since investment opportunities are nonstochastic, a first guess might be—following the logic set out above—that the optimal strategy is to hedge *all* of the N random cash flows. For example, if the cash flows represent revenues from oil wells that will deliver 100 million barrels in each of the next ten years, it might seem that the best thing to do is to sell short 100 million barrels worth of futures with delivery one year hence, 100 million barrels worth with delivery two years hence, and so on, with contract maturities running out to ten years.

However, this raises a problem, at least if futures contracts are used in the hedge. If oil prices rise in the first year, the margin call on the aggregate futures position—representing ten years' worth of production—will be very large, and will much more than offset the positive impact of oil prices on first-year revenues. In other words, hedging the whole future stream of production leads to enormous margin fluctuations and hence to enormous variations in the year-by-year level of cash available for investment.

This suggests that if futures are indeed to be used, the aggregate size of the position will have to be lowered somewhat. The optimal hedge will have to trade off insulating the present value of all cash flows versus insulating the level of cash at each point in time.

An alternative possibility might be for the firm to structure its hedge using a series of forward contracts (or other "forward-like" instruments, such as swaps or indexed debt) rather than futures contracts. In an intertemporal setting, forwards might represent a more desirable instrument, since they do not have to be settled until maturity and hence do not entail interim margin calls. However, there are reasons to believe that forward contracts, while potentially useful, may not completely "solve" the problem sketched above. Precisely because they are not settled until maturity, forwards can involve substantially more credit risk than futures.[31]

---

[31] If the oil production is literally certain to be 100 million barrels, then forward contracts do not involve credit risk, and would allow complete hedging. However, if, more realistically, production quantities are uncertain or subject to moral hazard problems, forward contracts *will* involve some credit risk, and therefore represent an imperfect hedging vehicle.

In effect, one can think of a forward contract as (loosely speaking) a combination of futures plus borrowing. In the context of our model, this means that a decision to use forwards may lower the firm's ability to raise external financing at any point in time. As a practical matter, it may simply be impossible for many firms to take very large positions in forwards because of the credit risks involved.

B. Capital Budgeting When Risks Are Not Marketable

We have assumed throughout that all risks impacting a firm's cash flows are marketable and thus can be hedged. However, this will not in general be true. For example, a firm's cash flows will be abnormally low if its new product introduction fails, but there may be no futures market in which this risk can be laid off.

If this is the case, such unmarketable idiosyncratic risks will (in a world with costly external finance) impose real costs on the firm. Capital-budgeting procedures should therefore take these costs into account. Consequently, the CAPM (or any other standard asset-pricing model) will no longer be universally valid as a capital-budgeting tool. In other words, when investment projects impose large idiosyncratic risks that cannot be directly sold off, a second-best risk management strategy will involve reducing the level of investment in these projects below that implied by a CAPM-type discounting procedure.

The *magnitude* of the deviation from traditional capital-budgeting principles should depend on the same sorts of factors that we identified above as determinants of the optimal hedging strategy. For example, if the unmarketable idiosyncratic risk on the investment currently being evaluated is closely correlated with the availability of future investment opportunities, then the logic developed in Section III.A suggests that there is relatively less reason to "hedge" by skimping on this investment. In contrast, if the investment in question is uncorrelated with the availability of future investment opportunities, it should be evaluated more harshly.

C. Hedging and Product-Market Competition

Our framework also has the implications for how companies' hedging strategies should depend on both (1) the nature of product market competition, and (2) their competitors' hedging strategies.[32] To see this, suppose that there are two firms and they compete à la Cournot—they each choose production quantities, q_i, $i = 1, 2$, holding fixed the other's quantity decision. One can interpret the quantity decision as investment I_i, so that $I_i = cq_i$, where c is the marginal cost of a unit of capacity.

Assume that both firms have no access to external finance, so that investment can never exceed cash flow. Suppose further that cash flow is perfectly

---

[32] Adler (1992) also considers the implications of product market competition for hedging policy.

correlated across firms and that its mean is equal to I^*, which we define as the investment level that would prevail in an unconstrained Cournot equilibrium.

The important feature of the Cournot model is that investment is less attractive the more a rival firm invests. In the terminology of Bulow, Geanakoplos, and Klemperer (1985), investment is a "strategic substitute." This contrasts with other models in which the strategic variables are "strategic complements"—firms want to invest more when their rivals invest more. Such might be the case in a research and development (R & D) model in which there are informational spillovers across firms.

Suppose that neither firm hedges. When their cash flows exceed I^*, the unconstrained Cournot equilibrium prevails—both firms invest I^*. However, when cash flow is less than I^*, both firms invest what they have. Both would like to increase their investment in these states—since investment/output is relatively low and prices are high—but cannot due to liquidity constraints.

Now suppose that just Firm 1 hedges, locking in a cash flow of I^*. When Firm 2's cash flows exceed I^*, the unconstrained Cournot equilibrium is achieved—just as it would be without hedging. But, when Firm 2's cash flows are less than I^*, Firm 2 invests only what it has, while Firm 1 (which has hedged) gets to invest more. Because investment is a strategic substitute, the additional investment that hedging makes possible is particularly attractive to Firm 1 in these states: Firm 2 is not investing much; prices are high; and so are the marginal returns to the investment. Thus Firm 1 is clearly better off hedging. Indeed, Firm 1 would like to go even further—adopting a hedge ratio greater than one—because the returns to investments are now higher when cash flow is low than when it is high. In the context of our model with changing investment opportunities, this is analogous to the case of $\alpha < 0$.

One can also show that there are benefits to Firm 1 from hedging in this model if Firm 2 *does* hedge, but they are not as high as in the previous example. The reasoning is that if Firm 2 hedges—ensuring that it can invest I^* in all states—its generally stronger position makes investment less appealing to Firm 1. Thus, there is less reason for Firm 1 to use hedging to lock in a high level of investment.

There are two related implications that follow from this example. First, hedging policy inherits the strategic substitutability feature of the product-market game—a firm will want to hedge more when its rival hedges less. Second, the overall industry equilibrium will involve some hedging by both firms.

We conjecture that we might get very different results if investment were a strategic complement, such as in the R & D example mentioned above. In this framework, if Firm 2 does not hedge, the marginal returns to Firm 1 R & D are low when cash flow is low and high when cash flow is high. This is because when cash flow is low, Firm 2 is constrained and does little R & D. And when cash flow is high, just the opposite is true. This is analogous to the case of a positive α—a positive correlation between investment opportunities and cash flow—so that less than full hedging is optimal.

Thus it would seem that hedging is generally less attractive when investment is a strategic complement. One might also conjecture that, like in the previous model, hedging policy inherits the strategic character of the product-market game. In this case, that would imply that hedging policies are strategic complements: a firm will want to hedge *more* when its rival hedges more.

VII. Empirical Implications

In this section we discuss some of the model's empirical implications. However, before doing so we should note two points. First, it is not at all clear that our theory should be interpreted solely as a positive one, i.e., as an accurate description of the actual status of corporate hedging policy. Even if empirical work were to find that few firms currently hedge according to our theory, we nevertheless think that the theory has a number of useful *prescriptive* implications.

Second, empirical work in this area is made difficult by the fact that most hedging operations are off balance sheet (and thus are not included in databases such as COMPUSTAT). This lack of a well-developed database has led researchers to collect survey data on firms' hedging policies. We begin with a review of some of this evidence. Next, we propose a new type of test for optimal hedging, one which has the advantage of not requiring direct measurement of hedging positions.

A. Anecdotal and Survey Evidence

That the coordination of financing and investment is the basis for at least some managers' hedging strategies seems evident from what they say. For example, a Unocal executive, Matthew Burkhart, argues that "one possible added value of hedging is to continue on a capital program without funding and defunding."[33] And Lewent and Kearney (1990), in explaining Merck's philosophy of risk management, note that a key factor in deciding whether to hedge is the "potential effect of cash flow volatility on our ability to execute our strategic plan—particularly, to make the investments in R&D that furnish the basis for future growth."

It is, of course, far more difficult to say whether the considerations we outline are those that drive hedging strategies more broadly. A recent study by Nance, Smith, and Smithson (1993) uses survey data to compare the characteristics of firms that actively hedge with those that do not. Some of their findings are consistent with our framework, while others cut less clearly. One noteworthy result is that high R&D firms are more likely to hedge. There are a couple of reasons why this might be expected in the context of our model. First, it may be more difficult for R&D-intensive firms

---

[33] The quote is from "Shareholders Applaud Risk Management," *Corporate Finance*, June/July 1992.

to raise external finance either because their (principally intangible) assets are not good collateral (see Titman and Wessels (1988)) or because there is likely to be more asymmetric information about the quality of their new projects. Second, R & D "growth options" are likely to represent valuable investments whose appeal is *not correlated* with easily hedgeable risks, such as interest rates. Thus, the logic of Section III.A would imply more hedging for R & D firms.

Nance, Smith, and Smithson (1993), as well as Block and Gallagher (1986) and Wall and Pringle (1989), also find weak evidence that firms with more leveraged capital structures hedge more. To the extent that such firms have fewer unencumbered assets, and hence more difficulty raising large amounts of external finance, this finding also fits with our model.

Finally, Nance, Smith, and Smithson (1993) also find that high-dividend-paying firms are more likely to hedge. It is not obvious how this fact squares with our model. One interpretation—which is inconsistent with our model—is that high-dividend payers are not likely to be liquidity constrained since they have chosen to pay out cash rather than use it for investment.[34] However, a second interpretation would be that high-dividend firms need to hedge more if they are to maintain both their dividends *and* their investment. This interpretation is more consistent with our model.[35]

B. A New Test for Optimal Hedging

The broadest implication of our model is that firms use hedging to lower the variability of the shadow value of internal funds. In the model of Section III.A, this was accomplished by choosing the hedge ratio, h, such that $cov(P_w, \epsilon) = 0$ (equation 19); in the model of Section V, it was done by setting P_w equal to a constant (equation (28)). Either way, the first-order condition of our model generates a clear testable restriction: that the shadow value of internal funds and ϵ ought to be uncorrelated.

Consider then the model of Section III.A, in which firm value is a function $P = (w(\epsilon), \epsilon)$. This means that the risk variable, ϵ, may affect P directly through its impact on investment opportunities *given* internal funds, w, and indirectly through its effect on w *given* investment opportunities. In addition, there is a third possible effect on P: changes in w that are unrelated to ϵ. This suggests a simple empirical specification of the form

$$P_{t,i} = \alpha + w_{t,i}(\alpha_1 + \alpha_2 \epsilon_t) + \alpha_3 \epsilon_t + \nu_{t,i}, \tag{31}$$

---

[34] This reasoning is certainly consistent with Fazzari, Hubbard, and Petersen (1988) who found that investment was least sensitive to cash flow for high-dividend firms.

[35] Nance, Smith, and Smithson also find that smaller firms are less likely to hedge. This fact is generally inconsistent with our model if one believes that smaller firms are more likely to be liquidity constrained due to greater informational asymmetries. However, the tendency toward greater information asymmetries may be offset by relationships with certain capital providers, such as banks. Also, if there are fixed costs of setting up a hedging program, the gains from hedging for small firms may not be enough to justify the cost.

where t denotes time and i denotes firm i. The error term, $v_{t,i}$, is interpreted as all other exogenous shocks to firm value. To get unbiased estimates of the coefficients involving ϵ, we would require that any unobserved shocks to P are independent of ϵ.

To implement this regression, we need to consider the choice of actual data. Take for example, a gold-mining firm. In this case, we would interpret: P as the market value of the firm: w as the amount of contemporaneous cash flow; ϵ as the price of gold. One also might want to scale value and cash flow by the book value of assets, or some other indicator of size, in order to facilitate cross-firm comparisons.

Equation (31) says that the marginal value of internal funds, P_w, is given by $\alpha_1 + \alpha_2 \epsilon_t$. The cross term thus allows ϵ_t to have an effect on the *marginal* value of internal funds. As discussed above, optimal hedging should eliminate this effect. Thus, according to the model's first-order condition, the null hypothesis that the firm is hedging optimally is given by $\alpha_2 = 0$.

To understand the intuition behind the test, imagine that we estimated α_2 to be significantly negative. This would mean that firm value is more sensitive to cash flow in low ϵ states, or, said differently, that liquidity constraints are more costly when ϵ is low. In this case, the firm could be made better off by shorting the source of ϵ risk.

Note that the model does *not* predict that α_3 should be zero. This is the point we made earlier: firm value should generally *not* be completely insulated from ϵ.

One possible problem with using firm value as a dependent variable in a regression of this sort is that firm value may respond to cash flow for reasons outside our model. For example, even if there are no liquidity constraints, α_1 is likely to be positive simply because cash flow is serially correlated and the dependent variable is forward looking. This will not create a problem in the estimation of α_2, however, unless the degree of serial correlation is a function of ϵ. For example, if current cash flows are a better predictor of future cash flows when ϵ is low, we will estimate a negative α_2 even when the firm is hedging optimally. Thus, a key identifying assumption of our methodology is that other exogenous variables which simultaneously drive w and P are independent of ϵ.

If this identifying assumption is not appropriate, a second-best alternative might be to use investment, rather than firm value, as the dependent variable and to add Tobin's Q as another explanatory variable. Here too, the test would involve checking to see whether α_2 is equal to zero. The benefit of such an approach is that it would be harder to argue here that a nonzero α_2 was spurious. The drawback, however, is that investment is not quite the right variable to be measuring. Such a specification implies that the impact of liquidity constraints on the *quantity* of investment should not vary with ϵ. In contrast, the theory implies that the impact of liquidity constraints on the *value* of investment should not vary with ϵ.

In fact, regressions very much like the latter set that we propose have been implemented in the literature. Gertler and Hubbard (1988), Hoshi,

Scharfstein, and Singleton (1993) and Kashyap, Lamont, and Stein (1993) all find that investment spending is more sensitive to liquidity during episodes of tight monetary policy, i.e., that liquidity constraints are more binding at these times. Subject to the above caveats, these regressions would seem to suggest that the firms in these samples could have benefitted by hedging more actively against the risk of tight monetary policy, say by using interest rate futures.

VIII. Conclusion

When external finance is more costly than internally generated sources of funds, it can make sense for firms to hedge. While this basic point seems to have already been recognized in the literature, its implications for optimal hedging strategy have not been fully developed. In this paper, we have argued that there is a rich set of such implications:

1. Optimal hedging strategy does not generally involve complete insulation of firm value from marketable sources of risk.
2. Firms will want to hedge less, the more closely correlated are their cash flows with future investment opportunities.
3. Firms will want to hedge more, the more closely correlated are their cash flows with collateral values (and hence with their ability to raise external finance).
4. In general, multinational firms' hedging strategies will depend on a number of additional considerations, including the exchange rate exposure of both investment expenditures and revenues. In some special cases, multinationals will want to hedge so as to "lock in" a fixed quantity of investment in each country in which they operate.
5. Nonlinear hedging instruments, such as options, will typically allow firms to coordinate investment and financing plans more precisely than linear instruments, such as futures and forwards.
6. In an intertemporal setting, there is a meaningful distinction between futures and forwards as hedging tools. In particular, the use of futures will involve a difficult tradeoff between insulating the present value of all cash flows versus insulating the level of cash at each point in time.
7. Optimal hedging strategy for a given firm will depend on both the nature of product market competition and on the hedging strategies adopted by its competitors.

Appendix

Derivation of Equation (24)

First, note that at the moment when the investments are made, ϵ has already been realized. It follows that the first-order condition of (22) with respect to domestic investment is

$$f_I^H = \frac{\theta}{\gamma} f_I^A, \tag{A1}$$

which says that the firm equalizes the marginal revenue product of an additional unit of domestic currency across investments. Second, note that the marginal return on domestic investment will always be set equal to the marginal cost of an additional unit (in domestic currency terms) of external finance,

$$f_I^H = C_e + 1. \tag{A2}$$

Together these equations, along with the budget constraint in (23), tie down the optimal choices for domestic and foreign investment, *for given wealth* of w. By applying the implicit function theorem to them, one can determine the sensitivity of optimal investment plans to changes in ϵ, $(dI^H/d\epsilon)$ and $(dI^A/d\epsilon)$.

Moving back to the initial period when the hedging decision is made, equation (22) must be maximized with respect to h. The first-order condition for this problem is identical to that given in equations (17) through (19). Applying the formula for covariance given in footnote 18, equation (19) can be rewritten

$$E\left[C_{ee}\left(\frac{dI^H}{d\epsilon} + \gamma\frac{dI^A}{d\epsilon} + \beta I^A - (1-h)w_0\right)\right] = 0. \tag{A3}$$

Substituting in the expressions for $(dI^H/d\epsilon)$ and $(dI^A/d\epsilon)$ derived above and simplifying yields equation (24).

Proof of Proposition 1: We start by hypothesizing that I^H and I^A are nonstochastic, and $h = 1 - \beta\bar{I}^A/w_0$. We then verify that this is optimal, i.e., that the first-order conditions for both hedging (equation (24)) and investment (equations (A1) and (A2) above) are satisfied.

First, note that I^H and I^A constant and $h = 1 - \beta\bar{I}^A/w_0$ together imply, from the budget constraint in (23), that $(de/d\epsilon) = 0$ — external financing is independent of the exchange rate. This implies that C_e is independent of ϵ. But, given the first-order condition in (A2), this in turn implies that it is optimal for I^H to be independent of ϵ. Similarly, when $\alpha = \beta$, the first-order condition in (A1) reduces to $f_I^H = f_I^A$. So if it is optimal for I^H to be constant, then it is optimal for I^A to be constant also.

This establishes that a constant I^H and I^A are optimal, given

$$h = \frac{1 - \beta\bar{I}^A}{w_0}.$$

We now must check that this hypothesized hedge ratio is itself optimal. This now follows immediately from (24), once we note that $E[I^A P_{ww}]$ can be simplified to $\bar{I}^A \bar{P}_{ww}$ when I^A is nonstochastic.

REFERENCES

Adler, Michael, 1992, Exchange rate planning for the international trading firm, Working paper, Columbia University.

——— and Bernard Dumas, 1983, International portfolio choice and corporation finance: A synthesis, *Journal of Finance* 38, 925-984.

Block, S. B., and T. J. Gallagher, 1986, The use of interest rate futures and options by corporate financial managers, *Financial Management* 15, 73-78.

Brealey, Richard A., and Stewart C. Myers, 1991, *Principles of Corporate Finance* (McGraw-Hill, New York).

Breeden, Douglas, and S. Viswanathan, 1990, Why do firms hedge? An asymmetric information model, Working paper, Duke University.

Bulow, Jeremy, John Geanakoplos, and Paul Klemperer, 1985, Multimarket oligopoly: Strategic substitutes and complements, *Journal of Political Economy* 93, 488-511.

DeMarzo, Peter, and Darrell Duffie, 1992, Corporate incentives for hedging and hedge accounting, Working paper, Northwestern University.

Diamond, Douglas, 1984, Financial intermediation and delegated monitoring, *Review of Economic Studies* 51, 393-414.

Fazzari, Steven M., R. Glenn Hubbard, and Bruce C. Petersen, 1988, Financing constraints and corporate investment, *Brookings Papers on Economic Activity* 2, 141-206.

Froot, Kenneth A., David S. Scharfstein, and Jeremy C. Stein, 1989, LDC debt: Foregiveness, indexation, and investment incentives, *Journal of Finance* 44, 1335-1350.

Gale, Douglas, and Martin Hellwig, 1985, Incentive-compatible debt contracts I: The one-period problem, *Review of Economic Studies* 52, 647-664.

Gertler, Mark, and R. Glenn Hubbard, 1988, Financial factors in business fluctuations, in *Financial Market Volatility* (Federal Reserve Bank of Kansas City, Kansas City).

Hoshi, Takeo, Anil Kashyap, and David Scharfstein, 1991, Corporate structure, liquidity, and investment: Evidence from Japanese industrial groups, *Quarterly Journal of Economics* 56, 33-60.

Hoshi, Takeo, David Scharfstein, and Kenneth Singleton, 1993, Japanese corporate investment and Bank of Japan guidance of commercial bank lending, in K. Singleton, ed., *Japanese Monetary Policy* (University of Chicago and NBER,Chicago).

Jensen, Michael C., and William H. Meckling, 1976, Theory of the firm: Managerial behavior, agency costs and ownership structure, *Journal of Financial Economics* 3, 305-360.

Kashyap, Anil K., Owen A. Lamont, and Jeremy C. Stein, 1993, Credit conditions and the cyclical behavior of inventories, Working paper, MIT.

Lessard, Don, 1990, Global competition and corporate finance in the 1990s, *Continental Bank Journal of Applied Corporate Finance* 1, 59-72.

Lewent, Judy C., and A. John Kearney, 1990, Identifying, measuring, and hedging currency risk at Merck, *Continental Bank Journal of Applied Corporate Finance* 1, 19-28.

Luehrman, Timothy A., 1990, Jaguar plc, 1984, Harvard Business School Case No. N9-290-005.

Myers, Stewart C., 1977, Determinants of corporate borrowing, *Journal of Financial Economics* 5, 147-175.

——— and Nicolas Majluf, 1984, Corporate financing and investment decisions when firms have information that investors do not have, *Journal of Financial Economics* 3, 187-221.

Nance, Deana R., Clifford W. Smith, and Charles W. Smithson, 1993, On the determinants of corporate hedging, *Journal of Finance* 48, 267-284.

Rawls, S. Waite, and Charles W. Smithson, 1990, Strategic risk management, *Continental Bank Journal of Applied Corporate Finance* 1, 6-18.

Rubinstein, Mark, 1976, The valuation of uncertain income streams and the pricing of options, *Bell Journal of Economics* 7, 407-426.

Smith, Clifford W., Charles W. Smithson, and D. Sykes Wilford, 1990, *Strategic Risk Management* (Institutional Investor Series in Finance) (Harper and Row, New York).

Smith, Clifford W., and René Stulz, 1985, The determinants of firms' hedging policies, *Journal of Financial and Quantitative Analysis* 20, 391-405.

Stulz, René, 1984, Optimal hedging policies, *Journal of Financial and Quantitative Analysis* 19, 127–140.

———, 1990, Managerial discretion and optimal financing policies, *Journal of Financial Economics* 26, 3–27.

Titman, Sheridan, and Roberto Wessels, 1988, The determinants of capital structure choice, *Journal of Finance* 43, 1–19.

Townsend, Robert M., 1979, Optimal contracts and competitive markets with costly state verification, *Journal of Economic Theory* 21, 265–293.

Wall, Larry D., and John Pringle, 1989, Alternative explanations of interest rate swaps: An empirical analysis, *Financial Management* 18, 59–73.

Disclosure Decisions by Firms and the Competition for Price Efficiency

MICHAEL J. FISHMAN and KATHLEEN M. HAGERTY*

ABSTRACT

This paper develops a model of the relationship between investment decisions by firms and the efficiency of the market prices of their securities. It is shown that more efficient security prices can lead to more efficient investment decisions. This provides firms with the incentive to increase price efficiency by voluntarily disclosing information about the firm. Disclosure decisions are studied. It is shown that firms may expend more resources on disclosure than is socially optimal. This is in contrast to the concern implicit in mandatory disclosure rules that firms will expend too few resources on disclosure.

THIS PAPER DEVELOPS A model of the relationship between firms' investment decisions and the efficiency of the market prices of their securities. It is shown that more efficient security prices can lead to more efficient investment decisions. This provides firms with the incentive to increase price efficiency by voluntarily disclosing information about the firm. Disclosure decisions are studied.

The costs of disclosure are twofold. First, there are costs of producing and disseminating the information. Included here are opportunity costs of firms' employees, auditing and legal expenses, costs of printing and distribution, and costs associated with the release of any proprietary information. Second, there are traders' costs of assimilating the information. For instance, while it is not very costly to obtain a firm's 8−K and 10−K (once produced), it is quite costly to understand the implications of their contents. While the former costs have been recognized in the literature on disclosure, the latter costs have not. That is, while traders are sometimes viewed as having access to some costly information, the information contained in firms' disclosures is typically taken to be costlessly observed by all (see for instance Diamond (1985) and Dye (1987)).[1]

Taking traders' costs of learning the information content of firms' disclosures into account leads to new conclusions regarding incentives to expend resources on disclosure. In particular, it is shown that firms may spend more on disclosure than is socially optimal. This overdisclosure results from firms competing for the attention of traders. This is an interesting result given the public policy concern that firms, on their own, will spend less on disclosure than is socially optimal—

---

* Kellogg Graduate School of Management, Northwestern University. We would like to thank Sugato Bhattacharyya, Doug Diamond, Bill Rogerson, Chester Spatt, and seminar participants at Columbia, MIT, Minnesota, and Wisconsin for helpful comments. The second author would like to thank the Banking Research Center at Northwestern University for financial support.

[1] The distinction between producing and assimilating information is also made by Merton (1987). It is used to motivate the idea that firms have "limited investor bases," and the implications for asset pricing are analyzed.

witness the enactment and survival of the Securities Act of 1933 and the Securities Exchange Act of 1934. These securities laws form the basis for mandatory disclosure for publicly-held firms.

The nature of the model is as follows. Managers of firms make investment decisions that are not observed by the market. This unobservability induces less investment than is efficient. This underinvestment problem is less severe the more efficient is a firm's stock price. More efficient prices are more sensitive to the chosen investment level, and thus provide greater incentives to invest. Interestingly, the information contained in the stock price is itself, of no use to the management. It is the presence of the information in the market, and the efficient pricing of shares that is beneficial.[2]

In an attempt to increase price efficiency, firms expend resources on disclosure. A disclosure is a signal that contains information on future cash flows, and the greater the expenditure on disclosure, the more informative the signal. Once firms have made their disclosure decisions, traders determine which firms' disclosures to observe. It is assumed that it is too costly for a trader to study the disclosures of every firm. After traders observe firms' disclosures, trading in a securities market takes place. In the securities market, price efficiency is increasing in both the informativeness of the signal made available to traders and the number of traders who observe the signal.

The incentive for firms to spend too much on disclosure arises as a result of the interaction between firms' disclosure decisions, traders' information acquisition decisions, and price efficiency. While a firm independently determines how informative its own disclosure is, the determination of the number of traders who study its disclosure depends on the disclosure decisions of other firms. Since traders cannot study every firm, firms must compete for the attention of traders. Other things equal, the more informative the disclosure of a given firm, the more profitable it is for a trader to study the disclosure and trade on the information. So a given firm can attract traders from other firms, and makes its own share price more efficient, by making a more informative disclosure.[3] This competition for traders may lead to an equilibrium in which firms provide more informative disclosures than is socially optimal.[4]

The remainder of the paper is organized as follows. Section I presents the model and the securities market equilibrium. Section II analyzes firms' investment incentives. Section III analyzes firms' disclosure decisions. Section IV concludes the paper.

---

[2] This investment problem is similar to that studied by Grossman and Hart (1982). In both analyses, investment decisions are unobservable. There it is shown that if the manager faces a bankruptcy cost, the issuance of debt induces the manager to make a more efficient investment decision. Here, an increase in the efficiency of the market's pricing of the firm's shares induces the manager to make a more efficient investment decision.

[3] This is in contrast to Diamond (1985), Fama and Laffer (1971), and Hakansson (1977) where disclosure deters traders from expending resources on information collection for speculative purposes. This is because traders observe a firm's disclosure costlessly and are deterred from expending resources on other information sources. In these studies, price efficiency offers no social benefit so discouraging information collection is beneficial. See also Hirshleifer (1971).

[4] For discussions of positive externalities associated with disclosure, see Beaver (1977) and Easterbrook and Fischel (1984). These may arise if one firm's disclosure provides information about another firm.

I. The Model and Securities Market Equilibrium

A. The Model

Consider a three-date model with an investment and disclosure decision by firms, information acquisition and trading decisions by traders, and a price determination by a market maker. First consider the firms. There are I all-equity firms, each with a manager whose objective is to maximize the expected wealth of current shareholders, who are risk neutral. At date 1, firm i consists of m_i in cash, observed only by the manager, and a project which pays θ_i at date 3, where $\tilde{\theta}_i$ is normally distributed with mean $\bar{\theta}_i$ and precision (inverse of the variance) h_θ. The manager of firm i chooses $\bar{\theta}_i$ by investing $C(\bar{\theta}_i)$, where $C' \geq 0$, $C'' > 0$, $C'(0) = 0$, and $C'(\bar{\theta}_i) = 1$ for some $\bar{\theta}_i$; the expected marginal product of investment is positive but decreasing. The choice of $\bar{\theta}_i$ is observed only by the manager.

In addition to making this investment decision, a manager releases information. Specifically, the signal $\tilde{s}_i = \theta_i + \tilde{\epsilon}_i$ is generated, where $\tilde{\epsilon}_i$ is normally distributed with mean 0, precision τ_i, and $\text{cov}(\tilde{\theta}_i, \tilde{\epsilon}_j) = \text{cov}(\tilde{\epsilon}_j, \tilde{\epsilon}_k) = 0$, for all $i, j, k \neq j$. The manager determines the precision of this disclosure. For simplicity, assume that τ_i takes one of two values, τ_H or τ_L where $\tau_H > \tau_L > 0$. The cost of precision τ_i is given by $D(\tau_i)$, where $D(\tau_H) > D(\tau_L) \geq 0$. The choice of τ_i is observed by all. The signal can be thought of as a corporate disclosure such as an annual report or quarterly earnings statement, whose informativeness increases as more resources are expended on its production.

The investment in the project and the expenditure on disclosure are made at date 1 out of the firm's cash holdings. Any remaining cash is distributed as a dividend to shareholders. Note that since initial cash holdings are unobservable, the market cannot directly infer the investment decision from the dividend. At date 2, after the investment and disclosure decisions are made, there is a market in firms' shares. Assume that in this market, current shareholders liquidate their positions in the firms. Thus a manager's objective is to maximize the dividend plus the expectation of the date 2 share price (discounting between dates is ignored).[5]

There are N risk-neutral traders who can study firms' disclosures prior to trading. Assume that a trader can observe the disclosure of one firm costlessly, but observing the disclosures of additional firms is prohibitively costly. This captures the idea that even though firms make their disclosures publicly available, it is increasingly costly to study these disclosures. If a trader studies firm i, he observes s_i. Note that all traders who study firm i observe the same signal. Traders decide which firm to study based on their ex ante assessments of the value of information, which is determined endogenously. Let n_i denote the number of traders who study firm i. After informed traders study firms' disclosures, they make trading decisions.

The modeling of the securities market follows Admati and Pfleiderer (1988) and Kyle (1984, 1985). Informed traders and liquidity traders (whose demands for shares are determined exogenously) submit market orders to a risk-neutral,

---

[5] If shareholders liquidate only a fraction of their holdings, then the manager would maximize the dividend plus a weighted average of the expectations of the date 2 and date 3 share values. The qualitative results of the analysis would be unchanged.

competitive market maker. The market maker observes the total order flow for the shares of each firm, takes the position that balances supply and demand, and sets the share prices. Prices are set so that the market maker earns a zero expected profit on all shares.

Assume that traders follow symmetric strategies. Let x_i denote the market order for the shares of firm i by a trader who studied firm i. (Informed traders trade only the shares of the firm that they have studied since trading the shares of other firms is unprofitable). Let z_i denote the net market order for the shares of firm i by the liquidity traders, where $\tilde{z}_i$ is normally distributed with mean zero, precision h_z, and $\text{cov}(\tilde{\theta}_j, \tilde{z}_i) = \text{cov}(\tilde{\epsilon}_j, \tilde{z}_i) = \text{cov}(\tilde{z}_i, \tilde{z}_k) = 0$ for all $i, j, k \neq i$. Let p_i denote the price of shares of firm i.

The sequence of events is summarized as follows:

Date 1: Manager i chooses $\bar{\theta}_i$ and τ_i, and pays out the dividend $m_i - C(\bar{\theta}_i) - D(\tau_i)$.

Date 2: (i) Informed traders observe $\tau_1, \tau_2, \cdots, \tau_I$, and choose which firm to study. Traders who choose to study firm i, observe s_i and submit market order x_i.

(ii) Liquidity traders submit net market order z_i.

(iii) The market maker takes the position that balances the supply and demand for the shares of firm i and sets a price of p_i. Original shareholders of firm i receive p_i.

Date 3: The value θ_i is realized.

An overall equilibrium consists of three parts: (i) a solution to the manager's optimization problem, i.e., maximize $E[\tilde{p}_i] - C(\bar{\theta}_i) - D(\tau_i)$, (ii) an equilibrium distribution of traders across firms, i.e., $n_1, n_2, \cdots, n_I$, and (iii) a securities market equilibrium. We first consider the securities market equilibrium, taking $\bar{\theta}_i, \tau_i$, and n_i, for all i, as given. Then we use the resulting securities market equilibrium to determine the equilibrium level of investment taking τ_i and n_i as given. Finally, we determine the equilibrium disclosure decisions by firms and the distribution of traders across firms.

B. *The Securities Market Equilibrium*

A Nash equilibrium among traders is considered. Let $X_i(s_i)$ denote an informed trader's trading strategy for the shares of firm i; X_i specifies the trader's market order as a function of the signal observed (x_i denotes the actual order). Let $P_i(n_ix_i + z_i)$ denote the pricing function used by the market maker; P_i specifies the share price as a function of the order flow (p_i denotes the actual price).

A securities market equilibrium in the shares of firm i consists of a trading strategy X_i and a pricing function P_i such that (i) X_i maximizes each informed trader's expected payoff taking the other traders' strategies and P_i as given, and (ii) P_i is the expected value of share i conditional on the information contained in the order flow. Note that informed traders take the effect of their trades on price into account (they take the pricing function, but not the price, as given).

The value of firm i's shares depends on $\bar{\theta}_i$. Since traders and the market maker do not observe the manager's choice of $\bar{\theta}_i$, they must form some conjecture about

Disclosure Decisions

its value. Let $\bar{\theta}_i^c$ denote their conjecture. Assume that the market's conjecture is rational in the sense that even though the market does not observe a firm's investment decision, in equilibrium, the conjecture is correct.

As shown by Admati and Pfleiderer (1988) and Kyle (1984), there is a unique securities market equilibrium in which (i) informed traders' strategies are symmetric, linear functions of the signals they observe, and (ii) the pricing function for firm i is linear in the order flow for the shares of firm i. Lemma 1 presents this equilibrium.

LEMMA 1: *There is a unique symmetric, linear equilibrium with*

$$X_i(s_i) = \beta_{0i} + \beta_{1i} s_i, \tag{1}$$

$$P_i(n_i x_i + z_i) = \lambda_{0i} + \lambda_{1i}(n_i x_i + z_i), \tag{2}$$

where

$$\beta_{1i} = \left\{ \frac{\tau_i h_\theta}{n_i h_z (\tau_i + h_\theta)} \right\}^{1/2},$$

$$\beta_{0i} = -\beta_{1i} \bar{\theta}_i^c,$$

$$\lambda_{0i} = \bar{\theta}_i^c,$$

$$\lambda_{1i} = \frac{1}{n_i + 1} \left\{ \frac{\tau_i n_i h_z}{h_\theta (\tau_i + h_\theta)} \right\}^{1/2}.$$

Proof: See Appendix.

Informed traders take a long (short) position in the shares of firm i if the signal, s_i, is higher (lower) than the prior mean of share value, $\bar{\theta}_i^c$. The price of the shares of firm i, for realizations of $\tilde{s}_i$ and $\tilde{z}_i$, is found by substituting (1) into (2). The resulting price is:

$$p_i = \bar{\theta}_i^c \frac{h_\theta}{h_\theta + \phi(\tau_i, n_i, h_\theta)} + \left(s_i + \frac{z_i}{n_i \beta_{1i}} \right) \frac{\phi(\tau_i, n_i, h_\theta)}{h_\theta + \phi(\tau_i, n_i, h_\theta)}, \tag{3}$$

where

$$\phi(\tau_i, n_i, h_\theta) = \frac{\tau_i n_i h_\theta}{\tau_i + h_\theta + n_i h_\theta}.$$

In equilibrium, the order flow for the shares of firm i is $n_i \beta_{1i}(\tilde{s}_i - \bar{\theta}_i^c) + \tilde{z}_i$. Since the market maker knows traders' strategies, observing the order flow is equivalent to observing $s_i + z_i/n_i \beta_{1i}$. The equilibrium price is a weighted average of $\bar{\theta}_i^c$, the market's prior expectation of share value, and the signal derived from the order flow. The precision of the posterior distribution of $\tilde{\theta}_i$ equals the sum of the precision of the prior distribution of $\tilde{\theta}_i$, h_θ, and the precision of the distribution of the signal generated by the order flow conditional on $\tilde{\theta}_i$, $\phi(\tau_i, n_i, h_\theta)$.

Increases in τ_i and n_i increase the precision $\phi(\tau_i, n_i, h_\theta)$. An increase in the informativeness of the signal observed by informed traders has two effects. First, it increases the responsiveness of informed traders' orders to a given s_i. This makes the aggregate order flow a less noisy signal on s_i, since the orders of the liquidity traders become a smaller fraction of the total. Second, s_i becomes a less noisy signal on θ_i. Both effects serve to increase $\phi(\tau_i, n_i, h_\mu)$. An increase in the number of informed traders also increases the responsiveness of the aggregate order flow to s_i (though individual traders' orders become less responsive). By (3), an increase in $\phi(\tau_i, n_i, h_\mu)$ increases the weight given to the signal generated by trading.

II. Investment Decisions

This section examines the effect of price efficiency on investment incentives. At date 1, managers make disclosure and investment decisions. Although the decisions are made simultaneously, it is easier to consider the managers' investment problem first, taking τ_i and n_i as given. This yields an optimal investment policy as a function of τ_i and n_i. Then firms' choices of τ_i and the determination of n_i is considered.

Consider manager i's investment problem taking τ_i, n_i, and the market's conjecture, $\bar{\theta}_i^c$, as given. His or her objective is to maximize expected share price less outlays. That is, using (3),

$$\max_{\bar{\theta}_i} \bar{\theta}_i^c \frac{h_\theta}{h_\theta + \phi(\tau_i, n_i, h_\theta)} + \bar{\theta}_i \frac{\phi(\tau_i, n_i, h_\theta)}{h_\theta + \phi(\tau_i, n_i, h_\theta)} - C(\bar{\theta}_i) - D(\tau_i). \quad (4)$$

The benefit of increasing $\bar{\theta}_i$ is that it raises the expected share price. The manager's optimal choice of $\bar{\theta}_i$ satisfies

$$\frac{\phi(\tau_i, n_i, h_\theta)}{h_\theta + \phi(\tau_i, n_i, h_\theta)} = C'(\bar{\theta}_i). \quad (5)$$

Let $\bar{\theta}^*(\tau_i, n_i)$ denote this optimal choice. The manager's choice is below the first-best level which satisfies $C'(\bar{\theta}_i) = 1$. The marginal benefit of investment equals the weight placed on the signal generated by the trading process. Since the signal is noisy, this weight is less than one. This is why price efficiency is important for investment decisions. The more sensitive share price is to investment, the greater is the incentive to invest. This is reflected in the fact that $\bar{\theta}^*$ is increasing in $\phi(\tau_i, n_i, h_\theta)$, and thus increasing in τ_i and n_i.

As mentioned above, the market's conjecture is rational. Therefore, for a given τ_i and n_i, the market's conjecture satisfies $\bar{\theta}_i^c = \bar{\theta}^*(\tau_i, n_i)$. The expected share price less outlays, given this investment policy, is found by substituting $\bar{\theta}^*(\tau_i, n_i)$ in for $\bar{\theta}_i^c$ and $\bar{\theta}_i$ in the objective function of (4). This yields

$$V(\tau_i, n_i) = \bar{\theta}^*(\tau_i, n_i) - C(\bar{\theta}^*(\tau_i, n_i)) - D(\tau_i). \quad (6)$$

Since investment is below the first-best level, and since $\bar{\theta}^*$ is increasing in τ_i and n_i, it follows from (6) that if a firm could costlessly increase the informativeness of its disclosure (holding the number of traders constant) it would benefit from doing so. Also, a firm benefits from more informed traders trading in its shares. Now consider firms' choices of τ_i and the determination of n_i.[6]

---

[6] This investment problem is similar to the incentive problem studied by Holmstrom (1982). There, a worker's output is a function of ability, effort, and a random shock. The market, however, only

III. Disclosure Decisions and the Competition for Price Efficiency

Prior to trading, informed traders decide which firm to study. Their decisions depend on the expected profitability of studying the various firms, which depends on the securities market equilibrium. Lemma 2 gives the expected trading profits as a function of τ_i and n_i.

LEMMA 2: *If n_i traders study firm i and the precision of $\tilde{\varepsilon}_i$ is τ_i, then the expected payoff to each of these traders equals*

$$\pi(\tau_i, n_i) = \frac{1}{n_i + 1} \left\{ \frac{\tau_i}{n_i(h_\theta + \tau_i)h_\theta h_z} \right\}^{1/2}.$$

Proof: See Appendix.

A trader's expected payoff is increasing in τ_i and decreasing in n_i. An increase in the precision of the disclosure augments the informational advantage of informed traders, and thus makes informed trading more profitable. The greater the number of informed traders, the more responsive the aggregate order flow is to the firm's disclosure. This links price more closely to the disclosure and thus makes informed trading less profitable.

In equilibrium, all traders study some firm and no trader has the incentive to study a different firm. Since $\pi(\tau_i, n_i)$ is decreasing in n_i and $\pi(\tau_i, 0) = \infty$, there is a unique equilibrium distribution of traders in which expected trading profits are equal across firms (ignoring the integer problem). That is, $\pi(\tau_i, n_i) = \pi(\tau_j, n_j)$ for all i and j, and $\sum n_i = N$. Let $n^*(\tau_i, I')$ denote the equilibrium number of traders that study a firm when it chooses τ_i and a total of I' firms choose τ_H. Notice that if firms make symmetric disclosure decisions, then informed traders evenly distribute across firms, i.e., $n^*(\tau_L, 0) = n^*(\tau_H, I) = N/I$. Also notice that holding other firms' disclosure decisions fixed, more traders study a given firm if it chooses τ_H as compared to τ_L, i.e., $n^*(\tau_H, I' + 1) > n^*(\tau_L, I')$. Finally, holding a given firm's disclosure decision fixed, more traders study that firm if fewer other firms choose τ_H, i.e., $n^*(\tau_i, I') > n^*(\tau_i, I'')$ if and only if $I' < I''$.

Consider a Nash equilibrium where each manager makes a disclosure decision taking other managers' disclosure decisions as given. In equilibrium, none of the firms that choose τ_H have an incentive to switch to τ_L and none of the firms that choose τ_L have an incentive to switch to τ_H. Formally, for $0 < I' < I$, it is a pure-strategy equilibrium for I' firms to choose τ_H and $(I - I')$ firms to choose τ_L if and only if

$$V(\tau_L, n^*(\tau_L, I')) \geq V(\tau_H, n^*(\tau_H, I' + 1)) \tag{7a}$$

and

$$V(\tau_H, n^*(\tau_H, I')) \geq V(\tau_L, n^*(\tau_L, I' - 1)). \tag{7b}$$

---

observes output and based on output, the market updates its beliefs about the worker's ability. The worker has the incentive to provide effort since it influences the market's beliefs about his ability. The greater the effect of output on the market's beliefs, the greater the incentive to work. Thus the worker works harder when there is more uncertainty about his ability. Here, the firm invests more when its cash flows are riskier, i.e., when h_θ is lower.

For $I' = 0$, only condition (7a) must be satisfied and for $I' = I$, only condition (7b) must be satisfied.

PROPOSITION 1: *There is always at least one pure-strategy equilibrium.*

Proof: Suppose there is no pure-strategy equilibrium. Then $V(\tau_L, n^*(\tau_L, 0)) < V(\tau_H, n^*(\tau_H, 1))$, or it would be an equilibrium for all firms to choose τ_L. This implies that (7b) is satisfied for $I' = 1$. Thus $V(\tau_L, n^*(\tau_L, 1)) < V(\tau_H, n^*(\tau_H, 2))$, or it would be an equilibrium for 1 firm to choose τ_H and $I - 1$ firms to choose τ_L. Repeating this argument $I - 2$ times leads to $V(\tau_L, n^*(\tau_L, I - 1)) < V(\tau_H, n^*(\tau_H, I))$. This implies that it is an equilibrium for all firms to choose τ_H, which is a contradiction. Q.E.D.

Equilibrium disclosure decisions can be compared to the social optimum. If I' firms choose τ_H and $I - I'$ choose τ_L, then the social surplus is given by

$$I' V(\tau_H, n^*(\tau_H, I')) + (I - I')V(\tau_L, n^*(\tau_L, I')). \tag{8}$$

Note that trading profits are not included in the social surplus since they are transfers between traders. Let I^* denote the value of $I' \in \{0, 1, \cdots, I\}$ that maximizes (8). Proposition 2 compares an equilibrium outcome to the social optimum.

PROPOSITION 2: *Firms' expenditures on disclosure either equal or exceed the socially optimal amount. That is, if it is an equilibrium for I' firms to choose τ_H and $I - I'$ firms to choose τ_L, then $I' \geq I^*$.*

Proof: If $I^* = 0$, then $I' \geq I^*$. Say $I^* > 0$. Since I^* is the social optimum,

$$I^* V(\tau_H, n^*(\tau_H, I^*)) + (I - I^*)V(\tau_L, n^*(\tau_L, I^*)) \geq IV(\tau_L, n^*(\tau_L, 0)),$$

which implies

$$I^* V(\tau_H, n^*(\tau_H, I^*)) + (I - I^*)V(\tau_L, n^*(\tau_L, 0)) > IV(\tau_L, n^*(\tau_L, 0)).$$

This implies that $V(\tau_H, n^*(\tau_H, I^*)) > V(\tau_L, n^*(\tau_L, 0))$. Thus, for $I' < I^*$, $V(\tau_L, n^*(\tau_L, I')) \leq V(\tau_L, n^*(\tau_L, 0)) < V(\tau_H, n^*(\tau_H, I^*)) \leq V(\tau_H, n^*(\tau_H, I' + 1))$. Therefore, it is not an equilibrium for I' firms to choose τ_H and $I - I'$ firms to choose τ_L. Q.E.D.

To understand this result, notice the negative externality. In choosing τ_i, manager i considers not only the direct effect of τ_i on $\phi(\tau_i, n_i, h_v)$, but also the indirect effect on $\phi(\tau_i, n_i, h_v)$ through n_i. A higher τ_i leads to more traders studying firm i, and fewer traders studying other firms. In effect, firms attempt to attract traders away from other firms. So while firm i's share price becomes more efficient with an increase in expenditure on disclosure, other firms' share prices become less efficient. This competition for price efficiency is responsible for the possible overdisclosure.[7]

---

[7] Similar effects would be obtained with more general specifications of traders' costs as long as the cost of studying additional firms is increasing. The specification used here, i.e., studying one firm is costless and studying additional firms is prohibitively costly, simplifies the analysis. The discussion of the social optimum would have to be modified though. If traders incur direct costs (here, a traders' cost of studying a firm is only the opportunity cost of not studying a different firm), these costs must be accounted for in the calculation of the social surplus.

For an example of overdisclosure, consider the two-firm case and suppose

$$V(\tau_H, n^*(\tau_H, 1)) > V(\tau_L, n^*(\tau_L, 0)) > V(\tau_H, n^*(\tau_H, 2)) > V(\tau_L, n^*(\tau_L, 1)).$$

Since $V(\tau_L, n^*(\tau_L, 0)) > V(\tau_H, n^*(\tau_H, 2))$, both firms would be better off if they choose τ_L as compared to both choosing τ_H. However, since $V(\tau_H, n^*(\tau_H, 1)) > V(\tau_L, n^*(\tau_L, 0))$, each firm has the incentive to choose τ_H if the other firm chooses τ_L. The only equilibrium is for both firms to choose τ_H.

Equilibria may be symmetric or asymmetric.[8] Since firms are ex ante identical, they all have the same value in a symmetric equilibrium. This is is not the case in an asymmetric equilibrium.

PROPOSITION 3: *In an asymmetric equilibrium, firms that spend more on disclosure have higher market values.*

Proof: Consider an asymmetric equilibrium in which I' firms choose τ_H. Condition (7b) and the fact that $V(\tau_L, n^*(\tau_L, I' - 1)) > V(\tau_L, n^*(\tau_L, I'))$, imply that $V(\tau_H, n^*(\tau_H, I')) > V(\tau_L, n^*(\tau_L, I'))$. Q.E.D.

This result is similar to a standard disclosure result that more valuable firms disclose more information than less valuable firms; see, for instance, Verrecchia (1983). The causality is reversed though. Here, firms are ex ante identical and more disclosure leads to a more valuable firm by inducing more efficient investment. In Verrecchia, firms are not ex ante identical, and more valuable firms choose to disclose more information.

In general, it is difficult to say much about the effect of parameter changes on the equilibrium. This is illustrated by the following examples. Consider the two-firm case, where $C(\bar{\theta}_i) = c\bar{\theta}_i^2/2$ and $c > 0$. For this case,

$$\bar{\theta}^*(\tau_i, n_i) = \frac{\phi(\tau_i, n_i, h_\theta)}{c(h_\theta + \phi(\tau_i, n_i, h_\theta))},$$

and

$$V(\tau_i, n_i) = \frac{\phi(\tau_i, n_i, h_\theta)}{c(h_\theta + \phi(\tau_i, n_i, h_\theta))}\left\{1 - \frac{\phi(\tau_i, n_i, h_\theta)}{2(h_\theta + \phi(\tau_i, n_i, h_\theta))}\right\} - D(\tau_i),$$

where $\pi(\tau_1, n_1) = \pi(\tau_2, n_2)$, and $n_1 + n_2 = N$. Figure 1 shows $V(\tau_L, N/2)$ and $V(\tau_H, N/2)$, firm values in symmetric equilibria, for $\tau_L = 1$, $\tau_H = 2$, $h_z = 1$, $c = 0.01$, $N = 50$, $D(\tau_L) = 1$, and $D(\tau_H) = 10$, and for a range of values of $1/h_\theta$. The equilibria are indicated. For low-risk firms (i.e., low values of $1/h_\theta$), the equilibrium is one in which both firms choose τ_L. For intermediate-risk firms, both firms choose τ_H. For high-risk firms, the equilibrium is again, one in which both firms choose τ_L.

Figures 2 and 3 show $V(\tau_L, N/2)$ and $V(\tau_H, N/2)$ and show how the equilibrium varies depending on the number of traders. In Figure 2, $\tau_L = 1.9$, $\tau_H = 2.8$, $h_\theta = 5$, $h_z = 1$, $c = 0.01$, $D(\tau_L) = 0.99$, and $D(\tau_H) = 6.65$, and in Figure 3, $\tau_L = 1.5$, $\tau_H = 3$, $h_\theta = 1$, $h_z = 1$, $c = 0.01$, $D(\tau_L) = 1$, and $D(\tau_H) = 6$. For the parameter values

---

[8] Since firms are ex ante identical, if there is an asymmetric equilibrium, then there are multiple equilibria. For in an equilibrium where I' firms choose τ_H, the identity of the I' firms does not matter. More fundamentally, there may exist multiple equilibria in which aggregate expenditures on disclosure differ.

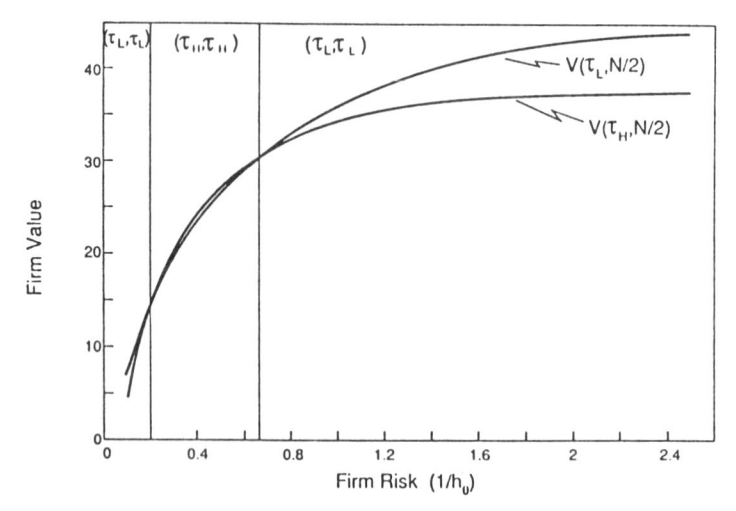

Figure 1. Two-firm example #1. Firm value as a function of the precision of its disclosure, $\tau_L = 1$ or $\tau_H = 2$, the number of traders who observe the disclosure, $N/2 = 25$, and firm risk, $1/h_v$, is shown. The equilibria for the various ranges of firm risk are indicated.

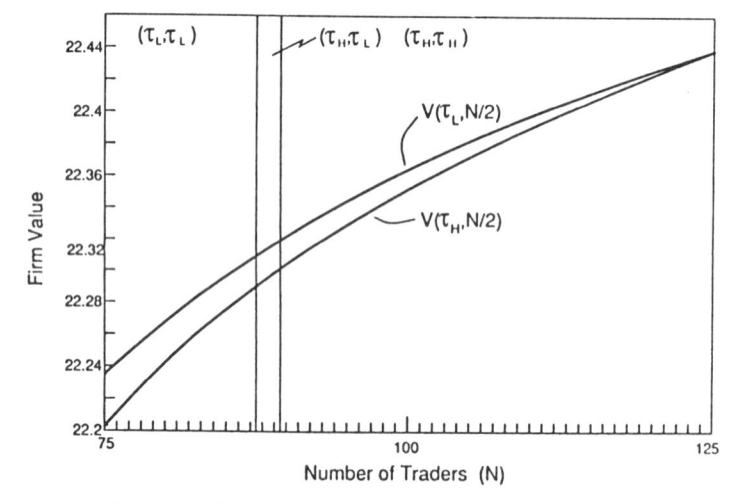

Figure 2. Two-firm example #2. Firm value as a function of the precision of its disclosure, $\tau_L = 1.9$ or $\tau_H = 2.8$, the number of traders who observe the disclosure, $N/2$, and firm risk, 0.2, is shown. The equilibria for the various ranges of the total number of traders, N, are indicated.

of Figure 2, when there are not many traders, both firms choose τ_L. For an intermediate range of traders, the equilibrium is asymmetric. When there are a large number of traders, both firms choose τ_H.

For the parameter values of Figure 3, it is almost the reverse situation. When there are not many traders, both firms choose τ_H. For an intermediate range of traders, there are two equilibria. It is an equilibrium for both firms to choose τ_L

Disclosure Decisions

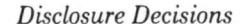

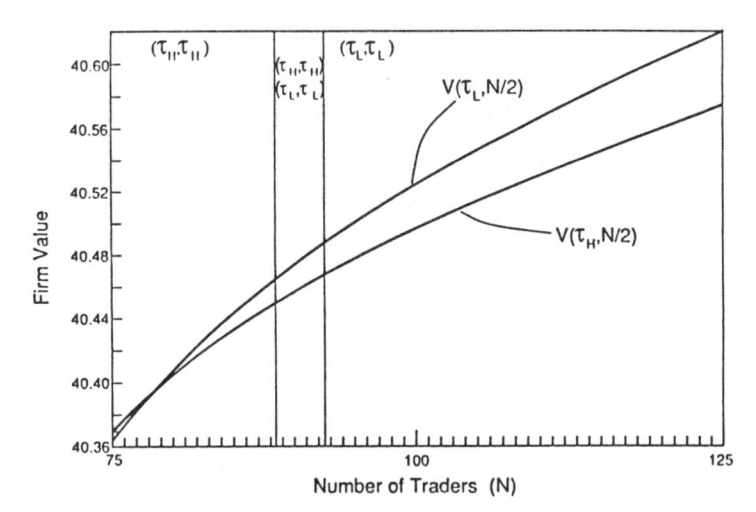

Figure 3. Two-firm example #3. Firm value as a function of the precision of its disclosure, $\tau_L = 1.5$ or $\tau_H = 3$, the number of traders who observe the disclosure, $N/2$, and firm risk, 1, is shown. The equilibria for the various ranges of the total number of traders, N, are indicated.

and it is an equilibrium for both firms to choose τ_H. When there is a large number of traders, both firms choose τ_L.

IV. Conclusion

Critics of mandatory disclosure regulations argue that firms have the incentive to disclose the appropriate amount of information—hence mandatory disclosure is a wasteful use of corporate resources. The main result of this paper reinforces this argument in the sense that firms may actually have the incentive to disclose too much information, and mandatory disclosure of additional information only aggravates the problem. Additional disclosure does increase the efficiency of prices, but the benefits do not justify the costs.[9]

The key feature of our model is a recognition of the costs traders incur when making use of publicly available information. It is assumed that traders face increasing costs in studying firms' disclosures. In practice, traders' costs may be more complicated. There may be costs of learning about a firm's industry as well as costs of learning about the firm itself. If so, then traders may face decreasing costs when studying firms in the same industry and increasing costs when studying firms in different industries. In such a case, both positive and negative externalities may be present. When one firm spends more on disclosure, other firms in the same industry may gain traders, while firms in other industries may lose traders.

[9] In practice, disclosure regulations not only specify the amount of information that should be disclosed, but also the type of information that should be disclosed. This paper deals only with the former issue. For an analysis of the latter issue, see Fishman and Hagerty (1989).

Appendix

Proof of Lemma 1: The subscript i, referring to firm i is suppressed in order to simplify the notation. Consider a pricing function

$$P(\textstyle\sum_j \tilde{x}_j + \tilde{z}) = \lambda_0 + \lambda_1(\textstyle\sum_j \tilde{x}_j + \tilde{z}), \tag{A1}$$

where λ_0 and λ_1 are constants, and trading strategies

$$X(\tilde{\theta} + \tilde{\varepsilon}) = \beta_0 + \beta_1(\tilde{\theta} + \tilde{\varepsilon}), \tag{A2}$$

where β_0 and β_1 are constants. Trader k, taking (A1) and (A2), for $j \neq k$, as given, solves the following problem:

$$\max_{x_k} E[x_k(\tilde{\theta} - \lambda_0 - \lambda_1((n-1)(\beta_0 + \beta_1(\tilde{\theta} + \tilde{\varepsilon})) + x_k + \tilde{z})) \mid \tilde{\theta} + \tilde{\varepsilon}],$$

which can be rewritten as

$$\max_{x_k} x_k \left[\frac{h_\theta \bar{\theta}^c + \tau(\tilde{\theta} + \tilde{\varepsilon})}{h_\theta + \tau} - \lambda_0 - \lambda_1((n-1)(\beta_0 + \beta_1(\tilde{\theta} + \tilde{\varepsilon})) + x_k) \right].$$

The solution to this problem is given by

$$x_k = \frac{\left[\dfrac{h_\theta \bar{\theta}^c}{h_\theta + \tau} - \lambda_0 - \lambda_1(n-1)\beta_0 \right] + \left[\dfrac{\tau}{h_\theta + \tau} - \lambda_1(n-1)\beta_1 \right][\tilde{\theta} + \tilde{\varepsilon}]}{2\lambda_1},$$

with the second-order conditions being satisfied if $\lambda_1 > 0$. The Nash equilibrium for the traders is found by setting

$$\beta_0 = \frac{\dfrac{h_\theta \bar{\theta}^c}{h_\theta + \tau} - \lambda_0 - \lambda_1(n-1)\beta_0}{2\lambda_1}$$

and

$$\beta_1 = \frac{\dfrac{\tau}{h_\theta + \tau} - \lambda_1(n-1)\beta_1}{2\lambda_1}.$$

Solving these two equations yields

$$\beta_0 = \frac{\dfrac{h_\theta \bar{\theta}^c}{h_\theta + \tau} - \lambda_0}{\lambda_1(n+1)}$$

and

$$\beta_1 = \frac{\dfrac{\tau}{h_\theta + \tau}}{\lambda_1(n+1)}. \tag{A3}$$

Disclosure Decisions

Now consider the market maker's problem. Since he or she is competitive, the pricing rule must satisfy, using (A2),

$$\lambda_0 + \lambda_1 \left(\sum_j \tilde{x}_j + \tilde{z} \right) = E[\tilde{\theta} \mid n(\beta_0 + \beta_1(\tilde{\theta} + \tilde{\varepsilon})) + \tilde{z}]. \quad (A4)$$

Substituting (A3) into (A4) and using Bayes' rule yields

$$\lambda_0 = \bar{\theta}^c$$

and

$$\lambda_1 = \frac{1}{n+1} \left[\frac{\tau n h_z}{h_\theta (h_\theta + \tau)} \right]^{1/2}. \quad (A5)$$

Substituting (A5) into (A3) yields

$$\beta_0 = -\bar{\theta}^c \left[\frac{h_\theta \tau}{n(h_\theta + \tau) h_z} \right]^{1/2}$$

and

$$\beta_1 = \left[\frac{h_\theta \tau}{n(h_\theta + \tau) h_z} \right]^{1/2}, \quad (A6)$$

which gives the unique linear symmetric equilibrium. Q.E.D.

Proof of Lemma 2: The proof follows directly from the substitution of β_{0i}, β_{1i}, λ_{0i}, and λ_{1i} into $E[(\beta_{0i} + \beta_{1i}(\tilde{\theta}_i + \tilde{\varepsilon}_i))(\tilde{\theta}_i - \lambda_{0i} - \lambda_{1i}(n_i(\beta_{0i} + \beta_{1i}(\tilde{\theta}_i + \tilde{\varepsilon}_i)) + \tilde{z}_i))]$. Q.E.D.

REFERENCES

Admati, A. R. and P. Pfleiderer, 1988, A theory of intraday patterns: Volume and price variability, *Review of Financial Studies* 1, 3–40.

Beaver, W. B., 1977, The nature of mandated disclosure, in: *Report of the SEC Advisory Committee on Corporate Disclosure* (U.S. Government Printing Office, Washington, D.C.).

Diamond, D. W., 1985, Optimal release of information by firms, *Journal of Finance* 40, 1071–1094.

Dye, R. A., 1987, Mandatory vs. voluntary disclosures: The cases of financial and real externalities, Working Paper, Northwestern University.

Easterbrook, F. H. and D. R. Fischel, 1984, Mandatory disclosure and the protection of investors, *Virginia Law Review* 70, 669–715.

Fama, E. F. and A. B. Laffer, 1971, Information and capital markets, *Journal of Business* 44, 289–298.

Fishman, M. J. and K. M. Hagerty, 1989, The optimal amount of discretion to allow in disclosure, Working Paper, Northwestern University.

Grossman, S. J. and O. D. Hart, 1982, Corporate financial structure and managerial incentives, in J. J. McCall ed.: *The Economics of Information and Uncertainty* (University of Chicago Press, Chicago, IL).

Hakansson, N. H., 1977, Interim disclosure and public forecasts: An economic analysis and a framework for choice, *Accounting Review* 52, 396–416.

Hirshleifer, J., 1971, The private and social value of information and the reward to inventive activity, *American Economic Review* 61, 561–574.

Holmstrom, B., 1982, Managerial incentive problems—A dynamic perspective, in: *Essays in Economics and Management in Honour of Lars Wahlbeck* (Swedish School of Economics, Helsinki).

Kyle, A. S., 1984, Market structure, information, futures markets, and price formation, in G. G. Storey, A. Schmitz, and A. Sarris eds.: *International Agricultural Trade: Advanced Readings in Price Formation, Market Structure, and Price Instability* (Westview Press, Boulder).

———, 1985, Continuous auctions and insider trading, *Econometrica* 53, 1315–1335.

Merton, R. C., 1987, A simple model of capital market equilibrium with incomplete information, *Journal of Finance* 42, 483–510.

Verrecchia, R. E., 1983, Discretionary disclosure, *Journal of Accounting and Economics* 5, 179–194.

[12]

Insider Trading: Should It Be Prohibited?

Hayne E. Leland
University of California, Berkeley

Insider trading moves forward the resolution of uncertainty. Using a rational expectations model with endogenous investment level, I show that, when insider trading is permitted, (i) stock prices better reflect information and will be higher on average, (ii) expected real investment will rise, (iii) markets are less liquid, (iv) owners of investment projects and insiders will benefit, and (v) outside investors and liquidity traders will be hurt. Total welfare may increase or decrease depending on the economic environment. Factors that favor the prohibition of insider trading are identified.

I. Introduction

Is insider trading good for financial markets? In 1934, the U.S. Congress decided "no," and insider trading in the United States has been regulated by the Securities and Exchange Commission since that time. Not all countries have followed the U.S. example, and the debate continues: some countries without regulation are now considering it, whereas in academic circles, the benefits of regulating insider trading are still being contested (see, e.g., Manne 1966; Carlton and Fischel 1983; Easterbrook 1985; Glosten 1988; Bajeux and Rochet 1989; Manove 1989).

The merits of insider trading have been debated on two levels: (i) Is it "fair" to have trading when individuals are differentially informed? (ii) Is it economically efficient to allow insider trading?

I thank the Laboratoire d'Econometrie for support during this research, and particularly Isabelle Bajeux and Patrick Bolton for their generous help. Gerard Gennotte, Pete Kyle, Ailsa Roell, and Michael Fishman also provided important insights. I retain credit for all mistakes.

The Securities Exchange Act of 1934 justifies the regulation of insider trading on the presumption that such activity is "unfair" to outside investors (see, e.g., Brudney 1979). Critics point out that trading is always unfair whenever one investor is better informed than another. Yet no one has advocated that all trading based on private information should (or could) be restricted. The line between what information is fair and what information is unfair has been the subject of considerable legal argument. Recent U.S. cases have emphasized breach of fiduciary duty by employees using privileged information rather than unfairness.

Because there is no commonly accepted definition of "unfair," this aspect of insider trading is not directly addressed. But the second aspect of insider trading, its impact on economic efficiency and welfare, is more susceptible to economic analysis. One can show which parties gain, which lose, and how much is gained or lost. When the sum of monetary gains and losses can be associated with economic welfare, this analysis also provides a measure of the net benefits (or costs) that result from prohibiting insider trading.[1]

To understand the nature of the current debate, it is useful to review the common arguments cited pro and con insider trading.

Pro.—(a) Insider trading will bring new and useful information into asset prices. Decision makers—both portfolio managers and firms making real investment decisions—can reduce risk and improve performance when prices reflect better information. (b) Because of reduced risk, asset prices will be higher and more real investment will occur.

Con.—(a) Outside investors will invest less because the market is "unfair." Asset prices will be lower and less real investment will occur. (b) Market liquidity will be reduced, thereby disadvantaging traders who must trade for life cycle or other reasons not related to information. (c) Insider trading will make current stock prices more volatile, further hurting traders with liquidity needs.

Note that all these points can be true simultaneously—with one exception. The pro-insiders argue that asset prices will rise when insider trading is permitted; the anti-insiders maintain that asset prices will fall.

Elements of a reasonable model to analyze these concerns should include the following: (i) Insiders, who by virtue of their privileged position have more precise information about future stock prices than

---

[1] If transfer payments are possible between parties, then the environment in which the sum of monetary benefits is greater will be Pareto superior to any alternative.

INSIDER TRADING

outside investors. It seems reasonable to presume that insiders will recognize the impact of their purchases on the current stock price. (ii) Outsiders, who have less precise information about future stock prices. Such investors recognize that the current price may reflect (at least partially) the information of insiders. Outsiders are risk averse and, being numerous, behave as perfect competitors. (iii) Liquidity traders who trade for exogenous reasons, such as intertemporal smoothing of income flows. (iv) Real investment, financed by a supply of new shares, which depends on the issuing price per share. A higher current stock price will lead to the issuance of a larger number of shares and to greater real investment.

A model is developed below that contains these elements in as simple a form as possible. The objective is to assess the validity of the arguments pro and con insider trading. Equilibrium prices and welfare are compared in markets in which insider trading is either permitted or restricted. It is assumed that if insider trading is prohibited, the inside information will not be reflected in prices or decisions.

The analysis begins with a model that includes differentially informed investors. The modeling draws from Grossman (1976), Grossman and Stiglitz (1980), Hellwig (1980), and Bray (1981). In recognition of the monopoly power of the inside trader, the model is similar in spirit to those of Grinblatt and Ross (1985) and Kyle (1985). However, there are important differences that permit a more appropriate analysis of insider trading.

First, the number of shares issued (and real investment) is endogenously determined. The amount of investment will be affected by prices, which in turn will be affected by information when insiders can trade. Endogenously determined and price-sensitive investment is required of any model that examines the full costs and benefits of insider trading.

Second, the model looks at the impact of insider trading on the welfare of each class of participants rather than simply on the degree to which prices reflect information. Informational efficiency is not an end in itself. It is generally thought to improve welfare, but, as Hirshleifer (1971) pointed out, this will not always be the case.

My model can be contrasted with other recent work addressing questions of insider trading. Glosten (1988) and Bajeux and Rochet (1989) have examined welfare in markets with insider trading but without production. They show that insider trading hurts liquidity traders. Their models, following Kyle (1985), assume that prices are set by risk-neutral market makers. But this assumption precludes consideration of an important aspect of insider trading: the impact of reduced future price volatility on the *level* of current asset prices.

These authors do not examine the potentially positive impact of insider trading on the efficiency of investment.[2]

Manove (1989) examines insider trading in which all participants are risk neutral. Manove's description of markets seems somewhat unusual: when information is favorable, rationing by lottery rather than price is assumed. Fishman and Hagerty (1989) examine a model in which all investors are risk neutral but recognize their influence on prices. They focus on the extent to which prices reflect information. In their model, insider trading is harmful only if it induces outsiders to gather less information, which in turn will be the case only if outsiders behave noncompetitively.

In contrast, my results suggest that insider trading may be undesirable even when investment is flexible, and risk-averse outsiders behave competitively and cannot alter their information. My results confirm that many of the arguments both pro and con insider trading are correct.

1. Stock prices will more fully reflect information when insider trading is permitted. Average stock price will rise, firms' average profits from financing new real investment will be higher, and the level of real investment may increase. However, this alone does not guarantee that welfare will increase.

2. Insider trading decreases both the expected return and risk to outsiders' investment. Under some circumstances, outside investors will demand more shares on average when insider trading is permitted. Nonetheless, I find that outside investors' welfare will always be lower, even when their average demand increases.

3. Liquidity of markets will be reduced when insider trading is permitted, and liquidity traders will suffer welfare losses.

4. Total welfare may increase or decrease with insider trading. Welfare will tend to increase when the amount of investment is highly responsive to the current stock price. In this case the gains from greater investment efficiency more than offset the costs to outside investors and liquidity traders. If investment is inflexible to current stock price, net welfare tends to be lower when insider trading is permitted.

Finally, I show that asymmetric information is likely to impose

---

[2] Interesting work by Dennert (1989) and Ausubel (1990) has come to my attention since this research was completed. Dennert addresses the impact of insider trading on investment using an overlapping generations model. In his model, as in Ausubel's, the proportion of inside investors affects investment levels, but the actual realization of their information does not. In contrast with my results, the level of investment in these models does *not* reflect information more fully when insiders are present. Their models also assume that insiders behave as perfect competitors.

greater welfare costs when the better-informed are employees of the firm itself rather than external investors. This distinction has escaped other economic models of insider trading.

II. Markets with Insiders and Endogenous Supply: An Overview

Investors choose a portfolio consisting of a risk-free asset (with interest rate normalized to zero) and shares of a risky asset. Investors maximize expected utility of future wealth, conditional on the information they possess when they make their choice.

Future price per share p is given by $p = \underline{p} + e$, where $\underline{p}$ is the mean future price, which is common knowledge, and e is a random variable with (unconditional) mean zero.

The current price p_0 is determined by the supply of and demand for shares. Demand for shares comes from three sources: insiders, outsiders, and liquidity traders.

i) Insiders observe e precisely and thus know future price exactly at the time they choose their portfolio.[3] However, their purchases or sales d_i will be tempered by the recognition that these activities will affect price. Insiders also observe the current price p_0.

ii) Outsiders cannot observe e. They can observe the current price p_0 and therefore can determine the net supply from this price. However, they cannot exactly infer e from insider trading since net supply depends on liquidity trading as well as insider trading. Thus the current price is a noisy signal of the future price, and outsiders will use this information to condition their expectations.

iii) Liquidity traders demand a random amount v, which is independent of price.[4] No market participants observe v directly, but insiders will be able to impute v from observing the current market price p_0. So it does not matter whether we allow them to observe v directly or not.

Supply comes from entrepreneurs or firms issuing shares:

iv) Firms offer an endogenously determined number of shares q, each share providing a random future value p. The cost of providing such shares, $C(q)$, is increasing and strictly convex. The firm chooses

---

[3] I could extend the model to include imperfect observation by insiders. This would reduce both the benefits and costs associated with insider trading, but the nature of the effects examined would not be affected.

[4] A more complex model would allow liquidity traders to reduce their activities as the cost of such trading rises. This would moderate the costs that insider trading imposes on liquidity traders, affecting the magnitude but not the nature of the results.

the number of shares issued to maximize its profit π from this activity, where $\pi = p_0 q - C(q)$.[5]

Let us presume that the firm behaves competitively and takes p_0 as given.[6] Note that whatever information the firm might have with respect to the future price p does not directly affect its decision to issue shares q: the current rather than the future price uniquely determines the share issuance decision. This assumption is relaxed in Section VII below.

A *rational expectations equilibrium* (REE) is a price function with the following properties.

i) It is a price function in which insider information enters only through insiders' demand. Since other participants cannot distinguish liquidity demand v from insider demand d_i, the price function must have the form

$$p_0 = f(v + d_i, \mathbf{w}), \qquad (1)$$

where $\mathbf{w}$ is the vector of all other commonly observed (or directly inferable) parameters.[7]

ii) Given the REE price function (1), d_i is chosen to maximize net insider wealth

$$W_i = (\underline{p} + e - p_0)d_i. \qquad (2)$$

Insiders behave as monopolists: they recognize that p_0 depends on d_i through (1).

---

[5] For example, consider an entrepreneur or firm that can produce a good in a competitive market with constant returns to scale (exclusive of the costs of installing capacity). Let q denote the number of units the firm chooses to produce and also the number of shares issued. The future profit per unit of production, and therefore per share, is random and equals p. The current price per share is p_0, implying that total revenue from issuing shares is $p_0 q$. The cost of installing capacity is $C(q)$, and the firm will issue a number of shares q that sets $p_0 = C'(q)$, where $C'(q)$ is the marginal cost of installing capacity. Profit to the original owner(s) is $\pi = p_0 q - C(q)$. Bray (1985) uses a related formulation in examining production decisions by farmers.

[6] In fact, the firm's choice of q will have a small impact on p_0 via the rational expectations price equilibrium. A change in q will have a much smaller impact on price than an unobserved change in supply d_i (or v) since the choice of q (unlike the choice of d_i) is known not to contain inside information. In the linear model examined subsequently, we could allow the firm's choice of q to affect price, with a resulting decrease in the variable z introduced below.

[7] We can think of the market as follows. Outside investors have a "willingness to pay" (inverse demand) function that depends on the supply of shares that must be absorbed. In the REE model developed below, this function has the form $p_0 = r - sq + tX$, where $X = v + d_i$, the sum of the (separately unobservable) demands from liquidity and informed traders. The term q is a linear, deterministic function of p_0 in this model. Substituting for q and rearranging terms give $p_0 = a + c(v + d_i)$. By requiring that price be measurable with respect to insiders' demand, this approach restricts the set of insiders' equilibrium strategies relative to those considered in Grinblatt and Ross (1985) and Laffont and Maskin (1989), who allow price functions in which e can enter the REE price function independent of insider demand d_i.

INSIDER TRADING

iii) Given the REE price function, outsiders choose to purchase a number of shares d_o that maximizes expected utility of future wealth, conditional on the price p_0. Thus p_0 serves two roles for outsiders: determining the cost of each share and influencing their expectations about future stock price $\underline{p} + e$.

iv) Firms choose to issue a number of shares q that maximizes the net proceeds to original shareholders, $p_0 q - C(q)$, where p_0 is the REE price.

v) The REE price function equates supply and demand for every possible value of the random variables e and v.

III. Markets with Inside Traders and Production: A Mean-Variance Rational Expectations Model

A simple model with mean-variance preferences is constructed along the lines suggested above. Ex ante distributions of future price shock e and liquidity demand v are given by

$$e: N(0, \Sigma_p),$$

$$v: N(0, \Sigma_v),$$

e, v are independent.

Let us postulate a linear REE price function of the form (1) above:

$$p_0 = a + c(v + d_i). \tag{3}$$

I shall show that for appropriate choices of a and c, (3) will indeed satisfy the earlier definition of a REE price function.

A. Demand

Assume a single inside investor (or cartel of investors), negligible in number relative to outside investors. Inside investors observe e precisely and thus have no uncertainty about the future price $p = \underline{p} + e$. They will choose d_i to maximize their final wealth, recognizing that their demand affects price through the equilibrium relationship (3):[8]

$$\text{maximize } W_i = (\underline{p} + e - p_0)d_i$$
$$= \{\underline{p} + e - [a + c(v + d_i)]\}d_i, \tag{4}$$

---

[8] Despite being few in number, insiders will have substantial investment demand because they face no risk and therefore act "risk neutrally."

using (3).[9] This implies

$$d_i = \frac{\underline{p} - a}{2c} + \left(\frac{1}{2c}\right)e - \tfrac{1}{2}v. \qquad (5)$$

Observe that the optimal d_i depends on both the inside information e and the liquidity demand v. Although v cannot be observed directly, the insider can impute v directly from observing p_0 and knowing the REE function (3).[10]

Substituting for d_i from (5) into (3) gives

$$p_0 = A + Be + Cv, \qquad (3')$$

where $A = (a + \underline{p})/2$, $B = \tfrac{1}{2}$, and $C = c/2$. The insiders' demand for stock (5) can be rewritten as

$$d_i = \frac{\underline{p} - A}{2C} + \left(\frac{1}{4C}\right)e - \tfrac{1}{2}v. \qquad (6)$$

Note that insider demand does not depend on risk aversion, since by assumption there is no risk at the time insiders choose d_i. While clearly an exaggeration, the assumption of perfect observability reflects the notion that insiders have a "sure thing" when they trade.

Outsiders can predict the insider's demand relation (6) and therefore recognize that (3') as well as (3) describes the REE price function. Outsiders do not observe e but can use (3') to form a probabilistic estimate for e given p_0, which in turn allows them to compute the conditional expectation and variance of the future price p given p_0:

$$E(p|p_0) = \underline{p} + \left[\frac{\text{cov}(p, p_0)}{\text{var}(p_0)}\right][p_0 - E(p_0)]$$

$$= \underline{p} + \left(\frac{K}{B}\right)(p_0 - A); \qquad (7)$$

$$\text{var}(p|p_0) = \Sigma_p(1 - K),$$

where

$$K = \frac{B^2 \Sigma_p}{B^2 \Sigma_p + C^2 \Sigma_v}.$$

---

[9] Final wealth is given by $W_i = \underline{W}_i + pd_i + y(1 + \rho)$, where $\underline{W}_i$ is initial wealth, y is the holding of the risk-free asset paying interest rate ρ, and the budget constraint is $p_0 d_i + y = \underline{W}_i$. Normalizing $\underline{W}_i = 0$ and $\rho = 0$ gives (4).

[10] Alternatively, we could postulate that the monopolist observes neither v nor p_0 at the time he makes his demand decision d_i. In this case, if the monopolist is risk neutral, it is easy to show $d_i = (\underline{p} + e - a)/2c$ and $p_0 = A + Be + Cv$, where $A = (a + \underline{p})/2$, $B = .5$, and $C = c$. (Compare with eq. [3'], in which the only difference is $C = .5c$.) The nature of the results will be little affected by the choice of what the monopolist observes.

INSIDER TRADING

Outsiders have mean-variance preferences over ending wealth W_o.[11] For any current price p_0, outsiders choose between investing in the stock and investing in a risk-free asset so as to maximize the certainty equivalent of W_o,

$$U(W_o|p_0) = E(W_o|p_0) - \left(\frac{R}{2}\right)\text{var}(W_o|p_0), \qquad (8)$$

where $W_o = (p - p_0)d_o$, d_o is outsiders' share purchase of the risky stock, and R reflects outsiders' aversion to risk.

Maximizing (8) with respect to d_o yields

$$d_o = \frac{E(p|p_0) - p_0}{R\,\text{var}(p|p_0)}. \qquad (9)$$

Using (7), rewrite (9) as

$$d_o = \frac{\underline{p} + (K/B)(p_0 - A) - p_0}{R\Sigma_p(1 - K)} \qquad (10)$$

$$= m + np_0,$$

where

$$m = \frac{\underline{p} - (KA/B)}{R\Sigma_p(1 - K)},$$

$$n = \frac{(K/B) - 1}{R\Sigma_p(1 - K)}.$$

Liquidity traders provide a third source of demand. While it is possible to endogenize aspects of their decisions (e.g., Bajeux and Rochet 1989), let us take the simplest possible route and assume that they demand a random amount v, whose distribution is exogenously given.

Summing the three sources of demand (6), (10), and v gives total demand as a function of the exogenous variables and the coefficients A, B, and C of the hypothesized REE price function (3'):

$$D = \frac{p - A}{2C} + \left(\frac{1}{4C}\right)e + \tfrac{1}{2}v$$

$$+ \frac{\underline{p} + (K/B)(p_0 - A) - p_0}{R\Sigma_p(1 - K)} \qquad (11)$$

Let us turn now to the supply of securities.

B. Supply

The firm (or entrepreneur) issues an endogenously determined number of shares q to the market. These shares promise an identical future value p per share, independent of the number of shares q that are offered. The cost of providing shares represents the real investment required to provide the returns to the q shares. Assume a convex cost function for providing additional shares, given by

$$C(q) = 0, \qquad 0 \le q \le Q,$$
$$= c_0 + c_1 q + .5 c_2 q^2, \quad q > Q,$$

where $c_1 = -Qc_2$, $c_0 = .5Q^2 c_2$, and $c_2 > 0$. This functional form has the following properties. Shares can be created without cost up to a level given by Q. Thereafter, marginal cost rises from zero with a speed that depends on the magnitude of c_2. The condition determining c_0 assures that the cost function is continuous at $q = Q$.

The firm must decide how many shares to supply. It can sell shares for p_0 per share, where p_0 is the current price. It issues shares to maximize profit (for its original shareowners)

$$\pi = p_0 q - C(q)$$
$$= p_0 q - c_0 - c_1 q - .5 c_2 q^2,$$

implying an optimal share issuance (supply) of

$$q = z p_0 + Q, \tag{12}$$

where $z = 1/c_2$.[12] Because the cost of providing shares is zero up to $q = Q$, the firm will always provide this level no matter how rapidly marginal cost increases beyond Q.[13] Note that the special case in which production is inflexible corresponds to the limiting case in which $z \to 0$ and $q = Q$ for all p_0.

C. The REE Price Function

Recall that an REE price function must equate supply and demand for each possible resolution of the random variables e and v. That is,

---

[12] Note that with this criterion the firm will make the same share issuance decision whether or not managers directly observe the inside information variable e. Nonetheless, e does affect investment through the REE price function p_0. For an alternative firm objective in which inside information can directly affect share issuance q, see Sec. VIIC below.

[13] I ignore the possibility of negative P_0, which technically is possible with normal distributions but for reasonable specifications of parameters (see table 1 below) is highly unlikely—a six- (or more) standard-deviation event.

INSIDER TRADING

total demand from (11) must equal total supply from (12), or

$$\frac{p-A}{2C} + \left(\frac{1}{4C}\right)e + \tfrac{1}{2}v$$
$$+ \frac{p + (K/B)(p_0 - A) - p_0}{R\Sigma_p(1-K)} - (zp_0 + Q) = 0, \qquad (13)$$

for all e, v. This equation can be solved for p_0, and the resulting constant term and coefficients of e and v must equal the coefficients $A, B,$ and C of the postulated REE function (3').

THEOREM 1. A linear REE exists in our model with

$$p_0 = A + Be + Cv, \qquad (14)$$

where

$$B = \tfrac{1}{2},$$

$$C = \frac{1}{2M},$$

$$A = \frac{p(z + 2g) - Q}{2(z + g)},$$

$$M = \left(\frac{R\Sigma_v}{2}\right)\left\{-1 + \left[\frac{1 + 4(z + g)}{R\Sigma_v}\right]^{.5}\right\},$$

$$g = \frac{1}{R\Sigma_p}.$$

Proof. See the Appendix.

Several conclusions can be drawn about prices in the REE setting: (i) The sensitivity B of price to inside information e is constant. Half of the future price surprise will be reflected in the current price, regardless of liquidity supply volatility Σ_v or future price uncertainty Σ_p. This constancy reflects the nature of the insiders' response to observations of e and v. (ii) The ex ante expected current price, A, is independent of the supply volatility Σ_v. It can readily be verified that the expected current price is decreasing in risk aversion R and in future price volatility Σ_p. (iii) The liquidity of the market (as measured by the inverse of C, the price impact of a liquidity trade) increases as production becomes more sensitive to price (z increases) and decreases as the volatility of future price (Σ_p) increases. For reasonable ranges of parameters, liquidity also increases with the volatility of liquidity trading Σ_v.

IV. Comparison of REE Prices: Markets with and without Insider Trading

My objective is to compare the REE price function with insider trading, as described in theorem 1, with the REE price function in a similar market that prohibits insider trading. Insiders now behave as outsiders, but since they have negligible mass, their trading, now limited by risk aversion, will be negligible.

Demand from the outside investors is given by

$$d'_o = \frac{p - p_0}{R\Sigma_p}$$
$$= m' + n'p_0, \qquad (10')$$

where $m' = \underline{p}/R\Sigma_p$ and $n' = -1/R\Sigma_p$. It can be readily verified that the REE price function in the absence of insider trading has the form

$$p'_0 = A' + B'e + C'v, \qquad (15)$$

where $A' = (\underline{p}g - Q)/(z + g)$, $B' = 0$, and $C' = 1/(z + g)$. Comparing this price function with (15), we obtain the following results.

1. The average stock price will be higher when insider trading is permitted. This can be seen immediately from

$$A - A' = \frac{\underline{p}z + Q}{2(z + g)} > 0.$$

The controversy of how insider trading affects the level of stock prices is resolved: prices will rise.

2. The average amount of real investment (or, equivalently, shares q issued) will be higher with insider trading. This follows immediately from (12) and the fact that the average stock price will be higher.

3. For "reasonable" parameter levels, the liquidity of the market is reduced by insider trading. Liquidity is greater when a liquidity trade has a smaller impact on price, that is, when the magnitude of C, the coefficient of v, is smaller. It can be shown that C exceeds C' (implying lower liquidity with insider trading) whenever

$$z + g > 2R\Sigma_v. \qquad (16)$$

This will be the most difficult to satisfy when $z = 0$ (no flexibility of production), in which case (16) reduces to

$$1 > 2R^2\Sigma_v\Sigma_p. \qquad (17)$$

Realistically, it is unlikely that the risk aversion factor R will exceed six, the volatility (standard deviation) of the liquidity supply will exceed 20 percent of total supply, or the volatility of prices will exceed

50 percent.[14] For such extremes, the right-hand side of (17) is .72, and the inequality is satisfied. We can conclude that, under reasonable parameter specifications, $C > C'$ and insider trading reduces market liquidity.[15]

4. For reasonable parameter levels, current prices will be more volatile when insider trading is permitted. Note that

$$\text{var}(p_0) = B^2\Sigma_p + C^2\Sigma_v > (C')^2\Sigma_v = \text{var}(p'_0).$$

This follows directly from the lower liquidity levels for reasonable parameters ($C > C'$) and the positive sensitivity of p_0 to e ($B > 0$) in the equilibrium with insider trading.

5. Future price volatility given current prices ($\text{var}[p|p_0]$) will be lower when insider trading is permitted. Note that

$$\text{var}(p|p_0) = \Sigma_p \left(1 - \frac{B^2\Sigma_p}{B^2\Sigma_p + C^2\Sigma_v}\right).$$

Since $B = 0$ when there is no insider trading, the result follows immediately.

These last two results show a key aspect of insider trading: it accelerates the resolution of uncertainty from the terminal period to the present period. A related consequence follows.

6. Current prices will be more highly correlated with future prices when insider trading is permitted. The actual correlation ρ is given by

$$\rho = \frac{B\Sigma_p}{(B^2\Sigma_p^2 + C^2\Sigma_p\Sigma_v)^{.5}}.$$

Without insider trading, the correlation is zero. For reasonable parameter values (see the example in Sec. VI), the correlation of current and future prices in the presence of insider trading will be on the order of .7.

The preceding results show that, in the presence of insider trading, investment (which depends on current price p_0) will be larger when

---

[14] Ibbotson and Sinquefield suggest that the Standard & Poors 500 return has averaged about 6–8 percent higher than the risk-free return, with a standard deviation of about 20 percent. The certainty equivalent of such a return would be consistent with an R of 1.5–2 in this model.

[15] Gennotte and Leland (1990) also show that the presence of a few asymmetrically informed investors (i.e., insiders) dramatically reduces the liquidity of markets in comparison to the case in which no insiders are present. Their model assumes that insiders behave competitively and that the supply of shares is fixed. It is interesting to note that additional insiders (behaving competitively) may improve liquidity relative to the case in which only a few insiders are present.

the future value p per unit of that investment is greater. This increased "informational efficiency" of investment is potentially desirable. It is desirable not for its own sake, however, but rather for how it contributes to the welfare of the economic agents. Welfare in the equilibria with and without insider trading is affected not only by investment decisions but by the distribution of risks and returns among the agents. Let us turn now to analyzing these issues.

V. Welfare

My objective is to examine the welfare of each class of participants in the rational expectations equilibria developed above. The question of welfare must be posed prior to knowledge of the random variables e or v. That is, let us ask the following question: Before knowing the actual information that insiders will receive, are participants better or worse off with insider trading? Assume that all classes of participants have mean-variance preferences of the form

$$U(W) = E(W) - \left(\frac{R}{2}\right)\text{var}(W).$$

Note that utility U can be interpreted as certainty equivalent wealth.

A. Inside Investors

At the time they make their decisions d_i, insiders can observe both e and p_0 (implying knowledge of v). Their wealth given these observations is

$$W_i = (\underline{p} + e - p_0)d_i$$

$$= (\underline{p} + e - p_0)\left(\frac{\underline{p} - A}{2C} + \frac{e}{4C} - .5v\right)$$

using (6). Substituting for p_0 from (14) allows us to express insider wealth (ex post) as

$$W_i = w_1 + w_2 e + w_3 v + w_4 e^2 + w_5 v^2 + w_6 ev, \tag{18}$$

where

$$w_1 = \frac{(\underline{p} - A)^2}{2C},$$

$$w_2 = \frac{(\underline{p} - A)(3 - 2B)}{4C},$$

$$w_3 = -(\underline{p} - A),$$

INSIDER TRADING

$$w_4 = \frac{1-B}{4C},$$

$$w_5 = \frac{C}{2},$$

$$w_6 = -\frac{3-2B}{4}.$$

While insider profits W_i are certain ex post, they are uncertain ex ante. From (18), we can immediately derive the ex ante mean and variance of insider wealth:

$$E(W_i) = w_1 + w_4 \Sigma_p + w_5 \Sigma_v,$$
$$\text{var}(W_i) = w_2^2 \Sigma_p + w_3^2 \Sigma_v + 2w_4^2 \Sigma_p^2 + 2w_5^2 \Sigma_v^2 + w_6^2 \Sigma_p \Sigma_v.$$

The certainty equivalent of ex ante random insider wealth is given by

$$U(W_i) = E(W_i) - \left(\frac{R}{2}\right) \text{var}(W_i).$$

B. Outsiders

Outsiders choose a risky investment d_o to maximize risk-adjusted final wealth, given that they observe p_0. Their final wealth will be

$$W_o = (p - p_0)d_o,$$

where d_o is given by (10). Recalling that

$$p - p_0 = \underline{p} + e - (A + Be + Cv)$$

allows us to write

$$W_o = s_1 + s_2 e + s_3 v + s_4 e^2 + s_5 v^2 + s_6 ev, \qquad (19)$$

where

$$s_1 = (\underline{p} - A)(m + nA),$$
$$s_2 = Bn(\underline{p} - A) + (1 - B)(m + nA),$$
$$s_3 = C[n(\underline{p} - A) - (m + nA)],$$
$$s_4 = nB(1 - B),$$
$$s_5 = -nC^2,$$
$$s_6 = nC(1 - 2B),$$

and m and n are defined in (10) when insider trading is permitted and in (10′) when insider trading is not permitted.[16] From (19) we derive the ex ante mean and variance of W_o:

$$E(W_o) = s_1 + s_4 \Sigma_p + s_5 \Sigma_v,$$
$$\text{var}(W_o) = s_2^2 \Sigma_p + s_3^2 \Sigma_v + 2s_4^2 \Sigma_p^2 + 2s_5^2 \Sigma_v^2 + s_6^2 \Sigma_p \Sigma_v \tag{20}$$

with certainty equivalent value

$$U(W_o) = E(W_o) - \left(\frac{R}{2}\right) \text{var}(W_o). \tag{21}$$

C. Liquidity Traders

Liquidity traders trade an amount v that is random ex ante. On average, liquidity traders expect neither to buy nor to sell: $E(v) = 0$. But when they do buy, they will tend to do so at a price greater than average. When they sell, they will tend to do so at a price lower than average. This creates both an expected cost and a volatility of cost.[17] Straightforward calculations yield

$$\text{cost} = -p_0 v$$
$$= -[(A + Be + Cv)v] \tag{22}$$
$$= m_1 + m_2 e + m_3 v + m_4 e^2 + m_5 v^2 + m_6 ev,$$

where $m_1 = m_2 = m_4 = 0$, $m_3 = -A$, $m_5 = -C$, and $m_6 = -B$. It follows immediately that

$$E(\text{cost}) = m_1 + m_4 \Sigma_p + m_5 \Sigma_v = -C\Sigma_v,$$
$$\text{var}(\text{cost}) = m_2^2 \Sigma_p + m_3^2 \Sigma_v + 2m_4^2 \Sigma_p^2 + 2m_5^2 \Sigma_v^2 + m_6^2 \Sigma_p \Sigma_v \tag{23}$$
$$= A^2 \Sigma_v + 2C^2 \Sigma_v^2 + B^2 \Sigma_p \Sigma_v,$$

$$U(\text{cost}) = E(\text{cost}) - \left(\frac{R}{2}\right) \text{var}(\text{cost})$$
$$= \left[-C - \left(\frac{R}{2}\right)(A^2 + B^2 \Sigma_p + 2C^2 \Sigma_v)\right] \Sigma_v. \tag{24}$$

---

[16] In the special case in which $z = 0$, it can be shown that $n = -1/2C$ and $n' = -1/C$. The terms for the weights s_j simplify accordingly.

[17] Alternatively, one could model the welfare of the liquidity trader as equivalent to an investor with future wealth $W_L = (p - p_0)v$ and estimate his utility as with other investors. This treats the liquidity trades as speculative; this approach is appropriate if trades are viewed as eliminating (hedging) prior positions. Such an alternative formulation would affect welfare levels but not the general nature of the results.

Note that costs are incurred in the first period. Assume the same risk aversion coefficient R here, although alternative formulations are possible.[18]

D. Stock Issuers: The Firm or Entrepreneur

The model considers equilibrium with an endogenous supply of new shares. The returns to the shares are created by real investment. A scenario consistent with this approach is an entrepreneur financing a new firm by selling equity. The amount he realizes as an entrepreneurial profit is $\pi = p_0 q - C(q)$.

Alternatively, one can think of the project as being undertaken by a firm with shares currently outstanding, but financing the new venture as a separate firm with its own equity financing. In this case it is the shareholders of the original firm who realize the increase in value π. This alternative becomes important if the shareholders of the new venture overlap with the shareholders of the original firm. This is discussed in Section VIIB below. Here, assume no overlap of ownership.

The expected profit and variance of profit to the original owners can be readily determined:

$$\pi = p_0 q - C(q)$$

$$= p_0(z p_0 + Q) - c_0 - c_1(z p_0 + Q) - \left(\frac{c_2}{2}\right)(z p_0 + Q)^2 \quad (25)$$

$$= \rho_1 + \rho_2 e + \rho_3 v + \rho_4 e^2 + \rho_5 v^2 + \rho_6 ev,$$

where $\rho_1 = (zA^2/2) + AQ$, $\rho_2 = zAB + BQ$, $\rho_3 = zAC + CQ$, $\rho_4 = zB^2/2$, $\rho_5 = zC^2/2$, and $\rho_6 = zBC$. It follows directly that

$$E(\pi) = \rho_1 + \rho_4 \Sigma_p + \rho_5 \Sigma_v,$$

$$\text{var}(\pi) = \rho_2^2 \Sigma_p + \rho_3^2 \Sigma_v + 2\rho_4^2 \Sigma_p^2 + 2\rho_5^2 \Sigma_v^2 + \rho_6^2 \Sigma_p \Sigma_v, \quad (26)$$

$$U(\pi) = E(\pi) - \left(\frac{R}{2}\right) \text{var}(\pi). \quad (27)$$

We have now assessed the welfare of the four different agents. Note that the formulas also hold for the expected utility of agents when inside trading is prohibited, provided that we substitute m', n', A', B', and C' for m, n, A, B, and C.

---

[18] Risk aversion to current wealth might be less than risk aversion to future wealth because consumption choice is more flexible when risks are revealed early. I examine the impact of differing group risk aversion in Sec. VIIA below.

TABLE 1

BASE CASE

Ex ante price volatility (variance Σ_p):	.04
This is consistent with an annual standard deviation of the stock price of 20%	
Ex ante expected future price ($\underline{p}$):	1.00
This is a normalization	
Volatility of liquidity supply (variance Σ_v):	.01
This is consistent with an annual standard deviation of liquidity supply equal to about 10% of total supply	
Risk aversion parameter (R):	2
This implies a return premium to stocks equal to twice the future price volatility given current price (in this example, a risk premium of 8% over the risk-free rate when supply is normalized to one)	
Costless supply (Q):	1
If production is inflexible to price ($z = 0$), then the production supply is normalized to one	

VI. Welfare Compared: Insider versus No Insider Trading

The complexity of the various expressions for utility of the four classes of agents precludes simple analytical results relating welfare with and without insider trading as a function of the exogenous parameters. Nonetheless, we can use numerical analysis to examine welfare effects. Let us start with a "base case" with parameters chosen to reflect average market data. The parameters chosen are given in table 1. Let us first consider agents' welfare as a function of the flexibility of production to price (the parameter z).

A. *No Production Flexibility ($z = 0$)*

In this case, $Q = 1$ is supplied to the market regardless of price p_0. Equilibrium values of expected demand, expected supply, and ex ante welfare follow: with no inside trading,

$$p_0 = A' + C'v$$
$$= .9200 + .0800v;$$

with inside trading,

$$p_0 = A + Be + Cv$$
$$= .9600 + .500e + 1.020v.$$

		Average Demand		Expected Utility (Certainty Equivalence)				
Average Price	Average Supply	Inside	Outside	Inside	Outside	Liquidity	Profit	Total
.9200	1.0000	.0000	1.0000	.00000	.04014	−.00927	.91994	.95081
.9600	1.0000	.0196	.9804	.01055	.01968	−.01973	.93959	.95010

The upper line refers to equilibrium without insider trading, and the lower line to equilibrium with insiders. Averages refer to the case in which $e = v = E(e) = E(v) = 0$. As implied by the earlier proposition, the average price is higher with insider trading. Supply is identical since by assumption supply is invariant to price.

Insider trading increases the welfare of insiders—quite naturally, since they are excluded in the other case. More interesting, the outsiders' utility (certainty equivalence) falls by more than half. While both expected returns and risk to outsiders fall, demand contracts only fractionally despite the substantial drop in their welfare.

Expected profit to original owners issuing the securities rises from .92 to .96. However, the increased riskiness of the issuing price in the case of insider trading reduces the expected utility of profits to .9396.[19] Profits to original owners when insider trading is prohibited are not very volatile, and their expected utility is .91994.

Because current prices are much more sensitive to random liquidity trades (i.e., markets are less liquid), the expected utility of liquidity traders drops from −.0093 to −.0197 when insider trading is permitted. The risk-adjusted cost to liquidity traders more than doubles in the presence of insider trading. Total utility (or certainty equivalence) declines slightly, from .9508 to .9501, when insider trading is permitted. *For the base case, with no production flexibility, insider trading decreases welfare.*

I varied the base-case parameters separately, with a range of ex ante price volatility from .01 to .08, volatility of liquidity supply from .001 to .10, and risk aversion from 1 to 4. In all cases, insider trading continued to diminish total utility as well as to increase the welfare of insiders and original owners, and to decrease the welfare of outsiders and liquidity traders.

The welfare advantage (increase in total certainty equivalent wealth) from prohibiting insider trading increases as (1) risk aversion increases, (2) liquidity trading is more volatile, and (3) volatility of future price increases over the range of parameters examined.

[19] This cost associated with greater variability of prices p_0 reflects Hirshleifer's (1971) observation that increased information can have negative as well as positive impacts on welfare.

A bit more insight into these results can be obtained in the case in which $z = 0$. Considerable algebraic manipulation shows that

$$s_4 + \rho_4 + m_4 + w_4 = 0,$$
$$s_5 + \rho_5 + m_5 + w_5 = 0,$$

both with and without insider trading. Furthermore, it can be shown that, when $z = 0$,

$$s_1 + \rho_1 + m_1 + w_1 = pQ,$$

regardless of whether insider trading is permitted or not.[20] Thus the *total expected wealth* (which depends only on terms with subscripts 1, 4, and 5) is invariant to the presence of insider trading when production is inflexible to price. This result implies that *total welfare* decreases in the presence of insider trading because of risk effects: The distribution of total risks is less favorable with insider trading.

B. Production Is Flexible ($z = 1$)

Let us now consider the case in which supply expands with price ($z = 1$). All other parameters remain at their base value. Equilibrium values of expected demand, expected supply, and ex ante welfare follow: with no inside trading,

$$p_0 = A' + C'v$$
$$= .8519 + .0740v;$$

with inside trading,

$$p_0 = A + Be + Cv$$
$$= .9259 + .500e + .981v.$$

Average Price	Average Supply	Average Demand Inside	Outside	Expected Utility Inside	Outside	Liquidity	Profit	Total
.8519	1.8519	.0000	1.8519	.00000	.13676	−.00800	1.2145	1.3433
.9259	1.9259	.0378	1.8882	.01249	.06992	−.01868	1.2914	1.3552

As before, the second line describes equilibrium with insiders.

In contrast with the earlier result, we can see that although each separate class of agents' welfare increases or decreases in the direction previously observed, the total welfare now increases rather than de-

---

[20] The comparison requires $w_1 = w_4 = w_5 = 0$ when insiders are prohibited, since their utility is presumed to be zero when prohibited.

creases with insider trading. This result continues to hold for the range of parameters studied earlier. Indeed, we find that when production flexibility z exceeds about .06, welfare in the base case will increase when insider trading is allowed. A relatively small amount of production flexibility will cause insider trading to help welfare.

These results suggest that certain kinds of better information might be more damaging to welfare than others. Information that affects price but not production decisions will in general have a more negative effect than information that affects production. For example, consider a situation in which inside information exists about the possibility of a takeover, but a change in stock price will not affect the firm's investment decisions. This example implies $z = 0$, and welfare would be negatively affected by insider trading. Contrast this with a situation in which an external investor knows that a firm's potential investment has a very high payoff. Permitting him to trade on this information will raise the share price and lead to cheaper (and therefore greater) financing. Welfare may be positively affected.

VII. Alternative Formulations and Interpretations

The results of this paper rest on a number of assumptions. In this section some alternative formulations and their likely impact on the conclusions are examined.

A. *Differing Risk Aversion Levels across Groups*

The equilibrium pricing function—with or without insider trading—depends only on the risk aversion of the outsider group. The reason is that other groups' behavior is not affected by their degree of risk aversion. But while the equilibrium itself does not depend on other groups' risk aversion, these groups' *welfare* in equilibrium is a function of their risk aversion. How are the welfare conclusions altered by allowing for differences in risk aversion parameters?[21]

Let us fix the risk aversion of the outsider group and therefore the REE price equilibria. Now consider increasing the level of risk aversion of any other group. These groups' risk is affected only by the variability of p_0, which increases when insider trading is permitted. Increased risk aversion will make the prohibition of insider trading more attractive to these groups.

If all *individual* investors have identical risk aversion, then groups with smaller numbers will have greater aggregate risk aversion. With

---

[21] I thank Michael Fishman for suggesting this line of inquiry.

preferences linear in the mean and variance of wealth, the risk aversion of the group (more exactly, of an aggregate investor representing the group) is inversely proportional to the number of investors in the group. Thus the aggregate risk aversion R_i of a group with N_i investors will be given by

$$R_i = R\left(\frac{N}{N_i}\right),$$

where R is the aggregate risk aversion of the outside investor group and N is the number of outside investors. Clearly R_i will be greater than R when there are more outsiders than investors in group i. Since this seems likely to be the case for insider, entrepreneur, and (perhaps) liquidity groups, the assumption of identical group risk aversions may bias results in favor of insider trading.

B. Uninformed or Informed Investors Are the Firm's Original Owners

It has been assumed that investors are a different group from the original owners. How does the analysis change when original owners are in fact the same group as the uninformed (outside) investors or, alternatively, the same group as the informed (inside) investors?

The combined investors/original owners will seek to

$$\underset{q,d}{\text{maximize}}\ U[W|I] = E[W|I] - \left(\frac{R}{2}\right)\text{var}[W|I],$$

where

$$W = (p - p_0)d + p_0 q - C(q),$$

$I = p_0$ if the original owners are uninformed, and $I = e$ if the original owners are informed.

Note that $W = W_o + \pi$: the wealth of the combined investor/owner group is equal to the sum of the separate groups' wealths. Of course there is no a priori reason to believe that the combined group will make the same portfolio and share issuance decisions as the groups when separated.

First-order maximizing conditions for the combined group are

$$d = \frac{E[p - p_0|I] + (\delta p_0/\delta d)(q - d)}{R\Sigma_{p|I}},$$

$$p_0 - C'(q) + \left(\frac{\delta p_0}{\delta q}\right)(d - q) = 0,$$

where $\delta p_0/\delta d$ and $\delta p_0/\delta q$ are the perceived marginal impact of decisions on current price. If the original owners are also uninformed investors, then given the competitive assumptions ($\delta p_0/\delta d = \delta p_0/\delta q = 0$), the combined investor/owner group will choose the same output q and demand d as when they were separate: see (9) and (12). Therefore, the assumption that uninformed investors and original owners are separate groups does not alter the equilibrium from the one that prevails when the two groups coincide.

Welfare, however, will be affected. If the groups are separated, the original owners will sell all their shares at a random price in the first period. This randomness reduces the certainty equivalent value of their shares. Similarly, outside investors purchase shares (from the original owners) at an ex ante random price, also affecting their risk. When the two groups are combined, outside investors coincide with the original owners. If, originally, outside investors purchased *all* issued shares when the groups were separate, all ex ante price risk associated with p_0 would disappear when the groups are combined. Even when outsiders purchase only a fraction of the issued shares, considerable price risk can be avoided.

Welfare can be analyzed by noting that wealth in the combined case is simply the sum of the wealths of the separate classes: outside (uninformed) investors and original owners. Thus define

$$t_1 = s_1 + \rho_1,$$
$$t_2 = s_2 + \rho_2,$$
$$\vdots$$
$$t_6 = s_6 + \rho_6.$$

Mean, variance, and expected utility of the combined class will be given by

$$E[W] = t_1 + t_4 \Sigma_p + t_5 \Sigma_v,$$
$$\text{var}[W] = t_2^2 \Sigma_p + t_3^2 \Sigma_v + 2t_4^2 \Sigma_p^2 + 2t_5^2 \Sigma_v^2 + t_6^2 \Sigma_p \Sigma_v,$$
$$U[W] = E[W] - \left(\frac{R}{2}\right) \text{var}[W].$$

This expression then replaces $U[W_o]$ and $U[\pi]$ in the previous analysis. Because the effect of the risky current price p_0 is reduced in this alternative, we find that welfare effects of insider trading are positive for the base case even with $z = 0$. The original owners/uninformed investors are slightly better off when insider trading is permitted:

Gains as original owners more than offset losses as uninformed investors.[22]

Insider trading does not benefit total welfare for all parameter levels in this case. For example, if the standard deviation of liquidity demand in the base case rises from 10 percent to 16 percent (or more), insider trading again lowers welfare when $z = 0$.

If informed investors are also the original owners, decisions (when insider trading is permitted) will not be identical to those made when owners and insiders are separate. Now the original owners realize that they can affect p_0, the price at which shares are originally sold, by their insider trading. This further exploitation of monopoly power is likely to create additional welfare costs when insider trading is permitted, although I have not formally modeled this more complex case.[23]

C. Managers Possess Inside Information

Let us return to the case in which investors and original owners are treated separately. The model assumes that original owners (or managers operating on their behalf) are interested only in maximizing the current net value of π of issued shares. With this formulation, it does not matter whether managers possess inside information or not, since π and therefore the optimal q are affected by e only through p_0. But a number of authors have asserted that, in the presence of asymmetric information, future as well as current stock value will affect managers' choice.[24] Assume now that the firm chooses share issuance q to maximize expected $U(\pi)$, where

$$\pi = [\alpha p_0 + (1 - \alpha)p]q - C(q),$$

with $0 < \alpha < 1$.[25] The optimal q will be responsive to information e even when insider trading is prohibited. Share issuance q will be less

---

[22] Note that in this case, the firm's shareholders would not vote to prohibit insider trading, since on net they gain. The losses to liquidity traders, however, may still cause insider trading to be detrimental to welfare. This refutes the argument that if shareholders do not prohibit insider trading, it must not be harmful (see, e.g., Carlton and Fischel 1983).

[23] In an alternative formulation, in which informed investors receive a noisy signal but behave as competitors (implying $\delta p_0/\delta d = \delta p_0/\delta q = 0$), the separation equivalence would continue to hold.

[24] Several authors (e.g., Ross 1977; Miller and Rock 1985) have assumed that in the presence of asymmetric information, managers choose to maximize a weighted average of current and future stock value.

[25] To remain consistent with the previous approach, we must now require that q is unobservable by outsiders. Otherwise, outsiders could use q to back out of the value of e. In the earlier approach, it did not matter whether q was observable or not, since q can be inferred from p_0.

INSIDER TRADING

sensitive to p_0 because (already knowing e) managers will not condition their expectation of p on p_0. In the limiting case in which $\alpha = 0$, q will be independent of p_0.

The information that the current price brings to share issuance (and investment) by firms is therefore less important when firms' managers already possess inside information. That is, z is smaller. But in the preceding section it was shown that smaller z causes insider trading to be less desirable. This suggests that it is not only legally appropriate but also economically useful to distinguish trading by a corporate insider from trading by an unaffiliated but informed investor. The former brings costs but little benefits (other than to himself), since the information he imparts through his price impact is already known by the firm; the latter may bring additional benefits to production decisions via his effect on price.

D. Outsiders Can Gather Information

When outsiders have the possibility of acquiring information, as in Fishman and Hagerty (1989), insider trading may affect this decision. We have seen that outsiders' expected utility suffers when inside trading is permitted. Following Fishman and Hagerty, assume that this reduces the amount of information outsiders gather, which in turn increases their ex ante future price volatility. But earlier examples showed that greater volatility of future prices implies a greater loss from insider trading. When outsiders can gather information, there is further reason to restrict insider trading.

VIII. Conclusions

The analysis of this paper suggests that insider trading may hurt or help markets, depending on the characteristics of those markets. This should not be surprising: the fact that controversy still exists on the issue suggests that there is no single "best" answer regardless of circumstances.

The analysis *does* indicate who gains and who loses. It also identifies the characteristics of those markets that are likely to gain from insider trading and those that are likely to lose.

Liquidity traders are major losers when insider trading is permitted. Markets become less liquid when insiders trade: prices move more in response to unobserved random supply shocks because investors believe that price movements might be coming from informed investor activity. If liquidity traders had a way to inform markets that their trades were indeed information-free, they would be less harmed.[26] However, liquidity traders who could not inform markets would suffer more, since market liquidity decreases as Σ_v becomes smaller.

Outside investors also are hurt when insider trading is permitted. Their expected return is reduced. Because they are trading against better-informed investors, they own, on average, more shares when expected returns are low and fewer shares when expected returns are high. But outside investors also have reduced risks: Because some risks are revealed through prices, the remaining risks are less. Both the mean and variance of outsiders' returns are reduced by insider trading. Outsiders' demand for stock may increase, but their welfare always decreases.

Gainers from insider trading of course include the insiders themselves. But owners of firms issuing shares also will, on average, benefit from insider trading. The average issuing price will be higher, and there are additional benefits when the firm's investment level is sensitive to future prospects, as reflected (when insider trading is permitted) in current price.[27]

The net impact of these separate consequences of insider trading can be positive or negative. The results indicate that insider trading is less desirable as (1) investment flexibility decreases, (2) investor risk aversion increases, (3) liquidity trading is more volatile, and (4) future price volatility increases.

The single most important factor is the sensitivity of investment to current price. If the sensitivity is great, insider trading is likely to be beneficial.

When firms themselves possess inside information, allowing insider trading for personal profit is likely to have negative effects. Firms will pay less attention to current market price if they already possess information superior to that price. Because the sensitivity of investment to current price is lower, the negative aspects of insider trading will tend to dominate the positive aspects. This may well explain why regulation has focused on prohibiting trading based on superior information emanating from *inside* the firm, as contrasted with superior information generated externally.

Typically, insider trading has been *more* tolerated in less developed financial markets. This is somewhat puzzling in light of the results

---

[26] See Admati and Pfleiderer (1990). The existence of basket securities could help (well-diversified) liquidity traders to the extent that trading a basket minimizes the likelihood that an investor has firm-specific information (see, e.g., Gorton and Pennacchi 1989).

[27] Note that I focus on producer surplus (from profit) but do not explicitly examine consumer surplus related to the output of the good being produced. Any possible increase in consumer surplus would favor insider trading.

INSIDER TRADING

above, if less developed markets are associated with greater future price volatility and, perhaps, greater investor risk aversion as well.

There are a number of possible explanations. First, liquidity trading is likely to be much more important in highly developed capital markets, where investors consider the stock market as a viable alternative for holding assets for retirement and other income-smoothing purposes. Insider trading is particularly harmful to liquidity traders. Second, it is possible (although not obvious) that less developed financial markets have a greater fraction of superior information that is generated outside the firm. Thus the investment level would be more sensitive to stock market price. Third, and most likely, less developed markets may be equally harmed by insider trading, but restrictions are simply impossible to enforce.

The model of this paper captures many of the key ingredients of the insider trading controversy, but it should be extended to multiple time periods. Insider trading "moves up" the resolution of uncertainty. This one-time benefit may be relatively more important in a two-period model than in a multiperiod model. If so, my results may overestimate the benefits of insider trading. But we must await the development of multiperiod rational expectations models to answer this question definitively.

Appendix

Proof of Theorem 1

From (13), we can group terms into coefficients—G of the future price surprise e, H of liquidity trading v, F of a constant, and M of price p_0—as follows:

$$Mp_0 = F + Ge + Hv, \qquad (A1)$$

where

$$M = z - \left(\frac{g}{1-K}\right)\left(\frac{K}{B} - 1\right),$$

$$F = \frac{\underline{p} - A}{2C} + \left(\underline{p} - \frac{AK}{B}\right)\left(\frac{g}{1-K}\right) - Q,$$

$$G = \frac{1}{4C},$$

$$H = \tfrac{1}{2},$$

$$g = \frac{1}{R\Sigma_p},$$

$$K = \frac{\Sigma_p}{\Sigma_p + (C/B)^2 \Sigma_v}.$$

For (A1) to be consistent with (14) for every possible e and v, it must be the case that

$$A = \frac{F}{M}, \tag{A2}$$

$$B = \frac{G}{M}, \tag{A3}$$

$$C = \frac{H}{M}. \tag{A4}$$

This yields three nonlinear equations in the unknowns A, B, and C. From (A4), $MC = H = \frac{1}{2}$, implying that $M = 1/2C$.

Substituting for G from (A1) and for M from above into (A3) gives $B = \frac{1}{2}$. Since $B = H = \frac{1}{2}$, it follows immediately from (A4) that $C/B = 1/M$, implying $(C/B)^2 = 1/M^2$ and $K = M^2 \Sigma_p / (M^2 \Sigma_p + \Sigma_v)$. Substituting for K and B into the equation for M in (A1) yields a quadratic equation with positive solution

$$M = \left(\frac{R\Sigma_v}{2}\right) \left\{ -1 + \left[1 + \frac{4(z+g)}{R\Sigma_v} \right]^{.5} \right\}.$$

We may now solve immediately for $C = 1/2M$ from (A4) and the expression above for M, and for

$$A = \frac{p(z + 2g) - Q}{2(z + g)}$$

from (A1), (A2), and the variables B, C, and K. Q.E.D.

References

Admati, Anat R., and Pfleiderer, Paul. "Sunshine Trading and Financial Market Equilibrium." Research Paper no. 2004. Stanford, Calif.: Stanford Univ., Grad. School Bus., September 1990.
Ausubel, Lawrence M. "Insider Trading in a Rational Expectations Economy." *A.E.R.* 80 (December 1990): 1022–41.
Bajeux, Isabelle, and Rochet, J.-C. "Opérations d'initiés: Une analyse de surplus." *Finance* 10 (June 1989): 7–19.
Bray, Margaret M. "Futures Trading, Rational Expectations, and the Efficient Markets Hypothesis." *Econometrica* 49 (May 1981): 575–96.
———. "Rational Expectations, Information and Asset Markets: An Introduction." *Oxford Econ. Papers* 37 (June 1985): 161–95.
Brudney, Victor. "Insiders, Outsiders, and Informational Advantages under the Federal Securities Laws." *Harvard Law Rev.* 93 (December 1979): 322–76.
Carlton, Dennis W., and Fischel, Daniel R. "The Regulation of Insider Trading." *Stanford Law Rev.* 35 (May 1983): 857–95.
Dennert, J. "Insider Trading and the Allocation of Risks." Manuscript. Basel: Univ. Basel, May 1989.
Easterbrook, Frank. "Insider Trading as an Agency Problem." In *Principals and Agents: The Structure of Business*, edited by John W. Pratt and Richard J. Zeckhauser. Boston: Harvard Bus. School Press, 1985.

Fishman, Michael J., and Hagerty, Kathleen M. "Insider Trading and the Efficiency of Stock Prices." Working Paper no. 65. Evanston, Ill.: Northwestern Univ., Kellogg Grad. School Management, Dept. Finance, 1989.

Gennotte, Gerard, and Leland, Hayne. "Market Liquidity, Hedging, and Crashes." *A.E.R.* 80 (December 1990): 999–1021.

Glosten, Lawrence R. "Insider Trading, Liquidity and the Role of the Monopolist Specialist." Working paper. Evanston, Ill.: Northwestern Univ., Kellogg Grad. School Management, 1988.

Gorton, Gary, and Pennacchi, George G. "Security Baskets and Index-linked Securities." Discussion Paper no. 29-89. Philadelphia: Univ. Pennsylvania, Wharton School, Dept. Finance, 1989.

Grinblatt, Mark S., and Ross, Stephen A. "Market Power in a Securities Market with Endogenous Information." *Q.J.E.* 100 (November 1985): 1143–67.

Grossman, Sanford J. "On the Efficiency of Competitive Stock Markets Where Traders Have Diverse Information." *J. Finance* 31 (May 1976): 573–85.

Grossman, Sanford J., and Stiglitz, Joseph E. "On the Impossibility of Informationally Efficient Markets." *A.E.R.* 70 (June 1980): 393–408.

Hellwig, Martin F. "On the Aggregation of Information in Competitive Markets." *J. Econ. Theory* 22 (June 1980): 477–98.

Hirshleifer, Jack. "The Private and Social Value of Information and the Reward to Inventive Activity." *A.E.R.* 61 (September 1971): 561–74.

Kyle, Albert S. "Continuous Auctions and Insider Trading." *Econometrica* 53 (November 1985): 1315–35.

Laffont, Jean-Jacques, and Maskin, Eric. "The Efficient Market Hypothesis and Insider Trading on the Stock Market." Working Paper no. 8909. Toulouse: Univ. Toulouse, GREMAQ-CRES, 1989.

Manne, Henry G. *Insider Trading and the Stock Market.* New York: Free Press, 1966.

Manove, Michael. "The Harm from Insider Trading and Informed Speculation." *Q.J.E.* 104 (November 1989): 823–46.

Miller, Merton H., and Rock, Kevin. "Dividend Policy under Asymmetric Information." *J. Finance* 40 (September 1985): 1031–51.

Ross, Stephen A. "The Determination of Financial Structure: The Incentive-Signalling Approach." *Bell J. Econ.* 8 (Spring 1977): 23–40.

Part IV
Taxes and Financial Policy

DEBT AND TAXES*

MERTON H. MILLER**

THE SOMEWHAT HETERODOX VIEWS about debt and taxes that will be presented here have evolved over the last few years in the course of countless discussions with several of my present and former colleagues in the Finance group at Chicago—Fischer Black, Robert Hamada, Roger Ibbotson, Myron Scholes and especially Eugene Fama. Charles Upton and Joseph Williams have also been particularly helpful to me recently in clarifying the main issues.[1] My long-time friend and collaborator, Franco Modigliani, is absolved from any blame for the views to follow not because I think he would reject them, but because he has been absorbed in preparing *his* Presidential Address to the American Economic Association at this same Convention.

This coincidence neatly symbolizes the contribution we tried to make in our first joint paper of nearly twenty years ago; namely to bring to bear on problems of corporate finance some of the standard tools of economics, especially the analysis of competitive market equilibrium. Prior to that time, the academic discussion in finance was focused primarily on the empirical issue of what the market *really* capitalized.[2] Did the market capitalize a firm's dividends or its earnings or some weighted combination of the two? Did it capitalize net earnings or net operating earnings or something in between? The answers to these questions and to related questions about the behavior of interest rates were supposed to provide a basis for choosing an optimal capital structure for the firm in a framework analogous to the economist's model of discriminating monopsony.

We came at the problem from the other direction by first trying to establish the propositions about valuation implied by the economist's basic working assumptions of rational behavior and perfect markets. And we were able to prove that when the full range of opportunities available to firms and investors under such conditions

---

* Presidential Address, Annual Meeting of the American Finance Association, Atlantic City, N.J., September 17, 1976.

** University of Chicago.

1. More than perfunctory thanks are also due to the many others who commented, sometimes with considerable heat, on the earlier versions of this talk: Ray Ball, Marshall Blume, George Foster, Nicholas Gonedes, David Green, E. Han Kim, Robert Krainer, Katherine Miller, Charles Nelson, Hans Stoll, Jerold Warner, William Wecker, Roman Weil, and J. Fred Weston. I am especially indebted (no pun intended) to Fischer Black.

2. To avoid reopening old wounds, no names will be mentioned here. References can be supplied on request, however.

are taken into account, the following simple principle would apply: in equilibrium, the market value of any firm must be independent of its capital structure.

The arbitrage proof of this proposition can now be found in virtually every textbook in finance, followed almost invariably, however, by a warning to the student against taking it seriously. Some dismiss it with the statement that firms and investors can't or don't behave that way. I'll return to that complaint later in this talk. Others object that the invariance proposition was derived for a world with no taxes, and that world, alas, is not ours. In our world, they point out, the value of the firm can be increased by the use of debt since interest payments can be deducted from taxable corporate income. To reap more of these gains, however, the stockholders must incur increasing risks of bankruptcy and the costs, direct and indirect, of falling into that unhappy state. They conclude that the balancing of these bankruptcy costs against the tax gains of debt finance gives rise to an optimal capital structure, just as the traditional view has always maintained, though for somewhat different reasons.

It is this new and currently fashionable version of the optimal capital structure that I propose to challenge here. I will argue that even in a world in which interest payments are fully deductible in computing corporate income taxes, the value of the firm, in equilibrium will still be independent of its capital structure.

I. Bankruptcy Costs in Perspective

Let me first explain where I think the new optimum capital structure model goes wrong. It is not that I believe there to be no deadweight costs attaching to the use of debt finance. Bankruptcy costs and agency costs do indeed exist as was dutifully noted at several points in the original 1958 article [28, see especially footnote 18 and p. 293]. It is just that these costs, by any sensible reckoning, seem disproportionately small relative to the tax savings they are supposedly balancing.

The tax savings, after all, are conventionally taken as being on the order of 50 cents for each dollar of permanent debt issued.[3] The figure one usually hears as an estimate of bankruptcy costs is 20 percent of the value of the estate; and if this were the true order of magnitude for such costs, they would have to be taken very seriously indeed as a possible counterweight. But when that figure is traced back to its source in the paper by Baxter [5] (and the subsequent and seemingly confirmatory studies of Stanley and Girth [36] and Van Horne [39]), it turns out to refer mainly to the bankruptcies of individuals, with a sprinkling of small businesses, mostly proprietorships and typically undergoing liquidation rather than reorganization. The only study I know that deals with the costs of bankruptcy and reorganization for large, publicly-held corporations is that of Jerold Warner [40]. Warner

---

3. See, among others, Modigliani and Miller [27]. The 50 percent figure—actually 48 percent under present Federal law plus some additional state income taxes for most firms—is an upper bound that assumes the firm always has enough income to utilize the tax shield on the interest. For reestimates of the tax savings under other assumptions with respect to availability of offsets and to length of borrowing, see Kim [21] and Brennan and Schwartz [12]. The estimate of the tax saving has been further complicated since 1962 by the Investment Tax Credit and especially by the limitation of the credit to fifty percent of the firm's tax liability. Some fuzziness about the size of the tax savings also arises in the case of multinational corporations.

tabulated the direct costs of bankruptcy and reorganization for a sample of 11 railroads that filed petitions in bankruptcy under Section 77 of the Bankruptcy Act between 1930 and 1955. He found that the eventual cumulated direct costs of bankruptcy—and keep in mind that most of these railroads were in bankruptcy and running up these expenses for over 10 years!—averaged 5.3 percent of the market value of the firm's securities as of the end of the month in which the railroad filed the petition. There was a strong inverse size effect, moreover. For the largest road, the costs were 1.7 percent.

And remember that these are the *ex post*, upper-bound cost ratios, whereas, of course, the *expected* costs of bankruptcy are the relevant ones when the firm's capital structure decisions are being made. On that score, Warner finds, for example, that the direct costs of bankruptcy averaged only about 1 percent of the value of the firm 7 years before the petition was filed; and when he makes a reasonable allowance for the probability of bankruptcy actually occurring, he comes up with an estimate of the expected cost of bankruptcy that is, of course, much smaller yet.

Warner's data cover only the *direct* costs of reorganization in bankruptcy. The deadweight costs of rescaling claims might perhaps loom larger if measures were available of the indirect costs, such as the diversion of the time and energies of management from tasks of greater productivity or the reluctance of customers and suppliers to enter into long-term commitments.[4] But why speculate about the size of these costs? Surely we can assume that if the direct and indirect deadweight costs of the ordinary loan contract began to eat up significant portions of the tax savings, other forms of debt contracts with lower deadweight costs would be used instead.[5]

An obvious case in point is the income bond. Interest payments on such bonds need be paid in any year only if earned; and if earned and paid are fully deductible in computing corporate income tax. But if not earned and not paid in any year, the bondholders have no right to foreclose. The interest payments typically cumulate for a short period of time—usually two to three years—and then are added to the principal. Income bonds, in sum, are securities that appear to have all the supposed tax advantages of debt, without the bankruptcy cost disadvantages.[6] Yet, except for a brief flurry in the early 1960's, such bonds are rarely issued.

The conventional wisdom attributes this dearth to the unsavory connotations that surround such bonds.[7] They were developed originally in the course of the railroad bankruptcies in the 19th century and they are presumed to be still associated with that dismal process in the minds of potential buyers. As an

---

4. For more on this theme see Jensen and Meckling [20].

5. A similar argument in a somewhat different, but related, context is made by Black [6, esp. pp. 330–31]. Note also that while the discussion has so far referred exclusively to "bankruptcy" costs fairly narrowly construed, much the same reasoning applies to the debt-related costs in the broader sense, as in the "agency" costs of Jensen and Meckling [20] or the "costs of lending" of Black, Miller and Posner [9].

6. Not quite, because failure to repay or refund the principal at maturity could trigger a bankruptcy. Also, a firm may have earnings, but no cash.

7. See Esp. Robbins [31], [27].

investment banker once put it to me: "They have the smell of death about them." Perhaps so. But the obvious retort is that bit of ancient Roman wisdom: *pecunia non olet* (money has no odor). If the stakes were as high as the conventional analysis of the tax subsidy to debt seems to suggest, then ingenious security salesmen, investment bankers or tax advisers would surely long since have found ways to overcome investor repugnance to income bonds.

In sum, the great emphasis on bankruptcy costs in recent discussions of optimal capital structure policy seems to me to have been misplaced. For big businesses, at least (and particularly for such conspicuously low-levered ones as I.B.M. or Kodak), the supposed trade-off between tax gains and bankruptcy costs looks suspiciously like the recipe for the fabled horse-and-rabbit stew—one horse and one rabbit.[8]

II. Taxes and Capital Structures: The Empirical Record

Problems arise also on the other side of the trade-off. If the optimal capital structure were simply a matter of balancing tax advantages against bankruptcy costs, why have observed capital structures shown so little change over time?[9]

When I looked into the matter in 1960 under the auspices of the Commission on Money and Credit (Miller [24]), I found, among other things, that the debt/asset ratio of the typical nonfinancial corporation in the 1950's was little different from that of the 1920's despite the fact that tax rates had quintupled—from 10 and 11 percent in the 1920's to 52 percent in the 1950's.[10] Such rise as did occur, moreover, seemed to be mainly a substitution of debt for preferred stock, rather than of debt for common stock. The year-to-year variations in debt ratios reflected primarily the cyclical movements of the economy. During expansions debt ratios tended to fall, partly because the lag of dividends behind earnings built up internally generated equity; and partly because the ratio of equity to debt in new financings tended to rise when the stock market was booming.

My study for the CMC carried the story only through the 1950's. A hasty perusal of the volumes of Statistics of Income available for the years thereafter suggests that some upward drift in debt ratios did appear to be taking place in the 1960's, at least in book-value terms. Some substantial portion of this seeming rise, however, is a consequence of the liberalization of depreciation deductions in the early 1960's. An accounting change of that kind reduces reported taxable earnings and, barring an induced reduction in dividend policy, will tend to push accumulated retained earnings (and total assets) below the levels that would otherwise have been

---

8. In this connection, it is interesting to note that the optimal debt to value ratio in the hypothetical example presented in the recent paper by E. Han Kim [21] turns out to be 42 percent and, hence, very substantially higher than the debt ratio for the typical U.S. corporation, even though Kim's calculation assumes that bankruptcy costs would eat up no less than 40 percent of the firm's assets in the event of failure.

9. A related question is why there appears to be no systematic cross-sectional relation between debt ratios and corporate tax rates in the countries of the European Economic Community. See Coates and Wooley [13].

10. The remarkable stability of corporate debt ratios in the face of huge increases in tax rates was noted by many other writers in this period. See, e.g., Sametz [22, esp. pp. 462-3] and the references there cited.

recorded.[11] Thus, without considerable further adjustment, direct comparison of current and recent debt ratios to those of earlier eras is no longer possible. But suppose we were to make the extreme assumption that all the rise in debt ratios genuinely reflected policy decisions rather than changes in accounting rules. Then that would still have meant that the average nonfinancial corporation raised its ratio of long-term debt from about one-fifth to only about one-fourth of total assets during the decade.[12]

Whatever may have been the case in the 1960's, the impression was certainly widespread in the early 1970's that corporate debt ratios were rising rapidly and ominously. This was a period, after all, in which *Business Week* could devote an entire and very gloomy issue (October 12, 1974) to the theme "The Debt Economy."

Looking back now, however, with all the advantages of hindsight, the increases in debt of such concern in 1974 can be seen to be a transitory response to a peculiar configuration of events rather than a permanent shift in corporate capital structures.[13] A surge in inventory accumulation was taking place as firms sought to hedge against shortages occasioned by embargoes or price controls or crop failures. Much of this accumulation was financed by short-term borrowing—a combination that led to a sharp deterioration in such conventional measures of financial health as "quick ratios" and especially coverage ratios (since little of the return on the precautionary inventory buildup was showing up in current earnings and since inflation *per se* will automatically reduce the ratio of earnings to interest payments even with no change in the interest burden in real terms).

But this inventory bubble burst soon after the famous doomsday issue of *Business Week* hit the stands—providing one more confirmation of Allen Wallis' dictum that by the time journalists become interested in an economic problem, the worst is already over. In the ensuing months, inventories have been pared, bank loans have been repaid and conventional measures of corporate liquidity have been restored to something closer to their old-time vigor. New common stock issues have been coming briskly to market as always in the past when the stock market was buoyant. Thus, when the returns for the first half of the 1970's are finally in, we are likely to be facing the same paradox we did in the 1950's—corporate debt ratios only marginally higher than those of the 1920's despite enormously higher tax rates.[14]

---

11. Also acting in the same direction were the liberalized rules for expensing rather than capitalizing outlays for research and development. On the other hand, debt ratios would tend to be understated by the growth during the decade of off-balance-sheet debt financing, such as leasing and unfunded pension liability.

12. For manufacturing corporations, Federal Trade Commission reports indicate that long-term debt rose during the 1960's from 12.2 percent of reported total assets to 16.6 percent. Short-term debt rose from about 7 percent to 12 percent of reported total assets over the same period. The corresponding figures for the end of 1975 were 17.9 percent for long-term debt and 10.2 percent for short-term debt. The figures here and throughout refer of course, to gross debt without allowing for the substantial amounts of debt securities that are owned by manufacturing and other nonfinancial corporations.

13. For an independent reading of these events that is similar in most essential respects, see Gilbert [16].

14. The discussion in the text has focused mainly on debt/asset ratios at book value, in the hope that

Actually, the cognitive dissonance is worse now than it was then. In the 1950's it was still possible to entertain the notion that the seeming failure of corporations to reap the tax advantages of debt financing might simply be a lag in adjustment. As corporate finance officers and their investment bankers sharpened their pencils, the tax savings they discovered would eventually wear down aversions to debt on the part of any others in the Boardroom still in a state of shock from the Great Depression. But hope can no longer be expected from that quarter. A disequilibrium that has lasted 30 years and shows no signs of disappearing is too hard for any economist to accept.[15] And since failure to close the gap cannot convincingly be attributed to the bankruptcy costs or agency costs of debt financing, there would seem to be only one way left to turn: the tax advantages of debt financing must be substantially less than the conventional wisdom suggests.[16]

III. THE TAX ADVANTAGES OF DEBT FINANCING REEXAMINED

That the solution might lie in this direction was hinted at, but alas only hinted at, in the original 1958 MM paper. If I may invoke the Presidential priviledge of being allowed to quote (selectively) from my earlier work, we said there in the 57th footnote:

> It should also be pointed out that our tax system acts in other ways to reduce the gains from debt financing. Heavy reliance on debt in the capital structure, for example, commits a company to paying out a substantial proportion of its income in the form of interest payments taxable to the owners under the personal income tax. A debt free company, by contrast, can reinvest in the business all of its (smaller) net income and to this extent subject the owners only to the low capital gains rate (or possibly to no tax at all by virtue of the loophole at death).

We alluded to the same line of argument again briefly in the correction paper in 1963.[17] The point was developed in a more extensive and systematic way by Farrar and Selwyn [15]. Further extensions were made by Myers [30], Stapleton [37],

---

book value measures might give better insight to corporate capital structure objectives than would market value measures of leverage, which are highly sensitive to changes in the level of stock prices. As of the end of 1975, tabulations prepared by Salomon Brothers in their volume *The Supply and Demand for Credit, 1976*, indicate a ratio of long-term debt to market value for all U.S. corporations (including public utilities) of 27.1 percent. (Actually, even this is a bit on the high side since the debt is measured at face value and thus does not reflect the substantial fall in the value of outstanding debt in the 1st half of the 1970's.) In 1972, at the height of the boom, the long-term debt ratio at market value was only about 17 percent. The highest recent level reached in recent years was 30 percent at the end of 1974 after a two-year fall of $500 billion in the market value of common and preferred stock.

15. There are certainly few signs that firms were rushing to close the gap by methods as direct as exchanges of debt for their common shares. Masulis [22] was able to find only about 60 such cases involving listed corporations in the 1960's and 1970's. Most of these were concentrated during an 18-month period after the drop in the stock market in 1973; and some of these, in turn, appear more to be attempts to "go private" than to adjust the capital structure.

16. The resolution of the paradox offered in the CMC paper [24] was essentially one of agency costs and, in particular, that the costs of monitoring risky debt made such debt uneconomic as a market instrument.

17. In that paper, the major weight in resolving the paradox was placed on what might be called a "precautionary" motive. Corporations were presumed to want to maintain substantial reserves of high-grade borrowing power so as not to be forced to float common stocks when they believe their stock to be undervalued. Such motives are by no means inconsistent with the explanation to be offered here.

Stiglitz [38], and in two important papers by Fischer Black [7], [8]—papers still unpublished but whose contents were communicated to me, sometimes in very forceful fashion, in the course of many arguments and discussions.

When the personal income tax is taken into account along with the corporation income tax, the gain from leverage, G_L, for the stockholders in a firm holding real assets can be shown to be given by the following expression:

$$G_L = \left[1 - \frac{(1-\tau_C)(1-\tau_{PS})}{1-\tau_{PB}}\right] B_L$$

where τ_C is the corporate tax rate, τ_{PS} is the personal income tax rate applicable to income from common stock, τ_{PB} is the personal income tax rate applicable to income from bonds and B_L is the market value of the levered firm's debt. For simplicity at this stage of the argument, all the taxes are assumed to be proportional; and to maintain continuity with the earlier MM papers, the expression is given in its "perpetuity" form.[18]

Note that when all tax rates are set equal to zero, the expression does indeed reduce to the standard MM no-tax result of $G_L = 0$. And when the personal income tax rate on income from bonds is the same as that on income from shares—a special case of which, of course, is when there is assumed to be no personal income tax at all—then the gain from leverage is the familiar $\tau_C B_L$. But when the tax rate on income from shares is less than the tax on income from bonds, then the gain from leverage will be less than $\tau_C B_L$. In fact, for a wide range of values for τ_C, τ_{PS} and τ_{PB}, the gain from leverage vanishes entirely or even turns negative!

Let me assure you that this result is no mere sleight-of-hand due to hidden trick assumptions. The gain evaporates or turns into a loss because investors hold securities for the "consumption possibilities" they generate and hence will evaluate them in terms of their yields net of all tax drains. If, therefore, the personal tax on income from common stocks is less than that on income from bonds, then the *before-tax* return on taxable bonds has to be high enough, other things equal, to offset this tax handicap. Otherwise, no taxable investor would want to hold bonds. Thus, while it is still true that the owners of a levered corporation have the advantage of deducting their interest payments to bondholders in computing their corporate income tax, these interest payments have already been "grossed up," so to speak, by any differential in the taxes that the bondholders will have to pay on their interest income. The advantage of deductibility at the one level thus merely

---

18. The expression can be derived in a number of ways of which the simplest is perhaps the following variant on the MM reply to Heins and Sprenkle [29]. Ownership of the fraction α of the levered corporation yields a return to the investor of $\alpha(\tilde{X} - rB_L)(1-\tau_C)(1-\tau_{PS})$ where $\tilde{X}$ is the uncertain return on firm's real (as opposed to financial) assets. This can be duplicated by the sum of (a) an investment of αS_U in the shares of the twin unlevered corporation, which yields $\alpha \tilde{X}(1-\tau_C)(1-\tau_{PS})$; plus (b), borrowing $\alpha B_L[(1-\tau_C)(1-\tau_{PS})/(1-\tau_{PB})]$ on personal account. Since interest is deductible under the personal income tax, the net cost of the borrowing is $\alpha r B_L(1-\tau_C)(1-\tau_{PS})$ and thus the original levered stream has been matched.

Here and throughout, the tax authorities will be presumed to have taken the steps necessary to prevent taxable individuals or firms from eliminating their tax liabilities or converting them to negative taxes by "tax arbitrage" dodges (such as borrowing to hold tax-exempt securities) or by large-scale short-selling.

serves to offset the disadvantages of includability at the other.[19] When the rates happen to satisfy the equation $(1-\tau_{PB})=(1-\tau_C)(1-\tau_{PS})$, the offset is one-for-one and the owners of the corporation reap no gain whatever from their use of tax-deductible debt rather than equity capital.

But we can say more than this. Any situation in which the owners of corporations could increase their wealth by substituting debt for equity (or vice versa) would be incompatible with market equilibrium. Their attempts to exploit these opportunities would lead, in a world with progressive income taxes, to changes in the yields on stocks and bonds and in their ownership patterns. These changes, in turn, restore the equilibrium and remove the incentives to issue more debt, even without invoking bankruptcy costs or lending costs as a *deus ex machina*.

IV. Taxes and Market Equilibrium

Like so many other propositions in financial economics this, too, is "obvious once you think of it." Let me belabor the obvious a bit, however, by a simple graphical example that will serve, I hope, both to illustrate the mechanism that brings the equilibrium about and to highlight some of the implications of that equilibrium.

Suppose, for simplicity that the personal tax rate on income from stock were zero (and we'll see later that this may be a less outrageous simplification than it looks). And suppose further, again strictly for simplicity of presentation, that all bonds are riskless and that there are no transaction costs, flotation costs or surveillance costs involved in their issuance. Then in such a world, the equilibrium of the market for bonds would be that pictured in Figure 1. The quantity of bonds outstanding is measured along the horizontal axis and the rate of interest along the vertical. The demand for bonds by the investing public is given by the upward sloping curve labeled $r_d(B)$. (Yes, it *is* a demand curve even though it slopes up.) Its intercept is at r_0 which measures the equilibrium rate of interest on fully tax-exempt bonds (such as those of state and local governments). The flat stretch of the curve immediately to the right represents the demand for fully taxable corporate bonds by fully tax-exempt individuals and organizations. Clearly, these investors would be the sole holders of corporate bonds if the market interest rate on corporate debts were only r_0. Any taxable investor who wanted to hold bonds in his or her portfolio would find it preferable to buy tax-exempt bonds.

To entice these taxable investors into the market for corporate bonds, the rate of interest on such bonds has to be high enough to compensate for the taxes on interest income under the personal income tax. More precisely, for an individual whose marginal rate of personal income tax on interest income is τ_{PB}^a, the "demand rate of interest" on taxable corporate bonds would be the rate on tax exempts grossed up by the marginal tax rate, i.e., $r_0(1/(1-\tau_{PB}^a))$. Since the personal income tax is progressive, the demand interest rate has to keep rising to pull in investors in

---

19. An analogous argument in the context of the lease-or-buy decision is given in Miller and Upton [26]. Reasoning of essentially this kind has also long been invoked to explain the otherwise puzzling survival of preferred stock (see, among many others, Miller [24, esp. note 40, p. 431]). The fact that 85 percent of any dividends received by a taxable corporation can be excluded in computing its taxable income, pushes down the yields on preferred stocks and thereby offsets the disadvantage of nondeductibility.

Debt and Taxes

Rate of Interest

$r_0 \dfrac{1}{1-\tau_C}$

r_0

$r_d(B) = r_0 \dfrac{1}{1-\tau_{PB}^{\alpha}}$

$r_s(B) = r_0 \dfrac{1}{1-\tau_C}$

B*

Quantity of Bonds Outstanding

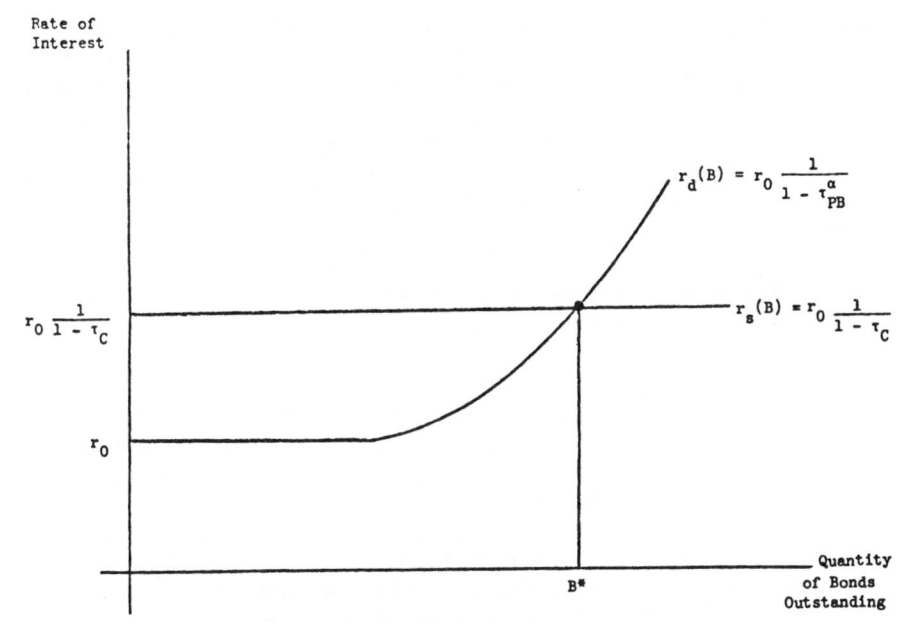

FIGURE 1. Equilibrium in the Market for Bonds

higher and higher tax brackets, thus giving the continuous, upward sloping curve pictured.

The intersection of this demand curve with the horizontal straight line through the point $r_0/1-\tau_C$, i.e., the tax-exempt rate grossed up by the corporate tax rate, determines the market equilibrium. If corporations were to offer a quantity of bonds greater than B^*, interest rates would be driven above $r_0/1-\tau_C$ and some levered firms would find leverage to be a losing proposition. If the volume were below B^*, interest rates would be lower than $r_0/1-\tau_C$ and some unlevered firms would find it advantageous to resort to borrowing.

The market equilibrium defined by the intersection of the two curves will have the following property. There will be an equilibrium level of aggregate corporate debt, B^*, and hence an equilbrium debt-equity ratio for the corporate sector as a whole. *But there would be no optimum debt ratio for any individual firm.* Companies following a no-leverage or low leverage strategy (like I.B.M. or Kodak) would find a market among investors in the high tax brackets; those opting for a high leverage strategy (like the electric utilities) would find the natural clientele for their securities at the other end of the scale. But one clientele is as good as the other. And in this important sense it would still be true that the value of any firm, in equilibrium, would be independent of its capital structure, despite the deductibility of interest payments in computing corporate income taxes.[20]

One advantage of graphical illustration is that it makes it so easy to see the

---
20. The details of corporate strategy and investor valuation at the micro level implied by this model are interesting in their own right, but further analysis is best deferred to another occasion.

answer to the following inevitable question: If the stockholders of levered corporations don't reap the benefits of the tax gains from leverage, who does? Professors of finance, of course—though only indirectly and only after cutting in their colleagues in other departments. As Figure 1 shows, universities and other tax exempt organizations, as well as individuals in low tax brackets (widows and orphans?) benefit from what might be called a "bondholders' surplus." Market interest rates have to be grossed up to pay the taxes of the marginal bondholder, whose tax rate in equilibrium will be equal to the corporate rate.[21] Note that this can cut both ways, however. Low bracket individuals (and corporations) have to *pay* the corporate tax, in effect, when they want to borrow.

An equilibrium of the kind pictured in Figure 1 does not require, of course, that the effective personal tax rate on income from shares of the marginal holder be literally zero, but only that it be substantially less than his or her rate on income from bonds. As a practical matter, however, the assumption that the effective rate at the margin is close to zero may not be so wide of the mark. Keep in mind that a "clientele effect" is also at work in the market for shares. The high dividend paying stocks will be preferred by tax exempt organizations and low income investors; those stocks yielding more of their return in the form of capital gains will gravitate to the taxpayers in the upper brackets.[22] The tax rate on such gains is certainly greater than zero, in principle. But holders need pay no taxes on their gains until realized and only a small fraction of accumulated gains are, in fact, realized and taxed in any year (see, e.g., Bhatia [4, esp. note 12] and Bailey [2]). Taxes on capital gains can not only be deferred at the option of the holder—and remember that by conventional folk wisdom, 10 years of tax deferral is almost as good as exemption—but until the recent Tax Reform Act of 1976, could be avoided altogether if held until death, thanks to the rules permitting transfer of the decedent's tax basis to his or her heirs.

To the extent that the effective tax rate on income from shares is greater than zero, the horizontal line defining the equilibrium interest rate will be above that pictured in Figure 1. In the limiting case where the tax concessions (intended or unintended) made to income from shares were either nonexistent or so small that $(1 - \tau_C)(1 - \tau_{PS})$ implied a value for τ_{PB}^a greater than the top bracket of the personal

---

21. In point of fact, the spread between municipals and corporates has typically been within shouting distance of the corporate rate, though comparisons are difficult because of differences in risk (including, of course, the risk that the tax status of municipals will be changed) and though, admittedly, mechanisms of a different kind might also be producing that result. The recent study of the yield curve of U.S. Government securities by McCulloch [23] gives estimates of the marginal tax rate of holders of such bonds that are close to, but usually somewhat below the corporate rate.

22. The data presented in the study of stock ownership by Blume, Crockett and Friend [11, esp. Table G, p. 40] are consistent with this form of clientele effect, though its magnitude is perhaps somewhat smaller than might have been expected *a priori*. They estimate, for example, that in 1971, the ratio of dividends to the market value of holdings was about 2.8 percent for individual investors with adjusted gross income of less than $15,000 as compared to 2.1 percent for those with adjusted gross incomes of $100,000 or more.

By invoking this dividend clientele effect, an argument analogous to that in Figure 1 can be developed to show that the value of a firm could be invariant to its dividend policy despite the more favorable tax treatment of capital gains than of dividends. Some gropings in that direction were made in the MM dividend paper [25, esp. pp. 431-2]. A more explicit analysis along those lines was given by Black and Scholes [10]. For a related model dealing with tax shelters on real investment see Bailey [3].

Debt and Taxes

income tax, then no interior market equilibrium would be possible. Common stock would indeed be a dominated security from the purely financial point of view, exactly as the standard micro model of the tax effect suggests. Common stock could continue to exist only by virtue of special attributes it might possess that could not be duplicated with bonds or with other forms of business organization, such as co-ops.

The analysis underlying Figure 1 can be extended to allow for risky borrowing, but there are complications. What makes things difficult is not simply a matter of risk *per se*.[23] Default risk can be accommodated in Figure 1 merely by reinterpreting all the before-tax interest rates as risk-adjusted or certainty-equivalent rates. The trouble is, rather, that bonds of companies in default will not, in general, yield the issuing stockholders their full tax shield (see MM [27, esp. note 5], Kim [21] and Brennan and Schwartz [12]). Unless the firm has past profits against which its current losses can be carried back, or unless it can escape the vigilance of the I.R.S. and unload the corporate corpse on a taxable firm, some of the interest deduction goes to waste. To entice firms to issue risky bonds, therefore, the risk-adjusted supply-rate would have to be less than $r_0(1/(1-\tau_C))$, and presumably the more so the greater the likelihood of default.[24]

An essentially similar effect will be produced by the bankruptcy costs discussed earlier. And this will imply, among other things, that the full burden of the bankruptcy costs or lending costs is not necessarily borne by the debtors as is frequently supposed. Part of the costs are shifted to the bond buyers in the form of lower risk-adjusted rates of interest in equilibrium.

A model of the kind in Figure 1 could, in principle, clear up most of the puzzles and anomalies discussed in Sections I and II above—the seeming disparity between the tax gains of debt and the costs of bankruptcy particularly for large low-levered corporations; the lack of widespread market interest in income bonds; and especially the failure of the average corporate debt ratio to rise substantially in response to the enormous increase in tax rates since the 1920's (because these increases in rates in the late 1930's as well as subsequent decreases and reincreases have generally moved both the corporate and individual rate schedules in the same direction). The model could also account as well for other of the stylized facts of corporate finance such as the oft-remarked dramatic transition of the bond market from an individual to an institution-dominated market in the late 1930's and early 1940's.[25] On the other hand, many questions clearly still remain to be answered.

---

23. For the specialists in these matters, suffice it to say that in the equilibrium of Figure 1, the capital markets are, of course, assumed to be "complete." For a discussion of some of the implications of corporate taxes the deductibility of interest payments under conditions of "incomplete markets" see Hakansson [18].

24. These effects, however, do not imply the existence of "super-premiums" for riskless bonds of the kind visualized recently by Glenn [17] and earlier by Durand [14]. Those were presumed to arise from the segmentation of the bond market and especially from the strong preferences of the institutional sector for low-risk securities. In terms of Figure 1, any such increase in the demand for safe securities would show up in the first instance as a lower value for r_0 and, hence, a lower value for the equilibrium corporate borrowing rate, $r_0/1-\tau_C$. (See the MM 1958 article [28, especially pp. 279–80]. See also Hamada's discussion of Glenn's paper [19].)

25. For an early account of that transition that stresses precisely the kind of tax effects that underlie Figure 1, see Shapiro [35].

What about cross-sectional variations in debt ratios, for example—a subject on which surprisingly little work has yet been done?[26] Can they be explained convincingly by the market equilibrium model presented here or some variant of it? Or do the variations observed reflect some systematic part of the equilibrating process that escapes the kind of aggregate market models discussed here? What about the distribution of stocks and bonds among investors? Does ownership sort out in terms of tax status as sharply as emphasized here? Or does the need for diversification swamp the tax differences and thereby throw the main burden of the equilibration onto other factors, such as agency costs?

The call for more research traditionally signals the approaching end of a Presidential Address; and it is a tradition that I know you will want to see preserved. Let me conclude, therefore, by trying to face up, as I promised in the beginning, to the kind of complaint so often raised against market equilibrium analysis of financial policy of the type here presented: "But firms and investors don't behave that way!"

V. Market Equilibrium and the Behavior of Firms and Individuals

If the phrase "don't behave that way" is taken to mean that firms and individuals don't literally perform the maximizing calculations that underlie the curves in Figure 1, then it is most certainly correct. No corporate treasurer's office, controller's staff, or investment banker's research team that I have ever encountered had, or could remotely be expected to have, enough reliable information about the future course of prices for a firm's securities to convince even a moderately skeptical outside academic observer that the firm's value had indeed been maximized by some specific financial decision or strategy. Given the complexities of the real-world setting, actual decision procedures are inevitably heuristic, judgmental, imitative and groping even where, as with so much of what passes for capital budgeting, they wear the superficial trappings of hard-nosed maximization. On this score, has there ever been any doubt that the Harvard cases (and the work of Herbert Simon and his followers) give a far more accurate picture of the way things really look and get done out on the firing line than any maximizing "model of the firm" that any economist ever drew?

Why then do economists keep trying to develop models that assume rational behavior by firms? They are not, I insist, merely hoping to con their business school deans into thinking they are working on problems of business management. Rather they have found from experience—not only in finance, but across the board —that the rational behavior models generally lead to better predictions and descriptions at the level of the industry, the market and the whole economy than any alternatives available to them. Their experience, at those levels, moreover, need involve no inconsistency with the heuristic, rule-of-thumb, intuitive kinds of decision making they actually observe in firms. It suggests rather that evolutionary mechanisms are at work to give survival value to those heuristics that are compat-

---

26. One of the few studies of cross-sectional differences in debt ratios is that of Schwartz and Aronson [34], but it really does little more than document the fact that utilities and railroads have substantially higher debt ratios than firms in manufacturing and mining.

ible with rational market equilibrium, however far from rational they may appear to be when examined up close and in isolation.[27]

But we must be wary of the reverse inference that merely because a given heuristic persists, it must have some survival value and, hence, must have a rational "explanation." The MM and related invariance propositions, for example, are often dismissed on grounds that corporate finance officers would surely not show so much concern over decisions that really "don't matter." The most, however, that we can safely assert about the evolutionary process underlying market equilibrium is that harmful heuristics, like harmful mutations in nature, will die out. Neutral mutations that serve no function, but do no harm, can persist indefinitely. Neither in nature nor in the economy can the enormous variation in forms we observe be convincingly explained in simple Darwinian terms.[28]

To say that many, perhaps even most, financial heuristics are neutral is not to suggest, however, that financial decision making is just a pointless charade or treat the resources devoted to financial innoviations are wasted. A mutation or a heuristic that is neutral in one environment may suddenly acquire (or lose) survival value if the environment changes. The pool of existing neutral mutations and heuristics thus permits the adaptation to the new conditions to take place more quickly and more surely than if a new and original act of creation were required. Once these types and roles of heuristics in the equilibrating process are understood and appreciated, the differences between the institutionalist and theorist wings of our Association may be seen to be far less fundamental and irreconcilable than the sometimes ferocious polemics of the last 20 years might seem to suggest.

REFERENCES

1. Victor L. Andrews. "Captive Finance Companies," *Harvard Business Review*, Vol. 42 (July-August 1964), 80–92.
2. Martin J. Bailey. "Capital Gains and Income Taxation," In *The Taxation of Income From Capital*. Edited by A. Harberger and M. Bailey. (Washington, D.C.: The Brookings Distribution, 1969).
3. ———. "Progressivity and Investment Yields under U.S. Income Taxation," *Journal of Political Economy*, Vol. 82, No. 6 (Nov./Dec. 1974), 1157–75.
4. Ku B. Bhatia. "Capital Gains and Inequality of Personal Income: Some Results From Survey Data," *Journal of the American Statistical Association*, Vol. 71, No. 355 (September 1976), 575–580.
5. Nevins Baxter. "Leverage, Risk of Ruin and the Cost of Capital," *Journal of Finance*, Vol. 22, No. 3 (September 1967), 395–403.
6. Fischer Black. "Bank Funds Management in an Efficient Market," *Journal of Financial Economics*, Vol. 2, No. 4 (December 1975).
7. ———. "Taxes and Capital Market Equilibrium." Working Paper No. 21A, Associates in Finance, Belmont, Massachusetts, April 1971 (mimeo).
8. ———. "Taxes and Capital Market Equilibrium under Uncertainty," Working Paper No. 21B, Chicago, May 1973 (mimeo).

---

27. Has anyone a better explanation for the puzzle of why the pay-back criterion continues to thrive despite having been denounced as Neanderthal in virtually every textbook in finance and accounting over the last 30 years?

28. Any experienced teacher of corporate finance can surely supply numerous examples of such neutral variations. My own favorite is the captive finance company. See, e.g., the perceptive discussion in Andrews [1].

9. ———, Merton H. Miller and Richard A. Posner. "An Approach to the Regulation of Bank Holding Companies," University of Chicago, April 1976 (multilith).
10. ——— and Myron Scholes. "The Effects on Dividend Yield and Dividend Policy on Common Stock Prices and Returns," *Journal of Financial Economics*, Vol. 1, No. 1 (May 1974), 1–22.
11. Marshall E. Blume, Jean Crockett and Irwin Frend. "Stock Ownership in The United States: Characteristics and Trends," *Survey of Current Business* (November 1974), 16–40.
12. M. J. Brennan and E. S. Schwartz. "Corporate Income Taxes, Valuation and the Problem of Optimal Capital Structure," University of British Columbia, Vancouver, B.C., Canada, multilith, August 1976 (revised).
13. J. H. Coates and P. K. Wooley. "Corporate Gearing in the E.E.C.," *Journal of Business Finance and Accounting*, Vol. 2, No. 1 (Spring 1975), 1–18.
14. David Durand. "The Cost of Capital, Corporation Finance and the Investment: Comment," *American Economic Review*, Vol. 49, No. 4 (Sept. 1959), 39–55.
15. Donald Farrar and Lee L. Selwyn. "Taxes, Corporate Policy, and Returns to Investors," *National Tax Journal*, Vol. 20, No. 4 (December 1967), 444–54.
16. R. Alton Gilbert. "Bank Financing of the Recovery," *Federal Reserve Bank of St. Louis Review*, Vol. 58, No. 7, 2–9.
17. David W. Glenn. "Super Premium Security Prices and Optimal Corporate Financial Decisions," *Journal of Finance*, Vol. 31, No. 2 (May 1976), 507–24.
18. Nils Hakansson. "Ordering Markets and the Capital Structures of Firms, with Illustrations," Working Paper No. 24, Institute of Business and Economic Research, University of California, Berkeley, October 1974 (multilith).
19. Robert Hamada. "Discussion," *Journal of Finance*, Vol. 31, No. 2 (May 1976), 543–46.
20. Michael C. Jensen and William H. Meckling. "Theory of the Firm: Managerial Behavior, Agency Costs and Capital Structure," University of Rochester, August 1975 (multilith).
21. Han E. Kim. "A Mean-Variance Theory of Optimum Capital Structure and Corporate Debt Capacity," Ohio State University, undated (multilith).
22. Ronald W. Masulis. "The Effects of Capital Structure Change on Security Prices," Graduate School of Business, University of Chicago, May 1976 (multilith).
23. J. Huston McCulloch. "The Tax Adjusted Yield Curve," *Journal of Finance*, Vol. 30, No. 3 (June 1975), 811–30.
24. Merton H. Miller. "The Corporation Income Tax and Corporate Financial Policies," In *Stabilization Policies*, Commission on Money and Credit, Prentice Hall, 1963.
25. ——— and Franco Modigliani. "Dividend Policy, Growth and the Valuation of Shares," *Journal of Business*, Vol. 34, No. 4 (October 1961), 411–33.
26. ——— and Charles W. Upton. "Leasing, Buying and the Cost of Capital Services." *Journal of Finance* (June 1976).
27. Franco Modigliani and Merton H. Miller. "Corporate Income Taxes and the Cost of Capital: A Correction," *American Economic Review*, Vol. 53, No. 3 (June 1963), 433–43.
28. ——— and ———. "The Cost of Capital, Corporation Finance and the Theory of Investment," *American Economic Review*, Vol. 48, No. 3 (June 1958), 261–97.
29. ——— and ———. "Reply to Heins and Sprenkle," *American Economic Review*, Vol. 59, No. 4, Part I (September 1969).
30. Stewart C. Myers. "Taxes, Corporate Financial Policy and the Return to Investors: Comment," *National Tax Journal*, Vol. 20, No. 4 (Dec. 1967), 455–62.
31. Sidney M. Robbins. "A Bigger Role for Income Bonds," *Harvard Business Review* (November-December 1955).
32. ———. "An Objective Look at Income Bonds," *Harvard Business Review* (June 1974).
33. Arnold W. Sametz. "Trends in the Volume and Composition of Equity Finance," *Journal of Finance*, Vol. 19, No. 3 (September 1964), 450–469.
34. Eli Schwartz and J. Richard Aronson. "Some Surrogate Evidence in Support of the Concept of Optimal Financial Structure," *Journal of Finance*, Vol. 22, No. 1 (March 1963), 10–18.
35. Eli Shapiro. "The Postwar Market for Corporate Securities: 1946–55," *Journal of Finance*, Vol. 14, No. 2 (May 1959), 196–217.

Debt and Taxes

36. D. T. Stanley and M. Girth. *Bankruptcy: Problem, Process, Reform.* (Washington, D.C.: The Brookings Institution, 1971).
37. R. C. Stapleton. "Taxes, the Cost of Capital and the Theory of Investment," *The Economic Journal,* Vol. 82 (December 1972), 1273-92.
38. Joseph Stiglitz. "Taxation, Corporate Financial Policy, and the Cost of Capital," *Journal of Public Economics,* Vol. 2, No. 1 (February 1973), 1-34.
39. James C. Van Horne. "Corporate Liquidity and Bankruptcy Costs," Stanford University, Graduate School of Business, Research Paper No. 205, undated (multilith).
40. Jerold Warner. "Bankruptcy Costs, Absolute Priority and the Pricing of Risky Debt Claims," University of Chicago, July 1976 (multilith).

Debt, Dividend Policy, Taxes, Inflation and Market Valuation

FRANCO MODIGLIANI*

I. Introduction

IN THIS CONTRIBUTION, I propose to go once more over two "core issues" of corporate finance—how do leverage and dividend policy affect market valuation? These are issues that were supposed to have been settled in the two contributions that students often refer to as MoMi (Modigliani and Miller [1958]) and MiMo (Miller and Modigliani [1961]). The basic message in these papers, was that with rational investors, well functioning markets, and no taxes (or at most, only of a certain type), financial policy does not matter!

But that conclusion did not carry over to a world with taxes, which have been, and still are, a continuing source of trouble. After a false start in MoMi, the MM "Correction" [1963], on the assumption that (i) all corporate returns are taxed equally at the personal level, and (ii) the tax saving from the use of debt can be regarded as a perpetual riskless flow, concluded that each dollar of debt in the capital structure should add to the market value of the firm at a rate equal to the corporate income tax.

The gain from leverage results, derived from the demand-side analysis, in turn created immediate problems. If debt is valuable, why should firms not be financed as nearly as possible by debt alone, with the optimum leverage representing a corner solution? This implication was disturbing because it was both counterfactual and against common sense. Accordingly, it has given rise to a good deal of work focussing on the supply side. This analysis has uncovered and analyzed four major ways in which leverage could unfavorably affect the market value of the firm: (i) the most obvious and traditional is through bankruptcy costs which reduce the expected flow to all concerned (numerous references, beginning with 1967, are provided in Williamson [1981], p. 18); (ii) a second is through agency costs, resulting from the arrangements needed to protect the creditors (Jensen

---

* Massachusetts Institute of Technology. The material for this paper is based upon work supported in part by the National Science Foundation under Grant SES 7926733. The author wishes to express his appreciation to Terry Marsh, Lucas Papademos, Julio Rotemberg and Robert Shiller for reading an earlier draft of the manuscript and making valuable suggestions. I have also benefited from the advice of Fischer Black, Robert Merton and Stewart Myers.

and Meckling [1976]; Chen and Kim [1979]); (iii) the third, and most sophisticated way, is what might be called moral hazard or foregone valuable opportunities (Myers [1977]) which would be particularly relevant for firms with true growth opportunities. A fourth and most recent argument for an interior solution relies on the consideration, first developed by Brennan and Schwartz [1978], that debt is valuable in so far as it serves to shelter income from taxes, though at a cost. As debt rises, there is a growing probability of income falling below a threshold level where the shelter can not be used. This argument has since been generalized by taking into account the availability of shelters other than debt and, in particular, tax credits (DeAngelo and Masulis [1980]; Cordes and Sheffrin [1981]).

In the midst of the efforts to explain why the supply of debt would be limited, even if leverage commanded a positive price, Miller [1977] took a radical turn on the demand side. He relies on the consideration that, contrary to the MM assumption, the personal taxation of equity returns is typically lower than that of interest—and the differential is larger the higher the tax bracket. As first shown by Farrar and Selwyn [1967], this implies that the *personal* value of leverage to any investor is a decreasing function of his income tax rate, becoming negative once that rate exceeds the corporate income tax rate by a factor depending on the capital gain rate. Now, Miller argues, the *market* valuation of leverage must reflect the personal tax of the *marginal* holder of corporate debt, and, given the availability of tax exempt securities, that marginal rate must rise continuously as the quantity of corporate debt outstanding rises. If the supply of debt is infinitely elastic and the top personal tax rate exceeds the corporate rate, as he assumes, then, in equilibrium the market value of leverage must be zero.

Ever since the appearance of Miller's 1977 paper, I have been skeptical of his conclusions. First, I found unconvincing his off-hand dismissal of factors limiting the supply of debt; if the supply of debt has costs, then the intersection of demand and supply can only come at a point where debt is valuable at the margin, and therefore leverage is a serious issue of financial policy. Second, I felt uneasy that his argument rested on tax exempt securities whose rate was taken as exogenously given, an approach that has generally been accepted by those who have since made use of his model, favorably or critically, (Lewellen, Stanley, Lease and Schlarbaum [1978]; Taggart [1980]). I suspected that the validity of his argument could not depend on the existence of tax exempt debt. Furthermore, his model implied a counterfactual coincidence between the ratio of tax exempt to fully taxed interest on the one hand, and the corporate tax rate on the other (Gordon and Malkiel [1981]; Skelton [1980]). But, in the process of validating these suspicions—a task which has since been at least partly accomplished by others (e.g., DeAngelo and Masulis [1980])-I discovered serious difficulties with Miller's framework, because of its tendency to lead to unstable corner solutions.

It soon became apparent that these counterfactual implications came from failure to properly take into account the role of diversification in a world of uncertainty and risk aversion. I was, thus, led to pursue the problem in the mean-variance framework, along lines first successfully considered in the pioneering contribution of Brennan [1970], and later extended to the analysis of individual portfolios by Elton and Gruber [1978] and Auerbach and King [1981].

In what follows, I propose to show that this framework can provide clear answers to a good number of long standing issues on the effect of alternative financial policies on market valuation and portfolio composition in the presence of various taxes and of (steady) inflation. Furthermore, the results, which coincide with MM in limiting cases, are intuitively appealing, and appear broadly consistent with empirical evidence, though with one important exception to be discussed presently, pertaining to the effects of inflation.

Because of space limitations, this paper concentrates on the demand side, taking the supply as largely given, though the concluding section outlines the integration of the demand with the supply side.

Some of the major conclusions can be summarized as follows:

1) We can expect, with great confidence, leverage to be valuable, but the value could be modest if, as one might expect, the market regards the tax saving flow as subject to risk, like the underlying profit stream, rather than as a sure perpetuity, as assumed in MM.

2) Inflation should increase the value of leverage and, through that route as well as others, also increase the *price-earnings ratio* (though not necessarily the *level* of stock prices).

3) The payment of dividends should, unequivocally, tend to reduce market value, but the effect could, again, be modest if the tax consequences are capitalized at a risky rather than at the sure rate.

4) Differential rates of taxation between investors as well as between sources of return, will result in clientele effects. That is, people having the same risk tolerance will have different portfolio compositions. Moving from the lowest brackets to the highest, one should find a steady rise in the share of the portfolio invested in stocks with low dividend yield (which generally accompany high true growth) and with relatively low betas, due in particular, to low leverage. However, the differences to be expected in the portfolio composition of a high versus a low tax bracket appear to be modest in contrast to Miller's corner type solutions.

5) Inflation can be expected to increase this polarization of portfolios.

II. Derivation of Market Equilibrium

1. *Individual demand*

In the spirit of the mean-variance model, we confine our attention largely to the market for equities and debt. We begin by deriving the demand for stocks and debt by individual investors from the maximization of the utility function, whose only arguments are portfolio mean and variance. We rely on the following notation: τ_c = corporate tax rate; τ_g = capital gain rate; τ_p = personal income tax rate; $\theta_x = 1 - \tau_x$; $x = c, g, p$; μ = cash flow (EBIT), $\mu^* = \theta_c \mu$; $[M]$ = variance-covariance matrix of tax adjusted cash flows, μ^*; S = market value of equity; D = net corporate debt; $V = S + D$ = market value of firm; Δ = dividend payment; R = nominal rate of interest; p = rate of inflation; $r = R - p$ = real rate of interest; $r_p = \theta_p R - p$ = real interest rate after personal taxes; $r_c = \theta_c R - p$. Finally, a letter superscript will characterize an investor, a subscript, a firm; the superscript $\sim$ denotes a random variable; and a bold letter stands for a column vector.

The expected return to the mth investor, y_i^m, from holding a fraction, n_i^m, of the equity of firm i, net of all corporate and personal taxes, and allowing for a fully anticipated, constant rate of inflation, p, can now be written as:

$$y_i^m = n_i^m\{[\mu_i - \tau_c(\mu_i - RD_i) - RD_i + pD_i - \Delta_i]\theta_g^m + \Delta_i\theta_p^m\}$$
$$= n_i^m[(\mu_i^* - r_cD_i)\theta_g^m + \Delta_i(\theta_p^m - \theta_g^m)] \qquad \text{II.1}$$

Making use of II.1 and the standard budget equation, we can express the total expected portfolio return to the mth individual, having wealth w^m, as:

$$y^m = (w^m - \sum_i n_i^m S_i)r_p^m + \sum_i n_i^m[(\mu_i^* - r_cD_i)\theta_g^m + \Delta_i(\theta_p^m - \theta_g^m)] \qquad \text{II.2}$$

where r_p^m is the after-personal-tax real rate, $\theta_p^m R - p$.

We will pursue first the implications of the "traditional" MM assumption that the flows associated with debt are both permanent and riskless. If we extend this assumption also to dividends, the only stochastic component of returns in II.2 is μ_i^*, and the variance of the portfolio return for the mth individual takes the form:

$$(\sigma_y m)^2 = E(\tilde{y}^m - y^m)^2 = (\theta_g^m)^2 \sum_i \sum_j n_i^m \mu_{ij}^* n_j^m \qquad \text{II.3}$$

where μ_{ij}^* is the covariance of $\tilde{\mu}_i^*$ with $\tilde{\mu}_j^*$.

Maximization of a utility function of the form:

$$u^m = u^m[y^m, (\sigma_y m)^2], \; u_1^m > 0, \; u_2^m < 0, \; \text{and} \; u_2^m/u_1^m = -\gamma^m/2$$

with respect to n_i^m, $i = 1, 2, \cdots, N$, subject to the budget constraint, leads to a system of first order conditions that can be expressed in vector notation as:

$$(\mu^* - r_cD)\theta_g^m - Sr_p^m - (\theta_g^m - \theta_p^m)\Delta = \gamma^m(\theta_g^m)^2[M]n^m \qquad \text{II.4}$$

where μ^* is a column vector of the μ_i^*'s, and similarly for D, S, etc., and $[M]$ is the variance-covariance matrix of the μ_i^*'s.

2. Market equilibrium

As shown by Brennan [1970], one can, from these conditions, obtain a general equilibrium solution for the price of all "firms" (or risk classes). To this end, multiply both sides of II.4 by:

$$\frac{\Lambda}{\gamma^m(\theta_g^m)^2}, \; \text{where} \; \Lambda = 1/\sum_m \frac{1}{\gamma^m(\theta_g^m)^2}$$

and then sum over all individuals. Taking into account the fact that:

$$\sum_m n_i^m = 1, \; \forall \, i$$

the result of this summation can be written as:

$$(\mu^* - r_cD)\theta_g - Sr_p - \Delta(\theta_g - \theta_p) = \Lambda[M]1 \qquad \text{II.5}$$

Here:

$$\theta_g = \sum_m \theta_g^m \times \frac{\Lambda}{\gamma^m(\theta_g^m)^2} \qquad \text{II.5A}$$

is an average of the θ_R^m, weighted by $\dfrac{1}{\gamma^m(\theta_R^m)^2}$, Λ being the inverse of the sum of the weights [and also $1/M$ the harmonic average of the quantities $\gamma^m(\theta_R^m)^2$]. Similarly, $r_p = \theta_p R - p$, with θ_p the same weighted average of the θ_p^m.

The market value of each firm's equity is obtained by solving II.5 for S. To obtain the market value of the firm as a whole, $V_i = S_i + D_i$, we can add and subtract Dr_p on the left hand side of II.5, rearrange terms, and solve for V to obtain:

$$V = \frac{1}{r_p}[\mu^*\theta_R - \Delta(\theta_R - \theta_p) - \Lambda[M]1] + lD \qquad \text{II.6}$$

where the ith row of $[M]1$ is $\mathrm{cov}(\mu_i\mu)$, and:

$$l = \left(1 - \frac{r_c}{r_p}\theta_R\right) \qquad \text{II.7}$$

is the "value of leverage" to be discussed presently.

Equations II.5 and II.6 can also be usefully restated in terms of risk premia and CAPM β's. To this end we sum the equations II.6 over all firms to obtain:

$$V - lD + \frac{\theta_R - \theta_p}{r_p}\Delta \equiv V^* = \frac{\mu^*\theta_R - \Lambda\,\mathrm{var}(\tilde\mu^*)}{r_p} \qquad \text{II.8}$$

Here, μ^*, Δ and V are the aggregate cash flow, dividend and total value respectively, $\mathrm{var}(\tilde\mu^*)$ is the variance of overall market returns, while V^* denotes that part of market value that is due to the risky return, and excludes the portion, if any, due to the capitalization of the government contribution through tax shields and treatment of dividends. Thus, V^* corresponds to the MM notion of the "value of an unlevered stream". II.8 implies:

$$\frac{\Lambda\,\mathrm{var}(\tilde\mu^*)}{V^*} = \frac{\mu^*\theta_R}{V^*} - r_p \equiv \pi \qquad \text{II.9}$$

and $(\mu^*/V^*)\theta_R$ is the after (average) tax rate of return on the unlevered market, in the absence of dividends. The expression after the first equality in II.9 can therefore be labeled the "tax adjusted excess return"—the difference between the market return and the interest rate, after both are adjusted by the weighted average tax rate defined by II.5A. II.9 tells us that this difference, or risk premium, which is denoted by π, is proportional to the variance of market returns adjusted for taxes (implicit in Λ), a generalization of the familiar CAPM result.

Using the above definition of π, one can express total market value as:

$$V = \frac{\mu^*\theta_R}{r_p + \pi} + lD - \frac{\theta_R - \theta_p}{r_p}\Delta \qquad \text{II.10}$$

Expressions analogous to II.10 can also be derived for individual stocks by defining:

$$V_i^* = V_i - lD_i + \Delta_i(\theta_R - \theta_p)/r_p \qquad \text{II.11a}$$

$$\beta_i = \mathrm{cov}\left(\frac{\mu_i^*}{V_i^*}, \frac{\mu^*}{V^*}\right) \qquad \text{II.11b}$$

Using II.11b and II.9, $\Lambda[M]1$ in the right hand side of II.6 can be replaced by $(V\beta)\pi$, and the equation can then be solved for V. For the ith firm, one obtains:

$$V_i = \frac{\mu_i^* \theta_g}{r_p + \beta_i \pi} + lD_i - \Delta_i \frac{\theta_g - \theta_p}{r_p} \qquad \text{II.12}$$

Subtracting the debt from both sides of II.12 yields an expression for the value of equity:

$$S_i = \frac{\mu_i^* \theta_g}{r_p + \beta_i \pi} - (1 - l)D_i - \Delta_i \frac{\theta_g - \theta_p}{r_p}$$

$$= \frac{(\mu_i^* - r_c D_i)\theta_g}{r_p + \beta_i^* \pi} - \Delta_i \frac{\theta_g - \theta_p}{r_p} \qquad \text{II.13}$$

where

$$\beta_i^* = \beta_i \left[1 + d_i' \frac{r_c \theta_g}{r_p} \right] \quad \text{and} \quad d_i' = D_i \bigg/ \left[S_i + \Delta_i \frac{\theta_g - \theta_p}{r_p} \right]. \qquad \text{II.13a}$$

The second equality is a rearrangement of the first for the purpose of expressing S in terms of stockholders' profits.

II.12 and II.13 are seen to be consistent with well known MM "Correction" formulae for the special case $\theta_g^m = \theta_p^m$ and no inflation (Modigliani and Miller [1963], equations (3) and (6) respectively), but they enable us to analyze the effect of financial policies under more general conditions, including inflation.

3. *The effect of financial policies in the absence of inflation*

i) *The value of leverage*

Remembering the definition of r_c and r_p, the value of leverage l, given in II.7, can be written in the following form, which separates out the effect of inflation:

$$l = q + (q - \tau_g)\frac{p}{r_p}; \quad q = 1 - \theta_c \theta_g / \theta_p \qquad \text{II.14}$$

For $p = 0$, l is seen to reduce to q, an expression made familiar by Farrar and Selwyn [1967]. It is consistent with the *MM* formulae and also with Miller's $l = 0$, if $\theta_g \theta_c = \theta_p$. But, according to our analysis, there is no reason why this equality should hold (at least for the U.S.). Indeed, with θ_c around 0.5, the value of $\theta_c \theta_g$ can not be appreciably in excess of 0.45, while the value of θ_p must, assuredly, be significantly higher, most likely around ⅔. This assessment of θ_p is supported by two considerations.

First, according to Miller, what insures the equality of θ_p and $\theta_c \theta_g$ is that θ_p represents the tax factor of the marginal holder of levered stock (i.e., the holder for whom leverage is least advantageous). Accordingly, θ_p decreases with the supply of leverage. An infinitely elastic supply together with sufficiently high tax brackets then insures that, in equilibrium, q must be zero. But once we take into account the benefits of diversification, the value of leverage, l, is *independent* of its supply and depends instead on the (weighted) *average* tax factors θ_p, and θ_g, and on θ_c.

The average value of τ_p^m, the personal tax rate, can probably be put at somewhat less than 0.4 (for some empirical evidence see, e.g. Lewellen, Stanley, Lease and Schlarbaum [1978]; Feldstein and Summers [1979]; Kim, Lewellen and McConnell [1979]). But the value of τ_p relevant in II.14 should be appreciably less than this average. In the first place, one should allow for tax exempt investors. Secondly, as long as there is a substantial market for tax exempt securities, the "effective" rate for any investor should be either his actual rate or $(1 - i/R)$, where i is the (nominal) rate on tax exempt securities, whichever is lower. For, clearly, regardless of his income, an investor always has the opportunity to invest in tax exempt securities yielding i, which is equivalent to investing in conventional debt at an "effective" rate, $\tau_p = 1 - (i/R)$. Thus, as long as i/R is larger than $\theta_c \theta_g$, corporate leverage is valuable to all investors, regardless of income. Now, at least for long maturities, i/R has consistently been well above one half. It has, in fact, tended to stay around 0.7 and uniformly above 0.6 (Mussa and Kormendi [1973]; Skelton [1980]). This suggests, therefore, that the average of the effective values of θ_p^m can be safely placed at no less than ⅔. If so, in the absence of inflation, l could be expected to be positive with a value around ⅓, compared with MM's τ_c or 0.5. Furthermore (as can be verified from II.12), if one can suppose that an expansion of interest payments is necessary and sufficient to enable the firm to cut dividends by an equal amount, then the (marginal) value of leverage is the full MM's τ_c (Brennan [1970]; Litzenberger [1980]).

An alternative way of assessing the value of leverage is to ask how much it can contribute to market value in relative terms. We find:

$$\frac{dV_i}{V_i} = \frac{q}{\theta_R} (r_p + \beta_i \pi) \, dd \qquad \text{II.15}$$

where $d = D_i/\mu_i^*$ and the derivative is evaluated at $D_i, \Delta_i = 0$. With q/θ_R estimated at below .4, the value of this expression for the "average" β of 1 can be put at between .02 and .03. Thus, a rise in d from 0 to as much as 10, and even neglecting any "cost" of leverage, would generate a rise in value of around 25 per cent—not negligible but not very large either.[1]

ii) *Valuation and dividend policy*

Since θ_R can be taken as larger than θ_p, at least for the U.S., from II.12 we can infer that the payment of dividends must unequivocally reduce the market value of the firm, at least within the set of cost-benefits explicitly modeled. This conclusion agrees with Brennan's result [1970] and with a widely held view, though it is hard to reconcile with prevailing payout policies.

If the market regarded the flow of extra taxes associated with dividends as fixed and perpetual as assumed in II.10, then the unfavorable effect of dividends on value would appear to be hefty. For instance, with the usual assumptions about the tax parameters, and assuming further that r_p is of the order of ½ π, one finds that an increase in the payout from zero to 10 percent would have the effect of reducing market value by some 8 percent, or even more for a high β stock. But

---

[1] II.15 suggests that the effect could be substantially larger, for high β stocks. But this implication is questionable—see section II.5 below.

this estimate is surrounded by considerable uncertainty. On the one hand, it might be argued that the value of τ_p applicable to dividends might be higher than that relevant to the leverage effect. But, on the other hand, Miller and Scholes [1981] have attempted to show (even if not entirely convincingly) that the relevant $\tau_p - \tau_R$ might be small or negative! Finally, the estimate would also be reduced if, as seems plausible, the market takes as given the payout policy rather than the dividend itself (see 5 below).

4. *The impact of inflation on valuation*

As is apparent from II.12, 13, and 14, inflation has an effect on valuation through, and only through, the real after tax rates r_p and r_c. Hence its impact depends critically on how these rates, particularly r_p, respond to inflation.

i) *Effect on interest rates*

Unfortunately, as is well known, the interest rate cannot be derived from the CAPM framework alone. We propose to handle this difficulty by relying on an approach which is appealing, at least if we are concerned with long run implications. It consists in adding an equation expressing the requirement that, in long run equilibrium, the market value of corporate capital must coincide with the reproduction cost of that capital (or, that Tobin's q should be one). Thus:

$$V = K$$

where K is the reproduction cost.[2]

Substituting K for V in II.8, we can solve that equation for the real rate, r. For present purposes, however, it turns out to be more convenient to solve for the real after tax rate, r_p. This yields:

$$r_p = \theta_p r - \tau_p p = \left[p\theta_R \frac{\theta_p - \theta_c}{\theta_p} d^* + \rho\theta_c\theta_R - \delta^*(\theta_R - \theta_p) - \Lambda\theta_c^2 \operatorname{Var}(\rho)K \right]/(1 - qd^*) \quad \text{II.16}$$

where $\rho = \mu/K$, $d^* = D/K$ and $\delta^* = \Delta/K$.

As one should expect, r_p rises with the net-of-tax return from assets and declines with the risk premium (the last term in the numerator). But, the effect of lowering θ_c or θ_R (raising taxes) is uncertain since it lowers the after tax return but it also lowers its variance (provided losses can be fully recouped).

The effects of inflation are captured primarily through the first term. Because θ_p exceeds θ_c, inflation should have a positive effect on r_p (through leverage). But, on the basis of our estimate of the tax coefficient, this effect is moderate: the tax factor comes to just over 0.2, so that with, say, a 25 percent average ratio of debt to total capital, 10 percent inflation would raise r_p by some 50 basis points.

The remaining terms do not involve p explicitly, but could nonetheless be systematically affected by inflation. In particular, even supposing that p is neutral

---
[2] As a result of tax effects, the market value may be taken as proportional rather than equal to reproduction cost.

with respect to K, the after tax return, $\rho\theta_c$, is likely to be systematically reduced through the taxation of paper profits from inflation. Suppose, for the moment, that the leverage and $\rho\theta_c$ effects roughly cancel. Then, II.16 says that inflation should leave unchanged the *after* (average) *tax, real* personal *rate* of return ($R\theta_p - p$). Thus it confirms the conclusion already reached by others (e.g., Feldstein [1976]; Summers [1981a]) that the nominal rate should *not rise* by p as stated by Fisher's Law, but rather p/θ_p (or, for the U.S., some one-and-a-half times as much as inflation), a proposition that may be labelled "Super Fisher's Law." Of course, even if r_p is inflation invariant, the after tax real rate will fall for those in above-average brackets, including corporations, and rise for low ones. In addition, the leverage and $\rho\theta_c$ effect need not offset each other precisely and, accordingly, the nominal and real rates might rise somewhat more or less than called for by the Super Fisher's Law. However, with significant inflation, one should definitely expect a nonnegligible rise in the (before-tax) real rate.

ii) Inflation and the value of leverage

To see what these results imply for the impact of inflation on the value of leverage, one can turn to II.14. Suppose inflation left roughly unchanged the after tax rate, r_p, as suggested by the result of the previous section. In this case, l can be seen to be a linear function of p. Furthermore, the coefficient of p/r_p is close to that of q, since τ_g is 0.1 or even less. Now, r_p is presumably a rather small number, say 2 to 3 percent. That implies a quite large response of l to inflation—a rise in p from zero to no more than 4 percent would be sufficient to double l! These results reflect the fact that, even if inflation does not increase the advantage of personal borrowing (r_p is constant), it will reduce r_c increasing the gains from corporate debt, and the gain is capitalized at a low rate. Even more dramatic effects should result if r_p declines—for example, because the *real* rate is constant.

iii) *Inflation and the stock market*

III.13 shows that the response of equity values to a (permanent) rise in the anticipated rate of inflation should reflect the effect of that rise on three components of S: (i) μ^*; (ii) l; and (iii) r_p. The effect on the first component unequivocally tends to lower S. But it might be more than offset by the effect on the remaining two components, which we have shown to push in an upward direction. This is true even if the higher tax burden, through the taxation of paper profits, has exceeded the lower burden due to the treatment of interest, and other effects, as has been maintained, e.g. by Feldstein and Summers [1979] (though the issue is by no means settled; see, e.g. Briden [1981]). For this development should have been offset by the fall in r_p, at least through the 70s, whether or not this fall is related to the higher tax burden claimed by Feldstein and Summers.

But whether S should have risen or not, one inference that can be clearly drawn from II.13 is that the price-earnings ratio (P/E) should have risen, and very substantially, during the rising inflation—for this effect depends only on components (ii) and (iii), both of which push unequivocally and strongly in an upward direction. Furthermore, the rise in P/E should be greater the higher the leverage.

To conclude, the model clearly implies that inflation should exert a pronounced upward thrust on the value of leverage and on P/E. However, there are grounds for discounting the implied large quantitative effects, especially those associated with possible near zero or even negative values of r_p, as a result of inflation. Actually, such values must be ruled out if r_p is to be interpreted as the "consol" rate. To be sure, a negative real rate is perfectly possible, but *not* if there exist *perpetual* positive real streams of returns (e.g., via tax saving).

This observation points to one important limitation of our analysis of the value of leverage and dividends, namely that the results are strictly applicable only when the relevant variables are expected to be *indefinitely* maintained and *certain*. This limitation must be kept in mind in interpreting all results, but particularly those associated with nominal quantities, such as R and p. There is no basis for the expectation that a high level of p and R would be preserved forever. Furthermore, if inflation is not neutral (notably because of nominal institutions or illusions), it is very doubtful that investors would, or should, act as though any given constellation of R, p, and institutions would last forever, especially if it gives rise to unusual advantages.

Another factor that could be counted on to reduce the magnitude of the response to inflation is the stochastic rather than deterministic nature of tax saving flows associated with alternative financial policies, to which we now turn.

5. *The implications of uncertain tax savings and dividends*

The implications of the market regarding the future stream of interest and dividend payments and the associated tax consequences as stochastic, rather than as certain, perpetual streams, depend on the stochastic properties of the expected streams. For the sake of illustration, we shall pursue the implications of the market taking as given, and nonstochastic, the debt-equity and payout policy, d_i and δ_i, rather than the interest and dividend flows. (This formulation has been suggested, with particular reference to debt and capital budgeting, by Miles and Ezzell [1980].)

The total return from firm i can now be written as:

$$\tilde{y}_i^m = \tilde{\mu}_i^*[\theta_K^m + (r_p^m - r_c\theta_K^m)d_i - \delta_i(\theta_K^m - \theta_p^m)]$$

where $d = D/\mu^*$, $\delta = \Delta/\mu^*$. Since equity holders are presumed to absorb all the risk, the variance associated with the equity must be $\text{var}(\tilde{y}_i)$.

By repeating the steps leading from II.4 to II.12, one obtains the following reformulation of equation II.12:

$$V_i = \mu_i^*[\theta_K + d_i(r_p - r_c\theta_K) - \delta_i(\theta_K - \theta_p)]/(r_p + \bar{\beta}_i\pi) \qquad \text{II.17}$$

Here the tax parameters are again averages of the individual investor's rates weighted by his shares of the market, $\bar{\beta}_i$ is a similarly weighted average of the β_i's of the individual portfolios, and π is the spread between the overall after tax rate of return on equity and the average after tax interest rate.[3]

---

[3] This proposition holds on the plausible assumption that $n_i^m\beta_i^m$ is not appreciably correlated with π^m across investors.

From II.17, the value of leverage becomes:

$$l^* = \frac{dV_i}{dD_i} = \frac{lr_p}{\beta_i \pi + r_p} \quad \text{or} \quad \frac{1}{V}\frac{dV}{dd^*} = \frac{qr_p}{\theta_g}$$

This suggests l^* can be put at roughly one-third the value of l implied by II.14, or at a bit above .10, and similarly for the relative change in value. The effect of dividend policy on value is also reduced by a factor of ⅔, to a fairly modest effect, suggesting that in setting dividend policy, tax considerations could well be swamped by other factors.

In summary, there can be little doubt that the estimate of l of ⅓ obtained under the assumption of perpetual, sure consequences suffers from serious upward bias, but there is little basis for pinpointing its magnitude. Even .10 need not provide a lower bound. It is interesting nonetheless, that the latter figure is not inconsistent with the recent estimates by Masulis [1981] relying on the ingenious technique of measuring the impact of various types of exchange offers on the price of common stock.[4]

It is much harder to assess the consistency with the evidence of our results for dividends, mainly because at present the evidence itself is so controversial. Some authors find no evidence in support of the hypothesis that dividends are valued significantly below other corporate returns,[5] while others report strong evidence consistent with that hypothesis, especially when allowing for the valuation to vary with the size of dividend yield, as implied by tax clientele effects.[6] In the latest application of the latter approach, Auerbach [1981] has estimated the effect of dividends on returns over a 15 year period for each of a large sample of firms. His average coefficient, .22, compared favorably with the value implied by II.17, $(\theta_g - \theta_p)/\theta_g$, or around .25.

At the same time, the implications of the model about the effects of inflation seem to be grossly inconsistent with the empirical evidence: (i) the after tax real rate has declined markedly, and even the real rate has hardly kept up during most of the last 15 years (for an analysis of earlier experiences, see Summers [1981a]); (ii) equity values, and most particularly price-earnings ratios, have declined dramatically, whereas they should have risen appreciably, especially in light of the decline in r_p; (iii) levered firms, instead of appreciating, have tended to lose value, at least according to one recent study;[7] and (iv) there is little

---

[4] While his "preferred" estimate is below .10, it should be remembered that it reflects also effects associated with the "cost of leverage" (see conclusions). In fact, if there is an interior optimum debt and the exchange were aimed at that optimum, the effect of the exchange on value would be appreciably smaller than l.

[5] See, e.g., Black and Scholes [1974], Gordon and Bradford [1980], and Miller and Scholes [1981].

[6] Elton and Gruber [1970]; Litzenberger and Ramaswamy [1980]. The Elton and Gruber results have been severely criticized and called in question by Kalay [1977], but it is not clear that his criticism applies to the other studies. It may be noted in this connection that even the results of Miller and Scholes, when they classify firms by dividend yield, are strikingly supportive of the hypothesis of a dividend effect, despite the authors' attempt at discrediting them by calling attention to outliers in one of the nine cells of the table.

[7] The study, carried out by myself and Richard Cohn, is still unpublished, but a short description is provided in Modigliani and Cohn [1982]. However, quite different results have been reported recently by Summers [1981b], using a somewhat different approach.

evidence of any significant increase in leverage, even though its profitability should have gone up.[8]

We suspect that this total failure can be attributed to the assumption of rational behavior, whereas in the presence of inflation, at least of a moderate size, the market may suffer from inflation illusion of the type hypothesized by Modigliani and Cohn [1979]. It can be verified that dropping the term p from II.1, and replacing R_p for r_p in equations like II.10 and II.12, as suggested by that hypothesis, would go a long way toward explaining the contradictions highlighted above.

III. Individual Portfolio Composition

1. *Taxes and portfolio allocation—basic characteristics*

It is well known that, in the absence of taxes, and with uniform assessments, the mean-variance approach implies that the optimum portfolio of every investor will hold the same fraction of every firm's equity.

As has been shown by a number of authors (Black [1971, 1973], Elton and Gruber [1978], Gordon and Malkiel [1981], Auerbach and King [1981]) this proposition no longer holds when investors are differently taxed. This conclusion can be verified by solving the equilibrium condition II.5 for S and substituting in the first order condition II.4. This yields, after some rearrangement:

$$(\mu^* - r_c D)\left(\theta_g^m - \frac{r_p^m}{r_p}\theta_g\right) - \Delta\left[(\theta_g^m - \theta_p^m) - \frac{r_p^m}{r_p}(\theta_g - \theta_p)\right] + \frac{r_p^m}{r_p}\Lambda[M]\mathbf{1}$$
$$= \gamma^m(\theta_g^m)^2[M]\mathbf{n}^m \qquad \text{III.1}$$

The system can be solved for $\mathbf{n}^m$ (assuming $[M]$ nonsingular) and the solution can be cast in the form:

$$\mathbf{n}^m = \frac{\Lambda}{\gamma^m}\left\{T_1^m \mathbf{1} + \frac{1}{\Lambda}[M]^{-1}[(\mu^* - r_c D)T_2^m - T_3^m \Delta]\right\} \qquad \text{III.2}$$

where

$$T_1^m = \frac{r_p^m/r_p}{(\theta_g^m)^2} \qquad \text{III.2a}$$

$$T_2^m = \frac{\theta_g^m - (r_p^m/r_p)\theta_g}{(\theta_g^m)^2} \qquad \text{III.2b}$$

$$T_3^m = [(\theta_g^m - \theta_p^m) - r_p^m/r_p(\theta_g - \theta_p)]/(\theta_g^m)^2 \qquad \text{III.2c}$$

---

[8] The evidence occasionally offered to support the proposition that leverage has increased dramatically, is uniformly based on measures which are irrelevant in the presence of inflation, such as using book value in the denominator or relying on market value, whose relevance is, at least, questionable in view of its dramatic decline (cf., for instance, Gordon and Malkiel [1981, Table 1]. If one relies on more suitable measures of the denominator, such as reproduction costs of assets, the association with inflation disappears (Gordon and Malkiel, ibid.), and the same tends to happen using a variable like *EBIT*.

In the absence of personal taxes, or, more generally, when everybody is taxed equally, III.2 implies the standard result, $n_i^m = \Lambda/\gamma^m$ for all i; every investor holds a share of the market, inversely related to the investor's risk aversion γ^m.

Next, if individuals were taxed differently, but (i) all property income was taxed at the *same* rate, or $\theta_g^m = \theta_p^m$ (as assumed implicitly in the MM "Correction" [1963]), and (ii) there was no inflation (or only real interest was taxed), then, since under those conditions $\theta_g = \theta_p$, and $r_p^m/r_p = \theta_p^m/\theta_p$, we find $T_2 = T_3 = 0$, and

$$n_i^m = \frac{\Lambda}{\gamma^m(\theta^m)^2} \; \forall \; i$$

Thus, each portfolio consists again of a share of the market, but that share now depends also on the investor's tax bracket, θ^m, relative to the average θ (implicit in Λ). Since θ^m is a decreasing function of the tax rate, for given risk preference, n^m is an increasing function of the investor's tax bracket. The reason, basically, is that a higher tax rate implies an equal decline in the (expected) return from equity and from debt, but it also implies a decline in the variance of the after tax outcome from equity, which makes equity relatively more attractive.

Finally, if, and only if, both individuals and sources of income are taxed differently, investors will hold different shares of any given firm depending on both their tax rates and their risk aversion. However, if any two investors, say, m and m', are subject to identical tax rates, then T_1, T_2, T_3 of III.2 will have the same value, and therefore: $n_i^m/n_i^{m'} = \gamma^{m'}/\gamma^m$, $\forall \; i$. Thus, it remains true that every investor could, in principle, secure his optimum portfolio by combining positive or negative debt with a share of a single appropriate "tax fund," which held shares in the relative quantities appropriate to his tax bracket, as given by III.2.

2. Firms' characteristics and portfolio composition

To examine how the portfolio composition of funds suited for different tax brackets should be expected to respond to various characteristics of the firm, it is convenient to consider first the special case where $[M]$ is diagonal. In this case, from III.2, the equation prescribing the holdings of the ith stock for a fund catering to investors with any given set of rates, say $\hat{\theta}_g$, $\hat{\theta}_p$, can be written as:

$$n_i = k[T_1 + x_i(T_2 - \delta_i T_3)] \qquad \text{III.3}$$

Here, T_1, T_2, and T_3, are the same as defined in III.2, but with θ_p^m, θ_g^m, r_p^m, replaced by $\hat{\theta}_p$, $\hat{\theta}_g$, $\hat{r}_p$; δ is the payout ratio and k is a proportionality factor that depends on the size of the fund. Finally:

$$x_i = \frac{(\mu_i^* - r_c D_i)}{\Lambda \mu_{ii}} = \frac{(\mu_i^* - r_c D_i)}{(\beta_i^* \pi S_i)} = \left(1 \, pl \, \frac{r_p}{\beta_i^* \pi}\right)(\theta_g)^{-1} \qquad \text{III.3a}$$

where β_i^* is the β of the rate of return to equity, defined in II.13a. The second equality in III.3a follows from II.9 and the fact that, with a diagonal matrix, $\text{var}(\tilde{\mu}_i) = \text{cov}(\tilde{\mu}_i, \tilde{\mu})$, while the last follows from II.13.

It is apparent from III.2 that both T_2 and T_3 are zero for the "average" tax fund which, therefore, holds the market, and that they are increasing functions of the tax rate, τ_p, as long as $d\tau_R/d\tau_p$ is well below unity, as is the case for the U.S. It then follows from III.3 that for a fund that caters to higher tax brackets, the relative share held of any stock will be higher the higher that stock's x (cf. Auerbach and King [1981]), and the lower its payout ratio (Elton and Gruber [1978])[9]. The converse is true for a below-average tax fund. Furthermore, the *variation* in the *relative* shares held of different equities will be larger the larger (in absolute value) the slope coefficient T_2, that is, the more the fund's target tax rates deviate from the average, in either direction.

It should be noted that though a high bracket portfolio will hold a *relatively* smaller share of low x firms, nonetheless, higher taxes will lead to holding a larger *absolute* share of every stock, including those with low x,[10] (provided their dividend rate is sufficiently low). This behavior reflects, in addition to the variance effect noted earlier, the favorable tax treatment of corporate returns, other than dividends, relative to interest.

3. *Extent of variation in optimum portfolios*

With the help of III.3, one can endeavor to go beyond these qualitative results and get some idea of just how sensitive portfolio composition might be to both taxes and firms' characteristics. One way to measure this sensitivity is to ask how much difference one should expect to find between the largest and smallest relative shares of firms held in the portfolio of funds for which the differences tend to be largest, namely those aimed at extreme tax brackets.

Ignoring inflation at first, and focussing on the role of x, from equation III.3, we obtain:

$$\frac{1}{\bar{n}} dn_i = \frac{k(T_2 - \delta_i T_3)}{\bar{n}} dx_i = \frac{kT_2(1 - \delta_i)}{\bar{n}} dx_i \qquad \text{III.4}$$

since, without inflation, $T_2 = T_3$ as can be seen from III.2b and c.

Thus, the range of variation of n_i depends on the range of x and on the "slope", $T_2(1 - \delta_i)$, which will be largest (in absolute value) when the payout is zero. Consider, then, the lowest possible tax class, $\theta_p = \theta_R = 1$. Relying on the earlier estimate of ⅔ for θ_p, and 0.9 for θ_R, one can put $kT_2/\bar{n}$ at just below 0.3.[11] For a very high tax fund, say, $\theta_p = .5$, $\theta_R = .85$, the slope is even lower, about .25. To estimate the relevant range of x, we can rely on III.3a. If, as seems reasonable, the bulk of the β's can be presumed to fall within the range of 0.5 to 2.0, the range of x is 1.4 to 2.2, or less than one. This implies that the variations in the relative shares of different stocks within one fund, or of the same stock between funds, arising from differences in x, would fall within a quite modest range of about 25 percent.

A second set of questions we can examine with the help of III.3 concerns the impact of leverage on the tax clientele of the firm. First, suppose we classify firms

---

[9] Elton and Gruber's result is actually stated in terms of the dividend yield, Δ_i/S_i.

[10] From III.2, for the smallest possible value of x which, from III.3a, is θ_R^{-1}, one finds:

$$n_i^m = \frac{\Lambda}{\gamma^m} \left[T_1 + \frac{T_2}{\theta_R} - \frac{T_3}{\theta_R} \delta_i \right] = \frac{\Lambda}{\gamma^m \theta_R} [(\theta_R^m)^{-1} - T_3 \delta_i]$$

which is an increasing function of the tax rate for sufficiently small values of δ_i.

[11] n/k is estimated from II.3 putting $x = 1.5$ (i.e., $\beta = 1$), and $\delta = .5$.

by debt-equity ratios and compute the average tax rate for each leverage class—how should the average tax rate change as leverage increases? In a well known contribution, Kim, Lewellen and McConnell [1979], have provided empirical evidence on this question, based on a large sample of portfolios. They find, as expected, that the estimated average tax rate of stockholders declines systematically as the debt-equity ratio rises from zero to roughly 2 in the highest class, but that the fall—roughly from 41 percent to 37 percent—is modest relative to the implications of Miller's model.

The implication of our model can be deduced from III.3 by examining how the relative share of firms characterized by different leverage differs in the portfolios of funds aimed at different tax brackets. It is apparent from III.2, III.3, and II.13a that leverage affects n_i through, and only through, β^*, and hence x. One can deduce from II.13a that, if leverage were uncorrelated with the asset's β, a rise in d' from zero to 2 would decrease x on the average from 1.5 to 1.2.[12] In light of III.4, this implies a very modest effect of leverage on relative shares. Even for the zero tax fund ($T_2 \simeq .3$) the difference between the relative holdings of unlevered and highly levered firms would be within 10 percent. In reality, there is substantial evidence that leverage is negatively correlated with risk and hence with β. Accordingly, the change in x, and hence n_i, between leverage classes should be even smaller. Clearly, these implications of the model can be easily reconciled with the results of Kim et al., cited above.

A related question concerns the effect that a change in debt policy could be expected to have on the tax clientele of a firm. Here, again, it is found that even for a relatively low β firm, and for a zero tax fund—the combination most sensitive to changes in leverage—the maximum swing in portfolio's relative shares might be within 20 percent, implying that changes in debt policy would not be a source of major shifts in clientele.

Turning finally to the effect of dividend policy, one can readily establish along the lines used above that its effect on portfolio composition should not be very large. But a comparison of the model's implications with empirical evidence is again complicated by the contradictory nature of this evidence. Our model seems to be broadly consistent with the systematic, though modest, association between dividend yield and average tax reported by Lewellen, Stanley, Lease, and Schlarbaum [1978][13] and by Blume, Crockett, and Friend [1974], but not with the rather large differentials that are implied by the results of Elton and Gruber [1970] and Auerbach [1981].[14]

4. The effect of inflation on portfolio allocation

How are these various conclusions affected by the presence of inflation? From III.3, one can see that inflation has an effect on n_i through the real after tax rates,

---

[12] This estimate is obtained by assigning to β in II.13a, the representative value of 1, and noting that the coefficient of d' in II.13a can be put at around ⅔.

[13] At least for tax 1, and dollar weighted positions, as reported in Table 5.

[14] One may suspect that the results of these authors, and others using a similar methodology, may be biassed by the fact that, the higher the dividend yield, the more likely it becomes that institutions that are tax exempt, or not taxed more heavily on dividends then on capital gains, will find it worth while to arbitrage the gains resulting from failure of the ex dividend price to fall commensurately with the dividend.

r_p^m, r_p, and r_c, which appear in T_1, T_2, and T_3, and also through the leverage component of x. The effect through the T coefficients is found to be:

$$\frac{d(n_i/\bar{n})}{dp} = \{-(x_i - \bar{x})[\hat{\theta}_g + (\delta\bar{x})(\hat{\theta}_p\theta_g - \hat{\theta}_g\theta_p)] + [\delta_i x_i - \delta\bar{x})]$$

$$\cdot [\hat{\theta}_g - \hat{\theta}_p + \bar{x}(\hat{\theta}_p\theta_g - \hat{\theta}_g\theta_p)]\} \frac{1}{\bar{n}^2} \frac{d}{dp}(\hat{r}_p/r_p) \quad \text{III.5}$$

where $\bar{x}$ and $(\delta\bar{x})$ are values x and δx that correspond to $n = \bar{n}$ and:

$$\frac{d}{dp}(\hat{r}_p/r_p) = \left(\frac{\hat{\theta}_p\tau_p - \theta_p\hat{\tau}_p}{r_p^2}\right)\left(1 - \frac{p}{r}\frac{dr}{dp}\right) \gtreqless 0, \quad \text{as } \hat{\theta}_p \gtreqless \theta_p \quad \text{III.6}$$

Conditions III.5 and III.6 are somewhat involved but their broad implications can be readily brought out. First, note that the coefficients of $(x_i - \bar{x})$ and $(\delta_i x_i - \delta\bar{x})$ can, both, be taken to be positive for all investors (or funds). We can then infer that for an *above average tax bracket*, for whom, according to III.6, $\hat{r}_p/r_p$ declines with p, there will be a tendency for inflation to increase the relative share of stock i if x_i is above average and the dividend, $\delta_i x_i$, is below average. Conversely, for a below-average tax bracket, will increase if x_i is below and $\delta_i x_i$ above average. But this means that inflation tends to increase n_i in portfolios where it was above average to begin with, and to reduce it when below average. In short, inflation has the effect of magnifying the difference between the portfolio composition of high and low tax funds.

If one tries to quantify the above effects, one runs again into the difficulty that the value of leverage appears unrealistically sensitive to the rate of inflation, especially if inflation is accompanied by a fall in the after tax real rate, r_p.

Inflation also tends to raise x through the leverage effect, but this increase does not seem to have systematic consequences for portfolio diversity (except through some increase in the range of x).

From these results one can infer that inflation should have an appreciable effect in increasing portfolio diversity between tax brackets. At the same time, the considerations stated in II.5 suggest that the numerical implications of III.3 and III.6 should be heavily discounted on the ground that nonneutral inflation effects should not, and will not, be taken as permanent by investors. As for empirical evidence, none seems presently available on this issue.

5. *Implications of a non-diagonal variance-covariance matrix*

In general, the variance-covariance matrix, $[M]$, will not be diagonal, and equation III.3 has to be replaced by:

$$n_i = k\left[T_1 + \frac{1}{\Lambda}\sum_{j=1}^{N} M_{ij}^{-1}(\mu_j^* - r_c D_j)(T_2 - \delta_j T_3)\right] \quad \text{III.7}$$

where M_{ij}^{-1} denotes the elements of the inverse.

Thus, n_i now depends not only on characteristics of stock i, but in principle, on those of all other stocks as well. The meaning of the additional terms in III.7 is readily understood. The first order condition requires that, at the margin, the risk premium for every stock held be equal to that stock's contribution to portfolio variance. But, except when $[M]$ is diagonal, raising n_i^m will contribute to variance (positively or negatively) through the covariance with every other stock in the portfolio, as shown by the last term of II.4; $[M]\mathbf{n}^m = n_i \mu_{ii} + \sum_{j \neq i} n_j \mu_{ij}^*$. The summation in III.7 corresponds precisely to the summation term above, but with n_j expressed in terms of its ultimate determinants, and thus allows for the dependence of each n on every other one.

To see the implications of this generalization, we note that III.7 requires no change in our conclusions about how a stock's own characteristics interact with tax rates in contributing to the attractiveness of that stock for a given tax bracket. As for the effect of all other stocks, we can think of them as falling into two classes: those which have a net positive correlation with, and may be thought of as substitutes for, stock i, and those, more rare, with a negative net correlation, which behave like complements of stock i. The demand for i declines with the attractiveness of its substitutes and rises with that of its complements.

Despite these indirect influences, one would normally expect n_i to be largely determined by the characteristics of stock i. But one cannot reach any definite conclusion unless one imposes restrictions on the variance-covariance matrix, as was done by Elton and Gruber [1978].

The same difficulty arises in analyzing the implications of the generalization III.7 for portfolio diversity. There is, nonetheless, one broad generalization that may be put forward in this case, suggesting a downward bias in our estimates of section III.3, namely that the prevalence of high substitution is likely to increase the extent of portfolio diversity and specialization until, in the limit, perfect correlation leads to the prevalence of corner solutions.[15]

Concluding Remarks and Agenda

In closing, attention must first be called to certain limitations of the current analysis of the demand side, mainly the failure to impose appropriate constraints on portfolios, such as limitations on short sales and on personal debt. This omission may be particularly serious in the case of debt, since it would appropriately give a greater role to wealth in portfolio composition. As one might expect, with such a constraint, it is no longer true that every portfolio includes every stock (in positive or negative amounts). Firms then have a clientele including only a subset of investors and the parameters of equations like II.12 or II.15 might differ between firms reflecting that clientele.

A second limitation is the failure to model explicitly the market for tax exempt securities, but this task is really trivial and the gap has no appreciable effect on the results.

Finally, closure of the model would require combining the demand analysis with an analysis of the forces limiting the supply of corporate debt. This has actually been done in good measure elsewhere (e.g., DeAngelo and Masulis [1980];

---

[15] This conclusion is illustrated by the result of Elton and Gruber [1978] for the case of equal correlation, equation (B.4); as ρ tends to unity, the fraction invested in stock j tends to plus or minus infinity.

Williamson [1981]). From the point of view of integration with the demand side, we note that the various supply limiting mechanisms which have been analyzed basically imply that an expansion of debt—total assets constant—must eventually either reduce the expected value of the flow, μ, produced by the firm, and/or cause lD to rise at a decreasing rate, because of decreasing probability of utilizing the costly tax shield. If II.12 is modified along the above lines, it turns into a nonlinear function of D_i with negative second derivative, and V will, in general, be maximized for some interior value of D_i, say $\hat{D}_i$. This maximization will fix the individual and aggregate supply of debt.

REFERENCES

Auerbach, Alan J., "Stockholder Tax Rates and Firm Attributes," forthcoming in *Journal of Public Economics*.
—— and Mervyn A. King, "Taxation, Portfolio Choice and Debt-Equity Ratios: A General Equilibrium Model," forthcoming in *Quarterly Journal of Economics*.
Black, Fischer, "Taxes and Capital Market Equilibrium," Working Paper 21A, Sloan School of Management, M.I.T., April 1971.
——, "Taxes and Capital Market Equilibrium Under Uncertainty," Working Paper 21B, Sloan School of Management, M.I.T., May 1973.
—— and Myron Scholes, "The Effects of Dividend Yield and Dividend Policy on Common Stock Prices and Returns," *Journal of Financial Economics*, Vol. 1, pp. 1-22, 1974.
Blume, Marshall E., Jean Crockett, and Irwin Friend, "Stockownership in the United States: Characteristics and Trends," *Survey of Current Business*, November 1974, pp. 16-40.
Brennan, M. J., "Taxes, Market Valuation and Corporate Financial Policy," *National Tax Journal*, Vol. XXIII, No. 4, 1970, pp. 417-427.
—— and E. Schwartz, "Corporate Income Taxes, Valuation, and the Problem of Optimal Capital Structure," *Journal of Business*, January 1978.
Briden, George, "The Effect of Inflation on Corporate Taxes," unpublished paper, Brown University, 1981.
Chen, A. H. and E. H. Kim, "Theories of Corporate Debt Policy: A Synthesis," *Journal of Finance*, June 1979.
Cordes, Joseph J. and Steven M. Sheffrin, "Taxation and the Sectoral Allocation of Capital in the U.S.," forthcoming in *National Tax Journal*, December 1981.
DeAngelo, H. and R. W. Masulis, "Optimal Capital Structure Under Corporate and Personal Taxation," *Journal of Financial Economics*, March 1980.
Elton, Edwin J. and M. Gruber, "Marginal Stockholder Tax Rates and the Clientele Effect," *Review of Economics and Statistics*, Vol. 52, 1970, pp. 68-74.
—— and ——, "Taxes and Portfolio Composition, *Journal of Financial Economics*, Vol. 6, 1978, pp. 399-410.
Farrar, Donald E. and Lee L. Selwyn, "Taxes, Corporate Financial Policy, and Returns to Investors," *National Tax Journal*, December 1967, pp. 444-454.
Feldstein, Martin, "Inflation and Income Taxes and the Rate of Interest: A Theoretical Analysis," *American Economic Review*, Vol. 66, December 1976, pp. 809-820.
—— and Lawrence Summers, "Inflation and the Taxation of Capital Income in the Corporate Sector," *National Tax Journal*, Vol. XXXII, No. 4, December 1979, pp. 445-470.
Gordon, R. H. and D. F. Bradford, "Taxation and the Stock Market Valuation of Capital Gains and Dividends," *Journal of Public Economics*, October 1980, pp. 109-136.
—— and B. G. Malkiel, "Corporation Finance," in H. J. Aaron and J. A. Pechman, eds. *How Taxes Affect Economic Behavior*, Washington, D.C.: The Brookings Institution, 1981.
Jensen, M. C. and W. H. Meckling, "Theory of the Firm: Managerial Behavior, Agency Costs, and Ownership Structure," *Journal of Financial Economics*, October 1976.
Kalay, A., "The Behavior of the Stock Price on the Ex-Dividend Day—A Reexamination of the

Clientele Effect," unpublished Ph.D. Dissertation, Graduate School of Management, University of Rochester, 1977.

Kim, E. Han, W. G. Lewellen and J. J. McConnell, "Financial Leverage Clienteles, Theory and Evidence," *Journal of Financial Economics*, Vol. 7, 1979, pp. 83-109.

Lewellen, Wilbur G., K. L. Stanley, R. C. Lease and G. G. Schlarbaum, "Some Direct Evidence on the Dividend Clientele Phenomenon," *The Journal of Finance*, Vol. XXXIII, No. 5, December 1978, pp. 1385-1399.

Litzenberger, Robert H., "Debt, Taxes and Incompleteness: A Survey," mimeo, 1980.

——— and K. Ramaswamy, "Dividends, Short Selling Restrictions, Tax-Induced Investor Clienteles and Market Equilibrium," *The Journal of Finance*, Vol. 35, 1980, pp. 469-482.

Miles, James A. and J. R. Ezzell, "The Weighted Average Cost of Capital, Perfect Markets, and Project Life: A Clarification," *Journal of Financial and Quantitative Analysis*, Vol. XV, No. 3, September 1980, pp. 719-730.

Miller, Merton H., "Debt and Taxes," *The Journal of Finance*, May 1977.

——— and Franco Modigliani, "Dividend Policy, Growth, and the Valuation of Shares," *Journal of Business*, Vol. 34, October 1961, pp. 411-433.

——— and Myron S. Scholes, "Dividends and Taxes: Some Empirical Evidence," Working Paper #55, University of Chicago, May 1981.

Modigliani, Franco and Richard Cohn, "Inflation and the Stock Market," *The Stock Market and Inflation*, eds., Anthony Boeckh and Richard T. Coghlan, Homewood, Il: Dow Jones-Irwin, 1982.

——— and ———, "Inflation, Rational Valuation and the Market," *Financial Analysts Journal*, March/April, 1979, pp. 24-44.

——— and Merton H. Miller, "The Cost of Capital, Corporation Finance and the Theory of Investment," *American Economic Review*, Vol. 48, June 1958, pp. 261-297.

——— and ———, "Corporate Income Taxes and the Cost of Capital: A Correction," *American Economic Review*, June 1963, pp. 433-443.

Myers, Stewart C., "Taxes, Corporate Financial Policy, and the Return to Investors: Comment," *National Tax Journal*, December 1967, pp. 455-462.

———. "Determinants of Corporate Borrowing," *Journal of Financial Economics*, November 1977.

Mussa, M., and R. Kormendi, *The Taxation of Municipal Bonds*, Washington, D.C.: American Enterprise Institute, 1973.

Skelton, Jeffrey L., "Bank Arbitrage and the Relative Pricing of Tax-Exempt and Taxable Bonds," mimeo, July 1981.

———. "The Relative Pricing of Tax-Exempt and Taxable Debt," mimeo, April 1980.

Summers, Lawrence H., "The Non-Adjustment of Nominal Interest Rates: A study of the Fisherian Effect," forthcoming in *Symposium in Honor of Arthur Okun*, eds., Peckman and Tobin, 1981a.

———, "Inflation and the Valuation of Corporate Equities," Working Paper No. 824, National Bureau of Economic Research, 1981b.

Taggart, Robert A., "Taxes and Corporate Capital Structure in an Incomplete Market," *The Journal of Finance*, June 1980.

Williamson, Scott H., "The Moral Hazard Theory of Corporate Financial Structure: Empirical Tests," Ph.D. Thesis, Massachusetts Institute of Technology, November 1981.

Debt and Taxes and Uncertainty

STEPHEN A. ROSS*

ABSTRACT

With a graduated personal tax schedule, Miller showed that there could be an equilibrium debt supply for the corporate sector as a whole. In the presence of uncertainty there is also a unique debt/equity ratio for each individual firm, and this ratio is related to the firm's operational risk characteristics. However, if firms merge and spin off in response to tax incentives, the identity of firms is ambiguous and only the corporate sector is a meaningful construct. These arguments are developed in both discrete and continuous models that employ extensions of the arbitrage-free pricing theory.

IN HIS FAMOUS PAPER, "Debt and Taxes" (1977), Merton Miller [11] showed that the original Miller-Modigliani propositions on the irrelevance of capital structure were not necessarily overturned by considerations of taxation. Miller argued that with a broad enough span of progressivity in personal income taxation, the corporate tax advantage to the issuance of debt would be offset by the disadvantage to investors of receiving ordinary income on personal account. In equilibrium, the differential rates of return on equity and debt would be such that the marginal investor would be indifferent between purchasing debt instruments or equity. The margin would be determined by the total amount of debt issued by the corporate sector, but in a competitive world it would be unaffected by the debt issued by any one firm. As a consequence, the total supply of corporate debt would be determined in equilibrium, increasing to the point where aggregate corporate value was not enhanced by further debt financing, but any individual firm would be looking at prices set at the margin and would find itself indifferent between issuing debt or equity.

The purpose of this article is to extend Miller's argument by recognizing the differences between debt and equity when the environment is not certain. We will not be concerned with what might be called corner questions, i.e., with whether or not there is a marginal investor or an internal equilibrium. To do so would obscure the basic points we have to make. Instead, we will examine models that have internal equilibria and ordinary neoclassical marginal interpretations. In related work, De Angelo and Masulis [5, 6] have also extended Miller's analysis, but their primary concern was with the effects of a more detailed treatment of the tax code and with the impact of bankruptcy. We will deal with such matters only in passing; our central concern is with the impact of uncertainty.

Our main result is the finding that there is a relationship between the capital structure of the firm—as induced by tax effects—and ordinary (beta) measures

---

* Yale University, School of Management. This paper is a version of an earlier one, and I am grateful to Richard Roll, Philip Dybvig, Jon Ingersoll, and Roger Ibbotson and to the members of the finance workshops at Hebrew Univerity, UCLA, and at Yale for helpful comments.

of risk. This relationship is particularly surprising because we will find that firms have optimal internal financial mixes in the absence of any bankruptcy costs or any agency, asymmetric information or signaling effects. It is a consequence solely of the interplay between uncertainty and taxes. This link has both empirical and theoretical implications. By tying the corporate financial structure to observable characteristics of the firm, we have a tool for relating financial structure to product market structure. This permits us to use the constructs of asset pricing, e.g., beta measures, to address such questions as whether, say, high-tech firms have high debt/equity ratios.

Unfortunately, though, the link we construct is not as strong as we would want; it really only throws the irrelevance question back a bit, but it does not eliminate it. If firms have nontax-related reasons for the particular forms they take, then our result holds, but if they merge and spinoff in an effort to minimize taxes or if intermediaries can accomplish the task for them, then Miller's irrelevance proposition will be reinstated. Furthermore, in some models, there are simple and appropriate modifications of the tax system itself that lead back to irrelevance. In particular, real indexing of taxation breaks the link.

The first section of the paper describes the tools and notation we will use and develops the basic model of pricing. The second section examines the optimal financial choice, while the third develops a diffusion model and uses it to study the cross-sectional relations. The fourth section describes some general limitations and caveats to the analysis and the fifth and final section briefly summarizes and concludes the paper with some suggestions for future research.

I. The Model

We will begin with a one-period world. In this world, equilibrium is reached today, at time 0, and cash flows are received one-period later, at time 1. (In Section III, we will examine a version with a richer dynamic structure.) A firm in such a world has cash flows at time 1 labelled as $x(\theta)$ or, simply, x. The cash flows, x, depend upon the state of nature, θ, that will be realized at time 1. Thus, x is a random variable, and θ is an element of an appropriately defined probability space.

Debt issued by the firm carries a face value of F. In the absence of taxes, the total payoff to the debt at time 1 will be given by

$$\min(F, x), \tag{1}$$

and the equity will receive the residual,

$$\max(x - F, 0), \tag{2}$$

which is equivalent to a call on the cash flows (or next period value) with an exercise price equal to the face value of the debt.

If we let D denote the current, time 0, market value of the debt and S the current value of the equity, then the market value of the firm, V, is given by

$$V \equiv D + S. \tag{3}$$

Debt and Taxes and Uncertainty

It is well known that in the absence of arbitrage there exists a positive linear valuation operator which values securities. Ross [12, 13] proved that such an operator exists and subsequent work, notably by Harrison and Kreps [9], Hansen and Richard [8], and Dybvig et al. [7] develop the martingale representation of this operator. Letting E^* denote the operator (and ignoring spanning issues) we have

$$V \equiv D + S$$
$$= E^*(\min(F, x) + \max(x - F, 0))$$
$$= E^*(x), \qquad (4)$$

independent of the amount of debt issued, F. This verifies the Miller-Modigliani theorem in this simple world.

To see what happens when taxes are introduced we will assume that the tax code takes a form that is simple enough to permit analysis, but rich enough to capture the essential elements.

We will first assume that taxes are collected from both firms and individuals on gross returns. At the corporate level, taxes will be paid on the returns to equity, and all debt payments will be deductible. Thus, if τ_c denotes the average tax rate of the firm, then the after tax returns to equity will be given by

$$(1 - \tau_c)\max(x - F, 0). \qquad (5)$$

Notice that no tax credits are given in bankruptcy. Notice, too, that we have avoided the complication of separating out the interest and principal repayment portions of the total debt payment, F. We will assume a constant corporate tax rate, τ_c. In general, though, we would expect firms—like individuals—to be inframarginal as well as marginal.

As for individual taxation, we will assume that equity returns and debt returns are taxed differentially with the latter being treated as ordinary income. For the moment, we can defer a more detailed discussion of exactly how this is done and move directly to the firm valuation. In Ross [14], it was shown that in the absence of arbitrage and with taxes there would exist a tax adjusted "before (personal) tax" margingale operator, E^*, or that could be used to value securities. In general, this operator would assign different values to cash flows with different tax characteristics. Thus, in the absence of arbitrage, the value of one firm will be given by

$$V(F) \equiv D + S$$
$$= E_0^*(\min(x, F)) + E_S^*((1 - \tau_c)\max(x - F, 0)), \qquad (6)$$

where E_0^* is the martingale operator used to value ordinary income receipts and E_S^* is the martingale operator used to value equity receipts. In general, though, these operators are not the same and they cannot be combined, as we did previously, to eliminate the influence of the debt level, F. To make this possibility explicit we have written the value, V, as $V(F)$.

Under a wide variety of circumstances, the valuation operator takes the form of tax-adjusted Arrow-Debreu state contingent claims prices, and this permits us to rewrite (6) in a more familiar form. Letting $Q_{g\theta}$ be the cumulative pricing distribution function for capital gains, i.e., for equity returns, and $Q_{0\theta}$ be the price distribution function for ordinary income, (6) becomes

$$V(F) = E_0^*(\min(x, F)) + E_{\$}^*((1 - \tau_c)\max(x - F, 0))$$

$$= \int \min(x, F) \, dQ_{0\theta} + \int (1 - \tau_c)\max(x - F, 0) \, dQ_{g\theta}$$

$$= \int_{|\theta|x(\theta)\leq F|} x(\theta) \, dQ_{0\theta} + F \int_{|\theta|x(\theta)>F|} dQ_{0\theta}$$

$$+ \int_{|\theta|x(\theta)>F|} (1 - \tau_c)(x(\theta) - F) \, dQ_{g\theta}. \tag{7}$$

If the state space is finite then (7) has the simple form

$$V(F) = \sum_{|\theta|x(\theta)\leq F|} x(\theta) \, q_{0\theta} + F \sum_{|\theta|x(\theta)>F|}^{q_{0\theta}} + \sum_{|\theta|x(\theta)>F|} (1 - \tau_c)(x(\theta) - F)q_{g\theta}, \tag{8}$$

where $q_{0\theta}$ and $q_{g\theta}$ are, respectively, the before personal tax prices of pure contingent claims to ordinary income and to capital gains.

Looking at the valuation formula (7) or its specialization to (8), it is at least plausible that the debt issued, F, will influence value, V. Indeed, since every set of positive before tax prices, $q_{0\theta}$ and $q_{g\theta}$, is consistent with (some) equilibrium (see Ross [14]), we need only assume some particular set of such prices and examine (7) or (8) to see how V changes with F in such a world. To say more about the qualitative properties of this dependence, though, we will have to specify the individual tax code in more detail. This will enable us to derive a particularly easy to interpret set of before tax state contingent prices.

To do so we will consider a very simple consumer problem with complete state markets for both ordinary income and capital gains. We are doing this primarily to aid our interpretation of the state prices. Such a model is not necessary for their existence—indeed they exist simply from the absence of arbitrage—rather, it is useful for interpreting our results. This distinction is an important one since we do not have to assume the completeness of markets for state contingent claims, let alone claims partitioned by tax characteristics.

Let c_θ denote consumption of the single consumption good in state θ, and let y_θ and g_θ denote the purchases of contingent claims entitling the holder to one unit of ordinary income or capital gains, respectively, in state θ. Let $U(\cdot)$ denote the von Neumann-Morgenstern utility function of the representative individual under consideration and let Π_θ denote the probability distribution of the states. (We will assume that the functions we use are smooth enough to validate our manipulations with them.)

We will represent the tax code by a function $T(\cdot)$ which is state independent, and maps adjusted gross income into taxes. Taxable income is defined as ordinary income minus a capital gain deduction of $1 - \gamma \in [0, 1]$ of capital gains. Thus, taxes in state θ are given by

$$T(y_\theta + \gamma g_\theta). \tag{9}$$

We will assume that $(\forall z)T(z) < z$, i.e., taxes are not confiscatory, and also that taxes are monotone, i.e., $T' > 0$.

The basic problem facing the consumer/investor in this world can be stated as

$$\max \int U(c_\theta) \, d\Pi_\theta$$

subject to

$$\int y_\theta \, dQ_{0\theta} + \int g_\theta \, dQ_{g\theta} = w$$

and

$$c_\theta = y_\theta + g_\theta - T(y_\theta + \gamma g_\theta), \tag{10}$$

where w is the individual's wealth.

Differentiating with respect to y_θ and g_θ, yields the first order conditions

$$\pi_\theta U'(c_\theta)(1 - \gamma T') = \lambda q_{g\theta},$$

and

$$\pi_\theta U'(c_\theta)(1 - T') = \lambda q_{0\theta}, \tag{11}$$

where λ is the marginal utility of wealth and π_θ, $q_{g\theta}$, and $q_{0\theta}$ are the densities of their respective distributions at θ.

Eliminating λ, we have

$$q_{g\theta} = \left[\frac{1 - \gamma T'}{1 - T'}\right] q_{0\theta}. \tag{12}$$

For any individual consumer facing prices $q_{g\theta}$ and $q_{0\theta}$, the interior conditions may not be satisfied, but, of course, given Inada conditions ($U'(0) = \infty$, $U'(\infty) = 0$) in the economy with an individual representative agent, prices will adjust at equilibrium to assure that (11) holds. Given relative prices

$$\frac{q_g}{q_0},$$

though, depending on adjusted gross income an individual will have

$$\psi \equiv \frac{1 - \gamma T'}{1 - T'} \gtreqless \frac{q_{g\theta}}{q_{0\theta}}.$$

With progressive taxes, i.e., T' increasing in taxable income and common utility functions, presumably there will be a cutoff wealth level, W_θ, associated with each state such that above that level

$$\psi \equiv \frac{1 - \gamma T'}{1 - T'} > \frac{q_{g\theta}}{q_{0\theta}},$$

and the individual will purchase only equity, with the converse result below W.

For every state, too, all individuals cannot be on one side of the margin since, then, prices would adjust, although it is possible for some to be on the margin and some off.

It follows, then, that there is a marginal investor for each state of nature and in these more complicated worlds we can interpret ψ as depending on the adjusted gross income of the marginal investor with the understanding that the identity of this investor may change with the state of nature.

Another point is worth mentioning. It is not the case that arbitrage would force

$$\psi \equiv 1,$$

nor does equilibrium require this. Of course, if firms can respond to differences in state prices by issuing state contingent claims then, in general, we must have

$$q_{0\theta} = (1 - \tau_c)q_{g\theta}.$$

De Angelo and Masulis [5] present this case, and while it is of theoretical interest, there are a variety of reasons why firms will not issue complete state contingent claims. For one thing, such claims require excessive monitoring expenditures. Perhaps less obviously and more interestingly, the tax code is not well defined for all such hybrid instruments. For example, how the IRS would treat state-dependent securities which collectively made up a classical bond instrument is not at all clear. Certainly the corporation's treatment as debt payments and, therefore, deductible of claims which began "if such and such a state occurs then holder is entitled to. . . ." would not go unchallenged. We will return to a somewhat more interesting version of this argument in Section IV.

The relative price of capital gains in terms of ordinary income,

$$\psi \equiv \frac{q_{g\theta}}{q_{0\theta}} = \frac{1 - \gamma T'}{1 - T'}, \qquad (13)$$

will play an important role in our analysis. Notice that ψ is an increasing function of the marginal tax rate, T', and that

$$\psi \geq 1, \qquad (14)$$

i.e., capital gains are no less valuable than ordinary income in each state.

In a general equilibrium, the taxes will be given back to consumers—assuming no government investment—in a lump sum redistribution, and we will assume that individual actions are unaffected by such transfers. Individuals take the lump sum transfers as part of their wealth, but we will assume that they ignore any responsiveness of the transfers to their own actions. In a representative agent world, the transfer will equal the taxes and we could take c_θ to be aggregate consumption. Of course, the breakdown into the y_θ and g_θ components is a function of the supply of these forms of income and that is the issue of interest in this paper.

To simplify (7) we can project all of the state-dependent variables onto the price standard—c in the above example. Let

$$G(x \mid c) \equiv \text{conditional distribution of } x \text{ given } c \qquad (15)$$

Debt and Taxes and Uncertainty

and

$$dQ_c \equiv E\{dQ_0 \mid c\}. \tag{16}$$

This permits us to rewrite (7) as

$$V(F) = \int \int_0^F x\, dG(x \mid c)\, dQ_c + F \int \int_F^\infty dG(x \mid c)\, dQ_c$$
$$+ \int \int_F^\infty (1 - \tau_c)(x - F)\psi\, dG(x \mid c)\, dQ_c, \tag{17}$$

where we have used the definition of ψ in (13) to eliminate dQ_g, and where we have also made use of the following assumption.

Assumption 1 (monotonicity): Taxable income is a monotonely increasing function of the pricing standard, with $T' \leq 1$.

In Assumption 1, we are using consumption as the pricing standard, but if we were to use prices themselves then, of course, the monotonicity would be reversed. Assumption 1 will be satisfied except in unusual circumstances. For example, suppose that there are only two firms, A and B, in the economy. Firm A is bankrupt and B is not. Now, suppose that a small increase in aggregate consumption is accompanied by a big increase in B's cash flows and an offsetting decline in A's flow. Since taxable income will be increased by only a fraction $\gamma < 1$ of the increase in B's capital gains while it decreases by the full amount of A's loss, the net effect can be that taxable income declines.

When the bulk of the cash flows respond positively to increases in consumption this unusual case cannot occur and it is what we are ruling out by our assumption.

II. The Debt/Equity Choice

To prevent arbitrage, the debt level of the firm must be set so as to maximize the value of the firm. This ignores spanning issues, but they are of limited interest in this analysis. Of course, it does not really matter whether the firm or its managers actually choose the optimum debt level themselves or whether the firm is refinanced by outsiders to accomplish this. We are also avoiding the somewhat ill-specified question of what the value will be if the firm chooses a debt level, F, which does not maximize V as defined by (17). Might not the value be bid up to the optimum anyway in anticipation of a refinancing? Depending on how we model the bidding and trading process it might well, in which case the choice of F will be, at least at the early stage of such a process, irrelevant. But, we will assume that to prevent tax losses the debt level is optimally set by the end of the process of trade. Presumably, too, equilibrium is achieved quite quickly and this is the value we would actually observe.

To analyze how $V(F)$ depends upon F, we begin by differentiating (17) with respect to F,

$$V'(F) = \int \int_F^\infty \left[1 - \frac{(1 - \tau_c)(1 - \gamma T')}{(1 - T')}\right] dG(x \mid c)\, dQ_c. \tag{18}$$

The integrand in (18) has been written out in full to make it easily recognizable as the criterion function derived by Miller [11]. Miller showed that at the margin, in the absence of uncertainty,

$$\varphi \equiv 1 - \frac{(1 - \tau_c)(1 - \gamma T')}{(1 - T)} = 0, \tag{19}$$

and the marginal investor finds after tax ordinary income of $1 - T'$ equivalent to after tax equity income of $(1 - \tau_c)(1 - \gamma T')$. Before tax, then, the investor is indifferent between $(1 - \tau_c)$ units of equity income or 1 unit of debt income and, therefore, the firm is indifferent as well. With uncertainty, though, the firm is not at the margin in all states.

We will assume that the tax structure is progressive in the sense that marginal rates increase.

Assumption 2 (progressivity): T is convex, i.e., $T'' \geq 0$.

It follows that in states associated with low levels of consumption—or whatever pricing standard is used—debt is relatively more valuable than equity, and, conversely, when consumption is high, equity income becomes relatively more valuable.

Proceeding analytically, from progressivity the integrand, φ, is a declining function of c. For c, sufficiently high φ will be negative provided that the marginal bracket can rise high enough. Letting c^* be defined as the lowest value of c which satisfies,

$$\varphi(c^*) = 1 - \frac{(1 - \tau_c)(1 - \gamma T')}{(1 - T')} = 0, \tag{20}$$

we have

$$\varphi \gtreqless 0 \quad \text{as} \quad c \lesseqgtr c^*. \tag{21}$$

If c^* fails to exist, then φ is always positive and the optimal debt level is infinite. Even in this case, though, and generally, $V'(F)$ approaches zero as F increases and,

$$V'(\infty) = 0. \tag{22}$$

From (17) we also have that

$$V(0) = \int \int_0^\infty (1 - \tau_c)\psi \, dG(x \mid c) \, dQ_c, \tag{23}$$

and

$$V(\infty) = \int \int_0^\infty x \, dG(x \mid c) \, dQ_c, \tag{24}$$

the values of the all equity and all debt firms, respectively.

Alternatively, we could have $c^* = 0$, in which case φ is never positive and even at the lowest brackets, equity income is preferred. If the marginal bracket for low levels falls to zero, though, we have

$$\varphi = 1 - (1 - \tau_c) = \tau_c > 0. \tag{25}$$

The interesting case to analyze, then, is one where the range of the tax code is broad enough to permit $c^* > 0$ to exist and where φ is positive for c below c^* and negative for c greater than c^*.

From (18), since φ does not depend on the firm's cash flow, x, but, rather, is an aggregate economic variable we have

$$V'(F) = \int \varphi \int_F^\infty dG(x|c) \, dQ_c$$

$$= \int \varphi \, \text{Prob}(x > F | c) \, dQ_c$$

$$= \int_F^\infty \left(\int \varphi(c) g(x|c) \, dQ_c \right) dx, \tag{26}$$

where $g(x|c)$ is the density function of $G(x|c)$.

In analyzing the firm's choice of a financial structure we will distinguish between two special cases.

Case 1: The "positive beta" case.

In this case, we assume that the conditional density function, $g(x|c)$ has the monotone likelihood ratio property (MLRP), i.e.,

$$c' > c'' \quad \text{implies that} \quad \frac{g(x|c')}{g(x|c'')} \tag{27}$$

is monotone increasing in x.

Milgrom [10] analyzes the MLRP is some detail. It is equivalent to the property that the larger c is, the more likely x is to be larger, i.e., the conditional distribution of x given c rises stochastically as c increases. This means that ($\forall K$)

$$\int_0^K dG(x|c') < \int_0^K dG(x|c''). \tag{28}$$

Conversely, the MLRP also implies that for $x' > x''$

$$\frac{g(x'|c)}{g(x''|c)}$$

is monotone increasing in c, and that the same monotonic properties hold for $g(c|x)$.

We refer to this condition as the positive beta case because it is sufficient to ensure that the regression coefficient of x on c,

$$\beta_{xc} \equiv \frac{\text{cov}(x, c)}{\text{var } c} > 0. \tag{29}$$

Continuing with the analysis, from (26) we have

$$V''(F) = -\int \varphi(c) g(F \mid c) \, dQ_c. \tag{30}$$

This enables us to verify the following result.

LEMMA 1. *If $V''(\hat{F}) > 0$, then $(\forall F > \hat{F}) V''(F) > 0$, and if $V''(\hat{F}) < 0$, then $(\forall F < \hat{F}) V''(F) < 0$.*

Proof: Suppose that $V''(\hat{F}) > 0$. From the MLRP $(\forall F > \hat{F})$

$$\frac{g(F \mid c)}{g(\hat{F} \mid c)} \equiv h(c) \tag{31}$$

rises monotonically in c. Hence, from (30),

$$V''(F) = -\int \varphi(c) g(F \mid c) \, dQ_c$$

$$= -\int \varphi(c) g(\hat{F} \mid c) h(c) \, dQ_c$$

$$= -\int_0^{c^*} \varphi(c) g(\hat{F} \mid c) h(c) \, dQ_c - \int_{c^*}^{\infty} \varphi(c) g(\hat{F} \mid c) h(c) \, dQ_c$$

$$> h(c^*) \left(-\int_0^{\infty} \varphi(c) g(\hat{F} \mid c) \, dQ_c \right)$$

$$> 0. \tag{32}$$

A similar argument proves the remainder of the lemma. Q.E.D.

This lemma has two immediate corollaries.

THEOREM 1. *The value function, V, has one of the following three forms:*

  (i) *V is everywhere concave and rises monotonically,*
  (ii) *V is everywhere convex and falls monotonically, and*
  (iii) *$(\exists \hat{F} > 0)$ such that V is concave on $[0, \hat{F}]$, convex on $(\hat{F}, \infty)$ and falls monotonically on the convex segment.*

Figure 1 illustrates the third form.

Proof: Follows immediately from the lemma and (22), $V'(\infty) = 0$. Q.E.D.

It follows, then, that we have shown that a unique optimal F^* exists. In form (i) $F^* = \infty$, in form (ii) $F^* = 0$, and in form (iii) F^* is either 0 or it is characterized by

$$V'(F^*) = 0, \tag{33}$$

for some $F^* < \infty$, as is illustrated in Figure 1.

Debt and Taxes and Uncertainty

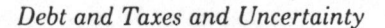

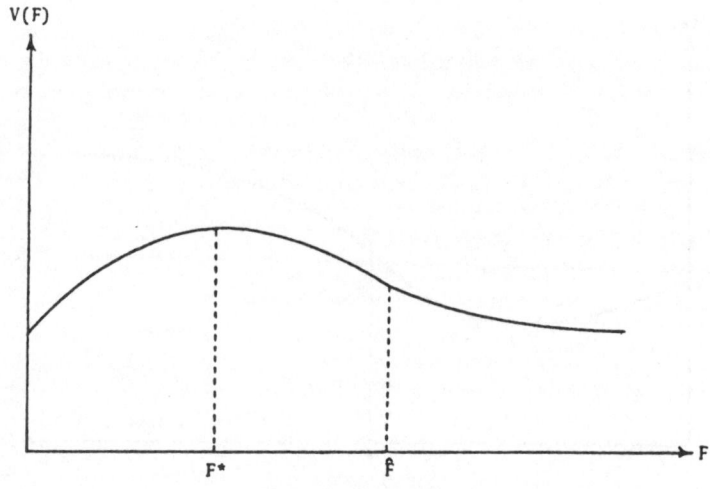

Figure 1. Positive Beta

Case 2: The "negative beta" case.

This case can be dealt with in precise analogy with the positive beta case. We simply reverse the monotonicity of (27), which implies that

$$h(x) \equiv \frac{g(x \mid c')}{g(x \mid c'')} \qquad (34)$$

declines monotonically in x for $c' > c''$. It is easily verified that

$$\beta_{xc} < 0. \qquad (35)$$

The conditions of the lemma are now reversed and we have

LEMMA 2. *If $V''(\hat{F}) < 0$, then $(\forall F > \hat{F})V''(F) < 0$, and if $V''(\hat{F}) > 0$, then $(\forall F < \hat{F})V''(F) > 0$.*

Proof: See the proof of Lemma 1, and use the monotonicity of (34). Q.E.D.

Figure 2 illustrates the general shape of $V(F)$ in the negative beta case and the following characterizes the possibilities.

THEOREM 2. *The value function, V, has one of the following three forms:*

  (i) *V is everywhere concave and rise monotonically,*
  (ii) *V is everywhere convex and falls monotonically, or*
  (iii) *$(\exists \hat{F} > 0)$ such that V is convex on $[0, \hat{F}]$, concave on $(\hat{F}, \infty)$ and rises monotonically on the concave segment.*

Proof: Immediate. Q.E.D.

We see, then, that the negative beta case must be characterized by an extreme

Figure 2. Negative Beta

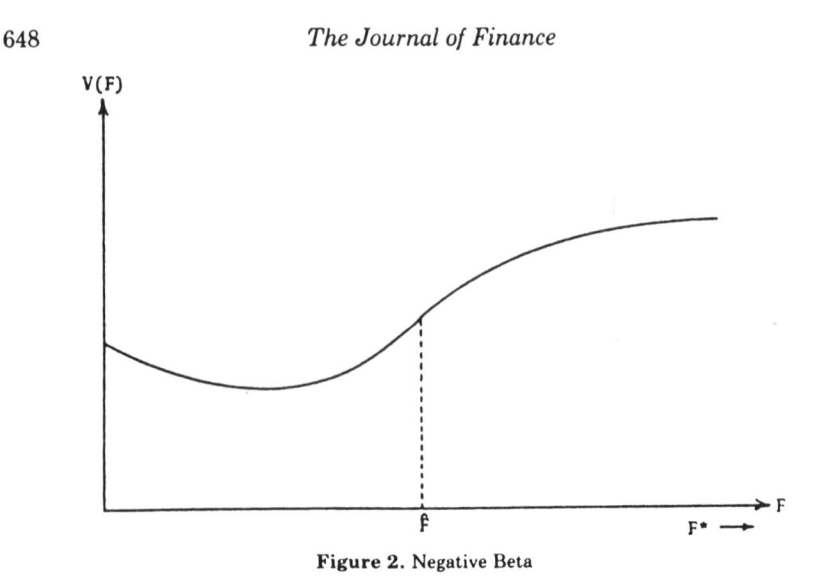

solution, i.e., either

$$F^* = 0$$

or

$$F^* = \infty.$$

Concluding this section, we have shown that as a general matter, the financial choice is not indifferent and that, in the positive beta case, an internal structure can be optimal. This occurs because firms face valuations for debt and equity income that favor equity income in "good" states of nature. Consequently, depending on the firm's responsiveness to (priced) general economic conditions, a firm that issues too little debt will find itself giving excessive equity income to its stockholders in moderate states where they place too little value on it. If debt is too high, though, they will give inadequate amounts of equity income, unnecessarily excluding states where it would be well valued by the market. In the next section, we will see how the optimal choice of a financial structure depends upon the firm's responsiveness or beta.

III. Cross-Sectional Relationships in a Diffusion Model

To examine the comparative statics properties of the debt choice, we will switch our analytical gears. While it would be possible to analyze the properties of the above one-period problem directly, it is extremely tedious to do so. Furthermore, it is useful to put the analysis into a more dynamic context so as to make the linkage with observables more direct.

To accomplish this, we first observe that the earlier section is a perfectly valid analysis of a firm which is making a debt decision for a fixed time period, T, where, in continuous time, x denotes the time T value of its assets. We will assume the same tax code and that there are no interim cash flows in the period $[0, T)$.

Debt and Taxes and Uncertainty

In continuous time, it is known that there is a continuous time martingale pricing standard, q, with the property that q follows a diffusion,

$$\frac{dq}{q} = -r\,dt + \sigma_q\,dz_q, \tag{36}$$

(where r is the riskless (constant) interest rate)[1] and such that the value of any asset with payoff of p_t is given by

$$p_0 = E\{q_t p_t\}; \quad q_0 = 1. \tag{37}$$

For the analysis of this see Dybvig et al. [7].

With taxation, the modification of the analysis is obvious (see Ross [14]). Letting interest income be ordinary and taxed at a rate T' where T' is independent on q,

$$T' = T'(q), \tag{38}$$

we can think of q as the pricing standard for ordinary income and

$$g = \psi q, \tag{39}$$

as the standard for capital gains income.

In our example above,

$$q_t = \frac{e^{-\delta t}(1 - T'(c_t))u'(c_t)}{u'(c_0)}, \tag{40}$$

where δ is a subjective rate of time preference. (This is clearly monotonely declining in c_t which verifies that T' is monotonely falling in q and that, by our previous analysis, ψ also falls monotonely in q.)

Using these results, we can write a dynamic form for the value of debt and equity as

$$D_t = E\{q_T \min(x_T, F)\}$$

and

$$S_t = E\{q_T \psi_T \max(x_T - F, 0)\}. \tag{41}$$

Writing these out in integral form with $h(q)$ denoting the densities of q yields

$$D_t = \int \int_0^F x g(x\mid q)\,dx q h(q)\,dq + F \int \int_F^\infty g(x\mid q)\,dx q h(q)\,dq$$

and

$$S_t = \int \int_F^\infty (1 - \tau_c)(x - F) g(x\mid q)\,dx \psi(q) q h(q)\,dq, \tag{42}$$

which are formally identical to Equation (17).

While we could analyze (42) directly, a more interesting approach is to return to the martingale analysis of (36) as modified by (40) to explicitly derive the local equations which describe the changes in the value for debt and equity.

[1] The constancy of the interest rate would generally have to be forced by the technology.

We will assume for purposes of analysis that all bond returns are taxed as ordinary income and that all expected returns, including those on stocks, are also taxed at ordinary rates. In this sense, it is as though the firm had adopted a dividend policy of paying out what would have been the deterministic portion of capital gains. The stochastic portion of capital gains, however, is taxed at the favorable capital gains rates. Finally, at the termination date, T, the payment on bonds is untaxed and the payment on equity is taxed at the corporate rate, τ_c.

To obtain explicit solutions, we will assume that the firm's terminal cash flow at time T is derived from the equation

$$\frac{dx}{x} = \mu \, dt + \sigma \, dz. \tag{43}$$

Under the assumptions, it is easy to see that the return of any asset must satisfy

$$(1 - T')E(dp) + (1 - T')c \, dt - (1 - T')rp \, dt = -E(dn \, dp), \tag{44}$$

where p is the asset's price, c is its cash flow, and n is the pricing standard. (For a different approach to the derivation of valuation equations with taxes, see Constantinides [1, 2] and Constantinides and Ingersoll [3].) The change in n, dn, is given by dq, from (40), for bonds and dg from (39) for stocks.

It is important to notice that while at any time t,

$$q_t = 1 - T'(c_t), \tag{45}$$

is the relative price of taxable ordinary income in terms of numeraire (after tax) consumption, the change in q for valuation purposes is given by (40) and includes the change in marginal utility as well as in tax rates.

Using (39) and (40) and taking Ito differentials, we have that the stochastic changes in the relevant pricing standards are given by

and
$$d\tilde{q} = \left[(1 - T')\frac{u''}{u'} - T''\right] \tilde{dc},$$

$$d\tilde{g} = \left[(1 - \gamma T')\frac{u''}{u'} - \gamma T''\right] \tilde{dc}. \tag{46}$$

To parametrize this system in the simplest possible fashion, we will make the following assumptions.

Assumption 3: The covariance between cash flow and the pricing standard for ordinary income is constant, i.e.,

$$E\left\{\frac{d\tilde{q}}{q} \, d\tilde{z}\right\} = \text{constant}. \tag{47}$$

This assumption is useful because it permits us to eliminate state variables from the analysis which would otherwise be needed to describe the development of the covariances. The next assumption serves a similar purpose.

Assumption 4: The covariance between cash flow and the pricing standard for

Debt and Taxes and Uncertainty

capital gains is proportional to ψ^{-1}, i.e.,

$$E\left\{\frac{d\tilde{g}}{g}\,d\tilde{z}\right\} = \text{constant} \cdot \psi^{-1}. \tag{48}$$

This latter assumption, then, implies that

$$E\left\{\frac{d\tilde{g}}{q}\,d\tilde{z}\right\} = \text{constant}. \tag{49}$$

From (46), Assumptions 3 and 4 establish a parametric relationship between the tax code and the utility function, i.e.,

$$\frac{(1 - \gamma T')u''/u' - \gamma T''}{(1 - T')u''/u' - T''} \equiv k, \text{ a constant}, \tag{50}$$

which, integrating, tells us that

$$T' = \left[\frac{1-k}{\gamma - k}\right] + \frac{b}{u'} \tag{51}$$

where b is an integration constant. Notice, too, that

$$k > 0 \tag{52}$$

and that from (46)

$$\frac{d\tilde{g}}{q} = k\,\frac{d\tilde{q}}{q}. \tag{53}$$

From (44), we now know that x is the only state variable for the system of equations governing the valuation changes for debt and equity. Letting β denote the cash flow beta of the firm,

$$\beta \equiv -\frac{\text{cov}\left(\dfrac{d\tilde{q}}{q}\,\sigma\,d\tilde{z}\right)}{\text{var}\left(\dfrac{d\tilde{q}}{q}\right)}$$

$$\equiv -\frac{\sigma\,\text{cov}\left(\dfrac{d\tilde{q}}{q}\,d\tilde{z}\right)}{\sigma_q^2} \tag{54}$$

and assuming that q is also lognormal we have the following result.[2]

THEOREM 3. *The following equations characterize debt, D, and equity, S.*

Debt

$$\tfrac{1}{2}\sigma^2 x^2 D_{xx} + (\mu - \beta\sigma_q^2)xD_x - D_\tau - rD = 0$$

$$D(x, 0) = \min(x, F), \tag{55}$$

---

[2] The reader may be worried that the system is overparametrized at this stage. However, since the consumption process is still unspecified, it is easy to see that this is not yet a problem.

and

Equity

$$\tfrac{1}{2}\sigma^2 x^2 S_{xx} + (\mu - k\beta\sigma_q^2)xS_x - S_\tau - rS = 0$$
$$S(x, 0) = (1 - \tau_c)\max(x - F, 0), \tag{56}$$

where τ is the time to receipt of the cash flow, x_T.

Proof: Follows immediately from (44) and Assumptions 3 and 4. Q.E.D.

Since these equations have been designed to be variations on simple diffusions (see Cox and Ross [4]), their solutions are variants of a well-known option formula. Let

$$\begin{aligned} C &\equiv c(\mu, x, F, \tau, \sigma^2, r) \\ &\equiv e^{-r\tau}\{xe^{\mu\tau}N(d_+) - FN(d_-)\}, \end{aligned} \tag{57}$$

where $N(\cdot)$ is the cumulative standard normal distribution function, and

$$d_+ \equiv \frac{\ln\frac{x}{F} + \left(\mu + \frac{1}{2}\sigma^2\right)\tau}{\sigma\sqrt{\tau}},$$

and

$$d_- \equiv d_+ - \sigma\sqrt{\tau}. \tag{58}$$

THEOREM 4. *The respective solutions to (55) and (56) are given by,*

$$D(x, \tau) = xe^{(\mu_D - r)\tau} - c(\mu_D)$$

and

$$S(x, \tau) = (1 - \tau_c)c(\mu_S), \tag{59}$$

where

$$\mu_D \equiv \mu - \beta\sigma_q^2,$$

and

$$\mu_S \equiv \mu - k\beta\sigma_q^2, \tag{60}$$

and where we have suppressed undifferentiated variables in this notation for c.

Proof: Follows directly from (55), (56), and (57). Q.E.D.

The positive beta case, $\beta > 0$, corresponds to our usual intuition about firms whose returns are positively correlated with aggregate consumption, and it is the one we will consider. Despite the different appearance of the model developed in this section, it is actually just a specific parameterization of the general analysis of Sections I and II. As a consequence, it is straightforward to verify that Theorem 1 applies and that if $k < 1$, there can be a determinate internal optimal debt level, F^*. We will analyze this case.

Debt and Taxes and Uncertainty

THEOREM 5. *The optimal debt level satisfies*

$$V'(F^*) = e^{-r\tau}\{N(d_-(\mu_D)) - (1 - \tau_c)N(d_-(\mu_S))\} = 0, \quad (61)$$

with the attendant second-order condition,

$$V''(F^*) = e^{-r\tau} \frac{1}{\sigma\sqrt{\tau}} \{(1 - \tau_c)n(d_-(\mu_S)) - n(d_-(\mu_D))\} < 0, \quad (62)$$

where $n(\cdot)$ is the unit normal density.

Proof: Simply differentiate (59). Q.E.D.

The first-order condition, (61), captures our original intuition describing how the optimal debt level is set. At the margin, an increase in F raises the value of debt by $N(d_-(\mu_D))$, the tax adjusted probability of paying off the debt. The loss to equity is the other side of this, but it is computed using a different tax adjustment for expected returns, $\mu_S > \mu_D$, which is what permits a nontrivial internal solution.

If $k > 1$, then from (61), $V'(F) > 0$ for all F, and an all debt firm is optimal. In this case, the tax code is not sufficiently progressive to confer any tax advantage to equity financing. The tax advantage to equity in this model comes from the difference between the change in its marginal capital gains tax and that on debt, $(1 - \gamma)T''$, which acts to offset its higher after tax beta. Interestingly, from (50) we can see that the condition $k < 1$ is equivalent to having the elasticity of taxation exceed risk aversion,

$$\frac{CT''}{T'} > -\frac{Cu''}{u'}. \quad (63)$$

Of course, the negative beta case will reverse this intuition.

We now move to our basic comparative statics results.

THEOREM 6. *The optimal debt level, F^*, is proportional to x, i.e.,*

$$\frac{x}{F^*} \frac{\partial F^*}{\partial x} = 1, \quad (64)$$

and independent of the interest rate, r, and exponential in μ, i.e.,

$$\frac{1}{F^*} \frac{\partial F^*}{\partial \mu} = \tau. \quad (65)$$

Proof: Follows from (61) directly. Q.E.D.

The independence of F^* and r may seem surprising, but keep in mind that μ is the return on a cash flow project and not on a capital asset. In the latter case, as for an option, μ would depend on r and that portion of Theorem 6 need no longer hold.

Lastly we can relate F^* to beta.

THEOREM 7. *In a cross-section of firms with the same total variance, σ^2, those* with higher (positive) cash flow betas will have lower debt levels, i.e.,

$$\left.\frac{\partial F^*}{\partial \beta}\right|_{\sigma^2} < 0. \tag{66}$$

Proof: Differentiating (61) and holding σ^2 constant—which means that the residual variability,

$$\sigma^2 - \beta^2 \sigma_q^2,$$

must pick up the slack—yields

$$\left.\frac{\partial V'}{\partial \beta}\right|_{\sigma^2} = e^{-r\tau} \left\{ n(d_-(\mu_D)) \left[-\frac{1}{c\sqrt{\tau}} \sigma_q^2 \tau \right] - (1 - \tau_c) n(d_-(\mu_S)) \left[-\frac{1}{\sigma\sqrt{\tau}} \sigma_q^2 k\tau \right] \right\}$$

$$= e^{-r\tau} \frac{\sigma_q^2 \sqrt{\tau}}{\sigma} \{ k(1 - \tau_c) n(d_-(\mu_S)) - n(d_-(\mu_D)) \}$$

$$< 0, \tag{67}$$

by the second-order condition, (62). Since $V''(F) < 0$.

$$\left.\frac{\partial F^*}{\partial \beta}\right|_{\sigma^2} = [-V''(F^*)]^{-1} \left.\frac{\partial V'}{\partial \beta}\right|_{\sigma^2} < 0. \quad \text{Q.E.D.} \tag{68}$$

The intuition underlying this result should be clear. Increasing beta lowers the marginal contribution to value of additional debt because it raises the expected return and, therefore, lowers the value of debt. It has a similar effect on equity, but it is mitigated by the capital gains offset. Hence, at the margin, debt must fall to accommodate its additional disadvantage relative to equity.

Further results are possible, but they remain to be explored. In particular, we would like to directly relate debt/equity ratios to ordinary equity betas,

$$\frac{xS_x}{S} \beta. \tag{69}$$

This would facilitate empirical testing. Nevertheless, we have succeeded in our initial goal of relating the choice of financial structure at the firm level to the characteristics of the firm's earnings stream.

IV. Robustness and Some Caveats

The above results obviously depend on our assumptions concerning taxation. But one particular adjustment for taxation is worth mentioning. The results hinge sensitively on the use of the financial structure to position the firm with respect to changes in marginal tax rates. An unanticipated increase in consumption, for example, is assumed to move the economy into a regime of higher marginal tax rates. Suppose, though, that progressivity in the tax regime is only relative and that the rates themselves are indexed against "bracket creep." In such circumstances, the impact on the firm will depend on the movement of investors across brackets, rather than on the movement in aggregate consumption. In a representative economy, there are no such distributional effects, and marginal tax rates will be fixed. In the above analysis, this means that T' will be fixed.

This brings us back, then, in the world of fixed rates, to Miller's analysis. In effect, by indexing the code the impact of uncertainty upon financial choice has been eliminated. In the absence of such complete real as well as nominal indexing, though, the effects we have examined will still play a role. This will be particularly true to the extent to which endogenous changes in the code itself are contemplated and firms position themselves in anticipation of such events.

Somewhat more interestingly, though, we are also assuming that firms have motives for taking the form we have given them other than simply tax considerations. In particular, if firms can merge and spin off in an arbitrary fashion, then tax considerations will again drive them to a form of Miller's world of indeterminancy at the individual firm level.

To see this suppose that there are two firms with cash flows of x_1 and x_2, and respective optimal debt levels of F_1 and F_2. Suppose that in some state of nature with capital gains more valuable than ordinary income, i.e., $(1 - \tau_c)q_{c\theta} > q_{0\theta}$, firm 1 is bankrupt and firm 2 is still paying its debt off. By transferring the income of firm 1 in this state to firm 2 we can increase their joint value, $V_1 + V_2$. In general, the corporate sector will solve the problem

$$\max_{\{F_1, \ldots, F_n\}} \sum_i V(x_i, F_i) \qquad (70)$$
$$\text{subject to } \sum_i x_i(\theta) = x(\theta),$$

the aggregate (before tax) earnings. Since, from (7), V is linear in x, the solution will be either a hyperplane of indifference or a corner. In this regime, the corporate sector has the ability to create pure state contingent claims. The only equilibrium, then, will be one in which each firm is always bankrupt or never bankrupt.

THEOREM 8. *If firms can form and combine in any fashion subject only to the constraint that*

$$\sum_i x_i(\theta) = x(\theta), \qquad (71)$$

and if taxes are the only consideration, then the equilibrium will be equivalent to one in which firms offer pure tax-contingent claims. Each firm can now be assumed to be always bankrupt or have zero debt.

Proof: Suppose that at the equilibrium for the corporate sector firm 1 has debt level F_1 and firm 2 has F_2. If the firms are not simultaneously bankrupt or solvent in all of the same states, then there will be a state, θ, where, say, firm 1 is bankrupt and firm 2 is not. In this state,

$$(1 - \tau_c)q_{c\theta} \gtreqless q_{0\theta}. \qquad (72)$$

If $(1 - \tau_c)q_{c\theta} > q_{0\theta}$, then transferring $x_1(\theta)$ to firm 2 will increase their joint value and if $(1 - \tau_c)q_{c\theta} < q_{0\theta}$, then transferring $x_2(\theta)$ to firm 1 will increase their joint value. Thus, the only equilibrium is where all equity income is realized in states for which $(1 - \tau_c)q_{c\theta} > q_{0\theta}$ and all debt income is realized in states for which

$(1 - \tau_c)q_{c\theta} < q_{0\theta}$. As a consequence, each firm will be either an all equity or an all debt firm. Q.E.D.

Depending on the structure of the market, and, in particular, whether short sales are permitted and what rules prevail on intercorporate offers the state contingent prices, $(1 - \tau_c)q_{c\theta}$ and $q_{0\theta}$ may or may not be equalized. But, even if they are not, in this world the financial structures are determinate but the firms themselves are not. In essence, then, Miller's indeterminacy returns since only the corporate sector as a whole can be identified. In particular, two firms which are all equity could combine or not with no impact on the equilibrium.

V. Conclusions

Using the force of taxation in a world of uncertainty we have linked the cash flows generated by the firm to its choice of a financial structure. We have also shown that such a structure can be determinate at the firm level and not just for the corporate sector as a whole. But, this result was not without exception; it took the industrial structure as given rather than as dependent on taxation itself. Perhaps, the most immediate task for future research, though, is the need to extend the analysis so as to establish a direct link amongst purely financial variables such as, for example, debt/equity ratios and systematic and nonsystematic equity risk measures.

Some other interesting extensions would be to inframarginal firms. It is clear that Miller's analysis can be extended to such a case with the margin defined by the marginal firm as well as the marginal investor. Inframarginal firms in a world of certainty would issue all debt or all equity, but in a world of uncertainty this need no longer be true. It remains to explore the robustness of such results to the considerations raised in Section IV, such as possibilities for redefining firms and the effects of financial intermediaries. It would also be worthwhile to consider the impact of uncertain changes in the code itself. To some extent, the results of this paper may be interpreted as applying to such problems.

REFERENCES

1. G. M. Constantinides. "Capital Market Equilibrium with Personal Tax." *Econometrica* 51 (May 1983), 611-36.
2. ———. "Optimal Stock Trading with Personal Taxes: Implications for Prices and the Abnormal January Returns." *Journal of Financial Economics* 13 (March 1984), 65-89.
3. ——— and J. Ingersoll. "Optimal Bond Trading with Personal Taxes." *Journal of Financial Economics* 13 (September 1984), 299-336.
4. J. C. Cox and S. Ross. "The Valuation of Options for Alternative Stochastic Processes." *Journal of Financial Economics* 3 (September 1976), 145-66.
5. Harry De Angelo and Ronald Masulis. "Optimal Capital Structure under Corporate and Personal Taxation." *Journal of Financial Economics* 8 (March 1980), 3-30.
6. ———. "Leverage and Dividend Irrelevancy under Corporate and Personal Taxation." *Journal of Finance* 35 (May 1980), 453-67.
7. P. Dybvig, J. Ingersoll, and S. Ross. "Martingales, Arbitrage and Valuation." Unpublished notes, November 1984.
8. L. Hansen and S. Richard. "Characterizing Asset Prices under Value Additivity." Mimeo, Carnegie-Mellon University, February 1983.

9. J. Harrison and D. Kreps. "Martingales and Arbitrage in Multiperiod Securities Markets." *Journal of Economic Theory* 20 (June 1979), 381–408.
10. P. Milgrom. "Good News and Bad News: Representation Theorems and Applications." *Bell Journal of Economics* 12 (Autumn 1981), 380–91.
11. Merton Miller. "Debt and Taxes." *Journal of Finance* 32 (December 1977), 261–75.
12. S. A. Ross. "Return, Risk and Arbitrage." In I. Friend and J. Bicksler (eds.), *Risk and Return in Finance*. Cambridge, MA: Ballinger, 1976.
13. ———. "A Simple Approach to the Valuation of Risky Streams." *Journal of Business* 51 (July 1978), 453–75.
14. ———. "Arbitrage and Taxes." Mimeo, Yale University, 1984.

Part V
Voting and Control

ONE SHARE–ONE VOTE AND THE MARKET FOR CORPORATE CONTROL*

Sanford J. GROSSMAN
Princeton University, Princeton, NJ 08544, USA

Oliver D. HART
Massachusetts Institute of Technology, Cambridge, MA 02139, USA

Received February 1987, final version received October 1987

This paper analyzes the optimality of the one share–one vote rule. We focus on takeover bids as a mechanism for allocating control. We assume two types of control benefits – benefits to security holders and private benefits to the controlling party. One share–one vote maximizes the importance of benefits to securityholders relative to benefits to the controlling party and hence encourages the selection of an efficient management team. However, one share–one vote does not always maximize the reward to securityholders in a corporate control contest. Sufficient conditions are given for one share–one vote to be optimal overall. The paper also includes a discussion of the empirical evidence.

1. Introduction

A corporation's securities give the holder claims to the firm's income stream and voting rights. These securities can be designed in various ways: one share of a given class may have a claim to votes disproportionately larger or smaller than its claim to income. In this paper we analyze some of the forces that make it desirable to set up the corporation so that all securities have votes in the same proportion as their claim to income (one share–one vote).

The literature on corporations has viewed security-voting structure as a response to the agency problems created by the delegation of control to management. For example, Easterbrook and Fischel (1983, p. 403) write: 'As the residual claimants, the shareholders are the group with the appropriate incentives (collective choice problems to one side) to make discretionary

---

*Both authors gratefully acknowledge research support from the National Science Foundation. The second author is also pleased to acknowledge financial support from the Guggenheim Foundation and the Center for Energy Policy Research at MIT. We also thank Harry DeAngelo, Douglas Diamond, Leo Herzel, Richard Ruback, and Michael Jensen (the editor) for their helpful comments on an earlier draft.

decisions.' The connection between agency problems and security-voting structure is not simple, however, for two reasons. First, although the delegation of control creates a conflict of interest between those who make decisions and those who bear the consequences, this agency problem does not bear directly on the security-voting structure; it implies only that management should receive performance-based compensation. Second, although it is clear that shareholders as a group have an incentive to monitor management – and hence tying votes to shares may be desirable to allow them to act on this incentive – in practice, monitoring by individual small shareholders will be limited because of free-rider problems [as Easterbrook and Fischel (1983) recognize].[1] That is, we would expect monitoring of management to be effective only when a single party becomes large enough to internalize the externalities of collective action, e.g., by making a takeover bid. This suggests that the main impact of a firm's security-voting structure will be in its influence on the market for corporate control – an influence the literature has so far not analyzed in detail.

The purpose of this paper is to analyze this influence. We will think of a corporation as a collection of assets; the key issue is who should manage them. At any moment, there is an incumbent management team, but it may not be the best group to run the corporation. We will view the corporation's security-voting structure as a mechanism for shifting control to a superior rival, if such a team exists.

We consider the following stylized scenario. We suppose that the corporate charter is written by an entrepreneur who wants to maximize the total market value of securities issued. The charter creates n classes of shares and specifies the share of dividends and total votes to which the ith class is entitled. The charter also specifies a fraction alpha of the outstanding votes a rival team must receive in an election for directors to replace existing management.

The charter is set up with the expectation that the corporation's securities will be widely held and in the belief that incumbent management cannot be relied upon to oversee future changes in control and in particular to fire itself if a superior management team becomes available (i.e., agency problems will exist). Thus takeover bids will be important in ensuring changes in control. We model a corporate control contest by assuming that a single buyer desiring control will appear and will compete against the incumbent management team

---

[1] Fischel (1986, p. 16) notes that large shareholders have better incentives to monitor management than do small shareholders and that 'one share/one vote recognizes this economic reality by assigning votes and thus the ability to monitor managers, in direct proportion to shareholders' stake in the venture'. DeAngelo and DeAngelo (1985, p. 37) recognize that a one share–one vote rule does not assign *effective* votes in direct proportion to shares, since under majority rule someone with 50.1% of the shares has 100% of the *effective* votes.

or its 'white knight'. It is also supposed that in an election small securityholders either do not vote or vote in favor of incumbent management.[2] Thus alpha = 0.5 refers to the situation in which there is majority rule and an acquirer must purchase at least 50% of the votes to take control.

Our analysis distinguishes between two classes of benefits from control: private benefits and security benefits. The private benefits of control are the benefits current management or the acquirer obtain for themselves, but that the target securityholders do not obtain. These include synergy benefits realized by the acquirer, the return from being able to freezeout minority shareholders at a price below the value of their shares; perquisites of control, and in extreme cases the diversion of resources from the securityholders to subsidiaries of management or the acquirer. The security benefits refer to the *total* market value of the income streams that accrue to the corporation's securityholders.

We show that the security-voting structure determines the extent to which a bidder with significant private benefits faces competition from parties who value the firm only for its security benefits. For example, in the absence of competition from another buyer, a voting claim with no dividend rights will be tendered by a securityholder to an acquirer at any positive price. The voteholder would fail to tender at such a price only if he faced a more attractive offer, but the only potential source of competition for pure votes comes from another party with private benefits. In contrast, if dividend rights are bundled with voting claims, some competition can come from parties with only security benefits of control, since such parties will have a positive willingness to pay for a bundle of dividends and votes.

Through this competition effect, the assignment of voting rights determines both whether control will rest in the hands of a high-private-benefit party or a high-security-benefit party and the value of income claims under the controlling management. Together these effects represent what we call the *allocative role* of the assignment of claims. The assignment of voting rights also determines the price an acquirer must pay voteholders for the private benefits of control, which we call the *surplus-extraction role*. In general, there can be a conflict between the two roles. In particular, while one share–one vote will be optimal if only the allocative role is important, deviations from one share–one vote may sometimes be desirable to take advantage of the surplus-extraction role. In practice, however, we argue that the surplus-extraction role is likely to

---

[2] This assumption is not unreasonable. If shareholders are small, each one has little incentive to vote, since it is very unlikely that he will be pivotal. Moreover, if a shareholder does vote, it may make sense for him to vote for a known incumbent rather than for an unknown outsider. Empirically it does seem that incumbent management usually receives the support of small shareholders in a proxy fight. However, outsiders do sometimes win proxy fights; see Dodd and Warner (1983).

be small, in which case one share–one vote will dominate all other security-voting structures. We also provide sufficient conditions for alpha to equal 0.5, i.e., for simple majority rule to be optimal.[3]

The paper is organized as follows. In section 2 we provide a summary and overview of our results. This section is designed to give the general flavor of our analysis, using numerical examples only. It can be skipped by those who are comfortable with the more formal analysis that follows. Section 3 describes the model. In section 4 we analyze first the case in which discriminatory restricted offers by a bidder are not feasible, i.e., if an offer is made for a fraction of the shares in a class, then the shares that are not acquired cannot be given payments worth less than those for the shares acquired. We provide conditions under which one share–one vote is optimal and explain that alpha is almost irrelevant when discriminatory restricted offers are not feasible. In section 5, we turn to the case in which discriminatory restricted offers are feasible, where there is a role for alpha as well as security structure. Extensions are discussed in section 6, the empirical evidence is discussed in section 7, and conclusions are presented in section 8.

2. Summary of results

2.1. Optimal security structure in the absence of restricted discriminatory offers and with one-sided private benefits

We begin our formal analysis in section 4 by considering the case in which discriminatory restricted offers are not feasible. We also start by assuming that at most one party can obtain substantial private benefits from control. This simplifies the analysis and brings out the following essential point. If the company has two classes of stock, each with voting and dividend rights, but a control change can be effected through the purchase of only the first class of shares, then securityholders can achieve a better outcome by shifting dividends to the first class so that a rival must buy more of the dividends to gain control.

For example, suppose the class A shares have a claim to all the votes and 50% of the dividends, while the class B shares have no voting rights and a claim to 50% of the dividends. Assume that the value of the dividends is 200 under the incumbent (i.e., class A and class B are each worth 100 per 100% of their respective class, exclusive of any expected tender premium) and that the total dividend stream is worth 180 under the rival's management (i.e., each

---

[3] Ours is not the first attempt to develop a model of security-voting structure. Blair, Gerard, and Golbe (1986) also analyze the effect of security-voting structure on takeover bids, but restrict attention to conditional tender offers and find that security-voting structure is irrelevant in the absence of taxes. Mention should also be made of the paper by Harris and Raviv (1988) written contemporaneously with this one. The Harris–Raviv paper is discussed briefly in section 6.

class is worth 90). Further assume that the rival is the only party with significant private benefits of control. Let the rival make a tender offer for all of class A at a total price of 101. Then in the absence of a counteroffer, a small holder of class A shares faces the choice of not tendering (and thus holding onto a claim worth 100 if the rival loses or 90 if he wins) or tendering to the rival and receiving 101. The shareholder therefore tenders and the rival obtains control for a price of 101. Holders of class B own shares that are now worth 90. The shareholders have lost by the takeover since the two classes combined receive only 191. The rival pays 101 for the class A shares, which will give him a dividend stream worth only 90. Nevertheless, if there is a synergy value (i.e., private benefit) of more than 11, the transaction will have been profitable for the rival.

Could the above value-reducing offer be blocked by another bidder? The answer is no, given our assumption that the rival is the only party with a private benefit from control. In the absence of a private benefit, a party would be willing to pay at most 100 for the class A shares, since that is the value of their dividend claims when the rival is defeated and the incumbent retains control. (This conclusion changes if the incumbent can use the target company's assets to pay for a counterbid, since this bestows a private benefit on incumbent management. For discussion of the use of company funds, see section 6.)

Now consider the same situation, except that the class A shares have a claim to 75% of the firm's total dividend stream. The class A shares would be worth 150 under the incumbent. If the rival made an offer for these shares at a price of 101, then a party representing the incumbent could make a counteroffer at a price of 150. Shareholders facing these two competing offers would tender to the higher bidder, and the rival would lose. Clearly, to deter the incumbent now, the rival must pay 151 for the class A shares. If he does this, the value of the firm will still fall, but by less than before: from 200 to (151 + 0.25 × 180) = 196. Moreover, the rival's capital loss increases from 11 to 16, since he now pays 151 for the class A shares, which yield a dividend stream worth only 135 to him. Hence the likelihood that the rival will make a bid is lower than previously: he will do so only if his synergy value exceeds 16.

What this example illustrates is that, when the rival is the only party with a private benefit, raising the dividend claims attached to the votes he must acquire makes him pay more for the benefits of control by intensifying the competition from a party who values the votes only for their dividend claims. The best outcome for shareholders is achieved when *all* the dividends are attached to the class A voting shares. In this case – which corresponds to one share–one vote – a rival must purchase the whole dividend stream to get the benefits of control. Further, since it is always possible for the incumbent or his supporters to offer shareholders the value of the status quo, the rival must pay the full value for this dividend stream. Hence, under one share–one vote, shareholder property rights are fully protected; value-reducing bids are impossible.

The above example is concerned with the case in which the rival will decrease the value of the dividend stream. If the rival increases the value of the dividend stream, one share–one vote is neither better nor worse than any other security-voting structure. In this case all shareholders can enjoy the benefits of the rival's improved management by holding onto their shares; furthermore, the rival does not have to pay a premium since, whatever the security-voting structure, an offer that values the firm according to its improved dividend stream cannot be resisted by an inferior incumbent with negligible private benefits of control. Putting the value-decreasing and value-increasing cases together yields the conclusion that one share–one vote dominates all other security-voting structures when the incumbent's private benefit of control is small.

An exactly analogous argument covers the situation in which the rival has negligible private benefits and the incumbent has substantial private benefits. That is, when the incumbent has private benefits, he may be willing to pay more for the class A shares than a value-increasing rival. In particular, the incumbent will defeat rivals who could increase the total dividend stream as long as his private benefit of control is larger than the share of dividends owned by class A multiplied by the increment in dividend value generated by the rival. To the extent that class A has larger dividend rights, the defeat of such a rival will be more expensive (i.e., occur in fewer situations), and this will increase the total value of the firm's securities when it first goes public.

2.2. Optimal security structure in the absence of restricted discriminatory offers and with two-sided private benefits

If both parties have private benefits, the security structure can affect securityholders' ability to extract some of the private benefit from the winning bidder. Since the security benefits are a public good to the security holders, a bidder's willingness to pay for control is determined by its private benefit. Therefore, if a class of shares has small dividend claims and large voting claims, both parties will compete for this class, and to win a party must pay the securityholders an amount close to the private benefit of the competing party. Thus securityholders may receive a large fraction of private benefits as compensation when votes are separated from dividend claims (the surplus-extraction effect). As a result, departures from one share–one vote may sometimes increase market value.

This possibility can be illustrated by an example. Suppose the value of dividends is 10 under the incumbent and 100 under the rival, and that the incumbent's private benefit is 1, while the rival's exceeds 1. This is a case in which the rival's public and private benefits are both greater than the incumbent's. Under one share–one vote the rival will win control by making an offer for all the shares at a price just above 100. Shareholders will tender because they are being offered more than the post-acquisition value of the company under either the rival or the incumbent. Moreover, the incumbent cannot resist this offer since the most he can afford to pay for 100% of the shares is 11 (comprising the value of the dividend stream under his management plus his private benefit of control). Hence, under one share–one vote the value of the corporation will be (just above) 100.

Suppose instead the charter specifies two classes of securities: class A has all the votes and none of the dividends and class B has all the dividends and none of the votes. Now the competition for control will take place over the class A securities (pure votes). The rival will still win since his willingness to pay for the votes (given by his private benefit of control) exceeds the incumbent's. To deter the incumbent, the rival will make an offer for the votes at just above 1. Thus class A securityholders receive 1, while class B holders have securities which are worth 100 under the rival's management. Therefore securityholders receive a total of 101 under a charter with voting and nonvoting shares, which exceeds the 100 they receive under one share–one vote.

To put it very simply, shareholders benefit when the rival and incumbent compete over products for which they have similar willingnesses to pay; in the example, pure votes qualify better for this than shares and votes together. (In more general examples, where neither party is dominant with respect to both public and private benefits, competition is maximized by a security structure lying somewhere between pure votes and one share–one vote.)

In this example, the surplus-extraction effect dominates the allocative role discussed previously and leads to a departure from one share–one vote. An important feature of the example is that securityholders are confident that both parties to the control contest have substantial private benefits; and that the party with high private benefits also has high security benefits. If high private benefits are not associated with high security benefits, shifting dividend claims away from voting claims may cause a bidder with low security benefits to win control, thus reducing market value overall. In practice we argue that the extraction of large private benefits from a public company is relatively unlikely, and so securityholders cannot be confident that both parties to a control contest will have substantial private benefits. Under these conditions we show that the allocative role will dominate the surplus-extraction role, and one share–one vote will be the optimal security structure.

2.3. Restricted offers and the determination of alpha

Section 5 discusses the determination of the voting rule alpha. The fraction of votes necessary to defeat the incumbent becomes important in situations in which a party can make an offer for less than 100% of a class and not provide equal treatment to those shareholders who tender but whose shares are not accepted. Restricted offers allow a party to acquire control by purchasing a fraction of the dividend stream of a class. Therefore the impact on the bidding process of restricted offers for a single class is very similar to the impact of unrestricted offers for a two-class firm where the bidder can acquire control by buying the votes of only one of the classes.

The choice of alpha affects the fraction of total dividends a rival must acquire to obtain control, as well as the fraction of dividends the incumbent needs to acquire to resist the rival (the latter is determined by one minus alpha). The former effect makes a high alpha optimal, whereas the latter effect makes a low alpha optimal. For example, if the corporate charter specifies that alpha = 0.95, then even under a one share–one vote security structure, the incumbent can easily block value-improving offers. In particular, if the dividend stream is worth 100 under the incumbent and 200 under the rival, the incumbent can resist an offer by the rival by making a counteroffer for 5% of the shares at a price of 201. If the rival has no private benefit he will not be willing to pay more than 200 for any shares, so the incumbent's offer will win. The incumbent pays 10.05 for shares that are worth 5 under his management, and this will be worthwhile if his private benefit exceeds 5.05.

Among other things, we show that one share–one vote and simple majority rule will be optimal when the incumbent's private benefits are substantially larger than the rival's.

3. The model

3.1. The corporate charter

We suppose that the corporate charter is written by an entrepreneur who wants to maximize the total market value of securities issued. The charter creates n classes of shares and specifies the share of dividends s_i and the fraction of total votes v_i to which the ith class is entitled. The charter also specifies a fraction alpha of the outstanding votes a rival team must receive to replace existing management, where $\frac{1}{2} \leq$ alpha ≤ 1.[4]

To simplify matters, we will concentrate on the case where there are only two classes of shares, A and B, with dividend and vote entitlements given by s_A, v_A and s_B, v_B, respectively (where $s_A + s_B = 1$, $v_A + v_B = 1$). However, all

---

[4] We assume alpha $\geq \frac{1}{2}$ for two reasons. First, in a more general model with several rival teams, alpha $< \frac{1}{2}$ could lead to ambiguous situations in which more than one team achieved the fraction alpha. Second, below we study a contest between the rival R and the incumbent I under the assumption that I requires $(1 -$ alpha$)$ votes to fight off R. If alpha $< \frac{1}{2}$, however, it would pay I to approach a white knight to fight the contest on his behalf; in this case he would require only alpha votes to win.

our results can be extended without difficulty to the case of n classes.[5] Without loss of generality we take A to be the superior voting stock, i.e., $v_A \geq v_B$. Note that one share–one vote is a special case of this dual-class structure where $s_A = v_A = 1$.

We suppose that there are only two candidates for the management position: the incumbent team, I, and a rival team, R. We represent by y^I (y^R) the market value of the income stream accruing to all the firm's securityholders under incumbent management (under the rival R), and by z^I (z^R) the present value of the incumbent's (the rival's) private benefits of control. (So all benefits are measured in current dollars.)

When the corporate charter is written, the market recognizes that the incumbent's characteristics, (y^I, z^I), and those of potential rivals, (y^R, z^R), cannot be known far into the future. The charter thus creates a mechanism that will work well in allocating control, averaging over the future random occurrences of (y^I, z^I) and (y^R, z^R). Below we analyze how the assignment of voting rights in the charter affects the allocation of management and shareholder benefits in the event of control changes.[6]

3.2. The corporate control contest

We suppose that to become large, a party must make a public tender offer. Some time after y^I, z^I, y^R, z^R are realized, the rival appears and either makes such an offer or doesn't. If R makes a bid, the incumbent will choose whether or not to resist it.[7]

Faced with one or two offers, securityholders will decide whether to tender to R, tender to I, or hold onto their shares. As a result of these tender decisions, R will either accumulate more than the fraction alpha of the corporation's votes necessary for him to win the election or he won't. If he does, R will replace I; if he doesn't, I will retain control. I will also retain control if R chooses not to bid.[8]

We assume that at the time of the control contest the characteristics (y^I, z^I, y^R, z^R) of the bidders are common knowledge and the securityholders

---

[5]For details, see Grossman and Hart (1987). Formal statements and proofs of many of the propositions in this paper will also be found there.

[6]We take (y, z) to be exogenous for R and I. In a richer model, (y, z) would depend on managerial actions. For an analysis of managerial agency problems in the presence of takeover bids, see Scharfstein (1986).

[7]The incumbent may finance the counterbid out of his own resources (e.g., as in a leveraged buyout) or he may find a 'friendly' firm to which the private benefit z^I can be transferred, and which will make the counteroffer (i.e., a white knight).

[8]Grossman and Hart (1987) consider a model in which I represents an arbitrageur who can attempt to accumulate enough shares to block R, and thus force R to negotiate a payment for I's shares. This model gives additional insights into the determination of security structure and the choice of alpha. In the present model, bargaining between I and R is assumed not to occur.

have rational expectations about the contest outcome. Since this outcome is deterministic (either R bids and receives more than alpha of the votes, in which case he wins, or in all other cases I wins), this means that securityholders predict the winner with certainty. We also suppose that each securityholder ignores his impact on this outcome. The latter assumption is reasonable, given that securityholders are individually small. The two assumptions together have the important implication that it never pays a bidder to make a losing tender offer. The reason is that a bidder cannot make a capital gain on any shares purchased, since if he offers less than $s_i y^W$ for class i (i = A or B), where y^W represents the value of the firm's dividend stream under the winning management team (W = R or I), individual shareholders in that class can do better by holding onto their shares and receiving their pro-rata share of the value $s_i y^W$ in the post-takeover company. Hence the only return a bidder can make is through the private benefits of control that he receives if he wins.[9]

3.3. Form of bid

The most general bid we consider is an unconditional, restricted (i.e., partial) offer (but see section 6). That is, the bidder offers to buy up to a fraction f_i of class i at a price of p_i per 100% of class i and will prorate equally if more than f_i is tendered. For example, if the bidder makes an offer for 50 class A shares at a price of $1 per share and 100 shares are tendered, then half of the shares tendered by each investor are returned, and the bidder pays out a total of $50. On the other hand, if 40 shares are tendered, the bidder takes them all and pays out $40.

It turns out that a restricted offer, which allows a bidder to pay a premium on only a fraction of the shares in a class, can be a very potent tool in a takeover contest. Such an offer may sometimes cause difficulties for the bidder, however. For example, in some circumstances it may be possible for a management team to realize its private benefits of control z only if it carries out a second-stage merger with another firm it operates. A problem with such a merger is that management may face allegations of 'unfair' treatment by minority shareholders who tendered shares that were not taken up in the original tender offer. In particular, if in its initial tender offer management bid for a fraction f of the class A shares, say, at a price p (per 100% of the class),

---

[9]This is the free-rider problem discussed in Grossman and Hart (1980). We ignore the possibility that the corporate charter explicitly allows a successful bidder to dilute minority shareholder property rights by diverting company profits to himself, e.g., in the form of salary (the private benefits z do, however, represent an implicit dilution of such property rights). Indeed there is a growing body of evidence that acquirers in hostile takeovers do not benefit significantly from the acquisition; see Jensen and Ruback (1983, p. 22). However, see Demsetz (1986) on the existence of large shareholders and Shleifer and Vishny (1986) on their role in reducing the free-rider problem.

then in the second-stage merger minority shareholders whose shares were returned might have good grounds for arguing that the 'fair' value of these shares is at least p and so this is what they should be paid.[10] If the courts accept this, management will be forced to buy up the whole class for p, which means that its attempt to pay a premium on only a fraction of shares in the class fails. In other words, under these conditions, a restricted offer within a class is impossible.

Of course, management will not always face this problem. In some cases, it will be able to realize the benefits z while maintaining the firm as a separate operation. Under these conditions restricted offers are presumably feasible. In what follows we therefore distinguish between the case in which restricted offers can be used and the case in which they cannot. It is also worth noting that it may be easier for the incumbent to realize z without a second-stage merger than for the rival. We therefore also look at the case in which the incumbent can take advantage of a restricted offer, but the rival cannot.[11]

4. The situation in which neither the incumbent nor the rival can benefit from a restricted offer within a class

Consider first the case in which neither R nor I can take advantage of a restricted offer within a class. In other words, each party must make an offer for 'any or all' of the shares of a class at a particular price. Note that quite different prices can be offered for the different classes; moreover, the bidder can choose not to buy any shares of one class or equivalently to offer such a low price that none are tendered.

To analyze the control contest, it is useful to start with the situation in which the incumbent's private benefit of control is insignificant. This situation

[10]Shareholders may be able to claim that the fair value exceeds p. In fact our assumption is that shareholders will be able to claim the fair value $s_i y^W$ if $s_i y^W > p$. In *Weinberger v. UOP*, 475 A.2d 701 (Del. ch., 1983), the Delaware Supreme Court clearly stated that the 'fair' value in an appraisal of a minority squeeze-out includes consideration of the future benefits to be expected from the merger. See Herzel and Colling (1984). Note however that federal law does not prohibit second-stage mergers at prices below the first-stage tender price: see *Radol v. Thomas*, 772 F.2d 244 (1985). However, see *A C Acquisitions v. Anderson, Clayton & Co.*, 519 A.2d 103 (Del. ch., 1986), pp. 113–114, for recognition of the 'coercive' nature of a restricted offer, where 'coercive' seems to refer to the fact that a restricted offer at a high price per share can lead shareholders to tender to a value-decreasing bidder. See Eisenberg (1976) for a discussion of fiduciary responsibility and Fischel (1983) for a discussion of the appraisal remedy and of *Weinberger v. UOP*.

[11]We have assumed that the corporate charter is designed by an entrepreneur who chooses the security-voting structure to maximize the market value of securities issued. From a social point of view, the appropriate objective function is the market value of securities plus the net present value of private benefits of control enjoyed by management. The divergence in objectives arises from our implicit assumption that the entrepreneur cannot charge management for its private benefits of control, e.g., by setting an entry fee. There are two justifications for this assumption. First, if management is risk-averse and private benefits are uncertain at the contracting date, management may not be prepared to pay a significant entry fee. Secondly, if management has limited initial wealth, it may not be able to afford a significant entry fee.

is equivalent to one in which I is an arbitrageur (rather than the incumbent) who holds a small amount of the company's securities before R's offer arrives, and can make a counteroffer such that if R loses, the status quo is maintained.

4.1. Situation 1: z^I is insignificant in relation to z^R, y^I, y^R

To see under what conditions R will make a bid, it is useful to consider how I will respond to such a bid. As argued above, it will not pay I to make a losing counteroffer. Now, in making a winning counterbid, I cannot profit from offering less than $s_i y^I$ for either class i, since then nobody from this class will tender (given that they expect I to win). On the other hand, I cannot afford to offer more than $s_i y^I$ for either class i, since his private benefit is negligible. Hence I's best (breakeven) response to a bid from R is to:

(*) offer exactly $s_A y^I$ for class A and $s_B y^I$ for class B.

The issue for R then is whether he can make a bid that (a) will win him more than the fraction alpha of the corporation's votes if it is unopposed, (b) will deter the best response (*) from I, i.e., if both these offers are made, R will win the necessary fraction of votes alpha, and (c) is profitable for R.

Consider first the case in which $y^R > y^I$, i.e., R is the superior management team (in terms of security benefits). Then the following bid by R satisfies (a)–(c): offer a price just above $s_A y^R$ for class A and just above $s_B y^R$ for class B. To see why, note that with only this bid on the table shareholders from both classes will tender to R because, whether they think R will win or not, they are being offered more than the post-acquisition value of the company. In addition, if I resists with the counteroffer (*), I will receive no shares since his offer is dominated by R's; hence R's bid does deter I. Finally, R makes a profit of z^R on his offer because he breaks even on the shares tendered to him (he pays what they are worth).

There is no more profitable bid for R that wins him control. This follows immediately from our previous observation that, since no bidder can make a capital gain on shares tendered to him, a bidder's return is bounded above by his private benefit of control.

Consider next the case in which $y^R < y^I$, i.e., I is the superior management team. Then to deter I, R must offer (slightly) more than $s_A y^I$ for the class A shares if $v_A > $ alpha (i.e., if the superior voting class by itself provides him with enough votes to win) and (slightly) more than $s_A y^I$ for class A shares and $s_B y^I$ for class B shares if $v_A \leq$ alpha (i.e., if he needs both classes to win). The reason is that, if R does not make such an offer, I can pick up the $(1 - \text{alpha})$ votes necessary to defeat R with the counteroffer (*). Now at the price $s_i y^I$, R makes a capital loss on the class i shares (their value to him is only $s_i y^R$), and so he will purchase as few shares as possible. Hence, if $v_A > $ alpha, R will purchase only the class A stock and his capital loss will be $L = s_A(y^I - y^R)$;

while, if $v_A \leq$ alpha, R will have to purchase both classes and his capital loss will be $L = (y^I - y^R)$. This loss must be weighed against R's private benefit of control, z^R. We may conclude that R will win control if and only if $z^R > L$.

Summary of situation 1

(1) If $y^R \geq y^I$, R wins control with an offer of (just above) $s_A y^R$ for class A shares and $s_B y^R$ for class B shares. All shareholders will tender and the market value of the firm will be y^R.[12]

(2) Given $y^R < y^I$, R will win control if and only if $z^R > L$, where $L = s_A(y^I - y^R)$ if $v_A >$ alpha and $L = (y^I - y^R)$ if $v_A \leq$ alpha. In the event $z^R > L$, R will offer (just above) $s_A y^I$ for the class A shares if $v_A >$ alpha (and the class B shares will be worth $s_B y^R$); while, if $v_A \leq$ alpha, R will offer (just above) $s_A y^I$ for the A shares and (just above) $s_B y^I$ for the B shares. Given $z^R > L$ (i.e., R does take control), the market value of the firm will therefore be $V = s_A y^I + s_B y^R$ if $v_A >$ alpha, and y^I if $v_A \leq$ alpha. We can rewrite this as $V = y^R + L$. On the other hand, if $z^R \leq L$ (i.e., the incumbent retains control), the market value of the firm will be y^I.

It is easy to see from the summary how the security-voting structure influences the outcome of the control contest. If $y^R \geq y^I$, it has no effect, since R wins regardless of the structure. However, if $y^R < y^I$, the security-voting structure does matter, since it determines the size of L and hence both whether R takes control and the value of the firm if R does take control. Shareholders never benefit when an inferior rival wins control, since the market value doesn't rise above y^I (its status quo value) and in some cases it falls (in particular, when R has to buy up only the A shares). Furthermore, the capital loss experienced by shareholders is decreasing in L. Therefore if $y^I > y^R$, shareholders want to make L large. This goal is accomplished by setting s_A large, alpha large, and v_A small. In particular, *either* one share–one vote (or, more generally, any structure with $s_A = 1$) *or* a dual-class structure with $s_A < 1$ but $v_A \leq$ alpha will dominate all other structures, since both force R to buy up 100% of the profit stream and so the firm's market value never falls below y^I. In contrast with any other structure there will be values of y^I, y^R, and z^R such that an inferior rival takes control by buying up less than 100% of the profit stream and reducing the value of the firm.

Under one share–one vote, alpha is irrelevant, since R has to buy 100% of the single class regardless (the same is true if $s_A = 1$). In contrast, alpha is important if $s_A < 1$ because it determines whether R has to buy up both classes or just class A shares. Further, the only optimal dual-class structure is

---

[12] Market value here refers to the value of the firm once the characteristics of the incumbent and rival become common knowledge.

one in which the winning bidder must buy 100% of all classes. This is really equivalent to a one share–one vote security structure.

One striking feature of situation 1 is that all security-voting structures allow a superior rival to win control at the price y^R. This is a consequence of the assumption that z^I is insignificant and so I cannot use his private benefit to fight off the rival. We now drop this assumption, considering first the polar opposite of situation 1: where z^I is significant but z^R is not.

4.2. Situation 2: z^R is insignificant in relation to z^I, y^I, y^R

Essentially we can adapt the analysis of situation 1, reversing the roles of R and I. It is now useful to start by considering the most aggressive bid that R can make for the firm. Given that he will win control, R is prepared to:

(**) offer $s_A y^R$ for the class A shares and $s_B y^R$ for the class B shares,

since this will allow him just to break even. R cannot offer more because his private benefit is insignificant; on the other hand, he cannot offer less and receive any shares, since given that he is expected to win, shareholders will prefer to hold on than to tender.

If $y^I \geq y^R$, it is clear that I can easily defeat this offer by bidding (just above) $s_A y^I$, $s_B y^I$ for the two classes, since then, whomever shareholders think will win, they will tender to I rather than to R. Hence in this case R will not make an offer at all and I will retain control.

On the other hand, suppose $y^I < y^R$. Now, to defeat R's offer, I must take a capital loss on the shares he purchases. Since $v_A \geq \frac{1}{2} \geq (1 - \text{alpha})$ (i.e., the class A shares provide enough votes for I to defeat R), I will minimize this loss either by offering (just above) $s_A y^R$ for the class A shares alone, or, if $v_B \geq (1 - \text{alpha})$ and $s_B < s_A$, by offering $s_B y^R$ for the class B shares alone. This makes I's capital loss $L_I = s_A(y^R - y^I)$ if $v_B < (1 - \text{alpha})$, and $L_I = \min(s_A, s_B)(y^R - y^I)$ if $v_B \geq (1 - \text{alpha})$. Of course, I will be prepared to incur this loss only if it is less than his private benefit. We may conclude that, given $y^I < y^R$, R will take control if and only if $z^I \leq L_I$.

We may summarize situation 2 as follows:

Summary of situation 2:

(1) If $y^I \geq y^R$, I retains control and the value of the firm is y^I.

(2) Given $y^I < y^R$, R wins control if and only if $z^I \leq L_I$, where $L_I = s_A(y^R - y^I)$ if $v_B < (1 - \text{alpha})$, and $L_I = \min(s_A, s_B)(y^R - y^I)$ if $v_B \geq (1 - \text{alpha})$. If $z^I \leq L_I$, R makes the offer (**) and the market value of the firm is y^R. If $z^I > L_I$, R does not make an offer and the market value of the firm is y^I.

One asymmetry between situations 1 and 2 should be noted. In situation 1, when $y^R < y^I$, the size of L affects both whether R takes control and the value of the firm in this event; in contrast, in situation 2, when $y^I < y^R$, L_I affects whether I retains control but the value of the firm is independent of L_I in this event. The difference stems from our assumption that in order to win control, R must make an offer that deters I and this offer will disgorge some of R's private benefits; on the other hand, when I retains control, R does not bid at all and so I is not forced to make a deterring offer; hence the value of the firm does not rise above y^I.

The effects of the security-voting structure on control contests in situation 2 are easy to discern. If $y^I \geq y^R$, security-voting structure has no effect since R wins regardless. However, if $y^I < y^R$, security-voting structure does have an effect by determining the size of L_I. When a superior rival takes control, this is good for shareholders because the value of the firm increases from y^I to y^R. Therefore a good security-voting structure is one that maximizes L_I. It follows that one share–one vote [or more generally, $s_A = 1$ and $v_B < (1 - \text{alpha})$] dominates all other structures. In particular, under such a structure $L_I = (y^R - y^I)$, whereas under all other structures $L_I < (y^R - y^I)$.

If we combine situations 1 and 2, we see that one share–one vote [more generally, a security structure with $s_A = 1$ and $v_B < (1 - \text{alpha})$] dominates all other security-voting structures. The intuition for this is that when only one party has a significant private benefit, competition between the two parties is maximized by having them fight over as large a fraction of the firm's profit stream as possible since this puts minimum weight on private benefits in relation to public benefits. Having one class of shares with votes attached is good in this regard because it forces each party to buy up 100% of the profit stream (in the absence of restricted offers). Any other security structure, in contrast, allows at least one party to gain control with a purchase of less than 100% of the profit stream.

When both parties' private benefits are significant, matters become more complicated. We turn next to this case.

4.3. Situation 3: z^I, z^R are both significant (in relation to y^I, y^R)

When both parties have significant private benefits, competition between them is no longer necessarily maximized by having them fight over 100% of the firm's profit stream. As a result, departures from one share–one vote may sometimes increase market value. An example of this possibility was given in section 2.2. In the example, the rival's public and private benefits are both greater than the incumbent's. Hence the rival wins control under any security structure. Under one share–one vote, however, shareholders extract none of R's private benefit. This is because, in the competition over bundles of public benefit y and private benefit z, R is sufficiently dominant in relation to I that

R can win by paying only y^R; which is what shareholders get by free-riding anyway. In contrast, under a pure votes system, the competition takes place over the pure private benefit, and this leads to the extraction of some of R's surplus.

The example shows that when both parties have private benefits, the surplus-extraction effect can dominate the allocative effect described previously. We discuss the importance of this possibility further below. First, however, we complete our analysis.

4.4. Situation 4: z^I, z^R are both insignificant (in relation to y^I, y^R)

This situation is very straightforward. If $y^R > y^I$, R wins control by making an offer at (just above) $s_A y^R$ for the A shares and $s_B y^R$ for the B shares. I cannot resist this offer because he would incur a large capital loss by doing so. On the other hand, if $y^R < y^I$, I retains control, because R cannot afford to bid $s_t y^I$ for either class and this would be required to deter I.

Hence, in situation 4, the superior management team always wins control regardless of the security-voting structure, because neither party can use its private benefit to offset any disadvantage in security benefit.[13] Although this conclusion is fairly obvious, it confirms the idea that private benefits of control are a crucial ingredient in determining optimal security-voting structure.

We may summarize the analysis for the case in which neither the rival nor the incumbent can take advantage of discriminatory restricted offers as follows. One share–one vote [more generally, $s_A = 1$ and $v_B < (1 - \text{alpha})$] dominates all other security-voting structures if either the incumbent's or the rival's private benefit of control is insignificant; if both private benefits are insignificant, one share–one vote is neither better nor worse than other structures; but one share–one vote may not be optimal if both private benefits are significant.

How important are the events described in situation 3 in predicting that firms will find it optimal to deviate from one share–one vote? Our feeling is that, although a high likelihood of situation 3 events may explain some observed departures from one share–one vote, in general the surplus-extraction effect is overwhelmed by the allocation effects identified in situations 1 and 2. As support for this position, note that while the potential private benefits z^R, z^I may sometimes be large (relative to y^R, y^I), corporate law will tend to make it difficult for the controlling party to realize these benefits. The corporation's directors have a fiduciary duty to all shareholders, and overt diversion of wealth to a controlling party at the expense of minority share-

---

[13] There is one case in which this conclusion does not hold and it occurs when there is a security consisting of pure votes ($s_t = 0$). This structure is inferior to all others in situation 4, however, and so will be disregarded.

holders would violate this duty. The controlling party can avoid the conflict of interest between itself and other shareholders by buying out the shareholders, but in this case the courts, in an appraisal proceeding, could decide that it is unfair for the controlling party to get a large benefit without compensating the shareholders. In particular, unless the corporate charter explicitly permits the majority to derive significant benefits from control [through the types of dilution discussed in Grossman and Hart (1980)], minority shareholders can assert and perfect claims against the private benefits enjoyed by the majority. Of course, the courts cannot always be relied upon to ensure that the majority and minority enjoy equal treatment, so the entrepreneur in writing a charter must take into account the possibility that z^R, z^I will sometimes be large. Arguably, however, the chance that both will be simultaneously large can be ignored.

We can sum up as follows:

Proposition 1. Suppose the situation in which both the incumbent's and the rival's private benefits of control are significant can be ignored. Then, if neither party can take advantage of restricted offers, one share–one vote [more generally, a structure in which the superior voting stock receives all the dividends and the inferior voting stock has less than a fraction $(1 - alpha)$ of the votes] dominates all other security-voting structures. Further, under one share–one vote, the choice of alpha is irrelevant.[14]

The conclusion that alpha is irrelevant is, of course, a direct consequence of the prohibition of restricted offers. We relax this assumption in the next section.

5. The situation in which restricted offers are possible

An important characteristic of a restricted offer is that it can defeat an unrestricted offer even when the latter is worth more. For example, under one share–one vote and majority rule, a restricted offer for 50% of the shares at a price per share of 70 will win over an unrestricted offer of 60. This is because, if it is thought that the restricted offeror is going to lose, he will not be prorating the shares he receives. Hence a shareholder will always prefer to tender to the restricted offeror when he is expected to lose. Thus, the restricted offeror wins and shareholders get less than 60 if $\frac{1}{2}70 + \frac{1}{2}y < 60$, where y is the value of dividends under the winner.

---

[14] We have not discussed the social optimality of different security-voting structures. However, it is worth noting that one share–one vote also leads to an efficient outcome. The reason is that a management team's willingness to pay for a single class of voting equity is given by $(y + z)$ and therefore under one share–one vote the corporate control contest will be won by the team with the higher social (i.e., security plus private) benefits.

We begin with a situation in which the incumbent can make a restricted offer, but the rival cannot. This might be because the rival has to undertake a second-stage merger to realize his private benefit of control, whereas the incumbent can realize his private benefit by operating the firm as an independent company.

A restricted offer is in fact useful to the incumbent only if his private benefit is significant. The reason is that only in this situation does I offer a premium. That is, if z^1 is insignificant, I cannot do better than make the breakeven offer $s_i y^1$ for class i, in which case he might as well accept all shares tendered to him.

Out of the four situations considered in the last section, therefore, the analysis changes only in situations 2 and 3. In situation 2, it is now cheaper for I to resist the bid (**) by R when $y^R > y^1$, since he needs to buy up only some of the class A or class B shares at the price $s_i y^R$. In fact, I may choose to buy a combination of A and B shares. To see what I's optimal strategy is, note that the effective cost of a class A vote is $(s_A/v_A)(y^R - y^1)$ since, in exchange for the payment $s_A y^R$ for class A, I receives v_A votes and gets a security worth $s_A y^1$. The corresponding cost of a B vote is $(s_B/v_B)(y^R - y^1)$. Therefore, if $(s_A/v_A) \leq (s_B/v_B)$, I will buy only class A shares – in fact the fraction $(1 - \text{alpha})/v_A$ of the class; while, if $(s_A/v_A) \geq (s_B/v_B)$, I will buy only class B shares if $v_B \geq (1 - \text{alpha})$; and all the B shares plus some A shares if $v_B < (1 - \text{alpha})$. I's capital loss is therefore now measured by

$$L_I = \begin{cases} (1 - \text{alpha})(s_A/v_A)(y^R - y^1) & \text{if } s_A/v_A \leq s_B/v_B, \\ (1 - \text{alpha})(s_B/v_B)(y^R - y^1) & \text{if } s_A/v_A > s_B/v_B \text{ and} \\ & v_B \geq (1 - \text{alpha}), \\ \{s_B + (1 - \text{alpha} - v_B)(s_A/v_A)\} \\ \times (y^R - y^1) & \text{if } s_A/v_A > s_B/v_B \text{ and} \\ & v_B < (1 - \text{alpha}). \end{cases}$$

Except for this change in L_I, everything else stays the same in the summary of situation 2 given in the last section.

Two points should be noted. First, under one share–one vote, $L_I = (1 - \text{alpha})(y^R - y^1)$ [since I must buy up a fraction $(1 - \text{alpha})$ of the single class of equity], whereas under any other structure $L_I \leq (1 - \text{alpha})(y^R - y^1)$. The latter observation follows from the fact that it is always feasible for I to accumulate the fraction $(1 - \text{alpha})$ of votes he requires by buying a fraction $(1 - \text{alpha})$ of each class A and B; the cost of this strategy is $(1 - \text{alpha})(y^R - y^1)$ and so the cost of the optimal strategy cannot be higher.[15] Since we observed in section 3 that a large value of L_I is good, it follows that (given

---

[15] In fact it will be strictly lower unless $(s_A/v_A) = (s_B/v_B)$.

alpha) one share–one vote again dominates all other security-voting structures.[16]

Second, L_1 is now strictly decreasing in alpha. It follows that alpha now matters in situation 2, and in fact alpha = 0.5 is optimal. Therefore, since alpha is irrelevant in situations 1 and 4 and, if we continue to ignore situation 3 on the same grounds as in section 4, we have:

Proposition 2. Suppose the possibility that the incumbent's and the rival's private benefits are simultaneously significant can be ignored. Then if only I can take advantage of a restricted offer, one share–one vote and alpha = 0.5 dominates all other security-voting structures.

We turn next to the case in which both the rival and the incumbent can take advantage of restricted offers. The only further change this makes is when z^R is significant, since restricted offers do not benefit R otherwise. Therefore it is now situation 1 that is altered. In particular, if $y^R < y^I$, then R, in making a bid that deters I's bid (*), now needs to buy only a fraction of class A or B shares. To see what R's optimal strategy is, note that the cost of a class A vote is $(s_A/v_A)(y^I - y^R)$ and the cost of a class B vote is $(s_B/v_B)(y^I - y^R)$. Therefore, if $(s_A/v_A) \leq (s_B/v_B)$, R will buy the fraction (alpha$/v_A$) of class A shares if $v_A \geq$ alpha, and all the class A shares plus a fraction (alpha $- v_A)/v_B$ of the class B shares if $v_A <$ alpha; while, if $(s_A/v_A) > (s_B/v_B)$, R will buy all the class B shares and a fraction (alpha $- v_B)/v_A$ of the class A shares. R's capital loss is therefore now measured by

$$L = \begin{cases} (s_A/v_A)(y^I - y^R)\text{alpha} & \text{if } s_A/v_A \leq s_B/v_B \text{ and} \\ & v_A \geq \text{alpha,} \\ \{s_A + (\text{alpha} - v_A)(s_B/v_B)\} \\ \times (y^I - y^R) & \text{if } s_A/v_A \leq s_B/v_B \text{ and} \\ & v_A < \text{alpha,} \\ \{s_B + (\text{alpha} - v_B)(s_A/v_A)\} \\ \times (y^I - y^R) & \text{if } s_A/v_A > s_B/v_B. \end{cases}$$

---

[16] To be precise, it strictly dominates all structures with $(s_A/v_A) \neq (s_B/v_B)$ and is equivalent to dual-class structures with $(s_A/v_A) = (s_B/v_B)$. This conclusion generalizes to the case of n classes of shares, where class i is assigned a fraction s_i of dividends and v_i of the votes. An incumbent who wants to buy up as small a fraction of the firm's profit stream as possible at the deterring price of y^R (per 100%), but who needs to acquire a fraction (1 − alpha) of the votes, will solve the linear programming problem: minimize $(f_1 s_1 + f_2 s_2 + \cdots + f_n s_n)$ subject to $(f_1 v_1 + f_2 v_2 + \cdots + f_n v_n) \geq (1 - \text{alpha})$, where f_i is the fraction of class i purchased. The value of this problem, S_1, satisfies $S_1 \leq (1 - \text{alpha})$ with equality if and only if $(s_1/v_1) = \cdots = (s_n/v_n)$. The first part of this statement follows from the fact that $f_1 = \cdots = f_n = (1 - \text{alpha})$ is a feasible solution. The second part follows from the fact that the first-order conditions for the linear programming problem imply that the solution cannot be interior unless $(s_1/v_1) = \cdots = (s_n/v_n)$. For further details, see Grossman and Hart (1987).

In the event that $z^R > L$, the value of the firm is given as before by

$$V = y^R + L.$$

For the same reasons as in section 4, a large value of L is good for shareholders. Therefore, one share–one vote continues to dominate all other structures in situation 1 (for a given alpha). In particular, one share–one vote yields $L = \text{alpha}(y^1 - y^R)$ (since I must buy up a fraction alpha of the single class of equity), whereas all other structures yield $L \leq \text{alpha}(y^1 - y^R)$ [since it is always feasible for R to win control by buying a fraction alpha of each class at a cost of $\text{alpha}(y^1 - y^R)$]. One important difference from section 4, however, is that L is increasing in alpha and so alpha = 1 (or arbitrarily close to 1) is now optimal in situation 1.

If we put situations 1, 2, and 4 together for the case in which R and I can both make restricted offers (continuing to ignore situation 3), we see that one share–one vote is optimal in all cases, but there is a conflict over alpha. The point is that, in situation 2, a low value of alpha is good, since it forces an incumbent with a significant private benefit to buy a large fraction of the firm's profit stream, thereby diluting the distorting effect of this benefit; whereas in situation 1, a high value of alpha is good for similar reasons concerning the rival. Where between 0.5 and 1 the optimal value of alpha should lie therefore depends on the relative importance of situations 1 and 2. We may summarize as follows:

Proposition 3. Suppose the possibility that the incumbent's and rival's private benefits are simultaneously significant can be ignored. Then, if both R and I can take advantage of restricted offers, one share–one vote is optimal.[17] *The optimal choice of alpha will be close to 0.5 if the likelihood of I's private benefit being significant is relatively high, and close to 1 if the likelihood of R's private benefit being significant is relatively high.*

Although one share–one vote continues to be an optimal security-voting structure in the presence of restricted offers, it no longer perfectly protects shareholder property rights. This is clear from the example at the beginning of this section. If $y^1 = 60$, $z^1 = 0$, $y^R = 40$, $z^R = 15$, and alpha = 0.5, R will win control with a restricted offer for 50% of the shares at just above 60. The point is that, even though the value of the firm falls to 50, I cannot resist this offer, because his best break-even counteroffer is an unrestricted bid at 60. Of course, it should not be surprising that value-reducing bids are possible in the

---

[17]To be precise, for each alpha one share–one vote dominates all structures with $(s_A/v_A) \neq (s_B/v_B)$. The situation $(s_A/v_A) = (s_B/v_B)$ is equivalent to one share–one vote in the presence of restricted offers by R and I. Again, this conclusion generalizes to the case of n classes of shares. See footnote 16 and Grossman and Hart (1987).

presence of restricted offers, since, as we have noted previously, there are close parallels between restricted offers and dual-class share structures.

6. Further remarks

6.1. Private benefits, freeze-out mergers, and self-tenders

It is sometimes argued that the ability of minority shareholders to free-ride on a bidder's improvement in a company is limited by the possibility of freeze-out mergers. We have already allowed for *partial* freeze-out mergers; in fact, the private benefit z can be interpreted as that part of total benefits $(y + z)$ that a management team can divert to itself using such a merger. In the case of an extreme freeze-out merger, however, where minority shareholders receive no benefits at all by not tendering, i.e., $y^R = y^I = 0$, security structure is irrelevant, and all that matters is the fraction of votes each party requires to win control.[18] If we combine the case of extreme freeze-out mergers with that of partial freeze-outs, we see that there is still a strong argument for one share–one vote. In particular, since one share–one vote is optimal when freeze-outs are limited and is not suboptimal when they aren't, one share–one vote continues to dominate all other security structures. It is also worth noting that the rival's ability to freeze-out is arguably different from the incumbent's. If the rival can engage in a complete freeze-out while the incumbent cannot, we are in the section 5 situation in which the rival's private benefit is likely to dominate the incumbent's, and we can apply Proposition 3 to conclude that one share–one vote and alpha = 1 is optimal. On the other hand, if the incumbent can engage in a complete freeze-out while the rival cannot, we are in the section 5 situation in which the incumbent's private benefit is likely to dominate the rival's, and we can apply Proposition 3 to conclude that one share–one vote and alpha = 0.5 is optimal.

Analogous comments can be made about defensive self-tenders by incumbent management. If the incumbent can use the firm's assets to finance a self-tender, the incumbent's offer becomes equivalent to an offer by a party with a large private benefit. For example, if $y^I = 100$, $z^I = 1$, and the incumbent can pledge 20% of the company's assets to finance a defensive self-tender, then the incumbent is capable of paying $1 + (0.2)100 = 21$ for

---

[18] To see this, note that a bidding party who tenders for a security class consisting of votes and dividends in a particular proportion is effectively tendering for the pure votes, since the dividends are worthless under his management. That is, all security structures are equivalent to one in which one security consists of pure votes and the other of pure dividends. The choice of alpha is still important, however. In particular, in the case in which both the incumbent and the rival can make restricted offers, the rival's willingness to pay for the fraction alpha of votes is (z^R/alpha) per vote, while the incumbent's willingness to pay for the fraction (1 − alpha) of votes is $(z^R/(1-\text{alpha}))$. Therefore, an increase in alpha will increase the degree of competition between the rival and incumbent to the extent that $(z^R/\text{alpha}) < (z^I/(1-\text{alpha}))$.

alpha of the votes. Thus the outcome of a control contest will be as if his private benefits are 21 rather than 1. If it is legally feasible for the incumbent to act as above, and this causes the incumbent effectively to have large private benefits in relation to the rival, then Proposition 3 can be applied to conclude that one share–one vote and alpha = 0.5 is optimal.[19]

6.2. More general offers

So far we have considered only different types of restricted offers a bidder might make. More complicated offers are theoretically feasible, however. For example, consider the case of one share–one vote. Then a rival with characteristics (y^R, z^R) could make the following offer: he will pay just above y^R (per 100%) if more than the fraction alpha of shares is tendered to him, and a large amount P (per 100%) if less than the fraction alpha of shares is tendered. Such an offer is more general than the restricted offers we have considered in that it makes the payment for shares a function of the fraction tendered.

It turns out that an offer like this – in which more is paid if the bidder loses than if he wins! – is remarkably powerful in deterring competition from the incumbent (or anyone else). The reason is that the only way for the incumbent to block this bid is by paying more than P (per 100%) for a fraction (1 − alpha) of the shares. In particular, if the incumbent makes any offer (however complicated or sophisticated) that cause him to pay out less than P (per 100%), this offer cannot win against R because, if shareholders expect it to win, they can do better by tendering to R and receiving P (which R has guaranteed in the event that he loses). It follows that I's losses will be at least $(1 - \text{alpha})(p - y^I)$, which will exceed his private benefit z^I if P is sufficiently large. Hence I will not make a counteroffer.[20]

Given that R's offer deters competition from the incumbent, R will, of course, win control, since all shareholders will tender to him at above y^R (this is better than holding on and receiving y^R). Hence the rival is able to obtain control at just above y^R and make a net profit of z^R, even if y^R is much smaller than y^I, i.e., even if the rival is far inferior to the incumbent. That is, with general offers like these, the rival will *always* gain control.

We see then that if general offers are allowed, a one share–one vote security structure no longer protects shareholder property rights. However, no other security structure does better: the rival can win at a price of y^R whatever the

---

[19]See *A C Aquisitions v. Anderson Clayton*, 519 A.2d 103 (Del. ch., 1986) for comments on the legality of defensive self-tender offers. See also Bradley and Rozensweig (1985) and Harris and Raviv (1988) for a discussion of self-tenders.

[20]R's offer to pay more if he loses than if he wins is akin to a firm's announcing that it will lower its output price if any other firm enters its market. It is hardly surprising that such an offer deters entry by another bidder.

structure. Hence to the extent that general offers like these are not always used (although they do not appear to be illegal, for some reason they are *not* used), one share–one vote still dominates all other security structures.

6.3. More complex security structures

So far we have analyzed the optimal security structure in a context in which all claims to income are proportional, i.e., each security is characterized by a share 's' of profit. We have thus excluded debt, warrants, convertible debentures, etc. To incorporate such securities in the model we would have to consider nonlinear sharing rules that, say, give the ith security a function $f_i(y)$ of total profit y. It can be shown that if these functions are restricted to be nondecreasing in profit, then (if private benefits are not simultaneously large) an optimal security-voting structure will consist of a combination of riskless debt and one share–one vote common stock.

Another restrictive assumption made is that the charter specifies voting rights to be independent of future information. This excludes risky debt where a default shifts control (i.e., votes) from equityholders to debtholders. It also excludes nonvoting preferred shares that obtain voting rights consequent to a series of low dividend payments. A careful analysis of such state-contingent voting rights would involve studying a multiperiod model, and this is deferred to future work. However, we think that the basic principle we have identified will still apply: tying votes to shares on a one-to-one basis is most likely to cause control to shift to an outsider who will raise the market value of the firm.

The preceding draws attention to a further restrictive assumption, namely that the security-voting structure is responsible for allocating control, while the managerial compensation scheme is responsible for assuring that management maximizes profit to the best of its ability. In reality, the allocation of control and the managerial compensation scheme are not completely separable. An entrepreneur who sets up a corporation will make various investments of time and other resources, for which adequate compensation may be impossible unless the entrepreneur possesses the residual rights inherent in control.[21] For this reason, parties to the initial capitalization of the corporation will try to allocate control changes in a manner that is as sensitive to public information as is feasible. For example, in the case of debt, the contract will explicitly define default events in which failure to make an immediate payment in full will shift control from management to debt holders. Presumable, the award of ordinary voting rights, which would allow the debtholders to achieve control

---

[21] See Grossman and Hart (1986) for an analysis of the determinants of the allocation of control rights.

independent of a default event, gives insufficient protection to the entrepreneur (and possibly other securityholders) in relation to its benefits.[22]

6.4. Vote selling

We have assumed throughout that it is illegal or infeasible for a party to make a tender offer for the irrevocable proxies of securityholders, in which he pays only for the votes and gets none of the dividend claims.[23] If an acquirer or an investment bank could profitably unbundle votes from shares and repackage a firm's security-voting structure, then securityholders would not be able to protect themselves from high-private-benefit but low-security-benefit acquisitions, and the outcome of any control contest would be as if the firm had all of its votes attached to non-dividend-paying securities.[24]

This assumption – that an acquirer can tender directly for votes no matter what type of security-voting structure is chosen by the firm – is made by Harris and Raviv (1988) in their analysis of optimal security-voting structures. Nevertheless, they reach conclusions similar to ours because *each* securityholder, in tendering his votes, assumes that he will be pivotal to the outcome of the control contest, and thus *his* tender decision will induce a change in the capital value of any dividend-paying securities he owns. In contrast, we assume that no shareholder thinks his tender decision will be pivotal, but the acquirer cannot separate votes from shares in his offer if the security structure has tied them together.

6.5. Several rivals

In section 4, we considered how the surplus-extraction role of the security-voting structure can conflict with the allocative role if the incumbent or the acquirer has private benefits of control. Our analysis and results would be essentially unchanged if, instead of considering competition between the acquirer and the incumbent, we had considered competition between two acquirers. One difference is that if we interpret I as another rival rather than the incumbent, then setting alpha > 0.5 no longer makes it easier for I to

---

[22] See Aghion and Bolton (1986) and Jensen and Meckling (1976) for a discussion of this and related points.

[23] Easterbrook and Fischel (1983) argue that a public market in votes separated from dividend claims is illegal.

[24] For example, an acquirer could make an offer to shareholders in a one share–one vote company that paid them a small cash amount $p and gave them one share of a new fund in exchange for each share of their existing securities. The new fund would pass through all dividends, but the acquirer would maintain voting control of the shares deposited in the fund. Acquirers who competed in this manner would, in effect, be making direct offers for votes, and the outcome would be as if the firm had a two-class voting structure in which one class had all the votes and none of the dividends.

attain control. The reason is that the acquisition of (1 − alpha) by I would not entitle him to the private benefits of control. Our analysis would have to be modified so that I makes an offer for alpha rather than (1 − alpha) when he competes against R. Our results on the optimality of one share–one vote, however, would be unchanged.

7. Empirical evidence on deviations from one share–one vote

Our theoretical results can be further clarified by reference to empirical evidence on deviations from one share–one vote. First, our model assumes that securities are widely held and that the market for corporate control is the important factor in allocating control. We thus have nothing to say about the much more complicated specific control agreements that are used in closely held corporations.[25] Second, since until very recently one share–one vote was a requirement for listing on the New York Stock Exchange, it is necessary to look elsewhere for widely held companies with different voting structures.

DeAngelo and DeAngelo (1985, p. 39) identified 78 companies publicly traded on the American Stock Exchange and over the counter (out of a universe of thousands of companies) that had classes of securities with differing voting rights. They found that in a majority of the cases that deviated from one share–one vote, the structure gave the incumbent enough votes so that a change in control was impossible without his approval. In particular, the observed deviation from one share–one vote did not create a situation in which widely held securities had differing effective voting rights; instead it created a situation in which the incumbent had all the effective votes necessary to maintain control, i.e., alpha was effectively equal to one. In our model this can occur when the benefits of preventing value-decreasing hostile control changes outweigh the costs of preventing value-increasing control changes, i.e., where the rival's private benefit is likely to be large, but his security benefits are likely to be less than those of the incumbent (see Proposition 3).

In sections 4 and 5, we emphasize that, when private benefits are small in relation to security benefits, one share–one vote and alpha < 1 are generally optimal. Empirically, as we noted earlier, management's fiduciary responsibility and the minority shareholders' appraisal remedy limit private benefits. The DeAngelo and DeAngelo study suggests that, when there is a deviation from

---

[25] Voting rights are most important to securityholders who are not promised a particular payout, but instead a claim to discretionary payments. Thus, our theory excludes default-free debt and preferred stock issues that are equivalent to such debt (but see section 6.3). Similarly, another deviation from one share–one vote involves mutual insurance companies, banks, and investment funds, where the takeover bid mechanism cannot operate to effect control changes. In such firms, the types of activities engaged in are more severely circumscribed by charter provisions than is the case in the typical common stock corporation. This, combined with industry regulation and competition, reduces somewhat the discretionary character of the payments given to securityholders. See Mayers and Smith (1986) for an analysis of mutual versus stock insurance companies.

alpha < 1 and one share–one vote, it is for the purpose of maintaining family control over an enterprise. Presumably in such cases the family receives significant private benefits from control. If the private benefits were small, the family would find it in its interest to allow the market to determine control changes, and be rewarded for these benefits by a compensation agreement that paid it following a change in control. Because the private benefits are large, however, the family prefers a charter that makes hostile bids impossible.[26]

Indeed, if the private benefits are available to compensate the family for the sunk investments in setting up the company, then it can be efficient for the charter to give the family the power to block hostile offers from other parties seeking to acquire these private benefits.[27] If the private benefits represent a return to sunk investments, it would not be efficient to have the voting securities widely held, as in our model, since the family would then have to compete against hostile offers and thus pay securityholders for the rights to their private benefits.

Therefore the DeAngelo and DeAngelo results are consistent with our theoretical results about optimal security structure. That is, though deviations from one share–one vote occasionally occur, they do so in situations in which private benefits are large.

8. Conclusions

We conclude with some remarks about the relevance of our model to the current policy debate on whether a corporation should be required to have a one share–one vote security structure as a condition for listing on various physical or electronic stock exchanges. First, our results show that deviations from one share–one vote can be a characteristic of a corporate charter that is in securityholders' best interest. We thus see no reason to interfere with the ability of a new company to choose a corporate charter and security structure that gives it the lowest cost of raising capital.

Our analysis has not dealt with the issue of a change in the security-voting structure by an old company which has a one share–one vote charter.

---

[26] If a compensation agreement were used when private benefits were large, the compensation ('golden parachute') would have to be large. Clearly, compensation that is a significant percentage of the market value creates moral hazards that might lead the incumbent to induce a control change even if it did not raise market value. More to the point, the best compensation rule would involve giving the incumbent a share of market value, but when the private benefits are large this has negative risk-bearing consequences, and hence can be a very costly method of inducing the incumbent to allow the market to decide who should have control.

[27] That is, private benefits may represent a return to activities for which the intial security-holders were willing to pay. Leo Herzel has suggested a type of private benefit that may lead to alpha = 1. A family may sink costs into setting up a newspaper because of its desire to enjoy the future benefits of editorial control. These benefits are a return to sunk investment, but a rival who took control could get these benefits (possibly by changing editorial style) without having sunk the costs.

Nevertheless, we would view such a change with suspicion. If such a corporation changes its structure so that incumbent management is entrenched and isolated from the market for corporate control, our result that one share–one vote is generally in securityholders' interest, and the fact that managerial entrenchment is in a manager's self-interest, leads us to believe that securityholders may be harmed. We would hold this view even if a majority (or two thirds) of shareholders voted for the change. The role of the market for corporate control derives from the fact that it is generally optimal for small shareholders to vote with management, and not devote the time and effort to read proxy statements and form an independent view. Hence, the fact that shareholders vote for a withdrawal from the corporate control market is only a weak defense of management's position.

The preceding observation may apply with less force to a corporation in which management already holds a majority of the votes, and wants to change the voting structure so that it may hold fewer shares of profit, yet still maintain voting control. For example, a family may wish to raise capital for other projects, or to diversify some of its wealth out of a company it founded. It does not necessarily want to sell its shares, since this would entail a loss of voting control, so it separates its shares from its votes by creating a class of shares with lower dividend claims but more votes than the common shares. If the initial shareholders expected management to maintain voting control, this change in security structure is consistent with the original desire to isolate the company from the corporate control market, and hence should not be interfered with. Of course, this conclusion would not be valid if shareholders instead expected that management would sell its combined shares and votes and relinquish control.

Even if it is undesirable to allow *ex-post* changes in security-voting structures, this has no particular implication for legislation on listing requirements. An exchange's listing requirements are an attempt to provide information to traders about the characteristics of the securities being traded. (Until recently, a trader of shares on the New York Stock Exchange would know, merely from the fact that the firm was trading on the NYSE, that all of the company's equity had one share–one vote.) We see no reason why traders cannot obtain information elsewhere on the voting structure of the firm. But we also see no reason why an exchange should be prevented from specializing in the trading of shares with a particular voting structure if it wishes to do so.[28]

If *ex post* changes in security-voting structure should be subject to further regulation, it would seem more appropriate to give shareholders dissenting rights of the type that they already have in mergers or other asset sales than to regulate listing rights. In particular, dissenting shareholders should be given appraisal rights allowing them to attempt to show that the value of their holdings has fallen under the proposed change in security-voting structure.

---

[28] See Gordon (1986) for an alternative point of view, however.

References

Aghion, P. and P. Bolton, 1986, An 'incomplete contracts' approach to bankruptcy and the optimal financial structure of the firm, Unpublished paper (Harvard University, Cambridge, MA).

Blair, Douglas, James Gerard and Devra Golbe, 1986, Unbundling the voting rights and residual profit claims of common shares, Unpublished paper (Rutgers University, New Brunswick, NJ).

Bradley, M. and Michael Rosenzweig, 1986, Defensive stock purchases, Harvard Law Review 99, 1377.

DeAngelo, Harry and Linda DeAngelo, 1985, Managerial ownership of voting rights: A study of public corporations with dual classes of common stock, Journal of Financial Economics 14, 33–69.

Demsetz, Harold, 1983, The structure of ownership and the theory of the firm, Journal of Law and Economics 26, 375–390.

Dodd, Peter and Jerold B. Warner, 1983, On corporate governance: A study of proxy contests, Journal of Financial Economics 11, 401–438.

Easterbrook, Frank H. and Daniel R. Fischel, 1982, Corporate control transactions, Yale Law Journal 91, 698–737.

Easterbrook, Frank H. and Daniel R. Fischel, 1983, Voting in corporate law, Journal of Law and Economics 26, 395–428.

Eisenberg, Melvin, 1976, The structure of the corporation: A legal analysis (Little Brown and Co., Boston, MA).

Fischel, Daniel R., 1983, Appraisal remedy in corporate law, American Bar Foundation Research Journal 4, 875–902.

Fischel, Daniel R., 1986, Organized exchanges and the regulation of dual class common stock, Monograph by Lexecon Inc.

Gordon, Jeffrey, 1986, Ties that bond: Dual class common and the problem of shareholder choice, Unpublished paper (New York University, New York, NY).

Grossman, Sanford J. and Oliver D. Hart, 1987, One share/one vote and the market for corporate control, Financial Research Center memorandum no. 76 (Princeton University, Princeton, NJ).

Grossman, Sanford J. and Oliver D. Hart, 1980, Takeover bids, the free-rider problem, and the theory of corporation, Bell Journal of Economics 11, 42–64.

Grossman, Sanford J. and Oliver D. Hart, 1986, The costs and benefits of ownership: A theory of vertical and lateral integration, Journal of Political Economy 94, 691–719.

Harris, Milton and Artur Raviv, 1988, Corporate governance: Voting rights and majority rules, Journal of Financial Economics 20, this issue.

Harris, Milton and Artur Raviv, 1988, Corporate control contests and capital structure, Journal of Financial Economics 20, this issue.

Herzel, Leo and Dale E. Colling, 1984, Squeeze-out mergers in Delaware: The Delaware Supreme Court decision in Weinberger v. UOP, Inc., The Corporation Law Review no. 7, 195–232.

Jensen, Michael C. and William H. Meckling, 1976, Theory of the firm: Managerial behavior, agency costs, and ownership structure, Journal of Financial Economics 3, 305–360.

Jensen, Michael C. and Richard Ruback, 1983, The market for corporate control: The scientific evidence, Journal of Financial Economics 11, 5–50.

Levy, Haim, 1983, Economic evaluation of voting power of common stock, Journal of Finance 38, 79–93.

Mayers, D. and C. Smith, Jr., 1986, Ownership structure and control: The mutualization of stock life insurance companies, Journal of Financial Economics 16, 73–98.

Scharfstein, David, 1985, The disciplinary role of takeovers, Unpublished paper (MIT, Cambridge, MA).

SEC, 1985, The economics of any-or-all, partial, and two-tier tender offers, A study by the office of the Chief Economist (Securities and Exchange Commission, Washington, DC).

Shleifer, Andrei and Robert W. Vishny, 1986, Large shareholders and corporate control, Journal of Political Economy 94, 461–488.

THE DESIGN OF SECURITIES*

Milton HARRIS
University of Chicago, Chicago, IL 60637, USA

Artur RAVIV
Northwestern University, Evanston, IL 60208, USA
Tel Aviv University, Tel Aviv, Israel

Received July 1988, final version received September 1989

This paper investigates the determinants of security design. We consider the assignment of both cash flows and voting rights, focusing on corporate control. We postulate that a conflict of interest exists between contestants for control and outside investors. The conflict arises because private benefits of control give contestants an incentive to acquire control even when this reduces firm value. Security design is a tool for resolving these conflicts and maximizing firm value. Our main result is that a single voting security is optimal.

1. Introduction

This paper investigates the determinants of security design. Why firms finance their investments using predominantly nonvoting debt and voting equity has puzzled economists for some years. For example, Jensen and Meckling (1976) state: 'The issue is... why [firms] obtain [capital] through the particular forms we have observed for such long periods of time' (p. 332). They continue: 'The fact is that no well articulated answer to this question currently exists in the literature of either finance or economics' (p. 332).[1]

---

*The authors gratefully acknowledge the research support of the National Science Foundation. Professor Harris would also like to thank Dimensional Fund Advisors for financial support. In addition, the current version has benefited from the comments of Richard Ruback (the editor), an anonymous referee, and participants in seminars at the University of Chicago, Northwestern, Stanford, Berkeley, the University of California at Los Angeles, Ohio State, Boston College, Wharton, New York University, and the University of British Columbia.

[1] Several attempts have been made to resolve the puzzle. See Alchian and Demsetz (1972), Townsend (1979), Diamond (1984), Gale and Hellwig (1985), Williams (1987), Allen and Gale (1988), and Zender (1988). The first model is based on differing expectations across investors. The next four models are based on private information, and Allen and Gale is based on incomplete markets and transaction costs. Zender focuses on wealth constraints and the transfer of control in bankruptcy. None of these models addresses the issue of voting rights and takeovers.

0304-405X/89/$3.50©1989, Elsevier Science Publishers B.V. (North-Holland)

In our view, security design involves the assignment both of cash flows and voting rights. Since we are interested in the allocation of votes, it is natural to base our approach on the idea that security design is driven by corporate control considerations. We postulate that a conflict of interest exists between contestants for control and outside investors. The conflict arises because contestants are assumed to have private benefits of control. These benefits give contestants an incentive to acquire control even when this reduces the value of the firm. In our approach, security design is a tool for resolving these conflicts and maximizing firm value.

We develop several important insights into the determinants of security design:

- *No cheap votes.* Cheap votes are votes attached to securities whose cash flows are not very sensitive to the outcome of control contests. Such votes enable an inferior candidate to gain control without suffering from the consequent reduction in firm value. Avoiding cheap votes, therefore, makes inferior takeovers more expensive and hence less likely. This increases firm value.
- *Securities are commitment devices.* Jensen and Meckling (1976), among others, emphasize that the entrepreneur or founder bears the agency costs when the firm goes public, because investors anticipate conflicts of interest with management and value the securities issued accordingly. Therefore, the entrepreneur maximizes his wealth by designing securities (including voting rights) that induce him to deviate as little as possible from total-value-maximizing resistance behavior.
- *Extraction of rival's surplus.* The security design affects the extent to which the entrepreneur can capture the rival's benefits of control when the rival takes over the firm. One way the entrepreneur can capture these rents is by keeping voting control of the firm and trading it to the rival for a direct payment. Alternatively, the entrepreneur can design securities that maximize outside investors' ability to extract the rival's benefits in return for their votes in the takeover contest. The entrepreneur captures these rents from investors in the issue price of the securities.

These considerations drive our results. Even more importantly, they will drive the results of any model of security design based on control considerations.

Our main results are:

- A single class of voting securities is strictly superior to multiple classes.
- When the entrepreneur relinquishes voting control upon going public, risky, nonvoting claims should not be sold to outside investors.
- Riskless debt should be *nonvoting* and should never be retained by the entrepreneur.

- It is optimal for the entrepreneur either to retain voting control when he takes the firm public or to retain no votes.
- Under certain sufficient conditions, the single voting security has cash flows that resemble those of levered common stock.

The intuition for having only one voting security follows directly from the insight that cheap votes are suboptimal. To win control, an inferior contestant must purchase securities with sufficient votes to assure victory. To purchase these securities, he must outbid the superior contestant, i.e., he must pay what the securities would be worth under the superior contestant. After the inferior contestant wins, however, the securities will be worth less. This loss constitutes the inferior contestant's cost of winning. If there is more than one class of voting securities, some classes will have less sensitive cash flows per vote than the average. In this case, the inferior contestant can win by purchasing these cheap votes, i.e., by purchasing voting securities whose value is relatively insensitive to the quality of management. The strategy of purchasing cheap votes results in a lower cost of winning control than if there were only one voting security. Therefore, issuing a single class of voting security maximizes the cost to the inferior contestant of winning control.

Selling risky, nonvoting securities to outsiders reduces the sensitivity of the voting security to the controlling party and therefore cheapens the votes. The cost to an inferior contestant of winning control can be raised if the cash flows to such securities are included with the voting security. Also, since no capital gain accrues to risk-free debt if a better manager takes over, no opportunity cost of purchasing this debt is incurred by an inferior contestant. Voting, risk-free debt is the extreme form of cheap votes, hence should not be issued. Moreover, risk-free debt cannot serve as a commitment and should not be held by the incumbent.

The model of this paper is similar to that of our previous papers, Harris and Raviv (1988a, b), and to that of Grossman and Hart (1988). In Harris and Raviv (1988a), we assume that the only securities available are nonvoting debt and a single class of voting equity. We investigate the use of capital structure as an antitakeover device. The models of Harris and Raviv (1988b) and Grossman and Hart (1988) *assume* the securities to be equity with endogenous voting rights. These papers investigate the optimality of one share–one vote (i.e., a single class of equity) and the simple majority rule. The current model makes endogenous both the cash flow characteristics of the securities and their voting rights, and thus analyzes the capital structure puzzle from a more fundamental perspective.

The paper is organized as follows. The model is introduced in section 2. In section 3, we prove the result that the optimal design of securities involves only one voting security. Section 4 provides the other results mentioned above. Section 5 shows that our results are robust to a modification of the basic model, and conclusions are given in section 6. All formal proofs are relegated to an appendix.

2. Model description

We view the design of corporate securities as solving the problem of raising funds while minimizing conflicts of interest arising from private benefits of control. Consequently, we model the choice of securities by an entrepreneur who recognizes that the securities' value will be affected by the extent to which they induce value-increasing takeovers. The model includes a firm, an entrepreneur who is also the firm's incumbent manager, a rival for control, and a set of outside investors. All agents are assumed to be risk-neutral. At the beginning of the model's single period, the entrepreneur takes the firm public, designing and issuing securities that are purchased by the outside investors. Subsequently, a rival for control appears and attempts to purchase voting securities. The incumbent may resist by also purchasing voting securities. The contest is decided by a vote of investors (including contestants). We now describe these elements in detail.

The firm is established and managed by an entrepreneur who owns a one-period project that requires external financing of $I > 0$. To make the problem nontrivial, we assume that I cannot be raised by selling only risk-free debt. At the end of the period, the project returns a nonnegative random cash flow $\tilde{y}$, and the firm is then liquidated. The distribution of $\tilde{y}$ depends on the ability, r, of the manager and is denoted $F(y|r)$. We normalize the ability level to be between zero and one and assume that $\tilde{y}$ takes values over the same range for every ability level. We also assume that larger values of r indicate higher ability in the sense that the conditional distributions $F(\cdot|r)$ are ordered by strict first-order stochastic dominance. We denote the expected cash flow of the project under manager r by $y(r)$ and assume that managers of similar ability produce similar returns, i.e., that $y(r)$ is a continuous function of r. Our ordering on $F(\cdot|r)$ implies that $y(r)$ is monotone increasing in r.

After the firm goes public, a rival considers mounting a control contest. Conflicts of interest between the contestants and outside investors arise, because the contestants derive private, noncontractible benefits from being in control of the firm. By noncontractible, we mean that the securities issued by the firm cannot depend directly on these benefits. Examples include psychic benefits derived from controlling a large enterprise, the ability to transfer resources to one's private use, and the ability to use one's position to further one's private goals. Because of these benefits, a contestant may wish to control the firm even though the other contestant produces higher expected returns.

To simplify the analysis, we consider just two polar cases: either the incumbent has private benefits and not the rival, or the reverse. We denote the benefits of control by B in either case. For the time being we confine our attention to the first case, in which only the incumbent has benefits of control. The other case is considered in section 5.

If the rival has no benefits of control and is less able than the incumbent, he will not initiate a control contest. Thus contests occur only when a more able rival appears. Consequently, we normalize the incumbent's ability to $r = 0$ and assume that a rival of ability $r > 0$ attempts to gain control of the firm. The rival's ability is assumed to be unpredictable when the securities are issued but is observable to everyone once the rival appears. The prior distribution of r is denoted by $F(r)$.

If the takeover is successful, the output distribution is $F(y|r)$; otherwise it is $F(y|0)$. The difference in expected returns between the superior manager and the inferior one is denoted $\Delta y(r)$ if the rival is of ability r, i.e., $\Delta y(r) = y(r) - y(0)$. This difference increases with the ability of the rival.

Outside investors are not contestants for control; they simply purchase and sell securities issued by the firm and vote these securities in corporate elections. In voting, each outside investor votes for the candidate who maximizes the value of his or her portfolio. In selling securities, each investor assumes that his or her decision will have no effect on the outcome of any control contest. Therefore, in any takeover contest, investors take the winner as given and sell to the highest bidder if and only if his offer is at least as high as the value of the security under the management of the given winner.

In a control contest, any rival must obtain more than the fraction α of the votes outstanding to unseat the incumbent. Equivalently, the incumbent must receive at least $\beta = 1 - \alpha$ votes to prevail.[2] The fraction α is taken as exogenously given [see Harris and Raviv (1988b) and Grossman and Hart (1988) for analyses of optimal majority rules].

In going public, the entrepreneur/incumbent designs securities to maximize the revenue he obtains from selling them plus his expected benefits of control. If, at the takeover stage, the incumbent owned the entire firm, he would resist only those takeovers that reduce the total output of the firm, including both private benefits and contractible returns. That is, he would resist only when $y(0) + B > y(r)$ or $B > \Delta y(r)$. For a sole owner, $\Delta y(r)$ can be interpreted as the opportunity cost of resisting a superior rival r. We denote by $\bar{r}$ the critical value of the rival's ability such that if the incumbent owned the entire firm, he would resist only when $r < \bar{r}$ (see fig. 1). We assume that a single-owner incumbent would resist some, but not all, rivals, i.e., that $\bar{r}$ is neither zero nor one. Therefore, by continuity of Δy, $\Delta y(\bar{r}) = B$. We refer to the strategy of resisting if and only if $r < \bar{r}$ as the *single-owner* solution.

---

[2] Charlie Kahn has suggested that a more general governance system would require the winner to obtain different fractions of the votes of each security. This interesting idea is beyond the scope of our investigation.

Firm Return, y

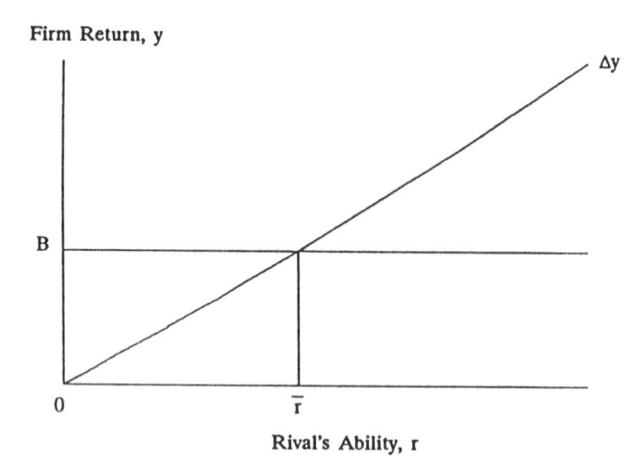

Fig. 1. The single-owner solution.

The curve labeled Δy is the difference in expected return between the rival and the incumbent and is, therefore, the incumbent's opportunity cost of resisting if he owns the entire firm. B is the incumbent's private benefit of control. The interval $(0, \bar{r})$ is the set of rivals against whom resistance is optimal in the single-owner solution, since for such rivals $B > \Delta y$.

Since the incumbent does not own the entire firm at the takeover stage, he will have an incentive to resist takeovers by rivals with abilities in excess of $\bar{r}$. This behavior is anticipated by investors, and therefore reduces the value of the firm when going public. Consequently, it is in the interest of the entrepreneur to make a commitment, insofar as possible, not to oppose highly able rivals (those with ability in excess of $\bar{r}$). The extent to which this is feasible depends on the commitment devices available. If, for example, the entrepreneur can sign a binding contract not to oppose highly able rivals, the problem is completely resolved. The problem can also be resolved if the manager can be paid a golden parachute equal to his private benefits if he chooses not to resist. Clearly, these simple devices will not work as well in reality as they do in our model, because, in reality, the rival's ability and the entrepreneur's private benefits are not verifiable. Consequently, we rule out such personalized contracts and concentrate on the use of standardized, marketable securities as the only commitment device available to the entrepreneur. Intuitively, the securities help to achieve the commitment by forcing the incumbent to acquire a significant share of the returns to capture enough votes to win.

More precisely, in taking the firm public, the entrepreneur can design any number n of securities. Once issued, these securities cannot later be modified. Each security is characterized by its cash flow and its voting rights. The aggregate cash flow of security i ($i = 1, \ldots, n$) can be any monotone increasing function of the contractible return, y, and is denoted $s_i(y)$. The fraction of votes assigned to security i is denoted by v_i. Each security is assumed to be infinitely divisible for the purpose of trading. The voting rights of a security cannot be traded separately from its cash flow. In addition, we assume that investors can store wealth in the form of cash, denoted as security 0. Of course, cash carries no voting rights in the firm. We define the feasible securities as follows:

Definition. A *feasible set of securities*, (s, v), where $s = (s_1, \ldots, s_n)$ and $v = (v_1, \ldots, v_n)$, satisfies:

(a) *Limited liability*: $s_i(y) \geq 0$, for all y, $i = 1, \ldots, n$,
(b) *Monotonicity and Continuity*: $s_i(y)$ is nondecreasing and continuous for all y, $i = 1, \ldots, n$,
(c) *Liquidation*: $\mathbf{1}s(y) \equiv y$,
(d) *Vote normalization*: $v_i \geq 0$, $i = 1, \ldots, n$, $\mathbf{1}v = 1$,

where $\mathbf{1}$ is a vector of n ones.

Although it would be interesting to explain why corporate securities always provide for limited liability, that is beyond the scope of this paper. To make the analysis tractable, we assume monotonicity, i.e., that securities are more valuable with more able management. [Continuity can be derived from monotonicity; see appendix, Lemma 1.] Without such an assumption, some investors will prefer inferior candidates. [This suggests that monotonicity can be derived; however, doing so does not seem worth the additional formalism.] Condition (c) simply states that, upon liquidation of the firm, the securities in total must pay out all of the returns. Condition (d) normalizes the votes to be nonnegative and sum to one.

We denote by $S_i(r)$ the value of security i to an outside investor under manager r, i.e., $S_i(r) = \mathrm{E}[s_i(\tilde{y})|r]$, $r \geq 0$, $i = 1, \ldots, n$. Let $S = (S_1, \ldots, S_n)$ and $\Delta S(r) = S(r) - S(0)$. Note that, because $F(\cdot|r)$ are ordered by first-order stochastic dominance and s_i is monotone increasing, the value of security i is increasing in the ability of the manager. Consequently, $\Delta S_i(r)$ is nonnegative and increasing in r. Also, it can be shown that S_i is continuous [see appendix, Lemma 1].

A *portfolio* is a vector (x_0, x), where x_0 represents cash balances, $x = (x_1, \ldots, x_n)$, and x_i is a fraction of security i. A *feasible portfolio* satisfies $x_0 \geq 0$, and $x_i \in [0, 1]$ for $i = 1, \ldots, n$, i.e., we assume that the incumbent cannot short any of the securities, including cash.

The sequence of events in the model is as follows. First, the incumbent takes the firm public, i.e., he designs securities that he sells to outside investors. He may retain a portfolio of securities. Second, the rival appears, his ability, r, becomes known, and the contestants bid for securities. Third, security holders vote. The rival wins if he obtains more than α votes, otherwise the incumbent wins. Finally, cash flows are generated and the firm is liquidated. We assume throughout that all model elements and decisions of the players are common knowledge. In the text we provide intuition for the results; all formal proofs are contained in the appendix.

3. The optimality of a single voting security

This section discusses our first major result: one voting security is optimal. This result can be interpreted as proving the optimality of one share–one vote in the sense that if one owns, say, 10% of this security, he is entitled to 10% of all votes outstanding. It generalizes the results of Grossman and Hart (1988) and Harris and Raviv (1988b), who proved the optimality of one share–one vote under the restriction that all securities specify cash flows that are proportional to total output. In general, observed corporate securities include claims whose cash flows are not proportional to output, e.g., debt and levered equity. Thus the current result comes closer to explaining the predominance of one share–one vote in actual practice. The result is stated formally as:

Theorem 1. One share–one vote. If potential rivals are sufficiently diverse, then the optimal security design requires one share–one vote.

We motivate this result in three stages. First, at the takeover contest, the incumbent weighs the minimum cost of resisting the rival against the benefits of control. We characterize this minimum cost of acquiring β votes. Second, we argue that, in designing securities, the incumbent wants to maximize his minimum cost of acquiring β votes. Third, we show that having one share–one vote maximizes this cost by preventing the incumbent from acquiring cheap votes in the takeover contest.

Stage 1: The minimum cost of acquiring β votes

Consider a takeover contest between the incumbent and a rival of given ability r. The securities (s, v) and the incumbent's initial portfolio (x_0, x) are taken as given. In section 4, we show that it is never optimal for the incumbent to retain a controlling stake when the firm goes public. [Recall that this result holds only when the rival has no benefits of control. We show in section 5 that the incumbent may choose to retain a controlling interest when rivals have benefits of control.] Consequently, we assume for the remainder of this section that the incumbent enters the contest with fewer than the β votes required for him to insure victory ($xv < \beta$), so he must choose whether to acquire enough votes to win or not. The incumbent chooses an optimal resistance strategy, i.e., for each security, he chooses an offer price and quantity to be purchased.

The incumbent's minimum winning offer price for security i is its value under the rival's management, $S_i(r)$. If the incumbent offers less than this value, the rival can bid more than the incumbent. Investors will tender their securities either to the rival at his price or not at all. Since the securities are worth more under the rival, securities retained by investors will be voted for the rival, and he will win. It follows that if the incumbent must purchase securities to maintain control, he must pay investors what these securities would be worth under the rival (plus a penny).

The incumbent's final portfolio is denoted by (z_0, z), where $z = (z_1, \ldots, z_n)$. If the incumbent chooses to acquire a controlling interest, i.e., he chooses $zv \geq \beta$, then his problem is to minimize the cost of doing so. As just argued, the incumbent's buying price for a voting security i is $S_i(r)$. The value of these securities under the incumbent's management is only $S_i(0)$. Therefore, his cost of acquiring β votes consists of the capital loss $\Delta S_i(r)$ on those securities he purchases and on his initial portfolio, x. We show that the incumbent can minimize the cost of obtaining β votes by bidding first for those securities whose capital loss per vote is low.

Letting $(z_i - x_i)^+ = \max(z_i - x_i, 0)$ be the amount of security i the incumbent buys or zero if he does not buy any i, and $(z_i - x_i)^- = \max(x_i - z_i, 0)$ be the amount sold or zero if he does not sell any i, we can state the incumbent's problem formally as

(P) $\qquad C(r, x, s, v) = \min_z \left[x + (z - x)^+ \right] \Delta S(r),$ \hfill (1)

subject to

$$zv \geq \beta, \tag{2}$$

$$z_i \in [0, 1] \quad \text{for} \quad i = 1, \ldots, n, \tag{3}$$

$$(z - x)^+ S(r) - (z - x)^- S(0) \leq x_0. \tag{4}$$

The objective function (1) represents the total cost of maintaining control. This cost consists of the opportunity cost on the initial portfolio x caused by foregoing the rival's incremental return, $x \Delta S(r)$, plus the direct cost of purchasing β votes, $(z - x)^+ \Delta S(r)$. Constraint (4) is the incumbent's budget constraint. Given that the incumbent will win the takeover contest, any securities he sells, $(z_i - x_i)^-$, are worth only their value under the incumbent's management, $S_i(0)$.

In analyzing this problem, we will ignore the budget constraint (4). Otherwise the problem is completely intractable. Thus we restrict our attention to situations in which the incumbent's resistance to takeovers depends on his capital loss and not on whether he can raise the funds necessary to purchase β votes using the loss-minimizing strategy. Although we would like to characterize these situations in terms of the exogenous elements, we are unable to do so.

Under these assumptions, the minimum cost of acquiring β votes [the solution of problem (P)] can be characterized as follows. The cost of purchasing security i is the difference $\Delta S_i(r)$ between what the incumbent pays, $S_i(r)$, and its value under his management, $S_i(0)$. The benefit of purchasing security i is its votes v_i. Obviously, the cheapest way to acquire β votes is to buy as much as possible of the security with the lowest cost per vote $\Delta S_i(r)/v_i$, then buy the second lowest, etc., until β votes are acquired.

Our result that a single voting security is optimal is driven by the preceding analysis. The cost of purchasing β votes can be increased by not offering cheap votes, i.e., securities with low cost per vote. Indeed, this cost is maximized when all voting securities have the same cost per vote, which occurs when there is only one voting security. Since it turns out to be beneficial to raise the cost as much as possible, our result on having a single voting security follows.

The incumbent chooses to acquire control if the benefits of control, B, exceed the minimum total cost, C. Let $w(x, s, v)$ denote the set of rivals the incumbent resists, i.e., r's for which $B > C(r, x, s, v)$ (see fig. 2). Since $C(r, x, s, v) \leq \Delta y(r)$ for all r, x, s, v, the incumbent will always contest a value-reducing takeover (when $r < \bar{r}$) and may oppose value-increasing takeover attempts. The objective in designing securities will be to increase the opportunity cost C of opposing each rival, thus reducing the set of highly able rivals the incumbent opposes. Of course, if it were possible to design securities so that, to acquire control, the incumbent is forced to bear the full opportunity cost of foregoing the rival's incremental return, i.e., if $C \equiv \Delta y$, the solution would be the same as the single-owner solution.

Stage 2: Optimal securities maximize the minimum cost of resisting

We now consider the incumbent's choice of securities and his initial portfolio, taking into account his behavior in the takeover contest. Since investors in this model engage only in zero net present value (NPV) transactions, the NPV of the firm accrues entirely to the entrepreneur. Therefore, his objective in issuing securities is to maximize this value.

When the incumbent successfully opposes the takeover, i.e., for r's in the winning region w (see fig. 2), the value of the firm is the return under the incumbent's management plus the private benefits of control, $y(0) + B$. The value of the firm when the incumbent does not contest the rival, i.e., for r's not in w, is $y(r)$. Letting l be the complement of w, we can write the incumbent's problem as choosing a portfolio x and a set of securities (s, v) to

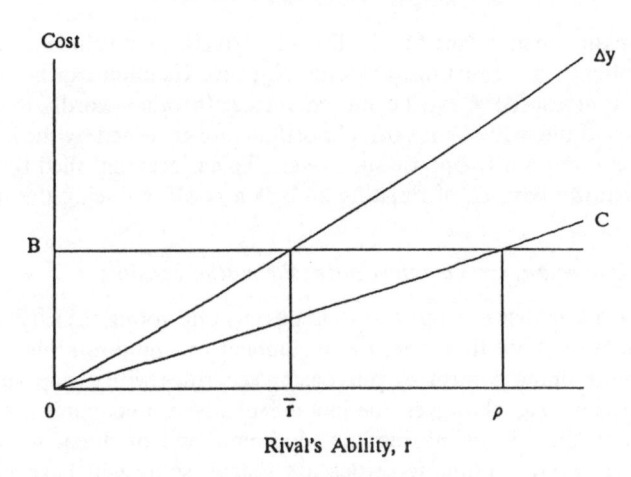

Fig. 2. Cost of maintaining control.

As in fig. 1, Δy is the rival's incremental expected output, B is the incumbent's private benefit of control, and the interval $(0, \bar{r})$ is the incumbent's winning region in the single-owner solution. The interval $(0, \rho)$ is the incumbent's winning region, w, when his minimum cost of maintaining control is given by the curve labeled C. Any security design that raises the incumbent's minimum cost of maintaining control makes the incumbent's winning region closer to that of the single-owner solution and increases firm value.

maximize the firm's NPV,

$$\text{(Q)} \quad V(x, s, v) = \int_w [y(0) + B]\, dF(r) + \int_l y(r)\, dF(r) - I, \tag{5}$$

subject to

$$xv < \beta, \tag{6}$$

$$R(x, s, v) - I \geq 0, \tag{7}$$

where $R(x, s, v)$ is the revenue raised if the incumbent chooses portfolio x and issues securities (s, v). We neglect discounting, since this would not affect the results. Constraint (6) is the condition that the incumbent does not retain a controlling interest, which we assume in this section. Constraint (7) is the budget constraint, which states that revenue from the sale of securities must at least cover the net investment cost. The incumbent holds the remainder as cash.

The analysis of the incumbent's problem (Q) is simplified by observing that the incumbent can increase the NPV if he can reduce the set of rivals he will oppose, w. To see this, note that $y(r) \geq B + y(0)$ if and only if $r \geq \bar{r}$. Although w will always include $(0, \bar{r})$, typically it will also include some rivals with abilities higher than $\bar{r}$ (see fig. 2). For such rivals, firm value is increased by the incumbent's not resisting. Thus the objective function can be increased if r's in w that exceed $\bar{r}$ can be moved into l. In other words, the choice of securities and the incumbent's initial portfolio are governed by the incumbent's desire to commit not to oppose such rivals. This is accomplished by increasing the opportunity cost, C, of resisting and, as a result, reducing the set w.[3]

Stage 3: One share–one vote maximizes the cost of resisting

We now argue that it is optimal to issue only one voting security. First recall that, if there is more than one, the incumbent can minimize his opportunity cost of maintaining control by purchasing securities with cheap votes. In the security design stage, however, the incumbent wishes to commit not to oppose rivals better than $\bar{r}$ by making the minimum cost of doing so as large as possible. If several voting securities are issued, some will have higher than average cost per vote ratios, and some will have lower than average ratios. The incumbent will choose to purchase those with lower than average ratios. He can raise his minimum cost by forcing himself to choose securities with the average cost per vote. This can be done only by issuing voting securities with a common cost per vote for any given rival. One way to insure that all voting securities have a common cost per vote for any rival is to issue only one voting security. This shows that having one voting security is optimal.

To establish Theorem 1, it remains only to show that this is the only way to eliminate cheap votes. Since the cost per vote depends on the expected value of the security for each rival, if the set of rivals is sufficiently diverse, the only way to equalize the cost per vote across securities for every possible rival is to have only one voting security. It is easy to see that some assumption that guarantees diversity of possible rival abilities is essential for this result by considering the case in which the rival's ability is known to be, say, $r = 0.5$. Let securities 1 and 2 be two voting securities with any cash flows. Suppose the incremental value of security 1 under the rival is $\Delta S_1(0.5) = 2$ and the incremental value of security 2 is $\Delta S_2(0.5) = 4$. We can still satisfy the requirement that the cost per vote be equalized across securities simply by allocating votes in proportion to the known opportunity costs $[\Delta S_i(0.5)]$ of the two securities, i.e., by letting $v_1 = 2/(4+2) = \frac{1}{3}$ and $v_2 = \frac{2}{3}$. In this case, the cost per vote is 6 for both securities. If the rival's ability is uncertain, this method of equalizing costs per vote will not be possible. Assigning votes in this way for one possible realization of the rival's ability, r, will not guarantee equal cost per vote for some other realization of r. The richer is the set of possible rival abilities, the more constraints are placed on the securities by the

---

[3] Increasing C and reducing w also increases revenue from the sale of securities, because the securities are more valuable if firm value increases.

requirement of equal cost per vote. For a rich enough set of rival abilities, the only way to equalize the cost per vote across securities for all rivals is to have only one voting security.

4. Other results on optimal security design

This section characterizes the cash flows of securities and the allocation of cash flows and votes to the incumbent and outside investors. While Theorem 1 extends results of Grossman and Hart (1988) and Harris and Raviv (1988b) on the assignment of voting rights, the issues addressed in this section have not previously been considered.

The basic insights described below are as follows: (i) the incumbent should retain securities that are as sensitive as possible to the quality of management, (ii) securities retained by the incumbent should be nonvoting, and (iii) the sensitivity of the voting security should not be reduced by the issuance of any nonvoting, risky securities to outside investors. These insights follow from the basic idea that the entrepreneur wants to commit, to the extent possible through the security design, not to oppose better rivals.

In section 3 we assumed that the incumbent did not retain voting control when the firm went public. We now argue that it is in fact optimal for the incumbent not to hold any voting securities when the firm goes public. Suppose he does retain voting securities when going public. This reduces the quantity of other securities he may keep without increasing the quantity of voting securities he must eventually obtain. Now consider an alternative solution in which we reallocate all the incumbent's votes to the outside investors' securities. The incumbent's opportunity cost of acquiring a controlling interest in the takeover contest will now consist of the capital loss on his initial portfolio as before, plus the additional capital loss on the voting securities he now must purchase. Therefore, the new solution commits the incumbent to oppose a smaller set of rivals than the original solution, and hence increases the value of the firm. Consequently, the incumbent should not retain voting securities.

Finally, suppose the nonvoting security held by the incumbent includes riskless cash flows, i.e., the security guarantees a positive minimum payoff. In this case, the incumbent's cost of retaining control can be increased by selling the riskless portion to outside investors and investing the proceeds in a risky security. This motivates:

Theorem 2. Incumbent's retention of control. When the firm goes public, the incumbent should not retain any votes or risk-free debt.

This result does not imply that the incumbent retains no stake in the firm when it goes public. Indeed, we show below that he should retain as large a stake as possible subject to the constraint that sufficient revenue is raised from outside investors. Generally, entrepreneurs do retain some voting securities when their firms go public. Often, however, they retain only an insignificant fraction of the votes. Moreover, vote retention could be a defense against inferior rivals who attempt takeovers because of their own benefits of control. This is discussed in section 5.

Our third result is that the incumbent should not sell nonvoting, risky securities. To see this, first observe that any nonvoting securities sold to outside investors can be relabeled as a single security. If this security contains any cash flows that are sensitive to the management in control, the incumbent's opportunity cost of opposing a takeover, C, can be increased by including these cash flows in the voting security. Thus, the nonvoting security can contain at most riskless cash flows, i.e., it must be a risk-free bond. We state this result as

Theorem 3. Nonvoting securities. The incumbent should not sell nonvoting, risky securities to outside investors.

From Theorem 3, we have that any nonvoting security sold to outside investors must be risk-free debt. Moreover, from Theorem 1, we have that any risk-free debt must be nonvoting, and, from Theorem 2, that this debt cannot be held by the incumbent. We summarize these implications in:

Corollary to Theorems 1–3. Any nonvoting security sold to outside investors must be risk-free debt, and any risk-free debt issued must be nonvoting and sold only to outside investors.

This result is the first to show that nonvoting debt is optimal.[4] Any riskless cash flows could also be included in the voting security, however, without affecting either the incumbent's opportunity cost of resisting or the revenue from the sale of securities, that is, without affecting the solution. Although we show only that issuing nonvoting risk-free debt as a separate security is weakly preferred, the model omits important features such as taxes that would make this preference strict. These features might also explain the existence of nonvoting risky debt. Although our analysis points out that issuing risky debt reduces the sensitivity of the voting securities to managerial quality, thus cheapening the votes, benefits of debt outside our model, such as tax shields, could outweigh this cost.

---

[4] Townsend (1979), Diamond (1984), Gale and Hellwig (1985), and Williams (1987) all show that risky debt can be part of an optimal security structure. As mentioned in footnote 1, these models are based on private information and do not address the issue of voting rights.

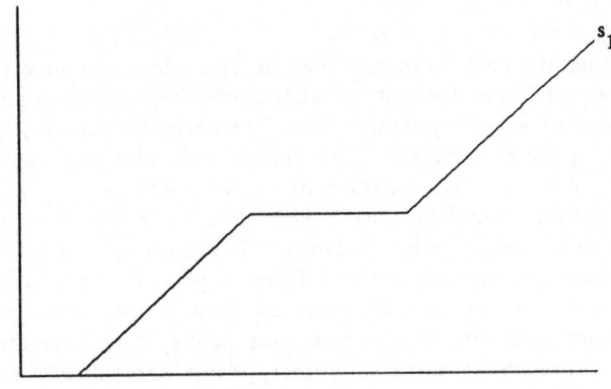

Payoff to the voting security

Fig. 3. Optimal pattern of cash flows to the voting security.

The kinked line shows a typical payoff, s_1, to the voting security. The upward sloping segments are 45° lines. Under certain conditions the optimal pattern would consist only of the initial horizontal segment and the first 45° line, i.e., would be the textbook form of levered equity.

Our fourth result characterizes the cash flows of the voting security and the security retained by the incumbent. We show that these securities consist of straight lines of slope one separated by horizontal segments, as shown in fig. 3. That is, any marginal increment in returns accrues entirely to one or the other security.

Some rough intuition for this result is as follows. First recall that we can assume there are only two securities. Let $s_1(y)$ be the voting security sold to outsiders and $s_2(y)$ be the incumbent's portfolio. Since all of the income is paid out and securities are monotone increasing, each security's marginal payoff must be between zero and one $[0 \le s_i'(y) \le 1]$. For each possible value of income, y, it is optimal to make s_1 as sensitive as possible to income ($s_1' = 1$) or as insensitive as possible ($s_2' = 1$). This 'bang-bang' solution is a consequence of the desire to make the incumbent's portfolio, s_2, as sensitive as possible to the fortunes of the firm and the quality of management while still raising the required revenue from selling s_1 to outsiders. Therefore, $s_1'(y)$ is either zero or one, as is s_2'. This result is summarized in:

Theorem 4. Cash flow properties. The cash flow to the optimal voting security as a function of earnings consists of straight lines of slope 1 separated by horizontal segments (see fig. 3). The same is true of the nonvoting security. That is, any increment in earnings accrues either entirely to the voting security or entirely to the nonvoting security.

Whether the cash flows described in Theorem 4 resemble those of actual voting equity raises the issue of what empirical regularities are found in the cash flows of actual equity securities. The pattern commonly associated with levered equity in textbooks is an initial horizontal segment followed by a segment of slope 1, i.e., a pattern of the form $\max\{y - D, 0\}$. It is not clear, however, that actual equity has precisely the textbook form. For example, if management compensation includes call options on the firm's equity, this equity does not have the textbook form. In general, the security described in Theorem 4 does not have the textbook form, but certain conditions on the distribution functions $F(y|r)$ guarantee that s_1 does have this form. These conditions, which are not readily interpretable economically, are given in the appendix.[5]

5. Rivals with benefits of control

Thus far we have considered only situations in which rivals have no benefits of control. In this case, the problem solved by optimal securities is how to encourage the incumbent not to resist takeovers by superior rivals. When the rival has benefits of control, the danger arises that an inferior rival will seek to gain control. In this case, the role of securities is to encourage resistance by the superior incumbent. This section considers the robustness of our results to this scenario. We restrict our attention to the situation in which only the rival has benefits of control. If the incumbent has no private benefits, he will not oppose superior rivals. Since security design is irrelevant in this case, we focus on the situation in which an inferior rival attacks the firm just because of his private benefits.

The model here is a mirror image of the one in section 2. All assumptions are maintained with the following exceptions. We normalize the incumbent's ability in this section to $r = 1$ and assume that he has no benefits of control. A rival with benefits of control $B > 0$ and of ability less than one attempts to gain control.

Unlike in the previous model, in this one it may be optimal for the incumbent to retain votes when the firm goes public. If the incumbent controls more than β votes, he may be able to extract some of the rival's benefits of control. Therefore, we split the analysis of this model into two cases, depending on whether it is optimal or not for the incumbent to retain voting control when the firm goes public.

---

[5] Under equally uninterpretable conditions, the voting security resembles the textbook form of debt, $\min\{y, D\}$.

When the incumbent has retained a controlling interest, the rival in a takeover contest must acquire some of the incumbent's votes, creating a bilateral bargaining situation. Rather than modeling the bargaining game explicitly, we assume that the incumbent can extract a fixed amount $b \leq B$. Our analysis would not be affected by including any explicit bargaining game or solution concept, such as the Nash bargaining solution. Suppose the expected payoff of the incumbent's portfolio is $S(r)$ as a function of the ability r of the management in control. Then the incumbent resists if and only if his payoff under his management exceeds his payoff under the rival's management plus the share of the rival's benefits he can extract, i.e., if and only if $S(1) > S(r) + b$ or $\Delta S(r) > b$, where we redefine $\Delta S(r) = S(1) - S(r)$. We can interpret $\Delta S(r)$ as the cost of surrendering to an inferior rival r. Since the cost of surrendering, $\Delta S(r)$, is generally less than the total reduction in expected returns due to a takeover, $\Delta y(r) \equiv y(1) - y(r)$, the incumbent will surrender to some rivals for whom the extracted benefits b do not compensate for the loss in expected returns, i.e., for whom $\Delta y(r) > b$. As in the previous model, there is no danger that the incumbent will resist a rival whose total return is higher. Therefore, in going public, it is optimal for the incumbent to design securities that commit him not to surrender when the extracted benefits are smaller than the loss in expected return. This is accomplished by increasing $\Delta S(r)$. What prevents the incumbent from simply setting $\Delta S(r) = \Delta y(r)$ is that he must raise at least I from outside investors. Consequently, the problem for the incumbent is identical to that considered in Theorem 4. The following result is immediate.

Theorem 5. If the incumbent chooses to retain a controlling interest when the firm goes public, the cash flow to his claim as a function of earnings consists of straight lines of slope 1 separated by horizontal segments (see fig. 3). The same is true of the other security. That is, any increment in earnings either accrues entirely to the incumbent's security or entirely to the other security.

As in the previous model, there are sufficient conditions under which the incumbent's claim takes the textbook form of levered equity.

Now consider the security design when the incumbent chooses to control less than β votes. In this case, he behaves in the takeover contest like any outside investor. Consequently, if the incumbent does not retain a controlling interest when the firm goes public, we do not distinguish between him and outside investors. The situation is exactly analogous to that of the previous model. The incumbent wants to maximize the cost of taking over by not providing cheap votes. Therefore, we can state the following result.

Theorem 6. If the incumbent chooses not to retain a controlling interest when the firm goes public and potential rivals are sufficiently diverse, the optimal security design requires a single class of voting equity, optionally levered by nonvoting, risk-free debt.

In this case, the incumbent may hold voting equity when the firm goes public, provided that he does not retain a controlling interest.

From Theorems 5 and 6, it is clear that when the rival has benefits of control while the incumbent does not, the major properties of optimal securities are preserved. For diffusely held firms, optimal design requires issuing a single voting security comprising all (risky) cash flows, i.e., equity in the usual sense.[6] This suggests that our basic insights, spelled out in the introduction, are robust to changes in the specification of conflicts of interest.

6. Conclusions

This paper focuses on capital structure in the broad sense: the design of cash flow contracts and the assignment of votes. This enquiry is more fundamental than the usual approach of explaining relative quantities of debt, equity, and, perhaps, other exogenously assumed securities.

Investigating both the design of cash flows and the assignment of voting rights leads to a research agenda that focuses on corporate governance and control contests. The current paper, our previous papers [Harris and Raviv (1988a, b)], and Grossman and Hart (1988) constitute a modest beginning on this agenda. One of the basic insights in these papers is that a single voting security does not allow the acquisition of (cheap) votes without corresponding cash flows, and therefore best allocates the consequences of control choices to the parties with the power to determine control. This suggests, and the current paper shows, that votes should not be allocated to riskless debt. In addition, we show that entrepreneurs/incumbents should either retain voting control or not hold any voting securities on going public, and that under certain conditions the voting security should resemble standard levered equity.

Two problems with the model should be pointed out. First, it predicts that only one risky security will be held by outside investors. It is thus inconsistent with the observation that outside investors typically hold both risky debt and equity. One modification of our model that could rectify this problem is to introduce wealth constraints on the contestants at the takeover stage. This would provide a reason for separating some risky cash flows from the voting security to make acquisition of control affordable for the superior candidate. Second, the conditions that guarantee that the voting security is levered equity are not easily interpretable in terms of observable firm characteristics. In

---

[6] Whether the incumbent decides when going public to retain a controlling interest depends on how much of the cash flow claims he can retain while raising the required investment from outside investors, as well as the amount he can extract from the rival, b, if he retains control. We do not pursue the determination of ownership structure here. See Israel (1988).

attempting to explain voting equity, we took the term 'levered equity' to mean a payoff pattern as a function of the firm's output of the form $\max\{y - D, 0\}$. As argued above, however, actual levered equity does not necessarily take this form. Therefore, even without the conditions just mentioned, our model may be consistent with the cash flow patterns of observed voting securities.

Although this paper addresses some of the issues raised by the research agenda described above, much remains to be done. In particular, although the basic insight mentioned above seems to be robust to the assumptions made in the current model, some of our specific results must be reexamined in more general settings. We have in mind relaxing the assumptions that only one takeover attempt can occur, that capital structure cannot be changed in response to a takeover attempt, and that the securities must specify cash flows that are functions only of the firm's output. In addition, it is important to consider more general corporate governance rules, e.g., requiring different fractions of the votes of different securities and allowing these fractions to vary according to the issue being voted on. Taking this agenda seriously will lead to an integration of the theories of capital structure, corporate governance, and managerial compensation.

Appendix

Lemma 1. For any feasible s, s_i must be continuous in y and $S_i \equiv E[s_i(\tilde{y})|r]$ must be continuous in r for each i.

Proof. First show that S_i is continuous in r. Fix r_0 and let $S_i^-(r_0)$ and $S_i^+(r_0)$ be the left and right limits of S_i as r approaches r_0 [if $r_0 = 0$, substitute $S_i(0)$ for $S_i^-(r_0)$]. By monotonicity of S_i, $S_i^-(r_0) \leq S_i^+(r_0)$. By monotonicity of $y(r) - S_i(r)$ and continuity of $y(r)$, $y(r_0) - S_i^+(r_0) \geq y(r_0) - S_i^-(r_0)$, or $S_i^-(r_0) \geq S_i^+(r_0)$. Therefore $S_i^-(r_0) = S_i^+(r_0)$. The proof for s_i is the same since the identity map is continuous. Q.E.D.

Solution of problem (P)

To write the solution formally, let K be the number of voting securities. Renumber securities so that within the voting securities $\Delta S_i(r)/v_i$ is increasing in i. This ordering, in general, depends on r. Let

$$k(r, x) = \min\left\{i \,\bigg|\, \sum_{j=1}^{i} v_j + \sum_{j=i+1}^{K} x_j v_j \geq \beta\right\}.$$

Then, assuming that the incumbent does not need to sell any voting securities to acquire β votes,

$$z_i^* = \begin{cases} 1, & 0 < i < k, \\ \left[\beta - v_1 - \cdots - v_{i-1} - \sum_{j=i+1}^{K} x_j v_j\right]/v_i, & i = k, \\ x_i, & i = k+1, \ldots, K, \\ 0, & i > K, \end{cases} \quad (A.1)$$

where $k(r, x)$ has been abbreviated to k.

Lemma 2. $z_k^*(r, x) > x_k$, for any r and x, where $k = k(r, x)$.

Proof. From (A.1),

$$z_k^* v_k = \beta - \sum_{i=1}^{k-1} v_i - \sum_{i=k+1}^{K} x_i v_i$$

$$> \sum_{i=1}^{k-1} v_i + \sum_{i=k}^{K} x_i v_i - \sum_{i=1}^{k-1} v_i - \sum_{i=k+1}^{K} x_i v_i, \quad \text{by definition of } k,$$

$$= x_k v_k,$$

or $z_k^* > x_k$ since $v_k > 0$. Q.E.D.

Analysis of (Q)

Using (5), we may write V as

$$V(x, s, v) = \int_{w^*} [B + y(0)] \, dF(r) + \int_{w \setminus w^*} [B + y(0)] \, dF(r)$$

$$+ \int_l y(r) \, dF(r) - I,$$

where $w \setminus w^*$ is the part of w not in $w^* = (0, \bar{r})$. Suppose that (x', s', v') and (x, s, v) are such that $w' \equiv w(x', s', v') \subseteq w(x, s, v) \equiv w$. Since w^* is independent of (x, s, v), this implies that $w' \setminus w^* \subseteq w \setminus w^*$. Since $y(r) > B + y(0)$ for $r \notin w^*$, we see that $V(x', s', v') \geq V(x, s, v)$. Moreover, it is clear that

$C(r, x', s', v') \geq C(r, x, s, v)$ for every r implies that $w' \subseteq w$. We have thus proved the following lemma:

Lemma 3. *Suppose (x, s, v) and (x', s', v') are such that*

$$C(r, x', s', v') \geq C(r, x, s, v), \quad \text{for all } r.$$

Then $w(x', s', v') \subseteq w(x, s, v)$. Hence $V(x', s', v') \geq V(x, s, v)$.

Using C, we can write the revenue associated with (x, s, v) as

$$R(x, s, v) = \int_w \left[(z^* - x)^+ S(r) + \left(1 - x - (z^* - x)^+\right) S(0) \right] dF(r)$$

$$+ \int_l (1 - x) S(r) dF(r)$$

$$= \int_w \left[C(r, x, s, v) - x \Delta S(r) + (1 - x) S(0) \right] dF(r)$$

$$+ \int_l (1 - x) S(r) dF(r)$$

$$= \int_w [C + y(0)] dF(r) + \int_l y(r) dF(r) - \int_0^1 x S(r) dF(r).$$

(A.2)

Lemma 4. *Suppose (x, s, v) and (x', s', v') are such that*

$$C'(r) \equiv C(r, x', s', v') \geq C(r, x, s, v) \equiv C(r), \quad \text{for all } r.$$

Also suppose that $xS(r) \geq x'S'(r)$ for all r. Then $R(x', s', v') \geq R(x, s, v)$. Moreover, this inequality is strict if $C' > C$ for a subset of $w(x, s, v)$ with positive probability, or $xS > x'S'$ with positive probability.

Proof. Let $w = w(x, s, v)$, $w' = w(x', s', v')$, and let l and l' be the respective complements. From the hypotheses of this lemma and from Lemma 3, $w' \subseteq w$.

Then, from (A.2),

$$R(x, s, v) = \int_w [C(r) + y(0)] \, dF(r) + \int_{l'} y(r) \, dF(r)$$
$$- \int x S(r) \, dF(r)$$
$$\leq \int_{w'} [C'(r) + y(0)] \, dF(r) + \int_{l'} y(r) \, dF(r)$$
$$- \int x' S'(r) \, dF(r)$$
$$= R(x', s', v').$$

The inequality follows from the hypotheses that $xS(r) \geq x'S'(r)$ for all r and $C'(r) \geq C(r)$ for all r and that this implies that $w' \subseteq w$. The inequality will be strict if $C' > C$ on a subset of w with positive probability, or $xS > x'S'$ with positive probability. The last equality uses (A.2) for (x', s', v'). Q.E.D.

Lemma 5. For any feasible solution (x, s, v) of (Q), we can construct another feasible solution (x', s', v') with $n' = 3$, $K' = 1$ $(v_1' = 1)$, $x_1' = 0$, $x_2' = 1$, and $x_3' = 0$ such that $V(x', s', v') \geq V(x, s, v)$ and $R(x', s', v') \geq R(x, s, v)$.

Proof. Number securities (s, v) so that $1, \ldots, K$ are the voting securities. Let n', x', and v' be as in the statement of the lemma, and let

$$s_1' = \sum_{i=1}^{K} (1 - x_i) s_i, \quad s_2' = \sum_{i=1}^{n} x_i s_i, \quad s_3' = \sum_{i=K+1}^{n} (1 - x_i) s_i.$$

Now it is easy to check that

$$C'(r) \equiv C(r, x', s', v')$$
$$= \beta \Delta S_1'(r) + \Delta S_2'(r)$$
$$= \sum_{i=1}^{K} \beta (1 - x_i) \Delta S_i(r) + x \Delta S(r)$$
$$= [x + (z - x)^+] \Delta S(r)$$
$$\geq C(r),$$

where $z_i = x_i + \beta(1 - x_i) = \beta + (1 - \beta)x_i$, for $0 < i \leq K$, $z_i = 0$, for $i = 0$ and $i > K$. Since it is easy to check that z is feasible for (P), given (x, s, v), for any r, the last inequality follows. Therefore, by Lemma 3, $w' \equiv w(x', s', v') \subseteq w(x, s, v) \equiv w$, so $V(x, s, v) \leq V(x', s', v')$. It remains only to show the feasibility of (x', s', v') and that the revenue associated with (x', s', v') is at least as large as that associated with (x, s, v). Clearly x' is a feasible portfolio and (s', v') is a feasible set of securities. Also $x'v' = 0 < \beta$. Finally, $xS(r) = x'S'(r)$ for all r, so, by Lemma 4, $R(x', s', v') \geq R(x, s, v) \geq I$.   Q.E.D.

Using Lemma 5, we can assume that the incumbent's first-stage problem involves choosing three securities, $s_1(y)$, $s_2(y)$, and $s_3(y) = y - s_1(y) - s_2(y)$, with only the first having votes, i.e., $v_1 = 1$, $v_2 = v_3 = 0$. Moreover, we can assume that the incumbent retains all of the second security and none of the others, i.e., his initial portfolio of securities $x = (0, 1, 0)$. It follows that C is given by

$$C(r, s) = \beta \Delta S_1(r) + \Delta S_2(r).$$

C is nondecreasing in r, since S_i are nondecreasing. Continuity of S implies that C is continuous in r. Let

$$\rho(s) = \sup\{r \in (0, 1] | C(r, s) < B\}.$$

Thus $\rho(s)$ is the least able rival the incumbent will not oppose and $w(s) = (0, \rho(s))$ and $l(s) = [\rho(s), 1]$.[7] If $\rho(s) < 1$, then $C(\rho(s), s) = B$. Also $\rho(s) \geq \bar{r}$ since $C(r, s) \leq \Delta y(r)$ for all r and s. It is thus clear that, to maximize NPV of the firm, V, the incumbent must minimize w, i.e., he must choose s to minimize ρ (see fig. 2).

We may restate problem (Q) as

(Q') $\min_{\rho, s} \rho,$

subject to

$\rho = \rho(s),$

$s_i \in [0, y]$ for all y, $i = 1, 2,$ (A.3)

$s_1 + s_2 \leq y$ for all y, (A.4)

s_i nondecreasing for all y, $i = 1, 2,$ (A.5)

$y - s_1 - s_2$ nondecreasing for all y, (A.6)

$R(\rho, s) \geq I,$ (A.7)

---
[7]These expressions are correct if $C(1, s) \geq B$. If not, then $w(s) = [0, 1]$ and $l(s) = \emptyset$. Henceforth, we will not make this distinction explicitly.

where $R(\rho, s)$ is the revenue associated with ρ and s, i.e.,

$$R(\rho, s) = \int_0^\rho [\beta \Delta S_1(r) + y(0) - S_2(0)] \, dF(r)$$

$$+ \int_\rho^1 [y(r) - S_2(r)] \, dF(r).$$

In this statement, we have replaced s_3 by $y - s_1 - s_2$. Also we have incorporated the definition of feasible securities into the statement of the problem, and suppressed the assignment of voting rights, since we showed that security one will have all the voting rights.

Lemma 6. Suppose (ρ, s) *is feasible for* (Q'), $\Delta y(\rho) > B$ (*i.e., the solution is not first best*), *and* $R(\rho, s) > I$. *Then there exists a feasible solution* (ρ', s') *such that* $\rho' < \rho$.

Proof. First note that $\Delta S_2(\rho) \le C(\rho, s) \le B < \Delta y(\rho)$. Therefore,

$$S_2(\rho) < y(\rho) + S_2(0) - y(0) \le y(\rho).$$

It follows that $s_2(y) < y$ on a set of positive probability relative to $F(\cdot | \rho)$. We wish to show that $\Delta S_2(\rho)$ can be increased without violating any constraints. Let Y be the common support of $F(y|r)$, and let $y_1 = \max Y$. By monotonicity of $y - s_2$, $s_2(y_1) < y_1$. If $s_2(y)$ is undefined for some $y < y_1$, we can define s_2 at y to be the linear interpolation of the original s_2 between the closest points on either side of y at which it is defined (s_2 must be zero at $y = 0$ and it must be defined at y_1 since $y_1 \in Y$). This will not affect the feasibility of (ρ, s). Using the redefined s_2, monotonicity of $y - s_2$ implies that

$$Y_1 \equiv \{ y \in [0, y_1] | s_2(y_1) - s_2(y) < y_1 - y \}$$

is nonempty. Let $y_0 = \sup Y_1$. For any $u \in [0, y_0)$, let

$$s_2(y, u) = \begin{cases} s_2(y) & \text{for } y \le u, \\ y - u + s_2(u) & \text{for } y \ge u. \end{cases}$$

It is easy to check that, for any $u < y_0$, $s_2(y, u) \ge s_2(y)$ for $y \in [u, y_1]$ with strict inequality over a set of positive probability relative to $F(\cdot | \rho)$. Let $s_1(y, u) = y - s_2(y, u)$. It is also easy to see that $s(\cdot, u)$ is a feasible set of securities and $s_2(\cdot, u)$ converges uniformly to s_2 as u approaches y_0.

Now

$$s_2(y,u) - s_2(y) = \begin{cases} 0 & \text{for } y \le u, \\ y - s_2(y) + s_2(u) - u & \text{for } y \ge u, \end{cases}$$

is monotone increasing in y on $[0, y_1]$ and strictly increasing over a set of positive probability relative to $F(\cdot|\rho)$. Therefore, by FOSD of $F(\cdot|\rho)$ over $F(\cdot|0)$,

$$\Delta S_2(\rho, u) - \Delta S_2(\rho) = \mathrm{E}[s_2(y,u) - s_2(y)|\rho]$$

$$- \mathrm{E}[s_2(y,u) - s_2(y)|0]$$

$$> 0.$$

Now

$$C(\rho, s(\cdot, u)) = \beta \Delta y(\rho) + (1 - \beta) \Delta S_2(\rho, u)$$

$$> \beta \Delta y(\rho) + (1 - \beta) \Delta S_2(\rho), \quad \text{since } \beta < 1,$$

$$\ge C(\rho, s).$$

By continuity of C in r, $\rho(s(\cdot, u)) < \rho(s)$ for all $u < y_0$. Also, note that

$$s_1(y, y_0) - s_1(y) = y - s_1(y) - s_2(y),$$

which is monotone increasing by (A.6). Therefore $\Delta S_1(\rho, y_0) \ge \Delta S_1(\rho)$. Consequently, $\rho(s(\cdot, y_0)) \le \rho(s)$. It is easy to check that R is decreasing in ρ for fixed s and increasing in ΔS_1 for fixed ρ and S_2. Therefore, since (A.7) is slack,

$$R(\rho(\cdot, y_0), s(\cdot, y_0)) \ge R(\rho, s) > I.$$

Also note that $R(\rho(\cdot, u), s(\cdot, u))$ approaches $R(\rho(\cdot, y_0), s(\cdot, y_0))$ as u approaches y_0 from below. It follows that, for u sufficiently close to y_0,

$$R(\rho(\cdot, u), s(\cdot, u)) \ge I.$$

Thus, for some $u < y_0$, $(\rho(s(\cdot, u)), s(\cdot, u))$ is feasible for (Q') and $\rho(s(\cdot, u)) < \rho$. Q.E.D.

Lemma 7. Suppose (x, s, v) is an optimal solution of (Q) and $w(x, s, v) \neq [0, 1]$. Then, for all i and j such that $v_i > 0$ and $v_j > 0$,

$$\Delta S_i(r)/v_i = \Delta S_j(r)/v_j \quad \text{for almost every} \quad r \in w(x, s, v). \tag{A.8}$$

Proof. Suppose not, i.e., suppose for some i and j with $v_i > 0$ and $v_j > 0$, $\Delta S_i(r)/v_i \neq \Delta S_j(r)/v_j$ on $u \subseteq w = w(x, s, v)$ with $\Pr(u) > 0$. We will construct a strictly superior solution. Define (x', s', v') as in Lemma 5 so that $V(x', s', v') \geq V(x, s, v)$. Let $\Delta C(r) = C(r, x', s', v') - C(r, x, s, v)$, and let z be as defined in Lemma 5. Now, for any given r, with $k = k(r, x)$,

$$\Delta C = \left[(z - x)^+ - (z^* - x)^+ \right] \Delta S$$

$$= -(1 - \beta) \sum_{i=1}^{k-1} (1 - x_i) \Delta S_i + \left[(\beta - z_k^*) + x_k(1 - \beta) \right] \Delta S_k$$

$$+ \sum_{i=k+1}^{K} \beta(1 - x_i) \Delta S_i.$$

Since $\Delta S_i \leq v_i \Delta S_k/v_k$ for $i < k$ and $\Delta S_i \geq v_i \Delta S_k/v_k$ for $i > k$, and at least one of these inequalities is strict for $r \in u$ according to our initial supposition,

$$\Delta C \geq \left[-(1 - \beta) \sum_{i=1}^{k-1} (1 - x_i) v_i + \left[(\beta - z_k^*) + x_k(1 - \beta) \right] v_k \right.$$

$$\left. + \sum_{i=k+1}^{K} \beta(1 - x_i) v_i \right] \frac{\Delta S_k}{v_k}$$

$$= \left[-\beta + \beta + (1 - \beta) \sum_{i=1}^{k-1} x_i v_i \right] \frac{\Delta S_k}{v_k}$$

$$\geq 0,$$

with the first inequality strict on u. Since $x'S' = xS$, it follows from Lemma 4 that revenue for solution prime is strictly greater than that for the original solution, hence strictly greater than I. Therefore, by Lemma 6, (x', s', v')

cannot be optimal. Since $V(x', s', v') \geq V(x, s, v)$, we have a contradiction.
Q.E.D.

Let Y be the common support of $F(\cdot | r)$, and let $y_1 = \max Y$.

Assumption. Diversity of rivals. For any $r \in (0, \bar{r})$ and for any subset A of $[0, y_1]$, there exists $\varepsilon \neq 0$ and $r' \in (0, \bar{r})$ such that

$$dF(y|r') = \begin{cases} (1 - \varepsilon) dF(y|r) & \text{for } y \in A, \\ [1 + \varepsilon \Pr(A|r)/(1 - \Pr(A|r))] dF(y|r) & \text{for } y \notin A, \end{cases}$$

where

$$\Pr(A|r) = \int_A dF(y|r).$$

Lemma 8. If (x, s, v) has voting securities $1, \ldots, K$ and satisfies $(A.8)$, then

$$s_i(y) = v_i h(y) \quad \text{for a.e. } y, \tag{A.9}$$

where $h(y) = s_1(y) + \cdots + s_K(y)$.

Proof. From (A.8), for almost every $r \in w(x, s, v)$,

$$\int [s_i(y) - v_i h(y)] dF(y|r) = S_i(0) - v_i H(0),$$

where $H(r) = E[h(\tilde{y})|r]$ for $r \in [0, 1]$. The above assumption implies that

$$s_i(y) = v_i h(y) + S_i(0) - v_i H(0)$$

with probability 1 for a.e. $r \in (0, \bar{r})$.

But $y \geq s_i \geq 0$ for all y implies $s_i(0) = 0$ and $h(0) = 0$. This implies that $S_i(0) = v_i H(0)$ and $s_i(y) = v_i h(y)$ with probability 1 for a.e. $r \in (0, \bar{r})$. Since $F(y|r)$ has common support, $s_i = v_i h$ for a.e. y. Q.E.D.

Lemma 9. Let (Q^*) be the same as (Q) without constraint (6). If (x, s, v) is a feasible solution of (Q^*) with $xv > \beta$, there is a solution, (x', s', v'), with $x'v' < \beta$ that is at least as good.

Proof. Without loss of generality we may treat the incumbent's portfolio as a single security with cash flows xs and votes xv and the complementary portfolio sold to outside investors as another security with cash flows $(1 - x)s$

and votes $(1-x)v$. Denote the outside investors' security as s_1 and the incumbent's security as s_2. With this relabeling, the solution now consists of two securities with $x = (0,1)$. The incumbent's opportunity cost of maintaining control in the takeover contest will consist simply of the capital loss on his portfolio, s_2, since he will not need to purchase any voting securities in the takeover contest. Now consider an alternative solution (x', s', v'), where $x' = x = (0,1)$, $s' = s$, but $v' = (1,0)$. The incumbent's opportunity cost of acquiring a controlling interest in the takeover contest will now consist of the capital loss on his initial portfolio (s_2), as before, plus the additional capital loss on the fraction β of the voting security, s_1, that he now must purchase. Therefore, the new solution results in a higher resistance cost than the original solution, and hence increases the value of the firm. The only remaining question is whether the new securities generate enough revenue. The new voting securities sold to outside investors are more valuable than the original ones, however, since the incumbent, in situations in which he wishes to maintain control, will be forced to buy voting securities at their value under the rival. Consequently, the new securities will raise more revenue than the original ones. Q.E.D.

Using Lemma 9, we henceforth consider only problems (Q) or (Q').

Theorem 1. One share–one vote. If potential rivals are sufficiently diverse, the optimal security design requires one share–one vote.

Proof. If the solution violates (A.9), i.e., does not exhibit one share–one vote, then, by Lemma 8, it also violates (A.8). Hence by Lemma 7, the solution cannot be optimal. Q.E.D.

Theorem 2. Incumbent's retention of control. When the firm goes public, the incumbent should not retain any voting securities or risk-free debt.

Proof. Suppose (x, s, v) is an optimal solution of (Q'). First, we claim that (x, s, v) cannot be a single-owner solution, for suppose it were. Then $C(\bar{r}, x, s, v) = \Delta y(\bar{r})$ or

$$\beta \Delta S_1(\bar{r}) + \sum_{i=2}^{n} x_i \Delta S_i(\bar{r}) = \Delta y(\bar{r}).$$

This implies that $\Delta S_1(\bar{r}) = 0$ and

$$\sum_{i=2}^{n} (1 - x_i) \Delta S_i(\bar{r}) = 0.$$

Therefore, since $F(y|\bar{r})$ strictly dominates $F(y|0)$, it follows that s_1 is constant on Y as is s_i for any i with $x_i < 1$. But this contradicts our assumption that the incumbent cannot finance the project by issuing only risk-free debt. This proves that (x, s, v) cannot be the single-owner solution.

Now suppose $x_1 > 0$. Construct another solution (x', s', v') as follows:

$$s_1' = (1 - x_1)s_1,$$

$$s_2' = x_1 s_1,$$

$$s_3' = x_2 s_2 + \cdots + x_n s_n,$$

$$s_4' = (1 - x_2)s_2 + \cdots + (1 - x_n)s_n,$$

$$v_1' = 1,$$

$$x_1' = 0, \quad x_2' = x_3' = 1, \quad x_4' = 0.$$

Let $C(r) = C(r, x, s, v)$, $C'(r) = C(r, x', s', v')$. Then

$$C'(r) = \beta \Delta S_1'(r) + \Delta S_2'(r) + \Delta S_3'(r)$$

$$= (1 - \beta)x_1 \Delta S_1(r) + C(r).$$

Since $x_1 > 0$, $C'(r) > C(r)$ for all r such that $\Delta S_1(r) > 0$. Since $C(r)$ is monotone increasing, $w(x, s, v) = [0, \rho)$ for some $\rho \geq \bar{r}$. Claim that $\Delta S_1(\rho) > 0$, for suppose not. Then $\Delta S_1(r) \equiv 0$ on w, $C(r) \equiv \Delta y(r)$ on w, and $\rho = \bar{r}$. But this contradicts the fact that (x, s, v) is not the single-owner solution. Therefore $\Delta S_1(\rho) > 0$, which implies that $\Delta S_1(r) > 0$ for all $r > 0$. Also $xS = x'S'$, so, by Lemma 4, revenue at (x', s', v') strictly exceeds that at (x, s, v). Therefore, (x', s', v') is a feasible solution of (Q) and, by Lemma 6, (x, s, v) is not optimal.

It remains to show that s_2 contains no riskless cash flows. This is done in the proof of Theorem 3. Q.E.D.

Theorem 3. Nonvoting securities. The incumbent should not sell nonvoting, risky securities to outside investors.

Proof. We must show that s_3 contains only riskless cash flows. In the process, we also show that s_2 contains no riskless cash flows. Suppose (ρ, s)

solves (Q'). Let D be the maximum risk-free debt that can be issued. Let

$$s_1' \equiv s_1 + s_3, \quad s_2' \equiv s_2 - s_2(D), \quad s_3' \equiv s_2(D).$$

We will first show that (ρ', s'), where $\rho' = \rho(s')$, is feasible for (Q'). Clearly, s' is a feasible set of securities, since $y \geq D$ with probability one. Moreover, $C(r, s') \geq C(r, s)$ since $\Delta S_1' = \Delta S_1 + \Delta S_3$, $\Delta S_2' \equiv \Delta S_2$. Also $x'S' = S_2' \leq S_2 = xS$. Therefore, by Lemma 4, $R(\rho', s') \geq R(\rho, s)$ with strict inequality if $\Delta S_3(r) > 0$ with positive probability on $[0, \rho)$. If s_3 is not constant on the common support of $F(y|r)$, then $\Delta S_3(r) > 0$ for all r and $R(\rho', s') > R(\rho, s)$. Moreover, even if s_3 is constant, $R(\rho', s') > R(\rho, s)$ if $s_2(D) > 0$ since, in that case, $x'S' < xS$. Therefore if either s_3 is not constant or $s_2(D) > 0$, $R(\rho', s') > R(\rho, s) \geq I$. Therefore, by Lemma 6, s_3 is constant and $s_2(D) = 0$, i.e., any optimal s_3 contains only risk-free debt and any optimal s_2 contains no risk-free debt. Obviously, if s_3 is constant and $s_2(D) = 0$, then (ρ, s') is also optimal and $s_3' \equiv 0$. Q.E.D.

Theorem 4. Cash flow properties. The cash flow to the optimal voting security as a function of earnings consists of straight lines of slope 1 separated by horizontal segments (see fig. 3). The same is true of the nonvoting security. That is, any increment in earnings accrues either entirely to the voting security or entirely to the nonvoting security.

Proof. Suppose s_1 is the voting security and (r^*, s^*) solves (Q'). If $r^* = 1$, any security design will result in the incumbent's resisting all rivals. In this case, security design is irrelevant, and the conclusion holds weakly. Henceforth, assume $r^* < 1$. Using Lemma 6 and Theorem 3, s_1^* solves the following 'dual' problem:

(D) $\quad \max_{s} R(r^*, s),$

subject to

$$s(y) \in [0, y], \quad s \text{ and } y - s \text{ monotone increasing}, \qquad (A.10)$$

$$\rho(s) = r^*.$$

Since we assume that $r^* < 1$, we may replace the constraint $\rho(s) = r^*$ by $C(r^*, s) = B$.

We now rewrite R and C using the definition of S:

$$R(\rho, s) = \int_0^\rho \int_Y s(y)[\beta \, dF(y|r) + (1-\beta) \, dF(y|0)] \, dF(r)$$

$$+ \int_\rho^1 \int_Y s(y) \, dF(y|r) \, dF(r)$$

$$= \int_Y s(y) \left\{ \int_0^\rho [\beta \, dF(y|r) + (1-\beta) \, dF(y|0)] \, dF(r) \right.$$

$$\left. + \int_\rho^1 dF(y|r) \, dF(r) \right\}$$

$$= \int_Y s(y) \, dF^*(y, \rho)$$

$$= s(y_1) - \int_Y F^*(y, r^*) s'(y) \, dy \quad \text{(using integration by parts),}$$

$$= \int_Y [1 - F^*(y, r^*)] s'(y) \, dy,$$

where

$$dF^*(y, \rho) = \int_0^\rho [\beta \, dF(y|r) + (1+\beta) \, dF(y|0)] \, dF(r)$$

$$+ \int_\rho^1 dF(y|r) \, dF(r).$$

Also

$$C(r, s) = \Delta y(r) + (1-\beta) \int_Y s(y) \, dG(y, r)$$

$$= \Delta y(r) - (1-\beta) \int_Y G(y, r) s'(y) \, dy,$$

where

$$dG(y, r) = dF(y|0) - dF(y|r).$$

Using this notation, we can rewrite (D) as

$$\max_{s} \int_Y s'(y)[1 - F^*(y, r^*)]\, dy,$$

subject to

$$s'(y) \in [0,1] \quad \text{for all } y,$$

$$\int_Y s'(y) G(y, r^*)\, dy = \text{constant}.$$

The solution to (D) can be characterized as follows. For some $\lambda > 0$, for each y, $s'(y) = 0$ if $1 - F^*(y, r^*) - \lambda G(y, r^*) < 0$ and $s'(y) = 1$ otherwise. Since s_1^* must solve (D), we have shown that it consists of straight lines of slope 1 separated by horizontal segments. Q.E.D.

s_1^* has the textbook form of levered equity if and only if $(1 - F^*)/G$ crosses λ once from below. A sufficient condition for this is that $(1 - F^*)/G$ be increasing in y.

Rivals with benefits of control

Theorem 5. If the incumbent chooses to retain a controlling interest when the firm goes public, the cash flow to his claim as a function of earnings consists of straight lines of slope 1 separated by horizontal segments (see fig. 3). The same is true of the other security. That is, any increment in earnings accrues either entirely to the incumbent's security or entirely to the other security.

Proof. It is easy to check, as in the previous model, that the outside investors' security, s, solves the same dual problem as in the proof of Theorem 4, except that, in this case, $C(r) = \Delta y(r) - \Delta S(r)$. The problem can be restated using s' exactly as in the proof of Theorem 4, except that now

$$dF^*(y, \rho) = dF(y|1) F(\rho) + \int_\rho^1 dF(y|r)\, dF(r),$$

$$dG(y, r) = dF(y|r) - dF(y|1).$$

This shows that the outside investors' security is such that, for some $\lambda > 0$, $s'(y) = 0$ whenever $1 - F^*(y, r^*) - \lambda G(y, r^*) < 0$, and $s'(y) = 1$ otherwise. Since the incumbent's security is $s_1(y) = y - s(y)$, the result follows. Q.E.D.

The incumbent's security will have the textbook form of levered equity if and only if $(1 - F^*)/G$ crosses λ once from above.

Theorem 6. *If the incumbent chooses not to retain a controlling interest when the firm goes public and potential rivals are sufficiently diverse, the optimal security design requires a single class of voting* equity, *optionally levered by nonvoting, risk-free debt.*

Proof. Redefining $\Delta y(r) = y(1) - y(r)$, all the relevant lemmas and theorems proved above go through, some with slight modifications of the proofs.

References

Alchian, Armen and Harold Demsetz, 1972, Production, information costs, and economic organization, American Economic Review 52, 777–795.
Allen, Franklin and Douglas Gale, 1988, Optimal security design, Review of Financial Studies 1, 229–263.
Diamond, Douglas, 1984, Financial intermediation and delegated monitoring, Review of Economic Studies 51, 393–414.
Gale, Douglas and Martin Hellwig, 1985, Incentive compatible debt contracts: The one-period problem, Review of Economic Studies 52, 647–663.
Grossman, Sanford J. and Oliver D. Hart, 1988, One share/one vote and the market for corporate control, Journal of Financial Economics 20, 175–202.
Harris, Milton and Artur Raviv, 1988a, Corporate control contests and capital structure, Journal of Financial Economics 20, 55–86.
Harris, Milton and Artur Raviv, 1988b, Corporate governance: Voting rights and majority rules, Journal of Financial Economics 20, 203–235.
Israel, Ronen, 1988, Capital and ownership structure, and the market for corporate control, Working paper (Department of Finance, Kellogg School, Northwestern University, Evanston, IL).
Jensen, Michael C. and William H. Meckling, 1976, Theory of the firm: Managerial behavior, agency costs and ownership structure, Journal of Financial Economics 3, 305–360.
Townsend, Robert, 1979, Optimal contracts and competitive markets with costly state verification, Journal of Economic Theory 21, 265–293.
Williams, Joseph, 1987, Bonds, stocks, and warrants as optimal contracts between corporate claimants, Working paper (Graduate School of Business, New York University, New York, NY).
Zender, Jaime F., 1988, Optimal financial instruments, Working paper (University of Utah, Salt Lake City, UT).

Part VI
Takeover Contests

[18]

Takeover bids, the free-rider problem, and the theory of the corporation

Sanford J. Grossman*

and

Oliver D. Hart**

It is commonly thought that a widely held corporation that is not being run in the interest of its shareholders will be vulnerable to a takeover bid. We show that this is false, since shareholders can free ride on the raider's improvement of the corporation, thereby seriously limiting the raider's profit. We analyze exclusionary devices that can be built into the corporate charter to overcome this free-rider problem. We study privately and socially optimal corporate charters under the alternative assumptions of competition and monopoly in the market for corporate control.

1. Introduction

■ In all but the smallest groups social choice takes place via the delegation of power from many to few. A fundamental problem with this delegation is that no individual has a large enough incentive to devote resources to ensuring that the representatives are acting in the interest of the represented. Since the representatives serve the Public Good, the social benefit to monitoring their activities is far larger than the private benefit to any individual. That is, the Public Good is a public good and each person attempts to be a free rider in its production.

It is often suggested that in a corporation the free-rider problem can be avoided by use of the takeover bid mechanism. Suppose that the current directors of the corporation are not acting in the shareholders' interest, but that each shareholder is too small for it to be in his interest to devote resources to overthrowing management.[1] It is argued that this situation will not persist because an entrepreneur (i.e., a "raider") can make a takeover bid: he can buy

---

* University of Pennsylvania.
** Churchill College, Cambridge.

We are grateful to Christopher Bliss, Frank Hahn, John Mitchell, Howard Sosin, Joseph Stiglitz, and members of the Cambridge SSRC project on "Risk, Information, and Quantity Signals in Economics" for useful suggestions. We would also like to thank an anonymous referee and the editors of the *Bell Journal* for helpful comments.

We are grateful for research support from the U.K. Social Science Research Council and N.S.F. Grant no. SOC76-18711.

[1] See Williamson (1964) for a discussion of the separation of ownership and control in the corporation.

the company at a low price, manage it well, and then sell it back at a high price.[2] We show that this argument is false. Any profit a raider can make from the price appreciation of shares he purchases represents a profit shareholders could have made if they had not tendered their shares to the raider. In particular, suppose each shareholder is so small that his tender decision will not affect the outcome of the raid. Then, if a shareholder thinks that the raid will succeed and that the raider will improve the firm, he will not tender his shares, but will instead retain them, because he anticipates a profit from their price appreciation. As a result, a takeover bid may not be profitable even though current management is not acting in the interest of shareholders. Hence, even in a corporation, the public good (of the shareholders) is a public good.[3]

There is a real resource cost in operating the takeover mechanism. A raid should take place if and only if the social benefit is larger than the social cost. The raider bears the full social cost, but because shareholders attempt to free ride by not tendering their shares, he may be able to get only a small part of the social benefit. As a result, there may be many raids which should take place, but which do not, because it is not profitable for a raider to execute them.

Shareholders can overcome this free-rider problem. Specifically, they can write a constitution for the firm which permits the raider to exclude minority shareholders (i.e., shareholders who do not tender their shares to the raider and who hold shares in the postraid company) from sharing in all the improvements in the firm brought about by the raider. One method is for the shareholders to permit a successful raider to sell the firm's assets or output to another company owned by the raider at terms which are disadvantageous to minority shareholders. The raider then receives more from the raid than just his share of the company's (increased) profits. This compensation comes at the expense of other shareholders and represents a voluntary dilution of their property rights.

In Section 2 of the paper, we discuss the role of such dilutions and focus on how the extent of permitted dilution affects the tender price the raider must pay, and hence the profitability of raids. The ease with which raids can take place will, of course, influence the actions of the incumbent management. We study this in Section 3. In Sections 4 and 5, we consider the optimal amount of dilution from the point of view of the firm's shareholders and from

---

[2] See Marris (1964) and Manne (1965) for a discussion of the role of takeover bids in ensuring that a director serves the interests of shareholders.

[3] The problem is similar to that which occurs in real estate deals involving urban renewal. It is sometimes suggested that if a few city blocks are dilapidated (because, e.g., there are filthy streets that are dark and unsafe, filled with houses that have unpainted ugly exteriors and uncut lawns, etc.), then an entrepreneur can buy the houses at a low price, clean the streets, etc., then sell the houses at a high price and make a profit. (The entrepreneur "internalizes" the externality.) However, if we own one of the houses on this street, then we shall surely not sell to the entrepreneur at a low price because, after the street is improved, our house will rise in value. In the case of real estate, this "unexcludability" is avoided by the use of secrecy or by making each house purchase contingent on the entrepreneur's acquiring *all* of the houses on the street (i.e., unanimity). The use of secrecy is difficult for firms traded in a stock market because: (A) in the United States the Williams Act requires potential raiders to disclose their intent publically after they purchase 5 percent of the stock and (B) the stock market is full of traders constantly looking for information that a stock will appreciate in value and thus secrecy is hard to maintain. The use of unanimity never occurs in takeovers of widely held companies, presumably because each shareholder would attempt to be the only "holdout" and thus anticipate a secret payment from the raider for his shares in addition to the tender price. With many small shareholders it would be very difficult to enforce a unanimous contract for the above reason.

the point of view of society. Section 6 comments on the role of competition among raiders. Finally, Section 7 contains concluding remarks. The Appendix contains the proofs of all the lemmas and propositions which are stated without proof in the text.

2. The role of dilution in takeover bids

■ In the Introduction we indicated that takeover bids may not ensure good management of corporations because of shareholders' attempts to free ride. The purpose of this section is to develop a formal model of this free-rider problem.

We assume that the profit of a typical firm is given by a function $f(a)$, where a is a description of activities engaged in by the firm (e.g., investment decisions, hiring decisions, and managerial effort). We suppose that there is no uncertainty about the firm's profit once the activity a has been selected. The number $f(a)$ may also be interpreted as the net present value of the future stream of profit generated by activity a or the market value of the firm's shares. (In this paper we shall not distinguish among profit, net present value, or market value.)[4] Let A denote the set of all feasible activities for the firm.

Consider a firm which is using activity $a_0 \in A$. Let $q = f(a_0)$ denote the current profit of the firm. Suppose now that an individual (henceforth known as the raider) announces his intention to take over the firm and announces a *tender price p* at which he is willing to buy unconditionally all shares tendered to him.

How will the shareholders of the target firm react to the tender offer? One of the most important factors influencing this reaction is the extent to which the shareholders believe the raider will improve the firm, should his takeover bid be successful. Because we wish to study the efficiency of the takeover bid process in the purest case, we shall assume that the raider is a profit maximizer:

For the sake of generality, however, we shall not suppose that the raider and the firm's current manager necessarily have the same ability in running the firm. Let $\max_{a \in A} f(a)$ be the maximum profit of the firm under current management. We write the profit of the firm under the raider's management as $v = \max_{a \in A} f(a) + \epsilon$, where ϵ is a measure of the differences in ability between the raider and the *status quo* manager. (We shall sometimes treat ϵ and thus v as random variables.) If the raider's bid is successful, the new profit of the firm is assumed to be given by v. We shall assume that both the raider and the shareholders know $\max_{a \in A} f(a)$, ϵ, and hence v at the time of the raid. This is a strong assumption, but it seems to provide a reasonable starting point for an analysis of takeover bids. Further, one might expect the takeover bid mechanism to work best when the shareholders and the raider are under no illusions about the quality of management.

The raider's takeover bid will be deemed successful if more than 50 percent of the shares are tendered to the raider. Suppose that the firm is owned by a large number of shareholders, each of whom owns a very small proportion of the firm. Under these conditions the probability that any shareholder's tender decision

---

[4] We shall assume that the market value of the firm's shares represents the total benefits which the shareholders get out of the firm. In other words, we assume that the demand curve for the firm's shares is infinitely elastic and hence shareholders get no consumer surplus from holding the firm's shares. A result of this is that the firm's initial shareholders will be unanimous that the firm should choose an action a to maximize $f(a)$.

will be decisive in determining the success or failure of the bid is negligible. Thus, each shareholder will ignore his impact on the outcome of the bid in making his tender decision.

We shall also assume that shareholders and the raider have rational expectations about the outcome of a bid. In this paper we shall not consider bids with stochastic outcomes, i.e., bids which succeed some fraction of the time and fail the remaining fraction of the time. Thus the only successful bids are those which are expected to be successful *with certainty*.

It is straightforward to show that under the above assumptions the commonly made argument that a poorly managed and hence low-priced firm can be taken over, managed well, and resold at a profit by an entrepreneur is incorrect. Suppose that the raider's tender price is p. Then any shareholder who thinks that the raid will succeed with certainty will *not* tender his shares if $p < v$. This results because, given that his tender decision has no impact on the outcome of the bid, he can do better by holding on (he gets v) than by tendering (he gets p). Since no shareholder tenders his shares, a bid with tender price $p < v$ will, of course, fail. It follows that for a raid to succeed, given that shareholders anticipate that it will succeed (this is the assumption of rational expectations), it is necessary that

$$p \geq v. \qquad (1)$$

But under these conditions the raider makes no profit, since he pays at least as much for the firm's shares as they are worth to him. In fact, if, as we would expect, raids are costly, the raider actually makes a loss! Thus no raids will take place, even if q is very low relative to v.[5]

Raids are unprofitable because each shareholder is in a position to free ride on a potentially successful raid. Any profit the raider can expect from the price appreciation of the shares he purchases can be captured by a shareholder if he does *not* tender. Therefore, individual rationality by shareholders concerning the tender decision leads to an outcome which is highly undesirable for all shareholders—there are no takeover bids and bad management is not penalized.[6]

In practice the free-rider problem is not so severe as in the model described above, and raids do take place. What changes are necessary to allow for this possibility? The most obvious modification is to introduce differences in valuation of the firm by the raider and the shareholders—as a result, say, of differences in risk preferences or information. Let us continue to assume that the raider values the raider-controlled firm at v, but let the shareholders' valuation be v_s, which may be different from v. That is, v_s is the value prospective minority shareholders put on 100 percent of the dividends in the raider-controlled corporation. Then, by the argument above, the lowest tender price at which the raider can get control of the firm is v_s. At this price we may assume that all shares are tendered to the raider, since shareholders are indifferent between

---

[5] We are assuming that the raider is not a shareholder before he makes the raid. Clearly, if the raider owns a fraction of the firm larger than $c/(v - q)$ before a successful raid is announced, where c is the cost of the raid, then the raider can make a profit. See footnote 3 for the reasons it is difficult to make purchases secretly.

[6] In Grossman and Hart (1979b), we analyze bids at prices p satisfying $q < p < v$ whose outcomes are stochastic. We show that stochastic bids do not change the nature of the free-rider problem. In particular, the result that the raider cannot make a profit from a takeover bid without dilution still holds (where profit must be interpreted in expected terms).

tendering and not tendering. Let c be the cost of the raid. The raider's profit is then

$$\pi = v - v_s - c. \tag{2}$$

If v_s is sufficiently small relative to v, raids will now occur.

While differences in valuation are undoubtedly important in permitting raids to take place, it would be unwise for shareholders to rely on luck to bring a raider who, for some exogenous reason, values the dividend stream of the firm more than shareholders do. It is better for shareholders to *create* a divergence between the value of the dividend stream to a raider and its value to shareholders who attempt to free ride on the raider's improvements of the firm.

This can be achieved as follows. Let initial shareholders write a corporate constitution or charter permitting any successful raider to reduce the value of the postraid company by a certain amount, which the raider is permitted to pay to himself. There are a number of ways to achieve such a reduction in value. For example, the raider can be allowed to pay himself a large salary or to issue a number of new shares to himself. Alternatively, the raider can be permitted to sell the target firm's assets at below their true value, via a merger or liquidation, to another company owned by the raider. (See Section 7 for further comments on this method.) A third possibility is for the raider to sell the target firm's output to one of the raider's other companies at an artificially low price. For example, suppose that company A, which produces automobiles, obtains control of company B, which produces automobile tires. Then the new directors of company B might sell tires to A at a low price so that most of the profits of the tire company accrue to the automobile company.

Whichever method is used, the result is the same: the value to shareholders of not tendering their shares to the raider and of becoming minority shareholders in the raider-run firm is reduced. A divergence between the shareholders' valuation and the raider's valuation of the postraid firm is introduced, and shareholders are excluded to some extent from free riding on the improvements brought about by the raider.

It is important to realize that this divergence corresponds to a voluntary dilution of shareholder property rights. When the firm is well managed, it is worth v, and hence the shareholders could with some justification claim that v is the "true" or "fair" value of their shares. By permitting the raider to reduce the value of the company and to pay the excess to himself, shareholders are depriving themselves of the full worth of their shares: that is, they are voluntarily diluting their property rights. Much of takeover bid law implicitly assumes that such dilutions are undesirable. The point of view taken in this paper, however, is that dilutions of this kind are essential if the takeover bid mechanism is to be effective in penalizing bad managers.

Let us consider how dilutions affect the price at which the raider can acquire control. Assume that the initial shareholders, when writing a corporate charter, can enforce a maximal level of dilution, given by ϕ dollars.[7] For simplicity, in what follows we shall ignore any exogenous differences in raider

---

[7] Though actual corporate charters do not specify a monetary limit on dilution, they do specify the extent to which minority shareholders are protected from dilution. See Grossman and Hart (1980) for an analysis of how monetary levels of dilution are related to the stringency of disclosure and appraisal requirements.

and shareholder valuations. Given the dilution factor ϕ, the value to a shareholder from retaining his shares in the event that a raid succeeds is $v_t \equiv v - \phi$. Thus, if the raider offers the tender price p, and shareholders think that the raid will succeed, they will tender as long as

$$p \geq v - \phi. \tag{3}$$

In this case, of course, the raid will indeed succeed (we assume as above that shareholders who are indifferent between tendering and not tendering do tender).

Equation (3) implies that if $v - \phi < q$, bids can take place at below the *status quo* market value $q = f(a_0)$. Note, however, that such bids will fail if they are expected to fail (shareholders will not tender, since tendering means getting p if the bid is unconditional, whereas not tendering means getting q).[8] For this reason, and also because bids at below market value are rarely observed in practice, we shall henceforth rule out bids at $p < q$. That is, we shall impose the condition $p \geq q$ in addition to (3).

It follows that the lowest tender price which enables the raider to get control, when dilution is restricted to ϕ, is

$$p = \max(v - \phi, q). \tag{4}$$

Thus, if the cost of the raid is c, the raider's profit will be

$$v - p - c = v - \max(v - \phi, q) - c = \min(\phi, v - q) - c. \tag{5}$$

This will be positive if ϕ and $(v - q)$ both exceed c, and raids will take place under these conditions.

It is important to realize that in our model the only effect of dilution is to reduce the price the raider has to pay the shareholders to get control of the firm. Given our assumptions, the raider who pays $p = \max(v - \phi, q)$ will get complete control of the firm, i.e., he will acquire 100 percent of the shares. (Since (3) holds, no shareholder will wish to retain any shares.) Once he owns 100 percent of the firm, the dilution which he extracts is a matter of complete indifference—every extra dollar he receives in dilution is one dollar less received in dividends. The point, however, is that it is precisely the *threat* that the raider can dilute up to ϕ, which reduces the value to shareholders of retaining their shares and allows the raider to get control. (In a more complicated model in which some shares are tendered and some are not, the raider will find it in his interest to carry out dilution.)

In the next section, we study the effect of dilutions on the current management's choice of *status quo* profit, q. Then in Sections 4 and 5 we analyze the optimal level of dilution for shareholders and for society.

3. The influence of takeover bids on the manager's choice of the status quo

■ We take as a premise that corporations have the following sort of life cycle. Initially, a very small group of shareholders writes the corporate charter and

---

[8] In other words, if $v - \phi < p < q$, there are two rational expectations equilibria. If the bid is anticipated to succeed, it will succeed. On the other hand, if the bid is anticipated to fail, it will fail. In contrast, when $p \geq \max(v - \phi, q)$, there is a single rational expectations equilibrium in which the bid succeeds.

decides to "go public," i.e., they sell part of their right to the company's earnings stream. Since these initial shareholders are large shareholders, who desire to sell their shares at the highest possible price, it is in their interest to devote resources to see that the corporation is organized to maximize the (expected) return to all potential shareholders. The initial shareholders realize that they will sell most of their shares in the future and that eventually the corporation will be owned by many small shareholders, none of whom will find it in his interest to collect information about the corporation. Hence, at the time the charter is written, initial shareholders try to devise self-enforcing mechanisms to ensure good management. One mechanism available to initial shareholders is to give directors salary incentives, e.g., stock options, warrants, etc. The initial shareholders recognize, however, that salary incentive schemes will not be perfect, because perfection would require the director's salary to be contingent on events which it would be quite costly for any small shareholder to verify. (For example, an optimal incentive scheme would attempt to distinguish between low earnings due to poor management and low earnings due to a general decline in the industry.)

Recognizing that there are many future states of nature in which the managerial salary incentive scheme will be so ineffective that directors will deviate significantly from profit maximization, initial shareholders write a corporate charter which encourages takeover bids. Initial shareholders realize that if deviations from profit maximization occur and if dilution is permitted, then a raider will find it in his interest to collect the appropriate information to discover how to revise the managerial incentive scheme so that profit maximization is again encouraged. That is, the raider can take over the firm at price $p = \max(v - \phi, q)$ and change the incentive scheme to incorporate all the new information available about the probability distribution of the firm's returns. The raider can then sell the company with the new incentive scheme in place at price v, and make a profit through the price appreciation of the target company's shares (assuming dilution is permitted).

When the raider takes over, he is in the same position as the initial shareholders were. In addition to revising the managerial salary incentive scheme, he may also modify the corporate charter. He then sells a large fraction of his shares so that the corporation is once again in the hands of many small shareholders. The whole life cycle then begins anew.

In this paper we shall analyze only one realization of this process; namely, assume the following sequence of events: (1) A single director-manager is assigned to the firm. (2) This manager chooses an action a_0 with resulting profit $q = f(a_0)$. (3) A potential raider arrives and decides whether or not to raid. (For the moment, we ignore the possibility that there is more than one raider; see, however, Section 6.) (4) If a raid is successfully carried out, the raider fires the current manager and replaces the action a_0 by a profit-maximizing action (it is assumed that the current manager has not yet had time to make any irreversible decisions); if no raid takes place, or if the raid is unsuccessful, the action a_0 is retained.

As in Section 2, the value of the firm under the raider's management is $v = \max_{a \in A} f(a) + \epsilon$. For reasons which will become clear, we assume that ϵ, and hence v, are stochastic. To indicate this we shall write $\tilde{v}$. We shall also assume that the cost of the raid is a random variable, denoted by $\tilde{c}$. The manager does not know the realizations of $\tilde{v}$ and $\tilde{c}$ when he chooses a_0. However, we assume that at the time of the raid, shareholders know the realization of $\tilde{v}$ and the raider knows the realization of $(\tilde{v}, \tilde{c})$.

The manager has well-defined preferences over the set of feasible actions of the firm, A. These preferences will be assumed to be representable by a utility function $\acute{U}: A \to R$, where R is the real line.[9] It is useful to express the manager's utility in terms of the profit q that he must achieve instead of the action a he takes. We denote this by $U(q)$ and assume that U is continuous in q.[10] We assume that the initial shareholders who write the corporate charter know the derived or indirect utility function $U(q)$.[11]

In this section we take the dilution factor ϕ to be fixed, and we analyze how the manager's choice of *status quo* profit q depends on ϕ.

Suppose the manager chooses a_0, giving rise to the profit $q = f(a_0)$. Let (v, c) be the realization of $(\tilde{v}, \tilde{c})$. We saw in Section 2 that if the raider decides to make a raid, he will have to offer at least the tender price max $(v - \phi, q)$ to be successful, so his profit will be $v - \max(v - \phi, q) - c = \min(\phi, v - q) - c$, where c is the cost of the raid. Thus, a raid will occur for realizations of $(\tilde{v}, \tilde{c})$ such that $\min(\phi, v - q) - c$ is positive and will not occur otherwise.

Let $\acute{U}$ be the utility that the manager receives if he is fired by the raider and must seek a job elsewhere. Without loss of generality, we set $\acute{U} = 0$. Then the manager's utility from the profit q is given by

$$\begin{cases} U(q) & \text{if} \quad \min(\phi, v - q) - c \leq 0, \quad \text{i.e., in the event of no raid;} \\ 0 & \text{if} \quad \min(\phi, v - q) - c > 0, \quad \text{i.e., in the event of a raid.} \end{cases} \quad (6)$$

We shall assume that the manager maximizes expected utility. Let $F(c, v)$ denote the distribution function of $(\tilde{c}, \tilde{v})$ and let $\pi(\phi, q) \equiv \text{Prob } [\min(\phi, \tilde{v} - q) > \tilde{c}]$ denote the probability of a raid.[12] Since the manager's final utility is given by (6) for the particular realization (c, v) of $(\tilde{c}, \tilde{v})$, it follows that the manager's expected utility from profit q is

$$W(q) = U(q)(1 - \pi(\phi, q)). \quad (7)$$

Hence, an optimal action for the manager is one that maximizes $W(q)$.

---

[9] The utility function $\acute{U}$ is understood to incorporate such factors as the salary of the manager, the amount of managerial effort required to implement the particular action a, the size of the firm, the manager's shareholding in the firm, and any salary incentive scheme that initial shareholders have devised for the manager. (For a discussion of these and other determinants of managerial "utility," see Baumol (1959), Marris (1964), and Williamson (1964). See also Ross (1977) and Mirrlees (1976) for discussion of salary incentive schemes.)

[10] Assume that the set of feasible profit levels $\{q | f(a) = q$ for some $a \in A\}$ equals the closed interval $[q_{min}, \max_{a \in A} f(a)]$ for some nonnegative numbers q_{min}, $\max_{a \in A} f(a)$. Define $U(q) = \max_{a \in A} \acute{U}(a)$ subject to $f(a) = q$, where $q_{min} \leq q \leq \max_{a \in A} f(a)$. Note that management may be attempting to maximize profit, but it may lack the ability or information to do so. This can be incorporated into our model if we think of $U(q)$ as being very low for values of q which the manager lacks the ability or information to produce. Thus, in particular, set $U(q) = -\infty$ for $q > \max_{a \in A} f(a)$.

[11] For simplicity, we have taken the profit function $q = f(a)$ to be deterministic. Of course, if this were really the case, there would exist a salary incentive scheme which gets the manager to maximize profit: "produce maximum profit $\max_{a \in A} f(a)$ or you are fired." A perfect incentive scheme of this sort would not exist, and none of our results would change, if we assumed that $q = f(a, \theta)$, where θ is a parameter unobserved by shareholders, but known to the manager and the raider. The need for dilution, furthermore, is just as great as in the deterministic model studied in this paper.

[12] We shall assume that $\tilde{v}$ is bounded from above and that $\tilde{c}$ and $\tilde{v}$ are nonnegative.

Note that the probability of a raid $\pi(\phi,q)$ is a nonincreasing function of q. Hence, the tradeoff for the manager is between choosing a high profit action with an associated low chance of being raided and choosing an action which provides high managerial utility but which is likely to lead to a successful takeover bid.

If $\tilde{v}$ and $\tilde{c}$ are nonstochastic, then for a given choice of q, either a raid occurs with certainty or no raid occurs, i.e., $\pi(\phi,q) = 1$ or $\pi(\phi,q) = 0$. It follows that as long as $U(v) > 0$, the manager will always choose q large enough so that no raids ever take place. However, when $\tilde{v}$ and $\tilde{c}$ *are* stochastic, it will not in general be optimal for the manager to choose q such that $\pi(\phi,q) = 0$, and hence takeover bids will generally occur.

4. Shareholders' optimal choice of the dilution factor, ϕ

■ In the last section we studied the manager's action for a fixed dilution factor ϕ. We consider now the optimal value of the dilution factor, ϕ, for the initial shareholders of the firm.

We shall assume that the market values the firm according to its expected return; that is, the market is risk-neutral with respect to the firm's activities.[13] Hence, the initial shareholders—who wish to get as high a value for their shares as possible—will choose a value of ϕ which maximizes the expected return from the firm's operations. This expected return is given by

$$r(\phi) \equiv q(1 - \pi(\phi,q)) + E[\max(\tilde{v} - \phi, q) | \min(\phi, \tilde{v} - q) > \tilde{c}]\pi(\phi,q), \quad (8)$$

since if there is no raid (which occurs when $\min(\phi, \tilde{v} - q) \le \tilde{c}$), the market value of the firm equals the profit of the firm, q; while if there is a raid (which occurs when $\min(\phi, \tilde{v} - q) > \tilde{c}$), the market value of shareholders' shares equals the tender price announced by the raider, $\max(\tilde{v} - \phi, q)$. It should be emphasized that $r(\phi)$ is the value at which the firm's shares sell in the market *before* it is known whether or not a takeover bid is going to occur.

Consider how changes in ϕ affect $r(\phi)$. As ϕ increases, the value of shares in the event of a raid (the tender price), $\max(\tilde{v} - \phi, q)$, decreases. At the same time, however, the probability of a raid, $\pi(\phi,q)$, increases. Hence an increase in ϕ reduces the *amount* shareholders gain from any particular raid, but it increases the *number* (the probability) of raids.

There is a further effect caused by a variation in ϕ which results from the fact that the *status quo* profit q depends on ϕ. In the last section we showed that the manager chooses q to maximize $W(q) = U(q)(1 - \pi(\phi,q))$. In general, we might expect that an increase in ϕ, by making raids easier, will lead the manager to choose a higher *status quo* profit. We shall demonstrate that this is indeed the case.

A difficulty that arises in the analysis of the relationship between *status quo* profit and ϕ is that there may be several actions which are optimal for the manager, and hence several possible optimal *status quo* profit levels, even if $U(q)$ is strictly concave. We shall assume that if the manager is indifferent between two actions, then he chooses the one with the higher profit level. This

---

[13] This is a reasonable assumption if the firm's return is independent of the returns of other firms, and shareholders hold well-diversified portfolios.

enables us to write *status quo* profit q as a function of ϕ, $q(\phi)$, and in the Appendix we prove:

Proposition 1: $q(\phi)$ is nondecreasing in ϕ.

An increase in ϕ therefore has three effects: (1) for a given *status quo* profit q, it reduces the tender price offered by the raider if he chooses to raid, and hence the amount that the shareholders receive from any particular raid; (2) it increases the number of raids that take place for any *status quo* profit q; (3) it increases the return to shareholders in the event there is no raid, i.e., it increases the *status quo* profit q. From the point of view of the shareholders, (2) and (3) are goods, while (1) is a bad.

Because of these three effects, general analysis of the optimal ϕ is quite difficult. However, much insight can be gained from the analysis of special cases. Consider first the case where $\tilde{c}$ is nonstochastic. Then the following can be established:

Proposition 2: Suppose $\tilde{c}$ is nonstochastic, i.e., $\tilde{c} = c$ with probability one.

(a) If $\tilde{v}$ is nonstochastic, i.e., $\tilde{v} \equiv v$, and $U(v) > 0$, then it is optimal for the initial shareholders to choose any ϕ such that $\phi > c$. At any optimal ϕ no raids take place.

(b) If $\tilde{v}$ is stochastic (i.e., the marginal distribution of $\tilde{v}$ is not degenerate), then: (i) Initial shareholders will want to choose ϕ to maximize the tender price in the event of a raid subject to $\phi > c$. This is accomplished by setting $\phi > c$, but as close to c as possible.[14] (ii) Raids will generally take place. (iii) $q(\phi)$ is constant for all $\phi > c$.

Proof:

(a) From (5), raids take place if and only if min $(\phi, v - q) > c$. Since $\tilde{c}$ and $\tilde{v}$ are nonstochastic, this means that a raid takes place with probability one or probability zero. The assumption $U(v) > 0$ implies that the manager would rather profit maximize—and hence avoid a raid—than choose an action which would lead him to lose his job with certainty. It follows that the manager will act so that no raids take place. Hence, the return to shareholders is given by *status quo* profit, $q(\phi)$. From Proposition 1 it follows that it is optimal for shareholders to set ϕ as large as possible. However, if $\phi > c$, then min $(\phi, v - q) > c$ iff $v - q > c$. Hence $\pi(\phi, q)$ is constant for all $\phi > c$, and therefore $r(\phi) = q(\phi)$ is constant for all $\phi > c$.

Note that since in this case there are never any raids, the factor which makes a large ϕ unattractive to shareholders (namely that a large ϕ will lead to a low tender price in the event of a raid) is absent.

(b) If $\phi \leq c$, then by (5) no raids take place so that in this case $r(\phi) = q(\phi)$. Since $r(\phi) \geq q(\phi)$ for $\phi > c$, it follows from Proposition 1 that $\phi \leq c$ is not optimal. If $\phi > c$, then min $(\phi, \tilde{v} - q) > c$ iff $\tilde{v} - q > c$. Hence $\pi(\phi, q)$ is constant for all $\phi > c$. Therefore, the manager's action $q(\phi)$ will be a constant for all $\phi > c$. However, for all $\tilde{v}$ such that $\tilde{v} - \phi > q$, the tender price $p = \max (\tilde{v} - \phi, q)$ will be reduced when ϕ is raised. Thus, by making ϕ as small as possible *but* larger than c, shareholders maximize the tender price without

---

[14] We denote such a situation by $\phi \cong c$. In general there is a trivial "openness problem" and no optimal ϕ exists in this case.

lowering managerial effort. In general, it will not be optimal for the manager to set q so high that the probability of a raid is zero (since with $\tilde{v}$ stochastic he can trade off low probability of raids against high managerial utility). Thus raids do in general take place. *Q.E.D.*

Proposition 2a illustrates the fact that permitting large levels of dilution, and thus a low tender price in the event of a raid, is good for shareholders if no raids ever occur. In Proposition 2b, however, raids do occur, and so shareholders wish to limit dilution to obtain a high tender price. In the case where $\tilde{c}$ is nonstochastic, this is achieved without any reduction in managerial effort because the threat of a raid, $\pi(\phi,q)$, will be constant for all $\phi > c$. The next proposition shows that if $\tilde{c}$ is stochastic, then there is a real tradeoff between the achievement of a high tender price and managerial efficiency.

Proposition 3: Suppose that $\tilde{v}$ is nonstochastic, i.e., $\tilde{v} = v$ with probability one, but that $\tilde{c}$ is stochastic (i.e., the marginal distribution of $\tilde{c}$ is not degenerate). Then it is optimal for the shareholders either (1) to put no restrictions on the raider's ability to dilute, i.e., to set $\phi = \infty$, which means that $p = \max(\tilde{v} - \phi, q) = q$; or (2) to choose ϕ to maximize

$$(v - \phi) \text{ Prob } (\phi > \tilde{c}) + q^* \text{ Prob } (\phi \le \tilde{c}), \qquad (9)$$

where q^* is the unconstrained utility-maximizing profit for the manager, i.e., q^* solves $\max_q U(q)$. (In case (2), the manager ignores the possibility of a raid and sets $q(\phi) = q^*$.)

The idea of the proof (which is given in the Appendix) can be seen by noting that if $\tilde{v} = v$ with certainty, then the raider's tender price is

$$p = \max(\tilde{v} - \phi, q) = \begin{cases} v - \phi & \text{if } q \le v - \phi \\ q & \text{if } q > v - \phi. \end{cases}$$

Consider a given value of ϕ. Then for each q, p is independent of either ϕ or q. Let ϕ^* be the optimal choice of ϕ for the shareholders. If $p = q$ at the optimum, then ϕ can be set equal to $+\infty$ without changing anything. This is case (1) of Proposition 3, and raids are encouraged as much as possible. In this case the manager maximizes $U(q)$ Prob $(v - q \ge \tilde{c})$. Let $\hat{q}$ denote the solution to this problem.

On the other hand, if $p = v - \phi > q(\phi)$ at the optimal ϕ, then by lowering q the manager will not increase the probability of a raid. Hence, he chooses $q = q^*$—the maximizer of $U(q)$. This is case (2) of Proposition 3. In this case shareholders know that for all ϕ such that $v - \phi > q^*$, the manager's action is unchanged, and hence their tradeoff is between increasing ϕ to increase the probability of a raid, Prob $(\phi > \tilde{c})$, or decreasing ϕ to increase the tender price $(v - \phi)$.

Case (1) of Proposition 3 will apply when $\hat{q}$ is close to v and $\hat{q}$ is much larger than q^*: if the threat of a raid provides very strong incentives for good management and if the salary incentive scheme embodied in $U(q)$ is not very effective. Case (2) applies, in contrast, when $\hat{q}$ is substantially lower than v and $\hat{q}$ is close to q^*: when the threat of a raid provides a weak incentive for managerial effort relative to the salary incentive scheme. In the latter case it is not optimal for the shareholders to set $\phi = \infty$ and to sacrifice the chance of getting a high tender price in the event of a raid. In fact, it is preferable for them to dispense with the takeover threat altogether.

When $\bar{v}$ is nonstochastic and $\bar{c}$ is stochastic, shareholders choose only between the profit levels $\hat{q}$ and q^*. If $\bar{v}$ and $\bar{c}$ are both stochastic, however, then $q(\phi)$ will take on more than two values as ϕ varies. In fact, it will vary smoothly with ϕ because for each ϕ and q, the tender price $p = \max(\bar{v} - \phi, q)$ will equal $\bar{v} - \phi$ for some realizations of $\bar{v}$, and it will equal q for other realizations of $\bar{v}$. Hence, changes in ϕ and q will always have some impact on the probability of a raid. In other respects, though, the case where $\bar{v}$ and $\bar{c}$ are both stochastic is very similar to the case where $\bar{c}$ alone is stochastic. In particular, there is a real tradeoff between achieving a high tender price and inducing managerial efficiency; shareholders' pursuit of the former leads to a (partial) sacrifice of the latter.

In summary, if shareholders know the costs of a takeover bid, then by setting $\phi > c$ they can compensate the raider for these costs. Proposition 2 shows that under these conditions it is optimal for shareholders to exploit fully the threat of raids: the optimal choice of ϕ leads to maximization of the *status quo* profit $q(\phi)$.[15] In contrast, when $\bar{c}$ is stochastic, Proposition 3(2) shows that shareholders may limit the disciplinary role of raids considerably in their efforts to ensure a high tender price.

Since the case where $\bar{c}$ is stochastic yields rather different results from that in which $\bar{c}$ is nonstochastic, it is worth considering the nature of takeover bid costs. A raider must face four main costs. The first is the cost of collecting information about possible improvements in the firm. Second, there is the cost of raising the funds to finance the purchase of the firm. Third, there are the administrative and litigation expenses of the takeover bid itself. Finally, there is the cost of reorganizing the firm if the raid is successful.[16] While it may be possible to estimate some of these costs quite accurately (e.g., the cost of running the tender offer), it may be very difficult to estimate others (e.g., the cost of information collection or reorganization). Furthermore, some of these costs may be raider-specific; they may be high for some raiders and low for others. Since the characteristics of the particular raider who will make a bid are not known *a priori*, this may create considerable uncertainty about cost levels. For these reasons it seems likely that the initial shareholders writing the corporate charter will perceive the raider's cost—his reservation price for carrying out a raid—as a random variable (with possibly high variance) rather than a determinate number. In other words, the case where $\bar{c}$ is stochastic would seem to be of greater practical significance than the case where $\bar{c}$ is nonstochastic.[17]

---

[15] In particular, $q(\phi) = q(\infty)$. One possibility which we have not considered is that shareholders subsidize raids. Under some conditions this can lead to higher *status quo* profit levels than $q(\infty)$. For example, suppose that $\bar{c}$ and $\bar{v}$ are nonstochastic. Let it be written into the corporate charter that anybody who carries out a raid will be given a subsidy equal to c. Then this forces the manager to set $q = v$, if he wants to avoid a raid. In contrast, if there is no subsidy and $\phi = \infty$, the manager can avoid a raid by setting $q = v - c$. There are obvious moral hazards involved with this scheme.

[16] For example, the raider may have to spend time working out how to devise an incentive scheme which will ensure that future managers of the firm carry out the profit-maximizing action.

[17] In the analysis we have lumped together the four above outlined costs. From a formal point of view, however, this is not really legitimate, since the cost of collecting information about the firm differs from the other costs in that it is a *sunk* cost by the time the raid occurs. Thus, while this cost will influence whether a raider investigates the firm in the first place, it will have no effect on the raider's decision to raid, once he has decided to become informed. See Grossman and Hart (1979a) for a model of takeovers which carefully distinguishes between the sunk and nonsunk costs.

5. The optimal choice of the dilution factor ϕ for society

■ So far we have looked at the initial shareholders' choice of the dilution factor. However, it is also interesting and important to consider society's perspective on this decision. This section will analyze the divergence between the shareholders' and society's views that is generated by the assumption that there is only one raider in the event of a takeover bid. The next section explains the reasons for this assumption.

We shall assume that society, like the shareholders, is risk neutral with respect to the activities of the firm. For a given value of ϕ, the return to society from the firm's activities is

$$R(\phi) \equiv q(\phi)(1 - \pi(\phi,q)) + E[\tilde{v} - \tilde{c} | \min(\phi, \tilde{v} - q(\phi)) > \tilde{c}]\pi(\phi,q)$$
$$= r(\phi) + E[\min(\phi, \tilde{v} - q(\phi)) - \tilde{c} | \min(\phi, \tilde{v} - q(\phi)) > \tilde{c}] \times \pi(\phi,q) \quad (10)$$

because when there is a raid, the efficiency gain is the increase in the profit of the firm minus the cost of resources used up in the raid. We are ignoring distributional effects—how much the raider gets versus how much the shareholders get—and we are also assuming that the social cost of resources consumed in the raid equals the private cost. Finally, we assume that perfectly competitive conditions prevail in the market for the firm's output(s), so that the social contribution of the firm to the economy is represented by its profit. (Thus we are not considering raids which take place to restrict competition.)

From (5) the raider's expected profit is $E[\min(\phi, \tilde{v} - q) - \tilde{c} | \min(\phi, \tilde{v} - q) > \tilde{c}] \times \pi(\phi,q)$. Hence, from (10) it is clear that the social return $R(\phi)$ will equal the private return $r(\phi)$ if the raider makes zero profit.[18] This will occur if there is competition by other raiders at the time of the raid. It will also occur if there are no realizations of $(\tilde{v},\tilde{c})$ for which a raid takes place. Recall from Proposition 2 that if $\tilde{v}$ and $\tilde{c}$ are nonstochastic, shareholders choose ϕ such that no raids take place. Hence we have:

Proposition 4: If $\tilde{c}$ and $\tilde{v}$ are nonstochastic and $U(v) > 0$, then it is optimal for society to choose any ϕ such that $\phi > c$.

Proposition 4 shows that, in particular, it is optimal for society to set $\phi = \infty$ when $\tilde{c}$ and $\tilde{v}$ are nonstochastic. We shall now show that, under our assumptions, this result generalizes: $\phi = \infty$ is socially optimal even when $\tilde{c}$ and $\tilde{v}$ are both stochastic. Recall from Section 4 that an increase in ϕ has three

---

[18] In measuring the firm's return to society, we have ignored the welfare of managers. In general, the manager gets consumer surplus out of his job. In fact, Calvo (1977) has emphasized that giving an employee consumer surplus in his present job is necessary if the threat of removal is to provide an incentive for good work. In our model this surplus depends on ϕ: $U(q)$ Prob $[\min(\phi, \tilde{v} - q) \le \tilde{c}]$. One justification for ignoring managerial welfare is that (1) shareholders remove managerial surplus by charging an entry fee; and (2) managers are sufficiently risk averse with respect to the possibility of losing their job that the maximum entry fee that they are prepared to pay is negligibly small. A second justification for ignoring managers is that managerial surplus is dissipated in the competition between prospective managers to get the managerial position. For example, managers may have to incur (opportunity) costs queueing for managerial positions, with the length of the queue adjusting until individuals are just indifferent between joining the queue and looking for a nonmanagerial position. It is important to note that, if managerial welfare is significant and is included in $R(\phi)$, then, while some of our specific results are altered, the principal conclusion reached in this section—that there is a deviation between the privately and socially optimal levels of dilution—stands.

effects: (1) it reduces the raider's tender price for a given value of q; (2) it increases the number of raids that take place for each value of q; (3) it increases *status quo* profit q. From the point of view of society, (2) and (3) are goods (the former because a raid only occurs if $\bar{v} - \bar{c} > p \geq q(\phi)$, i.e., if the firm's return under the raider is higher than under current management), while (1) is irrelevant since distributional effects are being ignored. Therefore, in contrast to shareholders, society will never wish to limit dilutions to increase the raider's tender price. In the Appendix we prove:

Proposition 5: $R(\phi)$ is nondecreasing in ϕ. In particular, $R(\phi)$ achieves a maximum at $\phi = \infty$. Furthermore, if Prob $[\bar{v} - q_{\min} - \bar{c} > 0] < 1$, a necessary condition for $R(\phi)$ to achieve a maximum also at $\phi' < \infty$ is that $q(\phi)$ achieves a maximum at $\phi' = \phi$.

As noted, Proposition 5 depends on the fact that from an efficiency point of view the division of the spoils between the raider and the shareholders is irrelevant. This is true, however, only because we have implicitly assumed that the amount invested by initial shareholders is independent of the rate of return which they earn, i.e., investment is interest-inelastic. We now show that if a low expected rate of return on investment leads shareholders to withhold investment funds, it is no longer true that society will desire to set $\phi = \infty$.

Suppose the profit function $f(a)$ of previous sections applies to a firm of unit scale. Assume that if an aggregate amount of investment or capital, K, is forthcoming, then it will be possible to set up exactly $g(K)$ firms of unit scale so that aggregate profits are $g(K)f(a)$, where a is the action of a typical firm. The function $g(K)$ is assumed to be twice differentiable and increasing with $g(0) = 0$, $g(1) = 1$, $\lim_{K \to \infty} g'(K) = 0$, $g'(0) = \infty$, and $g''(K) < 0$. The strict concavity of g indicates that there are decreasing returns to scale in establishing new firms.

Let $s > 0$ be the opportunity cost of capital, i.e., the social rate of return which can be earned from investing in the unincorporated sector. Then the social return from investing in the corporate sector is given by

$$g(K)R(\phi) - sK. \tag{11}$$

In a private ownership economy, however, K will be chosen by private investors not to maximize (11) but instead to maximize the private return on investment

$$g(K)r(\phi) - sK. \tag{12}$$

Note that we assume that the private rate of return from investing in the unincorporated sector equals the social rate of return, s.

Assume that the economy is decentralized so that the government can set legal limits on the dilution of property rights but cannot control investment directly.[19] Thus, the government attempts to maximize (11) subject to K's being chosen by private investors. If $r(\phi) \geq 0$, let $K(\phi)$ denote the unique K which maximizes $g(K)r(\phi) - sK$ so that $K(\phi)$ is the level of private investment which is forthcoming if the government sets the maximum amount of dilution equal to ϕ. The government's objective is to choose ϕ to maximize $g(K(\phi))R(\phi)$

---

[19] If the government controlled both K and ϕ directly, then from (11) ϕ would be chosen to maximize $R(\phi)$ and K would be chosen to maximize $g(K)R(\phi) - sK$.

$- sK(\phi)$.[20] We shall compare the resulting value of ϕ with what emerges when initial shareholders have control over dilution, in which case they choose ϕ and K simultaneously to maximize (12). In particular, this means that an optimal ϕ for shareholders is one which maximizes $r(\phi)$: our earlier analysis applies to the shareholders' choice of ϕ even when investment is interest-elastic.

It is clear that, in general, it will now no longer be optimal for the government to set $\phi = \infty$. Although permitting unlimited dilutions maximizes the social return *per unit* of investment, this entails diluting the property rights of initial shareholders by reducing the expected rate of return to them, which in turn reduces their incentive to invest. In Proposition 6 we show that while the government *will* wish to limit dilution when investment is interest-elastic, it will never wish to limit dilution to a greater extent than shareholders would: the socially optimal ϕ is no smaller than the privately optimal ϕ. The distortion caused by the existence of only a single raider implies that the government should encourage raids at least as much as the private sector would.

Proposition 6: Let ϕ_p be a maximizer of $r(\phi)$. Assume $r(\phi_p) > 0$. Then (i) there is a ϕ_s satisfying $\phi_s \geq \phi_p$ which maximizes $g(K(\phi))R(\phi) - sK(\phi)$. (ii) If ϕ_p is the unique maximizer of $r(\phi)$, then every ϕ_s which maximizes $g(K(\phi))R(\phi) - sK(\phi)$ satisfies $\phi_s \geq \phi_p$. (iii) A sufficient condition that ϕ_s can be chosen equal to ϕ_p is that ϕ_p be a maximizer of $R(\phi)$. (iv) If ϕ_p is a unique maximizer of $r(\phi)$, a sufficient condition that $\phi_s > \phi_p$ is that $r(\phi)$, $R(\phi)$ are differentiable functions of ϕ and that $R'(\phi_p) > 0$.

Parts (i)–(iii) of Proposition 6 are proved in the Appendix. Part (iv), which says that the socially optimal level of dilution exceeds the privately optimal level if $R'(\phi_p) > 0$, is sufficiently simple to establish here. We shall show that at $\phi = \phi_p$, the government's objective function $g(K(\phi))R(\phi) - sK(\phi)$ is increasing. The derivative of the objective function is $(g'R - s)K' + gR'$. Shareholders choose K to maximize $g(K)r(\phi) - sK$ for $\phi = \phi_p$, so that

$$g'(K)r(\phi_p) = s.$$

Differentiating, we get

$$g''(K)K'(\phi_p)r(\phi_p) + g'(K)r'(\phi_p) = 0.$$

But $\phi = \phi_p$ maximizes $r(\phi)$ so that $r'(\phi_p) = 0$ and hence $K'(\phi_p) = 0$. Thus, the derivative of the government's objective function becomes gR', which is positive because $R'(\phi_p) > 0$. Thus $\phi_s > \phi_p$, and the government will want to make raids easier than the private sector does.

Let us interpret the condition $R'(\phi_p) > 0$. It is clear from Proposition 5 that this condition will generally hold as long as ϕ_p is not a maximizer of $R(\phi)$, i.e., as long as there is a divergence between private and social optimality in the interest-*inelastic* investment case. But we know that there is generally such a divergence, for we showed in Section 4 that when $\tilde{c}$ is

---

[20] It is easy to show that if the distribution function of (c,v), $F(c,v)$, is a continuous function (this implies that $\tilde{c}$ and $\tilde{v}$ are both stochastic), then an optimal choice of ϕ exists for the government. Under the same conditions, it can be shown that there is a solution to the shareholders' problem: $\max_\phi r(\phi)$. The only difficulty in proving these results is that $q(\phi)$ may not be continuous in ϕ. This results from our assumption that if the manager is indifferent between two values of q, he chooses the higher one. However, $q(\phi)$ will be upper semicontinuous in ϕ, and this is all that is needed in the proofs.

stochastic, shareholders will in general limit the disciplinary role of raids in their efforts to ensure a high tender price, i.e., $q(\phi)$ will not be maximized at $\phi = \phi_p$ (see, in particular, Proposition 3(2)). It follows from Proposition 5 that $R(\phi)$ is also not maximized at $\phi = \phi_p$.[21]

If there is no divergence between private and social optimality in the interest-inelastic investment case, then Proposition 6(iii) tells us that there will also be no divergence in the interest-elastic investment case. Therefore, Proposition 6 may be summarized as follows: if privately and socially optimal levels of dilution are equal in the inelastic investment case, then they will also be equal in the elastic investment case; however, if the socially optimal level of dilution exceeds the privately optimal level of dilution in the inelastic investment case, then it will also in general exceed it (and certainly never fall short of it) in the elastic investment case.

6. Competition and the costs involved in a takeover bid

■ In this section we analyze the consequences of permitting competing raids. Suppose there are no sunk costs of a raid and there is perfect competition among raiders in the sense that the $(\tilde{v}, \tilde{c})$ pairs of different raiders are perfectly correlated. Then in the event $(\tilde{v}, \tilde{c}) = (v, c)$, raiders will compete and drive the tender price up to $v - c$ as long as $\phi > c$. Thus, if $\phi > c$, the raider's profit is zero, and the social and private benefits from a raid are equal. It follows that shareholders acting in their own (private) interests will choose the socially optimal amount of dilution, which is $\phi = \infty$. Note that the presence of competition among raiders does not in any way alter our conclusion that dilution is essential in permitting takeovers to occur.

This argument assumes that shareholders can rely on enough competition to protect them. Before giving some theoretical arguments why initial shareholders may not be able to rely on the existence of competing raiders at the time of a takeover bid, it is worth mentioning some empirical evidence in favor of our conclusion that ϕ is, in general, set sufficiently low to restrict raids. First, there is a class of corporations called "closed end mutual funds" for which it is clear that $v - c > q$.[22] These corporations have had many 5-year periods where if $\phi = \infty$, a raider could have made a profit of at least 15 percent (assuming $c/v = 5$ percent) by taking over at a price of q and then liquidating the corporation's assets for v. Second, there are many other companies for which

---

[21] Although a divergence between private and social optimality generally exists in the interest-inelastic investment case, and hence, by the argument just given, also in the interest-elastic investment case, in some special cases the divergence is absent. We already know that one such case is when $\tilde{c}$ and $\tilde{v}$ are both nonstochastic (see Propositions 2(a) and 4). In fact, the divergence is absent even when $\tilde{v}$ is stochastic, as long as $\tilde{c}$ is nonstochastic. For, by Proposition 2(b), $\phi_p \cong c$ under these conditions (see Proposition 2(b) and footnote 14). Furthermore, Proposition 2(b) shows that raising ϕ above ϕ_p neither increases *status quo* profit nor enlarges the set of raiding states, and hence has no effect on $R(\phi)$. Therefore, $\phi_p \cong c$ is also a maximizer of $R(\phi)$. Finally, if $\tilde{c}$ is stochastic, but $\tilde{v}$ is nonstochastic, Proposition 3(1) shows that it will sometimes be the case that $\phi = \infty$ is privately optimal. Again the divergence is absent in such cases.

[22] These corporations' only assets are shares of other corporations. The value of a particular closed end fund's assets can be calculated by checking the value of the shares it holds; the value of its assets is called its "net asset value." These corporations often sell at substantial discounts, i.e., the price of 100 percent of the closed end fund is often 20 percent lower than its net asset value; see Sharpe and Sosin (1974), Malkiel (1977), or any Monday issue of the *Wall Street Journal*.

there is some evidence that $v - c > q$.[23] The fact that companies can persist for long periods, operating publicly at profit levels substantially below maximum profit, is stong evidence in favor of the hypothesis that shareholders do not allow large levels of dilution; for, if they did, then surely some entrepreneur would take over these "discounted" companies. Presumably shareholders did not set $\phi = \infty$ because they were afraid that their property rights would be massively diluted because of a lack of competition at the time of a takeover bid.

As we noted at the end of Section 4, there are several types of costs which arise in a takeover bid. Some of these, e.g., the financing, administrative, litigation, and reorganization costs, are consistent with competition among raiders, since they are incurred at the time of the raid. However, the presence of *ex ante* costs of research and information collection, which are sunk by the time the raid takes place, will tend to limit *ex post* competition. This is so because generally one raider will be first to discover what changes should be made in a corporation, and since other raiders do not have this knowledge, they will not be able to compete effectively with the informed raider.

In fact, perfect competition, *ex post*, among raiders is inconsistent with any of their earning a return on their "sunk," *ex ante*, information costs. Therefore, not only will initial shareholders be unable to rely on *ex post* competition, but *ex post* competition will not always be desirable.[24] In particular, a corporate charter which (a) requires a raider to make public his information and intentions (thus transmitting the information for free to other potential raiders and encouraging competition) or (b) requires that the raider keep his tender offer outstanding for some fixed minimum amount of time (so shareholders can wait for a better offer from a competing raider) may be undesirable for initial shareholders. Instead, shareholders may prefer to protect their property rights by limiting the dilution level, ϕ. The Williams Act now makes (a) and (b) the law in the United States. The *ex post* competition it generates may in the long run discourage many raids from ever taking place. The decrease in managerial efficiency which is a consequence of the government-induced decrease in the probability of raids will not in general be socially desirable.[25]

---

[23] The *Value Line Survey*, published monthly by Arnold Bernhard Co., New York, lists companies which have stock market prices which are as much as 50 percent smaller than the value of liquid assets (like vault cash) less the value of debt liabilities. The *Value Line Survey* lists these companies as good investments because they are ripe for a takeover bid! Hearsay evidence indicates that these firms are rarely taken over. See Hindley (1970) for empirical work on a similar problem.

[24] This problem is similar to competition in product innovation. See Loury (1977) and Dasgupta and Stiglitz (1977) for an analysis of *ex ante* competition and its relationship to *ex post* monopoly power.

[25] Recently, incumbent directors have used the courts to delay a raider's takeover bid while they search for a "White Knight" (i.e., another firm which will offer a higher price for the target than did the initial raider, as well as a better position for incumbent directors in the reorganized firm). This appears to be good for both shareholders and the directors. However, the price paid by the "White Knight" is often only slightly higher than that offered by the original raider. Thus the *ex post* gain in the event of a raid may not be very large. The *ex ante* loss, however, may be enormous, because a potential raider (who considers incurring research and information costs) cannot possibly hope to earn a return if he knows that after he announces his takeover bid, the directors will find a competitor and freely give the competitor all the information that the original raider had to pay for. Thus, a regime conducive to the use of "White Knights" is not necessarily in shareholders' or society's best interest, since it may lower the long-run frequency of takeover bids. It gives incumbent directors an enormous threat to use against potential raiders.

7. Conclusions

■ The proper management of a common property is a public good to all the owners of the property. Our fundamental hypothesis is that there are significant costs in ensuring that directors/managers act in the interest of the owners. If one small shareholder devotes resources to improving management, then all shareholders benefit. This is the externality that the takeover bid mechanism attempts to "internalize."

The only way to create proper incentives for the production of a public good is to exclude nonpayers from enjoying the benefits of the public good.[26] A simple takeover bid does not exclude shareholders from benefiting from the improvements in their corporation. Any profit a raider can make through the price appreciation of the shares he purchases can also be made by a shareholder who free rides and does not sell his shares to the raider. Thus, a raider faces the same sort of externality that any shareholder would face if he devoted resources to improving management.

We are thus led to the conclusion that the initial shareholders who write the corporate charter will create some exclusionary device so that a raider can benefit from a takeover bid other than through the price appreciation of the shares he purchases. This can be accomplished by permitting the raider to treat the shares of those who have not tendered differently from the shares he owns. In practice, this is often achieved as follows. After a raid succeeds, the raider has voting control and can vote to liquidate or merge the corporation with a parent wholly owned by the raider. The raider sets the price of this merger or liquidation at a value he determines as "fair" to all shareholders. Of course, it is in his interest to underestimate the value of the corporation's assets, since in that case the parent company, which he wholly owns, gets the target corporation's assets at a discount.

The nontendering shareholders are in a minority after a successful raid and a merger or liquidation at an unfavorable price represents a dilution of their property rights. The law in some states in the United States (e.g., Delaware) sanctions this dilution, because it recognizes that the raider has no fiduciary responsibility to act in all of the shareholders' interests (Brudney and Chirelstein, 1978, p. 1367). However, it is essential to note that *ex ante*, the initial shareholders could have prevented this *ex post* dilution. For example, the corporate charter could require that outside appraisers, who would be approved by the *minority* shareholders, estimate the value of the corporation's assets before a merger or liquidation. Another *ex ante* method the initial shareholders could have used to prevent dilutions would require approval of say ⅔ of the *minority* shareholders in the event that a raider attempts to merge or liquidate the corporation after a successful raid.[27]

We have shown that if initial shareholders cannot rely on competition among raiders, then they will tend to choose low levels of dilution. Shareholders realize that by permitting more dilution they increase the threat of a raid, which

---

[26] The strengthening of class action laws so that the person bringing the class action can get a large portion of the improvements would be helpful in insuring good management of common property.

[27] These are the actual "antitakeover" provisions (Articles 8 and 9) of the Brunswick Corporation's (a corporation registered in Delaware) corporate charter.

is good because it makes *status quo* management more efficient, but they also lower the tender price they receive in the event of a raid, which is bad for them. From a social welfare point of view, permissible dilutions should be large, because this produces a large threat of a raid, which makes current management very efficient. The fact that this large threat is sometimes exercised and shareholders get a low price has no welfare consequence if investment is *interest-inelastic* because it then represents a mere redistribution of the gains from improvement from the shareholders to the raider. From this analysis we concluded that shareholders will tend to make takeover bids more difficult than they should be from a social welfare point of view. Where investment by initial shareholders is *interest-elastic* and where the low tender price received by shareholders has the socially undesirable consequence of reducing investment, the government will want to restrict raids to some extent. But the government will still want to encourage raids more than the private sector will.

What policy implications can be drawn from our analysis? This can be answered on two levels. On one level we can conclude that U.S. government policy on takeover bids from the Williams Act in 1968 to the present may have had certain undesirable consequences. The Act may have made raids more difficult, contrary to what our analysis suggests the government's objective should be. Alleged securities disclosure law violations are often used by current management to stall the raider in the courts and in general to increase the cost of takeover bids. Alleged antitrust violations are also used by *status quo* management to increase the costs of a raid via costly litigation and delays. *Status quo* management uses the shareholders' money to impose these litigation costs on raiders. Further, the disclosure provisions of the Williams Act, which force a raider to announce his intentions after buying 5 percent of the company, may be good in that competition from other raiders is encouraged, but may be bad in that shareholders in an attempt to free ride will compete against the raider.[28] Of course, to the extent that there are social benefits from preventing monopoly and increasing shareholder information via disclosure, the undesirable consequences of making takeover bids more difficult must be traded off against these benefits. A discussion of some of the benefits and costs of disclosure laws may be found in Grossman and Hart (1980) and Ross (1978).

On another level, however, the positive analysis of this paper has implications for the management of common property generally. In particular, we have developed a model which can predict how much deviation can persist between the *potential* benefits of collective action and the *actual* benefits of collective action. If the corporation is properly managed, shareholders get a benefit, which we have represented by $\max_{a \in A} f(a)$, from pooling their resources to take advantage of increasing returns to scale—this is a *potential* benefit. The *actual* benefit of collective action, which we have represented by $\max_\phi r(\phi)$, will be smaller because, in general, directors will not act in the shareholders' interest. We have suggested that the deviation depends on the amount of unpredictability in the benefits and cost of making takeover bids.

Throughout the paper we have used the stock market corporation as our example of common property. However, the fact that the Public Good is a public

---

[28] Recently the Securities and Exchange Commission has proposed amending the Williams Act, so that a raider must disclose intentions even *before* he buys up 5 percent of the shares (*Wall Street Journal*, February 1, 1979, p. 12). This will further exacerbate the free-rider problem.

good is true for all forms of common property and collective action. Further, in some forms of common property, for example local public goods, there are mechanisms which are analogous to takeover bids (see footnote 3). Our analysis of the resulting deviation between the actual benefits and the potential benefits of collective action is therefore likely to generalize beyond the stock market corporation.

Appendix

Proofs of theorems

□ **Proposition 1**: $q(\phi)$ is nondecreasing.

Proof (by contradiction): Suppose $\phi < \phi'$ and $q(\phi) \equiv q > q' \equiv q(\phi')$. By revealed preference and the assumption that a manager chooses the higher profit action if he is indifferent between two actions, we get

$$U(q) \text{ Prob } [\min(\phi, \tilde{v} - q) \leq \tilde{c}] \geq U(q') \text{ Prob } [\min(\phi, \tilde{v} - q') \leq \tilde{c}], \quad (A1)$$

and

$$U(q') \text{ Prob } [\min(\phi', \tilde{v} - q') \leq \tilde{c}] > U(q) \text{ Prob } [\min(\phi', \tilde{v} - q) \leq \tilde{c}]. \quad (A2)$$

Clearly, the strict inequality in (A2) implies that Prob $[\min(\phi', \tilde{v} - q') \leq \tilde{c}] > 0$. Hence Prob $[\min(\phi, \tilde{v} - q') \leq \tilde{c}] \geq$ Prob $[\min(\phi', \tilde{v} - q') \leq \tilde{c}] > 0$, since $\phi < \phi'$. Therefore, we may divide (A1) and (A2) to get

$$\frac{\text{Prob } [\min(\phi, \tilde{v} - q) \leq \tilde{c}]}{\text{Prob } [\min(\phi, \tilde{v} - q') \leq \tilde{c}]} \geq \frac{U(q')}{U(q)} > \frac{\text{Prob } [\min(\phi', \tilde{v} - q) \leq \tilde{c}]}{\text{Prob } [\min(\phi', \tilde{v} - q') \leq \tilde{c}]}. \quad (A3)$$

Define A = Prob $[\min(\phi, \tilde{v} - q) \leq \tilde{c}]$, A' = Prob $[\min(\phi', \tilde{v} - q) \leq \tilde{c}]$, B = Prob $[\min(\phi, \tilde{v} - q') \leq \tilde{c}]$, B' = Prob $[\min(\phi', \tilde{v} - q') \leq \tilde{c}]$, and $\Delta_1 = A - A'$, $\Delta_2 = B - B'$. Then we can rewrite (A3) as

$$\frac{A}{B} > \frac{A'}{B'} = \frac{A - \Delta_1}{B - \Delta_2}. \quad (A4)$$

Now $A \geq B$, since $q > q'$. Also

$$\Delta_1 = \text{Prob } [\min(\phi', \tilde{v} - q) > \tilde{c} \quad \text{and} \quad \min(\phi, \tilde{v} - q) \leq \tilde{c}]$$

$$= \text{Prob } [\phi \leq \tilde{c} < \phi' \quad \text{and} \quad \tilde{v} - q > \tilde{c}] \leq \text{Prob } [\phi \leq \tilde{c} < \phi'$$

$$\text{and} \quad \tilde{v} - q' > \tilde{c}]$$

$$= \text{Prob } [\min(\phi', \tilde{v} - q') > \tilde{c} \quad \text{and} \quad \min(\phi, \tilde{v} - q') \leq \tilde{c}] = \Delta_2.$$

But, by (A4), $AB - A\Delta_2 > AB - B\Delta_1$, i.e., $B\Delta_1 > A\Delta_2$, which is impossible if $A \geq B$, $0 \leq \Delta_1 \leq \Delta_2$. Q.E.D.

□ **Proposition 3**: For statement of Proposition 3, see Section 4 of the text.

Proof: Let ϕ^0 be an optimal value of ϕ, and let $q^0 = q(\phi^0)$. Either $v - \phi^0 \leq q^0$ or $v - \phi^0 > q^0$. In the first case, the tender price will equal q^0 for all $\phi \geq \phi^0$. Thus $\pi(\phi, q^0)$ is constant for $\phi \geq \phi^0$, and hence the *status quo* profit $q(\phi)$ and $r(\phi)$ are constant for $\phi \geq \phi^0$.

On the other hand, if $v - \phi^0 > q^0$, then q^0 must maximize $U(q)$. Suppose

62 / THE BELL JOURNAL OF ECONOMICS

there is a q' such that $U(q') > U(q^0)$. Then

$$U(q') \text{ Prob } [\min (\phi^0, v - q') \leq \tilde{c}] > U(q^0) \text{ Prob } [\min (\phi^0, v - q') \leq \tilde{c}]$$

$$\geq U(q^0) \text{ Prob } [\phi^0 \leq \tilde{c}] = U(q^0) \text{ Prob } [\min (\phi^0, v - q^0) \leq \tilde{c}],$$

which contradicts the fact that $q^0 = q(\phi^0)$. Thus $q^0 \equiv q^*$. Then (9) is equivalent to the shareholder objective given in (8) in Section 4. Q.E.D.

☐ **Proposition 5**: For statement of Proposition 5, see Section 5 of the text.

Proof of Proposition 5: We show first that R is nondecreasing in ϕ for a given value of q. We then show that R is nondecreasing in q for a given value of ϕ. These two facts combined with Proposition 1 will prove that R is nondecreasing in ϕ.

(a) For a given q, R is nondecreasing in ϕ. Let $S(\phi) = \{(c,v) | c < \min (\phi, v - q)\}$ and $Q(\phi) = \{(c,v) | c \geq \min (\phi, v - q)\}$. Assume $\phi' > \phi$; then noting that $Q(\phi) \supset Q(\phi')$ and $S(\phi') \supset S(\phi)$:

$$R(\phi') \equiv \int_{Q(\phi')} q dF(c,v) + \int_{S(\phi')} (v - c) dF(c,v);$$

$$R(\phi') \equiv \int_{Q(\phi)} q dF(c,v) - \int_{Q(\phi) \cap S(\phi')} q dF(c,v) + \int_{S(\phi)} (v - c) dF(c,v)$$

$$+ \int_{Q(\phi) \cap S(\phi')} (v - c) dF(c,v);$$

$$R(\phi') \equiv R(\phi) + \int_{Q(\phi) \cap S(\phi')} (v - c - q) dF(c,v) \geq R(\phi). \tag{A5}$$

(b) For a given ϕ, R is nondecreasing in q. Let $s(q) = \{(c,v) | c < \min (\phi, v - q)\}$ and $f(q) = \{(c,v) | c \geq \min (\phi, v - q)\}$. Assume $q' > q$. Then noting that $f(q') \supset f(q)$ and $s(q) \supset s(q')$:

$$R(q') = \int_{f(q')} q' dF(c,v) + \int_{s(q')} (v - c) d(c,v);$$

$$R(q') = \int_{f(q)} q' dF(c,v) + \int_{s(q) \cap f(q')} q' dF(c,v) + \int_{s(q)} (v - c) dF(c,v)$$

$$- \int_{s(q) \cap f(q')} (v - c) dF(c,v);$$

$$R(q') = \int_{f(q)} q' dF(c,v) + \int_{s(q)} (v - c) dF(c,v)$$

$$+ \int_{s(q) \cap f(q')} [q' - (v - c)] dF(c,v). \tag{A6}$$

Note that if $(c,v) \in s(q) \cap f(q')$, then $c < \min (\phi, v - q)$ and hence $c < \phi$; but $c \geq \min (\phi, v - q')$ since $(c,v) \in f(q')$; therefore $c \geq v - q'$. Thus $(c,v) \in s(q) \cap f(q')$ implies $q' - (v - c) \geq 0$. Whence from (A6)

$$R(q') \geq \int_{f(q)} q dF(c,v) + \int_{s(q)} (v - c) dF(c,v) = R(q).$$

To prove the last part of Proposition 5, note that $R(q') > R(q)$ as long as Prob $f(q) > 0$. This is guaranteed by the condition Prob $[\bar{v} - q_{\min} - \bar{c} > 0] < 1$.

☐ **Proposition 6**: For statement of Proposition 6, see Section 6.

Proof of Proposition 6: By contradiction. Suppose that ϕ_s is any optimal dilution for the government and that $\phi_s < \phi_p$. Then, by definition of ϕ_s, $g(K_s)R(\phi_s) - sK_s \geq g(K_p)R(\phi_p) - sK_p$, where $K_s \equiv K(\phi_s)$ and $K_p \equiv K(\phi_p)$. Therefore,

$$s(K_p - K_s) \geq g(K_p)R(\phi_p) - g(K_s)R(\phi_s) \geq g(K_p)R(\phi_p) - g(K_s)R(\phi_p), \quad (A7)$$

where the last inequality follows from Proposition 5 and $\phi_p > \phi_s$. Hence

$$s(K_p - K_s) \geq [g(K_p) - g(K_s)]R(\phi_p) \geq [g(K_p) - g(K_s)]r(\phi_p), \quad (A8)$$

where the last inequality follows from the fact that $R(\phi) \geq r(\phi)$ (i.e., the social return is always as large as the private return) as can be seen from equations (8) and (10). Now note that there are two possibilities:

(A) $r(\phi_s) < r(\phi_p)$ or (B) $r(\phi_s) = r(\phi_p)$, since ϕ_p is a maximum of $r(\phi)$.

(A) If $r(\phi_s) < r(\phi_p)$, then $K_s < K_p$, since investment has a higher nominal return under $r(\phi_p)$ for a given K. Hence $g(K_p)r(\phi_p) - sK_p > g(K_s)r(\phi_p) - sK_s$ or equivalently $[g(K_p) - g(K_s)]r(\phi_p) > s(K_p - K_s)$, which contradicts (A8).

(B) If $r(\phi_p) = r(\phi_s)$, then, by the definition of $K(\phi)$ in the statement of the proposition, $K_s = K_p$. Since $R(\phi)$ is nondecreasing, $R(\phi_p) \geq R(\phi_s)$. Therefore, ϕ_p would yield a social return at least as high as ϕ_s. That is, ϕ_p is an optimal dilution for the government to set and this contradicts the assumption that every optimal dilution for the government is strictly smaller than the private dilution ϕ_p.

This proves the first part of the proposition.

The proof of the second part follows from the fact that if there is *any* $\phi_s < \phi_p$, then by the argument in the above proof either (A) or (B) above obtains. But (A) is impossible by the same argument as above. (B) is impossible because $r(\phi)$ has a unique maximizer. Part (iii) follows from the fact that if ϕ_p is a maximizer of $R(\phi)$ and $\phi_s > \phi_p$, then $r(\phi_s) \leq r(\phi_p)$ and $R(\phi_p) = R(\phi_s)$. Hence, reducing ϕ_s to ϕ_p can only increase the private return on investment, which will improve things. Finally, Part (iv) was proved in the text. *Q.E.D.*

References

BAUMOL, W.J. *Business Behavior, Value and Growth*. New York: Macmillan, 1959.

BRUDNEY, V. AND CHIRELSTEIN, M.A. "A Restatement of Corporate Freezeouts." *Yale Law Journal*, Vol. 87, No. 7 (June 1978), pp. 1354–1376.

CALVO, G.A. "Supervision, Utility, and Wage Differentials across Firms." Mimeo, Department of Economics, Columbia University, 1978.

DASGUPTA, P. AND STIGLITZ, J. "Market Structure and the Nature of Incentive Activity." Mimeo, London School of Economics, 1977.

GROSSMAN, S. AND HART, O. "The Allocational Role of Takeover Bids in Markets with Asymmetric Information." Mimeo, Department of Economics, University of Pennsylvania, 1979a.

—— AND ——. "How to Make a Successful Takeover Bid." Mimeo, Department of Economics, University of Pennsylvania, 1979b.

—— AND ——. "Disclosure Laws and Takeover Bids." *Journal of Finance* (May 1980).

HINDLEY, B. "Separation of Ownership and Control in the Modern Corporation." *Journal of Law and Economics*, Vol. 13, No. 1 (April 1970), pp. 185–221.

LOURY, G. "A Nash Equilibrium Model of Research and Development." Mimeo, Department of Economics, Northwestern University, 1977.

MALKIEL, B. "The Valuation of Closed-End Mutual Investment-Company Shares," *Journal of Finance*, Vol. 32, No. 3 (June 1977), pp. 847–860.

MANNE, H.G. "Mergers and the Market for Corporate Control." *Journal of Political Economy* (April 1965), pp. 110–120.

MARRIS, R. *The Economic Theory of Managerial Capitalism*. Illinois: Free Press of Glencoe, 1964.

MIRRLEES, J.A. "The Optimal Structure of Incentives and Authority within an Organization." *Bell Journal of Economics*, Vol. 7. No. 1 (Spring 1976), pp. 105–136.

MULLANY, R. "Guarding against Takeovers—Defensive Charter Provisions." *Business Lawyer*, Vol. 25, No. 4 (July 1970), pp. 1441–1462.

ROSS, S. "The Determination of Financial Structure: the Incentive Signalling Approach." *Bell Journal of Economics*, Vol. 8, No. 1 (Spring 1977), pp. 23–40.

——. "Disclosure Regulation in Financial Markets: Implications of Modern Finance Theory" in F.P. Edwards, ed., *Key Issues in Financial Regulations*, Columbia University Center for Law and Economic Studies, 1978.

SHARPE, W. AND SOSIN, H. "Closed-End Mutual Funds." *European Finance Association Proceedings* (1974).

WILLIAMSON, O.E. *The Economics of Discretionary Behavior: Managerial Objectives in a Theory of the Firm*. Englewood Cliffs, N.J.: Prentice-Hall, 1964.

——. *Markets and Hierarchies: Analysis and Antitrust Implications*. New York: Free Press, 1975.

Preemptive Bidding and the Role of the Medium of Exchange in Acquisitions

MICHAEL J. FISHMAN*

ABSTRACT

The medium of exchange in acquisitions is studied in a model where (i) bidders' offers bring forth potential competition and (ii) targets and bidders are asymmetrically informed. In equilibrium, both securities and cash offers are observed. Securities have the advantage of inducing target management to make an efficient accept/reject decision. Cash has the advantage of serving, in equilibrium, to "preempt" competition by signaling a high valuation for the target. Implications concerning the medium of exchange of an offer, the probability of acceptance, the probability of competing bids, expected profits, and the costs of bidders are derived.

IN STRUCTURING ITS OFFER to acquire a firm, an acquirer must, among other things, determine the medium of exchange of the offer. That is, an acquirer must choose whether the payment will be in the form of cash, debt, equity, or some combination. With symmetric information, no transactions costs, and no taxes, the medium of exchange is irrelevant. This is not the case, though, if these assumptions are not satisfied. This paper studies the role of the medium of exchange in acquisitions in a setting in which there is asymmetric information between a target and competing bidders.

The focus of the paper is on the role of the medium of exchange in preempting competition. Consider a bidder that studies the profitability of an acquisition. If it makes a bid, other potential bidders will observe the bid, learn of the potentially profitable acquisition, and perhaps compete for it. A preemptive bid may be a way to eliminate this competition. Suppose a competing bidder's expected payoff is decreasing in the initial bidder's valuation for the target. When bidding against an initial bidder with a high valuation, a competitor may face a low probability of winning the bidding and a low expected payoff given that it does win. In this case, if the initial bidder could signal a sufficiently high valuation, it could deter the competition. As Fishman [7] and P'ng [18] have shown, a high bid can signal a high valuation and thus serve to preempt competition. Both studies, however, deal only with cash offers. (See also Giammarino and Heinkel [9] and Khanna [14].)

A key difference between a cash offer and a (risky) securities offer is that a security's value depends on the profitability of the acquisition, while the value of cash does not. In the studies cited above, bidders, but not the target, have private

---

* Kellogg Graduate School of Management, Northwestern University. This is a revised version of a chapter of my Ph.D. thesis at the University of Chicago. I am grateful to Doug Diamond, Ron Giammarino, Sandy Grossman, Milt Harris, Robert Heinkel, Merton Miller, René Stulz, an anonymous referee, and an anonymous Associate Editor for helpful comments and discussions.

information on the profitability of the acquisition, and thus on the value of securities offers. Since no party has private information on the value of cash, all bidders offer cash. This is because an equity or risky debt offer would be presumed to have a low value, for, if the bidder knew the securities had a high value, it would have offered cash. The analysis here allows the target, in addition to bidders, to observe private information on the profitability of an acquisition. This is an important possibility to consider. Target management would likely have the best information on the target's physical assets and contractual commitments.

Securities offers then become a relevant alternative to cash offers. Consider offering a high payment if the target's information indicates a profitable acquisition, and a low payment otherwise. This would induce the target to make an efficient, given its information, accept/reject decision. If, however, the target's information is not verifiable, this offer is not feasible. An alternative, though, is a securities offer. Rather than making the offer contingent on the target's information about future cash flows, a securities offer's value is contingent on the cash flows themselves. If structured properly, a securities offer also induces the target to make an efficient accept/reject decision. In contrast, the value of a cash offer is not contingent on the future cash flows of the acquired target. Thus, the target can make its accept/reject decision independently of any information on these cash flows, and a cash offer cannot induce an efficient accept/reject decision.

A model of preemptive bidding is developed. In equilibrium, securities are offered by lower valuing bidders and cash by higher valuing bidders. The advantage of a securities offer is its ability to induce an efficient accept/reject decision on the offer. The advantage of a cash offer is that, in equilibrium, it serves to preempt potential competition by signaling a high valuation. Among the implications of the analysis are:

1. An initial bidder's expected payoff is lower if the medium of exchange of its initial offer is securities as compared to cash.
2. The probability that competing bids will be observed is higher after an initial securities offer as compared to an initial cash offer.
3. The probability that target management will reject an offer is higher if the medium of exchange is securities as compared to cash.
4. The higher the cost of studying a target, the more likely that an initial bidder's offer is cash and the less likely that there is a multiple bidder contest.

Hansen [12] (in independent work) also studies the choice of medium of exchange in acquisitions. As is the case here, the benefit of a securities offer is that it offers a state-contingent payment to the target. The benefit of a cash offer, however, differs between models. In Hansen, bidders have private information on their own premerger values, and, in equilibrium, bidders offer cash if their equity is relatively undervalued. Here, cash offers are made to signal a high valuation for the target, in order to preempt a potential competing bidder. A difference in predictions between the two models concerns a target's share price response to the outcome of an offer. The model here predicts a target share price increase (decrease) if an offer is accepted (rejected), while, in Hansen, the reverse is predicted. Empirically, Dodd [5] reports results that are consistent with the predictions here. In addition, the analysis here addresses issues concerning the degree of competition in acquisitions markets. Whether an initial bidder faces competition for the target is endogenously determined. (In Hansen, there is assumed to be one bidder.) This leads to predictions on the interrelationships between the medium of exchange of an offer, the number of bidders, the profits from an acquisition, and the costs of studying a target.

Section I sets out the model, and Section II analyzes the equilibrium. Section III discusses the possibility of advance disclosure of the target's private information. If bidders are not deterred from studying the target altogether, a target's expected payoff is higher with advance disclosure. Section IV discusses some additional implications of the model.

I. The Model

For a given target there are two potential bidders. Assume that the target and both bidders are all-equity firms with risk-neutral shareholders. Also, target and bidder managements are assumed to maximize the wealth of their shareholders, and there is no collusion.[1] It is assumed that the target accepts the offer with the highest value if it is at or above a known reservation price. Though the analysis goes through with any reservation price, it is assumed equal to the target's prebid market value, denoted v_0.[2]

At a known cost $k_i > 0$, bidder i can observe a private signal, s_i, which conveys information on its own valuation for the target but is independent of the other bidder's valuation. In addition, the target costlessly observes a private signal, s_0, which conveys information on both bidders' valuations. Assume that $\tilde{s}_0$, $\tilde{s}_1$, and $\tilde{s}_2$ are mutually independent. Also, assume that there is no private information on the target value if unacquired. Let $f_i(\cdot)$ denote the density function of $\tilde{s}_i$ ($i = 1, 2$), where $f_i(s_i) > 0$ if and only if $s_i \in [l, h]$. Assume that $\tilde{s}_0$ has a two-point distribution: $\tilde{s}_0 = \alpha(\beta)$ with probability $1 - \gamma(\gamma)$, where $0 < \gamma \leq 1$. Denote bidder i's valuation for the target as $v_i = v^\alpha(s_i)$, for $s_0 = \alpha$, and $v_i = v^\beta(s_i)$, for $s_0 = \beta$. It is assumed that $v^\alpha(s_i)$ and $v^\beta(s_i)$ are increasing in s_i, and $v^\beta(s_i) > v^\alpha(s_i) \geq 0$, for

---

[1] If target management has private information on the value of a securities offer (the case studied here), a conflict of interest between management and shareholders may provide an additional (to this analysis) benefit to cash offers. Say target management has some unobserved preference for control. Then it may reject a securities offer, claiming it has a low value when it actually has a high value. Cash has the advantage that shareholders need not rely on management to value it for them. For related work, see Baron [2].

[2] Suppose the problem is repeated, period after period, until the target is acquired. With an infinite horizon and stationary environment, the market value of the target, v_0, is the same at the start of every period. Further, this is the target's reservation price in a take-it-or-leave-it offer. Note that, in an auction, the target receives the second highest valuation and the high bidder receives the difference in bidders' valuations. If it were the case that the target and high bidder would bargain over this difference in valuations, then the signaling stage of the problem would become more complicated. An initial bidder would be simultaneously signaling to both the potentially competing bidder and the target. The target's beliefs become important because they affect the outcome of the later-stage bargaining game.

all s_i. Moreover, assume that $v''(h) < v_0$. Thus, since v_0 is the minimum acquisition price, neither bidder can profitably acquire the target if $s_0 = \alpha$. Also assume that $Ev^\beta(\tilde{s}_i) < v_0$. This implies that it is not profitable for bidder i to bid without observing s_i.

The problem unfolds as follows. Bidder 1 exogenously learns of a potentially profitable acquisition. Assume that only a few firms are potentially profitable acquisitions, so that studying random firms is not profitable. Once bidder 1 learns of a target, it can pay k_1 to observe s_1, and then perhaps make an offer. If bidder 1 does not make an offer, the problem ends with the target remaining known only to bidder 1. If bidder 1 does make an offer, the target is identified. Bidder 2, after observing this offer, determines whether to compete for the target. After bidder 2 makes its decision, the target costlessly observes s_0. (The possibility of observing and disclosing s_0 prior to any bidding is discussed in Section III.)

If bidder 2 competes, it pays k_2 to observe s_2. Then a competitive open auction follows: i.e., the high offer rises until one bidder remains. If bidder 2 does not compete, bidder 1's initial offer is the high offer. In either case, the target accepts the high offer if its value equals or exceeds v_0, and rejects it otherwise. If an offer is accepted, control of the target changes, and the new target value is realized.

The mediums of exchange considered are cash and debt, and offers are for all target shares. If a cash offer p from bidder i is accepted, bidder i receives $v_i - p$, and the target receives p. The debt considered is discount debt backed by the target's assets. If a debt offer from bidder i with face value p is accepted, bidder i receives $\max\{v_i - p, 0\}$, and the target receives $\min\{v_i, p\}$. If the target under bidder i's control is worth p or more, the debt liability is satisfied, and, if it is worth less than p, the bidder defaults on the debt and turns over the assets. In what follows, offers of cash or debt with face value $p < v_0$ can be ignored, since they would always be rejected. Also, assume that bidder i never offers debt with face value $p > v''(s_i)$.[3]

A debt offer with face value p is worth $\min\{v^\beta(s_i), p\} \geq v_0$ if $s_0 = \beta$, and $\min\{v''(s_i), p\} < v_0$ if $s_0 = \alpha$. Thus, the target will accept (reject) the offer if $s_0 = \beta$ ($s_0 = \alpha$). This is an efficient decision rule in that the target accepts the offer only if its private information indicates a profitable acquisition. In contrast, since a cash offer's value is independent of s_0, a target would not need to consult its private information in deciding whether to accept or reject it. Thus, a cash offer cannot induce the target to make an efficient accept/reject decision.[4]

---

[3] Bidder i receives zero with certainty from such an offer. This assumption eliminates the strategy of never dropping out of the bidding. A rigorous way to exclude such offers is to assume a cost (no matter how small) either of bidding or of defaulting on debt.

[4] The cash and debt offers are equivalent to offers explicitly contingent on s_0. An offer with $p(s_0) \geq v_0$ for $s_0 = \alpha, \beta$, is equivalent to a cash offer, and an offer with $p(\alpha) < v_0 \leq p(\beta)$ is equivalent to a debt offer. In practice, securities offers commonly include equity of the merged entity. As the model stands, the debt offer dominates any offer that includes equity. This is because equity induces an adverse selection problem. Suppose, though, it is assumed that (i) bidders have no private information on the value of their assets in place and (ii) after bidder 2 makes its entry decision, $\tilde{s}_1$ and $\tilde{s}_2$ are observable by all. Then the equilibrium outcome to be derived can be obtained with cash and mixed cash/equity offers. The assumptions ease the adverse selection problem. In Hansen [12], securities offers consist of equity of the merged entity. This, however, is by assumption. The optimal securities offer there is also one backed only by target assets. Further, if allowed, such offers would dominate cash, and, thus, cash offers would not be observed.

Let (p, θ) denote bidder 1's initial offer, where $p \in [v_0, v''(s_1)]$ is the face value and $\theta \in \{C, D\}$ is the medium of exchange—cash or debt, respectively. Let e denote bidder 2's decision, where $e = 1$ (0) denotes competing (not competing). Finally, let $\pi_i(s_1, s_2, s_0, p, \theta, e)$ denote bidder i's payoff as a function of the specified arguments. We will first state and then explain the payoffs for the case when bidder 1 studies the target and bids. Define l_0 such that $v^\beta(l_0) = v_0$. Since the reservation price is v_0, bidder 1 only bids if $s_1 \geq l_0$. For $s_1 \geq l_0$, bidder 1's payoffs, gross of the sunk cost k_1, are as follows. If bidder 1 makes an initial debt offer (p, D), its payoffs are given by

$$\pi_1(s_1, s_2, s_0, p, D, 0) = \begin{cases} 0 & \text{if } s_0 = \alpha, \\ v^\beta(s_1) - p & \text{if } s_0 = \beta; \end{cases}$$

$$\pi_1(s_1, s_2, s_0, p, D, 1) = \begin{cases} 0 & \text{if } s_0 = \alpha, \\ v^\beta(s_1) - \min\{\max(p, v^\beta(s_2)), v^\beta(s_1)\} & \text{if } s_0 = \beta. \end{cases} \quad (1a)$$

If bidder 1 makes an initial cash offer, (p, C), its payoffs are given by

$$\pi_1(s_1, s_2, s_0, p, C, 0) = \begin{cases} v^\alpha(s_1) - p & \text{if } s_0 = \alpha, \\ v^\beta(s_1) - p & \text{if } s_0 = \beta; \end{cases}$$

$$\pi_1(s_1, s_2, s_0, p, C, 1) = \begin{cases} v^\alpha(s_1) - p & \text{if } s_0 = \alpha, \\ v^\beta(s_1) - \min\{\max(p, v^\beta(s_2)), v^\beta(s_1)\} & \text{if } s_0 = \beta. \end{cases} \quad (1b)$$

If bidder 1 makes an initial offer, (p, θ), bidder 2's payoffs are given by

$$\pi_2(s_1, s_2, s_0, p, \theta, 0) = 0;$$

$$\pi_2(s_1, s_2, s_0, p, \theta, 1) = \begin{cases} -k_2 & \text{if } s_0 = \alpha, \\ v^\beta(s_2) - \min\{v^\beta(s_1), v^\beta(s_2)\} - k_2 & \text{if } s_0 = \beta. \end{cases} \quad (2)$$

Say bidder 1 initially offers (p, D). If bidder 2 competes, an auction follows. Note that, once in an auction, there is no incentive to offer cash since debt can promise the same payment as cash if $s_0 = \beta$ but can also promise a low payment if $s_0 = \alpha$. The face value of the ultimately highest valued offer is determined as follows. If $v''(s_2) \leq p$, bidder 2 will not top the initial bid. If $v''(s_2) > p$, the high bid is bid up to the second highest valuation. So the high bid is a debt offer with face value $\min\{\max(p, v''(s_2)), v''(s_1)\}$ if bidder 2 competes and is the initial offer (p, D) otherwise. Whichever it is, the target accepts (rejects) it if $s_0 = \beta$ ($s_0 = \alpha$). Say bidder 1 initially offers (p, C). If bidder 2 does not compete, the target accepts this offer regardless of s_0. If bidder 2 competes, an auction follows, and, if $s_0 = \beta$, the payoffs are the same as with an initial debt offer. If, however, $s_0 = \alpha$, the target has no incentive to await the outcome of an auction, for, as discussed above, once in an auction, all bids consist of debt; so, if $s_0 = \alpha$, the target accepts the initial cash offer.

Notice that bidder 2's expected payoff from competing is decreasing in s_1. Also notice that, for a given decision as to whether or not to compete, bidder 2's payoff does not depend on bidder 1's initial offer. In making this decision, however, bidder 2 may find bidder 1's offer to be important as it may convey information on s_1.

Two final assumptions are made. Assume that

$$E[\pi_2(\hat{s}_1, \hat{s}_2, \hat{s}_0, p, \theta, 1) | \hat{s}_1 \geq l_0] > 0. \qquad (3)$$

The minimum learned from bidder 1's initial bid is that $s_1 \geq l_0$. Assumption (3) posits that this information is not sufficient to deter bidder 2. Define r such that $E[\pi_2(\hat{s}_1, \hat{s}_2, \hat{s}_0, p, \theta, 1) | \hat{s}_1 > r] = 0$; r is the minimum value for which, if bidder 2 knew that s_1 exceeded this value, bidder 2 would not find it profitable to compete. Assumption (3) implies that $l_0 < r < h$. Also assume that

$$E\pi_1(r, \hat{s}_2, \hat{s}_0, v_0, C, 0) > E\pi_1(r, \hat{s}_2, \hat{s}_0, v_0, D, 1). \qquad (4)$$

As will be seen, (4) implies that a cash offer equal to v_0 is not sufficient to deter bidder 2. Deterrence requires a positive premium bid. (Relaxation of (3) and (4) is discussed in footnote 9.)

Before proceeding, a few comments are in order. The target value if acquired depends both on factors specific to the target, i.e., s_0, and factors specific to the bidder, i.e., s_1 or s_2. Target-specific factors may represent the condition of the target's physical assets, and bidder-specific factors may repesent the bidder's talent in managing resources in the target's industry. It has been assumed that $\hat{s}_1$ and $\hat{s}_2$ are independent. This implies (see (2)) that bidder 2's expected payoff from competing is decreasing in s_1. It is more profitable to compete against a less talented bidder since a less talented bidder cannot afford to bid as much. This is a necessary condition for the results that follow, though independence of $\hat{s}_1$ and $\hat{s}_2$ is not necessary. If this condition does not hold, bidder 1 has no incentive to signal that it has a high valuation for the target. Such information would not be a deterrent. Consider also the assumption that target management has private information on each bidder's valuation but not on target value in the absence of a change in control. This allows for a known target reservation price. One interpretation is as follows. As with bidders, suppose that target value under current management depends on factors specific to itself and factors specific to the target assets. Suppose also that the target cash flow history is observable. Then, target value under current management may be observable, even though the factors specific to current management and assets are not.

Pure strategy equilibria are considered. Denote bidder 1's strategy as $\sigma_1 = (\sigma_p, \sigma_\theta)$; σ_p and σ_θ specify the face value and medium of exchange, respectively, of bidder 1's initial offer, each as a function of s_1. Denote bidder 2's strategy as σ_2; σ_2 specifies bidder 2's response as a function of bidder 1's initial offer. Let the density function $g(s_1 | p, \theta)$ denote bidder 2's updated beliefs on s_1, conditional on bidder 1's initial offer.

The definition of equilibrium is based on the concept of Perfect Sequential Equilibrium (PSE).[5] Let $\hat{S}(p, \theta; \sigma_1) = \{s_1 | \sigma_1(s_1) = (p, \theta)\}$; $\hat{S}$ denotes the set of s_1 for which bidder 1 would make a given offer when using a particular strategy. For a nonempty $S \subset [l_0, h]$, let

$$\hat{g}(s_1; S) = \begin{cases} \dfrac{f_1(s_1)}{\int_{s_1 \in S} f_1(s_1) \, ds_1} & \text{if } s_1 \in S, \\ 0 & \text{otherwise.} \end{cases}$$

---
[5] See Grossman and Perry [11].

Definition: The triple (σ_1, σ_2, g) constitutes a PSE if and only if:

(*Sequentially Rational Strategies*) taking g as given,

(i) σ_1 maximizes bidder 1's expected payoff given σ_2,

(ii) for all (p, θ), σ_2 maximizes bidder 2's expected payoff;

(5)

(*Credible Beliefs*) taking (σ_1, σ_2) as given, for all (p, θ),

(i) if $\hat{S}(p, \theta; \sigma_1)$ is nonempty, then $g(s_1 \mid p, \theta) = \hat{g}(s_1; \hat{S}(p, \theta; \sigma_1))$,

(ii) if $\hat{S}(p, \theta; \sigma_1)$ is empty, and if there is a unique nonempty set $S \subset [l_0, h]$ such that $E\pi_1(s_1, \hat{s}_2, \hat{s}_0, p, \theta, \hat{\sigma}_2(S)) > E\pi_1(s_1, \hat{s}_2, \hat{s}_0, \sigma_p(s_1), \sigma_\theta(s_1), \sigma_2(\sigma_p(s_1), \sigma_\theta(s_1)))$ if and only if $s_1 \in S$, where $\hat{\sigma}_2(S)$ is an optimal response for bidder 2 given beliefs $\hat{g}(s_1 \mid S)$, then $g(s_1 \mid p, \theta) = \hat{g}(s_1; S)$.

(6)

Conditions (5) and (6i) are based on the concept of Sequential Equilibrium.[6] Bidders must always follow an optimal strategy given beliefs, and, in equilibrium, bidder 2's beliefs must be consistent with bidder 1's strategy and Bayes' rule. Condition (6ii), the additional condition required by a PSE, restricts the extent to which beliefs can be formed in response to out-of-equilibrium offers. Suppose that, for an out-of-equilibrium offer, (p, θ), there is a set S that satisfies (6ii). Then, first bidders for which $s_1 \in S$, and only those first bidders, will prefer to deviate from the proposed strategy and offer (p, θ) if it will induce bidder 2 to believe $s_1 \in S$. In such a case, credibility requires bidder 2 to believe $s_1 \in S$.

II. Analysis of Equilibrium

Bidder 1, in making its initial offer, takes into account the effect of the offer on the beliefs of bidder 2, for, if bidder 2 believes bidder 1 has a sufficiently high valuation, it chooses not to compete. This is the strategic interaction characterized in equilibrium. Sequentially rational strategies for a fixed updating rule (for bidder 2) are derived first. Then, a credible updating rule given sequentially rational strategies is characterized. Combining these results yields the unique PSE outcome.

Upon observing bidder 1's offer, bidder 2 updates its beliefs and computes its expected payoff from competing. Bidder 2's optimal strategy is to compete if this expected payoff is positive and not to compete otherwise. For an updating rule g, and $\theta \in \{C, D\}$, let $Q(\theta; g)$ denote the set of p for which the offer (p, θ) induces bidder 2 to expect a nonpositive payoff from competing, and suppose $Q(\theta; g)$ is nonempty. Let $q(\theta; g)$ equal the minimum element of $Q(\theta; g)$; $q(C; g)$ and $q(D; g)$ represent the minimum cash and debt offers that deter bidder 2.[7] Bidder 1's optimal strategy is to offer either $(q(D; g), D)$, $(q(C; g), C)$, or (v_0, D)—either a (minimum) preemptive offer or a zero premium debt offer (i.e., an offer of the

---

[6] See Kreps and Wilson [15].

[7] If $Q(\theta; g)$ contains no minimum element, let $q(\theta; g) = \inf(Q(\theta; g)) + \epsilon$, where ϵ is positive and very small.

reservation value, contingent on a profitable acquisition). All other offers are dominated.

To determine which first bidders make which offer, the expected payoffs from these three offers must be compared. First compare preemptive with nonpreemptive offers. For $s_1 \in [l_0, h]$, define

$$p_D(s_1) = E \min\{\max(v_0, v''(\tilde{s}_2)), v''(s_1)\},$$

$$p_C(s_1) = \gamma E \min\{\max(v_0, v''(\tilde{s}_2)), v^\beta(s_1)\} + (1 - \gamma)v''(s_1),$$

and let $s_D(\cdot)$ and $s_C(\cdot)$ denote the respective inverse functions. Using (1), it can be verified that, for $\theta \in \{C, D\}$, bidder 1's expected payoff from the preemptive offer $(q(\theta; g), \theta)$ exceeds the expected payoff from the offer (v_0, D) if $q(\theta; g) < p_v(s_1)$ or, equivalently, if $s_v(q(\theta; g)) < s_1$. High valuing bidders make preemptive offers. The reason is as follows. For a given offer (p, θ), the value to bidder 1 of deterring bidder 2 equals

$$E\pi_1(s_1, \tilde{s}_2, \tilde{s}_0, p, \theta, 0) - E\pi_1(s_1, \tilde{s}_2, \tilde{s}_0, p, \theta, 1)$$
$$= \gamma[E \min\{\max(p, v^\beta(\tilde{s}_2)), v''(s_1)\} - p],$$

the difference between bidder 1's expected payoff if bidder 2 is deterred and bidder 1's expected payoff if bidder 2 is not deterred. This difference is increasing in s_1. Higher valuing first bidders stand to lose more in an auction and thus have a greater incentive to deter competition.

Now compare the two preemptive offers. Let $z(s_1, p^D, p^C) = \gamma p^D + (1 - \gamma)v''(s_1) - p^C$, and define $s_{DC}(p^D, p^C)$ as follows. If there is an $s \in [l_0, h]$ such that $z(s, p^D, p^C) = 0$, then $s_{DC}(p^D, p^C) = s$. Otherwise, if $z(l_0, p^D, p^C) < 0$, then $s_{DC}(p^D, p^C) = l_0$, and, if $z(h, p^D, p^C) < 0$, then $s_{DC}(p^D, p^C) = h$. Using (1), it can be verified that bidder 1's expected payoff is higher with the preemptive cash (debt) offer if $s_1 > (<) s_{DC}(q(D; g), q(C; g))$. Of the bidders that make preemptive bids, the high-valuing ones use cash and the low-valuing ones use debt. The reason is as follows. A debt offer is only accepted if $s_0 = \beta$, while a cash offer is always accepted. Thus, a cash offer is a commitment to acquire the target if $s_0 = \alpha$, that is, even when the acquisition is unprofitable. For an offer with a given face value p, the expected cost of this commitment equals

$$E\pi_1(s_1, \tilde{s}_2, \tilde{s}_0, p, D, e) - E\pi_1(s_1, \tilde{s}_2, \tilde{s}_0, p, C, e) = (1 - \gamma)[p - v''(s_1)],$$

the difference between bidder 1's expected payoff if it offers debt and bidder 1's expected payoff if it offers cash. This difference is decreasing in s_1. The commitment is cheaper for higher valuing bidders, and, for given preemptive offers, if any bidders use cash it is the higher valuing ones.

These results on optimal strategies are summarized in Lemma 1.[8]

---

[8] The following conventions are adopted. If bidder 1 is indifferent between a preemptive and nonpreemptive offer, it makes a nonpreemptive offer, and, if it is indifferent between a preemptive cash offer and a preemptive debt offer, it makes a preemptive debt offer. If bidder 2 is indifferent between competing and not competing, it does not compete. Also, if $Q(\theta; g)$ is empty, let $q(\theta; g) = p_*(h)$ (for $\theta \in \{C, D\}$).

LEMMA 1: *For an updating rule g, the strategies that satisfy* (5) *are*

$$\sigma_1(s_1) = \begin{cases} (v_0, D) & \text{if } l_0 \leq s_1 \leq \min\{s_D(q(D;g)), s_C(q(C;g))\}, \\ (q(D;g), D) & \text{if } s_D(q(D;g)) < s_1 \leq s_{DC}(q(D;g), q(C;g)), \\ (q(C;g), C) & \text{if } s_1 > \max\{s_C(q(C;g)), s_{DC}(q(D;g), q(C;g))\}; \end{cases} \quad (7a)$$

$$\sigma_2(p, \theta) = \begin{cases} 1 & \text{if } E[\pi_2(\tilde{s}_1, \tilde{s}_2, \tilde{s}_0, p, \theta, 1) | p, \theta] > 0, \\ 0 & \text{if } E[\pi_2(\tilde{s}_1, \tilde{s}_2, \tilde{s}_0, p, \theta, 1) | p, \theta] \leq 0. \end{cases} \quad (7b)$$

A credible updating rule given such strategies is now characterized. Recall that r is defined such that $E[\pi_2(\tilde{s}_1, \tilde{s}_2, \tilde{s}_0, p, \theta, 1) | \tilde{s}_1 > r] = 0$.

LEMMA 2: *If* (σ_1, σ_2, g) *constitutes a PSE, then* (i) $q(D; g) \geq p_D(r)$ *and* (ii) $q(C; g) = p_C(r)$.

Proof: See the Appendix.

In equilibrium, preemptive offers must be sufficiently high so that only first bidders with valuations high enough to deter second bidders have the incentive to make them. No debt offer below $p_D(r)$ preempts bidder 2, and the minimum preemptive cash offer is $p_C(r)$. Notice that, if $\gamma = 1$, the target effectively possesses no private information. In this case, $p_D(r) = p_C(r)$ since cash is then equivalent to debt. If $\gamma < 1$, the target does possess private information, and, in this case, $p_D(r) > p_C(r)$. The cash offer required to deter bidder 2 is below the face value of the debt offer required to do the same. As shown in Lemma 1, for any given minimum preemptive bids, bidders with higher values of s_1 are the ones that find it profitable to preempt with cash. Thus, the face value needed to signal that s_1 is at or above any given level is lower with cash as compared to debt.

Combining the characterization of sequentially rational strategies with the characterization of credible beliefs yields Proposition 1.

PROPOSITION 1:
(i) *There exists a PSE.*
(ii) *If* $(\sigma_1^*, \sigma_2^*, g^*)$ *constitutes a PSE, then*

$$\sigma_1^*(s_1) = \begin{cases} (v_0, D) & \text{if } l_0 \leq s_1 \leq r, \\ (p_C(r), C) & \text{if } s_1 > r; \end{cases} \quad (8a)$$

$$\sigma_2^*(p, \theta) = \begin{cases} 1 & \text{if } p < p_D(r) \text{ and } \theta = D, \\ 1 & \text{if } p < p_C(r) \text{ and } \theta = C, \\ 0 & \text{if } p = p_C(r) \text{ and } \theta = C. \end{cases} \quad (8b)$$

Proof: See the Appendix.

In equilibrium, low-valuing bidders offer debt and high-valuing bidders offer cash. The information signaled by the cash offer preempts bidder 2, while the information signaled by the debt offer does not.[9] Note that, as γ, the probability that the acquisition is profitable (i.e., $s_0 = \beta$), increases, bidder 2 becomes more difficult to deter and there are fewer preemptive bids (r, the threshold between preempting and nonpreempting bidders, is increasing in γ). As a result, as γ increases, even though securities offers afford protection against the decreasingly likely event of an unprofitable acquisition (i.e., $s_0 = \alpha$), they are made more frequently.[10]

Using the equilibrium strategies from Proposition 1, equilibrium expected payoffs can be computed. Bidder 1's equilibrium expected payoff from studying the target equals (note that, if bidder 2 competes, $p_D(s_1)$ is the expected acquisition price for a given s_1 and for $s_0 = \beta$)

$$E\pi_1(\tilde{s}_1, \tilde{s}_2, \tilde{s}_0, \sigma_p^*(\tilde{s}_1), \sigma_u^*(\tilde{s}_1), \sigma_2^*(\sigma_p^*(\tilde{s}_1), \sigma_u^*(\tilde{s}_1))) - k_1$$
$$= E[\gamma(v^\beta(\tilde{s}_1) - p_D(\tilde{s}_1)) \mid l_0 \le \tilde{s}_1 \le r]\mathrm{pr}(l_0 \le \tilde{s}_1 \le r)$$
$$+ E[\gamma v^\beta(\tilde{s}_1) + (1-\gamma)v''(\tilde{s}_1) - p_C(r) \mid \tilde{s}_1 > r]\mathrm{pr}(\tilde{s}_1 > r) - k_1$$
$$= \gamma E[v^\beta(\tilde{s}_1) - p_D(\min\{\tilde{s}_1, r\}) \mid \tilde{s}_1 \ge l_0]\mathrm{pr}(\tilde{s}_1 \ge l_0)$$
$$+ (1-\gamma)E[v''(\tilde{s}_1) - v''(r) \mid \tilde{s}_1 > r]\mathrm{pr}(\tilde{s}_1 > r) - k_1. \qquad (9)$$

Bidder 1 initially studies the target if (9) is positive. If this is the case, bidder 2's equilibrium expected payoff equals

$$E\pi_2(\tilde{s}_1, \tilde{s}_2, \tilde{s}_0, \sigma_p^*(\tilde{s}_1), \sigma_u^*(\tilde{s}_1), \sigma_2^*(\sigma_p^*(\tilde{s}_1), \sigma_u^*(\tilde{s}_1)))$$
$$= E[\gamma v^\beta(\tilde{s}_2) - \gamma \min\{v^\beta(\tilde{s}_1), v^\beta(\tilde{s}_2)\} - k_2 \mid l_0 \le \tilde{s}_1 \le r]\mathrm{pr}(l_0 \le \tilde{s}_1 \le r), \qquad (10)$$

and the target's equilibrium expected payoff equals

$$E[\tilde{\pi}_0] = v_0 \mathrm{pr}(\tilde{s}_1 < l_0)$$
$$+ E[\gamma p_D(\tilde{s}_1) + (1-\gamma)v_0 \mid l_0 \le \tilde{s}_1 \le r]\mathrm{pr}(l_0 \le \tilde{s}_1 \le r)$$
$$+ p_C(r)\mathrm{pr}(\tilde{s}_1 > r)$$
$$= v_0 \mathrm{pr}(\tilde{s}_1 < l_0) + \gamma E[p_D(\min\{\tilde{s}_1, r\}) \mid \tilde{s}_1 \ge l_0]\mathrm{pr}(\tilde{s}_1 \ge l_0)$$
$$+ (1-\gamma)[v_0 \mathrm{pr}(l_0 \le \tilde{s}_1 \le r) + v''(r)\mathrm{pr}(\tilde{s}_1 > r)]. \qquad (11)$$

---

[9] In a Sequential Equilibrium, Lemmas 1 and 2(i) are unchanged. However, a Sequential Equilibrium only implies that $q(C; g) \ge p_C(r)$. This weaker result implies the existence of a continuum of Sequential Equilibrium outcomes characterized by the particular values of $q(C; g)$ and $q(D; g)$.

Say (3) is not satisfied. In equilibrium, if $s_1 \ge l_0$, bidder 1 offers (v_0, D), which preempts bidder 2. Say (3) is satisfied, but (4) is not. Noting that (4) is equivalent to $p_C(r) > v_0$, say $p_C(r) \le v_0 < p_C(h)$. In equilibrium, low-valuing first bidders offer (v_0, D) and bidder 2 competes, and high-valuing first bidders offer (v_0, C), which preempts bidder 2. There may also be a range of intermediate valuations for which bidder 1 offers (p, D), where $p > p_D(r)$, which also preempts bidder 2. Say $p_C(h) \le v_0$. In equilibrium, if $l_0 \le s_1 \le r$, bidder 1 offers (v_0, D) and bidder 2 competes, and, if $s_1 > r$, bidder 1 offers $(p_D(r), D)$, which preempts bidder 2.

[10] The analysis suggests some interesting implications for contract theory. An important question is why certain contracts are (seemingly) "incomplete" in that there appear to be relevant and observable variables that are not contracted upon. The results here suggest that incomplete contracts may be agreed upon in an attempt to signal private information.

Consider the implications of a decrease in bidder 2's cost of studying the target. Since bidder 2's cost of competing is lower, its expected payoff is higher. Bidder 1's expected payoff is lower since a higher valuation must be signalled to deter bidder 2, and this is more costly. In addition, bidder 1 is more likely to offer securities. Consider now the target. Bidder 2 is preempted less often, and, when it is preempted, the bid is higher. Both effects benefit the target, and its expected payoff is higher. Note that these results require bidder 1's expected payoff to remain positive. Otherwise no bidder will study the target initially.

Figure 1 illustrates the determination of r, the critical value of s_1 that separates first bidders that offer cash ($s_1 > r$) from first bidders that offer securities ($l_0 \leq s_1 \leq r$). In the example, $\hat{s}_i$ is uniformly distributed on [0, 1], $v_0 = 1$, $v^a(s_i) = 0.49 + s_i$ (thus $l_0 = 0.51$), and $v''(s_i) = s_i/1.01$. As is shown, r is decreasing in k_2, bidder 2's information cost, and increasing in γ, the probability that the acquisition is profitable.

III. Advance Disclosure of the Target's Information

It has been assumed that the target observes s_0, its private information on the profitability of an acquisition, after bidder 1 bids. Suppose, though, that the target observes and (truthfully) discloses s_0 prior to bidder 1's initial offer. This section discusses the effects of such a disclosure. It is shown that bidder 1's expected payoff is decreased, and, provided that bidder 1 is not deterred, bidder 2's and the target's expected payoffs are increased.

If the target discloses s_0 after bidder 1 studies the target but before it bids, the

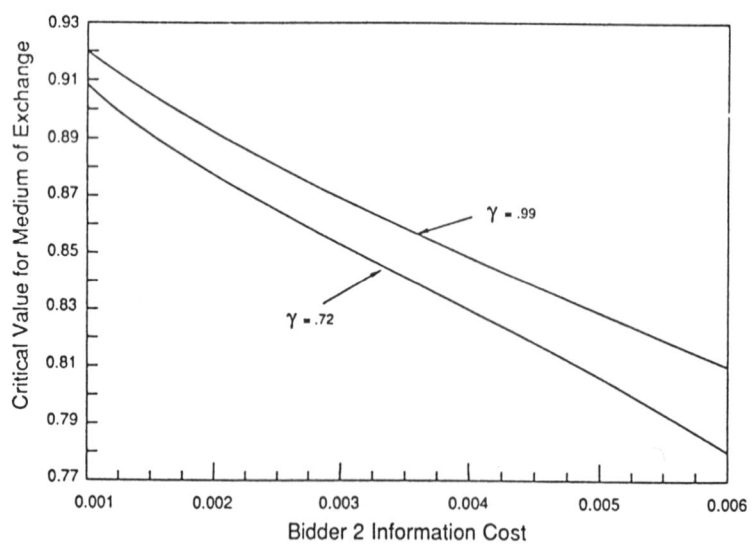

Figure 1. Preemptive Bidding Examples. The critical value separating first bidders that offer cash (those with valuations above the critical value) from first bidders that offer securities (those with valuations below the critical value), as a function of bidder 2's information cost, is shown. γ denotes the probability that the acquisition is profitable.

nature of the bidding problem is unchanged, with the exception that s_0 is known. With probability $1 - \gamma$, $s_0 = \alpha$ is disclosed, and there is no bidding. Bidder 1's payoff is $-k_1$, bidder 2's payoff is zero, and the target's payoff is v_0. With probability γ, $s_0 = \beta$ is disclosed, and the expected payoffs for bidders 1 and 2 and the target are given by (9), (10), and (11), respectively, evaluated at $\gamma = 1$. Define r' such that $E[\pi_2(\tilde{s}_1, \tilde{s}_2, \beta, p, \theta, 1) | \tilde{s}_1 > r'] = 0$; if it is known that $s_0 = \beta$, then r' is the minimum value for which, if bidder 2 knew that s_1 exceeded this value, bidder 2 would not find it profitable to compete. If $\gamma < 1$, then $r' > r$. Advance disclosure of $s_0 = \beta$ makes bidder 2 more difficult to deter.

Bidder 1's expected payoff with advance disclosure equals

$$E[\tilde{\pi}_1^d] - k_1 = \gamma E[v^d(\tilde{s}_1) - p_D(\min\{\tilde{s}_1, r'\}) | \tilde{s}_1 \geq l_0]\text{pr}(\tilde{s}_1 \geq l_0) - k_1. \quad (12)$$

If $\gamma < 1$, (9) exceeds (12). That is, bidder 1's expected payoff is lower with advance disclosure. There are two reasons. The first is that bidder 2 observes the target's information prior to deciding whether to compete, and this makes competing more profitable for bidder 2. Thus, preemption by bidder 1 now requires signaling a higher valuation, and this is more costly. The second reason is that bidder 1 observes the target's information prior to its own bidding. Since bidder 1 can make a debt offer, which is contingent on the target's information, observing this information prior to bidding yields no benefits. Further, the benefit of a noncontingent cash offer is eliminated. Cash establishes a commitment to acquire the target even if it turns out that the target's information indicates an unprofitable acquisition. In equilibrium, high-valuing bidders find it profitable to establish this commitment in order to signal. With advance disclosure of the target's information, the cost of such a commitment is zero, and the efficacy of cash in signaling is eliminated. This lowers bidder 1's expected payoff.

If bidder 1 will still study the target initially, then bidder 2's expected payoff with advance disclosure equals

$$E[\tilde{\pi}_2^d] = \gamma E[v^d(\tilde{s}_2) - \min\{v^d(\tilde{s}_1), v^d(\tilde{s}_2)\} - k_2 | l_0 \leq \tilde{s}_1 \leq r']\text{pr}(l_0 \leq \tilde{s}_1 \leq r'), \quad (13)$$

and the target's expected payoff with advance disclosure equals

$$E[\tilde{\pi}_0^d] = \gamma[v_0\text{pr}(\tilde{s}_1 < l_0) + E[p_D(\min\{\tilde{s}_1, r'\}) | \tilde{s}_1 \geq l_0]\text{pr}(\tilde{s}_1 \geq l_0)] + (1 - \gamma)v_0. \quad (14)$$

If $\gamma < 1$, (13) exceeds (10) and (14) exceeds (11). That is, both bidder 2's and the target's expected payoffs are higher with advance disclosure. Bidder 2's expected payoff is higher because the chance that it studies the target when the target's information indicates an unprofitable acquisition is eliminated. The target's expected payoff is higher because there are fewer preemptive bids, and any preemptive bids that do occur are higher.[11]

---

[11] Milgrom and Weber [16] present results of a similar nature in a study of auctions. It is shown that a seller with access to private information may raise its expected selling price by disclosing this information. Key to this result is that bidders' valuations not be independent. (With independent valuations and risk neutrality, disclosure has no effect on expected selling price.) Here, even if there were independent valuations, the results would go through. Suppose that, instead of the target having private information common to both bidders' valuations, it has private information specific to each bidder. That is, suppose the target observes the independent random variables $\tilde{s}_{01}$ and $\tilde{s}_{02}$, and suppose s_{0i} conveys information only on bidder i's valuation. If advance disclosure is taken to mean the disclosure of both s_{01} and s_{02}, then the qualitative results of this section will be unchanged.

This is an interesting rationale for firms to continually release information. It can make preemptive bids more costly and thus raise a firm's expected payoff in the event it becomes a candidate for acquisition. More generally, bidders will seek to lower the costs of preemption and targets will seek to raise these costs. An interesting question for future work concerns what other actions may derive from such incentives.

IV. Further Implications

An implication of the model is that target management is more likely to reject a securities offer as compared to a cash offer. Dodd [5] reports that, for a sample of merger offers rejected by target management, the target's share price dropped. One conclusion that might be drawn is that this is evidence of a firm's management acting contrary to the interests of its shareholders. The theory here suggests another possibility. Rejection of a securities offer indicates that the proposed acquisition is not profitable—and thus the drop in share price. (The price will have risen at the offer's announcement.) It would have been worse for target shareholders, though, had the offer been accepted. It would be interesting to examine rejected offers conditional on the medium of exchange.[12]

The model also predicts that competing bidders are more likely to be observed following an initial securities offer as compared to an initial cash offer. This is because cash is only used in preemptive bids.[13]

Share price responses to acquisition announcements, conditional on the medium of exchange, can be considered. If $l_0 \leq s_1 \leq r$, bidder 1 offers securities and faces competition. Thus, the market's expectation of bidder 1's payoff, conditional on its making a securities offer, equals (note that the market observes the initial offer, but not s_1)

$$\gamma E[v^a(\tilde{s}_1) - p_D(\tilde{s}_1) | l_0 \leq \tilde{s}_1 \leq r] - k_1. \tag{15}$$

If $s_1 > r$, bidder 1 offers cash and the competition is deterred. Thus, the market's expectation of bidder 1's payoff, conditional on its making a cash offer, equals

$$E[\gamma v^a(\tilde{s}_1) + (1 - \gamma)v^n(\tilde{s}_1) - p_C(r) | \tilde{s}_1 > r] - k_1. \tag{16}$$

---

[12] Travlos [19] reports that, for a sample of merger offers and tender offers, the chance of success is lower if the medium of exchange is cash. It would be useful to examine the results for merger offers only. This is because the key to the model here is the assumption that the accept/reject decision is made by a party with private information on the target. This party is more reasonably interpreted as management rather than shareholders, and, thus, the model is best viewed as a model of merger offers. Further, there is likely to be a hostile/friendly distinction that is relevant between tender offers and merger offers, and tender offers generally consist of cash. Huang and Walkling [13] report that, in a sample of thirty-three cash merger offers, one (3.0 percent) was opposed by target management, and, in a sample of fifty-five merger offers that included securities, four (7.3 percent) were opposed.

[13] Franks, Harris, and Mayer [8] report cases when initial bidders revise their bids but no competing bids are observed. A scenario in which the model would be consistent with this is one in which an intitial bidder does not know whether there is a potentially competing bidder. Then it offers securities initially, and, if a competitor is observed, it may make a revised, preemptive cash offer. They also report that bidding contests in which the final offer is cash are more likely to have had revised bids or been met by competing bids than are contests in which the final offer includes securities. The likelihood of competing bids is not reported separately (from revised bids); nor is the likelihood as a function of the initial offer.

It can be verified that (16) exceeds (15). Thus, the share price revaluation for bidder 1 will be higher if it offers cash as compared to securities. Consistent with this prediction, Asquith, Bruner, and Mullins [1], Franks, Harris, and Mayer [8] (for the U.S., but not U.K.), Gordon and Yagil [10], and Travlos [19] report higher share price revaluations for bidders that made cash-only as compared to combination cash and securities merger offers.

Whether a target's share price revaluation is also higher given a cash offer as compared to a securities offer depends on the parameters of the model. Since there is competition following a securities offer, the market's expectation of a target's payoff given a securities offer equals

$$\gamma E[p_D(\tilde{s}_1) | l_0 \leq \tilde{s}_1 \leq r] + (1 - \gamma)v_0.$$

Since there is no competition following a cash offer, a target's payoff from a cash offer is $p_C(r)$. If the preemptive offer is high enough, a target's share price revaluation will be higher given a cash offer. Asquith, Bruner, and Mullins [1], Franks, Harris, and Mayer [8], Gordon and Yagil [10], Huang and Walkling [13], and Wansley, Lane, and Yang [20] study target returns to merger offers, conditional on the medium of exchange. All report higher share price revaluations for targets of cash-only offers as compared to combination cash and securities offers.

As discussed in Section II, bidder 1's expected payoff decreases and the target's expected payoff increases, with a decrease in k_2, bidder 2's information cost. Consider the effect on share price responses to acquisition announcements, conditional on the medium of exchange. It follows from (15) that bidder 1's share price revaluation, conditional on its offering securities, increases if k_2 decreases. This is because r, the critical value of s_1 that separates first bidders that offer cash from those that offer securities, is decreasing in k_2. That is, first bidders that offer securities now have a higher average valuation. Using (16), it can be shown that bidder 1's share price revaluation, conditional on its offering cash, may also increase if k_2 decreases. Though the preemptive bid is higher, first bidders that offer cash also have a higher average valuation, so, while a first bidder's expected payoff decreases if k_2 decreases, share price revaluations for a first bidder, conditional on securities offers and cash offers, may both increase. For the target, share price revaluations, conditional on both cash and securities offers, increase if k_2 decreases.

These implications were derived in a model based on informational asymmetries. A prominent competing model is tax based; bidders structure offers to minimize the total tax liability of bidder and target shareholders.[14] Such a model also predicts higher premiums for cash offers as compared to securities offers. Target shareholders must realize any capital gain from a cash offer immediately, whereas a capital gain from a securities offer can be deferred until the securities are sold. Thus, for a given after-tax reservation price, target shareholders require a higher premium to sell their shares for cash. Franks, Harris, and Mayer [8], however, report higher premiums for cash offers in the U.K. for a time period before the introduction of a capital gains tax. Thus, while tax considerations may

---

[14] See Carleton et al. [4] and Niden [17] for accounting/tax-based analyses and Brown [3] and Dreyfus [6] for strategic, tax-based analyses of the structure of offers in acquisitions.

help in understanding the choice of medium of exchange, they do not provide the complete explanation.

Appendix

Proof of Lemma 2: Let $\Pi_1(s_1, p, \theta, e) = E\pi_1(s_1, \tilde{s}_2, \tilde{s}_0, p, \theta, e)$, and, for a nonempty set $S \subset [l_0, h]$, let $w(S) = E[\pi_2(\tilde{s}_1, \tilde{s}_2, \tilde{s}_0, p, \theta, 1) | \tilde{s}_1 \in S]$.

(i) Establish $q(D; g) \geq p_D(r)$.

Say $q(D; g) < p_D(r)$. There are two cases to consider.

(a) $s_{DC}(q(D; g), q(C; g)) \leq s_D(q(D; g))$.
In this case, $s_{DC}(q(D; g), q(C; g)) \leq s_D(q(D; g)) < s_D(p_D(r)) = r$.
Therefore, $\gamma p_D(r) + (1 - \gamma)v''(r) - q(C; g) > \gamma q(D; g) + (1 - \gamma)v''(s_{DC}(q(D; g), q(C; g))) - q(C; g) \geq 0$.
This implies $q(C; g) < p_C(r)$, which implies $s_C(q(C; g)) < s_C(p_C(r)) = r$.
Using Lemma 1, $\hat{S}(q(C; g), C; \sigma_1) = (\max\{s_C(q(C; g)), s_{DC}(q(D; g), q(C; g))\}, h]$, and (6i) requires $g(s_1 | q(C; g), C) = \hat{g}(s_1; \hat{S}(q(C; g), C; \sigma_1))$.
However, $w((\max\{s_C(q(C; g)), s_{DC}(q(D; g), q(C; g))\}, h]) > w((r, h]) = 0$, and, thus, $q(C; g) \notin Q(C; g)$, which is a contradiction.

(b) $s_{DC}(q(D; g), q(C; g)) > s_D(q(D; g))$.
Using Lemma 1, $\hat{S}(q(D; g), D; \sigma_1) = (s_D(q(D; g)), s_{DC}(q(D; g), q(C; g))]$, and (6i) requires $g(s_1 | q(D; g), D) = \hat{g}(s_1; \hat{S}(q(D; g), D; \sigma_1))$.
However, $w((s_D(q(D; g)), s_{DC}(q(D; g), q(C; g))]) > w((s_D(p_D(r)), h]) = w((r, h]) = 0$, and, thus, $q(D; g) \notin Q(D; g)$, which is a contradiction.

Thus, $q(D; g) \geq p_D(r)$.

(ii) Establish $q(C; g) = p_C(r)$.

Say $q(C; g) < p_C(r)$.
Then, $s_C(q(C; g)) < s_C(p_C(r)) = r$ and $s_{DC}(q(D; g), q(C; g)) < s_{DC}(p_D(r), p_C(r)) = r$.
Using Lemma 1, $\hat{S}(q(C; g), C; \sigma_1) = (\max\{s_C(q(C; g)), s_{DC}(q(D; g), q(C; g))\}, h]$, and (6i) requires $g(s_1 | q(C; g), C) = \hat{g}(s_1; \hat{S}(q(C; g), C; \sigma_1))$.
However, $w((\max\{s_C(q(C; g)), s_{DC}(q(D; g), q(C; g))\}, h]) > w((r, h]) = 0$, and, thus, $q(C; g) \notin Q(C; g)$, which is a contradiction.

Say $q(C; g) > p_C(r)$.
Using Lemma 1, $\hat{S}(p_C(r), C; \sigma_1)$ is empty. It will be shown that there exists an S that satisfies (6ii) for the offer $(p_C(r), C)$. There are two possibilities to consider.

(a) Say $S \subset [l_0, h]$ and $w(S) > 0$.
For $s_1 \in [l_0, h]$, $\Pi_1(s_1, p_C(r), C, \hat{\sigma}_2(S)) = \Pi_1(s_1, p_C(r), C, 1) < \Pi_1(s_1, v_0, D, 1) = \Pi_1(s_1, v_0, D, \sigma_2(v_0, D)) \leq \Pi_1(s_1, \sigma_p(s_1), \sigma_\theta(s_1), \sigma_2(\sigma_p(s_1), \sigma_\theta(s_1)))$, and there exists no such S that satisfies (6ii).

(b) Say $S \subset [l_0, h]$ and $w(S) \leq 0$.
For $s_1 \in [l_0, h]$, $\Pi_1(s_1, p_C(r), C, \hat{\sigma}_2(S)) = \Pi_1(s_1, p_C(r), C, 0) > \Pi_1(s_1, q(C; g), C, 0) = \Pi_1(s_1, q(C; g), C, \sigma_2(q(C; g), C))$.

Using $s_C(p_C(r)) = r$, for $s_1 \in (r, h]$, $\Pi_1(s_1, p_C(r), C, \hat{\sigma}_2(S)) = \Pi_1(s_1, p_C(r), C, 0) > \Pi_1(s_1, v_0, D, 1) = \Pi_1(s_1, v_0, D, \sigma_2(v_0, D))$.
For $s_1 \in (s_{DC}(q(D;g), p_C(r)), h]$, $\Pi_1(s_1, p_C(r), C, \hat{\sigma}_2(S)) = \Pi_1(s_1, p_C(r), C, 0) > \Pi_1(s_1, q(D;g), D, 0) = \Pi_1(s_1, q(D;g), D, \sigma_2(q(D;g), D))$.
Thus, since $\sigma_1(s_1)$ equals (v_0, D), $(q(D;g), D)$, or $(q(C;g), C)$, we have that, for $s_1 \in ([l_0, h] \cap (r, h] \cap (s_{DC}(q(D;g), p_C(r)), h])$, $\Pi_1(s_1, p_C(r), C, \hat{\sigma}_2(S)) > \Pi_1(s_1, \sigma_p(s_1), \sigma_\theta(s_1), \sigma_2(\sigma_p(s_1), \sigma_\theta(s_1)))$.
Lemma 2(i) implies $s_{DC}(q(D;g), p_C(r)) \le s_{DC}(p_D(r), p_C(r)) = r$.
Therefore, $[l_0, h] \cap (r, h] \cap (s_{DC}(q(D;g), p_C(r)), h] = (r, h]$.
Using $s_C(p_C(r)) = r$, for $s_1 \in [l_0, r]$, $\Pi_1(s_1, p_C(r), C, \hat{\sigma}_2(S)) = \Pi_1(s_1, p_C(r), C, 0) \le \Pi_1(s_1, v_0, D, 1) = \Pi_1(s_1, v_0, D, \sigma_2(v_0, D)) \le \Pi_1(s_1, \sigma_p(s_1), \sigma_\theta(s_1), \sigma_2(\sigma_p(s_1), \sigma_\theta(s_1)))$.
Finally, $w((r, h]) = 0$, and we have that $S = (r, h]$ satisfies (6ii). Therefore, $g(s_1 | p_C(r), C) = \hat{g}(s_1; (r, h])$.
However, $w((r, h]) = 0$, and, thus, $p_C(r) \in Q(C; g)$, which is a contradiction.
Thus, $q(C; g) = p_C(r)$. Q.E.D.

Proof of Proposition 1:

(i) It can be verified that the updating rule

$$g(s_1 | p, \theta) = \begin{cases} \hat{g}(s_1; [l_0, r]) & \text{if } \theta = D, \\ \hat{g}(s_1; (s_C(p), h]) & \text{if } \theta = C, \end{cases}$$

combined with strategies given by (8), constitutes a PSE.

(ii) Suppose $(\sigma_1^*, \sigma_2^*, g^*)$ constitutes a PSE.
That σ_2^* satisfies (8b) follows directly from Lemma 2.
Using Lemma 2, $s_D(q(D;g)) \ge s_D(p_D(r)) = r$, $s_C(q(C;g)) = s_C(p_C(r)) = r$, and $s_{DC}(q(D;g), q(C;g)) \le s_{DC}(p_D(r), p_C(r)) = r$.
Therefore, $\min\{s_D(q(D;g)), s_C(q(C;g))\} = r$, $s_D(q(D;g)) \ge s_{DC}(q(D;g), q(C;g))$, and $\max\{s_C(q(C;g)), s_{DC}(q(D;g), q(C;g))\} = r$.
That σ_1^* satisfies (8a) then follows directly from Lemma 1. Q.E.D.

REFERENCES

1. P. Asquith, R. Bruner, and D. Mullins. "Merger Returns and the Form of Financing." Unpublished paper, Harvard University and University of Virginia, 1986.
2. D. P. Baron. "Tender Offers and Management Resistance." *Journal of Finance* 38 (May 1983), 331–43.
3. D. T. Brown. "The Construction of Tender Offers: Capital Gains Taxes and the Free Rider Problem." *Journal of Business* 61 (April 1988), 183–96.
4. W. T. Carleton, D. K. Guilkey, R. S. Harris, and J. F. Stewart. "An Empirical Analysis of the Role of the Medium of Exchange in Mergers." *Journal of Finance* 38 (June 1983), 813–26.
5. P. Dodd. "Merger Proposals, Management Discretion and Stockholder Wealth." *Journal of Financial Economics* 8 (June 1980), 105–37.
6. J. F. Dreyfus. "Essays on the Theory of Takeover Bids and Firm Behavior in Incomplete Markets." Unpublished Ph.D. dissertation, University of Pennsylvania, 1985.

7. M. J. Fishman. "A Theory of Preemptive Takeover Bidding." *RAND Journal of Economics* 19 (Spring 1988), 88–101.
8. J. R. Franks, R. S. Harris, and C. Mayer. "Means of Payment in Takeovers: Results for the United Kingdom and the United States." In A. J. Auerbach (ed.), *Corporate Takeovers: Causes and Consequences*. Chicago and London: The University of Chicago Press, 1988.
9. R. M. Giammarino and R. L. Heinkel. "A Model of Dynamic Takeover Behavior." *Journal of Finance* 41 (June 1986), 465–80.
10. M. J. Gordon and J. Yagil. "Financial Gain from Conglomerate Mergers." In H. Levy (ed.), *Research in Finance*. Greenwich, CT: JAI Press, Inc., 1981.
11. S. J. Grossman and M. Perry. "Perfect Sequential Equilibrium." *Journal of Economic Theory* 39 (June 1986), 97–119.
12. R. G. Hansen. "A Theory for the Choice of Exchange Medium in Mergers and Acquisitions." *Journal of Business* 60 (January 1987), 75–95.
13. Y. Huang and R. A. Walkling. "Target Abnormal Returns Associated with Acquisition Announcements: Payment, Acquisition Form, and Managerial Resistance." *Journal of Financial Economics* 19 (December 1987), 329–49.
14. N. Khanna. "Optimal Bidding for Tender Offers." Mimeo, University of Michigan, Graduate School of Business Administration, 1987.
15. D. Kreps and R. Wilson. "Sequential Equilibria." *Econometrica* 50 (July 1982), 863–94.
16. P. Milgrom and R. Weber. "A Theory of Auctions and Competitive Bidding." *Econometrica* 50 (September 1982), 1089–1122.
17. C. M. Niden. "The Role of Taxes in Corporate Acquisitions: Effects on Premium and Type of Consideration." Unpublished Ph.D. dissertation, University of Chicago, 1988.
18. I. P. L. P'ng. "Facilitation of Competing Bids and the Price of a Takeover Target." Business Economics Working Paper No. 87-10, UCLA Graduate School of Management, 1987.
19. N. G. Travlos. "Corporate Takeover Bids, Methods of Payment, and Bidding Firms' Stock Returns." *Journal of Finance* 42 (September 1987), 943–63.
20. J. W. Wansley, W. R. Lane, and H. C. Yang. "Abnormal Returns to Acquired Firms by Type of Acquisition and Method of Payment." *Financial Management* 12 (Autumn 1983), 16–22.

[20]

Share Tendering Strategies and the Success of Hostile Takeover Bids

David Hirshleifer and Sheridan Titman

University of California, Los Angeles

This paper presents a model of tender offers in which the bid perfectly reveals the bidder's private information about the size of the value improvement that can be generated by a takeover. We argue that bidders with greater improvements will offer higher premia to ensure that sufficient shares are tendered to obtain control. The model relates announcement date returns and takeover success or failure to the amount bid, the initial shareholdings of the bidder, the number of shares the bidder attempts to purchase, the dilution of minority shareholders, and managerial opposition. We show that managerial defensive measures will sometimes increase the probability of the offer's success, either by raising the incentive to bid high or by decreasing the asymmetry of information about the improvement.

When a hostile bidder makes a tender offer for a widely held firm, target shareholders must evaluate competing claims to decide whether or not to tender their shares. Bidders typically accuse the incumbent management of mismanaging the firm and claim that they are offering a fair price for its shares that reflects the higher value of the target under their direction. Management, on the other hand,

---

We especially thank the referee of this *Journal*, Milton Harris, and Robert Vishny for extremely helpful comments. We also thank Michael Brennan, Peter Carr, Julian Franks, Ron Giammarino, David Levine, Ivan Png, Eric Rasmusen, Avanidhar Subrahmanyam, Brett Trueman, and participants at seminars at University of British Columbia, University of California at Berkeley and Los Angeles, Carnegie-Mellon University, Columbia University, Northwestern University, Stanford University, Vanderbilt University, University of Washington, and the Symposium on Financial Contracting at Indiana University for helpful comments.

[*Journal of Political Economy*, 1990, vol. 98, no. 2]
© 1990 by The University of Chicago. All rights reserved. 0022-3808/90/9802-0003$01.50

often accuses the bidder ("raider") of trying to buy shares on the cheap, offering insufficient compensation given the true value of the firm's assets.

The target shareholders' assessment of these claims generally cannot be known in advance. Furthermore, shareholders may have specific attributes such as liquidity or tax considerations that affect their tendering decisions. For these reasons, the outcome of an offer is generally uncertain. This is evidenced by the observed negative price reactions of target shares on announcements of the failure of an offer (Bradley, Desai, and Kim 1983; Samuelson and Rosenthal 1986; Ruback 1988) and by the positive reactions of the bidder's stock price to success and negative reactions to failure (Bradley 1980).

Grossman and Hart (1980) were the first to explain that, because of a free-rider problem, target shareholders may rationally turn down bids that offer substantial premia over the current market price. They argued that if atomistic shareholders of the target firm are able to share fully in the improvements brought about by a successful takeover without tendering their own shares, they will not accept an offer unless the price equals or exceeds the posttakeover value of the shares. They further argued that if takeovers are to be profitable, bidders must be able to dilute the posttakeover value of the shares that are not tendered. The threat of dilution induces target shareholders to tender at a price that allows the bidder to cover his costs associated with the takeover.

Shleifer and Vishny (1986) pointed out that takeovers may still be profitably undertaken without dilution if the bidder had accumulated a large fraction of the target firm's shares prior to publicly announcing the offer. Although these large shareholders cannot on average profit from the additional shares they purchase, they realize gains on the shares they owned prior to the tender offer that are at least sufficient to cover their costs. An important innovation in the Shleifer and Vishny paper is the introduction of an informational asymmetry between the purchaser, who knows the posttakeover value of the target firm, and the target shareholders, who do not. Given this asymmetry, target shareholders cannot be certain whether it is in their interest to tender their shares.

Although the Grossman and Hart and Shleifer and Vishny papers provide important intuition about why shareholders might view some offers as inadequate, in their analyses no observed bid ever fails. With the reservation prices of the target shareholders known with certainty, a given offer either is high enough to succeed or else will fail with certainty. Since bids that fail with certainty are obviously unprofitable, the bids in these models will be made only at the minimum acceptable price.

SHARE TENDERING STRATEGIES

This paper provides a model in which observed tender offers sometimes do fail. The argument above indicates that for offers to fail, the bidder must be uncertain about the prices at which shareholders will tender. This type of uncertainty will arise if shareholders have some personal costs and benefits of tendering (e.g., transaction costs and tax or liquidity considerations) that are not known by the bidder. Even if these costs are zero, bidders may still be uncertain about the outcome of an offer if shareholders follow mixed strategies (i.e., randomize) when they are indifferent about whether or not to tender their shares. We show that similar results can be obtained with either setting. However, since the mixed-strategy equilibrium is more tractable, we relegate the development of the model with random tendering costs to Appendix B.[1]

A fundamental property of the bidding game we describe is that shareholders are more likely to accept high bids than low ones. In consequence, bidders with low potential gains from the takeover can bid low to separate themselves credibly from high-gain bidders. A high-gain bidder will not find it in his interest to offer as low a bid because rejection is more costly to him. The greater willingness of low-value bidders to make low offers leads to an equilibrium in which the offer perfectly reveals the information of the bidder, with the bid exactly equaling the posttakeover value of the shares.

A positive relation between the bid premium and the probability of offer success is also a feature of recent takeover models with multiple bidders (e.g., Giammarino and Heinkel 1986; Fishman 1988; Hirshleifer and Png 1990).[2] These papers differ from those of Grossman and Hart and of Shleifer and Vishny in assuming that offers are made to *management*, rather than directly to shareholders. This assumption is more relevant for friendly merger bids, in which the target behaves as a unit, than for hostile tender offers, which are subject to a free-rider problem among shareholders.[3]

This paper also examines scenarios that allow for a free-rider problem among target shareholders and yet also allow managers to affect

---

[1] Harsanyi (1973) has shown that in some games, as private shocks to player-specific costs and benefits become arbitrarily small, the behavior of the players can be described by a mixed-strategy equilibrium.

[2] The model is also similar to the recent work by Giammarino and Lewis (1988) that analyzes the decision of a firm to issue new shares to finance a known investment project. In their separating equilibrium, the higher-valued firm offers shares at a higher price, taking the risk that the issue will be rejected. Because their cost of failure is higher, lower-valued firms do not mimic this action.

[3] Berkovitch and Khanna (1988) examine the choice of friendly and hostile takeover methods in a single model. Morck, Shleifer, and Vishny (1988) have provided evidence that tender offers are used in hostile takeovers to discipline poorly performing management, while merger bids are more likely to be associated with friendly takeovers.

the success or failure of bids by resisting offers. We show that the managerial defensive measures affect the success of takeovers not only by affecting the strategies of bidders but also by affecting how shareholders interpret the bid. In particular, some defensive actions can potentially increase the likelihood of the bid's success, either by raising the incentive to bid high or by decreasing the asymmetry of information about the improvement. As a result, defensive measures can potentially improve welfare as well as increase the value of the target firm. However, defensive strategies can also be designed to entrench management and thereby reduce welfare.

I. Offer Prices as Signals of Posttakeover Value

A. *The Basic Model*

This section presents the model in its simplest form. We assume that, with the exception of one potential acquirer who owns the fraction α of the firm's shares, shareholders of the target firm are atomistic and hence view the success of the tender offer as independent of their individual tendering decisions. These holdings are determined exogenously and are unrelated to the posttakeover value of the firm. If the potential acquirer can successfully purchase the fraction $0.5 - \alpha$ of the firm's shares, he can gain control of the firm and improve its value by the amount z per share. This amount, which is bounded above by $\bar{z}$, is known only to the potential acquirer.[4] To simplify the notation we assume that the firm's value under the incumbent management is zero. If the potential acquirer attempts to take over the firm, a conditional tender offer is made for a controlling portion of the firm's shares. In other words, the bidder makes no purchase unless the number of shares tendered is at least as large as the number he has chosen to bid for; otherwise the offer fails.[5] We assume that the po-

---

[4] The model may be expanded so as to make $\bar{z}$ endogenous. Suppose that the range of possible positive values of z is unbounded. We assume that the manager maximizes his own expected wealth and possesses initial shareholdings γ in the firm. He obtains perquisites with value Q from control of the firm, but in deciding whether to accept or reject a friendly *merger* bid (rather than a tender offer), he balances this against the profit he obtains from selling his shares, $x^m\gamma$, and allowing the merger to take place, where x^m is the premium per share in a merger bid. This implies a critical value for the improvement, called $\bar{z}$, above which the bidder prefers to make a friendly merger bid, which will be accepted, rather than a hostile tender offer.

[5] We have also examined unconditional or "any and all" tender offers. Although the analysis is somewhat more complex, it yields essentially the same substantive results. Currently, a large proportion of tender offers are made unconditionally. However, since these offers can be withdrawn prior to the expiration date if the bidder believes that an insufficient number of shares will be tendered, we think our characterization of conditional offers probably offers a realistic description of unconditional offers as well. See Bagnoli and Lipman (1988) for further analysis of "any and all" tender offers.

SHARE TENDERING STRATEGIES

tential acquirer gets only one opportunity to bid: if it is rejected, there is no opportunity for later upward revisions. The critical aspect of this assumption is that the bidder's loss from being rejected is increasing with the size of his improvement. At the end of this section, we shall discuss ways in which the assumption of just a single bid can be relaxed. It is assumed that all market participants are risk neutral.

Up to this point, the assumptions are essentially identical to those in Shleifer and Vishny (1986). They imply that shareholders will turn down all bids that are less than the expected posttakeover value of the nontendered shares and accept all bids that exceed this value. Shleifer and Vishny further assume that shareholders always accept bids that make them indifferent. Given this assumption, they show that in equilibrium all bidders make the same bid, and shareholders always tender because the equilibrium bid equals the expected value as assessed by shareholders given that bid. Hence, observed bids never fail.

To construct an alternative equilibrium in which bids sometimes do fail, we begin by describing the problem faced by a bidder. Let x be the amount per share bid, and let ω be the fraction of the outstanding shares for which he bids. Let $P(x; \alpha, \omega)$ be the probability that at least ω shares are tendered to a potential acquirer who bids x and begins with an initial shareholding of α in the target. Let C be the cost of making a bid. Although C is known to the bidder, it need not be known to target shareholders. If more than ω shares are tendered, the shares are prorated, so that the bidder still pays x per share for ω shares.

We shall propose an equilibrium in which the potential acquirer, if he chooses to bid, makes an offer for exactly $\omega = 0.5 - \alpha$ shares, independent of the level of z. If a bid is made, the level of the bid is chosen to maximize his expected gain,

$$\max_{x} \; [\alpha z + (z - x)\omega] P(x; \alpha, \omega) - C. \qquad (1)$$

If we assume that $P(x; \alpha, \omega)$ is twice differentiable with respect to the amount of the bid, the sufficient first- and second-order conditions with respect to x are

$$P'[\alpha z + (z - x)\omega] - P\omega = 0 \qquad (2)$$

and

$$P''[\alpha z + (z - x)\omega] - 2P'\omega < 0. \qquad (3)$$

We assume that for each z there exists an x such that (2) and (3) obtain to ensure an interior optimum.[6] Then the following proposition holds (all proofs are in App. A).

---

[6] A rather mild condition on the probability schedule that ensures this is that $P(0) =$

PROPOSITION 1. If the probability of success $P(x; \alpha, \omega)$ is strictly increasing in the level of the bid, then the optimal bid $x(z)$ is a strictly increasing function of the improvement z.

The intuition is fairly straightforward. Bidders who can realize higher improvements are willing to bid higher to increase the probability that the offer succeeds because they have more to gain from a successful takeover. Proposition 1 suggests that the pooling equilibrium of Shleifer and Vishny may be sensitive to the assumptions of their model that permit the probability schedule to make a discontinuous jump from zero to one. For example, if we perturb the model by making y, the information about z possessed by the target shareholders, imperfectly known to the bidder, then the shareholders' tendering decisions cannot be foreseen with certainty by the bidder. The Shleifer-Vishny equilibrium is based on shareholders' inference about z, $E(z|y, x)$, not rising too rapidly with x, so that if y is a known constant, any bid greater than or equal to $E(z|y, x)$ is accepted with certainty. But with y stochastic, there will be a probability that x exceeds or is smaller than $E(z|\bar{y}, x)$, so that the offer may succeed or fail. Hence, the probability that the offer succeeds, instead of a step function, will be smoothly increasing in the bid. As proposition 1 demonstrates, a smoothly increasing probability schedule will induce bidders to reveal their levels of improvement through their bids, that is, a separating rather than a pooling outcome.[7]

If bids are to be accepted probabilistically, there must be uncertainty about the prices at which shareholders will tender. Such uncertainty arises in our model as a result of target shareholders' random choice of whether or not to tender their shares when they are indif-

---

0 and that the percentage rate of increase in probability with the bid is decreasing in the bid:

$$\frac{\partial}{\partial x}\left[\frac{P'(x; \alpha, \omega)}{P(x; \alpha, \omega)}\right] < 0.$$

[7] Even in the original game, the Shleifer and Vishny equilibrium is sensitive to the specification of beliefs. The belief that supports their equilibrium is that all bidders who would profit from an accepted low bid are *equally likely* to make the error of bidding too low. Under these beliefs, the low bid is below the conditional expected value of the gain from takeover, so shareholders will always reject. This is in contrast to the Banks and Sobel (1987) criterion of universal divinity, which requires that the likelihood of an off-equilibrium low bid be assessed to be lower for types for whom such a move is desirable under a more restricted set of responses by shareholders. It should be noted that the pooling equilibrium is *not* removed by some other well-known refinement concepts, such as the intuitive criterion of Cho and Kreps (1987) and perfect sequential equilibrium of Grossman and Perry (1986). However, we believe that the arguments breaking the equilibrium are intuitively appealing. Since the risk of having a bid rejected is less costly to a low-z bidder than to a high-z bidder, shareholders should infer that low bids are more likely to be associated with low z's. This tends to promote the acceptance of low bids, so that the pool evaporates.

SHARE TENDERING STRATEGIES

ferent, that is, when $x = E(z|x)$. If they are indifferent, we follow the convention that the target shareholders' tendering strategies are chosen so that the probability of the offer's success at different levels of the bid supports the proposed equilibrium behavior of the bidders.[8] The intuitive justification for a mixed-strategy equilibrium is that if the bid makes shareholders very nearly indifferent about whether to tender, then from the bidder's perspective the actions of the shareholders will seem random (see n. 1). In Appendix B, we model this explicitly, assuming that the shareholders' tendering decisions are deterministic functions of characteristics unknown to the bidder. The mixed-strategy model we develop in this section may be viewed as a metaphor for a situation with unknown characteristics of shareholders; it has the advantage of being far more tractable than the model of Appendix B, while yielding the same basic intuitions.

In a mixed-strategy separating equilibrium, the bid must make target shareholders indifferent between tendering and not tendering. This is the case in the proposed equilibrium in which the bid is fully revealing with $x = z$. To demonstrate that such an equilibrium exists and to solve for the probability schedule that supports it, we substitute the inference schedule $\hat{z}(x) = x$ for z into (2) and rewrite the equation in terms of x as

$$\frac{P'}{P} = \frac{\omega}{\alpha x}. \qquad (4)$$

Integrating both sides of (4) over x and rearranging terms yields a schedule that expresses the probability of the tender offer's success as an increasing function of the level of the bid, that is, $P(x; \alpha, \omega) = kx^{\omega/\alpha}$, where k is a constant of integration. The constant k is determined by noting that shareholders will accept any bid greater than $\bar{z}$ with certainty since they can do no better by retaining their shares. It follows that $P(\bar{z})$ must equal one (otherwise, the bidder would raise the bid by one cent), so the probability schedule is

$$P(x; \alpha, \omega) = \left(\frac{x}{\bar{z}}\right)^{\omega/\alpha}. \qquad (5)$$

This applies when the expected net profit from bidding,

$$\alpha x P(x; \alpha, \omega) - C = \alpha x^{(\omega+\alpha)/\alpha} \bar{z}^{-(\omega/\alpha)} - C,$$

is positive. The expected profit is increasing in x, so there exists a

---

[8] For a given bid x, shareholders do not need to coordinate their actions to generate a probability of $P(x)$ of offer success. With a large finite number of shareholders, any arbitrary probability of success may be achieved when shareholders select independent tendering probabilities close to ½. For an analysis of how stochastic outcomes can result from a continuum of random variables, see Judd (1985).

critical value z^c below which no offer is made, determined by equating the expected profit to zero. There is also a minimum value of α consistent with profitable bidding, $\alpha^* = C/\bar{z}$.[9] The preceding results can be summarized in the following proposition.

PROPOSITION 2. In the tender offer game described above, a mixed-strategy Bayesian equilibrium exists with the following properties: (1) The bid equals z (and hence perfectly reveals the bidder's private information) for all $z \geq z^c$, where $z^c = (C/\alpha)^{\alpha/(\omega+\alpha)}(\bar{z})^{\omega/(\omega+\alpha)}$. For $z < z^c$, no bid is made. (2) The tender offer will be successful with probability $P(x; \alpha, \omega) = (x/\bar{z})^{\omega/\alpha}$, $x \in [z^c, \bar{z}]$. (3) The bidder will offer to buy $\omega = 0.5 - \alpha$ shares, the minimum needed to obtain control.

In this analysis a bidder with a high z is induced to submit a high bid by the dependence on the bid of the likelihood that the tender offer will succeed.[10] Since a bidder with a low z gains less from a successful offer, he is less willing than a high-z bidder to increase his bid. Similarly, because of a higher opportunity cost associated with the failure of an offer, a bidder with high z is not motivated to bid low. Finally, there is no incentive to bid for more shares than the minimum needed to gain control because, by (5), bidding for more shares reduces the probability of success.[11]

B. *Empirical Implications of the Basic Model*

The following points summarize a number of empirical implications of proposition 2.

---

[9] For example, if the cost of bidding is 5 percent of the maximum possible improvement, the minimum initial shareholding needed to make bidding profitable is 5 percent of the target. Poulsen and Jarrell (1986) report a range of initial holdings of bidders varying from 0 percent to nearly 50 percent. The minimum α needed will be smaller and can easily be zero if dilution of target shareholders is possible (as in Sec. IC).

[10] If shareholders do not know the size of C, every sensible bid (i.e., $x \in (0, \bar{z}]$) is viewed by shareholders as possible in the equilibrium. Hence, if the number of shares bid for ω is taken as given, the separating equilibrium is robust to all the standard refinements (e.g., intuitive criterion, divinity, and perfect sequential equilibrium), for the simple reason that it does not require shareholders to draw inferences from out-of-equilibrium moves.

[11] Although we have confirmed that the mixed tendering strategy supports a Bayesian equilibrium, one may wonder whether the belief revisions are credible in the face of deviants who bid for a greater number of shares, $\omega > 0.5 - \alpha$. For example, consider the alternative belief that those who did so had low values of $z < x$. Then their bids would always be accepted. This high acceptance rate would encourage bids for more than $0.5 - \alpha$ shares. However, this deviant belief is not consistent because if a bid of $x < \bar{z}$ were always accepted, then those with $z > x$ would also find it profitable to bid x. On intuitive grounds, it is not plausible that bidding for more shares is a signal of low $z < x$. It is when the bidder intends to bid below his value, $z > x$, that he profits from his share purchases and has something to gain by buying a greater number of shares. So the proposed belief, which rules out using high share purchases as a way of signaling low size of improvements, seems reasonable.

SHARE TENDERING STRATEGIES

IMPLICATION 1. *The probability of an offer's success increases with the bid premium and with the initial holdings of the bidder in the target, and it is decreasing in the number of shares required to obtain control.*

The intuition is that when, for example, a supermajority provision forces the bidder to make an offer for more shares, the marginal savings from underbidding are greater, so a steeper slope of the probability schedule is required to deter the highest type of bidder with $z = \bar{z}$ from underbidding. The effect of α on the probability of success arises because lower α implies relatively lower potential profits from originally owned shares compared with purchased shares, which increases the incentive to underbid. So if the bidder has a smaller initial holding, it takes a larger drop in probability to deter a high-valuation type from underbidding. This is shown in figure 1, where for the highest possible bid $\bar{x} \equiv \bar{z}$, $P(\bar{x}; \alpha, 0.5 - \alpha) = 1$ for both high

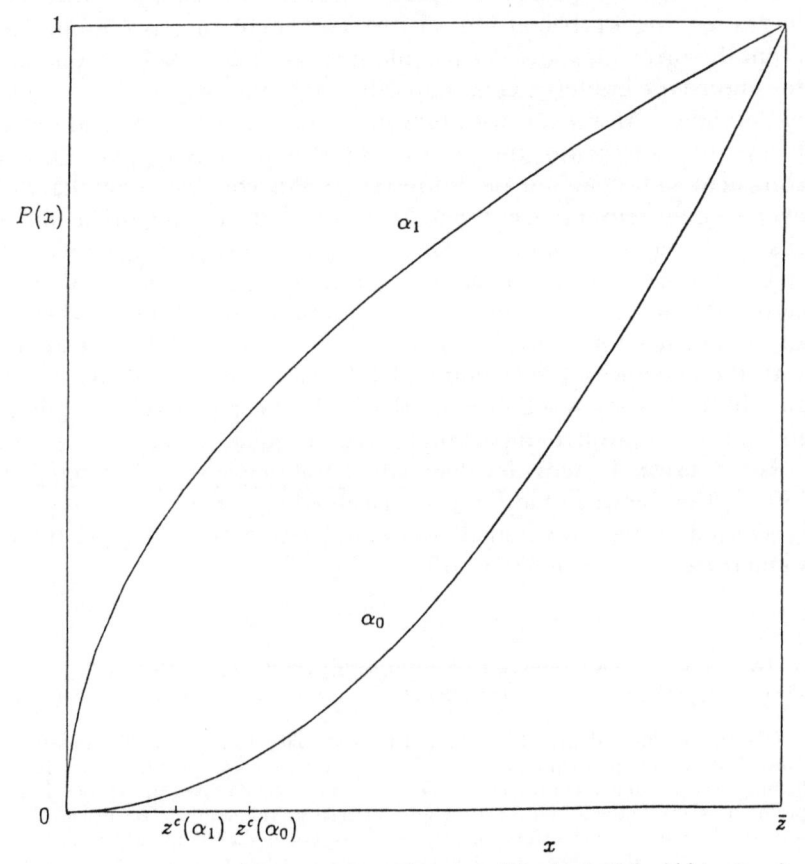

FIG. 1.—Probability of offer success as a function of the level of the bid ($\alpha_1 > \alpha_0$)

and low α, so that for lower α, the schedule is steeper at the right endpoint. The result that the probability of success rises with the bid premium and with the bidder's initial holdings is consistent with the evidence of Walkling (1985).

IMPLICATION 2. The ratio of the stock price reaction at the announcement of the bid to the bid premium is increasing in both the level of the bid and the initial shareholdings of the bidder, and it is decreasing in the number of shares required to obtain control.

This implication is due to the impact of these parameters on the probability of an offer's success.

It is also of interest to examine the effect of varying parameters on z^c. This leads to the following prediction.

IMPLICATION 3. The average bid premium declines with the size of the bidder's initial holdings in the target and increases with the number of shares needed to obtain control.

An increase in α raises the expected profit from making an offer by increasing the probability of success and increasing profits in the event the offer succeeds. As a result, increasing α makes it profitable for lower-type bidders to make an offer, so z^c and, hence, the average bid decline.[12] Moreover, with bids more likely to be made and more likely to be successful, the preoffer market price is higher. This is consistent with Walkling and Edmister (1985), who document that the average bid premium over the market price is decreasing in the initial shareholding of the bidder.[13] Similarly, an increase in the number of shares needed to win control, by reducing the probability of success, causes z^c to increase, raising the expected premium. If the number of shares needed for control varies across firms, this is also consistent with the evidence of Walkling and Edmister, who found that a 0-1 variable indicating whether more than $0.5 - α$ shares were sought in the bid had a positive impact on average premia.

IMPLICATION 4. Activities that reduce the degree of asymmetry of information between bidder and shareholders, such as the payment of solicitation fees to persuade shareholders to tender, are predicted to increase the probability of offer success.

---

[12] Algebraically, the formula for z^c in proposition 2 declines as long as $α > C/e\bar{z}$, where e is Euler's constant. This must hold in the relevant range of $z^c \leq \bar{z}$, which implies $α \geq C/\bar{z}$.

[13] However, the evidence of Franks and Harris (1988) is only partially supportive. Consistent with the prediction, they find that the premium is lower if the initial shareholding exceeds 30 percent than if it is positive but less than 30 percent. However, the premium is also lower in the third category of zero shareholdings. This is consistent with the hypothesis that offers made without an initial shareholding are made by bidders with a credible threat to dilute target shares, leading to lower bid premia (see Sec. IC).

SHARE TENDERING STRATEGIES

A reduction in the degree of asymmetry of information, that is, a mean-preserving inward shift in the distribution of z that lowers $\bar{z}$, the maximum possible value of the improvement, will, by proposition 2, raise the probability of offer success at any given level of the bid. In consequence, the bidder will be motivated to take actions to communicate information about the source of and likely magnitude of the improvement to target shareholders. This could be one function of hiring brokers to solicit shares. Consistent with our analysis, Walkling finds that the payment of solicitation fees does increase the probability of takeover success.

C. *The Solution with Dilution*

Grossman and Hart (1980), in a model with only small shareholders, stress that for tender offers to be profitable some means by which a successful bidder can dilute the value of minority holdings is needed.[14] Shleifer and Vishny pointed out that if there is a large shareholder, he can profitably initiate a bid without dilution. In this subsection we examine a solution in which the potential bidder has large shareholdings and also has the power to engage in some dilution of minority shareholders.

Suppose that the amount by which minority shares may be diluted contains a fixed component δ_0 and a proportional component δ_1, where δ_0 and $\delta_1 < 1$ are known constants. A dilution by $\delta_0 + z\delta_1$ means that after obtaining control, the bidder can reduce the value per share, so that the posttakeover value of minority shares is $z(1 - \delta_1) - \delta_0$.[15] Since target shareholders do not know z, this assumption implies that they also do not know the posttakeover value of their shares.

In a perfectly revealing equilibrium, shareholders will be just indifferent about whether to tender if they receive a bid they believe to be equal to the posttakeover value,

$$x = z(1 - \delta_1) - \delta_0. \tag{6}$$

---

[14] Dilution refers not just to expropriation of assets of the target, but to sharing some of the gain from the improvement. We therefore view dilution as widely prevalent, and despite the connotation of the word, it need not indicate any malfeasance or predatory behavior on the part of the bidder.

[15] More generally, one might allow δ_0 and δ_1 to be random. However, this would change the solution radically because the probability needed to persuade a bidder to bid "truthfully"—$x = z(1 - \delta_1) - \delta_0$—will in general depend separately on the bidder's z and on his δ_1; for a given $z(1 - \delta_1) - \delta_0$, the gains to success are greater for a bidder with higher z since his profit on his own shares is larger. We conjecture that this should lead to a solution in which bidders sometimes overbid and sometimes underbid but in which the bid is equal to $E[z(1 - \delta_1) - \delta_0|x]$ (to keep the shareholders indifferent).

The probability schedule will depend on δ_0 and δ_1, but we suppress all arguments except for x and write the probability of success as $P(x)$. The bidder's objective function is then

$$\max_x [\alpha z + \omega(z - x) + 0.5(\delta_0 + \delta_1 z)]P(x). \quad (7)$$ [16]

Following steps that parallel the previous section, we may take the first-order condition of the bidder's problem, invert the bidding function (6) to obtain the inference schedule $\hat{z}(x) = (x + \delta_0)/(1 - \delta_1)$, and substitute $\hat{z}(x)$ for z in the first-order condition to obtain a differential equation for $P(x)$. Shareholders will always accept the highest possible bid, $\bar{x} \equiv (1 - \delta_1)\bar{z} - \delta_0$, so $P(\bar{x}) = 1$. This boundary condition implies the probability schedule

$$P(x) = \left(\frac{x + \beta_0\beta_1}{\bar{x} + \beta_0\beta_1}\right)^{\beta_1}, \quad (8)$$

where $\beta_0 \equiv \delta_0/\omega(1 - \delta_1) > 0$, and $\beta_1 \equiv \omega(1 - \delta_1)/[\alpha + \delta_1(1 - \alpha)] > 0$. As x is linearly related to z, the probability of success is indirectly a function of the improvement z,

$$P^*(z) = \left(\frac{z + d}{\bar{z} + d}\right)^{\beta_1},$$

where, by its definition, $\beta_1 < \omega/\alpha$, and $d = (\beta_0\beta_1 - \delta_0)/(1 - \delta_1) > 0$. Since the displacements $\beta_0\beta_1, d > 0$ are increasing in δ_0 and δ_1, while β_1 is decreasing, the probability of success is uniformly higher than it is in the basic model and increases with the amount of dilution.

Profits increase with dilution both directly in (7) and as an indirect result of the increased probability of success. As a result, z^c decreases. Dilution therefore raises the probability that a bid will be made, as well as raises the probability of success of an outstanding offer. It remains the case with dilution that higher initial shareholdings α increase the probability of offer success and reduce the critical value z^c.

The intuition for why the probability of success increases with the amount of dilution (δ_0 and δ_1) is roughly that the effect of being able to dilute is similar to the effect of raising α described in Section IA. Higher dilution increases the cost to underbidding because a given

---

[16] The term $0.5(\delta_0 + \delta_1 z)$ may be interpreted in two ways. Finally, if dilution has no deadweight costs, it reflects the profit to the bidder when he can successfully appropriate resources from the minority shareholders. Alternatively, if dilution is costly, after obtaining a majority of shares from a tender offer, with the value of the improvement revealed, the bidder can make a cleanup offer for the remaining shares, setting the bid in the cleanup offer equal to $z(1 - \delta_1) - \delta_0$. Since the bidder would profitably dilute the minority were this offer to fail, the remaining shareholders are all willing to tender.

SHARE TENDERING STRATEGIES 307

drop in probability reduces the expected gain arising from the term $0.5\delta_1 z$ by a greater amount. When z is high, this implies a shallower slope of the probability schedule when δ_1 is high. But when z is low, the differential in probabilities between a low- and high-δ_1 bidder becomes larger, increasing the benefit for a bidder to underbid if δ_1 is high.

The model predicts that dilution threats will be reflected in the "first tier" of the offer, so that minority shareholders do no worse than those who tender. However, in Section II*B*2 we shall see that when managers take defensive measures, "overbidding" is possible, so that the bid can potentially exceed the postoffer share price.

D. *Costs of Bid Failure*

The preceding model assumes that if target shareholders reject the bid, the bidder will lose the target with certainty and hence will suffer costs that are increasing in the size of his improvement. In reality a bidder who is rejected by shareholders may be able to revise his bid and ultimately succeed. If a first failure were entirely costless, then a low-type bidder would be unable to separate from a high-type bidder on the first bid.

There are a number of reasons why rejection of an initial bid may ultimately result in a failed or at least a less profitable acquisition. For example, the rejection may result in the loss of a window of opportunity, such as a reduction of synergies. Alternatively, failure of the initial bid may give management or labor unions more time to mobilize legal or asset structure defensive activities. If the management response blocks the takeover, it leads to a loss to the bidder that is consistent with the assumptions of the basic model. A failed bid may also give management the opportunity to learn about and take steps to *preempt* the policies planned by the bidder, increasing the firm's pretakeover stock price and making the takeover unprofitable. If the bidder profits only on his initial stake (α), this could in principle help him as much as an actual acquisition. However, if incumbent management cannot implement the improvements or synergies efficiently, or if (as will normally be the case) the bidder can appropriate some positive fraction of a takeover improvement through dilution, then the attempt to preempt the improvement imposes an opportunity cost on the bidder that increases with the size of the improvement.

Another important consideration is that rejection may give competing bidders time to enter. Again, this would involve a loss of the gains associated with dilution. If we set $\alpha = 0$ in the model with dilution, the solution is identical to that of an alternative model in which a failed offer always results in the appearance of a competing bidder who can successfully purchase the firm by matching the initial bid. The objective function of the first bidder is then just (7) with $\alpha = 0$, and the probability schedule is precisely (8) with $\beta_1 = \omega(1 - \delta_1)/\delta_1$. This illustrates simply that a separating equilibrium can be enforced by a cost of failure arising from a competing bidder who appropriates the potential dilution.[17]

II. Management Defensive Actions

There has been a great deal of debate about whether managerial defensive measures are in shareholders' interests or whether they are a means of entrenching managers pursuing their own objectives (see, e.g., Easterbrook and Fischel 1981; Gilson 1981; Bebchuk 1982). In the next two subsections we examine three categories of defensive measures: contingent cost defensive strategies, which impose costs on the bidder only in the event that he is successful; pretakeover costs, which are imposed on the bidder prior to the outcome of the offer; and blocking defensive strategies, which increase the likelihood that the bid will be disallowed for legal reasons. Our analysis takes these defensive measures as exogenous and examines their effects on the amount that the bidder offers, the tendering strategies of target shareholders, and the probability of offer success. We show that while some defensive measures reduce shareholder value, others can increase both the amount bid and the probability of the offer's success.

A. Contingent Defensive Costs

A number of defensive strategies impose costs on the bidder only in the event that a tender offer succeeds. These strategies may redistribute wealth from the successful bidder to the nontendering shareholders; they may impose deadweight costs on the bidder without affecting the value of untendered shares or they may reduce the posttakeover value of the remaining shares as well. These distinctions are important since the type of cost imposed affects both the shareholders' tendering decisions and the bidder's strategy.

The following is a general model that incorporates all three possibilities. As a special case, in Section IIA1, we examine "poison pills," in which the loss to the bidder, should the pill be triggered, is fully redistributed to the remaining target shareholders; in Section IIA2, we examine value-reducing measures ("sale of the crown jewels"), in

---

[17] A competing bidder model in which the initial stake of the first bidder is positive is available from the authors on request.

SHARE TENDERING STRATEGIES

which the shareholders who do not tender are also hurt by the defensive measure.[18]

Let $h(z)$ be the cost per share imposed on the shares either originally held or purchased by the bidder should the bid succeed. If the takeover succeeds, the value per minority share is increased by an amount $z + eh(z)$, where $-1 \leq e \leq 1$, $h(z) > 0$, and $h'(z) \geq 0$. Here $h(z)$ will generally be increasing in the improvement. For example, in a discriminatory rights offering to all shareholders but the bidder (a poison pill), the rights will be worth more when the firm is worth more. The term e is a redistributive parameter that reflects the fact that the target shareholders may not fully appropriate the costs imposed on bidders.

In a mixed-strategy separating equilibrium, the bidder must bid the value of the target shares should the takeover succeed, inclusive of the redistribution, so that

$$x = z + eh(z). \qquad (9)$$

Given the costs imposed on the bidder, his problem is

$$\max_x [\alpha z + (z - x)\omega - 0.5h(z)]P(x). \qquad (10)$$

If h is linear, that is, $h(z) = a + bz$, where $b < 1$, the equilibrium is derived from the first-order condition of (10) by substituting for z using (9) and solving the differential equation for $P(x)$. Imposing the boundary condition of certain success at the highest bid, $P(\bar{x}) = P[\bar{z} + eh(\bar{z})] = 1$, we obtain

$$P(x) = \left[\frac{x - (B/A)}{\bar{x} - (B/A)}\right]^{\omega(1 + eb)/[\alpha - b(\omega e + 0.5)]}, \qquad (11)$$

where $A = [\alpha - b(\omega e + 0.5)]/\omega(1 + eb)$, and $B = [0.5a(1 + e)]/\omega(1 + eb)$. Insight into particular forms of managerial defensive measures may be derived by examining special cases of this model. The following subsections examine cases in which $e = -1$ and 1.[19]

---

[18] A sale of valuable assets prior to a bid can still be considered a "contingent" cost, in the sense that the bidder's wealth is reduced by this action more if his offer succeeds than if it fails. Of course, from the target shareholders' point of view, a measure that becomes operative only if the takeover succeeds (such as legislation limiting investment changes by new management) may be very different from a sale of assets that becomes operative regardless of whether a takeover occurs.

[19] The intermediate case of $e = 0$ corresponds to defensive measures that, while imposing costs on the bidder in the event of success, do not affect the wealth of the minority target shareholders. This may approximate the effects of charter amendments providing for staggered terms of directors. When a bid succeeds, these amendments may force the bidder to suffer further litigation costs, or the costs of a proxy fight, before implementing his program. In our model, such measures imply a uniform reduction in the probability of offer success.

1. Poison Pills: Redistributive Defensive Measures

A poison pill is a defensive measure that redistributes wealth from the bidder to the shareholders who do not participate in the tender offer if the bidder accumulates a sufficient number of shares. Such a redistribution corresponds to $e = 1$ in (11), implying that the probability schedule is identical in form to the schedule in the model with dilution, with $\delta_0 = -a$ and $\delta_1 = -b$. In other words, poison pills can be viewed as mechanisms that generate negative dilution. In consequence, the poison pill unambiguously reduces the probability of success and increases the bid for a given level of the improvement. Ryngaert (1988) and Malatesta and Walkling (1988) found a negative average stock price reaction to the announcement of poison pills. This is consistent with our model to the extent that the reduction in the probability of takeover outweighs the benefit to shareholders of being able to extract a higher premium.

2. Value-Reduction Strategies

We now examine defensive measures that impose costs on the target shareholders as well as the bidder, should the takeover succeed. One such measure is to lobby for legislation that outlaws the investment changes the bidder wishes to make. Other examples are the "scorched earth" or "sale of crown jewels" defensive measures, in which the firm sells off those divisions or assets whose values can be improved.

A value-reducing strategy is reflected in the current model by a negative e, so that reductions in bidder wealth are associated with reductions in the improvement in target shareholder wealth; we examine the pure case in which $e = -1$. It should be stressed that we are considering a defensive measure that reduces the size of the improvement from a takeover. The sale, at below the market price, of an asset that cannot be improved by the acquirer or any other measure that reduced firm value without altering the amount by which it could be improved would have no effect on the probability schedule or on the premium (x) offered above the firm's value under current management. When $e = -1$, the reduction in value per share is the same for the bidder and for the nontendering shareholders. This case is equivalent to a reduction in z at all its values. Hence, by (11),

$$P(x) = \left(\frac{x}{\bar{x}}\right)^{\omega/\alpha}, \tag{12}$$

as in the basic model. Note that since $\bar{x} = \bar{z} - h(\bar{z}) < \bar{z}$, the probability of acceptance *as a function of the amount bid* rises. This is not surprising since a given bid becomes more attractive when compared with a

SHARE TENDERING STRATEGIES

reduced value of the improvement. However, the amount bid will also be reduced, so the probability of success of a bidder with a given improvement of z may or may not be reduced. The level of the bid is

$$x = z - h(z) = -a + (1 - b)z, \quad (13)$$

which when substituted into (12) gives the probability schedule in terms of z of

$$P^*(z) = \left\{ \frac{z - [a/(1 - b)]}{\bar{z} - [a/(1 - b)]} \right\}^{\omega/\alpha}. \quad (14)$$

A value-reducing defensive strategy can either increase or decrease the severity of the information asymmetry between the bidder and the other target shareholders, depending on the values of a and b. A *fixed* reduction in the size of the improvement, that is, $a > 0$ and $b = 0$, makes the improvement more uncertain relative to its mean and hence reduces the probability of success as well as the profits in the event of success. Alternatively, with $a = 0$ the probability of offer success is unchanged. The prior uncertainty about the improvement relative to its mean is unaffected by such a measure; however, both the level of the bid and the profits of the bidder are reduced. Therefore, such a strategy can deter a potential bidder from attempting the takeover.[20]

Perhaps most interesting, if $a < 0$ and $b > 0$, the asymmetry of information about the increase in the value of target shares (net of defensive costs) that the takeover will bring about is diminished.[21] By (14), it follows that this value-reduction measure *increases* the probability of offer success. Intuitively, it is asymmetry of information that leads to bid failure, and to the extent that this can be reduced, the frequency of acceptance is raised.[22]

The results of Section IIA can be summarized by the following proposition.

PROPOSITION 3. For poison pills ($e = 1$), the probability of success as

---

[20] Dann and DeAngelo (1988) examine a number of cases in which targets sell assets for defensive purposes, and they provide evidence that stock prices decline on average.

[21] To illustrate, let $z = \bar{z}_1 + z_2$, where $\bar{z}_1$ is an improvement of known value and z_2 is an improvement whose value is unknown to target shareholders. These may be viewed as two projects that the bidder could undertake. Consider a measure that imposes costs $b'z_2$ that are proportional to z_2, so that $h(z) = b'z_2 = b'(z - \bar{z}_1) = b'z - b'\bar{z}_1$. Hence, this measure is subsumed by our general framework with $b = b'$ and $a = -b'\bar{z}_1 < 0$. It is worth noting that in this example, $z \geq \bar{z}_1 > 0$; i.e., the improvement is bounded from zero. Otherwise, the specification would imply that the defensive measure could be value increasing for small z, which does not seem plausible.

[22] For similar reasons, a value-*increasing* strategy such as preemption by the target management of the planned improvement could decrease the probability of success. This corresponds precisely to the fixed reduction in the improvement, $a > 0$ and $b = 0$, discussed in the paragraph above.

a function of either the level of the bid or the size of the improvement (z) is lowered. For value-reducing defensive measures ($e = -1$), the probability of success as a function of the bid is higher than in the basic model without defensive measures; however, the probability of success as a function of the bidder's improvement can be greater, lower, or the same as when there are no defensive measures. A value-reducing defense can either raise, lower, or leave unchanged the probability that an offer will be made.

B. Litigation

Litigation by incumbent management imposes costs on the bidder and can in some cases directly block a takeover. Any legal costs undergone by the bidder prior to the outcome of the offer are uncontingent in that they are expended even if the bid should later fail. We examine separately the effect on the bidder's strategy of the uncontingent legal costs that are imposed (Sec. IIB1) and of the possibility of blocking the bid (Sec. IIB2).

1. Defensive Costs Imposed prior to the Offer Outcome

The analysis that follows assumes that the magnitude of defensively imposed costs depends on the amount bid.[23] In this case, the bidder's objective is

$$\max_{x} \ [\alpha z + (z - x)\omega]P(x) - h(x), \qquad (15)$$

where $h(x)$ is the cost imposed on the bidder by the managerial defensive action prior to the offer outcome, $h'(x) \leq 0$. Taking the first-order condition of (15) and substituting the condition for a fully revealing equilibrium that $z = x$ gives a linear first-order differential equation for the probability schedule as a function of x. The following proposition, which assumes that the model parameters are such that a mixed-strategy equilibrium exists (i.e., $x = z$), can be proved by solving this equation subject to the initial condition $P(\bar{z}) = 1$.

PROPOSITION 4. In the tender offer game with costs imposed by management defensive litigation, when a separating equilibrium exists, (1) the probability of an offer's success in the mixed-strategy

---

[23] The assumption that the legal cost of the offer is decreasing in the size of the bid arises from the possibility that courts may be more sympathetic to defensive suits if a low price has been offered to shareholders; e.g., the statutes of a number of states give target shareholders appraisal rights. Alternatively, management may not fight high bids as hard as low bids.

SHARE TENDERING STRATEGIES

signaling equilibrium is

$$P(x) = P_0(x)\left[1 + \int_z^x \frac{h'(t)}{\alpha t}\left(\frac{t}{\bar{z}}\right)^{-(\omega/\alpha)} dt\right],$$

if this quantity is uniformly less than or equal to one, where $P_0(x)$ is the probability schedule that applies when $h' \equiv 0$, as in the model without target-imposed costs; (2) if $h' < 0$, defensive measures increase the probability of an offer's success.

To see that part 2 is true, note that the integrand is a negative quantity ($h' < 0$) and the limits indicate a backward interval ($\bar{z} \geq x$), so $P(x)$ is higher under the new solution than under the old one. This is intuitive: if we start from the endpoint $x = \bar{z}$ and reduce x, the probability may fall less and still deter a lower bid since a lower bid would lead to higher litigation costs. So when a litigation strategy is pursued, the probability of takeover success, given that a bid is made, can actually *increase!*

Litigation by the target can also lead to offers that exceed the magnitude of the improvement, $x > z$. For example, if the manager is able to impose high costs on all bids below $\bar{z}$, some bidders with improvements below $\bar{z}$ increase their bids to $x = \bar{z}$. In consequence, it is possible that imposing costs on bidders may be in the target shareholders' interest for two reasons: first, because this can raise the probability of an offer's success and, second, because it can increase the pressure to make a higher bid. Jarrell (1985) provides evidence that litigation increases the takeover price and, hence, can sometimes be in the interest of target shareholders.

2. Blocking Defensive Measures

In addition to imposing a cost on bidders, management opposition may be able to force the bidder to withdraw his offer for legal reasons. Let $T(x)$ equal the probability that $0.5 - \alpha$ shares are tendered, and let $U(x)$ equal the probability that the offer is not blocked by the courts. It is assumed that the two sources of failure occur independently. Let $P(x)$ be defined as the overall probability that a bid succeeds,

$$P(x) = T(x)U(x). \tag{16}$$

The objective of the potential acquirer, if he chooses to bid, is still (1), leading as before to the first-order condition (2). Any solution to this differential equation for which $x = z$, consistent with the randomization of shareholders, satisfies

$$T(x)U(x) = kx^{\omega/\alpha}. \tag{17}$$

When we solve for $P(x)$, the difference between this problem and that of Section IA is that, with $T(x) \leq 1$, the additional constraint $P(x) \leq U(x)$ is imposed.

Sometimes the ability to block the bid is not based on the level of the bid (e.g., "antitrust" defensive lawsuits), in which case the blocking probability $U(x)$ is a constant. Then since $P_0(\bar{z}) = 1$, the schedule $P(x)$ is necessarily lower at the right endpoint, as illustrated in figure 2. The resulting schedule may be determined by applying the initial condition $P(\bar{z}) = U$ to (17). This yields the solution

$$P(x) = \left(\frac{x}{\bar{z}}\right)^{\omega/\alpha} U. \tag{18}$$

A comparison of (18) with (5) illustrates that in this case the blocking defensive measure uniformly reduces the probability of the offer's success.[24]

In other cases, the probability of the success of a legal action is decreasing in the amount of the offer, that is, $U'(x) \geq 0$.[25] If in addition $U(x)$ is never below $P_0(x)$, then the boundary condition for $P(x)$ in the basic model may be applied to (17) without modification. Hence, the resulting probability schedule is the same as that in the basic model, implying that the direct loss in probability due to defensive action is precisely offset by an increased willingness to tender! Moreover, as the payoffs to the bidder are exactly the same as before, z^c also does not change. So the defensive measure will be entirely ineffective in promoting either shareholders' goals or those of an entrenched management. This extreme case illustrates the more general point that shareholders may compensate for blocking measures by increasing their willingness to tender their shares.

The intuition can be seen by imagining that the tendering probabilities of shareholders were unchanged. Then opposition would increase the incentive of a bidder with a given z to bid high to avoid being blocked. A given bid would thus become more attractive to shareholders. The increased willingness of shareholders to tender at a given bid can offset the direct probability-reducing effect of management defensive measures.[26]

---

[24] More generally, if $U(x) < (x/\bar{z})^{\omega/\alpha}$ for any $x \in (0, \bar{z}]$, then the original schedule $P_0(x)$ becomes infeasible. The reduction in probability of success imposed by the defensive action is binding because for some x, even were shareholders to tender with certainty, the probability of legal success would be less than $P_0(x)$. However, the reduction in probability that results could be slight.

[25] This assumption may be justified by arguments similar to those in n. 23.

[26] Further insight into the source of the greater willingness to tender arises from the model of App. B. There, defensive measures can give the bidder an incentive to bid higher, and the higher bidding not only makes shareholders less skeptical in their assessments of z but also raises the probability that the excess of x over the assessed z is

SHARE TENDERING STRATEGIES

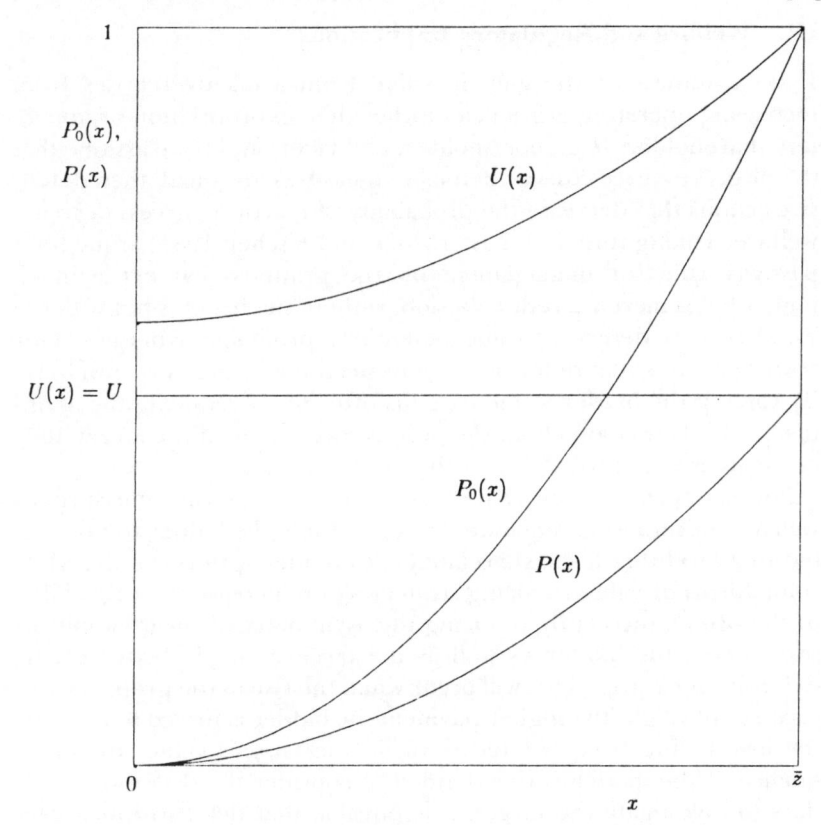

FIG. 2.—Effect of binding defensive measures on the probability of offer success

A sufficiently steep $U(x)$ schedule may lead to overbidding, thereby rendering infeasible a mixed-strategy equilibrium in which bidders offer the true value of the improvement. Under the conditions of proposition 1, bidders still separate because the slope of the $U(x)$ schedule provides an incentive for high-z bidders to make higher offers than low-z bidders. In this case the threat of defensive actions increases the bids and can thus increase the probability of takeover success. Overbidding in some acquisitions is consistent with the evidence of Bradley (1980) that the posttakeover value of those shares not tendered is on average lower than the tender price.[27]

---

large enough to outweigh the costs of tendering. Here, with shareholders just indifferent, the willingness to tender is infinitely elastic with respect to the bid, so the compensation in tendering probabilities is brought about without any rise in the bid at all.

[27] As a simple illustration, suppose that z can take on just two values, $\bar{z}$ and $\underline{z}$. Suppose that $U(\bar{z}) = 1$ but $U(x) = 0$ for all $x < \bar{z}$. Then if α and $\underline{z}$ are sufficiently high, it will pay for the lower-value bidder to overbid, $x = \bar{z}$, to be accepted with certainty, since the gain on his own shares will exceed the loss on the shares he purchases.

III. Welfare and Regulatory Implications

If we assume that the gain in value from a takeover arises from increasing operating efficiencies rather than expropriation of nonequity shareholders (e.g., bondholders and labor) and if we assume that the direct resource costs of defensive measures are small, then defensive actions that decrease the probability of takeover success decrease welfare. Taking this view, Easterbrook and Fischel (1981) argue for a passivity rule for management on the grounds that extracting a higher bid is merely a redistribution, without net benefits but with the social cost of deterring some potentially profitable synergies. Our model suggests that defensive actions need not reduce social welfare. By forcing the bidder to increase his offer or by reducing the asymmetry of information about the posttakeover value of the target, they can increase the probability of the offer's success.

For example, we show that certain blocking defensive measures as well as cost-imposing litigation strategies force the bidder to raise his bid to a level that leads shareholders to tender with certainty, while some forms of value-reducing strategies also increase the probability of the offer's success by reducing the asymmetry of information. In some cases, the bidder as well as the target is made better off by defensive measures. This will occur when the rise in the probability of success outweighs the higher payment the bidder is forced to make or the loss arising from the reduction in the target's value. In consequence, if the model were extended to consider the decision of bidders to investigate the target, it is possible that defensive measures could lead to a higher overall probability of takeover and higher social welfare.

However, some defensive measures such as poison pills act to reduce dilution and thereby increase the offer price while lowering the probability of offer success. As in Grossman and Hart (1980), our model implies that managers that act in shareholders' interest will take defensive actions to reduce dilution in order to raise the bid above the socially optimal level. Shareholders will support this activity because they bear only part of the social cost associated with the reduced probability of an offer's success and capture a transfer gain from raising the offer price.

This suggests that there may be some role for regulations that limit the use of defensive measures. However, it should be stressed that this argument takes the investment decisions of the target as given. If there exist preoffer investments that a target can make that increase synergies, then to encourage investment it may be socially preferable to allow targets to take actions to capture more of the synergistic benefits.

SHARE TENDERING STRATEGIES

Our analysis further suggests that the Williams Act, by facilitating defensive actions, may have promoted overbidding in hostile takeover contests. The risk in bid premia subsequent to the Williams Act described by Jarrell and Bradley (1980) is consistent with this hypothesis. An alternative truncation hypothesis is that a rise in the cost of bidding will raise the average bid premium by deterring profitable takeovers with relatively lower gains.[28] Overbidding can explain not only the higher premia paid to targets but also the lower abnormal returns to bidders, found by Jarrell and Bradley, after the Williams Act and later state acts.[29] Malatesta and Thompson (1988) provide evidence that a wealth transfer from bidders to targets (i.e., higher bids) was more important than truncation of the sample in causing the rise in target mean premia and lower abnormal returns to bidders.

The discussion above suggests that regulation that facilitates defensive action can potentially increase welfare, but need not do so. Our analysis indicates that a necessary but not sufficient condition for a defensive strategy to increase welfare is that it benefits target shareholders. A recent paper by Jarrell and Poulsen (1987) indicates that, on average, antitakeover amendments lead to negative target stock price reactions, suggesting that they may, in general, be welfare decreasing. However, the price reaction is not always negative and is on average more positive in those cases in which a large fraction of the firm is held by institutional shareholders, who are presumably better able to block amendments that oppose their interests. This suggests that antitakeover amendments sometimes are in the interest of target shareholders and thus may sometimes improve social welfare.

Our analysis of the desirability of defensive measures may be sensitive to the assumptions about the effects of offer failure. The possible welfare gains arise from forcing up the bid or reducing informational asymmetry, which leads the bidder to succeed with higher probability. In practice, however, a failed first bid can be followed by a revised bid or a competing bid. If the target does not take defensive actions, it is likely to be taken over eventually, either by the initial bidder or, if he fails, by another bidder. This suggests that although defensive actions can increase the probability that an initial bid will succeed, it is unlikely that they will increase the probability that the firm will ultimately be taken over.

If an initial failure leads to less efficient implementation of the

---

[28] Our model is also consistent with the truncation effect. Jarrell and Bradley's discussion combines features of both explanations.

[29] Lower bidder returns could also be due to the increased costs imposed by defensive measures.

improvement, because management either preempts the planned changes inefficiently or finds a white knight who does so, then implications similar to our analysis apply. On the other hand, if an initial failure does not prevent the target from ultimately being acquired by either the first bidder or a competing bidder with either an equal or a greater improvement, then our argument must be modified. In this case, defensive measures that reduce the probability of initial success can be socially beneficial if they give higher-improvement bidders more time to make offers.

IV. Conclusion

This paper presented a model of tender offers in which the bid perfectly reveals the bidder's private information about the size of the gain that can be generated by a takeover. The magnitude of the tender offer premium affects the probability that a bid succeeds, so that bidders with high-valued improvements who have more to gain from the offer's success make higher bids than those bidders with lower gains. The model provides a number of testable implications relating to the determinants of an offer's success. For example, we have shown that both high initial holdings by the bidder and the possibility of dilution of minority shareholders increase the probability that an offer will succeed.

Our analysis has also demonstrated that the tendency of target shareholders to participate in a tender offer is affected by the management's defensive strategies. Some defensive actions can actually raise the probability of the offer's success. These strategies may benefit shareholders. In addition, even defensive measures that could potentially cause the bid to be disallowed can benefit shareholders ex ante, by inducing bidders to make higher offers. Furthermore, there is a tendency for shareholders to raise their probabilities of tendering in response to managerial defensive actions in an offsetting manner, so that in some cases the defensive measure will not lead to any net reduction in the overall probability of an offer's success. Of course, defensive measures can also be designed to reduce the probability of an offer's success in ways that can reduce shareholder value.

The model suggests that a key determinant of the outcome of tender offers is whether target shareholders know as much as the bidder about the posttakeover value of the target's shares. If information is symmetric, then a bidder can always purchase as many shares as he seeks by bidding one cent above the posttakeover value in a tender offer. With asymmetric information, even the strategy of overbidding will not necessarily assure the success of the offer because target shareholders will interpret the higher bid as an indication that the posttakeover value of the shares is higher. This effect may be more apparent in the model presented in Appendix B in which the equilibrium bid is strictly lower with asymmetric than with symmetric information.

As shareholders become better informed about the size of the posttakeover value, the likelihood of a bid that is prone to failure (i.e., a bid far below the bidder's maximum improvement $\bar{z}$) becomes small. For bids in which a merger is expected or for management buy-outs, the posttakeover value of minority shares is often determined by a court decision about the fairness of the price. In this case, the bidder's information may be little better than that of target shareholders. Therefore, in the absence of management defensive actions and competing bids, we expect takeover bids for merger usually to succeed. On the other hand, in takeovers initiated to change the policy of the target without merger (e.g., Carl Icahn's takeover of Trans World Airlines), the bidder may have superior information about the prospects for increasing firm value. In such cases, failure of the bid becomes more likely. Our model suggests that future empirical studies should examine samples of these different kinds of takeovers separately.

Like most theoretical work on this topic, our model has assumed that the bidder is rational and profit maximizing. However, others (e.g., Roll 1986) have suggested that bidders may be afflicted with "hubris," systematically overestimating their ability to improve firm value. In our model, a bidder would have his bids accepted with certainty if target shareholders believed that he was overly confident and had a tendency to overbid. This suggests that "rational" bidders may have an incentive to develop and maintain reputations for hubris. Hence, in a repeated game, it may pay a rational bidder to overbid, to persuade future targets that he too is prone to hubris.[30] This suggests that future empirical work should also try to analyze separately those bidders that make a number of bids.

Appendix A

Proof of Proposition 1

Parametrically differentiating (2) with respect to z and solving for dx/dz yields an expression that is strictly positive, by (3).

---

[30] See Kreps et al. (1982) for a reputation model in which rational players mimic irrational ones. Our argument for overbidding contrasts with the model of Leach (1988), in which merger bidders make low offers to gain the reputation for being tough bargainers.

Proof of Proposition 2

Let us propose as off-equilibrium behavior by shareholders that if a bid of $\omega > 0.5 - \alpha$ is made, then shareholders will still mix their actions to satisfy (5). Hence, regardless of ω the bid $x = z$ will satisfy the first-order condition (2). Direct calculation verifies that with the proposed probability schedule, the second-order condition for an interior global optimum (as well as the first-order condition [2]) is satisfied by setting the bid $x = z$. At this bid, shareholders are indifferent between accepting and rejecting, which is consistent with randomization.

Only part 3 remains to be verified. Note that for a given x, $P(x; \omega)$ is decreasing in ω. Regardless of what value for ω is selected by the bidder, his optimal bid is $x = z$. Therefore, his profit on the shares he purchases is zero, and his entire gain is due to his gain on the original α shares. He maximizes expected wealth by choosing ω to maximize the probability of the offer's success. This occurs with the minimum value of ω consistent with obtaining control, $\omega = 0.5 - \alpha$.

Appendix B

Unobserved Tendering Costs

In this Appendix we provide a model in which shareholders possess a common cost of tendering that is unknown to the bidder. This is meant to describe, more explicitly, situations in which the bidder does not know perfectly the costs and benefits to the target shareholders of tendering. In this case, the success of the offer is determined by whether

$$x > \hat{z}(x) + c, \tag{B1}$$

where c is the cost of tendering, and $\hat{z}(x)$ is the shareholders' evaluation of z given a bid of x. The bidder solves the same optimization problem as in the text, (1), and therefore has the same first-order condition with respect to his bid, (2). Each value of z generates a corresponding optimal bid $x(z)$. Furthermore, in a perfectly revealing equilibrium, each value of z corresponds to a different value of x, so that $z = \hat{z}(x)$. The probability of success is then the likelihood that c falls in the range at which (B1) holds,

$$P(x) = \int_0^{z - \hat{z}(x)} f(c) dc. \tag{B2}$$

Differentiating (B2) with respect to x gives

$$P'(x) = f(x - \hat{z}(x))[1 - \hat{z}'(x)]. \tag{B3}$$

Substituting for $P'(x)$ in (2) yields

$$\omega \int_0^{z - \hat{z}(x)} f(c) dc = f(x - \hat{z}(x))[1 - \hat{z}'(x)](0.5z - x\omega). \tag{B4}$$

For an exogenously given distribution of c, this integral equation can be solved to give the equilibrium inverse bidding schedule $\hat{z}(x)$, which from (B2) also gives the probability of success schedule.

We shall develop our analysis under the assumption of a uniform distribu-

SHARE TENDERING STRATEGIES 321

tion for the tendering cost. We have shown that similar results can be obtained assuming a power density as well.[31] Substituting the uniform density

$$f(c) = \frac{1}{\bar{c}}, \quad c \in [0, \bar{c}], \tag{B5}$$

into (B4) and letting $\hat{z}(x) = z(x)$, the inverse of the bidding schedule $x(z)$, gives

$$\omega(x - z) = [1 - z'(x)](0.5z - x\omega). \tag{B6}$$

Symmetric Information Case

A special case of interest is the one in which information about z is symmetric (i.e., z is known to all target shareholders). We refer to this as the "symmetric information" case, even though c is still assumed unknown to the bidder. In this case, the inference schedule is $\hat{z}(x) \equiv z$ for all x (equilibrium or not), so that $\hat{z}'(x) \equiv 0$. Substituting into (B6) gives the symmetric information bidding function,

$$x^s(z) = \left(\frac{0.5 + \omega}{2\omega}\right)z. \tag{B7}$$

Note that since $\omega < 0.5$, this solution satisfies the fundamental property that $x^s > z$, so that (when the tendering cost is nonnegative) there is a positive probability of offer success.

Asymmetric Information Case

When z is unknown to the target shareholders, the bidding schedule solves the differential equation (B6). Let x^a denote the asymmetric information bid. A boundary condition that the equilibrium schedule must satisfy is that the highest-type bidder $\bar{z}$ must make a maximum bid $\bar{x}^a$ equal to $x^s(\bar{z})$ of the symmetric information case.

To see why, suppose that the maximum bid $\bar{x}^a > \bar{x}^s$. Then it would pay for the $\bar{z}$ type to reduce his bid to $\bar{x}^s$ because of two benefits. First, if he were viewed as type $\bar{z}$, then by revealed preference, since he preferred to bid $\bar{x}^s$ to $\bar{x}^a$ under symmetric information, he would still rather do so. Second, he may be viewed as a lower type, $z < \bar{z}$. If so, his gains from bidding $\bar{x}^s$ are even greater since his probability of success is greater.

Suppose, on the other hand, that $\bar{x}^a < \bar{x}^s$. Then it would pay for type $\bar{z}$ to raise his bid to $\bar{x}^s$, for essentially the same reasons as above. By revealed preference, if his type is still viewed as $\bar{z}$ since he chose $\bar{x}^s$ under symmetric information, he will still prefer it here. Second, if changing his bid were to lead to a lower inference of his type, his probability of success would rise and his gains would be even greater.

Having established this, we now show that the level of the bid under asymmetric information for any type below $\bar{z}$ is smaller than the bid under symmetric information. We may rewrite (B6) as

$$x^a(z) = \left(\frac{0.5 + \omega}{2\omega}\right)z - z'_a\left(\frac{0.5z - \omega x^a}{2\omega}\right), \tag{B8}$$

---

[31] A power density function for costs may be written as $f(c) = (1 - \beta)\bar{c}^{\beta-1}c^{-\beta}, \beta < 1.$

where z'_a is the derivative of the inference schedule with respect to x under asymmetric information. Subtracting (B7) from (B8), we see that

$$x^a - x^s = -z'_a\left(\frac{0.5z - \omega x^a}{2\omega}\right). \quad (B9)$$

In a separating equilibrium, by proposition 1, $z'_a > 0$. The term in parentheses is proportional to the bidder's profit from winning, which must be positive. So $x^a < x^s$. It follows immediately from (B2) that in equilibrium a given type has a lower probability of success under asymmetric than under symmetric information, $P^*_a(z) < P^*_s(z)$.

Suppressing a superscripts, we can solve the differential equation (B6) by the substitution $v \equiv z/x$, which gives a separable differential equation in v and x. Imposing the appropriate boundary conditions gives the solution in implicit form of

$$(x - z)^{(1 - 2\omega)/(4\omega - 1)}(4\omega x - z)^{-2\omega/(4\omega - 1)} = (0.5 - \omega)^{(1 - 2\omega)/(4\omega - 1)}(2\omega)^{-1/(4\omega - 1)}\bar{z}^{-1} \quad (B10)$$

if $\omega \neq \frac{1}{4}$ and

$$2e^{-3/2}(x - z) = \bar{z}e^{x/2(x - z)} \quad (B11)$$

if $\omega = \frac{1}{4}$.

We have extended this model to include a managerial defensive action that imposes costs on the bidder prior to the outcome. In this case, the bidder's objective is

$$\max_x \, (0.5z - x\omega)P(x) - h(x),$$

$h'(x) < 0$. Under the specific functional form $h(x) = k(x - \bar{x})^2$, $k > 0$, we have verified a "compensation effect" similar to that described in the text. This is that the cost-imposing measure encourages higher bidding and hence raises the probability of offer success.

References

Bagnoli, Mark, and Lipman, Barton L. "Successful Takeovers without Exclusion." *Rev. Financial Studies* 1 (Spring 1988): 89–110.
Banks, Jeffrey S., and Sobel, Joel. "Equilibrium Selection in Signaling Games." *Econometrica* 55 (May 1987): 647–64.
Bebchuk, Lucian A. "The Case for Facilitating Competing Tender Offers." *Harvard Law Rev.* 95 (March 1982): 1028–56.
Berkovitch, Elazar, and Khanna, Naveen. "A Theory of Acquisition Markets—Mergers vs. Tender Offers; Golden Parachutes and Greenmail." Manuscript. Ann Arbor: Univ. Michigan, 1988.
Bradley, Michael. "Interfirm Tender Offers and the Markets for Corporate Control." *J. Bus.* 53 (October 1980): 345–76.
Bradley, Michael; Desai, Anand; and Kim, E. Han. "The Rationale behind Interfirm Tender Offers: Information or Synergy?" *J. Financial Econ.* 11 (April 1983): 183–206.
Cho, In-Koo, and Kreps, David M. "Signaling Games and Stable Equilibria." *Q.J.E.* 102 (May 1987): 179–221.

Dann, Larry Y., and DeAngelo, Harry. "Corporate Financial Policy and Corporate Control: A Study of Defensive Adjustments in Asset and Ownership Structure." *J. Financial Econ.* 20 (January/March 1988): 87–127.

Easterbrook, Frank H., and Fischel, Daniel R. "The Proper Role of a Target's Management in Responding to a Tender Offer." *Harvard Law Rev.* 94 (April 1981): 1161–1204.

Fishman, Michael J. "A Theory of Pre-emptive Takeover Bidding." *Rand J. Econ.* 19 (Spring 1988): 88–101.

Franks, Julian, and Harris, Robert. "Shareholder Wealth Effects of Corporate Takeovers: The U.K. Experience, 1955–85." Manuscript. London: London Bus. School, 1988.

Giammarino, Ronald M., and Heinkel, Robert L. "A Model of Dynamic Takeover Behavior." *J. Finance* 41 (June 1986): 465–80.

Giammarino, Ronald M., and Lewis, Tracy. "A Theory of Negotiated Equity Financing." *Rev. Financial Studies* 1 (Fall 1988): 265–88.

Gilson, Ronald J. "A Structural Approach to Corporations: The Case against Defensive Tactics in Tender Offers." *Stanford Law Rev.* 33 (May 1981): 819–91.

Grossman, Sanford J., and Hart, Oliver D. "Takeover Bids, the Free-Rider Problem, and the Theory of the Corporation." *Bell J. Econ.* 11 (Spring 1980): 42–64.

Grossman, Sanford J., and Perry, Motty. "Perfect Sequential Equilibrium." *J. Econ. Theory* 39 (June 1986): 97–119.

Harsanyi, John C. "Games with Randomly Disturbed Payoffs: A New Rationale for Mixed-Strategy Equilibrium Points." *Internat. J. Game Theory* 2, no. 1 (1973): 1–23.

Hirshleifer, David, and Png, I. P. L. "The Information Conveyed by a Tender Offer and the Takeover Price of a Target Firm." *Rev. Financial Studies* 2, no. 4 (1990).

Jarrell, Gregg A. "The Wealth Effects of Litigation by Targets: Do Interests Diverge in a Merge?" *J. Law and Econ.* 28 (April 1985): 151–77.

Jarrell, Gregg A., and Bradley, Michael. "The Economic Effects of Federal and State Regulations of Cash Tender Offers." *J. Law and Econ.* 23 (October 1980): 371–407.

Jarrell, Gregg A., and Poulsen, Annette. "Shark Repellents and Stock Prices: The Effects of Antitakeover Amendments since 1980." *J. Financial Econ.* 19 (September 1987): 127–68.

Judd, Kenneth L. "The Law of Large Numbers with a Continuum of IID Random Variables." *J. Econ. Theory* 35 (February 1985): 19–25.

Leach, J. Chris. "Repetition, Reputation, and Raiding." Manuscript. Ithaca, N.Y.: Cornell Univ., 1988.

Kreps, David M.; Milgrom, Paul; Roberts, John; and Wilson, Robert. "Rational Cooperation in the Finitely Repeated Prisoners' Dilemma." *J. Econ. Theory* 27 (August 1982): 245–52.

Malatesta, Paul H., and Thompson, Rex. "Government Regulation of the Corporate Acquisitions Market: The Williams Act." Manuscript. Seattle: Univ. Washington, 1988.

Malatesta, Paul H., and Walkling, Ralph A. "Poison Pill Securities: Stockholder Wealth, Profitability, and Ownership Structure." *J. Financial Econ.* 20 (January/March 1988): 347–76.

Morck, Randall; Shleifer, Andrei; and Vishny, Robert W. "Characteristics of

Targets of Hostile and Friendly Takeovers." In *Corporate Takeovers: Causes and Consequences*, edited by Alan J. Auerbach. Chicago: Univ. Chicago Press (for NBER), 1988.

Poulsen, Annette, and Jarrell, Gregg A. "Stock Trading before the Announcement of Tender Offers: Insider Trading or Market Anticipation." Washington: Securities and Exchange Comm., 1986.

Roll, Richard. "The Hubris Hypothesis of Corporate Takeovers." *J. Bus.* 59, no. 2, pt. 1 (April 1986): 197–216.

Ruback, Richard S. "Do Target Shareholders Lose in Unsuccessful Control Contests?" In *Corporate Takeovers: Causes and Consequences*, edited by Alan J. Auerbach. Chicago: Univ. Chicago Press (for NBER), 1988.

Ryngaert, Michael. "The Effect of Poison Pill Securities on Shareholder Wealth." *J. Financial Econ.* 20 (January/March 1988): 377–417.

Samuelson, William, and Rosenthal, Leonard. "Price Movements as Indicators of Tender Offer Success." *J. Finance* 41 (June 1986): 481–99.

Shleifer, Andrei, and Vishny, Robert W. "Large Shareholders and Corporate Control." *J.P.E.* 94, no. 3, pt. 1 (June 1986): 461–88.

Walkling, Ralph A. "Predicting Tender Offer Success: A Logistic Analysis." *J. Financial and Quantitative Analysis* 20 (December 1985): 461–78.

Walkling, Ralph A., and Edmister, Robert O. "Determinants of Tender Offer Premiums." *Financial Analysts J.* 41 (January–February 1985): 27–37.

Part VII
Corporate Bankruptcy

[21]

The Resolution of Financial Distress

Ronald M. Giammarino
University of British Columbia

Most models of financial structure embody an assumption about financial distress that causes debt to be costly to the issuing firm. This approach has been criticized on the grounds that the assumed costs could be avoided by a costless financial reorganization. In this article we show that despite the possibility of costless reorganization, it may be rational for firms to incur significant costs in the resolution of financial distress. The main assumptions that give rise to our results are the existence of asymmetric information and of judicial discretion that allows courts to impose a reorganization on the claimants of a firm.

Most models of financial structure embody an assumption about financial distress that causes debt to be costly to the issuing firm.[1] In some the assumption is that it is costly to have a firm legally declared bankrupt; in others the costs result from suboptimal investment and operating decisions that may be induced by the agency problems associated with financial distress. Both types of model have been criticized on the grounds that the costs that are central to the analysis could be avoided in practice by a relatively costless financial reorgani-

---

This article is based on my PhD thesis. The financial support of the SSHRCC, CMIIC, Center of International Business Studies, and Institute of International Relations is gratefully acknowledged. I thank the members of my committee, I. G. Morgan, D. D. Purvis, and especially my supervisor, E. H. Neave. I also received helpful comments from Jim Brander, Michael Brennan, David T. Brown, Rob Heinkel, David Hirshleifer, Tracy Lewis, Bentley MacLeod, John Moore, Ed Nosal, Ivan P'ng, Bill Scott, Chester Spatt, Sheridan Titman, and David Webb. Address reprint requests to Ron Giammarino, Faculty of Commerce, University of British Columbia, Vancouver, BC V6T 1Y8, Canada.

[1] For the purpose of this article, a firm enters financial distress when it is unable to meet a condition of its debt contract. Financial distress ends with either a financial reorganization or with the legal extinction of the firm through the declaration of bankruptcy by a court of law.

zation. In this article we show that despite the possibility of costless reorganization it may be rational for firms to incur significant deadweight costs in the resolution of financial distress.

Despite their central role in models of corporate financing, there is little theoretical justification for the existence of these assumed debt-related costs.[2] In fact there is an apparently compelling argument that they must be insignificant: In well-functioning markets agents who face a conflict of interest will reorganize the capital structure so as to avoid any deadweight costs. Fama and Miller (1972), for instance, argue that the capital structure decision of the firm will not affect the welfare of security holders if agents insist on protective covenants or "me-first" rules ex ante and are allowed to make side payments ex post. In this context, bankruptcy laws can be thought of as me-first rules and a financial reorganization can be thought of as a way of implementing an ex post cost-avoiding side payment. A slightly different argument is found in Stiglitz' (1974) generalization of the Modigliani-Miller theorem in which an intermediary is assumed to be able to costlessly repackage suboptimal capital structures in order, for example, to avoid costly conflicts of interest.

The most direct attack on the existence of significant costs, however, is made by Haugen and Senbet (1978, 1988). They argue that it would pay debt holders and equity holders to agree to an informal reorganization of the firm before any deadweight costs are incurred. To illustrate, suppose that a firm has defaulted on a debt payment but that it is costly for debt holders to have the equity extinguished by a bankruptcy court. Instead of proceeding with the costly legal action, the debt holders could offer to reduce the debt claim so as to avoid bankruptcy and the associated costs. If the proposed reorganization leaves the equity with a value less than the costs avoided then the debt holders are better off. At the same time the equity holders are also better off. Consequently, both agents should agree to a cost-avoiding reorganization.[3]

Despite this argument, costly financial distress is a common assumption in financial economics. For instance, many analyses of capital structure rest on the assumption that financial distress generates significant deadweight costs which, in equilibrium, are balanced by the tax advantage of debt.[4] Other studies have analyzed the way in which debt-related costs can be used to explain investment and output decisions in an imperfectly com-

---

[2] Exceptions include Aivazian and Callen (1983) and Webb (1987).

[3] Haugen and Senbet (1978) also argue that if the present claimants to the firm did not undertake the appropriate reorganization, then a third party could do so by purchasing all existing claims in the market, eliminating the conflict, and earning a riskless profit in the process. However, Allen (1986) and Haugen and Senbet (1988) recognize that this process is likely to be impeded by the free-rider problem identified by Grossman and Hart (1980). Haugen and Senbet (1988) suggest that the free-rider problem can be circumvented by, among other means, charter amendments which "give the bond trustee the right to accept or reject bids on behalf of all the debt holders." In our analysis we eliminate the free-rider problem by assuming that there is only one debt holder and one equity holder.

[4] For example, Kraus and Litzenberger (1973), Scott (1976), Kim (1978).

Resolution of Financial Distress

petitive product market.[5] Finally, the literature on optimal contracting with costly state verification develops the optimal contract form under the assumption that agents incur deadweight costs in verifying the realized state.[6] While these studies reflect an increasingly elaborate treatment of financial distress, they are all subject to the criticism outlined above.

In this article we take a step toward the development of a positive theory of the cost of financial distress by modeling the resolution of financial distress as a noncooperative game of incomplete information played by a firm and its creditor. Although we assume that debt contracts are complete in that they specify a state-contingent resolution of financial distress, the bargaining problem remains interesting because enforcement of the contract is costly and agents are asymmetrically informed about the state that has obtained. Under certain conditions, we are able to extend the argument of Haugen and Senbet to a world with asymmetric information. However, this is not a general result since we are also able to characterize equilibria in which agents, acting rationally, decide to incur deadweight costs.

An important difference between our analysis and previous work is that we explicitly address the question of whether or not agents will decide to incur costs given the existence of the costless alternative of renegotiation. A second important feature of our analysis is that we allow for strategic interaction between the different claimants to the firm. The combination of these features is not found in earlier contributions. For example, Van Horne (1976) examined the optimal initiation of bankruptcy essentially as a game against nature in which the firm passively accepts the decision made by the creditors. This, by assumption, precludes cost-avoiding reorganizations as well as learning and strategic behavior. Bulow and Shoven (1978) analyze the coalition that might form between the firm and a bank in the process of expropriating wealth from debt holders during financial distress. By assumption, however, debt holders and equity holders are not allowed to renegotiate. Aivazian and Callen (1983) and Brown (1986) look at questions that relate to coalition formation within the context of a cooperative game under symmetric information. Bergman (1986) assumes that me-first rules do not exist and considers the case in which equity holders force a reorganization on the debt holders by threatening to slowly destroy the firm. In a paper which is closest in spirit to ours Webb (1987) considers the question of whether or not agents will incur costs during financial distress. However, Webb assumes that agents act on the basis of their prior information only and therefore there is no learning or strategic behavior involved.[7]

---

[5] For example, Myers (1977), Bulow and Shoven (1978), Green and Shoven (1983), Titman (1984), Maksimovic (1984), Brander and Lewis (1986), and Allen (1987).

[6] For example, Townsend (1979), Diamond (1984), and Gale and Hellwig (1985).

[7] The bargaining environment that we posit is more closely related to the literature dealing with the economics of out of court settlements. The literature in this area includes contributions by Gould (1973), Shavell (1982), P'ng (1983, 1987), Salant (1984), and Reinganum and Wilde (1986). However, our treatment

In the following section we discuss U.S. bankruptcy law and the way in which it affects the bargaining problem surrounding an informal reorganization of the firm. This is followed by a description of our model in Section 2. The analysis and discussion of resulting equilibria are presented in Section 3. Concluding remarks are found in Section 4. To enhance the readability of the paper, most of the formal results are placed in the Appendix.

1. Bankruptcy Law and a Statement of the Problem

An informal reorganization of the firm involves a bargaining problem in which the payoffs that will result if bargaining fails (i.e., the conflict point) are determined by the formal procedures and rights set out in bankruptcy law. In this section we briefly outline some of the features of bankruptcy law and discuss ways in which they affect the bargaining problem.[8]

It is often argued that the main purpose of bankruptcy law is, as Jackson (1986) states, "... to ameliorate the common pool problem." This refers to inefficiencies in the operations of a financially distressed firm brought about by the conflicting claims that are triggered by default on a debt contract. For example, if upon default secured creditors begin procedures to recover their security, it may be that unsecured creditors and/or equity holders who have claim to other assets of the firm suffer significant losses. This may arise from synergies within the firm or transaction-specific investments which become worthless without the secured property.[9]

Bankruptcy law mitigates the common pool problem by imposing an automatic stay on all creditor actions when a bankruptcy petition is filed. Effectively, the stay protects the firm from creditor harassment and allows it full use of all assets, subject only to the supervision of a trustee, until a reorganization plan is formulated and ultimately confirmed by the courts. The bankruptcy petition may be filed by either the debtor firm (voluntary bankruptcy) or by the creditors (involuntary bankruptcy).

While the model which we employ in this study is quite general, it is perhaps most consistent with chapter 11 of the U.S. Bankruptcy Reform Act. Under a chapter 11 filing the debtor is typically allowed to act as the trustee in which case he is referred to as the debtor in possession and retains complete control over the operations of the firm. Furthermore, the debtor alone is entitled to file a reorganization plan during the first 120

---

is distinguished by the following features: (1) We introduce communication possibilities by allowing the relatively better informed agent to make the initial offer to which the relatively uninformed agent responds. (2) The settlement offer that is presented as an alternative to going to court is determined endogenously rather than exogenously. (3) We assume that the court protects agents from frivolous legal action through the mechanism by which the incurred costs are allocated. (4) Since we are dealing with financial distress, we do not allow cash settlement offers. As a result, the value of the settlement offer is based on the firm-specific value of a financial contract.

[8] For a more detailed account of the bankruptcy process see Newton (1981) or Baird and Jackson (1984).

[9] Cases in which court rulings reflect this line of thinking can be found in Baird and Jackson (1984).

days following the filing of a bankruptcy petition and has an additional 60 days to obtain acceptance by the creditors. Only after this time and only if acceptance has not been obtained can other parties file a reorganization plan. Hence, despite having defaulted on a debt contract, a firm can remain in control of its assets for at least six months and possibly longer.[10]

A reorganization plan offers each class of claimants new securities in exchange for those currently held. If the reorganization is rejected by the creditors the case goes to "cram down" where the court imposes a plan on all claimants. In so doing, however, the court must rule that the reorganization being imposed is "fair and equitable." This essentially requires that the court be convinced that the reorganization provides claimants to the firm with new securities that are worth as much as the securities surrendered or, if they are not, that no junior security holder receives payment if senior security holders have not received the value of the securities surrendered. Critical to this process is the ability of the court to interpret and verify evidence presented to it regarding the firm's economic value.

The following hypothetical example illustrates the importance of the court's valuation and the role which this valuation plays in the prepetition negotiations between debtor and creditor. Consider a firm that has an outstanding liability with a face value of 100 that is currently due in full. Suppose that its only asset is a claim to a future cash flow that will be either 180 or 0, each with equal probability. Assume that all agents are risk-neutral, the discount rate is zero, and therefore that the asset value is 90. Since this is less than the outstanding debt value, the firm is economically insolvent.

Suppose that creditors can have the firm liquidated through bankruptcy but that this will generate costs of 15. Prior to any action being taken, however, the firm and the creditor attempt to settle out of court so as to avoid costs. In bargaining, both agents will anticipate that if the case goes to cram down the court would require that the debt holders receive securities worth at least 75 (the net liquidation value of the firm) before the equity holders are allowed to receive anything. Since this is exactly what the firm will be worth, net of costs, the only reorganization plan which the court would confirm is one which gave full asset value to the debt holders.

The projected outcome of the court resolution provides a basis for the informal reorganization of the firm. In particular, since the value of the firm is reduced by the bankruptcy costs, there exists a new debt contract that, if accepted in an informal reorganization, would leave the debt holders as well off as they would have been if the dispute had been resolved formally. In the example just presented, having the court declare the firm bankrupt would reduce the value of the firm to 75. Alternatively, equity holders can offer to exchange existing debt for new debt with a face value

---

[10] The extension will be longer if other delay tactics are successfully employed. In this regard, it is interesting to note that the average time taken to resolve railroad bankruptcy cases in Warner's (1977) study is 13 years!

of 150. The new debt would have an economic value of 75, as much as would be received from the court, while the equity holders would have claims worth 15, an amount equal to the avoided costs.

In a world with symmetrically informed agents, a cost-avoiding reorganization of this type would be expected to emerge. However, an important source of disagreement in chapter 11 negotiations concerns the true value of the firm's assets, or, more precisely, the court's view of the true value. To see how this affects negotiations, suppose that the firm argues that it has inside information that can be used to convince the court that the worst possible payoff is 100 instead of 0. If the claim is valid, then, when the case goes to cram down, a reorganization in which debt holders were promised 100 would, since the court sees the debt as riskless, be considered a fair and equitable reorganization. If this outcome is expected by both debt holder and creditor, then, in bargaining to avoid bankruptcy costs, the creditor's position is weakened in that the minimum acceptable offer is reduced from 150 to 100.

In practice, courts hear evidence on the firm's prospects in a valuation hearing and adopt a valuation based on their interpretation of the often conflicting information provided. In prepetition bargaining, debtors and creditors must form opinions about the outcome of the court case and in so doing may view the outcome as a random variable, the distribution of which is refined by their own knowledge of the facts and their understanding of the facts available to their opponent.

In the model set out below we assume that the firm is better informed about the likely outcome of a valuation hearing than is the debt holder. This assumption is made because it is likely that managers have better information about the value of the firm than does the debt holder and that the court has the power to evaluate (perhaps imperfectly) claims made by either party.

2. A Model of Financial Distress

Consider a firm in financial distress that has no cash but has outstanding debt with a face value of B, currently payable in full. Assume that the firm's equity is entirely owned by a single risk-neutral individual and that the firm's debt is held entirely by a single risk-neutral debt holder.[11]

We impose the following structure on the problem. We assume that the equity holder has no resources with which to make the required payment and is unable to raise money by selling securities to new investors. As a result, the equity holder must offer a new debt contract to the debt holder

---

[11] The manager can be thought of as the owner manager of the firm or as the manager of a widely held firm who acts in the best interest of the firm's shareholders. Similarly, the debt holder can be thought of as a single creditor or as an agent acting on behalf of all creditors. We recognize that this assumption eliminates interesting agency problems but we make it in order to focus on the bargaining problem that remains when such problems have been taken care of.

Resolution of Financial Distress

in exchange for the old debt contract.[12] The debt holder must then either accept the offer or reject it. If the offer is rejected then total costs of C are incurred and the court resolves the issue either by declaring the firm bankrupt (legally extinguishing the equity claim), or by imposing a reorganization under which the firm will continue to operate. In either case the court also rules on the allocation of costs in a manner specified below.

The firm, while having no cash, has assets in place with a state-contingent value of $V(\theta)$, where $\theta \in \{S, I\}$ is the current state of the world. There are only two possible states in our model: the solvent state S in which $V(S) \geq B$, and the insolvent state I in which $V(I) < B$. In keeping with common practice, we will refer to the state of the world as the firm's type. Hence a solvent firm is one that is experiencing short-run cash flow problems only, whereas an insolvent firm is one with more substantial difficulties.

Given that the firm is in financial distress, the equity holder is required to offer a new debt contract to the debt holder. The offer is characterized by the face value of the new debt contract F which can be drawn from a discrete set of possible values contained in the interval $(0, \nu)$, $\nu < \infty$. The economic value of a particular informal reorganization to the debt holder, $D(F, \theta)$, is a nondecreasing concave function of the face value F. Conversely, the economic value of the equity claim is $E(F, \theta) \equiv (V(\theta) - D(F, \theta))$, a nonincreasing convex function of F.

Once the offer is made, the debt holder must either accept or reject it. Acceptance allows the firm to continue operating with the new debt contract in place. If the offer is rejected we assume that the court, which knows the state, strictly adheres to the following rules:

- If the firm is *insolvent* then it is declared bankrupt: The equity holder receives nothing and the debt holder receives $V(I) - C$.[13]
- If the firm is *solvent* and an offer F has been presented and turned down then:
  - If the value of the offered contract is at least as large as the surrendered contract [i.e., if $D(F, S) \geq B$], the court considers the action to be frivolous and protects the firm from creditor harassment. Thus, the rejected contract is imposed on the litigants and deadweight costs C are recovered from the debt holder who then receives $D(F, S) - C$ while the equity holder receives $E(F, S)$.
  - If the offered contract is worth less than the surrendered contract [i.e., if $D(F, S) < B$], the court imposes F_s, where F_s is defined implicitly by

$$D(F_s, S) = B$$

---

[12] The assumption that only debt is allowed in the reorganization is one of convenience. If a straight equity reorganization were involved, then the bargaining would involve the fraction of the firm which must be surrendered instead of the face value of the debt. If both debt and equity are allowed, the analysis would be similar but more complex. In particular, explicit assumptions about the distribution of underlying cash flows would have to be made. This is discussed further in Section 4.

[13] For convenience, these rules incorporate the assumption that $V(I) \geq C$ and $V(S) \geq B + C$. This implies that the deadweight costs will be paid by the litigants.

Since the court does not consider the legal action launched by the debt holder to be frivolous, costs are recovered from the equity holder. Hence the debt holder receives $D(F_s, S) = B$ while the equity holder receives $E(F_s, S) - C = V(S) - (B + C)$.

We have simplified the problem by assuming that unavoidable costs of C are incurred when an offer is rejected. Clearly, however, the process is more complex than this. For instance, in practice rejection of a reorganization offer might be followed by an attempt by creditors to seize assets which in turn might induce the firm to seek protection under chapter 11. During the time required to formally resolve the dispute, costly litigation will generate direct costs while the distraction of management, the impact on the firm's reputation, and risk-increasing production changes will generate indirect costs. We ignore these complexities as they would add little insight while obfuscating the main points of our analysis.

In addition, the assumed behavior of the court imposes a special cost allocation mechanism on the negotiation and deserves some explanation. Our treatment of costs in the insolvent state seems quite natural since limited liability implies that equity holders cannot be forced to bear costs. However, a large number of allocation schemes are possible in the solvent state. The mechanism that we have imposed is intended to eliminate the incentive to engage in frivolous legal action. We do this for two reasons. First, even though U.S. bankruptcy courts do not recover costs,[14] there is legal recourse through tort law. Second, we wish to focus on cases in which the only incentives agents have for going to court stem from the financial contracting problems that arise under asymmetric information. Hence, we assume away the potentially significant frivolous suit motives which an imperfect cost collection mechanism would introduce.

Given the assumed structure it is clear that if all agents were symmetrically informed about the firm's type the resolution of this problem would be simple and efficient. To see this, define F_I as the face value of a debt contract that would have a value to the debt holder exactly equal to the amount that would be received if an insolvent firm were taken to court. That is, F_I satisfies

$$D(F_I, I) = V(I) - C$$

Hence an insolvent firm would offer F_I to the debt holder who would accept the offer and, in so doing, avoid costs. The debt holder receives the value of the firm less costs while the equity holder receives the foregone costs.[15]

On the other hand, if the firm is solvent, the equity holder will offer F_S, the minimum that the debt holder would accept. Offering any less would lead to costly court action while offering any more is, from the equity

---

[14] Although to some extent Canadian and British courts do collect costs.

[15] We follow the convention of assuming that, when indifferent, the debt holder will accept the offer since in practice acceptance could be ensured by an offer that is even one cent higher.

holder's point of view, wasteful. In both cases the resolution is efficient in that it does not involve actions which bring about deadweight costs.

A more interesting and realistic scenario, however, has agents that are asymmetrically informed about the firm's type. In particular, we assume that the equity holder and the court are both aware of the firm's type while the debt holder, prior to receiving an offer, is only aware that the firm is solvent with probability P_s and insolvent with probability $P_I = 1 - P_s$. Once the offer has been received, however, the debt holder uses the structure of the game and the magnitude of the offer to revise his beliefs about the firm type. The precise nature of this revision is analyzed in the following section.[16]

Under this scenario, the equity holder's optimal offer and the debt holder's optimal response are no longer as simple to determine. Clearly, the debt holder will reject an offer that is less than min $\{F_I, F_s\}$ since it is less than the minimum acceptable from either a solvent or an insolvent firm. On the other hand, if an offer that at least equals max $\{F_I, F_s\}$ is received, it will be accepted since it is at least as valuable as taking a solvent or insolvent firm to court. Hence, only offers within the interval [min $\{F_s, F_I\}$, max $\{F_s, F_I\}$] need be considered in our analysis. When an offer is in this interval, acceptance or rejection depends on the beliefs formed by the equity holder that in turn depend on the strategies being followed by the debt holder. This problem is analyzed in the next section.

3. Analysis

We view the model developed in the previous section as an extensive form game of incomplete information and employ the sequential equilibrium concept of Kreps and Wilson (1982) to identify equilibria. A sequential equilibrium requires that, for each information set, the equilibrium strategies are sequentially rational with respect to beliefs and that beliefs are consistent with the informational structure of the game. An important feature of this approach is that it explicitly deals with off-equilibrium-path information sets and rules out dynamically inconsistent strategies in which the debt holder precommits to arbitrary actions.

The equity holder's strategy is described by the probability that each feasible offer is made. Let $\pi_\theta(F)$ denote the probability that a firm of type θ will offer F in exchange for the existing debt contract. On the other hand, the debt holder's strategy is simply the probability, denoted $\rho(F)$, with which an offer is rejected. This formulation is quite general in that it allows both mixed- and pure-strategy equilibria. Finally, beliefs, defined as the revised probabilities attached to the possibility that an offer has been

---

[16] An alternative interpretation of this structure is that the agents are asymmetrically informed about the evidence they will present to the court but that the information can be revealed at a cost. In either case, it is not essential that the court be perfectly informed about the value of the firm but only that the manager be better informed about the distribution of the possible outcomes of the valuation hearing.

presented by each type, incorporate expectations about the strategy which the equity holder is following and the prior probability of the firm being of a particular type. We let $P_s(P_I)$ denote the prior probability that the firm is solvent (insolvent) and denote the revised probabilities by $\mu(S|F)$ for a solvent firm and $\mu(I|F) = 1 - \mu(S|F)$ for an insolvent firm.

Our procedure will be to identify strategies which define $\pi_s(F)$, $\pi_I(F)$, and $\rho(F)$ for all possible offers and demonstrate that these satisfy the requirements of a sequential equilibrium. Our main interest is to determine whether or not the strategies imply that deadweight costs will be incurred, that is, whether or not offers will be made that, with positive probability, will be turned down.

In deriving the equilibria to this game we make two further assumptions about the behavior of the players. First, we introduce the concept of a dominated action.

Definition. *An action is dominated if the largest payoff possible from the action does not exceed the smallest payoff possible from another feasible action.*[17]

Throughout this article we assume that players will not select an action that is dominated and that beliefs reflect this.

Our second assumption concerns the response of debt holders to offers which are "unexpected" in the sense that they are given 0 probability in the equilibrium strategies of both types. Although these offers would not be observed in equilibrium, the construction of equilibrium strategies for the players requires that we specify optimal responses to all conceivable offers. In some cases (for instance, Propositions 1 and 2 below) the refinement afforded by the elimination of dominated strategies is sufficient. In others, however, such a procedure is of little help.[18]

Since our goal is to illustrate why debt holders may insist on a costly reorganization, it suffices to consider a particular set of beliefs under which this will occur. Specifically, we assume that off-equilibrium-path offers are believed to have been presented by the solvent firm if $F_I < F_S$ and by the insolvent firm if $F_S < F_I$. However, for each equilibrium we also indicate whether or not the intuitive criterion due to Cho and Kreps (1987) is satisfied. In the context of our model, an equilibrium offer is said to fail this criterion (and hence to be supported by unreasonable beliefs) if we can identify an off-equilibrium-path offer that satisfies the following condition. First, we define a set S of types who would not prefer to make the off-equilibrium-path offer relative to the equilibrium regardless of the debt

---

[17] For a more formal discussion of dominance and its role in refining off-equilibrium-path beliefs see McLennan (1985), or Cho and Kreps (1987).

[18] The problem of how players react and the types of conjectures they form when confronted with disequilibrium behavior is still an unresolved issue in games with asymmetric information. Discussion of various approaches that one may adopt in dealing with this problem is contained in Banks and Sobel (1987), Cho and Kreps (1987), McLennan (1985), and the references cited therein.

Resolution of Financial Distress

holder's response. Then we define the set $\bar{S}$ to be the complement of S in the set of all possible types. The equilibrium is said to *fail* the intuitive criterion if there is a type in $\bar{S}$ that would be better off presenting the off-equilibrium-path offer rather than the equilibrium one given that the debt holder believes the firm to be any one of the types contained in the set $\bar{S}$. Clearly the power of these criteria is in eliminating from consideration types who cannot be made better off by presenting the off-equilibrium-path offer.

Our analysis identifies two main types of equilibria; those which imply that deadweight bankruptcy costs will be avoided despite the fact that agents are asymmetrically informed, and those which imply that costs will not be avoided. It turns out that the actual types of equilibria that exist depend on whether or not $F_I < F_S$. This in turn depends on the relative size of the incentives to take a particular type of firm to court. The incentive to take an insolvent firm to court increases with the size of the debtor's assets (as these are transferred to the creditor through bankruptcy), but decreases with the costs incurred. Accordingly, the size of the promised payment that would be needed to induce the debt holder to accept if the firm was thought to be insolvent, F_I, increases with $V(I)$ but decreases with C. On the other hand, the incentive to take a solvent firm to court is increasing in the face value of the unpaid debt contract, B, and hence F_S is increasing in B.

When $F_S < F_I$, both solvent and insolvent firms would like to convince their creditors that they are solvent and that the inability to meet contractually specified payments reflects a temporary cash flow problem. There are two mutually exclusive equilibria in this case; one in which costs are avoided (Proposition 1) and one in which they are not (Proposition 2). When $F_I < F_S$ both solvent and insolvent firms wish to convince the debt holder that they are insolvent and that the terms of the reorganization should reflect the bankruptcy costs that their proposal would avoid. We find that equilibria exist in which costs are avoided by a reorganization that on average is appropriate from the creditor's point of view (Proposition 3). However, the same conditions also give rise to equilibria in which expected deadweight costs are positive (Propositions 4 and 5).

3.1 $F_s < F_I$

We will define a *solvency claim* strategy set as a set in which both solvent and insolvent firms claim to be solvent by offering F_S with probability 1, while the debt holder rejects all offers except F_S and F_I.

Proposition 1. *A solvency claim strategy set forms a sequential equilibrium if and only if $F_S < F_I$ and*

$$P_I(D(F_I, I) - D(F_S, I)) \leq P_s C \tag{1}$$

Proof. See the Appendix. ∎

The equilibrium may be interpreted as follows. Given that $F_S < F_I$ the solvent firm will not offer more than F_S: If the offer is rejected, cram down will lead to the court imposing the contract F_S on the debt holders (see Lemma A1 in the Appendix). Realizing this, the debt holder believes that any other offer that is received is presented by an insolvent firm. Accordingly all offers except F_S and F_I are rejected.

The difficult problem facing the debt holder is in deciding how to respond to an offer of F_S. While it is true that a solvent firm will present only this offer, it is also true that an insolvent firm might "bluff" by also presenting F_S. The cost of acceptance of F_S is the payoff reduction from not going to court if the firm turns out to be insolvent [i.e., $D(F_I, I) - D(F_S, I)$]. The cost of rejection is the court costs incurred when the firm turns out to be solvent (i.e., C).

If condition (1) holds, then even when the insolvent firm bluffs with probability 1, the expected cost of acceptance is less than the cost of rejection. Hence the offer is always accepted. Anticipating acceptance, both firm types present F_S with probability 1. In this case costs are avoided because they exceed the maximum gain available to the debt holder from more stringent enforcement of the debt contract.

The other strategy set of interest when $F_S < F_I$ will be referred to as a *solvent semiseparating* or SSS set and is defined by

1. The solvent firm offers F_S with probability 1.
2. The insolvent firm randomizes between offering F_S and F_I (the probability with which each offer is presented is given in the Appendix).
3. The debt holder accepts an offer of F_I with probability 1 but rejects offers of F_S with positive probability (the exact rejection probability is given in the Appendix).

Proposition 2. *SSS strategies form a sequential equilibrium if and only if $F_S < F_I$, and*

$$P_I(D(F_I, I) - D(F_S, I)) \geq P_s C \qquad (2)$$

Proof. See the Appendix. ∎

Condition (2) ensures that if the insolvent firm bluffs with probability 1 by offering F_S, then the cost of rejection is no greater than the cost of acceptance. As a result, a semiseparating equilibrium exists in which the insolvent firm bluffs by offering F_S with a probability that is large enough to make the debt holder indifferent to accepting or rejecting the offer. The debt holder imposes discipline on the insolvent firm by rejecting F_S with positive probability. Hence agents decide to incur deadweight costs because, while the "pie" shrinks by doing so, their expected share of the pie is maximized.[19]

---

[19] Both the solvency claim and solvent semiseparating equilibria are supported by the belief that off-equilibrium-path offers are presented only by the insolvent firm. These beliefs satisfy the intuitive criteria for

Resolution of Financial Distress

3.2 $F_I < F_S$

We define a *pooling* strategy set to be a set that implies that a pooled offer, denoted by F^*, is offered by both solvent and insolvent firms with probability 1, and accepted with probability 1, while all offers except F^* and F_S are rejected.

Proposition 3. *A pooling strategy set forms a sequential equilibrium if and only if $F_I < F_S$ and the pooled offer F^* is such that $\bar{F} \leq F^* \leq F_S$, and $\bar{F}$ is implicitly defined by*

$$P_s(D(F_S, S) - D(\bar{F}, S)) = P_I(D(\bar{F}, I) - D(F_I, I)) \quad (3)$$

Proof. See the Appendix.[20] ∎

In this equilibrium the only offer presented with positive probability by either type is F^*, an offer that, given equilibrium beliefs, provides the debt holder no incentive to reject. Hence deadweight costs are avoided. Under the equilibrium beliefs, the left-hand side of Equation (3) is the expected opportunity cost of not taking a solvent firm to court when $F^* = \bar{F}$, while the right-hand side is the expected gain from not taking the case to court when the firm is insolvent and $F^* = \bar{F}$. Since $\bar{F}$ is the face value at which these two terms offset each other the debt holder is as well off accepting any $F^* \geq \bar{F}$.

Proposition 3 establishes that whenever $F_I < F_S$ there exists an equilibrium in which costs are avoided. Under these conditions, the Haugen-Senbet argument that bankruptcy costs are insignificant can be extended to the case of asymmetric information. However, Propositions 4 and 5, presented below, demonstrate that, under the same conditions, other equilibria exist in which expected costs are positive.

The equilibria described in these propositions are referred to as semi-separating and are characterized by the fact that only two offers are presented with positive probability. One of the offers, referred to as the pooled offer, is presented by both solvent and insolvent firms while the other offer is presented only by one type and hence reveals the firm's type to the debt holder.

In order to motivate and interpret the equilibria presented in Propositions 4 and 5 we will first set out some preliminary results. Consider two arbitrary offers, denoted F_L and F_H, that either a solvent or an insolvent firm might present with positive probability. We will adopt the convention that $F_L < F_H \leq F_S$.

---

reasonableness since they are consistent with the elimination of dominated actions: For the solvent firm, all off-equilibrium-path offers are dominated by the equilibrium offer.

[20] This equilibrium satisfies the intuitive criterion. To see this, note that for both types $F > F^*$ is dominated by F^*. On the other hand off-equilibrium-path offers $F < F^*$ would, if accepted, be preferred to the equilibrium by both types so that the set $\tilde{S}$ contains both solvent and insolvent types. However, the best response of the debt holder based on beliefs that the firm is solvent is to reject the offer. Based on this response, neither type in $\tilde{S}$ would defect from the equilibrium.

Lemma 1. *Strategies in which a separating and a pooled offer are both presented will form an equilibrium only if the separating offer exceeds the pooled offer in magnitude.*

Proof. Suppose to the contrary that F_L is the separating offer. Since the offer is separating it will reveal the firm's type. If the firm is solvent then the offer will be rejected since it is less than F_S and F_S will be imposed by the courts. Consequently, the solvent firm will prefer to offer F_S rather than F_L. If the separating offer is presented by the insolvent firm it will be optimal for the debt holder to accept the offer with probability 1. However, based on this response the solvent firm will also present the offer, thereby destroying the separating equilibrium. ∎

Lemma 2. *If $F_I < F_S$ then in equilibrium the only separating offer which a solvent firm will present is F_S.*

Proof. A separating offer is one which reveals the firm's type. Hence the minimum acceptable offer that a solvent firm can present is F_S. Since the outcome from offering F_S is greater than the outcome from offering $F < F_S$ if the offer is rejected with probability 1, the solvent firm will only present F_S as a separating offer. ∎

Lemmas 1 and 2 establish the fact that in equilibrium the magnitude of the separating offer must exceed that of the pooled offer. In characterizing the equilibrium we must also examine the question of which type will present the separating offer and which will present the pooled offer. If we view the separating offer as a signal, the answer can be seen to depend on the relative advantage of signaling. This advantage for the solvent firm will be denoted by Δ_S and is defined as the payoff from having F_H accepted with probability 1, minus the expected payoff from offering F_L and having it accepted with probability ρ^*.

$$\Delta_S(\rho^*) = [V(S) - D(F_H, S)] - ((1 - \rho^*)[V(S) - D(F_L, S)]$$
$$+ \rho^*[V(S) - (B + C)])$$
$$= \rho^*[B + C - D(F_L, S)] - [D(F_H, S) - D(F_L, S)]$$

A solvent firm will prefer F_H over F_L if $\Delta_S > 0$, will have the opposite preference if $\Delta_S < 0$, and will be indifferent if $\Delta_S = 0$. Note that in order for the solvent firm to randomize between F_H and F_L it is necessary that $\Delta_S = 0$.

Similarly, we can define Δ_I by

$$\Delta_I(\rho^*) = \rho^*[V(I) - D(F_L, I)] - [D(F_H, I) - D(F_L, I)]$$

Let ρ_S^* and ρ_I^* be defined such that $\Delta_S(\rho_S^*) = 0$ and $\Delta_I(\rho_I^*) = 0$, respectively. That is,

$$\rho_S^* = \frac{D(F_H, S) - D(F_L, S)}{B + C - D(F_L, S)}$$

and

$$\rho_I^* = \frac{D(F_H, I) - D(F_L, I)}{V(I) - D(F_L, I)}$$

Thus if in equilibrium a solvent firm randomizes over F_H and F_L then it is necessary that the rejection probability be ρ_S^*. If this is the case then the behavior of the insolvent firm will be determined by the sign of $\Delta_I(\rho_S^*)$ which in turn can be shown to be given by the sign of $(\rho_S^* - \rho_I^*)$. Hence, ignoring the knife-edge case in which $\rho_I^* = \rho_S^*$, if the solvent firm plays a mixed strategy over F_H and F_L then the insolvent firm will play a pure strategy of presenting F_H with probability 1 if $\rho_S^* > \rho_I^*$, or a pure strategy of presenting F_L if $\rho_S^* < \rho_I^*$.

By using a similar argument it can be shown that if an insolvent firm randomizes, implying that the pooled offer is rejected with probability ρ_I^*, the solvent firm will prefer to offer F_H if $\rho_I^* > \rho_S^*$ and will prefer to offer F_L if $\rho_I^* < \rho_S^*$. These features of a semiseparating equilibrium are summarized in the following lemma:

Lemma 3.
1. A semiseparating equilibrium in which the insolvent firm randomizes while the solvent firm pools exists only if $\rho_I^* < \rho_S^*$.
2. A semiseparating equilibrium in which the solvent firm randomizes while the insolvent firm pools exists only if $\rho_I^* > \rho_S^*$.

Proof. See the Appendix. ∎

Proposition 4 refers to a *solvent randomization* strategy set which is defined by

1. The insolvent firm only offers the pooled offer F_L.
2. The solvent firm randomizes between offering F_L and a higher separating offer F_S (the probability with which each offer is selected is found in the Appendix).
3. The debt holder accepts the separating offer with probability 1 and rejects F_L with probability ρ_S^*.

Proposition 4. *The solvent randomization strategy forms a sequential equilibrium if and only if $F_I < F_S$, and $\rho_S^* < \rho_I^*$.*

Proof. See the Appendix. ∎

In this equilibrium the solvent firm will either imitate an insolvent firm in demanding the lower reorganization F_L, realizing that the offer will be rejected with positive probability, or it will make an acceptable fully revealing offer F_S. An insolvent firm will always present F_L even though this will be rejected with positive probability since the expected payoff from doing so is larger than it would be if it imitated a solvent firm [i.e., $\Delta_I(\rho_S^*) < 0$].

Recognizing the incentives that the firm faces, the debt holder is willing to accept a separating offer knowing that it has been presented by the solvent firm, but will reject the pooled offer with positive probability. In this case, rejection is required to impose the appropriate level of discipline on the solvent firm.

Proposition 5 deals with an *insolvent randomization* strategy set which is defined by

    1. The solvent firm offers the pooled offer F_L with probability 1.

    2. The insolvent firm randomizes between the pooled offer and the separating offer F_{II} (the equilibrium probabilities with which each offer is selected are found in the Appendix).

    3. The debt holder accepts the separating offer with probability 1, and rejects the pooled offer with probability ρ_I^*.

Proposition 5. *The insolvent randomization strategy set forms a sequential equilibrium if and only if $F_I < F_S$ and $\rho_I^* < \rho_S^*$.*

In contrast to the solvent randomization strategies, the insolvent randomization requires that the solvent firm present offer F_L only, while the insolvent firm randomizes by selecting either F_L or separating itself by selecting F_{II}. Again rejection with positive probability is optimal for the debt holder implying that costs are incurred.

It turns out that the equilibrium described in Proposition 4 satisfies the intuitive criterion whereas that dealt with in Proposition 5 does not.[21]

4. Conclusions

The purpose of this study has been to address the question of whether or not financial distress-related costs will, in all cases, be avoided through a costless reorganization. Our conclusion is that costs may not always be avoided: We have identified equilibria in which the debt holder would rather appeal to a costly arbitrator than trust the equity holder to present an appropriate reorganization. Hence, private information interferes in the efficiency of ex post recontracting.

Our results show that the type of equilibrium that results will depend

---

[21] To see how the criterion eliminates the insolvent randomization strategy of Proposition 5 note that, by construction, the insolvent type is indifferent to presenting F_{II} which is sure to be accepted and presenting F_I which is rejected with positive probability while the solvent firm strictly prefers to offer F_L even though it will be rejected with positive probability. This implies that there is an offer $\tilde{F}$, where $F_L < \tilde{F} < F_{II}$, which if accepted with probability 1 would provide the same expected payoff as the solvent firm receives in equilibrium but more than the insolvent firm would. Consider now an off-equilibrium-path offer F that satisfies $\tilde{F} < F < F_{II}$. If this offer were accepted it would be preferred to the equilibrium by the insolvent firm but not by the solvent firm, so that the set $\tilde{S}$ contains only the insolvent firm. However the best response to the set of types in $\tilde{S}$ is to accept the offer. If accepted, then it would induce the insolvent firm to defect. Hence the equilibrium fails the intuitive criteria.

When a similar argument is applied to Proposition 4, the set $\tilde{S}$ contains both types and hence the set of best responses includes rejection, which implies that the types in $\tilde{S}$ would not defect to the equilibrium so that the criterion is satisfied.

Resolution of Financial Distress

upon the setting within which negotiations take place. In our first case, the parameters of the problem are such that both solvent and insolvent firms have an incentive to claim that their economic prospects are favorable and that the inability to meet contractually specified payments reflects temporary cash flow problems. This will come about when the outstanding debt is small relative to the size of the solvent firm or when the enforcement costs are small relative to the size of the insolvent firm. The equilibria in this case (Propositions 1 and 2) survive several of the recently advanced refinements of the sequential equilibrium concept because the only restriction which must be placed on off-equilibrium-path beliefs is that they attach a 0 probability to strategies that are dominated for one of the agents.

The second case involves conditions under which both the solvent and insolvent firms wish to convince the creditor that they are insolvent and that the acceptable reorganization should reflect the costs avoided through the proposed reorganization. This will occur when financial distress costs are relatively large so that F_I is small or when the outstanding debt is large so that F_s is large. While a cost-avoiding pooled equilibrium exists under these conditions (Proposition 3), we are also able to show that there exist other equilibria in which costs are incurred (Propositions 4 and 5).

There are several ways in which the analysis could be extended. For instance, intermediaries may specialize in assessing the status of a financially distressed firm in such a way that the informational asymmetry is reduced. Suppose further that the intermediary's abilities in this respect are type specific and unknown to the firm. This situation could be dealt with as a game of repeated transactions with two-sided informational asymmetry in which the intermediary deals with a number of debtors sequentially. Reputation, which is absent from our analysis, would be an important part of this extension. A second extension would be to allow reorganizations that involve more complex capital structures. For example, suppose that both debt and equity are allowed and an explicit distribution for the underlying cash flows is specified. It is conceivable that, to the extent that the distributions have distinct type-specific features, there could be more scope for signaling than exists in our framework.

The major assumptions upon which our analysis is built are that courts attempt to reorganize the firm in a manner consistent with their assessment of firm value and that agents are asymmetrically informed about the assessment that will be formed. We recognize that the entire problem disappears if there is no judicial discretion to interpret contracts and if agents engage in contracts written solely on observables so that asymmetric information would not be a problem. An example of such a contract would be what Brennan (1986) refers to as a reverting consol bond which automatically becomes equity when the value of the firm falls to a particular point. In practice, however, even when contracts are contingent on observables only, interested parties appeal to a court of law to suspend these terms for various reasons. Judicial discretion, which provides the court the power to rule on these appeals, is widespread and makes every contract essentially ambiguous. It is this discretion which drives our results.

Appendix

In this appendix we derive the results presented in the text.

Lemma A1. *If $F_s < F_i$ then offering F_s with probability 1 dominates all other strategies for a solvent firm.*

Proof. The assumed protection from frivolous court action implies that the payoff from offering $F > F_s$ is independent of the response of the debt holder: If the offer is rejected it will be imposed on the debt holder by the court at no cost to the equity holder. However, since the payoff to the equity holder is nonincreasing in the offered face value all offers which exceed F_s are dominated by F_s. Thus, F_s dominates all other offers. ∎

Proof of Proposition 1

Sufficiency. Consider first the behavior of the debt holder. If the equilibrium offer is presented, the conditional expected payoff as a function of ρ, denoted $U(\rho|F)$, is

$$\begin{aligned} U(\rho|F_s) &= \rho[\mu(S|F_s)(D(F_s, S) - C) + \mu(I|F_s)(V(I) - C)] \\ &\quad + (1-\rho)[\mu(S|F_s)D(F_s, S) + \mu(I|F_s)D(F_s, I)] \\ &= \mu(S|F_s)D(F_s, S) + \mu(I|F_s)D(F_s, I) \\ &\quad + \rho[\mu(I|F_s)(V(I) - C - D(F_s, I)) - \mu(S|F_s)C] \end{aligned} \quad \text{(A1)}$$

Equilibrium beliefs can be formed according to Bayes' rule along the equilibrium path and would, in this case, be $\mu(I|F_s) = P_I$ and $\mu(S|F_s) = P_S$, reflecting the fact that the pooled offer is uninformative. Substituting these beliefs into Equation (A1) and using the fact that $D(F_I, I) = V(I) - C$ we obtain

$$U(\rho|F_s) = P_S D(F_s, S) + P_I D(F_s, I) + \rho[P_I(D(F_I, I) - D(F_s, I)) - P_S C] \quad \text{(A1a)}$$

Clearly, $U(\rho|F_s)$ is decreasing in ρ if $P_I(D(F_I, I) - D(F_s, I)) < P_S C$, implying that acceptance is the optimal response to the equilibrium offer. If $P_I(D(F_I, I) - D(F_s, I)) = P_S C$, then $U(\rho|F_s)$ is unaffected by ρ and hence the debt holder has no incentive to defect from the equilibrium strategy.

Beliefs for all off-equilibrium-path offers are based on dominance. Since $F_s < F$ are dominated by F_s for a solvent firm (see Lemma A1) but not for the insolvent firm all offers in this range would be treated as if they were presented by an insolvent firm. This means that all offers except F_I would be rejected, as is required by the equilibrium strategies.

Next consider the behavior of the equity holder. Lemma A1 establishes that, since $F_s < F_I$, only the equilibrium strategy is undominated for the

42

Resolution of Financial Distress

solvent firm. Given the equilibrium response of the debt holder and the fact that the payoff to the equity holder is decreasing in F, the insolvent firm would only be worse off by defecting from the equilibrium, regardless of the debt holder's response.

Necessity. If $F_I < F_S$ then both the solvent and insolvent firms would defect from the equilibrium strategies by presenting F_I with probability 1 since $\rho(F_I) = 0$. If $P_I(D(F_I, I) - D(F_S, I)) > P_S C$, $U(\rho | F_S)$ would be increasing in ρ implying that the debt holder would reject F_S. ∎

Proposition 2 refers to a solvent semiseparating strategy set (SSS), which is formally defined as follows:

1. $\pi_S(F_S) = 1, \pi_I(F_S) = P_S C/(P_I(D(F_I, I) - D(F_S, I))), \pi_I(F_I) = (P_I(D(F_I, I) - D(F_S, I)) - P_S C)/(P_I(D(F_I, I) - D(F_S, I)))$
2. $\rho(F_I) = 0, \rho(F_S) = (V(I) - D(F_S, I) - C)/(V(I) - D(F_S, I)), \rho(F) = 1 \; \forall F \neq F_S, F_I$

Proof of Proposition 2

Sufficiency. Consider first the debt holder's response to the equilibrium path offers. Since F_I is a separating offer, the debt holder will conclude that the firm is insolvent and therefore will have no incentive to reject. On the other hand, if the offer is F_S then the payoff is given by Equation (A1). Given the equilibrium beliefs, this expression is independent of the value of ρ and may be written as

$$U(\rho | F_S) = \frac{P_S}{P_S + P_I \pi_I(F_S)} D(F_S, S) + \frac{P_I \pi_I(F_S)}{P_S + P_I \pi_I(F_S)} D(F_S, I) \quad \text{(A1b)}$$

Since $U(\rho | F_S)$ is independent of ρ, there is no reason for the debt holder to defect from the equilibrium mixed strategy.

As with Proposition 1, off-equilibrium-path beliefs are based on dominance. Hence all off-equilibrium-path offers are treated as having been made by an insolvent firm and are therefore rejected.

We now demonstrate that the firm will not defect from the equilibrium strategies. Lemma A1 establishes this for a solvent firm that will present F_S with probability 1. The equilibrium requires that an insolvent firm randomize between F_S and F_I. In order for there to be no incentive for the equity holder to defect from this it must be the case that the payoff from offering F_I and having it accepted with probability 1 is equal to the expected payoff from presenting F_S and having it rejected with probability $\rho(F_S)$. That is, $\rho(F_S)$ must satisfy

$$V(I) - D(F_I, I) = [1 - \rho(F_S)][V(I) - D(F_S, I)]$$

Since this is satisfied in equilibrium, the insolvent firm has no incentive to prefer F_S over F_I. Finally, since all off-equilibrium-path offers are rejected with probability 1, there is no incentive for agents to defect from the equilibrium offers.

Necessity. If $F_I < F_S$, then both the solvent and insolvent firms would prefer to present F_I with probability 1, thereby destroying the equilibrium.

If $P_I(D(F_I, I) - D(F_S, I)) < P_S C$ then the value of $\pi_I(F_S)$ specified in the strategy description exceeds one and is therefore not feasible. ∎

Note that both Propositions 1 and 2 satisfy the intuitive criteria by virtue of the fact that beliefs are based on dominance.

Proof of Proposition 3

Sufficiency. The debt holder's payoff given that the equilibrium offer has been presented is

$$U(\rho|F^*) = [\mu(S|F^*)D(F^*, S) + \mu(I|F^*)D(F^*, I)] \\ + \rho[\mu(S|F^*)(D(F_S, S) - D(F^*, S)) \\ - \mu(I|F^*)(D(F^*, I) - D(F_I, I))] \quad (A2)$$

By substituting in equilibrium beliefs and rearranging terms we obtain

$$U(\rho|F^*) = P_S D(F^*, S) + P_I D(F^*, I) \\ + \rho[P_S(D(F_S, S) - D(F^*, S)) - P_I(D(F^*, I) - D(F_I, I))] \quad (A2a)$$

If $F^* = \bar{F}$, then by Equation (3) we have that

$$U(\rho|\bar{F}) = P_S D(F^*, S) + P_I D(F^*, I)$$

which implies that the debt holder has no incentive to reject the offer. For $F^* > \bar{F}$, $U(\rho|F^*)$ is decreasing in ρ so that acceptance of the offer is optimal.

Neither the solvent nor the insolvent firm has an incentive to offer any more than F^*. Furthermore, since offering any less would lead to rejection, such offers would not be presented.

Necessity. If $F_S < F_I$ then the solvent firm would offer $F_S < F^*$ only (see Lemma A1) and the equilibrium would be destroyed. ∎

Proof of Lemma 3

1. Suppose that an insolvent firm randomizes so that F_L is rejected with probability ρ_I^*. If $\rho_S^* < \rho_I^*$ then $\Delta_S(\rho_I^*) > 0$ and the solvent firm will prefer to present F_H. However, this implies that F_L is a separating offer and, given Lemma 1, these strategies cannot be a separating equilibrium.

2. The proof of (2) is similar to the proof of (1) and is therefore omitted. ∎

Proposition 4 deals with the solvent randomization strategy set which is defined formally as follows:

Resolution of Financial Distress

1. $\pi_I(F_L) = 1$, $\pi_S(F_L) = [P_I(D(F_L, I) - D(F_I, I))]/[P_S(D(F_S, S) - D(F_L, S))]$, $\pi_S(F_S) = 1 - \pi_S(F_L)$
2. $\rho(F_S) = 0$, $\rho(F_L) = \rho_S^*$, $\rho(F) = 1 \ \forall \ F \neq F_S, F_L$

where F_L can be any element from the set of all F for which $0 \leq \pi_S(F_L) < 1$.

Proof of Proposition 4

Sufficiency. The assumed off-equilibrium-path beliefs (i.e., that off-equilibrium-path offers are made by the solvent firm) ensure that all offers except F_L and F_S would be rejected. Hence, neither firm type would be willing to present such offers.

Since F_S is a separating offer, $\mu(S|F_S) = 1$ and acceptance is optimal. If F_L is presented, then the conditional payoff to the debt holder is

$$U(\rho|F_L) = \frac{P_S \pi_S(F_L)}{P_I + P_S \pi_S(F_L)} D(F_L, S) + \frac{P_I}{P_I + P_S \pi_S(F_L)} D(F_L, I)$$

$$+ \frac{\rho}{P_I + P_S \pi_S(F_L)} [P_S \pi_S(F_L)(D(F_S, S)$$

$$- D(F_L, S)) - P_I(D(F_L, I) - D(F_I, I))] \quad (A3)$$

Equation (A3) reflects beliefs which incorporate the fact that an insolvent firm selects F_L with probability 1 while the solvent firm makes this selection with probability $\pi_S(F_L)$. With the equilibrium value of $\pi_S(F_L)$ substituted in, Equation (A3) becomes

$$U(\rho|F_L) = \frac{P_S \pi_S(F_L)}{P_I + P_S \pi_S(F_L)} D(F_L, S) + \frac{P_I}{P_I + P_S \pi_S(F_L)} D(F_L, I) \quad (A3a)$$

Given that the equilibrium strategies followed by the solvent and insolvent firms have neutralized the impact of ρ on $U(\rho|F_L)$, the debt holder has no incentive to defect from the equilibrium strategy.

Since ρ_S^* is defined so that the solvent firm is indifferent between presenting F_S and F_L there will be no reason for the solvent firm to defect from the equilibrium mixed strategy. Lemma 3 also establishes that if $\rho_S^* < \rho_I^*$ then the insolvent firm strictly prefers presenting F_L rather than F_S. Thus neither firm type has an incentive to defect from the equilibrium strategies. Finally, neither firm type would present an off-equilibrium-path offer since such an offer would be rejected.

Necessity. If $F_S < F_L$ a solvent firm would offer F_S with probability 1, thereby destroying the equilibrium. If $\rho_I^* < \rho_S^*$ then, the insolvent firm would prefer to offer F_S instead of F_L, thereby destroying the equilibrium. ∎

Proposition 5 involves the insolvent randomization strategy set which is defined formally as follows:

1. $\pi_S(F_L) = 1$, $\pi_I(F_L) = [P_S(D(F_S, S) - D(F_L, S))]/[P_I(D(F_L, I) - D(F_I, I))]$, $\pi_I(F_H) = 1 - \pi_I(F_L)$
2. $\rho(F_H) = 0$, $\rho(F_L) = \rho_I^*$, $\rho(F) = 1 \ \forall \ F \neq F_H, F_L$

The proof of Proposition 5 is similar to that of Proposition 4 and is omitted.

References

Aivazian, V. A., and J. L. Callen, 1983, "Reorganization in Bankruptcy and the Issue of Strategic Risk," *Journal of Banking and Finance*, 7, 119-183.

Allen, F., 1986, "The Insignificance of Bankruptcy Costs to the Theory of Capital Structure: A Comment," working paper, The Wharton School, University of Pennsylvania.

Allen, F., 1987, "Capital Structure and Imperfect Competition in Product Markets," Rodney White Working Paper 1187, The Wharton School, University of Pennsylvania.

Baird, D., and T. Jackson, 1984, *Cases, Problems, and Materials on Security Interests in Personal Property*, Foundation Press, Mineola, N.Y.

Banks, J. S., and J. Sobel, 1987, "Equilibrium Selection in Signalling Games," *Econometrica*, 84, 647-661.

Bergman, Y. Z., 1986, "On Debt Renegotiation: A Strategic Analysis," working paper, Department of Economics, Brown University.

Brander, J., and T. Lewis, 1986, "Oligopoly and Financial Structure: The Limited Liability Effect," *American Economic Review*, 76, 956-970.

Brennan, M. J., 1986, "Costless Financing Policies Under Asymmetric Information," working paper, University of California at Los Angeles.

Brown, D. T., 1986, "Claimholder Incentive Conflicts in Reorganization: A Game Theoretic Analysis of the Role of Bankruptcy Law," working paper, University of Florida, Gainesville.

Bulow, J., and J. Shoven, 1978, "The Bankruptcy Decision," *Bell Journal of Economics*, 9, 437-456.

Cho, I., and D. M. Kreps, 1987, "Signalling Games and Stable Equilibrium," *Quarterly Journal of Economics*, 102, 179-221.

Diamond, D. W., 1984, "Financial Intermediation and Delegated Monitoring," *Review of Economic Studies*, 51, 393-414.

Fama, E. F., and M. H. Miller, 1972, *The Theory of Finance*, Dryden Press, Hinsdale, Ill.

Gale, D., and M. Hellwig, 1985, "Incentive Compatible Debt Contracts: The One-Period Problem," *Review of Economic Studies*, 52, 647-665.

Gould, J., 1973, "The Economics of Legal Conflicts," *Journal of Legal Studies*, 14, 279-300.

Green, J. R., and J. B. Shoven, 1983, "The Effects of Financing Opportunities and Bankruptcy on Entrepreneurial Risk Bearing," in J. Ronen (ed.), *Entrepreneurship*, D.C. Heath and Company, Toronto.

Grossman, S., and O. Hart, 1980, "Takeover Bids, the Free-Rider Problem, and the Theory of the Corporation," *Bell Journal of Economics*, 11, 42-64.

Haugen, R. A., and L. W. Senbet, 1978, "The Insignificance of Bankruptcy Costs to the Theory of Optimal Capital Structure," *Journal of Finance*, 33, 383-393.

Haugen, R. A., and L. W. Senbet, 1988, "Bankruptcy and Agency Costs: Their Significance to the Theory of Optimal Capital Structure," *Journal of Financial and Quantitative Analysis*, 23, 27-38.

Jackson, T. H., 1986, *The Logic and Limits of Bankruptcy Law*, Harvard University Press, Cambridge, Mass.

Kim, E. H., 1978, "A Mean Variance Theory of Optimal Capital Structure and Corporate Debt Capacity," *Journal of Finance*, 33, 45-63.

Resolution of Financial Distress

Kraus, A., and R. Litzenberger, 1973, "A State-Preference Model of Optimal Financial Leverage," *Journal of Finance*, 28, 911–922.

Kreps, D. M., and R. Wilson, 1982, "Sequential Equilibria," *Econometrica*, 50, 863–894.

Maksimovic, V., 1984, "Capital Structure in a Stochastic Oligopoly," working paper, University of British Columbia.

McLennan, A., 1985, "Justifiable Beliefs in Sequential Equilibrium," *Econometrica*, 53, 889–904.

Myers, S. C., 1977, "Determinants of Corporate Borrowing," *Journal of Financial Economics*, 5, 147–175.

Newton, G. W., 1981, *Bankruptcy and Insolvency Accounting: Practice and Procedure* (2d ed.), Wiley, New York.

P'ng, I. P. L., 1983, "Strategic Behavior in Suit Settlement and Trial," *Bell Journal of Economics*, 14, 539–550.

P'ng, I. P. L., 1987, "Liability, Litigation, and Incentives to Take Care," *Journal of Public Economics*, 34, 61–85.

Reinganum, J. F., and L. L. Wilde, 1986, "Settlement, Litigation, and the Allocation of Litigation Costs," *Rand Journal of Economics*, 17, 557–566.

Salant, S. W., 1984, "Litigation of Settlement Demands Questioned by Bayesian Defendants," Social Science Working Paper 516, Division of Humanities and Social Sciences, California Institute of Technology.

Scott, J. H., Jr., 1976, "A Theory of Optimal Capital Structure," *Bell Journal of Economics*, 7, 33–54.

Shavell, S., 1982, "Suit, Settlement and Trial: A Theoretical Analysis under Alternative Methods for the Allocation of Legal Costs," *Journal of Legal Studies*, 11, 55–81

Stiglitz, J. E., 1974, "On the Irrelevance of Corporate Financial Policy," *American Economic Review*, 64, 851–866.

Titman, S., 1984, "The Effect of Capital Structure on a Firm's Liquidation Decision," *Journal of Financial Economics*, 13, 137–151.

Townsend, R., 1979, "Optimal Contracts and Competitive Markets with Costly State Verification," *Journal of Economic Theory*, 21, 1–29.

Van Horne, J. C., 1976, "Optimal Initiation of Bankruptcy Proceedings by Debt Holders," *Journal of Finance*, 31, 897–910.

Warner, J. B., 1977, "Bankruptcy Costs: Some Evidence," *Journal of Finance*, 32, 337–347.

Webb, D. C., 1987, "The Importance of Incomplete Information in Explaining the Existence of Costly Bankruptcy," *Economica*, 54, 279–288.

A Theory of Workouts and the Effects of Reorganization Law*

ROBERT GERTNER and DAVID SCHARFSTEIN

ABSTRACT

We present a model of a financially distressed firm with outstanding bank debt and public debt. Coordination problems among public debtholders introduce investment inefficiencies in the workout process. In most cases, these inefficiencies are not mitigated by the ability of firms to buy back their public debt with cash and other securities—the only feasible way that firms can restructure their public debt. We show that Chapter 11 reorganization law increases investment, and we characterize the types of corporate financial structures for which this increased investment enhances efficiency.

DURING THE LATE 1980S there was a dramatic increase in the leverage of U.S. corporations, raising concerns about the corporate sector's financial stability.[1] Indeed, by June 1990, 156 (24%) of the 662 companies that issued high-yield bonds between 1977 and 1988 had either defaulted, gone bankrupt, or restructured their public debt. The face value of these distressed bonds amounts to nearly 21 billion dollars.[2]

The central question raised by these distressed firms is easy to put but hard to answer: What is the effect of financial distress on a firm's operating performance? There are two competing views. The first, an application of the

---

*This is a greatly revised version of "The Effects of Reorganization Law on Investment Efficiency." Gertner is with the Graduate School of Business and the Law School, University of Chicago; Scharfstein is with the Sloan School of Management, Massachusetts Institute of Technology, and with the National Bureau of Economic Research. We thank Ian Ayres, Doug Baird, Walter Blum, Keith Cohon, Doug Diamond, Ken Froot, Bob Gibbons, Steve Kaplan, Ron Masulis, Kevin Murphy, Randy Picker, Mark Roe, Jeremy Stein, René Stulz, Robert Sydow, Rob Vishny, an anonymous referee, and seminar participants at the NBER, University of Chicago, the Federal Reserve Bank of Richmond, Ohio State, University of Michigan, Boston University, and Princeton for helpful comments. We especially thank Paul Asquith for comments and providing the data for some of the summary statistics. Gertner is grateful to the John M. Olin Foundation Fellowship in Law and Economics at The University of Chicago Law School, the NSF, Grant SES-8911334, and the IBM Faculty Research Fund at the Graduate School of Business, University of Chicago for financial support. Scharfstein is grateful for fellowships from the Olin Foundation and Batterymarch Financial Management and for financial support from the International Financial Services Research Center at MIT.

[1] Bernanke and Campbell (1988) and Bernanke, Campbell, and Whited (1990) document the increases in corporate leverage in the 1980s. The most significant increase occurs in the leverage of the most highly indebted companies.

[2] These numbers were calculated from data made available to us by Paul Asquith. For a more complete analysis of default rates on high-yield bonds, see Asquith, Mullins, and Wolff (1989).

Coase Theorem, holds that there are no real effects of financial distress.[3] Critical to this view is the distinction between financial and economic distress. Admittedly, most firms in financial trouble also suffer from poor operating performance. But, no financial maneuvering can save these economically distressed firms. If, however, a firm's capital structure prevents it from pursuing its value-maximizing operating strategy, creditors will restructure their claims to maximize firm value. We should expect financially distressed firms to do poorly on average, but no worse than if they had no leverage.

The second view—implicit in the leading theory of capital structure—is that financial distress hampers operating performance. In this view, the Coase Theorem fails; financial renegotiation is inefficient and operating distortions are introduced.

Distinguishing between these two views is important for understanding a variety of issues: capital structure decisions; the costs of tax policies which affect the level of corporate debt; the impact of wide-scale financial distress during a recession; and the role and effects of specific provisions of bankruptcy law.

Unfortunately, it is difficult to distinguish empirically between financial and economic distress. Is a financially distressed firm liquidated because renegotiation is inefficient or because the firm is not economically viable? Is a firm's poor operating performance the result of underlying business problems or an inappropriate capital structure? Unfortunately, the empirical attempts to distinguish between financial and economic distress are limited to specific environments in which it is relatively easy to make such a distinction.[4]

The theoretical distinction between financial and economic distress emerges in the important work of Bulow and Shoven (1978) and the follow-up work of White (1980, 1983).[5] These models demonstrate how conflicts among creditors can lead to inefficiencies when a firm is in financial distress. The impediment to efficient renegotiation in these models is the assumption that

---

[3] This view has been argued by Haugen and Senbet (1978), Roe (1983), Baird (1986), and Jensen (1986).

[4] Cutler and Summers (1988) study the stock price reactions to the events following Pennzoil's successful 10 billion dollar lawsuit against Texaco. Events which should have zero-sum effects resulted in a larger market value loss to Texaco than gain to Pennzoil. They interpret this finding as evidence that Texaco's financial distress was costly; Texaco was in financial but not economic distress. Hoshi, Kashyap, and Scharfstein (1990) show, in a sample of distressed Japanese firms, that those with financial structures that are easier to renegotiate a priori—those which borrow a lot from a single bank—invest more and have higher sales than firms with more complex financial structures.

[5] More recent contributions include Aivazian and Callen (1983), Titman (1984), Brown (1989), Giammarino (1989), Bergman and Callen (1990), and Baird and Picker (1991). With the exception of Titman, which assumes it is impossible to negotiate with customers who rely on the firm for product maintenance and Giammarino which analyzes a signaling model of debt restructuring, these papers assume efficient renegotiation and therefore focus on how value is divided.

the firm cannot renegotiate with public debtholders, although they can renegotiate efficiently with a bank. There are two types of inefficiencies that can result. On the one hand, because public debtholders claim part of the cash flows from new investment, distressed firms can have difficulty issuing equity or debt for new investment. Thus, they may pass up positive net present value investments.[6] On the other hand, a distressed company may actually overinvest because shareholders receive much of the upside benefits of risky investment but bear little of the downside costs. As a result, they may take negative net present value projects which increase the riskiness of the firm's cash flow.[7]

There are two primary contributions of this paper. The first is to show that these investment inefficiencies are still a problem even when firms can renegotiate with public debtholders. We analyze the implicit renegotiation that takes place when firms offer a package of new securities and cash in exchange for the original public debt. Public debt restructurings almost always take this form because the Trust Indenture Act of 1939 requires unanimous debtholder consent before a firm can alter the principal, interest, or maturity of its public debt. Exchange offers effectively alter these features but, since nontendering public debtholders maintain their original claim for payments from the firm, the Trust Indenture Act is not violated.

Despite the frequency with which exchange offers have been made—73 of 156 distressed junk bond issuers have successfully completed exchanges between 1977 and 1990—there is at least one substantial obstacle to successfully completing an exchange.[8] Those debtholders who do not tender can see the value of their bonds rise if the exchange offer is successful since tendering creditors forgive some of the debt and reduce the default risk of the original debt. Although public debtholders as a group would be better off if the exchange offer goes through, those with small stakes have an incentive to hold out. Thus, it can be very difficult to complete an exchange.

This free-rider problem can be, and often is, mitigated by offering a more senior security in exchange for the public debt, one with shorter maturity, or, when it is available, cash. Moreover, in these types of exchanges public debtholders may be willing to tender at below-market prices because they fear that holding out will make them effectively junior to the new securities. But, the important point is that even though these types of offers enable firms to restructure their public debt profitably, they do not, in general, result in efficient investment. The problem is that in deciding whether to tender, public debtholders take the firm's investment policy as given. Thus, individual debtholders—each with small stakes—fail to take into account their effect on the firm's investment decision, despite the fact that their decisions, taken as a whole, affect investment behavior.

---

[6] This is the effect first analyzed by Myers (1977).
[7] This risk-taking effect is analyzed in detail by Jensen and Meckling (1976).
[8] Of the 73 firms that successfully completed exchange offers 23 have subsequently filed for bankruptcy. Also, many firms have attempted exchange offers which failed.

The second principal contribution is to analyze the effects of reorganization law on investment. We show that key features of the law—the automatic stay, the voting rules for plan approval, and the power of equity holders to retain value for themselves—all act to increase investment both in and out of Chapter 11. Whether this increases efficiency depends on whether the firm would otherwise have underinvested or overinvested as a result of financial distress. We characterize the aspects of the firm's debt structure—the priority of bank debt relative to public debt, the maturity structure, and the existence of covenants restricting senior debt issues—that lead to underinvestment or overinvestment. We are then able to identify the situations in which Chapter 11 increases or decreases investment efficiency.

Our paper is organized as follows. Section I presents our benchmark model of workouts when public debt restructurings are not possible and bankrupt firms are liquidated, not reorganized. We build on the Bulow and Shoven model to analyze the effects of priority and maturity on investment after the onset of financial distress. Section II introduces the possibility of public debt restructurings through exchange offers and compares the results of this model to those of Section I's benchmark model. We show that if there is no restriction on senior debt issues, exchange offers do not affect the costs of financial distress but do place more of the burden of distress on public debtholders. If there are covenants restricting senior debt issues, however, exchange offers can be used to eliminate them and thereby increase investment. In this case, exchange offers may reduce the debt burden so much that they lead to overinvestment and actually exacerbate inefficiencies. We show that it is sometimes efficient to eliminate seniority covenants, but investment efficiency is greater if a firm can only remove them with a vote that is separate from an exchange offer. Section III introduces the possibility of reorganization rather than liquidation upon default. We review some of the key features of Chapter 11 reorganization law and analyze their effects on investment. We conclude in Section IV.

I. A Simple Model of Workouts and Investment

In this section, we consider a simple model of a financially distressed firm with both privately-placed debt and publicly-traded debt. We think of the private debt as bank debt (although it could be held by any large creditor) and the public debt as debentures.[9] We model the idea that it is easier to renegotiate with a bank (or a small syndicate of banks) than with numerous public debtholders by assuming at first that the firm cannot renegotiate with public debtholders. We relax this assumption in Section II where we present a model of exchange offers.

An important issue is how the debt's maturity structure affects the ability of firms to work out of distress. We assume that all of the bank debt, with face value B, is short-term, maturing at date 1. By contrast, fraction q of the

---

[9] We model public debt as unsecured, so we use the term debentures to distinguish them from bonds, which in the legal literature exclusively refers to secured debt.

face value of the public debt D, is due at date 1, and fraction $1 - q$ is due at a later date 2. This timing reflects the fact that bank debt generally has a shorter maturity than public debt.

The firm has two assets: cash and/or liquid assets of Y; and an investment project which requires an investment of I at date 1 and returns a stochastic cash flow of X at date 2 distributed over the support $[0, \infty)$. We denote the cumulative distribution of X as $F(X)$, the density as $f(X)$, and the mean as $\bar{X}$. For simplicity, we assume the firm has no fixed assets such as plant and equipment. All parties are risk neutral, and the riskless interest rate is zero.

Finally, we assume that the firm is in financial distress at date 1; its assets in place are worth less than the face value of its debt obligations: $Y < B + D$. Thus, if the firm is liquidated, and if absolute priority rules are followed, shareholders receive nothing, and public debtholders and the bank share Y between them. Assuming equal priority of bank and public debt in liquidation, the bank gets $[B/(B + D)]Y$, which we denote L_B and the public debtholders get $[D/(B + D)]Y$, which we denote L_D.[10] If the firm is liquidated, the public debt maturing at date 2 is accelerated to date 1, consistent with the Bankruptcy Code. In this section, we assume that bankruptcy is equivalent to liquidation; reorganization in Chapter 11 is ruled out. In Section III, we analyze how reorganization law affects investment incentives in this model.

The central question is whether the financially distressed firm invests in the project at date 1. If $Y > I + B + qD$, the firm has enough cash to invest in the project and pay off both the bank debt and the public debt maturing at date 1. In this case, the firm invests regardless of whether the project has positive or negative net present value: if the firm does not invest, equity gets nothing; if the firm does invest, there is some chance that equity's payoff would be positive. We assume instead that $Y < I + B + qD$ so that the firm needs an additional $I + B + qD - Y$ to meet its date-1 obligations and invest in the project.

The firm has several options in meeting its cash shortfall. It can try to raise new funds by issuing debt or equity, or it can try to restructure its existing bank debt or public debt. We focus here on debt restructurings—first on bank debt restructurings and, in Section II, on public debt restructurings. We show later that the firm prefers to restructure than to issue new debt or equity.

A. Bank Debt Restructurings

We consider bank debt restructurings first because they are substantially easier to organize than public debt restructurings.[11] Indeed, the Trust Indenture Act of 1939 *prohibits* public debtholders from changing the principal,

---

[10] In bankruptcy, creditors do not have a claim for unmatured interest. So, for simplicity, we assume that the contractual interest rate on the public debt is zero.

[11] Gilson, John, and Lang (1990) show empirically that the existence of public debt is the most significant determinant of whether a financially distressed firm restructures successfully out of court or files for Chapter 11 reorganization.

interest, or maturity of public debt without public debtholders' unanimous consent. Even without the Trust Indenture Act, free rider problems can impede successful renegotiation. For example, if some public debtholders forgive part of their debt, the value of the remaining debt rises. If each public debtholder is small, and thus has no effect on the outcome of the negotiations, then each will refuse to restructure his portion of the debt. We discuss these issues in detail in Section II.

In a bank debt restructuring the firm effectively rolls over its initial loan of B and borrows an additional $I + qD - Y$ for the investment and to pay off the public debt due at date 1. Our analysis is simplified if we assume that the interest on this loan has lower priority than all outstanding debt while the principal has equal priority. This assumption is not realistic since bankruptcy law does not distinguish between principal and matured interest. But, any other assumption complicates the analysis because the fraction of the firm that the public debtholders get depends on the interest rate on the new loan. On the other hand, if we assume the new interest has lower priority, the combined return to the bank and the firm is independent of the interest rate. This permits us to complete the analysis without determining the interest rate on the bank debt. The issue this raises for the ability to renegotiate with the bank is interesting, but it is an unnecessary complication for the basic analysis.

If the firm invests, and $X < I + B + D - Y$, the bank receives

$$\frac{I + B + qD - Y}{I + B + D - Y} X.$$

If $X > I + B + D - Y$, the shareholders and the bank together get to split $X - (1 - q)D$. The bank agrees to finance the firm provided:

$$\int_0^Z \frac{I + B + qD - Y}{I + B + D - Y} Xf(X) \, dX$$
$$+ \int_Z^\infty [X - (1 - q)D] f(X) \, dX - (I + qD - Y) \geq L_B, \quad (1)$$

where $Z \equiv I + B + D - Y$.

The right-hand side of inequality (1) is what the bank receives in liquidation. There are two important assumptions implicit in this formulation. First, the firm liquidates and cannot invest in bankruptcy. In Section III, we introduce the possibility of investment in Chapter 11 bankruptcy proceedings. Second, we assume that if the bank does not lend money, the firm goes bankrupt; the firm cannot raise the necessary cash from an outside source. We will see below that, although it may be possible to raise outside funds, the bank has a greater incentive to provide funds than any outsider. Since we wish to derive conditions under which investment occurs, not how the gains from the investment are split, our analysis is unaffected by this assumption.

Inequality (1) is equivalent to:

$$\bar{X} - I \geq qD + \int_0^Z \frac{(1-q)D}{Z} Xf(X)\,dX$$
$$+ \int_Z^\infty (1-q)Df(X)\,dX + L_B - Y. \quad (2)$$

The first three terms on the right-hand side sum to the market value of the public debt conditional on bank lending and investment. Thus, we write (2) as:

$$\bar{X} - I \geq V_D - L_D, \quad (3)$$

where V_D is the market value of the public debt in this case.

Inequality (3) captures a simple but important idea. V_D is the value of the public debt conditional on investment while L_D is its value if no investment occurs. So the difference of the two measures the transfer from the bank and equity holders to public debtholders if the firm invests. If the net present value of the project, $\bar{X} - I$, is greater than this transfer, then the firm restructures its bank debt and invests.

Interestingly, this transfer can be positive or negative. If it is positive, the firm will tend to forego positive NPV projects, those with NPV between zero and $V_D - L_D$; the debt obligations act as a tax on the project, discouraging investment. If it is negative, the firm may adopt negative NPV projects, those with NPV between $V_D - L_D$ and zero; creditors effectively subsidize the project, encouraging investment. So, inefficiencies can involve either under-investment or overinvestment.

This wedge is introduced because the value of the public debt conditional on investment can be greater or less than its liquidation value. If, for example, Y is close to zero, public debt is worth almost nothing in a liquidation, so public debtholders benefit from investment. In this case, the existence of public debt discourages investment. By contrast, if Y is close to $B + D$, public debtholders would get paid off nearly in full if the firm is liquidated. But, if it is not liquidated, public debtholders own a risky claim, the value of which could well be below D. Here, public debt promotes investment, though it may be inefficient.

The discussion suggests that there are two effects at work. On the one hand, the debt obligations tend to make investment look unattractive because existing creditors can siphon off cash flow from the project. This is Myers' (1977) well-known argument; the existence of a "debt overhang" discourages investment. On the other hand, debt obligations can lead the firm to take excessive risks: equity receives nothing if the firm is liquidated but has some value if the firm invests, even if it is in a negative NPV investment, a point made clear by Jensen and Meckling (1976).

The maturity structure of the debt has important effects on the efficiency of investment. As the maturity of the public debt shortens (q increases), its value increases because the date-1 portion is safe and the date-2 portion is risky: $dV_D/dq > 0$. This increases the transfer to public debtholders and reduces the firm's incentive to invest. In the limit as all the public debt becomes due at date 1, the transfer approaches $D - L_D > 0$. In this case, the firm may pass up positive NPV investments but will never choose negative NPV investments. The efficiency effect of shortening the public debt's maturity is ambiguous. The increase in q may force the firm to pass up positive NPV projects, but it also may deter investment in negative NPV projects.

An increase in bank debt, holding fixed the total amount of indebtedness, $B + D$, has an unambiguously positive effect on efficiency. The increase in B decreases the right-hand side of expression (3) if it is positive and increases it if it is negative. So, the shift toward bank debt away from public debt can either induce the firm to take positive NPV projects it would not have taken or turn down negative NPV projects it would have taken. Clearly, if all debt were held by the bank, investment would always be efficient; bank renegotiation is assumed to be costless so the conditions of the Coase Theorem are satisfied.

B. New Capital Infusions

Instead of restructuring its bank debt, the firm could try to raise new money from another bank or by issuing equity. Neither of these alternatives is as attractive as a restructuring. Like a restructuring, the new bank lends $I + B + qD - Y$ and receives the same date-2 payoffs. But, unlike a restructuring, some of the new money goes to pay off the existing bank debt of B at face value. One can show that the firm will be able to raise new debt financing provided

$$\overline{X} - I \geq V_D - L_D + B - L_B, \qquad (4)$$

or, in words, if the net present value of the investment exceeds the sum of the transfer to the public debtholders, $V_D - L_D$, and the transfer to the bank, $B - L_B$. The condition differs from a bank debt restructuring because in a restructuring the bank takes into account the fact that its debt is worth only $L_B < B$ in a liquidation. With a new loan the bank receives a transfer of $B - L_B > 0$. This subsidy means that the set of investment projects that can be financed without outside debt is a strict subset of those which can be financed with a bank debt restructuring.

Investment is even less attractive if the firm issues equity rather than debt. The bank continues to receive a subsidy of $B - L_B$, but the transfer to the public debtholders rises. The public debt conditional on investment is worth more because the date-2 portion of the debt is paid off before equity is paid anything. By contrast, when the firm issues debt, the public debtholders and the new debtholders are on equal footing at date 2. So, the condition for investment takes the same form as inequality (4) except that V_D is greater when the firm issues equity.

The analysis implies that the firm never issues equity since an equity issue transfers value to public debtholders not transferred by a debt issue. The prediction is less clear about the choice between debt issues and a bank loan restructuring. Clearly, when inequality (3) is satisfied but inequality (4) is not, the firm will restructure its bank debt. But, if both inequalities are satisfied the model has no prediction. The bank knows that if there is no restructuring, the firm will issue new debt and the bank will receive B. So, in a debt restructuring, the bank will settle for nothing less than B. As a result, equity holders are indifferent between a debt issue and a bank debt restructuring because they must transfer B to the bank in both situations.

C. Effects of Priority

So far, we have assumed that all debt has equal priority in bankruptcy. However, firms can explicitly contract for certain debts to be paid before others in bankruptcy. There are two ways in which priority can affect the ability of distressed firms to raise capital in our model. First, the seniority of the existing bank debt affects what the bank would get in bankruptcy liquidation if it did not lend new money, thereby determining the value of the bank's next best alternative. The more junior the existing bank debt, the worse off the bank is in liquidation, so the more willing it is to lend. Second, the seniority of the new bank debt affects what the bank can get if it lends new money. In general, the more senior the new bank debt, the better off the bank is at any chosen interest rate. Thus, if they could, the firm and the bank would like to issue debt that is senior to the existing public debt. Of course, there are often constraints on their ability to do so; the public debt may contain covenants restricting the issuance of any debt senior to the public debt. These covenants may prohibit such issuance altogether, may limit the amount, or may allow it if certain cash flow and net worth conditions are satisfied.

To see this more formally, suppose there is no covenant prohibiting a senior debt issue. Then the interest rate on the new bank debt can be set so high that the firm always defaults at date 2 and the senior debt gets all of the date-2 cash flow X. This means that the value of the public debt conditional on new senior lending is just qD and public debtholders only receive their date-1 payment. The value of the public debt if the firm is liquidated is L_D, assuming, as before, that the existing bank debt and public debt have equal priority. Based on the previous section we know that the project's net present value must exceed the net subsidy to public debtholders from investment. So the bank will be willing to lend provided

$$\bar{X} - I \geq qD - L_D. \tag{5}$$

The right-hand side of (5) is strictly less than the right-hand side of expression (3) since $qD < V_D$; the firm is more prone to invest when there is no covenant restricting senior debt issuance.[12] It can have positive or negative efficiency effects by reducing the underinvestment problem or exacerbating the overinvestment problem.

This analysis can tell us something about the interaction between maturity structure and seniority covenants. If the public debt has a relatively short maturity (q near 1), the firm is likely to underinvest. In this case, a seniority covenant tends to worsen the problem, making it more difficult for the firm to raise capital. If the firm leaves out the covenant, we would expect to see the bank lend new money that is senior to the old debentures. The ability to issue such debt can counteract the inefficiency created by the short maturity of the public debt. In contrast, if the debt has a relatively long maturity, the firm is more prone to overinvest. In this case, a seniority covenant makes it more difficult to raise capital and could eliminate the tendency toward overinvestment. Thus, if capital structure is chosen partly to minimize the costs of financial distress, we would expect long-term public debt to contain seniority covenants in the indentures and short-term public debt to omit such covenants.

This framework can also tell us something about the interaction between public debt maturity and the priority of the existing debt. Suppose that there is no seniority covenant. Then if the original public debt is pari passu (equal priority) with the bank debt, the investment condition is given by expression (5). But, if the initial bank debt is senior to the public debt, the condition becomes

$$\overline{X} - I \geq qD - \max(Y - B, 0) \tag{6}$$

because the value of the junior public debt in liquidation is now $\max(Y - B, 0)$. Since this is less than $L_D \equiv [D/(B + D)]Y$, the value of the public debt if it is pari passu with the old bank debt, the firm is now less prone to invest; the bank does better in liquidation, so financing new investment is less attractive.

The shorter the maturity of the public debt, the more likely the firm is to underinvest. Thus, the model suggests that when the public debt is relatively short term, existing senior bank debt is likely to worsen the underinvestment problem. But, when the public debt is long term, the seniority of bank debt can be a useful way of curbing the overinvestment problem. If the costs of financial distress drive capital structure choices, our model predicts that the bank debt will be senior if the public debt is long term and junior if it is short term.

---

[12] Stulz and Johnson (1985) develop this point in a model where the ability to use secured debt for new borrowing mitigates the Myers (1977) underinvestment problem. Berkovitch and Kim (1990) analyze how priority structure affects investment efficiency under both symmetric and asymmetric information.

Although the model predicts that the bank debt will be junior if the public debt is short term, in a more realistic formulation, it is difficult to make short-term bank debt effectively junior. To see this, suppose that if the firm does not invest and is not liquidated at date 1, it nevertheless has positive, stochastic cash flows at date 2. Thus, unlike the model above, if the firm pays off its debts at date 1, the value of equity is positive even if the firm does not invest. The firm has three alternatives: invest, continue without investing, or be liquidated.

Now suppose that $Y \geq qD + B$ so that it is feasible for the firm to meet its date-1 debt obligations and continue in operation without investing. The value of the bank debt is B, which is what it is worth in liquidation if the bank debt is senior. The bank refuses to provide new funds for investment, but demands payment of B in period 1. This is more than $\max(Y - D, 0)$, the bank's payoff if the firm is liquidated and the bank is junior to the public debt. Thus, even though the bank debt is contractually junior to the public debt, the bank acts as if it is senior. This makes the bank reluctant to lend new money, a more efficient outcome. So, in this model, if q is small enough so that $Y > qD + B$, the bank acts as a senior lender. But, if q is very close to one, it is possible to induce the bank to act as if it was junior to the public debt.

II. Distressed Exchange Offers for Public Debt

So far, we have assumed that it is impossible to renegotiate with public debtholders. This assumption is not too far off the mark; the Trust Indenture Act's prohibitions on changes in the timing or amount of public debt payments forces public debt restructurings to take the form of exchange offers.[13] Firms offer cash and/or a package of debt and equity securities, with the offer typically contingent on the acceptance of a specified fraction of the debt.[14]

In this section, we analyze the extent to which this limited form of renegotiation affects the inefficiencies discussed in the previous section. The key assumption of the model is that each debtholder's stake is small enough that he ignores the effect of his tender decision on both the firm's investment decision and the value of the firm's securities. This assumption is unrealistically strong for firms with a large portion of their debt held by just a few institutional investors, an admittedly common situation. We make this assumption to highlight the problems that arise when creditors cannot fully

---

[13] There are some similarities between corporate debt exchange offers and buybacks of developing country debt. See Froot (1989) and Bulow and Rogoff (1989) for analyses of developing country debt exchanges.

[14] For example, in early 1990, AP Industries offered $50 in cash, one share of common stock, and $340.91 principal amount of new zero-coupon senior subordinated notes due in 1997 in exchange for each $1000 principal amount of its 12 $^3/_8$% subordinated debentures due in 2001. The offer was conditioned on 95% of the outstanding principal amount being tendered.

coordinate their actions. We believe that similar effects would be present in a model in which debtholders have substantial stakes.[15]

We proceed in two stages. First, we analyze the profitability of exchanges assuming that the firm has ample cash to finance the investment even without a debt restructuring. We will show that an exchange is profitable only if the debt is exchanged for cash or for debt that has higher priority than the original debt. Although this analysis has no efficiency implications—the firm invests even without an exchange—it is helpful in answering the second more interesting question: when can an exchange reduce cash obligations and enable the firm to invest? We will show that the bank is generally better off if the firm can exchange its debentures, that investment incentives are unaffected by the ability to exchange debt in most circumstances, and that the ability to exchange is not equivalent to efficient renegotiation of the public debt.

A. Exchanges Assuming No Cash Shortage

In this subsection we assume that, while the firm is in financial distress, it does not need an exchange or a bank concession in order to invest and meet its date-1 debt obligations: $Y > I + B + qD$. We first consider an exchange for debt due at date 2 with a face value of p for each dollar in face value of the existing debt. Let X_b be the breakeven value of X, so the firm defaults at date 2 for all $X < X_b$. Shareholders receive nothing if $X < X_b$ and receive $X - X_b$ otherwise. Thus, an exchange is profitable if and only if it lowers X_b.

Let β denote the fraction of public debt the firm exchanges. Without an exchange, $X_b = I + D + B - Y$. By contrast, if the firm exchanges, it owes the nontendering debtholders $(1 - \beta)D$ and the tendering debtholders βpD, so $X_b = I + (1 - \beta)D + \beta pD + B - Y$. Here, X_b is decreasing in β if and only if $p < 1$, i.e., the firm can exchange a dollar of old debt for less than a dollar of new debt. So if $p < 1$ an exchange is profitable and if $p > 1$ an exchange is unprofitable.

Proposition 1: *It is unprofitable to offer an exchange for new debt with equal priority to the old public debt.*

Proof: See Appendix.

The exchange is unprofitable because of a classic holdout problem.[16] If other debtholders tender, the value of the existing debt rises, creating an incentive to hold out. To see this, consider the decision facing the holder of $1 of debt who is offered $1 of the new debenture ($p = 1$) due at date 2.[17] Will the holdout have an incentive to tender, assuming that all the other

---
[15] Gertner (1990) analyzes a bargaining model in which one party needs to reach agreement with two others under asymmetric information. Holdout problems similar to those analyzed here are also present. In addition, he shows that it may not be in the private interest of bargaining parties to form coalitions, even though the coalitions improve overall bargaining efficiency.
[16] Roe (1987) contains the first discussion of this holdout problem.
[17] We assume that $1 is a negligible portion of the overall public debt.

debtholders tender? If so, then it is an equilibrium for all debtholders to exchange.

The answer depends on the payoffs of the two debentures when the firm is in default at date 2. If the firm does not default, the debtholder is just as happy with the new debentures as with the old debentures. But if the firm does default at date 2, the payoffs are quite different. Those who tender receive their pro rata share of the firm at date 2, $(X + Y - I - B)/D$, but the holdout receives q at date 1 and receives a pro rata share of the firm at date 2, $(1 - q)(X + Y - I - B)/D$. Since $(X + Y - I - B)/D < 1$, the debtholder is better off holding out.

The holdout is better off because the earlier payment on the old debenture is effectively senior to the new debenture. Tendering debtholders share ratably in a risky date-2 claim. But, by holding out, the debtholder receives a safe date-1 payment while still sharing pro rata in the date-2 portion of payoffs.

This logic rests crucially on the assumption that the debtholders do not act collectively. Suppose they could. Then the question becomes: are we all better off if we all tender than if we all hold out? This is quite different from the individual question: am I better off if I tender than if I hold out assuming everyone else tenders? In the collective case, if everyone tenders then the payoff is again $(X + Y - I - B)/D$ when the firm defaults. But, if no one tenders then the payoff is q at date 1 and $(X + Y - I - B - qD)/D$ at date 2. This is equal to the payoff from tendering, so debtholders as a group are indifferent between the two options when $p = 1$.

The holdout problem is even more pronounced if the firm offers to exchange junior debt or equity for the old debentures. There are now two reasons why debtholders want to hold out. As before, holdouts are senior in that some of their claim is paid at date 1 before the uncertainty is realized and tendering debtholders are paid. In addition, holdouts also have seniority at date 2 since the new security is junior debt or equity. If all debtholders tender, a holdout's claim would be riskless since the holdout gets q at date 1, and the $1 - q$ that is owed at date 2 is senior to the claims of all tendering debtholders, making it riskless as well. Thus, a corollary of Proposition 1 is that exchange offers for junior debt or equity are also unprofitable.

Quite the opposite result holds if the firm can offer a more senior debenture in exchange for the old debt. These types of exchanges are quite common. In a sample of 169 exchange offers by 67 companies, we discovered at least 48 instances in which a firm offered a debenture that is senior to the old debentures.[18]

---

[18] These 67 companies are a subsample of the 73 original issue high-yield debt companies that completed exchange offers between 1977 and June 1990. We found information on the exchange offers from two sources: *First Boston High Yield Handbook*, 1988 and 1989, and the S&P Called Bond Record, 1977–1990. We could not find detailed information on the exchange offers of the remaining 6 companies. This may be an underestimate of the frequency of exchanges for senior securities because classification is based on a security's title. In some case cases, the new security may have the same title but be senior.

Proposition 2: *It is profitable to offer an exchange for new debt which is senior to the old public debt.*

Proof: See Appendix.

There are two competing effects at work. Again, the difference in the payoffs from tendering and holding out depends on the payoffs of the old and new debentures when the firm is in default at date 2. As before, consider the decision facing the holder of $1 of debt, assuming that all others tender when $p = 1$. On the one hand, the holdout's date-2 claim is worthless when the firm defaults. Since the new debt is senior, each new debenture holder is paid $(X + Y - I - B)/D$ and there are insufficient funds to pay the old junior debenture holder. On the other hand, the portion q of the holdout's claim is paid at date 1, making it effectively senior to the new debentures. On the whole, given our assumptions that $X > 0$ and $Y > I + B + qD$, the increased seniority at date 2 is worth more than the earlier maturity of the q portion of the claim. Instead of a holdout problem there is a *hold-in* problem; debt holders would tender for $p < 1$ despite the fact that they are made worse off as a group.

The hold-in problem is more severe when the public debt is relatively long term. Very short maturity debt is paid off almost in full at date 1. So only a small portion of the debt can be leapfrogged in the capital structure. The short maturity of the debt effectively gives it a degree of seniority that cannot be erased by a senior debt issue. Indeed, one can show that as the debt becomes shorter-term, p increases and exchanges become less attractive to the firm.[19]

We have shown that the firm prefers exchanges for senior debt to exchanges for pari passu or junior debt. But in many cases there are seniority covenants in the public debt prohibiting senior debt issues. Yet firms with such covenants do issue more senior debt in exchanges.[20] How is this possible? The indenture for the debt issue typically specifies that covenants can be changed or eliminated by either a simple or super majority vote of the

---

[19] The property of longer maturity debt that makes the hold-in problem relevant is that a greater fraction of promised payments come after the resolution of uncertain cash flows. Extending maturity from date 1 to date 1.5 would have no effect if there were no chance of insolvency before date 2.

[20] For example, in March 1987, Michigan General offered $500 principal amount of 6% Increasing Rate Senior Subordinated Notes due in 1992, $200 principal amount of Zero Coupon Delayed Convertible Senior Subordinated Notes due in 1997, and 12 shares of $2 Delayed Convertible Preferred Stock in exchange for each $1000 principal amount of 10 $3/4$% Senior Subordinated Debentures due in 1998. Both new Senior Subordinated Notes were made senior to the old debentures even though there was a covenant in its indenture stating, "the Company will not incur, create, issue, assume or guarantee any full recourse indebtedness which is both senior in right of payment to the Debentures and subordinate or junior in right of payment to any other Senior Indebtedness." This covenant protects the public debtholders from being leapfrogged by new public debt but does not, by itself, restrict issuing new senior bank debt. The bank loan agreement or other covenants in the public debt indenture may restrict the amount of new senior bank debt.

face value of the debt.[21] The exchange is then made contingent on a so-called *exit consent* in which the required fraction of the debt votes to strip the old debenture of the seniority and perhaps other covenants. The act of tendering consists of two actions: first, a vote to strip the debt of its covenant protection, and second, an acceptance of the exchange for the now legally-issued senior debt.[22] In Section II.B below, we discuss the efficiency consequences of tying the covenant waiver to the exchange offer via an exit consent.

There are at least two other ways firms commonly structure an exchange. One is to offer cash instead of a security such as debt or equity. Another is to offer debt with a shorter maturity than the existing debt. It turns out that in our two-period model these alternatives are equivalent. Debt due at date 1 is paid off with certainty, so exchanges for short-term debt are equivalent to cash exchanges.[23]

Proposition 3: *It is profitable to offer an exchange for cash.*

Proof: See Appendix.

Exchange offers for cash are profitable for similar reasons that senior debt exchanges are profitable. As more debtholders tender, more cash is paid out at date 1, reducing the value of the old debt at date 2. Tendering debtholders are paid cash for the $1 - q$ portion of their claim at date 1. Since this is paid before a holdout receives payment on the $1 - q$ portion of his claim, the tendering debtholders are effectively senior to the nontendering debtholders. As a result, the date-2 portion of the old debt claim is less valuable. Faced with this hold-in problem, old debtholders are willing to tender at a low price.

Recall that throughout the analysis we have assumed that the firm does not have a cash shortage. If the firm does not have sufficient cash, it will use all of its cash in excess of $B + I$ to buy back debt. It is important to note that the firm would not find it profitable to issue outside equity or debt (with equal or junior priority to the old debt) in order to buy back the public debt. The outside capital would not be senior to the untendered debt, so the required interest rate on the outside capital would more than make up for the savings on the exchange offer.

In this model, the ability to exchange for cash does not lead to any added inefficiencies since the firm will always invest in the single project. However, in a model in which there are either several projects or the level of investment is a choice variable, significant inefficiencies can result. The firm may choose to use cash which could be invested in positive net present value

---

[21] Since the vote does not change the timing or amount of payments it is not prohibited by the Trust Indenture Act. See Roe (1987).

[22] The legal status of exit consents is quite uncertain. Although an exit consent was upheld in Katz versus Oak Industries Inc. 508 A.2d 873 (Del. Ch. 1986), several potential legal arguments against them have not been tried. See Coffee and Klein (1990).

[23] Both alternatives are quite common. In our sample of 169 exchange offers, 39 involved some cash. Of the 101 cases in which a debt security was offered, 74 offered debt with a shorter maturity than the old debt.

projects to buy back public debt if the reduction in payments to creditors exceeds the NPV of a project. But, this inefficiency is limited in scope; financially distressed firms tend not to have a great deal of excess cash available for this type of activity.

As we discussed above, there is no difference between an exchange for cash and an exchange for shorter maturity debt of any priority in this model. In a model with more than two periods, there may be a difference because the firm may not have enough cash to exchange all the debt for cash immediately but may be able to achieve a similar effect with an exchange for shorter maturity debt. Our analysis suggests that an exchange for shorter maturity debt is profitable when the firm can make the debtholders who tender effectively senior to those who do not tender. This is possible if the realization of the risky project occurs after the new debt matures, but there are some relatively certain cash flows before the new debt matures. This allows the new debt to have low default risk and be paid off before the old debt matures.

B. *Exchanges When There Is a Cash Shortage*

The above analysis assumes that the firm does not need to restructure its debt in order to invest at date 1. Exchanges have no effect on efficiency; they just redistribute value from public debtholders to shareholders. We now suppose the firm needs a concession from either the bank or public debtholders to invest at date 1. We start by assuming that $I + B < Y < I + B + qD$; the firm needs some concession to invest but has enough cash to pay off the bank and invest.

We explicitly model bank renegotiation and public debt exchanges. The firm first approaches the bank seeking a concession. It makes a take-it-or-leave-it offer to postpone some or all of B until date 2, perhaps along with some debt forgiveness. The firm then has the option of offering an exchange for the public debt. This timing captures the idea that a firm is unable to commit to the bank not to pursue a profitable exchange offer.

Suppose the bank refuses to give the firm a concession. At this point, the firm can propose to exchange the public debt for a more senior debenture. (As we saw in the previous section this is preferred to offering a debenture that is pari passu with the old debt.) We assume for the moment that there is no seniority covenant. Because the new debt is senior to the old, the firm can set p, the face value of the new debenture, so that it is paid all of the date-2 cash flows. Thus, the maximum value of a unit of the new debenture is $(\overline{X} - Y - I - B)/D$, provided the firm buys back all of the debt.[24] If a debtholder does not tender, he receives only the date-1 payment q. So, if $(\overline{X} + Y - I - B)/D > q$ or, equivalently, if

$$\overline{X} - I \geq B + qD - Y \tag{7}$$

---

[24] The proof that the firm will wish to buy back all of the debt applies in this case as well.

an exchange offer for senior debt is feasible. In this case, the firm will want to buy back its public debt because the alternative is liquidation in which case shareholders get nothing.

Now consider the first stage of the model in which the firm approaches the bank to receive a concession. The bank knows that if it turns down the firm's offer, the firm will be able to exchange its debentures provided expression (7) is met. In this case, the bank receives B. So, the bank will turn down any offer which has an expected value less than B.

It is possible that the firm might prefer to renegotiate with the bank to receive some date-1 debt relief rather than restructure its public debt. As long as it can defer enough of its bank debt to pay off the date-1 portion of the public debt, this strategy is feasible. So, suppose the bank extends the maturity of its loan but requires the firm to pay B' at date 2. Assume for the moment that there is no public debt covenant prohibiting the issuance of senior debt; B' can be senior to the date-2 payments on the public debt. In addition, if $Y < I + qD$ the bank has to provide a cash infusion of $I + qD - Y$. If $Y > I + qD$, the remaining cash of $Y - I - qD$ is available to pay off the bank at date 1. Since the new bank debt is senior, the minimum B' that the bank would accept satisfies

$$\int_0^{B'} Xf(X)\,dX + \int_{B'}^{\infty} B'f(X)\,dX + Y - I - qD = B. \tag{8}$$

The question is whether the firm prefers renegotiating with the bank or renegotiating with the public debtholders via an exchange offer. Proposition 4 establishes that, when feasible, the firm prefers a public debt restructuring to a bank debt restructuring.

Proposition 4: *If $I + B < Y < I + B + qD$ and there are no contractual restrictions on issuing senior debt, the firm prefers a public debt exchange to a bank debt restructuring.*

Proof: See Appendix.

In both an exchange offer and a bank debt restructuring, the bank ends up with a claim worth B. However, the exchange is less costly because the firm can take advantage of the hold-in problem; by exchanging for senior debt and leaving holdouts with a junior security, the firm induces public debtholders to tender for a claim that the bank would not accept.

Now suppose instead that $\overline{X} - I < B + qD - Y$, so expression (7) is violated. In this case, an exchange offer is not feasible without a bank concession. Thus, if the bank turns down the firm's take-it-or-leave-it offer, the firm is liquidated and the bank gets L_B. This means that the firm can offer the bank a claim worth L_B, and the bank will accept the offer. Note also that when $Y < I + B$ the bank would also accept an offer of L_B because without such a writedown the firm would be unable to invest at date 1.

Given an offer worth L_B and the bank's acceptance, the firm may be able to exchange its public debt. In an exchange, the maximum value of each new senior debenture is $(\overline{X} + Y - I - L_B)/D$, while each untendered debenture is worth q because there will no funds available at date 2 to pay off the untendered junior debt. Thus, the firm can complete an exchange provided

$$\overline{X} - I \geq qD - L_D. \tag{9}$$

Note that if the exchange is successful, the firm will be able to make its date-1 bank payment of L_B and invest I since we have assumed that $Y > I + B > I + L_B$. If (9) is violated, however, the firm does not offer to exchange and thus is liquidated at date 1.

There will tend to be underinvestment if the current portion of the public debt qD exceeds its liquidation value L_D and overinvestment if the current portion is less than its liquidation value. The minimum transfer to the public debtholders from investment is the least that they can be given with investment qD minus what they get in liquidation L_D. If the transfer is positive, there is underinvestment, and if the net subsidy is negative, there is overinvestment.

The condition for investment is exactly the same as in the model of Section I in which exchange offers were ruled out, but it is possible for the firm to issue senior bank debt. In both cases, investment occurs if the net present value of the project exceeds $qD - L_D$. Although investment behavior is no different, the parties who pay for the investment are different. If (9) is a strict inequality, the public debtholders are worse off with an exchange than with a bank debt restructuring. In the bank debt restructuring, they keep their old securities, while in an exchange the hold-in problem leads public debtholders to accept a lower value security. Since, in both cases, the bank gets a claim worth L_B, equity is the beneficiary of the exchange offer.

Thus, exchange offers can be profitable for the firm if it is able to exchange the debt for more senior securities or has excess cash it can use to exchange the debt for cash. But note the ability to exchange does nothing to improve the efficiency of investment decisions of financially distressed firms if there is no seniority covenant in the public debt; it just affects who bears the costs of financial distress.[25] The reason is that public debtholders take the success of the exchange as given in making their tender decision. Therefore, they do not consider how a change in operating policy made possible by the exchange, affects their claim.

We summarize these results in the following proposition.

Proposition 5: If the firm has insufficient cash to invest, there are three possible outcomes. If the NPV of the investment $\overline{X} - I$ is sufficiently large, the bank is paid in full, the public debtholders accept an exchange, and the firm invests. For intermediate NPVs, the bank debt is forgiven to L_B, the public debtholders accept an exchange, and the firm invests. If the NPV is suffi-

---

[25] Although the basic idea that exchange offers give limited possibilities to increase investment incentives is quite robust, the strong result of no effect is somewhat model-specific. For example, if management were only willing to invest if equity value exceeded some threshold level, the concessions from public debtholders would increase the ability to invest.

ciently small, the firm is liquidated and does not invest. The possibility of a public debt exchange does not alter investment when there are no covenants prohibiting senior debt issues.

The analysis assumes that there is no covenant in the public debt prohibiting a senior debt issue. As discussed in Section II.A, however, firms can get around this covenant through an exit consent in which debtholders simultaneously tender their debentures for more senior ones and, as a condition of the exchange, vote to remove the seniority covenant on the original debt issue. The condition for investment continues to be given by inequality (9).

Thus, exchange offers combined with exit consents can be used to strip seniority covenants that would otherwise prevent a public debt restructuring and constrain investment; in this case, exchange offers have real investment effects. But, the firm can go too far; exit consents and exchange offers can reduce the value of the public debt so much that the firm actually overinvests. Coffee and Klein (1990) have argued that the "coercive" character of exit consents leads to inefficiencies and have called for a ban on exit consents. As a result of a ban, debtholders would still be able to vote to remove covenants, but the vote would not be a condition for tendering in an exchange.

Such a ban on exit consents is efficient in our model. To see this, suppose there is a seniority covenant in the public debt. The interesting case is where the firm cannot raise new bank financing that is pari passu with the existing debt: $\bar{X} - I < V_D - L_D$ and $V_D - L_D > 0$, so that the firm potentially underinvests. If the firm could renegotiate directly with public debtholders they would be willing to reduce the value of their debt conditional on investment to L_D through a reduction of principal or interest. Of course, the Trust Indenture Act does not permit public debtholders to reduce V_D in this way. But, they can effectively reduce V_D by voting to waive the seniority covenant. At the same time, the bank lends new money senior to the public debt, and the interest rate is chosen so that the value of the public debt V'_D is anywhere from a minimum of qD to a maximum of V_D. (Note that V'_D cannot be below qD because if the firm invests the payment of qD is required.)

Public debtholders will accept a covenant waiver only if they know they will receive at least L_D as a result of the restructuring. If $qD < L_D$, the firm can offer L_D, and the public debtholders will accept; if $qD > L_D$, the value of the debt cannot be reduced all the way to L_D, and the offer will be qD. So $V'_D = \max\{qD, L_D\}$. Thus, the condition for investment with a covenant waiver is

$$\bar{X} - I \geq \max\{qD, L_D\} - L_D = \max\{qD - L_D, 0\}. \qquad (10)$$

Contrast this condition to inequality (9) which determines investment when exit consents are possible. The two conditions are the same when $qD > L_D$. In both cases underinvestment may result because there are limits on how much debt reduction is feasible via exit consents or covenant waivers. But, when $qD < L_D$, exit consents allow some negative NPV projects to be taken while covenant waivers do not. The firm can reduce the value of the public debt to below its liquidation value when exit consents are possible but cannot do this when debtholders vote separately on the covenant waiver. Thus, in some situations, exit consents go too far in lowering the debt burden. We have only focused on the case where $\bar{X} - I < V_D - L_D$ and $V_D - L_D > 0$, but in the other cases covenant waivers also lead to weakly more efficient investment outcomes than exit consents.[26]

The conclusion is that exchange offers only alter investment behavior when there is a covenant in the public debt prohibiting senior debt issues. In these cases, firms can use exit consents to remove covenants, issue senior debt, and increase investment. But, exit consents can result in excessive investment. By contrast, if the firm is prohibited from using exit consents and instead must ask for a separate vote to waive a seniority covenant, investment decisions are improved.

The results of this section indicate that the firm would never propose an exchange for more junior securities. This is difficult to reconcile with empirical observations. There are two promising explanations. First, if the firm has private information, it may signal its information by the type of security offered in an exchange. As Myers and Majluf (1984) show, equity issues can signal that the firm's value is low. The firm may then offer an exchange for equity so that debtholders lower the value of the claim they require in exchange.[27] This may offset the losses the firm incurs from the holdout problem created by an exchange for a more junior security.

A second reason why firms may offer junior securities is that public creditors are not really atomistic. In this case, the firm may be able to convince a sufficient number of large debtholders that their acceptance of equity is necessary for a successful restructuring. Equity may be preferred because it reduces the cash drainage from the firm.

Finally, we note two recent developments that have made exchanges less attractive. In the LTV bankruptcy, Judge Lifland disallowed a portion of the claims of public debtholders who participated in a previously completed exchange. He ruled that the admissible claim was the market value of the debentures at the time of the exchange, not its face value. Thus, there may be some reluctance to exchange for fear that the firm would file for Chapter 11 in the future. In addition, the tax treatment of exchanges was changed as part of the Revenue Reconciliation Act of 1990, requiring the firm to recognize cancellation of debt income based on the market value of new securities, not their face value. Firms may be able to avoid this tax liability in Chapter 11.

---

[26] For completeness, consider the case where $\bar{X} - I < V_D - L_D < 0$. In this case the public debtholders would never agree to lower the value of their debt further below its liquidation value. In contrast, an exit consent could allow negative NPV projects to be taken. Also consider the case where $\bar{X} - I > V_D - L_D$. Neither covenant waivers nor exit consents change investment behavior. Public debtholders reject any covenant waiver, but an exit consent can be used to extract value from public bondholders.

[27] See Gertner (1990) and Brown, James, and Mooradian (1991). The latter paper provides empirical evidence consistent with the signaling view.

III. Reorganization Law and Investment

In the U.S., financially distressed companies often seek court protection under the provisions of Chapter 11 of the Bankruptcy Code. These provisions in the Code are intended to promote reorganization of economically viable firms as going-concerns and thereby avoid inefficient liquidation of distressed firms. When a firm files for bankruptcy, all of its debts become due, but an *automatic stay* is invoked stopping all principal and interest payments, and secured creditors lose the right to take possession of their collateral.

In Chapter 11, control of a firm, known as the *debtor in possession*, typically remains with the current management and board of directors. This contrasts with Chapter 7 bankruptcy proceedings in which a trustee takes control and manages the company while organizing a piecemeal liquidation or sale of the firm as a going concern. Creditors are paid in accordance with the absolute priority rule, so equity gets nothing unless all creditors are paid in full. In Chapter 11, management is permitted to continue operating the firm, but all significant decisions are subject to court review and legal motions by creditors to disallow the proposed policy.[28] In reviewing the debtor's policies, the court's objective is to approve policies which maximize the value of the estate. The court has the charge of promoting "equitable" resolutions. This gives the court significant latitude in overseeing the debtor's operations. In addition, the fiduciary responsibility of management is to maximize the value of the estate, not the value of equity.

Operations proceed with court oversight until a reorganization plan is approved through a voting procedure of creditors or the firm is liquidated (piecemeal or as a going concern) either in Chapter 11 or after a conversion to Chapter 7. A reorganization plan specifies a new capital structure for the firm, delineating how creditors are paid in terms of cash or securities of the reorganized firm.

In this section, we focus on three aspects of Chapter 11 that we believe are fundamental for understanding its effect on operating and investment decisions: the automatic stay, the voting rules that determine whether a reorganization plan is approved, and the maintenance of equity value despite the fact that creditors are not paid in full. In general, Chapter 11 has ambiguous effects on efficiency, but the analysis characterizes the situations in which efficiency is enhanced or diminished.

A. The Automatic Stay

The automatic stay increases the firm's incentive to invest. To see this suppose the firm files for Chapter 11 and that the automatic stay is the only feature of Chapter 11. The public debtholders' claims are delayed until date 2, at which time they are either paid in full or share the firm's assets with the bank if the firm is unable to make its debt payment.

---

[28] Control of the corporation can be given to a trustee if creditors can show that current management has acted fraudulently.

Effectively, the automatic stay extends the maturity of the public debt from $q > 0$ to $q = 0$. As we have seen, the firm has a greater incentive to invest when the debt has longer maturity. There are two separate effects. First, the firm may now have the cash needed for investment, so it may not have to borrow funds at date 1: Y may be less than $I + B + qD$ but greater than $I + B$. And even if the firm must borrow ($Y < I + B$), investment is more attractive because the automatic stay forces public debtholders to bear more risk.

The firm may be more willing to invest, but it is not necessarily efficient for it to do so. Public debtholders may be forced to bear too much risk, leading the firm to overinvest. The oversight of the court and the ability of public debtholders to object to the firm's investment plans may prevent large abuses of this type.

This analysis assumes that the new money comes from the bank and is pari passu with the outstanding public debt. But, the debtor will generally try to get the court to approve financing senior to all existing debt. Such financing—known as *debtor in possession (DIP) financing*—is considered an administrative cost which is paid ahead of all other creditors. The court can even make post-petition debt senior to other administrative costs. In addition, the court can approve a *cash collateral* agreement, allowing the debtor to use liquid assets to finance its operations even if these assets are pledged as collateral to a creditor. Thus, the court can effectively strip seniority covenants and security from existing debt. This leads to even greater investment incentives, although the junior creditors who are potentially hurt by the new senior investment can try to petition the court to reject the new financing.

The automatic stay also affects the incentives of the bank to lend outside of bankruptcy. Since the subsidy to the public debtholders from investment is reduced by the automatic stay, the bank and the firm have an incentive to restructure inside bankruptcy rather than outside bankruptcy. If the deadweight losses associated with bankruptcy are less than the reduction in the net subsidy to debtholders, firms will file for bankruptcy even though they could have successfully restructured outside of bankruptcy. In this case, the Chapter 11 option can reduce efficiency. Investment is unchanged by the filing, but the firm is willing to incur a deadweight cost to extract value from public debtholders.[29]

B. Chapter 11 Voting

Investment inefficiencies arise in our model because of the inability to negotiate directly with public debtholders. Exchange offers do little to improve investment efficiency. The underlying problem is that unlike the bank,

---

[29] This implicitly assumes that a firm which defaults must file for bankruptcy. However, in this situation, if bankruptcy proceedings are costly, public bondholders may choose not to force the firm into bankruptcy despite default. They know that bankruptcy results in imposition of the automatic stay which may delay payment as much as default. In this case, the automatic stay can effectively be achieved without an actual filing.

public debtholders do not take into account their effect on the firm's investment policy.

Chapter 11 voting rules can get around this problem. Reorganization plans must be approved by all classes of creditors and the court. Classes are determined by grouping creditors with essentially equivalent claims. So, for example, secured and unsecured creditors are always assigned to different classes. A class approves a plan if two-thirds of the allowed monetary interests and a majority in number within the class accepts the plan. A dissenting member of a class can object to a plan if he gets a claim worth less than his claim in liquidation.

To see how the voting procedure affects restructuring and investment, suppose that the firm files for Chapter 11 reorganization and immediately proposes a reorganization plan that gives public debtholders a claim on the reorganized company which, conditional on investment, is worth $L_D + \varepsilon$, a little more than the return to public debtholders under liquidation. Furthermore, suppose that this is a take-it-or-leave-it offer and that if the plan is rejected the firm is liquidated. In deciding how to vote, a public debtholder compares his return if the plan is successful with his return if it is not. If the plan is successful, all public debtholders share $L_D + \varepsilon$. If the plan is unsuccessful, all public debtholders share L_D in liquidation. Thus, they all vote for the plan. The debtor can offer the holders of the public debt a claim just above its liquidation value, so there is no subsidy to or from public debtholders. The result is efficient investment.

Why does this voting mechanism work while an exchange offer does not? The answer is that the voting procedure does not allow public debtholders to be treated differently depending on their vote, whereas tendering and nontendering public debtholders are treated differently. In an exchange offer, a public debtholder compares the value of the new claim with the value of the old claim *conditional on success* of the exchange offer because it is possible for the debtholder to keep his old claim even if the tender offer is successful. But if the conditions for acceptance under the voting procedure are met, those who do not vote for the plan are compelled to accept the offer.[30] Thus, the voting procedure can be used to internalize the effects of the investment decision and get around the holdout and hold-in problems, thereby improving investment efficiency.[31]

The voting procedure is unlikely to work as smoothly as we have modeled it. In practice, the debtor does not have all the bargaining power. The threat to liquidate the firm if the plan is rejected may not be credible; the debtor may choose to continue operating the firm in Chapter 11. Asymmetric

---

[30] A dissenting member of an approving class who gets less than the liquidation value of its claim can object to the plan. If successful, this will cause the plan to be defeated. This does not accomplish the same thing as holding out in a successful exchange offer. In that situation, other creditors make concessions while the holdout's claim is unchanged.

[31] A similar problem arises in the context of takeovers. Shareholders that do not tender may be able to free-ride on the acquirer's value gains. One way around this problem has been proposed by Bebchuk (1985): let the shareholders vote whether to accept the offer and make a successful vote binding on all shareholders. This reduces inefficiency for the same reason it does here.

information may lead to inefficiencies through strategic behavior and delay. Nevertheless, an important feature of voting is its capacity to overcome the holdout and hold-in problems.

This analysis raises a natural question: if Chapter 11 voting procedures enhance efficiency, why can the firm not include in its debt covenants a provision that mimics the Chapter 11 voting procedures for exchange offers by the firm. The answer is that, as discussed above, the Trust Indenture Act of 1939 prohibits it.[32]

This voting rule can help the firm to obtain concessions from public debtholders. Even if the bank is willing to lend outside Chapter 11, the firm may be better off filing for bankruptcy and taking advantage of the voting procedure to obtain a transfer from public debtholders. This is more likely to be the best strategy when these concessions are large. Thus, if the public debt is relatively short term, senior, or protected by seniority covenants, the public debt is generally more valuable outside Chapter 11 than inside. In these cases, we would expect firms to file.

C. Maintenance of Equity Value

One of the most salient features of Chapter 11 reorganizations is that shareholders typically retain a stake in the firm, even though debtholders are not paid in full. Franks and Torous (1989) find that, in a sample of 28 Chapter 11 filings, equity holders retain some equity in the reorganized firm in 21 cases.

The debtor's bargaining power in Chapter 11 is derived from a number of procedural rules on the formation and acceptance of a reorganization plan. The *debtor in possession* has the exclusive right to propose a plan for the first 120 days after filing the bankruptcy petition. This exclusivity period can be, and often is, extended by the judge for long periods. Only once exclusivity is lifted can creditors propose a plan.

The debtor's threat to delay a plan is often credible; the debtor wishes to protract bankruptcy proceedings on the chance that the debtor will turn solvent and that shareholders will receive a larger payoff in the liquidation or reorganization. These debtor bargaining powers help explain why shareholders typically retain a stake in the reorganized firm even though creditors are not paid in full.

---

[32] "The Act was initially promoted to protect public debtholders from being exploited by the firm. The fear was that a large shareholder would have an incentive to secretly buy up the bonds and vote to eliminate principal and interest payments. Roe (1987) argues that this provision of the Trust Indenture Act no longer serves any useful purpose and is inconsistent with the voting procedures used in Chapter 11 reorganizations. Fraud statutes can be used to avoid manipulation by large shareholders. The Act may force firms to file for bankruptcy with all its other baggage in order to restructure its public debt. Currently, "pre-packaged" or "1126b" plans, in which reorganization plans are already approved when the firm files for bankruptcy, are becoming popular. They are used mainly to compel holdouts to go along with other members of their creditor class. Republic Health used a pre-package plan successfully."

This threat is damaging to creditors because they usually want the proceedings to end as soon as possible in order to receive principal and interest payments on their debt. In addition, all creditors face the risk that the estate's value will decline dramatically during bankruptcy. Secured creditors also face the risk that the secured assets will depreciate during Chapter 11.

Clearly, the decision to accept or reject a plan depends on what happens if the plan is not approved, i.e., on the threat points in this game.[33] One threat point of a plan's sponsor is that the plan will be approved by the court even in the presence of a dissenting class of creditors. The procedure is referred to as *cramdown*. Section 1129 of the Bankruptcy Code provides for cramdown if a class receives a claim with value equivalent to full payment or if every class junior to the dissenting class receives nothing.[34]

Creditors also have threats. They can propose a plan of their own which can be crammed down on the equity holders. Perhaps, even more important, secured creditors can try to lift the automatic stay.[35] They can also file for dismissal of the case or conversion to Chapter 7 liquidation.[36] Creditors can fight management's operating and investment decisions. They can refuse to lend new money, and they can try to block asset sales.

The fact that equity retains value in many reorganizations even if creditors are not paid in full can have important implications for behavior outside of Chapter 11, in particular for incentive to lend new money outside of bankruptcy. In our model, the firm has only two alternatives: to obtain new funds and invest, or to go bankrupt and liquidate the firm. In practice, however, there is generally a third option: to file for Chapter 11 protection, invoke the automatic stay, and maintain control, continuing in operation without new funds for investment. This threat is often both harmful to creditors and perfectly credible: in liquidation equity value is almost certain to be wiped out, while in Chapter 11 equity value is positive if there is any possibility of solvency. Faced with this threat, the creditors' best alternative may be to extend further funds for investment. Thus, reorganization law provides a distressed firm with a credible threat that increases the creditors' incentives to provide new funds. In essence, the law affects the bargaining

---

[33] See Brown (1989) and Baird and Picker (1991) for analyses of how various bankruptcy rules affect the way in which firm value is divided between shareholders and creditors.

[34] Some jurisdictions have allowed equity to maintain value in cramdown even if all creditors are not paid in full. This rule, known as the *new value exception*, permits old equity holders to maintain control as long as it pays creditors the liquidation value of the assets and the old equity holders contribute new capital equal to the value of the equity of the reorganized company. The existence of the new value exception under the Bankruptcy Code is a controversial and unsettled legal issue. See Norwest Bank Worthington versus Ahlers 485 U.S. 197 (1988) and the discussion in Baird and Jackson (1990).

[35] Causes to lift the automatic stay include lack of adequate protection, or a showing that the creditor is undersecured and the collateral is not necessary for an effective reorganization.

[36] The court can convert a Chapter 11 case to Chapter 7 if it is in the best interest of the creditors and the estate as long as certain conditions are met. These conditions, listed in Section 1112 of the Code, include continuing losses with "no reasonable likelihood of rehabilitation," unreasonable delay by the debtor, and failure to consummate a plan.

process outside of bankruptcy, changing not just how surplus is split but the efficiency of outcomes as well.

To develop this idea in more detail, we consider the following simple extension of our model in Section I. Suppose that if the firm continues in operation without investing, it receives a stochastic date-2 payoff of X_c (with mean $\bar{x}_c$) in addition to the date-1 liquidation value of Y. In order to focus on continuation as a threat rather than a value-maximizing strategy, we assume that continuation is inefficient; total value is higher if the firm liquidates than if it continues without investment, $\bar{X}_c < 0$. The value of the public debt if the firm follows the continuation strategy is V_D^c. The bank and the firm together get $\bar{X}_c + Y - V_D^c$ if the firm continues without investing. If the firm invests, their combined payoff, as before, is $\bar{X} - I + Y - V_D$. Finally, if the firm is liquidated, their combined payoff is L_B, with equity getting nothing.

Suppose that among these three alternatives liquidation is the most attractive to the bank and equity combined, so that

$$L_B > \max(\bar{X} - I + Y - V_D, \bar{X}_c + Y - V_D^c) \tag{11}$$

Then, absent Chapter 11 reorganization, the firm will be liquidated.

But, now suppose the firm can file in Chapter 11, invoke the automatic stay, defer debt payments until date 2, and stay in control of the firm. This is collectively inefficient for the bank and shareholders since $L_B > \bar{X}_c + Y - V_D^c$. The bank would like to pay the firm to liquidate instead of continue, but it cannot. Any payment from the bank to the firm cannot go to shareholders before it goes to the firm's other creditors; this would be a fraudulent conveyance and declared illegal. Given this restriction, the firm's threat is credible; shareholders are better off continuing in operation in the hope that X_c is sufficient to pay creditors at date 2, thereby giving equity a positive return, which exceeds equity's zero return in liquidation.

So the bank has two options. It can let the firm file Chapter 11 or it can provide new money for investment. If the joint returns from investing are larger than those from continuation in Chapter 11, i.e.,

$$\bar{X} - I - V_D \geq \bar{X}_c - V_D^c, \tag{12}$$

the bank will lend money for investment. If not, the firm will file for Chapter 11 protection.

The option to file for Chapter 11 protection can increase efficiency. If (12) is satisfied, the firm will be more prone to invest. This is efficient if $V_D - L_B > 0$, the case in which the firm underinvests without Chapter 11. If, however, $V_D - L_D < 0$, the firm would otherwise overinvest, and Chapter 11 merely exacerbates the inefficiency. By contrast, if (12) is violated, Chapter 11 always reduces efficiency since the firm continues rather than liquidates, and $\bar{X}_c < 0 < Y$.

The overall efficiency effects of this aspect of Chapter 11 are ambiguous, but we can identify the situations in which it is likely to be helpful or harmful. First, when the public debt is short term, the bank debt is senior, and the public debt is protected by seniority covenants, underinvestment is likely to be a problem, and Chapter 11 can be helpful. Second, when investment is risky relative to continuation, investment tends to be more attractive to the bank and equity because the public debt is worth less. In this case, the likely effect of Chapter 11 is to promote investment rather than to give the firm an easy way of avoiding efficient liquidation.

Another out-of-bankruptcy effect of the maintenance of equity value in Chapter 11 is to reduce the incentives to take risk. In a Chapter 7 liquidation, shareholders generally receive nothing, making Chapter 7 very unattractive to shareholders and management. So, as the firm's financial position gradually deteriorates, management has a strong incentive to take risk-increasing investments and to pay out as much firm value as possible to themselves. This incentive is obviously diminished the higher the return to equity and management in Chapter 11. Of course, if public debtholders are aware of the law, they must be promised a higher interest rate to compensate them for their lower return when the firm is in distress. If the investment decisions of a financially distressed firm are more efficient, there will be more than enough increased value to pay the higher interest rates and yet increase equity value.

IV. Concluding Remarks

This paper outlines some of the characteristics of corporate financial structure that can make financial distress more or less costly. We focus on coordination problems among numerous public debtholders as the main source of inefficiency. This problem can lead to underinvestment when bank debt is senior, when public debt is short term, or when it is protected by seniority covenants. Overinvestment tends to be a problem with junior bank debt, long-term public debt, and when a firm can strip seniority covenants with exit consents.

Exchange offers can be used to restructure public debt, but they do not, in general, lead to efficient investment. So, financial distress may result in inefficient operating policy even though banks are perfectly informed and exchanges are possible with public creditors. If there are no seniority covenants in the public debt, exchange offers do not change the firm's investment behavior but simply force public debtholders to bear more of the burden of financial distress. If there is a seniority covenant, however, investment can be increased through an exchange offer that strips public debt of its covenant and enables a firm to issue senior debt to finance investment. However, such exchange offers can go too far, resulting in overinvestment in some cases. Efficiency is increased if exit consents are not allowed, and, instead, debtholders vote separately to eliminate seniority covenants.

The Trust Indenture Act gives rise to investment inefficiencies because it forces firms to make exchange offers rather than bargain directly with public debtholders. In our model, all investment inefficiencies would be eliminated if the Trust Indenture Act was repealed. Of course, this result follows from our assumption of complete information in which case bargaining is efficient in the absence of transaction costs. In a more realistic model with asymmetric information and other transaction costs, investment inefficiencies are likely to result.

There are a number of empirical implications of our model. First, the model predicts that, conditional on an out-of-court workout, distressed firms with senior bank debt, short-term public debt, and effective seniority covenants will invest less. Second, the model predicts that exchanges are more likely when the public debt is relatively long term. And, when possible, exchanges should shorten the maturity of public debt, strip existing covenants, and offer more senior securities.

Our model is also a useful starting point to think about the tradeoffs firms face in deciding whether to file for Chapter 11 rather than seek an out-of-court restructuring. We have outlined how debt structure affects the payoffs from an out-of-court restructuring. To complete the theory, we need a model of the reorganization process, one that tells us how debt structure affects investment behavior and the division of firm value in Chapter 11.

We conclude by noting that while we have analyzed the effects of Chapter 11 on distressed firms, we have sidestepped an important point made by legal scholars. Roe (1983), Baird (1986), and Jackson (1986) have all argued that the manipulation that is possible in Chapter 11 can be avoided by eliminating Chapter 11 reorganization altogether and relying on Chapter 7.

The basic thrust of the argument is as follows. Consider a firm in financial distress much like the firm we have modeled. Suppose the firm goes into Chapter 7 and the trustee sells the firm in its entirety, either through an auction or through negotiations with investors and other firms. The proceeds from the sale are then used to pay off creditors using the same priority rules that apply if the assets are sold piecemeal. Any funds that are left after paying off all the creditors in full go to the original shareholders. The newly created firm has none of its previous debts and should be able to invest efficiently. If the original managers of the firm are essential for the investment project, the new owners can hire them to run the company, or the old managers could buy the firm themselves, borrowing against the firm's now unencumbered assets. In effect, the Chapter 7 effects a swap of all the outstanding debt for a package of new securities.

Our analysis suggests that the issues are more complex than these authors suggest. The important point is that the maintenance of equity value in Chapter 11 affects both investment and bargaining outside of bankruptcy. It makes creditors more willing to lend, and it can reduce managerial moral hazard outside of bankruptcy. Moreover, if the market for the sale of distressed firms is thin and inefficient, the buyer will get some rents. This will inefficiently increase the firm's ex ante cost of capital since neither original shareholders nor creditors receive these rents. And, the forced sale envisioned by these authors can lead to different operating and investment policies. So, the normative question of whether a forced sales regime is more or less efficient than some form of reorganization law is an empirical one, given the potential allocative distortions of both systems.

Appendix

Proof of Proposition 1: For a given p and β, the value of the firm in default is: $X + Y - I - B - (1 - \beta)qD$. Total outstanding claims at date 2 are $(1 - \beta)(1 - q)D + \beta pD$ of which tendering debtholders collectively receive a fraction $\beta pD/[(1 - \beta)(1 - q)D + \beta pD]$. Thus, the value of each of the βD tendered debentures is:

$$\int_0^{X_b} \frac{p}{(1 - \beta)(1 - q)D + \beta pD} [X + Y - I - B - (1 - \beta)qD] f(X) \, dX$$

$$+ \int_{X_b}^{\infty} pf(X) \, dX. \quad (A1)$$

Each nontendering debtholder receives a certain payment of q at date 1 and a risky claim at date 2 comprised of his share of the insolvent firm if $X < X_b$ and full payment of $(1 - q)$ if $X > X_b$:

$$q + \int_0^{X_b} (1 - q) \frac{X + Y - I - B - (1 - \beta)qD}{(1 - \beta)(1 - q)D + \beta pD} f(X) \, dX$$

$$+ \int_{X_b}^{\infty} (1 - q) f(X) \, dX. \quad (A2)$$

Equating (A1) and (A2) determines, for any given β, the p at which debtholders are just indifferent between tendering and not tendering. This equation can be rewritten as:

$$\int_0^{X_b} \frac{(X + Y - I - B)(1 - q - p) + pqD}{(1 - \beta)(1 - q)D + \beta pD} f(X) \, dX$$

$$+ \int_{X_b}^{\infty} (1 - p) f(X) \, dX = 0. \quad (A3)$$

At $p = 1$, the left-hand side is

$$\int_0^{X_b} \frac{q[D - (X + Y - I - B)]}{(1 - \beta)(1 - q)D + \beta pD} f(X) \, dX. \quad (A4)$$

The integrand is 0 at $X = X_b$ and positive for $X < X_b$, so (A4) is positive at $p = 1$. Since the left-hand side of (A3) is decreasing in p, the p that solves (A3) is greater than one. Q.E.D.

Proof of Proposition 2: The value of the old debentures given β and p when the firm exchanges for senior debt is given by:

$$q + \int_{X_1}^{X_b} \frac{X + Y - I - B - (1-\beta)qD - \beta pD}{(1-\beta)D} f(X)\,dX$$

$$+ \int_{X_b}^{\infty} (1-q)f(X)\,dX, \quad (A5)$$

where $X_1 \equiv I + B + (1-\beta)qD + \beta pD - Y$ is the cutoff value of X above which the new debentures are paid in full and $X_b \equiv I + B + (1-\beta)D + \beta pD - Y$ is the cutoff value of X above which the old debt is paid in full and the firm is solvent; $X_1 \le X_b$, with equality if and only if $\beta = 1$. Since the new debt is senior to the old debt, for X between X_1 and X_b, holdouts share $X + Y - I - B - (1-\beta)qD - \beta pD$, the cash left after date-1 payments and date-2 payments of βpD to the new senior debt.

Tendering debtholders do not receive q at date 1 but do receive a senior claim at date 2. The value of their debt is

$$\int_0^{X_1} \frac{X + Y - I - B - (1-\beta)qD}{\beta D} f(X)\,dX + \int_{X_1}^{\infty} pf(X)\,dX. \quad (A6)$$

We now show that the value to the firm of an exchange is increasing in β. Equating (A5) and (A6) and combining terms gives,

$$\int_0^{X_1} \frac{X + Y - I - B - qD}{\beta D} f(X)\,dX - \int_{X_1}^{X_b} \frac{X + Y - I - B - pD}{(1-\beta)D} f(X)\,dX$$

$$- \int_{X_b}^{\infty} (1-p)f(X)\,dX = 0. \quad (A7)$$

Since $X_b = I + B - Y + (1-\beta)D + p\beta D$,

$$\frac{dX_b}{d\beta} = D\left[\beta \frac{\partial p}{\partial \beta} - (1-p)\right]. \quad (A8)$$

Differentiating (A7),

$$\frac{\partial p}{\partial \beta} = \frac{\displaystyle\int_0^{X_1} \frac{X + Y - I - B - qD}{\beta^2 D} f(X)\,dX + \int_{X_1}^{X_b} \frac{X + Y - I - B - pD}{(1-\beta)^2 D} f(X)\,dX}{\displaystyle\int_{X_1}^{X_b} \frac{1}{1-\beta} f(X)\,dX + \int_{X_b}^{\infty} f(X)\,dX}. \quad (A9)$$

Multiplying by β and substituting from (A7),

$$\beta \frac{\partial p}{\partial \beta} = \frac{\frac{1}{1-\beta}\int_{X_1}^{X_b} \frac{X+Y-I-B-pD}{(1-\beta)D} f(X)\,dX + \int_{X_b}^{\infty}(1-p)f(X)\,dX}{\int_{X_1}^{X_b}\frac{1}{1-\beta}f(X)\,dX + \int_{X_b}^{\infty}f(X)\,dX},$$

(A10)

and

$$\beta \frac{\partial p}{\partial \beta} - (1-p) = \frac{\frac{1}{1-\beta}\int_{X_1}^{X_b} \frac{X+Y-I-B-pD}{(1-\beta)D} f(X)\,dX - \int_{X_1}^{X_b}\frac{1-p}{1-\beta}f(X)\,dX}{\int_{X_1}^{X_b}\frac{1}{1-\beta}f(X)\,dX + \int_{X_b}^{\infty}f(X)\,dX}.$$ (A11)

The denominator is clearly positive. The numerator is equal to

$$\frac{1}{(1-\beta)^2 D}\int_{X_1}^{X_b}[X+Y-I-B-D(1-\beta+\beta p)]f(X)\,dX.$$

At X_1 the integrand is $(1-\beta)(q-1)D$, which is negative. Since the integrand is increasing in X, the numerator is negative, and X_b is decreasing in β. Thus, one can determine whether an exchange offer is profitable by checking to see whether p is greater or less than one at $\beta = 1$.

If we set $\beta = 1$, $X_1 = X_b$ and we can rewrite (A7) as

$$\int_0^{X_b}\frac{X+Y-I-B-qD}{D}f(X)\,dX - \int_{X_b}^{\infty}(1-p)f(X)\,dX = 0. \quad (A13)$$

Since $Y > I + B + qD$ by assumption, the first term in (A13) is positive. Thus, to satisfy (A13), p must be less than one. Q.E.D.

Proof of Proposition 3: Suppose the firm offers to exchange each dollar of old debt for V dollars of cash or new short-term debt. Debtholders will be indifferent between tendering and not for any V and β provided,

$$q + \int_0^{X_b}\frac{X+Y-I-B-(1-\beta)qD - V\beta D}{(1-\beta)D}f(X)\,dX$$

$$+ \int_{X_b}^{\infty}(1-q)f(X)\,dX = V, \quad (A14)$$

where $X_b \equiv I + B + (1 - \beta)qD + V\beta D - Y$. We can rewrite (A14) as

$$\int_0^{X_b} \frac{X + Y - I - B - VD}{(1 - \beta)D} f(X) \, dX + \int_{X_b}^{\infty} (1 - V) f(X) \, dX = 0. \quad (A15)$$

Totally differentiating (A15) yields,

$$\frac{dV}{d\beta} = \frac{\int_0^{X_b} \frac{X + Y - I - B - VD}{(1 - \beta)^2 D} f(X) \, dX}{F(X_b) + (1 - \beta)[1 - F(X_b)]} \quad (A16)$$

$$= \frac{-(1 - V)[1 - F(X_b)]}{\beta \{ F(X_b) + (1 - \beta)[1 - F(X_b)] \}}, \quad (A17)$$

where the second equality follows from substituting (A15) into (A16). From (A14), $V < 1$, so (A17) implies that $V'(\beta) < 0$. The cost to the firm of the exchange is $\beta D V(\beta)$. Since debtholders are indifferent between tendering and not, the expected payments to the nontendering debtholders must be $(1 - \beta) DV(\beta)$. Adding, the expected payments to all public debtholders is $V(\beta)D$. So, the firm maximizes profits by choosing β to minimize $V(\beta)$. Since $V'(\beta) < 0$, an exchange for cash is profitable. Q.E.D.

Proof of Proposition 4: From (A13), the exchange offer terms for senior debt are determined by

$$\int_0^{X_b} (X + Y - I - B - qD) f(X) \, dX - \int_{X_b}^{\infty} (1 - p) Df(X) \, dX = 0, \quad (A18)$$

where $X_b = X + Y - I - B - pD$.

In an exchange, the shareholders receive $X - X_b$ if it is positive and zero otherwise. In a bank renegotiation, shareholders receive $X - B' - (1 - q)D$ if it is positive and zero otherwise. So an exchange is more profitable provided $X_b < B' + (1 - q)D$.

To show that this is indeed the case, we assume, to the contrary, that $X_b \geq B' + (1 - q)D$. Thus, let $B' \equiv X_b - (1 - q)D - \varepsilon$, $\varepsilon \geq 0$. Then equation (8) can be rewritten as

$$\int_0^{X_b - (1-q)D - \varepsilon} Xf(X) \, dX + \int_{X_b - (1-q)D - \varepsilon}^{\infty} [X_b - (1 - q)D - \varepsilon] f(X) \, dX$$

$$+ Y - I - qD - B = 0. \quad (A19)$$

Using the definition of X_b and rearranging, (A19) becomes

$$\int_0^{X_b - (1-q)D - \varepsilon} (X + Y - I - qD - B) f(X) \, dX$$

$$- \int_{X_b - (1-q)D - \varepsilon}^{\infty} (1 - p) D = 0. \quad (A20)$$

Now compare (A20) and (A18). The only difference is the limits of integration. Note that the left-hand side of (A18) is increasing in X_b and since $X_b - (1 - q)D - \varepsilon < X_b$, the left-hand side of (A20) is less than that of (A18). Thus, if (A18) is satisfied with equality, (A20) must be violated. Thus, B' must be greater than $X_b + (1 - q)D$. Q.E.D.

REFERENCES

Aivazian, V. and J. Callen, 1983, Reorganization in bankruptcy and the issue of strategic risk, *Journal of Banking and Finance* 7, 1989, 119-133.

Asquith, P., D. Mullins, and E. Wolff, 1989, Original issue high yield bonds: Aging analyses of defaults, exchanges, and calls, *Journal of Finance* 44, 923-952.

Baird, D., 1986, The uneasy case for corporate reorganization, *Journal of Legal Studies* 15, 127-147.

―――― and T. Jackson, 1990, *Cases, Problems, and Materials on Bankruptcy*, 2nd Edition (Little Brown and Company, Boston).

―――― and R. Picker, 1991, A simple noncooperative bargaining model of corporate reorganizations, *Journal of Legal Studies*, Forthcoming.

Bebchuk, L., 1985, Towards an undistorted choice and equal treatment in corporate takeovers, *Harvard Law Review* 98, 1693-1808.

Bergman, Y. and J. Callen, 1990, Opportunistic behavior in debt renegotiations and an interior optimal capital structure of the firm without deadweight costs, Unpublished manuscript, Brown University Department of Economics.

Berkovitch, E. and E. H. Kim, 1990, Financial contracting and leverage induced over- and under-investment incentives, *Journal of Finance* 45, 765-794.

Bernanke, B. and J. Campbell, 1988, Is there a corporate debt crisis? *Brookings Papers on Economic Activity*, pp. 83-139.

――――, J. Campbell, and T. Whited, 1990, U.S. corporate leverage: Developments in 1987 and 1988, *Brookings Papers on Economic Activity*, pp. 255-278.

Brown, D., 1989, Claimholder incentive conflicts in reorganization: The role of bankruptcy law, *The Review of Financial Studies* 2, 109-123.

――――, C. James, and R. Mooradian, 1991, The information content of exchange offers made by distressed firms, Unpublished manuscript, Graduate School of Business, University of Florida.

Bulow, J. and J. Shoven, 1978, The bankruptcy decision, *Bell Journal of Economics* 9, 437-456.

―――― and K. Rogoff, 1989, Sovereign debt repurchases: No cure for overhang, Working paper 2850, National Bureau of Economic Research.

Coffee, J. and W. Klein, 1990, Protection of bondholders from unfair constrained-choice tender offers, Unpublished manuscript, UCLA Law School.

Cutler, D. and L. Summers, 1988, The costs of conflict resolution and financial distress: Evidence from the Texaco-Pennzoil litigation, *Rand Journal of Economics* 19, 157-172.

Franks, J. and W. Torous, 1989, An empirical investigation of firms in reorganization, *Journal of Finance* 44, 747-779.

Froot, K., 1989, Buybacks, exit bonds, and the optimality of debt and liquidity relief, *International Economic Review* 30, 49-70.

――――, D. Scharfstein, and J. Stein, 1989, LDC debt: Forgiveness, indexation, and investment incentives, *Journal of Finance* 44, 1335-1350.

Gertner, R., 1990, Inefficiency in three-person bargaining, Unpublished manuscript, University of Chicago, Graduate School of Business.

Giammarino, R., 1989, The resolution of financial distress, *The Review of Financial Studies* 2, 25-47.

Gilson, S., K. John, and L. Lang, 1990, Troubled debt restructurings: An empirical study of private reorganization of firms in default, *Journal of Financial Economics* 27, 315-354.

Haugen, R. and L. Senbet, 1978, The insignificance of bankruptcy costs to the theory of optimal capital structure, *Journal of Finance* 33, 383–393.

Hoshi, T., A. Kashyap, and D. Scharfstein, 1990, The role of banks in reducing the costs of financial distress in Japan, *Journal of Financial Economics* 27, 67–88.

Jackson, T., 1986, *The Logic and Limits of Bankruptcy Law*. (Harvard University Press, Cambridge.)

Jensen, M., 1986, Agency costs of free cash flow, corporate finance, and takeovers, *American Economic Review* 76, 323–329.

—— and W. Meckling, 1976, Theory of the firm: Managerial behavior, agency costs, and ownership structure, *Journal of Financial Economics* 3, 305–360.

Myers, S., 1977, "Determinants of corporate borrowing, *Journal of Financial Economics* 5, 147–175.

—— and N. Majluf, 1984, Corporate financing and investment decisions when firms have information that investors do not have, *Journal of Financial Economics* 13, 187–221.

Roe, M., 1983, Bankruptcy and debt: A new model for corporate reorganization, *Columbia Law Review* 83, 528–602.

——, 1987, The voting prohibition in bond workouts, *The Yale Law Journal* 97, 232–279.

Stulz, R. and H. Johnson, 1985, An analysis of secured debt, *Journal of Financial Economics* 14, 501–521.

Titman, S., 1984, The effect of capital structure on a firm's liquidation decision, *Journal of Financial Economics* 13, 137–151.

White, M., 1980, Public policy toward bankruptcy: Me-first and other priority rules, *Bell Journal of Economics* 11, 550–564.

——, 1983, Bankruptcy costs and the new bankruptcy code, *Journal of Finance* 38, 477–487.

The Effect of Bankruptcy Protection on Investment: Chapter 11 as a Screening Device

ROBERT M. MOORADIAN*

ABSTRACT

Asymmetric information and conflicts of interest between equity and debt holders can force a distressed but efficient firm to liquidate and may enable a distressed inefficient firm to continue. In the extreme, if it is costless for an inefficient firm to mimic an efficient firm in a debt restructuring, efficient and inefficient firms are equally likely to continue or liquidate. This article shows that Chapter 11 procedures impose costs on inefficient firms that would otherwise mimic efficient firms. This separation induces voluntary filing for bankruptcy by inefficient firms and consequently enables efficient firms to continue when they would otherwise be liquidated.

FINANCIALLY DISTRESSED FIRMS OFTEN seek court protection under Chapter 11 of the U.S. Bankruptcy Code. Chapter 11 is both the most prominent and controversial feature of the corporate bankruptcy law. Considerable debate over Chapter 11 appears in both the law and financial economics literature. Some authors even advocate the repeal of Chapter 11.[1]

The fundamental question in the debate over Chapter 11 is one of efficiency: what is the effect of Chapter 11 bankruptcy reorganization on the restructuring and investment of financially distressed firms? There are two competing views. The first view is that bankruptcy laws exacerbate the incentive to overinvest.[2] In the model of Gertner and Scharfstein (1991), Chapter 11 increases investment, which reduces the incentive to underinvest but exacerbates the incentive to overinvest. In the extreme, Chapter 11 encourages corporate managers to reorganize when liquidation is efficient.[3]

The second view, espoused by Baird (1991), Bebchuk and Picker (1992), Berkovich and Israel (1991), and Harris and Raviv (1993), is that Chapter 11 enhances efficiency. Harris and Raviv (1993) suggest that Chapter 11 inhibits the inefficient liquidation of firms in default. Baird (1991) argues that Chapter 11 provides shareholders with the incentive to seek bankruptcy

---

*College of Business Administration, Northeastern University. Thanks to David T. Brown, Stephen Buser, Mark Flannery, Joel Houston, Christopher James, René Stulz, and an anonymous referee for helpful comments.

[1] See Aghion, Hart, and Moore (1992), Bebchuk (1988), and Bradley and Rosenzweig (1992).

[2] Bebchuk (1994) argues that the availability of Chapter 11 has adverse effects on investment decisions made prior to the period of financial distress, although Chapter 11 has beneficial effects on investment decisions made during the period of financial distress.

[3] See Bradley and Rosenzweig (1992) and White (1994).

proceedings rather than delay the resolution of financial distress. Finally, in Berkovich and Israel's (1991) model, firms seek Chapter 11 rather than overinvest.

This article analyzes the effect of Chapter 11 bankruptcy reorganization on the restructuring and investment of financially distressed firms. In contrast to Bradley and Rosenzweig (1992), this article is not limited to the investigation of financially distressed firms that file for Chapter 11. I consider the impact of Chapter 11 reorganization law on not only a distressed firm's bankruptcy decision but also on out-of-court debt restructurings. Furthermore, I analyze the effect of Chapter 11 on the investment of all financially distressed firms, those that file for Chapter 11 and those that renegotiate outside bankruptcy. When all distressed firms are considered, in contrast to Bradley and Rosenzweig (1992), reorganization law does not diminish economic efficiency.

There are two primary contributions of this article. First, it introduces asymmetric information into a model of public debt restructurings; debt holders do not observe whether a firm is economically efficient or inefficient. The starting point for the analysis is the model of Gertner and Scharfstein (1991). Firms have outstanding public debt that they have to restructure via an exchange offer; direct renegotiation is essentially prohibited by the Trust Indenture Act. The inability of public debt holders to coordinate their exchange offer tender decisions can result in investment inefficiencies. This article begins with the coordination problem among debt holders, introduces asymmetric information, and shows that without a collective reorganization mechanism like Chapter 11, economically efficient and inefficient firms are equally likely to continue or liquidate. Although debt holders would agree to renegotiate with efficient firms, they are unwilling to renegotiate with inefficient firms. Inefficient firms pool with efficient firms, because otherwise inefficient firms are liquidated and equity holders receive nothing. Hence, one of two investment inefficiencies occurs: inefficient firms continue when they should be liquidated or efficient firms are liquidated when they should continue.

The second and principal contribution of the article is to introduce Chapter 11 bankruptcy reorganization into the model. The existing models of debt renegotiation assume that firms are liquidated when bankrupt (a Chapter 7 outcome) and equity holders receive nothing. In fact, in Chapter 11 firms are often reorganized and shareholders retain some valuable equity in the firm.[4] The shareholders of an inefficient firm forego the equity in the firm that they can extract in Chapter 11 if the firm mimics an efficient firm's offer to debt holders in a debt restructuring because the offer determines the shareholders' residual value.

The result is that inefficient firms no longer have such a strong incentive to pool with efficient firms. Inefficient firms can file for Chapter 11 and share-

[4] See Franks and Torous (1989), Eberhart, Moore, and Roenfeldt (1990), Weiss (1990), and LoPucki and Whitford (1992).

holders retain some valuable equity in the firm because of the nature of the Chapter 11 process. As a result of Chapter 11, inefficient firms still continue when they should be liquidated, although inefficient firms may only get to continue in Chapter 11. However, efficient firms, instead of being liquidated, renegotiate and continue outside Chapter 11.[5] Chapter 11 increases efficiency to the extent that it allows efficient firms to renegotiate and continue, but decreases efficiency to the extent that economically inefficient firms file for bankruptcy under Chapter 11 rather than liquidate.

A number of economists have argued that Chapter 11 is inefficient because it allows bad or inefficient firms to continue in operation. And, indeed many of the firms in Chapter 11 look like very bad firms.[6] But, a key point of this article is that one cannot assess the welfare effects of Chapter 11 simply by looking at what happens in Chapter 11; Chapter 11 has consequences for out-of-court restructuring as well. Allowing shareholders to retain some valuable equity in firms in Chapter 11 has some value for firms restructuring outside of Chapter 11.[7] In the model, Chapter 11 is beneficial in that it separates inefficient firms from efficient firms, enabling efficient firms to renegotiate and continue where they would otherwise be liquidated. In effect, Chapter 11 serves as a mechanism for screening inefficient firms.

A contemporaneous paper, White (1994), also examines bankruptcy as a screening mechanism. In an investigation limited to financially distressed firms that file for bankruptcy, White (1994) develops a model of the interaction between the two corporate bankruptcy procedures, Chapter 7 (liquidation) and Chapter 11, where creditors act collectively. In contrast to White (1994), this article provides a model of the Chapter 11 process in the context of out-of-court debt restructurings where debt holders are subject to a coordination problem. This article focuses not only on the impact of Chapter 11 reorganization law on a distressed firm in bankruptcy, but also on the consequences of Chapter 11 for out-of-court debt restructurings.

The existing literature makes inferences concerning the welfare implications of Chapter 11 largely through the examination of firms experiencing Chapter 11. In particular, in interpreting their empirical findings, Bradley and Rosenzweig (1992) argue that Chapter 11 rewards self-interested management to the detriment of all security holders. This article suggests an alternative interpretation of Bradley and Rosenzweig's empirical evidence; managers of economically inefficient firms, acting in the interest of equity

---

[5] In a Townsend (1979) costly state verification framework, Heinkel and Zechner (1991) demonstrate that deviations from the absolute priority rule, as in Chapter 11, can lead to value-increasing capital structure renegotiations. The basic problem in Heinkel and Zechner (1991) is that high-cash-flow firms have the incentive to mimic low-cash-flow firms in order to obtain debt forgiveness. However, in this article, the basic problem is that inefficient firms have the incentive to mimic efficient firms.

[6] See Bradley and Rosenzweig (1992) and Hotchkiss (1992).

[7] This point seems to have been missed by authors such as Bebchuk (1988), Bradley and Rosenzweig (1992), and Aghion, Hart, and Moore (1992) who seem to think that preserving absolute priority should be an inherently valued objective.

holders, choose the best of a set of bad alternatives, reorganization under Chapter 11.

The article is organized as follows: Section I presents the basic model of distressed firms when debt restructurings are not possible and bankrupt firms are liquidated, not reorganized. Section II permits public debt restructurings through exchange offers, which, given symmetric information, will always take the form of a senior debt for debt exchange offer. Section III models the public debt restructurings of distressed firms with asymmetric information. Debt holders are uninformed about whether the firm is economically efficient or inefficient. Bankrupt firms are liquidated. I find that economically efficient and inefficient firms are equally likely to continue or liquidate. In Section III, there is no separation of economically efficient firms from inefficient firms. In Sections IV and V, I review some important features of Chapter 11 bankruptcy reorganization law and analyze their effects on investment. Chapter 11 reorganization reduces the incentive for economically inefficient firms to mimic efficient firms in out-of-court debt restructurings. Section VI concludes and provides a discussion of the limitations of Chapter 11.

I. A Simple Model of a Distressed Firm

This section presents a simple model of a financially distressed firm with unsecured public debt. For now I assume that a firm cannot renegotiate its public debt. Because the firm cannot renegotiate its debt, debt holders have no avenue through which to influence liquidation and investment decisions. The remainder of the article allows for debt restructurings by means of exchange offers for public debt. However, I show in the next section that even allowing for exchange offers for public debt, public debt holders have very little, if any, influence over liquidation and investment decisions.

A firm has two assets at time 1: cash and/or liquid assets of value Y and a growth option or investment project which requires an investment of I at time 1. The liquid assets at time 1 can be used to meet current obligations to debt holders and/or to take advantage of the growth opportunity. The firm may or may not have sufficient liquid assets to do both at time 1. If the firm does not invest at time 1, the firm is liquidated. A proportion q, $q \in (0, 1)$, of the face value of the public debt, D, is due at time 1, and proportion $(1 - q)$ is due at time 2.

There are two types of firms, good and bad. The fraction λ are good firms and the fraction $1 - \lambda$ are bad firms, where $0 < \lambda < 1$. For a good firm the investment project returns cash flow of $X|g$ at time 2, and for a bad firm the project returns $X|b$ at time 2. The stochastic cash flow of $X|i$, $i \in \{b, g\}$, is distributed over the interval $[0, \infty)$. The density of $X|g$ is $f(X|g)$, and the density of $X|b$ is $f(X|b)$. Let $F(X|i)$ be the cumulative distribution function corresponding to the density $f(X|i)$. Cumulative distribution functions are ordered by the following first-order stochastic dominance (FOSD) relationship: g FOSD b. The mean of $X|i$ is $E(X|i)$, where $E(X|b) < I < E(X|g)$. Thus, it is efficient for good firms to invest at time 1, and efficient for bad firms to liquidate at time 1. I assume that if all firms invest, aggregate investment is zero net present value (NPV), i.e., $(1 - \lambda)E(X|b) + \lambda E(X|g) = I$. I assume the firm has no other assets such as plant or equipment, the riskless interest rate is zero, and all agents are risk neutral.

I assume the firm is in financial distress at time 1; as in Gertner and Scharfstein (1991), this is defined by liquid assets (representing all assets in place) that are worth less than the face value of the firm's total debt obligations, i.e., $Y < D$. If the firm is liquidated and if the absolute priority rules are observed, then public debt holders receive Y and equity holders receive nothing. In this section bankruptcy and liquidation are equivalent; there is no reorganization in bankruptcy.

The principal question of this article is whether a distressed firm, good or bad, invests in the project at time 1. Since the public debt cannot be restructured, the firm can only invest at time 1 if the firm has sufficient cash flow at time 1 to cover the cost of the investment and meet current obligations to creditors. Consequently, if $Y \geq I + qD$, the firm has sufficient cash flow to invest and meet current obligations at time 1. Equity has positive (option) value if the firm invests, but equity holders receive nothing if the firm is liquidated at time 1. Therefore, whether investment is efficient or inefficient, i.e., whether firm type is good or bad, the firm invests at time 1 given the conflict between debt and equity. Alternatively, if $Y < I + qD$, the firm has insufficient cash flow to invest and meet current obligations at time 1, and, by assumption, its debt cannot be restructured. Therefore, whether investment is efficient or inefficient, i.e., firm type is good or bad, the firm is liquidated at time 1. Liquidation and investment decisions depend on cash flow but are unrelated to investment efficiency.

II. Public Debt Restructurings with Symmetric Information

The remainder of this article allows the firm to renegotiate with public debt holders under the restrictions imposed by the Trust Indenture Act of 1939. The Trust Indenture Act requires that each public debt holder must agree to any change in the timing or amount of public debt payments made to him. A public debt holder may not be bound to a vote of public debt holders authorizing a change in the timing or amount of public debt payments. Therefore, public debt restructurings are modeled as, and do in practice take the form of, exchange offers. Firms may offer any combination of cash, debt, or equity in exchange for public debt.

The article now examines the effect of debt renegotiation on the investment inefficiencies described in Section I that occur when renegotiation is impossible. Each public debt holder's claim on the firm is assumed to be sufficiently small that he disregards the effect of his tender decision on both the firm's investment decision and on the value of the firm's securities. In making a tender decision, debt holders consider only the value of the claims offered relative to the value of the existing claims if all debt holders tender. Debt holders do not consider the value of the existing claims if no debt holders tender. Clearly this assumption may not apply to firms whose public debt is held by a small number of investors. However, this assumption allows for a simple exposition of the problems that arise when creditors cannot fully coordinate their actions.

I now address the principal question of this article, whether a distressed firm, good or bad, invests in the project at time 1. In Section I, a firm with a cash flow shortage at time 1 (i.e., a firm with insufficient cash flow to cover the cost of the investment and meet current obligations to creditors) must liquidate. In contrast, a firm with a cash flow shortage can now invest at time 1 if the firm can restructure its public debt.

Public debt holders decide whether to tender or reject the offer and retain the original claim on the firm based on the value of the claim offered relative to the value of the claim currently held conditional on the creditors' beliefs about the success of the offer. If other public debt holders are offered and accept pari passu or junior claims, holdouts benefit.[8] Suppose each public debt holder has a claim with a face value of $1, which is small relative to the total public debt outstanding. If other public debt holders tender, the holdout is paid q at time 1 and has a claim of equal priority or senior to the claim of the tendering public debt holders at time 2. On the other hand, suppose the firm offers senior debt.[9] The payment of q at time 1 is still effectively senior to all other claims; however, the holdouts have a junior claim at time 2.

If the firm makes a senior debt offer, the firm must offer senior claims worth at least qD to public debt holders in order for the offer to succeed. Therefore, as long as the firm value is greater than the firm's current obligations to debt holders, i.e., $Y + E(X|i) - I > qD$, $i \in \{b, g\}$, the firm can make a senior debt offer that public debt holders will accept. In fact, it follows from Gertner and Scharfstein (1991) that if $Y + E(X|i) - I > qD$, $i \in \{b, g\}$, the firm will offer to exchange senior debt for the public debt outstanding. The exchange is accepted by all debt holders and transfers wealth from debt holders to equity holders. Gertner and Scharfstein (1991) show that an offer of senior claims (as opposed to an offer of pari passu or junior claims) maximizes the wealth transfer from debt holders to equity holders.

With symmetric information, investment efficiency has some impact on the success of a debt restructuring. Investment efficiency affects firm value, which determines the success of an exchange offer. Since a successful exchange offer allows a firm to invest, investment bears some relationship to investment efficiency. However, inefficient firms, for which firm value is

---

[8] For earlier discussions of this holdout problem see Bulow and Shoven (1978), Allen (1985, 1986), Roe (1987), Coffee (1990), and Gertner and Scharfstein (1991).

[9] Even if the public debt indenture contains a seniority covenant, the covenant can be stripped through the use of an exit consent. For a discussion of exit consents see Roe (1987), Coffee (1990), or Gertner and Scharfstein (1991).

greater than current obligations to debt holders, successfully restructure their debt and invest, and efficient firms for which firm value is less than current obligations to debt holders cannot restructure their debt and liquidate.

III. Public Debt Restructurings with Uninformed Debt Holders

In this section I allow both the collective action problem discussed above and an information asymmetry to affect investment efficiency. I assume that public debt holders do not know a priori firm type and hence whether investment at time 1 is efficient. While management knows its own firm type, public debt holders know only the distribution of firm types. Debt holders' (common) prior belief is that fraction λ are good firms and $(1 - \lambda)$ are bad firms, and $(1 - \lambda)E(X|b) + \lambda E(X|g) = I$. Given public debt holders' prior beliefs, firm value is Y. Since investment efficiency is independent of public debt holders' prior beliefs about firm value, the success of a debt restructuring is unrelated to investment efficiency unless efficient firms can separate from inefficient firms. Therefore, without separation, a firm's liquidation and investment decisions are unrelated to investment efficiency.

A perfect Bayesian equilibrium (PBE) of this game consists of strategies (offers to renegotiate with debt holders) for a firm as a function of firm type, a strategy for public debt (accept or reject the offer as a function of its beliefs), and a specification of public debt holders' beliefs (as a function of any possible exchange offer). I also use the refinement of PBE developed by Farrell (1983) and Grossman and Perry (1986), which restricts public debt holders' beliefs should they receive an out-of-equilibrium offer.[10] The refinement requires that there are no deviations with consistent interpretations.

I assume that the firm has sufficient cash flow at time 1 to invest, i.e., $Y > I$. Hence, a firm that renegotiates with debt holders at time 1 has sufficient cash flow to invest at time 1. In this section, I maintain the assumption that if the firm does not invest at time 1, the firm is liquidated at time 1. The firm always prefers to invest at time 1 rather than liquidate, since equity has option value if the firm invests. In a liquidation, public debt holders have claims of D regardless of any negotiation with debt holders the firm may attempt just before the firm liquidates at time 1.[11] Since $Y < D$, equity holders receive nothing in a liquidation.

Firms that have cash flow, Y, greater than current obligations, qD, at time 1 and those that have cash flow less than current obligations at time 1 are

---

[10] See Gertner (1991) and Gertner, Gibbons, and Scharfstein (1988) for a discussion of this refinement.

[11] See "Financially Troubled Firms Get More Freedom to Restructure Debts," *Wall Street Journal* p. B11, April 16, 1992, which reports the reversal of the LTV decision. If a firm undertakes a debt restructuring and subsequently files for bankruptcy, creditors may make a claim for the face value of the debt before the restructuring.

examined in turn. Unless the firm can signal its true type to the public debt holders, the debt holders believe expected firm value is identical to cash flow Y since by assumption $\lambda E(X|g) + (1 - \lambda)E(X|b) = I$. Therefore, for $Y > qD$, public debt holders believe (a priori) firm value is greater than the firm's current obligations at time 1; and for $Y < qD$, public debt holders believe (a priori) firm value is less than the firm's current obligations.

A. Current Obligations Exceed Cash Flow

Suppose that current obligations, qD, exceed cash flow, Y, at time 1. If the firm invests at time 1, the value of a good firm is $Y - I + E(X|g)$ and the value of a bad firm is $Y - I + E(X|b)$. Since $Y < qD$ and $E(X|b) < I$, $Y - I + E(X|b) < qD$. Whether the firm renegotiates with public debt holders at time 1 depends on the debt holders' beliefs about firm type and therefore their beliefs about firm value.

Unless debt holders believe firm value is at least qD, the firm cannot renegotiate with public debt holders. To see that this is a necessary condition, suppose debt holders believe firm value is less than qD at time 1, and each debt holder has a claim with face value $1. For any offer the firm makes to public debt holders, holdouts receive at least $q at time 1, which is greater than the value of any security that the firm could offer with a payoff at time 2. Debt holders will hold out, since each debt holder is better off with $q at time 1 rather than a claim on cash flow at time 2 that is worth less than $q regardless of the tendering decisions of other debt holders.[12]

If $Y - I + E(X|g) < qD$, then even if the public debt holders believe the firm is good with probability 1, the firm is liquidated at time 1. Since debt holders know firm value is less than qD for all firms, debt holders will not accept any offer from the firm to renegotiate.

If $Y - I + E(X|g) > qD$, there is no pooling equilibrium in which both types of firms renegotiate and invest and no separating equilibrium in which at least one type of firm renegotiates and invests at time 1. To see that there is no pooling equilibrium in which both types of firms renegotiate and invest, suppose bad firms are pooled with good firms. Since $Y < qD$, public debt holders will not accept any offer from the firm to renegotiate unless the offer reveals the firm is a good firm. Furthermore, there cannot be a separating equilibrium in which a good firm renegotiates with debt holders and a bad firm liquidates, since bad firms would always mimic good firms. Since $Y - I + E(X|b) < qD$, bad firms are liquidated in any separating equilibrium and equity value is zero. Good firms for which $Y - I + E(X|g) > qD$ cannot credibly convey their firm type, because bad firms always have the incentive to mimic any offer the good firms make.[13]

---

[12] Since firm value is less than qD, each debt holder who tenders has a claim worth less than $qD/D = q$.

[13] This is in contrast with models presented in Brown, James, and Mooradian (1993) or Gertner (1991). In these models bad firms have an incentive to signal their type in order to reduce the uninformed debt holder's reservation value in a debt renegotiation. These models assume no coordination problem among debt holders.

For $Y < qD$, the only equilibrium that exists is one in which all firms liquidate at time 1.

PROPOSITION 1: *When current obligations exceed cash flow, both good and bad firms liquidate at time 1.*

Proof: See Appendix.

For $Y < qD$, where $Y - I + E(X|g) > qD$ or $Y - I + E(X|g) < qD$, the firm cannot renegotiate with debt holders. Debt holders receive Y and equity holders receive nothing. This outcome is efficient for a bad firm but inefficient for a good firm.

First-best investment implies that all good firms invest and all bad firms liquidate at time 1. Aggregating over all firms, first-best investment at time 1 implies a NPV of $(E(X|g) - I)\lambda N$, where N is the total number of firms and λ is the proportion of good firms. Therefore, the social opportunity loss from the outcome that all firms liquidate at time 1 is $(E(X|g) - I)\lambda N$, where $E(X|g) - I > 0$. The social opportunity loss results from the fact that all good firms forego an economically efficient investment opportunity.

The result that all firms for which $Y < qD$ are liquidated depends on both the imperfect coordination among debt holders and the information asymmetry. Without the information asymmetry good firms could successfully renegotiate with public debt and invest at time 1 if $Y - I + E(X|g) > qD$. However, if $Y - I + E(X|g) < qD$, without the information asymmetry but because of the imperfect coordination among debt holders, good firms could not renegotiate with public debt and would be liquidated even though a liquidation is inefficient.

B. Current Obligations Less than Cash Flow

Now suppose that current obligations, qD, are less than cash flow, Y, at time 1. If the firm invests at time 1, the value of a good firm is $Y - I + E(X|g)$ and the value of a bad firm is $Y - I + E(X|b)$. Since $Y > qD$ and $E(X|g) > I$, $Y - I + E(X|g) > qD$. Whether the firm renegotiates with public debt holders at time 1 depends on the debt holders' beliefs about firm type and therefore their beliefs about firm value. If the public debt holders believe the firm is worth $Y > qD$, the firm can make an offer that public debt holders accept, which allows the firm to invest at time 1. The firm can offer senior claims that debt holders believe to be worth at least qD, and therefore the firm can offer senior claims that public debt holders prefer to their existing claims.

If $Y - I + E(X|b) > qD$, then even if the public debt holders believe the firm is bad with probability 1, the debt is renegotiated and the firm invests at time 1. Since debt holders know firm value is greater than qD for all firms, the firm can renegotiate with debt holders.

If $Y - I + E(X|b) < qD$, there cannot be a separating equilibrium in which a good firm renegotiates with debt holders and a bad firm liquidates. Since $Y - I + E(X|b) < qD$, bad firms are liquidated in any separating equilibrium and equity value is zero. Good firms for which $Y - I + E(X|g) > qD$ cannot credibly convey their firm type, because bad firms always have the incentive to mimic any offer good firms make.

If $Y - I + E(X|b) < qD$, there does not exist an equilibrium in which both good and bad firms are liquidated. To see that this would not satisfy the refinement because there is a pooling-consistent deviation, consider public debt holder beliefs that a firm that deviates (a firm that makes an offer) is good with probability λ and bad with probability $1 - \lambda$. Given debt holder beliefs and the assumption that $(1 - \lambda)E(X|b) + \lambda E(X|g) = I$, debt holders believe that a firm making an offer has value Y. Because $Y > qD$, all firms can make an offer that debt holders will accept. Since the firms are not liquidated, equity value is positive rather than zero, i.e., equity holders of either firm type are better off. Therefore, there is a deviation with a consistent interpretation.

For firms in which $Y > qD$ and $Y - I + E(X|b) < qD$, there are no separating equilibria and no equilibria in which both good and bad firms liquidate. However, there exists a pooling equilibrium in which firms of either type renegotiate and invest. To see this, suppose bad firms are pooled with good firms. Since $Y > qD$, given debt holder beliefs that the firm is good with probability λ, the firm is able to renegotiate with public debt holders. The debt will be renegotiated and the firm will invest at time 1.

PROPOSITION 2: *When current obligations are less than cash flow, both good and bad firms renegotiate and invest at time* 1.

Proof: See Appendix.

For $Y > qD$, whether $Y - I + E(X|b) > qD$ or $Y - I + E(X|b) < qD$, all firms regardless of firm type renegotiate with debt holders and invest at time 1. For good firms, investment is efficient. But for bad firms, liquidation is efficient. Bad firms overinvest. Therefore, the social opportunity loss from the outcome that all firms invest at time 1 is $(I - E(X|b))(1 - \lambda)N$, where $I - E(X|b) > 0$. The social opportunity loss results from the fact that all bad firms make an inefficient investment.

Both types of firms invest because of the imperfect coordination among debt holders and because of the information asymmetry. Without the information asymmetry bad firms could not successfully renegotiate with public debt and invest at time 1 if $Y - I + E(X|b) < qD$. However, if $Y - I + E(X|b) > qD$, without the information asymmetry but because of the imperfect coordination among debt holders, the bad firms could still renegotiate with public debt and invest even though investment is inefficient.

C. Discussion

Bad firms can either liquidate or mimic good firms. Since equity value is zero in a liquidation, the reservation value of a bad firm is zero. Bad firms forego nothing to mimic good firms.

The relationship between cash flow and current obligations determines whether the firm liquidates or renegotiates and invests. Since bad firms will always mimic the good firms whenever liquidation is the alternative, good firms cannot credibly signal their type. Debt holders learn nothing about firm type or firm value from offers to renegotiate. Moreover, debt holders' a priori belief about firm value is equivalent to cash flow. Since debt holders will accept an offer to renegotiate if they believe firm value is greater than current obligations, the firm can renegotiate if cash flow is greater than current obligations. Firms that are insolvent on a flow basis are liquidated.

First-best investment requires that good firms invest and bad firms liquidate at time 1. However, firms liquidate if and only if they are insolvent on a flow basis. Therefore, the social opportunity loss is $(E(X|g) - I)\lambda N$ if $Y < qD$, and $(I - E(X|b))(1 - \lambda)N$ if $Y > qD$. Insolvent good firms forego efficient investment, and solvent bad firms undertake inefficient investment.

Even though I permit debt restructurings by means of exchange offers for public debt, given asymmetric information, liquidation and investment decisions are unrelated to investment efficiency. In fact, the investment inefficiencies in this section are the same kind of inefficiencies described in Section I that occur when renegotiation is impossible.

IV. Chapter 11 Reorganization and Investment

In order to analyze the effect of Chapter 11 bankruptcy reorganization on the restructuring, liquidation, and investment of financially distressed firms, I modify the model presented in Section III to permit Chapter 11 reorganization at time 1. The essence of the model's insights are best conveyed using a simplified characterization of the bankruptcy game, which is presented here. However, these simplifications are in no way central to the results. For the interested reader, I provide a more detailed description of Chapter 11 and a more rigorous treatment of the bargaining in Chapter 11 in Section V.

In this section I take the outcome of the bankruptcy process as given and model the choice to renegotiate outside Chapter 11 or file for Chapter 11. In doing so, I assume two general results from both theoretical and empirical work[14] in this area. First, a Chapter 11 reorganization results in the maintenance of equity value. Equity holders receive valuable claims on the reorganized firm even though creditor claims are not satisfied in full. Second, management does not follow an investment policy (detrimental to debt holders) that maximizes equity value. In fact, Lopucki and Whitford (1992) find that 1) management does not expand into new lines of business, expand existing business, or engage in high-risk activity that would favor equity holders in Chapter 11, and 2) management avoids any quick liquidations of major assets that would favor senior debt holders in Chapter 11.

---

[14] See Franks and Torous (1989), Eberhart, Moore, and Roenfeldt (1990), Weiss (1990), and LoPucki and Whitford (1992).

Investment policy and the maintenance of equity value in Chapter 11 are related. The Bankruptcy Code promotes bargaining in Chapter 11 among management, equity holders, and debt holders and effectively defines the bargaining position of each group. To the extent that management's incentives are tied to equity holders' payoff in Chapter 11, management acts on their behalf.[15] Franks and Torous (1994) find that equity holders' payoff in Chapter 11 depends on the extent to which equity holders can bargain on their own behalf and the extent to which management bargains with debt holders on behalf of equity holders. Furthermore, a major source of management bargaining power is its control over investment policy. Thus, investment policy as well as the reallocation of claims on the firm are subject to bargaining in Chapter 11. Management may trade off an investment policy more favorable to creditors for a larger claim on the firm for equity holders. In this section, the results of the bargaining are taken as given; however, in Section V I endogenize the bargaining in Chapter 11.

For now, I assume that the bargaining in Chapter 11 allows stockholders to retain some valuable equity in the firm. The stockholders of an inefficient firm forego the equity in the firm that they can extract in Chapter 11 if the firm mimics an efficient firm's offer to debt holders in a debt restructuring, because the offer determines the stockholders' residual value. Inefficient firms voluntarily file for bankruptcy. Although inefficient firms reorganize in Chapter 11, liquidation is optimal. However, management gives up its bargaining power if it liquidates immediately. Therefore, I assume an investment policy that is inefficient but not completely in equity holders' interest. In Section V, investment policy is endogenized, which enables a discussion of the efficiency of investment in Chapter 11.

The maintenance of equity value in Chapter 11 and investment in Chapter 11 are defined as follows: first, the cost of investment in Chapter 11 is I at time 1. However, the present value of investment is equal to $\{\alpha(E(X|i)) + (1 - \alpha)I\}$, where $i \in \{b, g\}$ and $0 < \alpha < 1$. For both good and bad firms, investment in Chapter 11 results in an opportunity loss. For good firms the opportunity loss is $(1 - \alpha)(E(X|g) - I)$, and for bad firms the opportunity loss is $\alpha(I - E(X|b))$. Second, the equity holders' share of a firm reorganized in Chapter 11 depends on the reorganization plan that is confirmed. I assume that the expected value of the equity claims of a bankrupt firm at time 1 are $E^i_{file} > 0$, $i \in \{b, g\}$, where E^i_{file} is a function of firm type, cash flow at time 1, and the face value of the debt outstanding at time 1.[16]

The alternative to a Chapter 11 filing is to renegotiate with debt holders outside Chapter 11. Let π_i, $i \in \{b, g\}$, be the face value of the senior debt that must be offered (for each unit of debt outstanding) to creditors who believe

---

[15] In practice, management may not always act on behalf of equity holders. Gilson and Vetsuypens (1993) provide evidence of distressed firms in which CEO compensation is tied to creditor payoffs.

[16] The assumption is consistent with Betker (1992) who finds that deviations from absolute priority in favor of equity in Chapter 11 are significantly lower the more insolvent the firm.

firm type is i with probability 1. Let π_p be the face value of the senior debt that must be offered to creditors who believe firm type is good with probability λ. Let $E^i_{\pi_p}$, $i \in \{b, g\}$, be the value of the equity of a type i firm that 1) renegotiates (i.e., makes a senior debt for debt exchange offer) with debt holders, who believe the firm to be good with probability λ and 2) invests at time 1. Let $E^i_{\pi_j}$, $i, j \in \{b, g\}$, be the value of the equity of a type i firm that 1) renegotiates (i.e., makes a senior debt for debt exchange offer) with debt holders who believe the firm to be type j with probability 1 and 2) invests at time 1. It follows that

$$E^g_{\pi_p} = \int_{\pi_p D - Y + I}^{\infty} (X - \pi_p D + Y - I) f(X|g) \, dX, \tag{1}$$

and

$$E^g_{\pi_g} = \int_{\pi_g D - Y + I}^{\infty} (X - \pi_g D + Y - I) f(X|g) \, dX. \tag{2}$$

To induce separation of firm types, a necessary condition is that good firms prefer to renegotiate with debt holders outside Chapter 11 rather than file for bankruptcy. For simplicity, I assume[17] that

$$E^g_{file} = \min\{E^g_{\pi_p}, E^g_{\pi_g}\} \tag{3}$$

and that if good firms are indifferent between 1) filing for bankruptcy and 2) renegotiating with debt holders and investing, good firms will renegotiate and invest if debt holders will accept their offer.

At time 1, the firm may now 1) renegotiate with debt holders and invest, 2) file for Chapter 11 bankruptcy and invest in Chapter 11, or 3) liquidate. Since the firm has the option to file for Chapter 11 bankruptcy at time 1, equity value is positive in Chapter 11, and equity value is zero in a liquidation, the firm will never choose immediate liquidation at time 1. Therefore, the remaining discussion only considers the choice between an informal reorganization (renegotiating and investing at time 1) and a Chapter 11 filing. In order to analyze the effect of Chapter 11 reorganization on investment, as in Section III, I divide firms into two categories: those that have cash flow, Y, greater than current obligations, qD, at time 1 and those that have cash flow less than current obligations at time 1.

A. *Current Obligations Exceed Cash Flow*

Suppose that current obligations, qD, exceed cash flow, Y, at time 1. Unless debt holders believe firm value is at least qD, the firm cannot renegotiate

---

[17] I relax this assumption in Section V.

with debt holders. As shown in the previous section, holdouts are always better off than debt holders who tender regardless of the offer to debt holders.

If $Y - I + E(X|g) < qD$, then, even if the public debt holders believe the firm is good with probability 1, the firm cannot renegotiate with debt holders. Since debt holders know firm value is less than qD for all firms, the firm files for bankruptcy at time 1 and invests in Chapter 11 regardless of whether the firm is good or bad.

Now let $Y - I + E(X|g) > qD$. There is no pooling equilibrium in which both types of firms renegotiate and invest at time 1. Since $Y < qD$, given beliefs that the firm is good with probability λ, debt holders will not accept any offer from the firm to renegotiate.

PROPOSITION 3: *Let $Y < qD$ and $Y - I + E(X|g) > qD$. Then at time 1 either 1) there exists a separating equilibrium in which good firms renegotiate and invest and bad firms file for bankruptcy, or 2) all firms file for bankruptcy.*

Proof: See Appendix.

Given equation (3), good firms are at least as well off renegotiating and investing at time 1 as they are filing for bankruptcy. Therefore, there exists a separating equilibrium if bad firms are better off filing for bankruptcy than mimicking the offer good firms make to debt holders. Chapter 11 permits the maintenance of equity value (which was absent in Section III) and consequently increases equity holders' reservation value in a debt restructuring. Furthermore, the reservation value of the equity holders of a bad firm may now be greater than their expected payoff from mimicking good firms.

Let $Y < qD$. If $Y - I + E(X|g) > qD$ and bad firms prefer to file rather than mimic good firms, only bad firms file for Chapter 11. Good firms make efficient investment decisions at time 1 but bad firms invest in Chapter 11 at time 1. Bad firms overinvest. Therefore, the social opportunity loss is $\alpha\{(I - E(X|b))(1 - \lambda)N\}$. However, if $Y - I + E(X|g) < qD$ or bad firms prefer to mimic good firms, all firms file for bankruptcy and invest in Chapter 11. The social opportunity loss is $(1 - \alpha)(E(X|g) - I)\lambda N + \alpha(I - E(X|b))(1 - \lambda)N$. This differs from the social opportunity loss of $(E(X|g) - I)\lambda N$ without Chapter 11 in Section III. Recall that without Chapter 11, all firms are liquidated immediately. Thus, for $Y < qD$, Chapter 11 increases investment. Either all firms invest in Chapter 11 or good firms renegotiate and invest outside Chapter 11 and bad firms invest in Chapter 11.

B. *Current Obligations Less than Cash Flow*

Now suppose that $Y > qD$ at time 1. Recall that if debt holders believe firm value is at least qD, the firm can renegotiate with debt holders. However, the maintenance of equity value in Chapter 11 provides an incentive for bad firms to file. Whether there is a separating equilibrium in which bad firms file for bankruptcy that satisfies the refinement depends on whether bad firms prefer to file for bankruptcy or renegotiate and invest at time 1.

PROPOSITION 4: *Let $Y > qD$. Then at time 1 either* 1) *there exists a separating equilibrium in which good firms renegotiate and invest and bad firms file for bankruptcy or* 2) *all firms renegotiate and invest.*

Proof: See Appendix.

If bad firms prefer to file for bankruptcy, there exists a separating equilibrium. Given equation (3), good firms are at least as well off renegotiating and investing at time 1 as they are filing for bankruptcy, but bad firms are better off filing for bankruptcy than mimicking the offer good firms make to debt holders. However, if bad firms prefer to renegotiate and invest at time 1, all firms renegotiate and invest rather than file for bankruptcy. Moreover, given $Y > qD$, there exists an offer that debt holders will accept.

For $Y > qD$, good firms make efficient investment decisions at time 1, but bad firms overinvest. It is efficient for bad firms to liquidate immediately, but bad firms either invest in Chapter 11 or renegotiate and invest at time 1.

For $Y > qD$, the social opportunity loss is either $\alpha\{(I - E(X|b))(1 - \lambda)N\}$ or $(I - E(X|b))(1 - \lambda)N$. Good firms renegotiate and invest at time 1, but bad firms either invest in Chapter 11 or renegotiate and invest at time 1. However, recall that all firms renegotiate and invest at time 1 without Chapter 11 in Section III. The social opportunity loss without Chapter 11 is $(I - E(X|b))(1 - \lambda)N$. Thus, for $Y > qD$, Chapter 11 reduces overinvestment.

C. Discussion

The model illustrates the effect of public debt restructurings and bankruptcy law on investment by financially distressed firms. If public debt holders cannot fully coordinate their actions and cannot observe whether investment is efficient, investment is not first-best for all financially distressed firms. Under a bankruptcy law that liquidates bankrupt firms and applies the absolute priority rule strictly, efficient financially distressed firms, i.e., firms for which investment is efficient, cannot credibly convey their type. Inefficient distressed firms, i.e., firms for which liquidation is efficient, always have the incentive to mimic efficient firms because equity holders of distressed firms receive nothing in a liquidation. However, Chapter 11 reorganization permits the equity holders of inefficient firms to receive valuable claims on the reorganized firm, which reduces the incentive for inefficient firms to mimic efficient firms.

Given bankruptcy law without Chapter 11 reorganization, efficient and inefficient firms invest or liquidate in equal proportions. However, to the extent that Chapter 11 makes possible separation by firm type, there is a broader range of parameter values in which 1) efficient firms renegotiate with debt holders and invest and 2) inefficient firms file for bankruptcy.

Bankruptcy law with Chapter 11 permits the maintenance of equity value. To the extent that the maintenance of equity value induces separation, efficient financially distressed firms avoid bankruptcy and investment efficiency improves for efficient firms. However, if one considers only inefficient firms, neither bankruptcy law with Chapter 11 nor bankruptcy law without Chapter 11 improves efficiency. With Chapter 11, a larger proportion of inefficient firms file for bankruptcy, but firms in Chapter 11 delay liquidations.

The most important empirical prediction of this model is that a larger proportion of distressed firms in Chapter 11 are inefficient rather than efficient. Although this does not imply that bankruptcy law without Chapter 11 dominates bankruptcy law with Chapter 11, the prediction does suggest that maintaining equity value in bankruptcy but reducing the incentive for firms to delay liquidations enhances efficiency.

To gain a better understanding of how investment in Chapter 11 differs across firm type and the extent to which the maintenance of equity value in Chapter 11 induces separation by firm type, I present a simple model of Chapter 11 in the next section of this article. In this model, management has some discretion over investment in Chapter 11. Moreover, debt holders may now bargain with management over investment policy as well as over the reorganization plan.

V. The Model of Chapter 11

In this section, I provide a model of Chapter 11 in the context of the analysis presented thus far. I analyze the bargaining and investment in Chapter 11 given the alternative of a renegotiation outside Chapter 11. I find that the more inefficient the investment of the firm, the more likely the firm voluntarily chooses to file for bankruptcy rather than mimic efficient firms in a renegotiation outside Chapter 11. Given a larger investment inefficiency, the surplus over which claim holders bargain in Chapter 11 is larger. This implies that management, on behalf of equity holders, is more likely to trade off a reduction in overinvestment for a larger claim on the firm for equity holders in a Chapter 11 reorganization. Chapter 11 reduces overinvestment for bad firms that file for Chapter 11 and allows more good firms to renegotiate with debt holders outside Chapter 11, reducing underinvestment.

This section proceeds as follows: Section V.A provides a description of the Chapter 11 process. In Section V.B, I examine management's choice to enter Chapter 11 and the bargaining in Chapter 11 and discuss the implications of Chapter 11 pertaining to investment efficiency.

A. A Summary of the Chapter 11 Process

The legislative intent of Chapter 11 of the Bankruptcy Code is to avoid the inefficient liquidation of distressed firms and to promote the reorganization of economically viable firms as ongoing concerns. In contrast to Chapter 7 of the Bankruptcy Code, in which a trustee is appointed to undertake immediate liquidation, filing for bankruptcy under Chapter 11 allows for a renegotiation between equity and debt holders over the allocation of claims on the firm.

Moreover, the Bankruptcy Code defines each claim holder's rights, which establishes the threat points under which the negotiation takes place.[18]

The Bankruptcy Code permits management to remain in control of the debtor firm in Chapter 11 bankruptcy and allows management considerable power to initiate the reorganization plan. The Bankruptcy Code defines a period in which management has an exclusive right to propose a plan of reorganization.[19] Management may threaten to delay the reorganization and reduce the value of creditor claims.[20] Moreover, management determines investment policy, subject to court review.[21]

The Bankruptcy Code grants the court considerable power to impose a settlement of claims in Chapter 11. However, except in extreme cases (see LoPucki and Whitford (1992), Franks and Torous (1989), or Eberhart, Moore, and Roenfeldt (1990)), the court promotes bargaining among claim holders to reach a consensual reorganization plan. Bargaining and settlement rather than adjudication determines the outcome of a Chapter 11 reorganization.

Although the Bankruptcy Code restricts some creditor rights in Chapter 11, creditors do acquire additional rights in Chapter 11 and derive considerable bargaining leverage from the requirement that each creditor committee must consent to the reorganization plan.[22] The automatic stay effectively extends the maturity of all outstanding debt. However, creditors can object to management's investment decisions and request court intervention. Creditors can request that the court remove management and appoint a trustee, and can request that the court require immediate liquidation. While creditors can move for court intervention, creditors also bargain directly with management. Since management needs creditor approval of a reorganization plan,[23] creditors, in practice, can exert considerable influence over investment policy as well as over the reorganization plan (see LoPucki and Whitford (1992)). Bargaining over the reorganization plan induces and interacts with bargaining over investment policy.

The Bankruptcy Code requires that a reorganization plan be approved by each class of claimants, with approval of a two-thirds majority of the securities required within the class. In Chapter 11, the voting mechanism forces a minority to exchange their debt. All debt holders are treated the same regardless of their vote. Public debt holders accept a plan of reorganization if and only if it is in the debt holders' collective interest. With one class of debt holders, in contrast to outside Chapter 11, there is no coordination problem in Chapter 11. Therefore, as in Bebchuk and Chang (1992), Baird and Picker (1991), and Brown (1989), I assume that public debt holders act as a single agent in Chapter 11.

---

[18] Brown (1989) and Baird and Picker (1991) provide models of the negotiation in Chapter 11.
[19] Bankruptcy Code (11 U.S.C.) §1121(d).
[20] See Bergman and Callen (1991).
[21] Bankruptcy Code (11 U.S.C.) §§1107(a) and 1108.
[22] The only exception to this requirement is a costly cramdown, Bankruptcy Code (11 U.S.C.) §1129(b).
[23] Bankruptcy Code (11 U.S.C.) §1126.

B. Management's Decision to Enter Chapter 11

In this section, I focus on the following fundamental aspects of Chapter 11. First, the automatic stay, together with management control of the debtor firm, grants equity "option value." Management can invest in Chapter 11, and equity captures the "upside" to the investment. The "option value" defines equity's threat point in the renegotiation. Second, if the management of an inefficient firm invests in Chapter 11, investment reduces the value of the firm and hence reduces the value of creditor claims. Management (acting on behalf of equity holders) can reduce investment and save the cost of overinvestment in exchange for a share of the savings (for equity holders). Moreover, if creditors believe that investment reduces the value of the firm, creditors agree to share the cost savings with equity holders. Thus, the surplus over which management (on behalf of equity holders) and creditors bargain in Chapter 11 is the savings from reducing overinvestment.[24] Finally, although creditors possess countervailing power, management derives bargaining power from its considerable power of initiation and control over investment policy. Therefore, I define γ as the maximum proportion of the surplus that management can capture for equity in a renegotiation with creditors, where $0 < \gamma \leq 1$.

In Chapter 11, I assume that there is an initial period before bargaining takes place between management and debt holders. In this initial period, debt holders organize in order to act as a single creditor once bargaining begins. Moreover, management operates the firm under court supervision. I assume that management must decide whether to invest before Chapter 11 bargaining begins. Management will invest because equity value is zero given an immediate liquidation. The cost of the investment is I. The present value of the investment is $\{\alpha(E(X|i)) + (1 - \alpha)I\}$, where $i \in \{b, g\}$ and $0 < \alpha < 1$. However, management may alter the investment after bargaining with creditors begins; management has discretion over α, where $0 < \alpha \leq \bar{\alpha} < 1$. For a firm in Chapter 11, the only investment choice variable is α. Increasing α increases option value and increases the value of a good firm, but decreases the value of a bad firm.

For a firm in Chapter 11, equity's reservation value is its option value, and management maximizes option value if it selects $\alpha = \bar{\alpha}$. Therefore, equity's reservation value[25] is

$$R(i) = \int_{D-Y+\bar{\alpha}I}^{\infty} (\bar{\alpha}X - D + Y - \bar{\alpha}I)f(X|i)\,dX, \quad i \in \{b, g\}. \qquad (4)$$

If creditors believe that a firm is good with probability 1, they believe investment in Chapter 11 increases firm value. Moreover, if creditors believe

---

[24] This is similar to Bebchuk and Chang (1992) and Bergman and Callen (1991).

[25] In this section, I do not assume equation (3). I no longer assume that good firms prefer to renegotiate with debt holders outside Chapter 11 rather than file for bankruptcy. Good firms may choose to file.

that a firm is good with probability λ (creditors' prior beliefs), by assumption[26] they believe investment in Chapter 11 has no effect on firm value. Creditors believe that there is no surplus over which they may bargain with management. No renegotiation takes place and equation (4) defines equity's payoff in Chapter 11.

If management can credibly convey that the firm is bad, then creditors believe that there is a surplus over which to bargain. The surplus is $(1 - \alpha)(I - E(X|b))$ and is maximized if management chooses $\alpha \to 0$. Therefore, given management bargaining power of γ, equity's payoff in a renegotiation is a fixed payoff (since the firm is effectively liquidated), F, such that

$$F = R(b) + \gamma(I - E(X|b)). \tag{5}$$

The first term of equation (5) is equity's reservation value, and the second term represents equity's share of the surplus.

Given equations (4) and (5), bad firms will not mimic good firms in Chapter 11 since bad firms only get more than their reservation value, $R(b)$, if they credibly signal their true type. However, good firms mimic bad firms if equity's share of the surplus is sufficiently large, i.e., if the fixed payoff, F, in a Chapter 11 renegotiation is larger than the largest alternative payoff to the equity holders of a good firm. A good firm's alternatives are its reservation value in Chapter 11, $R(g)$, and the value of the equity of a good firm that renegotiates outside of Chapter 11, $E^g_{\pi_R}$. To credibly convey its true type, a bad firm cannot propose a reorganization plan in Chapter 11 that gives equity more than a good firm's largest alternative payoff. Therefore, a bad firm selects $\alpha \to 0$ and offers a reorganization plan in which equity's payoff is

$$E^b_{file} = \min\left\{\max\left\{R(g), E^g_{\pi_R}\right\}, F\right\}. \tag{6}$$

Creditors accept such an offer because they believe that the firm is bad and that the offer will accomplish an increase in the value of the creditors' claims.

If bad firms choose to file for bankruptcy, equity's payoff is E^b_{file}. However, bad firms must first choose whether to file for bankruptcy or mimic good firms outside bankruptcy. As the surplus going to equity in a bankruptcy increases, E^b_{file} increases until it equals $\max\{R(g), E^g_{\pi_R}\}$. Since $E^b_{\pi_g}$, the payoff to a bad firm that mimics a good firm in a renegotiation outside Chapter 11, is strictly less than $E^g_{\pi_R}$ given FOSD, bad firms prefer to file.

PROPOSITION 5: *A sufficient condition for the existence of an equilibrium in which bad firms are liquidated (though not immediately) in Chapter 11 and good firms invest either in Chapter 11 or outside Chapter 11 is that the equity value of a bad firm that files for bankruptcy is greater than the equity value of a bad firm that mimics a good firm in a renegotiation outside Chapter 11.*

Proof: See Appendix.

If bad firms choose to file for bankruptcy, investment efficiency improves since management agrees to liquidate in Chapter 11 when creditors agree to

---

[26] Recall the assumption that $\lambda E(X|g) + (1 - \lambda)E(X|b) = I$.

an equity payoff of E^b_{file}. Chapter 11 reduces bad-firm overinvestment. Moreover, good firms either renegotiate and invest outside Chapter 11 or invest in Chapter 11. For a good firm, investment outside Chapter 11 is efficient, but investment is inefficient inside Chapter 11 since $\bar{a}$ is less than 1. However, to the extent that good firms invest (inside or outside Chapter 11) rather than liquidate, Chapter 11 reduces good-firm underinvestment.

Bad firms are more likely to choose to file for bankruptcy, the larger the surplus that the bad firm equity holders can capture in Chapter 11. Equity's payoff in bankruptcy in excess of its reservation value is a function of equity's bargaining power, γ, and the magnitude of the total surplus, $I - E(X|b)$. Taking equity's bargaining power as given, whether bad firms voluntarily file for bankruptcy is directly related to the absolute value of the NPV (NPV < 0) of the investment. Therefore, bad firms are more likely to choose to file for bankruptcy, the more inefficient the investment.

C. Discussion

The model assumes frictionless bargaining always occurs in Chapter 11 and, as a result, Chapter 11 brings about the liquidation of inefficient firms. In practice, Chapter 11 does not typically result in liquidation. However, whether Chapter 11 brings about liquidation is unimportant in making the point that Chapter 11 induces voluntary filing for bankruptcy by inefficient firms.

In the absence of Chapter 11, some inefficient investment takes place that does not take place when Chapter 11 is available. Even though the firm is allowed to continue in Chapter 11, the preservation of equity value means that the firm will avoid risky investment activity that it would otherwise undertake. Chapter 11 results in a shift in investment policy away from high-risk activity (see LoPucki and Whitford (1992)) and allows shareholders to retain valuable equity in the firm. Furthermore, as long as equity holders extract a share of the surplus from avoiding inefficient investment in Chapter 11, inefficient firms have a greater incentive to file for bankruptcy than efficient firms.

VI. Concluding Discussion

A. Private versus Public Debt

In this section I will comment on the assumption in the model that all debt is public and diffusely held. The assumption motivates the focus on exchange offers with their associated free-rider problems. In the model, public debt holders cannot fully coordinate their actions. However, for a firm with a single creditor, there is no coordination problem.

Given a well-informed private creditor, there are no restrictions on out-of-court restructurings. Private creditors can distinguish between economically efficient and inefficient firms. Given the gain from allowing an efficient firm to invest, private creditors renegotiate with an economically efficient firm and the firm invests. Moreover, to the extent that an inefficient firm can invest without renegotiating with the private creditor outside bankruptcy, the private creditor renegotiates with the firm and the firm liquidates. In general, investment is efficient, regardless of the bankruptcy law, as long as the firm can renegotiate with the well-informed private creditor outside bankruptcy.

If the private creditor is uninformed, then (in the absence of Chapter 11) renegotiation, investment, and liquidation depend on the creditor's prior beliefs about investment efficiency and the extent to which the firm can invest without renegotiating with the creditor outside bankruptcy. If the firm has sufficient cash flow to meet current debt obligations and invest, the firm renegotiates with the creditor if there is a surplus over which the creditors can bargain. If the firm is inefficient, the surplus is equal to the reduction in firm value if the firm invests. The inefficient firm renegotiates with the creditor and liquidates. If the firm is efficient, there is no renegotiation and the firm invests. Therefore, if the firm has sufficient cash flow to meet current debt obligations and invest, investment is first-best.

If the firm must renegotiate with the creditor in order to invest, the renegotiation depends on the creditor's prior beliefs about investment efficiency. In the absence of Chapter 11, an inefficient firm always mimics an efficient firm. If the creditor believes the firm is inefficient, the creditor refuses to renegotiate with the firm, the firm liquidates, and the equity holders' payoff is zero. The efficient firm cannot signal its type. Therefore, the only possible equilibria are two pooling equilibria. First, the creditor believes (a priori) that investment is on average (but not always) efficient, renegotiates with the firm, and permits investment. The alternative is that the creditor believes (a priori) that investment is on average (but not always) inefficient, refuses to renegotiate with the firm, and the firm liquidates. Therefore, either inefficient firms overinvest or efficient firms underinvest.

In contrast, Chapter 11 procedures impose costs on inefficient firms that would otherwise mimic efficient firms. All firms now have an incentive to reveal their type. In a separating equilibrium, efficient firms renegotiate with the creditor and invest. Inefficient firms either file for Chapter 11 (as in Berkovich and Israel (1991)) or renegotiate with the creditor outside Chapter 11 and liquidate. In a renegotiation outside Chapter 11, each claim holder's expected payoff in Chapter 11 serves as his reservation value in the renegotiation. In a separating equilibrium, investment is first-best.

Because Chapter 11 provides an incentive for an economically inefficient firm to reveal its type, investment efficiency improves relative to investment efficiency with bankruptcy laws that do not allow Chapter 11. This result is similar to the result in the model with public debt holders. However, with Chapter 11 and a single uninformed private creditor, a firm benefits from Chapter 11 but never enters Chapter 11 (if it can renegotiate outside Chapter 11). I focus on distressed firms with public debt, because the voting mechanism in Chapter 11 eliminates the public debt holder coordination problem present outside Chapter 11 and motivates filing for Chapter 11. Therefore, firms with public debt outstanding are more likely to use Chapter 11.

Gilson, John, and Lang (1990) find that distressed firms with public debt outstanding are disproportionately large users of Chapter 11. To the extent that this article addresses empirical evidence about firms that file for Chapter 11, I assume the debt is public debt in order to motivate filing for Chapter 11. With a private creditor rather than public debt, the maintenance of equity value in Chapter 11 provides the same incentive for the inefficient firm to reveal its type but does not explain Chapter 11 filings.

B. The Limitations of Chapter 11

This article outlines the features of corporate financial structure that can make financial distress costly. I focus on both information asymmetry and coordination problems among public debt holders as the sources of inefficiency. Information asymmetry and coordination problems can lead to underinvestment by economically efficient firms and overinvestment by economically inefficient firms.

In the model presented in the article, Chapter 11 works well when inefficient firms file and has good incentive effects outside of Chapter 11. However, in practice, with respect to firms that file, there are limitations to what Chapter 11 can achieve because of conflicts between claim holders or between management and claim holders.

The model assumes that management bargains on behalf of equity holders in Chapter 11. Management liquidates an inefficient firm in exchange for a more valuable claim on the firm for equity holders. However, in practice, managers may care more about protecting their jobs than they care about shareholder wealth (see Bradley and Rosenzweig (1992)). Unless creditors can bribe managers to liquidate the firm, managers avoid liquidation. To the extent that managers of inefficient firms in Chapter 11 avoid liquidation, managers destroy value.

An alternative explanation for why inefficient firms are not completely liquidated in Chapter 11 is consistent with managers acting on behalf of equity holders. When the firm is completely liquidated in Chapter 11, creditors cannot credibly commit to permit the maintenance of equity value. Creditors have the incentive to offer valuable claims on the firm to equity holders in exchange for agreement to liquidate the firm. As soon as the firm is liquidated, the firm becomes just a collection of liquid assets. Creditors can then argue for the application of the absolute priority rule leaving equity holders with nothing (see Brown (1989)). Therefore, managers of inefficient firms acting on behalf of equity holders avoid a complete liquidation to maintain equity value in Chapter 11.

Hotchkiss (1992) presents evidence consistent with both of the above hypotheses, which suggests that managers of economically inefficient firms avoid liquidation in Chapter 11 and destroy firm value. Hotchkiss (1992) finds that, for bankrupt firms, the relationship between the fraction of managers retained after filing and firm performance is significantly negative.

Bradley and Rosenzweig (1992) and others argue that the operating and investment inefficiencies possible in Chapter 11 can be avoided by eliminating Chapter 11 reorganization altogether and relying on Chapter 7. In a Chapter 7, a trustee sells the firm in its entirety, either through an auction or through negotiations with investors and other firms. In effect, Chapter 7 shifts control of a bankrupt firm to creditor-oriented managers. However, Hotchkiss (1992) finds no evidence that factors associated with increased creditor influence can be tied to improved firm performance.

The normative question of whether a forced sale regime is more or less efficient than some form of reorganization law is largely an empirical one given the potential allocative distortions of both systems. However, any thorough analysis of bankruptcy law cannot ignore the consequences of bankruptcy law for out-of-court restructurings. Since the maintenance of equity value in Chapter 11 has value for restructurings outside of Chapter 11, any reform of bankruptcy law should preserve this feature of Chapter 11. However, it follows from this article that firms filing for Chapter 11 are disproportionately economically inefficient. Given management's incentive to avoid liquidation in Chapter 11, one can expect economically inefficient firms to emerge from Chapter 11. In fact, Hotchkiss (1992) documents the postbankruptcy poor performance of firms reorganized in Chapter 11. Therefore, it follows that a logical first step in reforming bankruptcy law is an actively enforced requirement that firms reorganized in Chapter 11 emerge with a financial structure conducive to operating and investment efficiency.

Appendix

Proof of Proposition 1: I set the off-the-equilibrium path beliefs of the probability the firm is good at λ everywhere. Debt holders believe firm value is $Y < qD$, and will reject all offers to renegotiate. Therefore, since debt holders will not accept any restructuring, neither type firm can deviate. The proposed equilibrium is a PBE.

I need to check that the equilibrium satisfies the refinement. There is no good-firm-consistent deviation, because any offer that a good firm prefers, a bad firm also prefers. There is no bad-firm-consistent deviation, because debt holders reject any offer if they believe the firm is a bad firm. There is no pooling-consistent deviation, because debt holders reject any offer if they believe the firm is good with probability λ. Q.E.D.

Proof of Proposition 2: Firms offer senior debt with a face value π' such that debt holders accept the offer but reject any offer of senior debt with face value less than π', given debt holder beliefs that a firm is good with probability λ. I set the off-the-equilibrium-path beliefs of the probability the firm is bad at one everywhere. Since $Y - I + E(X|b) < qD$, debt holders will not accept any deviation. Because both good and bad firms get nothing if the offer is rejected, neither type of firm will deviate. The proposed equilibrium is a PBE.

I need to check that the equilibrium satisfies the refinement. There is no good-firm-consistent deviation, because any offer that a good firm prefers, a bad firm also prefers. A good firm would only prefer to offer senior debt with a lower face value, i.e., an offer a bad firm would also prefer. There is no bad-firm-consistent deviation, because debt holders reject any offer if they believe the firm is a bad firm. There is no pooling-consistent deviation: any offer that both good and bad firms prefer, debt holders will reject with beliefs that the firm is good with probability λ. Both good and bad type firms are worse off with an offer that is rejected. Q.E.D.

Proof of Proposition 3: Because $Y < qD$, $Y - I + E(X|b) < qD$ and debt holders would not accept an offer to renegotiate with the firm if they believe that the firm is bad with probability 1. There cannot be a separating equilibrium in which only bad firms renegotiate and invest at time 1.

Because $Y < qD$, debt holders would not accept an offer to renegotiate with the firm if they believe that the firm is good with probability λ. There cannot be a pooling equilibrium in which both types of firms renegotiate and invest at time 1.

Define $\hat{\pi}$ such that

$$\int_{\hat{\pi}D-Y+I}^{\infty} (X - \hat{\pi}D + Y - I)f(X|b)\,dX = E_{file}^{b} + \varepsilon, \tag{7}$$

where $\varepsilon \to 0$. Let $\bar{\pi} = \max\{\hat{\pi}, \pi_g\}$.

Suppose

$$E_{file}^{b} \geq \min\left\{\int_{\pi_p D-Y+I}^{\infty} (X - \pi_p D + Y - I)f(X|b)\,dX, \right.$$

$$\left. \int_{\pi_g D-Y+I}^{\infty} (X - \pi_g D + Y - I)f(X|b)\,dX\right\}. \tag{8}$$

A possible equilibrium is one in which both types of firms file for bankruptcy. However, this is not an equilibrium that satisfies the refinement, because there exists a good-firm-consistent deviation. Given equation (3), good firms will offer to renegotiate with debt holders. Good firms will offer senior debt with face value $\bar{\pi}$. Given equation (8), bad firms will not mimic the offer. Debt holders believe only good firms will offer to renegotiate, and debt holders will accept an offer of senior debt with face value $\bar{\pi}$. Good firms will deviate, and debt holders believe only good firms deviate. Thus, there does not exist a pooling equilibrium that satisfies the refinement.

The only equilibrium is a separating equilibrium in which good firms renegotiate with debt holders and bad firms file for bankruptcy. I set the off-the-equilibrium path beliefs of the probability the firm is good at λ everywhere. If given a deviation, debt holders believe the firm is good with probability λ, believe firm value is $Y < qD$, and reject the offer to renegotiate. If debt holders believe only good firms offer senior debt with face value $\tilde{\pi}$, given equation (8), bad firms will prefer to file. Given equation (3), good firms will offer $\tilde{\pi}$, and debt holders believe that a firm that offers $\tilde{\pi}$ is good. Since neither type of firm wishes to deviate, the proposed equilibrium is a PBE.

I now show that the separating equilibrium satisfies the refinement. First, there is no good-firm-consistent deviation: if $\tilde{\pi} = \pi_g$ and debt holders believe the firm is good, debt holders reject any offer that a good firm prefers. If $\tilde{\pi} > \pi_g$, any offer that a good firm prefers, a bad firm also prefers. There is no bad-firm-consistent deviation, because any offer that a bad firm prefers, a good firm also prefers. Last, there is no pooling-consistent deviation because debt holders will not accept an offer if they believe the firm is good with probability λ.

Now suppose

$$E^b_{file} < \min\left\{\int_{\pi_p D - Y + I}^{\infty} (X - \pi_p D + Y - I) f(X|b)\, dX, \right.$$

$$\left. \int_{\pi_g D - Y + I}^{\infty} (X - \pi_g D + Y - I) f(X|b)\, dX \right\}. \quad (9)$$

There is no separating equilibrium in which good firms renegotiate with debt holders and bad firms file for bankruptcy. Any offer that good firms prefer to filing for bankruptcy, bad firms also prefer given equations (3) and (9). Bad firms will mimic the offer. Given equation (9), bad firms deviate.

The only equilibrium is one in which both types of firms file for bankruptcy. I set the off-the-equilibrium path beliefs of the probability the firm is good at λ everywhere. If given a deviation, debt holders believe the firm is good with probability λ, believe firm value is $Y < qD$, and reject the offer to renegotiate.

I now show that the equilibrium satisfies the refinement. First, there is no good-firm-consistent deviation, because any offer that a good firm prefers, a bad firm also prefers given equation (9). There is no bad-firm-consistent deviation, since debt holders reject any offer if they believe the firm is bad. Last, there is no pooling-consistent deviation because debt holders will not accept an offer if they believe the firm is good with probability λ. Q.E.D.

Proof of Proposition 4: There cannot be a separating PBE in which only bad firms renegotiate and invest at time 1. If $\pi_b > \pi_p > \pi_g$, $E^g_{file} = E^g_{\pi_g}$. There is a pooling consistent deviation. Moreover, if $\pi_b < \pi_g$, $E^g_{file} = E^g_{\pi_g} < E^g_{\pi_b}$. Good firms mimic bad firms.

There is no pooling equilibrium in which both types of firms file for bankruptcy. Given equation (3), either good firms deviate or both types of firms deviate. There is a pooling PBE in which both types of firms renegotiate and invest, or a separating PBE in which good firms renegotiate and invest and bad firms file for bankruptcy.

If equation (8) is satisfied, following the same reasoning as in the proof of proposition 3, there is a separating PBE in which bad firms file for bankruptcy with no good-firm- or bad-firm-consistent deviations. Furthermore, given equation (8), there is no pooling-consistent deviation. Given debt holder beliefs that a firm is good with probability λ, bad firms prefer to file for bankruptcy rather than pool with good firms. Therefore, if equation (8) is satisfied, the separating PBE satisfies the refinement.

If equation (9) is satisfied, bad firms deviate. Following the same reasoning as in the proof of proposition 3, there are no separating PBE.

Suppose equation (9) is satisfied. Given equation (9), both good and bad firms prefer to renegotiate and invest at time 1 rather than file for bankruptcy. The existence of Chapter 11 has no impact on bad-firm behavior. Therefore, the problem reverts back to Section III.B of this article. From Section III.B it follows that both good and bad firms renegotiate and invest at time 1. Q.E.D.

Proof of Proposition 5: Given equation (6), good firms do not mimic bad firms in Chapter 11. Therefore, $E^g_{file} = R(g)$.

Suppose

$$R(g) \leq \min\{E^g_{\pi_p}, E^g_{\pi_g}\}. \tag{10}$$

Equation (8) implies that $E^b_{file} \geq E^b_{\pi_g}$. Therefore, it follows from the proofs of Propositions 3 and 4 that there exists a separating PBE that satisfies the refinement.

Now suppose

$$R(g) > \min\{E^g_{\pi_p}, E^g_{\pi_g}\}. \tag{11}$$

There exists an equilibrium in which both types of firms file for bankruptcy. I set the off-the-equilibrium path beliefs of the probability the firm is good at 1 everywhere. Since both types of firms prefer to file for bankruptcy rather than make an offer that debt holders would accept, neither type firm deviates. The proposed equilibrium is a PBE.

The PBE satisfies the refinement: given equation (11), there is no good-firm-consistent deviation, because good firms prefer to file rather than make an offer that debt holders will accept. Given equations (5) and (6), there is no bad-firm-consistent deviation. Any offer a bad firm prefers, a good firm also prefers. Finally, there is no pooling-consistent deviation. Given equations (5), (6), and (11), both types of firms prefer to file rather that make an offer that debt holders will accept. Q.E.D.

REFERENCES

Aghion, P., O. Hart, and J. Moore, 1992, The economics of bankruptcy reform, NBER Working paper No. 4097.

Allen, F., 1985, Capital structure and imperfect competition in product markets, Working paper, The Wharton School, University of Pennsylvania.

———, 1986, The insignificance of bankruptcy costs to the theory of capital structure: A comment, Working paper, The Wharton School, University of Pennsylvania.

Baird, D., 1991, The initiation problem in bankruptcy, *International Review of Law and Economics* 11, 223–232.

———, and R. Picker, 1991, A simple noncooperative bargaining model of corporate reorganizations, *Journal of Legal Studies* 20, 311–349.

Bebchuk, L., 1988, A new approach to corporate reorganization, *Harvard Law Review* 101, 775–804.

———, 1994, The effects of Chapter 11 and debt renegotiation on ex ante corporate decisions, *Journal of Finance*, Forthcoming.

———, and H. Chang, 1992, Bargaining and the division of value in corporate reorganization, *Journal of Law, Economics, and Organization* 8, 253–279.

Bebchuk, L., and R. Picker, 1992, Bankruptcy rules, managerial entrenchment, and management human capital, Working paper, Harvard University and University of Chicago.

Bergman, Y., and J. Callen, 1991, Opportunistic underinvestment in debt renegotiation and capital structure, *Journal of Financial Economics* 29, 137–171.

Berkovich, E., and R. Israel, 1991, The bankruptcy decision and debt contract renegotiations, Working paper, University of Michigan.

Betker, B., 1992, Management changes, equity's bargaining power and deviations from absolute priority in Chapter 11 bankruptcies, Working paper, Ohio State University.

Bradley, M., and M. Rosenzweig, 1992, The untenable case for Chapter 11, *The Yale Law Journal* 101, 1043–1095.

Brown, D., 1989, Claimholder incentive conflicts in reorganization: The role of bankruptcy law, *The Review of Financial Studies* 2, 109–123.

———, C. James, and R. Mooradian, 1993, The information content of distressed restructurings involving public and private claims, *Journal of Financial Economics* 33, 93–118.

Bulow, J., and J. Shoven, 1978, The bankruptcy decision, *Bell Journal of Economics* 9, 437–456.

Coffee, J., 1990, Coercive debt tender offers: The problem of distorted choice revisited, Working paper, The Center for Law and Economic Studies, School of Law, Columbia University.

Eberhart, A., W. Moore, and R. Roenfeldt, 1990, Security pricing and deviations from the absolute priority rule in bankruptcy proceedings, *Journal of Finance* 45, 1457–1470.

Farrell, J., 1983, Communication in game I: Mechanism design without a mediator, Working paper, Massachusetts Institute of Technology.

Franks, J., and W. Torous, 1989, An empirical investigation of U.S. firms in reorganization, *Journal of Finance* 44, 747–770.

———, 1994, Equity's bargaining power and deviations from absolute priority in Chapter 11 bankruptcies, *Journal of Financial Economics*, Forthcoming.

Gertner, R., 1991, Capital structure signalling in distressed debt restructurings, Working paper, University of Chicago.

———, R. Gibbons, and D. Scharfstein, 1988, Simultaneous signalling to the capital and product markets, *Rand Journal of Economics* 19, 173–190.

Gertner, R., and D. Scharfstein, 1991, A theory of workouts and the effects of reorganization law, *Journal of Finance*, 46, 1189–1222.

Gilson, S., K. John, and L. Lang, 1990, Troubled debt restructurings: An empirical study of private reorganization of firms in default, *Journal of Financial Economics* 27, 315–354.

Gilson, S., and M. Vetsuypens, 1993, CEO compensation in financially distressed firms: An empirical analysis, *Journal of Finance* 48, 425–458.

Grossman, S., and M. Perry, 1986, Perfect sequential equilibrium, *Journal of Economic Theory* 39, 97–119.

Harris, M., and A. Raviv, 1993, The design of bankruptcy procedures, Working paper, University of Chicago and Northwestern University.

Heinkel, R., and J. Zechner, 1991, Debt payment structure, optimal default decisions and capital structure renegotiation, Working paper, Faculty of Commerce, University of British Columbia.

Hotchkiss, E., 1992, The post-bankruptcy performance of firms emerging from Chapter 11, Working paper, New York University.

LoPucki, L., and W. Whitford, 1992, Corporate governance in the bankruptcy reorganization of large publicly held companies, Working paper, University of Wisconsin Law School.

Roe, M., 1987, The voting prohibition in bond workouts, *The Yale Law Journal* 97, 232–279.

Townsend, R., 1979, Optimal contracts and competitive markets with costly state verification, *Journal of Economic Theory* 21, 265–293.

Weiss, L., 1990, Bankruptcy resolution: Direct costs and violation of priority of claims, *Journal of Financial Economics* 38, 477–488.

White, M., 1994, Corporate bankruptcy as a screening device, *Journal of Law, Economics, and Organization*, Forthcoming.

Name Index

Abel, A. 20
Admati, A. 206, 257, 259
Aivazian, V.A. 497
Alchian, A. 6
Alderson, M. 92
Allen, B. 206
Allen, F. 20
Anderson, R. 206
Antle, R. 155
Aronson, J. 16
Asquith, P. 459
Auerbach, A.J. 317, 326, 327, 329, 330
Ausubel, L. 206

Bailey, M.J. 310
Baird, D. 44, 545, 552, 568
Bajeux, I. 269, 271
Baskin, J. 20
Baxter, N. 4, 302
Bebchuk, L.A. 476, 552, 568
Beekhuesen, T. 20
Bergman, Y.Z. 497
Berkovich, E. 552, 572
Bernanke, B. 43, 63, 130
Bhagat, S. 63
Bhatia, K.B. 310
Bierman, H. 105
Black, F. 159, 161, 163, 167, 301, 307, 327
Blair, R.D. 20
Block, S.B. 249
Blume, M.E. 330
Bogue, M.C. 105
Bradley, M. 20, 464, 483, 485, 553, 554, 573, 574
Brander, J. 20, 68
Bray, M.M. 271
Breeden, D. 226, 228
Brennan, M.J. 105, 107, 109, 130, 158, 160–62, 174, 185, 311, 317, 319, 322, 511
Briden, G. 324
Brock, W.A. 108
Brown, D. 497, 568, 573
Brudney, V. 270, 440
Bruner, R. 92, 459
Bulow, J. 247, 497, 519
Burkhart, M. 248

Callen, J.L. 497
Campbell, J.Y. 43, 63
Carlton, D.W. 269
Castanias, R. 20
Chan, K.C. 59
Chang, H. 568
Chen, A.-H. 317
Chen, K.C. 92
Chen, N.F. 59
Chirelstein, M.A. 440
Cho, I. 103, 504
Coffee, J. 536
Cohn, R. 101, 327
Constantinides, G.M. 105, 107, 348, 355
Cordes, J.J. 317
Cox, J.C. 113, 123, 132, 159, 161, 163, 167, 350
Crockett, J. 330

Dean, J. 105
DeAngelo, H. 317, 332, 335, 340, 355, 383, 384
DeMarzo, P.M. 200, 201, 228
Demsetz, H. 6
Desai, A. 464
Diamond, D.W. 46, 255
Diamond, P.A. 201, 219, 220
Dodd, P. 448, 458
Donaldson, G. 79
Dothan, U. 107
Drèze, J.H. 201
Duffie, D. 201, 228
Dybvig, P. 337, 355
Dye, R.A. 255

Easterbrook, F. 44, 269, 359, 360, 476, 484
Eberhart, A. 568
Edmister, R.O. 472
Ekern, S. 130, 201
Elton, E.J. 317, 327, 329, 330, 332
Eppen, G. 155
Ezzell, J.R. 325

Fama, E. 301, 496
Farrar, D. 306, 317
Farrell, J. 558
Feldstein, M. 322, 324

Fershtman, C. 68
Fischel, D.R. 269, 359, 360, 476, 484
Fischer, E. 161, 192
Fisher, I. 105
Fishman, M.J. 272, 293, 446, 465
Flannery, M. 72
Fleming, W.H. 113
Franks, J. 459, 541, 563, 568
Friend, I. 330
Froot, K.A. 228
Fudenberg, D. 68, 75

Gale, D. 72, 232
Gallagher, T.J. 249
Geanakoplos, J. 201, 247
Gertler, M. 250
Gertner, M. 57
Gertner, R. 552, 553, 557
Giammarino, R.M. 446, 465
Gilson, R.J. 476
Gilson, S. 573
Girth, M. 302
Glosten, L.R. 269, 271
Golbe, D.L. 62
Gordon, M.J. 459
Gordon, R.H. 317, 327
Grinblatt, M.S. 271
Grossman, S.J. 271, 375, 389, 391, 394, 399, 404, 441, 464, 465, 473, 484, 558
Gruber, M. 317, 327, 329, 330, 332

Hagerty, K.M. 272, 293
Hamada, R. 301
Hansen, L. 337
Hansen, R.G. 447, 448
Harrington, D.R. 92
Harris, M. 45, 46, 160, 382, 389, 391, 394, 399, 404, 552
Harris, R.S. 459
Harrison, J. 337
Hart, O. 45–7, 49, 50, 57, 375, 389, 391, 394, 399, 404, 441, 464, 465, 473, 484
Haugen, R. 4, 496
Heinkel, R. 161, 192, 446, 465
Hellwig, M. 72, 232, 271
Hermalin, B. 72
Hirshleifer, D. 465
Hirshleifer, J. 271
Holland, M. 58
Holmström, B. 155
Hoshi T. 250
Hotchkiss, E. 573, 574
Huang, Y. 459
Hubbard, R.G. 250

Ibbotson, R. 301
Icahn, C. 487
Ingersoll, J.E. 113, 123, 132, 348
Israel, R. 552, 553, 572

Jackson, T. 498, 545
Jarrell, G. 20, 481, 485
Jarrow, R.A. 123
Jensen, M. 6, 46, 57, 72, 184, 187, 200, 317, 387, 388, 524
John, K. 573
Judd, K. 68

Kaldor, N. 109
Kane, A. 161
Kaplan, S.N. 58, 64, 184
Kashyap, A. 251
Katz, M. 68
Kearney, A.J. 248
Khawna, N. 446
Kim, E.H. 311, 317, 322, 330, 464
Kim, H. 3, 20
King, M.A. 317, 327, 329
Klein, A. 91
Klein, W. 536
Klemperer, P. 247
Kraus, A. 3
Kreps, D. 103, 337, 503, 504
Kyle, A.S. 257, 259, 271

Lamont, O.A. 251
Lane, W.R. 459
Lang, L. 573
Lease, R.C. 317, 322, 330
Leland, H. 184, 201, 223
Lessard, D. 226–8
Lewellen, W.G. 317, 322, 330
Lewent, J.C. 248
Lewis, T. 20, 68
Litzenberger, R. 3, 322
Long, M.S. 20
Lopucki, L. 562, 568, 571
Lynch, M. 58

Magill, M. 201
Majluf, N. 45, 57, 537
Maksimovic, V. 20, 68
Malatesta, P.H. 478, 485
Malitz, E.B. 20
Malkiel, B.G. 317, 327
Manne, H.G. 269
Manove, M. 269, 271
Marcus, A. 161
Marglin, S. 130

Marshall, S.B. 92
Martin, J. 16
Masulis, R.W. 317, 326, 332, 335, 340, 355
Mayer, C. 459
McAllister, P. 206
McConnell, J.J. 91, 322, 330
McDonald, R. 130, 161
Meckling, W. 6, 57, 187, 200, 317, 387, 388, 524
Merton, R. 113, 133, 134, 159, 160
Meza, D. de 20, 21
Miles, J.A. 325
Milgrom, P. 69, 75, 343
Miller, M.H. 3, 20, 33, 108, 157, 159–61, 200, 304, 316, 317, 321, 323, 335, 355, 496
Modigliani, F. 3, 101, 157, 159–61, 200, 301, 316, 321, 327
Moore, J. 45, 46
Moore, W. 568
Mullins, D. 459
Muscarella, C.J. 91
Myers, S.C. 45, 47, 228, 306, 317, 524, 537
Myerson, R. 68

Nance, D.R. 248, 249

Oldfield, G.S. 123

Paddock, J.L. 108
Perry, M. 558
Pfleiderer, P. 257, 259
Picker, R. 552, 568
Pindyck, R.S. 107
Png, I.P.L. 446, 465
Poulsen, A. 485
Pringle, J. 249

Quinzii, M. 201

Raviv, A. 45, 46, 160, 382, 389, 391, 394, 399, 404, 552
Remmers, L. 20
Richard, S.F. 123, 337
Rishel, R.W. 113
Roberts, J. 69, 75
Rochet, J.-C. 269, 271
Roe, M. 545
Roenfeldt, R. 568
Roll, R. 105, 487
Rosenthal, L. 464
Rosenzweig, M. 553, 554, 573, 574
Ross, S.A. 83, 113, 123, 132, 200, 271, 337, 338, 350, 355, 441

Rothschild, M. 108, 152, 209
Ruback, R.S. 464
Ryngaert, M. 478

Sahlman, W. 72
Samuelson, W. 464
Sappington, D.E.M. 73
Scharfstein, D.S. 57, 228, 251, 552, 553, 557
Schlarbaum, G.G. 313, 322, 330
Scholes, M. 301, 323
Schwartz, E. 16, 85, 107, 130, 158, 160–62, 174, 185, 311, 317
Scott, D. 3, 16
Selwyn, L.L. 306, 317
Senbet, L. 4, 496
Shafer, W. 201
Sheffrin, S.M. 317
Shleifer, A. 464, 465, 467, 473
Shoven, J. 497, 519
Siegel, D.R. 108, 130
Singleton, K. 251
Skelton, J.L. 317
Smidt, S. 105
Smith, C.W. 57, 226, 228, 248, 249
Smith, J.L. 108
Smithson, C.W. 226, 228, 248, 249
Solow, R.M. 120
Sonnenschein, H. 206
Stanley, D.T. 302
Stanley, K.L. 317, 322, 330
Stapleton, R.C. 306
Stein, J.C. 64, 228, 251
Stiglitz, J.E. 26, 72, 108, 152, 209, 271, 307, 496
Stonehill, A. 20
Stulz, R. 45, 46, 226–8
Summers, L.H. 322, 324, 326
Sundaresan, M. 123

Taggart, R.A. 317
Telser, L.G. 109
Thompson, R. 98, 485
Tirole, J. 68, 75
Titman, S. 6, 20, 130, 249
Torous, W. 541, 563, 568
Tourinho, O.A.F. 108
Townsend, R. 72, 232
Turnbull, S.M. 105

Upton, C.W. 108, 301

Van Horne, J.C. 302, 497
Vanderhei, J. 92
Verrecchia, R.E. 263

Vickers, J. 68
Vishny, R.W. 464, 465, 467, 473
Viswanathan, S. 226, 228

Walkling, R.A. 459, 472, 478
Wall, L.D. 249
Wansley, J.W. 459
Warner, J. 4, 57, 302
Warshawsky, M. 43, 63
Webb, D.C. 497
Weiss, A. 72
Weiss, L. 155
Wessels, R. 20, 249
White, L.J. 62
White, M. 519, 554

Whitford, W. 562, 568, 571
Wilford, D.S. 226
Williams, J. 107, 301
Williamson, O.E. 43, 45, 59
Williamson, S.H. 316, 333
Wilson, R. 201, 503
Working, H. 109
Wright, R. 20

Yagil, J. 459
Yang, H.C. 459
Yannelis, N. 207

Zechner, J. 161, 192